GENERAL MOTORS | CAVALIER/SUNBIRD/SKYHAWK/FIRENZA 1982-94 REPAIR MANUAL

Covers all U.S. and Canadian models of Buick Skyhawk, Cadillac Cimarron, Chevrolet Cavalier, Oldsmobile Firenza and Pontiac 2000/Sunbird

by Matthew E. Frederick, A.S.E., S.A.E.

CHILTON *Automotive Books*

PUBLISHED BY **HAYNES NORTH AMERICA**. Inc.

APAA
AUTOMOTIVE
PARTS &
ACCESSORIES
ASSOCIATION MEMBER

Manufactured in USA
© 1996 Haynes North America, Inc.
ISBN 0-8019-9113-7
Library of Congress Catalog Card No. 99-072293
4567890123 9876543210

Haynes Publishing Group
Sparkford Nr Yeovil
Somerset BA22 7JJ England

Haynes North America, Inc
861 Lawrence Drive
Newbury Park
California 91320 USA

ABCDE FGHIJ K

6E2

Contents

1 GENERAL INFORMATION AND MAINTENANCE

1-2 HOW TO USE THIS BOOK
1-3 TOOLS AND EQUIPMENT
1-6 SERVICING YOUR VEHICLE SAFELY
1-7 FASTENERS, MEASUREMENTS AND CONVERSIONS
1-11 SERIAL NUMBER IDENTIFICATION
1-15 ROUTINE MAINTENANCE
1-36 FLUIDS AND LUBRICANTS
1-45 TRAILER TOWING
1-46 TOWING THE VEHICLE
1-46 JUMP STARTING A DEAD BATTERY
1-47 JACKING

2 ENGINE ELECTRICAL

2-2 HIGH ENERGY IGNITION (HEI) SYSTEM
2-7 DIRECT IGNITION SYSTEM (DIS) AND ELECTRONIC IGNITION (EI) SYSTEMS
2-10 FIRING ORDERS
2-11 CHARGING SYSTEM
2-15 STARTING SYSTEM
2-18 SENDING UNITS AND SENSORS

3 ENGINE AND ENGINE OVERHAUL

3-2 ENGINE MECHANICAL
3-52 EXHAUST SYSTEM
3-55 ENGINE RECONDITIONING

4 DRIVEABILITY AND EMISSIONS CONTROLS

4-2 AIR POLLUTION
4-3 AUTOMOTIVE EMISSIONS
4-4 EMISSION CONTROLS
4-11 ELECTRONIC ENGINE CONTROLS
4-18 TROUBLE CODES
4-23 COMPONENT LOCATION DIAGRAMS
4-28 VACUUM DIAGRAMS

5 FUEL SYSTEM

5-2 BASIC FUEL SYSTEM DIAGNOSIS
5-2 FUEL LINES AND FITTINGS
5-2 CARBURETED FUEL SYSTEM
5-10 MODEL 300 AND 500 THROTTLE BODY (TBI) INJECTION SYSTEMS
5-14 MODEL 700 THROTTLE BODY INJECTION (TBI) SYSTEM
5-18 BOTTOM FEED PORT (BFP) INJECTION SYSTEM
5-20 MULTI-PORT (MFI) & SEQUENTIAL (SFI) FUEL INJECTION SYSTEMS
5-27 FUEL TANK

6 CHASSIS ELECTRICAL

6-2 UNDERSTANDING AND TROUBLESHOOTING ELECTRICAL SYSTEMS
6-7 BATTERY CABLES
6-7 SUPPLEMENTAL INFLATABLE RESTRAINT (SIR) SYSTEM
6-9 HEATING AND AIR CONDITIONING
6-13 CRUISE CONTROL
6-14 ENTERTAINMENT SYSTEMS
6-16 WINDSHIELD WIPERS AND WASHERS
6-19 INSTRUMENTS AND SWITCHES
6-22 LIGHTING
6-27 TRAILER WIRING
6-27 CIRCUIT PROTECTION
6-31 WIRING DIAGRAMS

Contents

7-2 MANUAL TRANSAXLE   **7-27** AUTOMATIC TRANSAXLE

7-23 CLUTCH

DRIVE TRAIN 7

8-2 WHEELS   **8-13** REAR SUSPENSION

8-4 FRONT SUSPENSION   **8-17** STEERING

SUSPENSION AND STEERING 8

9-2 BRAKE OPERATING SYSTEM   **9-18** PARKING BRAKE

9-9 DISC BRAKES   **9-19** ANTI-LOCK BRAKE SYSTEM (ABS)

9-13 REAR DRUM BRAKES

BRAKES 9

10-2 EXTERIOR   **10-10** INTERIOR

BODY AND TRIM 10

10-20 GLOSSARY

GLOSSARY

10-25 MASTER INDEX

MASTER INDEX

SAFETY NOTICE

Proper service and repair procedures are vital to the safe, reliable operation of all motor vehicles, as well as the personal safety of those performing repairs. This manual outlines procedures for servicing and repairing vehicles using safe, effective methods. The procedures contain many NOTES, CAUTIONS and WARNINGS which should be followed, along with standard procedures to eliminate the possibility of personal injury or improper service which could damage the vehicle or compromise its safety.

It is important to note that repair procedures and techniques, tools and parts for servicing motor vehicles, as well as the skill and experience of the individual performing the work vary widely. It is not possible to anticipate all of the conceivable ways or conditions under which vehicles may be serviced, or to provide cautions as to all possible hazards that may result. Standard and accepted safety precautions and equipment should be used when handling toxic or flammable fluids, and safety goggles or other protection should be used during cutting, grinding, chiseling, prying, or any other process that can cause material removal or projectiles.

Some procedures require the use of tools specially designed for a specific purpose. Before substituting another tool or procedure, you must be completely satisfied that neither your personal safety, nor the performance of the vehicle will be endangered.

Although information in this manual is based on industry sources and is complete as possible at the time of publication, the possibility exists that some car manufacturers made later changes which could not be included here. While striving for total accuracy, the authors or publishers cannot assume responsibility for any errors, changes or omissions that may occur in the compilation of this data.

PART NUMBERS

Part numbers listed in this reference are not recommendations by Haynes North America, Inc. for any product brand name. They are references that can be used with interchange manuals and aftermarket supplier catalogs to locate each brand supplier's discrete part number.

SPECIAL TOOLS

Special tools are recommended by the vehicle manufacturer to perform their specific job. Use has been kept to a minimum, but where absolutely necessary, they are referred to in the text by the part number of the tool manufacturer. These tools can be purchased, under the appropriate part number, from your local dealer or regional distributor, or an equivalent tool can be purchased locally from a tool supplier or parts outlet. Before substituting any tool for the one recommended, read the SAFETY NOTICE at the top of this page.

ACKNOWLEDGMENTS

Portions of materials contained herein have been reprinted with the permission of General Motors Corporation, Service Technology Group.

HOW TO USE THIS BOOK 1-2
WHERE TO BEGIN 1-2
AVOIDING TROUBLE 1-2
MAINTENANCE OR REPAIR? 1-2
AVOIDING THE MOST COMMON
 MISTAKES 1-2
TOOLS AND EQUIPMENT 1-3
SPECIAL TOOLS 1-4
SERVICING YOUR VEHICLE SAFELY 1-6
DO'S 1-6
DON'TS 1-6
**FASTENERS, MEASUREMENTS AND
 CONVERSIONS 1-7**
BOLTS, NUTS AND OTHER THREADED
 RETAINERS 1-7
TORQUE 1-7
 TORQUE WRENCHES 1-8
 TORQUE ANGLE METERS 1-10
STANDARD AND METRIC
 MEASUREMENTS 1-10
SERIAL NUMBER IDENTIFICATION 1-11
VEHICLE 1-11
ENGINE 1-11
TRANSAXLE 1-15
ROUTINE MAINTENANCE 1-15
AIR CLEANER 1-17
 REMOVAL & INSTALLATION 1-17
FUEL FILTER 1-17
 REMOVAL & INSTALLATION 1-17
PCV VALVE 1-18
 REMOVAL & INSTALLATION 1-18
EVAPORATIVE CANISTER 1-19
 FUNCTIONAL TEST 1-20
BATTERY 1-20
 PRECAUTIONS 1-20
 GENERAL MAINTENANCE 1-20
 BATTERY FLUID 1-20
 CABLES 1-21
 CHARGING 1-22
 REPLACEMENT 1-22
STANDARD DRIVE BELTS 1-22
 INSPECTION & ADJUSTMENT 1-22
 REMOVAL & INSTALLATION 1-22
SERPENTINE DRIVE BELTS 1-23
 INSPECTION & ADJUSTMENT 1-23
 REMOVAL & INSTALLATION 1-23
TIMING BELT 1-23
 SERVICING 1-23
HOSES 1-23
 INSPECTION 1-23
 REMOVAL & INSTALLATION 1-23
CV-BOOT 1-24
 INSPECTION 1-24
SPARK PLUGS 1-24
 SPARK PLUG HEAT RANGE 1-25
 REMOVAL & INSTALLATION 1-25
 INSPECTION & GAPPING 1-25
SPARK PLUG WIRES 1-27
 TESTING 1-27
 REMOVAL & INSTALLATION 1-27
DISTRIBUTOR CAP AND ROTOR 1-27
 REMOVAL & INSTALLATION 1-27
 INSPECTION 1-27
IGNITION TIMING 1-28
 GENERAL INFORMATION 1-28
 INSPECTION & ADJUSTMENT 1-29
VALVE LASH 1-29
IDLE SPEED AND MIXTURE
 ADJUSTMENTS 1-29
 CARBURETED ENGINES 1-29
 FUEL INJECTED ENGINES 1-29
AIR CONDITIONING SYSTEM 1-31
 SYSTEM SERVICE & REPAIR 1-31
 PREVENTIVE MAINTENANCE 1-31

SYSTEM INSPECTION 1-32
WINDSHIELD WIPERS 1-32
 ELEMENT (REFILL) CARE &
 REPLACEMENT 1-32
TIRES AND WHEELS 1-33
 TIRE ROTATION 1-33
 TIRE DESIGN 1-34
 TIRE STORAGE 1-34
 INFLATION & INSPECTION 1-34
 CARE OF SPECIAL WHEELS 1-35
FLUIDS AND LUBRICANTS 1-36
FLUID DISPOSAL 1-36
FUEL AND ENGINE OIL
 RECOMMENDATIONS 1-36
 FUEL 1-36
 ENGINE OIL 1-36
ENGINE 1-37
 OIL LEVEL CHECK 1-37
 OIL & FILTER CHANGE 1-37
MANUAL TRANSAXLE 1-38
 FLUID RECOMMENDATIONS 1-38
 LEVEL CHECK 1-38
 DRAIN & REFILL 1-38
AUTOMATIC TRANSAXLE 1-39
 FLUID RECOMMENDATION 1-39
 LEVEL CHECK 1-39
 DRAIN & REFILL (INCLUDES PAN
 & FILTER SERVICE) 1-40
COOLING SYSTEM 1-40
 FLUID RECOMMENDATIONS 1-41
 LEVEL CHECK 1-41
 DRAIN & REFILL 1-42
 FLUSHING & CLEANING THE
 SYSTEM 1-42
BRAKE MASTER CYLINDER 1-42
 FLUID RECOMMENDATION 1-42
 LEVEL CHECK 1-43
CLUTCH MASTER CYLINDER 1-43
 FLUID RECOMMENDATIONS 1-43
 LEVEL CHECK 1-43
POWER STEERING PUMP 1-43
 FLUID RECOMMENDATIONS 1-43
 LEVEL CHECK 1-43
STEERING GEAR 1-43
CHASSIS GREASING 1-44
BODY LUBRICATION 1-44
 TRANSAXLE SHIFT LINKAGE 1-44
 HOOD LATCH & HINGES 1-44
 DOOR HINGES 1-44
 PARKING BRAKE LINKAGE 1-45
 ACCELERATOR LINKAGE 1-45
WHEEL BEARINGS 1-45
TRAILER TOWING 1-45
GENERAL RECOMMENDATIONS 1-45
TRAILER WEIGHT 1-45
HITCH WEIGHT 1-45
COOLING 1-45
 ENGINE 1-45
 TRANSMISSION 1-45
HANDLING A TRAILER 1-45
TOWING THE VEHICLE 1-46
JUMP STARTING A DEAD BATTERY 1-46
JUMP STARTING PRECAUTIONS 1-46
JUMP STARTING PROCEDURE 1-46
JACKING 1-47
COMPONENT LOCATIONS
 UNDERHOOD COMPONENT
 LOCATIONS 1-16
SPECIFICATIONS CHARTS
 VEHICLE IDENTIFICATION CHART 1-12
 ENGINE IDENTIFICATION 1-14
 TUNE-UP SPECIFICATIONS 1-30
 MAINTENANCE INTERVALS 1-48
 CAPACITIES 1-50

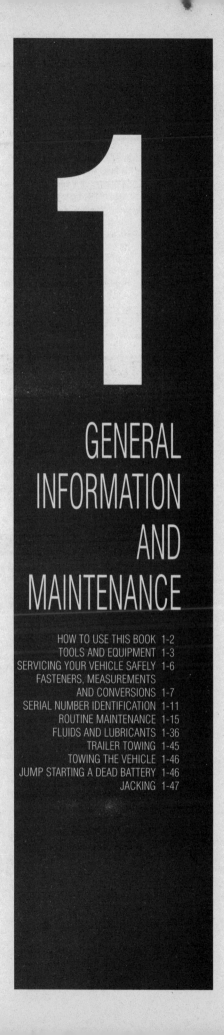

1

GENERAL
INFORMATION
AND
MAINTENANCE

HOW TO USE THIS BOOK 1-2
TOOLS AND EQUIPMENT 1-3
SERVICING YOUR VEHICLE SAFELY 1-6
FASTENERS, MEASUREMENTS
 AND CONVERSIONS 1-7
SERIAL NUMBER IDENTIFICATION 1-11
ROUTINE MAINTENANCE 1-15
FLUIDS AND LUBRICANTS 1-36
TRAILER TOWING 1-45
TOWING THE VEHICLE 1-46
JUMP STARTING A DEAD BATTERY 1-46
JACKING 1-47

HOW TO USE THIS BOOK

Chilton's Total Car Care for the Chevrolet Cavalier, Buick Skyhawk, Cadillac Cimarron, Pontiac 2000/Sunbird, and the Oldsmobile Firenza is intended to help you learn more about the inner workings of your vehicle and save you money on its upkeep and operation.

The beginning of the book will likely be referred to the most, since that is where you will find information for maintenance and tune-up. The other sections deal with the more complex systems of your vehicle. Operating systems from engine through brakes are covered to the extent that the average do-it-yourselfer becomes mechanically involved. This book will not explain such things as rebuilding a differential for the simple reason that the expertise required and the investment in special tools make this task uneconomical. It will, however, give you detailed instructions to help you change your own brake pads and shoes, replace spark plugs, and perform many more jobs that can save you money, give you personal satisfaction and help you avoid expensive problems.

A secondary purpose of this book is a reference for owners who want to understand their vehicle and/or their mechanics better. In this case, no tools at all are required.

Where to Begin

Before removing any bolts, read through the entire procedure. This will give you the overall view of what tools and supplies will be required. There is nothing more frustrating than having to walk to the bus stop on Monday morning because you were short one bolt on Sunday afternoon. So read ahead and plan ahead. Each operation should be approached logically and all procedures thoroughly understood before attempting any work.

All sections contain adjustments, maintenance, removal and installation procedures, and in some cases, repair or overhaul procedures. When repair is not considered practical, we tell you how to remove the part and then how to install the new or rebuilt replacement. In this way, you at least save labor costs. "Backyard" repair of some components is just not practical.

Avoiding Trouble

Many procedures in this book require you to "label and disconnect . . ." a group of lines, hoses or wires. Don't be lulled into thinking you can remember where everything goes—you won't. If you hook up vacuum or fuel lines incorrectly, the vehicle may run poorly, if at all. If you hook up electrical wiring incorrectly, you may instantly learn a very expensive lesson.

You don't need to know the official or engineering name for each hose or line. A piece of masking tape on the hose and a piece on its fitting will allow you to assign your own label such as the letter A or a short name. As long as you remember your own code, the lines can be reconnected by matching similar letters or names. Do remember that tape will dissolve in gasoline or other fluids; if a component is to be washed or cleaned, use another method of identification. A permanent felt-tipped marker or a metal scribe can be very handy for marking metal parts. Remove any tape or paper labels after assembly.

Maintenance or Repair?

It's necessary to mention the difference between maintenance and repair. Maintenance includes routine inspections, adjustments, and replacement of parts which show signs of normal wear. Maintenance compensates for wear or deterioration. Repair implies that something has broken or is not working. A need for repair is often caused by lack of maintenance. Example: draining and refilling the automatic transmission fluid is maintenance recommended by the manufacturer at specific mileage intervals. Failure to do this can shorten the life of the transmission/transaxle, requiring very expensive repairs. While no maintenance program can prevent items from breaking or wearing out, a general rule can be stated: MAINTENANCE IS CHEAPER THAN REPAIR.

Two basic mechanic's rules should be mentioned here. First, whenever the left side of the vehicle or engine is referred to, it is meant to specify the driver's side. Conversely, the right side of the vehicle means the passenger's side. Second, screws and bolts are removed by turning counterclockwise, and tightened by turning clockwise unless specifically noted.

Safety is always the most important rule. Constantly be aware of the dangers involved in working on an automobile and take the proper precautions. See the information in this section regarding SERVICING YOUR VEHICLE SAFELY and the SAFETY NOTICE on the acknowledgment page.

Avoiding the Most Common Mistakes

Pay attention to the instructions provided. There are 3 common mistakes in mechanical work:

1. Incorrect order of assembly, disassembly or adjustment. When taking something apart or putting it together, performing steps in the wrong order usually just costs you extra time; however, it CAN break something. Read the entire procedure before beginning disassembly. Perform everything in the order in which the instructions say you should, even if you can't immediately see a reason for it. When you're taking apart something that is very intricate, you might want to draw a picture of how it looks when assembled at one point in order to make sure you get everything back in its proper position. We will supply exploded views whenever possible. When making adjustments, perform them in the proper order. One adjustment possibly will affect another.

2. Overtorquing (or undertorquing). While it is more common for overtorquing to cause damage, undertorquing may allow a fastener to vibrate loose causing serious damage. Especially when dealing with aluminum parts, pay attention to torque specifications and utilize a torque wrench in assembly. If a torque figure is not available, remember that if you are using the right tool to perform the job, you will probably not have to strain yourself to get a fastener tight enough. The pitch of most threads is so slight that the tension you put on the wrench will be multiplied many times in actual force on what you are tightening. A good example of how critical torque is can be seen in the case of spark plug installation, especially where you are putting the plug into an aluminum cylinder head. Too little torque can fail to crush the gasket, causing leakage of combustion gases and consequent overheating of the plug and engine parts. Too much torque can damage the threads or distort the plug, changing the spark gap.

There are many commercial products available for ensuring that fasteners won't come loose, even if they are not torqued just right (a very common brand is Loctite®. If you're worried about getting something together tight enough to hold, but loose enough to avoid mechanical damage during assembly, one of these products might offer substantial insurance. Before choosing a threadlocking compound, read the label on the package and make sure the product is compatible with the materials, fluids, etc. involved.

3. Crossthreading. This occurs when a part such as a bolt is screwed into a nut or casting at the wrong angle and forced. Crossthreading is more likely to occur if access is difficult. It helps to clean and lubricate fasteners, then to start threading the bolt, spark plug, etc. with your fingers. If you encounter resistance, unscrew the part and start over again at a different angle until it can be inserted and turned several times without much effort. Keep in mind that many parts, especially spark plugs, have tapered threads, so that gentle turning will automatically bring the part you're threading to the proper angle. Don't put a wrench on the part until it's been tightened a couple of turns by hand. If you suddenly encounter resistance, and the part has not seated fully, don't force it. Pull it back out to make sure it's clean and threading properly.

Be sure to take your time and be patient, and always plan ahead. Allow yourself ample time to perform repairs and maintenance. You may find maintaining your car a satisfying and enjoyable experience.

TOOLS AND EQUIPMENT

♦ **See Figures 1 thru 15**

Naturally, without the proper tools and equipment it is impossible to properly service your vehicle. It would also be virtually impossible to catalog every tool that you would need to perform all of the operations in this book. Of course, It would be unwise for the amateur to rush out and buy an expensive set of tools on the theory that he/she may need one or more of them at some time.

The best approach is to proceed slowly, gathering a good quality set of those tools that are used most frequently. Don't be misled by the low cost of bargain tools. It is far better to spend a little more for better quality. Forged wrenches, 6 or 12-point sockets and fine tooth ratchets are by far preferable to their less expensive counterparts. As any good mechanic can tell you, there are few worse experiences than trying to work on a vehicle with bad tools. Your monetary savings will be far outweighed by frustration and mangled knuckles.

Begin accumulating those tools that are used most frequently: those associated with routine maintenance and tune-up. In addition to the normal assortment of screwdrivers and pliers, you should have the following tools:
- Wrenches/sockets and combination open end/box end wrenches in sizes from ⅛ –¾ in. or 3–19mm, as well as a ¹³⁄₁₆ in. or ⅝ in. spark plug socket (depending on plug type).

➡**If possible, buy various length socket drive extensions. Universal-joint and wobble extensions can be extremely useful, but be careful when using them, as they can change the amount of torque applied to the socket.**

- Jackstands for support.
- Oil filter wrench.
- Spout or funnel for pouring fluids.

Fig. 1 All but the most basic procedures will require an assortment of ratchets and sockets

Fig. 2 In addition to ratchets, a good set of wrenches and hex keys will be necessary

Fig. 3 A hydraulic floor jack and a set of jackstands are essential for lifting and supporting the vehicle

Fig. 4 An assortment of pliers, grippers and cutters will be handy for old rusted parts and stripped bolt heads

Fig. 5 Various drivers, chisels and prybars are great tools to have in your toolbox

Fig. 6 Many repairs will require the use of a torque wrench to assure the components are properly fastened

Fig. 7 Although not always necessary, using specialized brake tools will save time

Fig. 8 A few inexpensive lubrication tools will make maintenance easier

Fig. 9 Various pullers, clamps and separator tools are needed for many larger, more complicated repairs

Fig. 10 A variety of tools and gauges should be used for spark plug gapping and installation

Fig. 11 Inductive type timing light

Fig. 12 A screw-in type compression gauge is recommended for compression testing

Fig. 13 A vacuum/pressure tester is necessary for many testing procedures

Fig. 14 Most modern automotive multimeters incorporate many helpful features

Fig. 15 Proper information is vital, so always have a Chilton Total Car Care manual handy

• Grease gun for chassis lubrication (unless your vehicle is not equipped with any grease fittings—for details, please refer to information on Fluids and Lubricants, later in this section).

• Hydrometer for checking the battery (unless equipped with a sealed, maintenance-free battery).

• A container for draining oil and other fluids.

• Rags for wiping up the inevitable mess.

In addition to the above items there are several others that are not absolutely necessary, but handy to have around. These include Oil Dry® (or an equivalent oil absorbent gravel—such as cat litter) and the usual supply of lubricants, antifreeze and fluids, although these can be purchased as needed. This is a basic list for routine maintenance, but only your personal needs and desire can accurately determine your list of tools.

After performing a few projects on the vehicle, you'll be amazed at the other tools and non-tools on your workbench. Some useful household items are: a large turkey baster or siphon, empty coffee cans and ice trays (to store parts), ball of twine, electrical tape for wiring, small rolls of colored tape for tagging lines or hoses, markers and pens, a note pad, golf tees (for plugging vacuum lines), metal coat hangers or a roll of mechanic's wire (to hold things out of the way), dental pick or similar long, pointed probe, a strong magnet, and a small mirror (to see into recesses and under manifolds).

A more advanced set of tools, suitable for tune-up work, can be drawn up easily. While the tools are slightly more sophisticated, they need not be outrageously expensive. There are several inexpensive tach/dwell meters on the market that are every bit as good for the average mechanic as a professional model. Just be sure that it goes to a least 1200–1500 rpm on the tach scale and that it works on 4, 6 and 8-cylinder engines. The key to these purchases is to make them with an eye towards adaptability and wide range. A basic list of tune-up tools could include:

• Tach/dwell meter.
• Spark plug wrench and gapping tool.
• Feeler gauges for valve adjustment.
• Timing light.

The choice of a timing light should be made carefully. A light which works on the DC current supplied by the vehicle's battery is the best choice; it should have a xenon tube for brightness. On any vehicle with an electronic ignition system, a timing light with an inductive pickup that clamps around the No. 1 spark plug cable is preferred.

In addition to these basic tools, there are several other tools and gauges you may find useful. These include:

• Compression gauge. The screw-in type is slower to use, but eliminates the possibility of a faulty reading due to escaping pressure.
• Manifold vacuum gauge.
• 12V test light.
• A combination volt/ohmmeter
• Induction Ammeter. This is used for determining whether or not there is current in a wire. These are handy for use if a wire is broken somewhere in a wiring harness.

As a final note, you will probably find a torque wrench necessary for all but the most basic work. The beam type models are perfectly adequate, although the newer click types (breakaway) are easier to use. The click type torque wrenches tend to be more expensive. Also keep in mind that all types of torque wrenches should be periodically checked and/or recalibrated. You will have to decide for yourself which better fits your pocketbook, and purpose.

Special Tools

Normally, the use of special factory tools is avoided for repair procedures, since these are not readily available for the do-it-yourself mechanic. When it is possible to perform the job with more commonly available tools, it will be pointed out, but occasionally, a special tool was designed to perform a specific function and should be used. Before substituting another tool, you should be convinced that neither your safety nor the performance of the vehicle will be compromised.

Special tools can usually be purchased from an automotive parts store or from your dealer. In some cases special tools may be available directly from the tool manufacturer.

DIAGNOSTIC TEST EQUIPMENT

Digital multimeters come in a variety of styles and are a "must-have" for any serious home mechanic. Digital multimeters measure voltage (volts), resistance (ohms) and sometimes current (amperes). These versatile tools are used for checking all types of electrical or electronic components

Modern vehicles equipped with computer-controlled fuel, emission and ignition systems require modern electronic tools to diagnose problems. Many of these tools are designed solely for the professional mechanic and are too costly and difficult to use for the average do-it-yourselfer. However, various automotive aftermarket companies have introduced products that address the needs of the average home mechanic, providing sophisticated information at affordable cost. Consult your local auto parts store to determine what is available for your vehicle.

Sensor testers perform specific checks on many of the sensors and actuators used on today's computer-controlled vehicles. These testers can check sensors both on or off the vehicle, as well as test the accompanying electrical circuits

Trouble code tools allow the home mechanic to extract the "fault code" number from an on-board computer that has sensed a problem (usually indicated by a Check Engine light). Armed with this code, the home mechanic can focus attention on a suspect system or component

Hand-held scanners represent the most sophisticated of all do-it-yourself diagnostic tools. These tools do more than just access computer codes like the code readers above; they provide the user with an actual interface into the vehicle's computer. Comprehensive data on specific makes and models will come with the tool, either built-in or as a separate cartridge

SERVICING YOUR VEHICLE SAFELY

▶ **See Figures 16, 17, 18 and 19**

It is virtually impossible to anticipate all of the hazards involved with automotive maintenance and service, but care and common sense will prevent most accidents.

The rules of safety for mechanics range from "don't smoke around gasoline," to "use the proper tool(s) for the job." The trick to avoiding injuries is to develop safe work habits and to take every possible precaution.

Do's

- Do keep a fire extinguisher and first aid kit handy.
- Do wear safety glasses or goggles when cutting, drilling, grinding or prying, even if you have 20–20 vision. If you wear glasses for the sake of vision, wear safety goggles over your regular glasses.
- Do shield your eyes whenever you work around the battery. Batteries contain sulfuric acid. In case of contact with the eyes or skin, flush the area with water or a mixture of water and baking soda, then seek immediate medical attention.
- Do use safety stands (jackstands) for any undervehicle service. Jacks are for raising vehicles; jackstands are for making sure the vehicle stays raised until you want it to come down. Whenever the vehicle is raised, block the wheels remaining on the ground and set the parking brake.
- Do use adequate ventilation when working with any chemicals or hazardous materials. Like carbon monoxide, the asbestos dust resulting from some brake lining wear can be hazardous in sufficient quantities.
- Do disconnect the negative battery cable when working on the electrical system. The secondary ignition system contains EXTREMELY HIGH VOLTAGE. In some cases it can even exceed 50,000 volts.
- Do follow manufacturer's directions whenever working with potentially hazardous materials. Most chemicals and fluids are poisonous if taken internally.
- Do properly maintain your tools. Loose hammerheads, mushroomed punches and chisels, frayed or poorly grounded electrical cords, excessively worn screwdrivers, spread wrenches (open end), cracked sockets, slipping ratchets, or faulty droplight sockets can cause accidents.
- Likewise, keep your tools clean; a greasy wrench can slip off a bolt head, ruining the bolt and often harming your knuckles in the process.
- Do use the proper size and type of tool for the job at hand. Do select a wrench or socket that fits the nut or bolt. The wrench or socket should sit straight, not cocked.
- Do, when possible, pull on a wrench handle rather than push on it, and adjust your stance to prevent a fall.
- Do be sure that adjustable wrenches are tightly closed on the nut or bolt and pulled so that the force is on the side of the fixed jaw.
- Do strike squarely with a hammer; avoid glancing blows.
- Do set the parking brake and block the drive wheels if the work requires a running engine.

Don'ts

- Don't run the engine in a garage or anywhere else without proper ventilation—EVER! Carbon monoxide is poisonous; it takes a long time to leave the human body and you can build up a deadly supply of it in your system by simply breathing in a little every day. You may not realize you are slowly poisoning yourself. Always use power vents, windows, fans and/or open the garage door.
- Don't work around moving parts while wearing loose clothing. Short sleeves are much safer than long, loose sleeves. Hard-toed shoes with neoprene soles protect your toes and give a better grip on slippery surfaces. Jewelry such as watches, fancy belt buckles, beads or body adornment of any kind is not safe working around a vehicle. Long hair should be tied back under a hat or cap.
- Don't use pockets for toolboxes. A fall or bump can drive a screwdriver deep into your body. Even a rag hanging from your back pocket can wrap around a spinning shaft or fan.
- Don't smoke when working around gasoline, cleaning solvent or other flammable material.
- Don't smoke when working around the battery. When the battery is being charged, it gives off explosive hydrogen gas.
- Don't use gasoline to wash your hands; there are excellent soaps available. Gasoline contains dangerous additives which can enter the body through a cut or through your pores. Gasoline also removes all the natural oils from the skin so that bone dry hands will suck up oil and grease.
- Don't service the air conditioning system unless you are equipped with the necessary tools and training. When liquid or compressed gas refrigerant is released to atmospheric pressure it will absorb heat from whatever it contacts. This will chill or freeze anything it touches.
- Don't use screwdrivers for anything other than driving screws! A screwdriver used as an prying tool can snap when you least expect it, causing injuries. At the very least, you'll ruin a good screwdriver.
- Don't use an emergency jack (that little ratchet, scissors, or pantograph jack supplied with the vehicle) for anything other than changing a flat! These jacks are only intended for emergency use out on the road; they are NOT designed as a maintenance tool. If you are serious about maintaining your vehicle yourself, invest in a hydraulic floor jack of at least a 1½ ton capacity, and at least two sturdy jackstands.

TCCS1020

Fig. 16 Screwdrivers should be kept in good condition to prevent injury or damage which could result if the blade slips from the screw

TCCS1021

Fig. 17 Power tools should always be properly grounded

TCCS1022

Fig. 18 Using the correct size wrench will help prevent the possibility of rounding off a nut

TCCS1023

Fig. 19 NEVER work under a vehicle unless it is supported using safety stands (jackstands)

FASTENERS, MEASUREMENTS AND CONVERSIONS

Bolts, Nuts and Other Threaded Retainers

▶ **See Figures 20, 21, 22 and 23**

Although there are a great variety of fasteners found in the modern car or truck, the most commonly used retainer is the threaded fastener (nuts, bolts, screws, studs, etc.). Most threaded retainers may be reused, provided that they are not damaged in use or during the repair. Some retainers (such as stretch bolts or torque prevailing nuts) are designed to deform when tightened or in use and should not be reinstalled.

Whenever possible, we will note any special retainers which should be replaced during a procedure. But you should always inspect the condition of a retainer when it is removed and replace any that show signs of damage. Check all threads for rust or corrosion which can increase the torque necessary to achieve the desired clamp load for which that fastener was originally selected. Additionally, be sure that the driver surface of the fastener has not been compromised by rounding or other damage. In some cases a driver surface may become only partially rounded, allowing the driver to catch in only one direction. In many of these occurrences, a fastener may be installed and tightened, but the driver would not be able to grip and loosen the fastener again. (This could lead to frustration down the line should that component ever need to be disassembled again.)

If you must replace a fastener, whether due to design or damage, you must ALWAYS be sure to use the proper replacement. In all cases, a retainer of the same design, material and strength should be used. Markings on the heads of most bolts will help determine the proper strength of the fastener. The same material, thread and pitch must be selected to assure proper installation and safe operation of the vehicle afterwards.

Fig. 20 Here are a few of the most common screw/bolt driver styles

POZIDRIVE PHILLIPS RECESS TORX® CLUTCH RECESS

INDENTED HEXAGON HEXAGON TRIMMED HEXAGON WASHER HEAD

TCCS1037

BOLTS
GRADE 0 GRADE 2 GRADE 5 GRADE 6 GRADE 7 GRADE 8 ALLEN CARRIAGE

NUTS
PLAIN JAM CASTLE (CASTELLATED) SELF-LOCKING SPEED

SCREWS
ROUND PAN FILLISTER HEXAGON SHEET METAL

LOCKWASHERS
INTERNAL TOOTH EXTERNAL TOOTH SPLIT PLAIN

STUD

TCCS1036

Fig. 21 There are many different types of threaded retainers found on vehicles

A - Length
B - Diameter (major diameter)
C - Threads per inch or mm
D - Thread length
E - Size of the wrench required
F - Root diameter (minor diameter)

TCCS1038

Fig. 22 Threaded retainer sizes are determined using these measurements

T - INTERNAL DRIVE
E - EXTERNAL

TCCS1016

Fig. 23 Special fasteners such as these Torx® head bolts are used by manufacturers to discourage people from working on vehicles without the proper tools

Thread gauges are available to help measure a bolt or stud's thread. Most automotive and hardware stores keep gauges available to help you select the proper size. In a pinch, you can use another nut or bolt for a thread gauge. If the bolt you are replacing is not too badly damaged, you can select a match by finding another bolt which will thread in its place. If you find a nut which threads properly onto the damaged bolt, then use that nut to help select the replacement bolt. If however, the bolt you are replacing is so badly damaged (broken or drilled out) that its threads cannot be used as a gauge, you might start by looking for another bolt (from the same assembly or a similar location on your vehicle) which will thread into the damaged bolt's mounting. If so, the other bolt can be used to select a nut; the nut can then be used to select the replacement bolt.

In all cases, be absolutely sure you have selected the proper replacement. Don't be shy, you can always ask the store clerk for help.

✳✳ WARNING

Be aware that when you find a bolt with damaged threads, you may also find the nut or drilled hole it was threaded into has also been damaged. If this is the case, you may have to drill and tap the hole, replace the nut or otherwise repair the threads. NEVER try to force a replacement bolt to fit into the damaged threads.

Torque

Torque is defined as the measurement of resistance to turning or rotating. It tends to twist a body about an axis of rotation. A common example of this would be tightening a threaded retainer such as a nut, bolt or screw. Measuring torque is one of the most common ways to help assure that a threaded retainer has been properly fastened.

When tightening a threaded fastener, torque is applied in three distinct areas, the head, the bearing surface and the clamp load. About 50 percent of the measured torque is used in overcoming bearing friction. This is the friction between the bearing surface of the bolt head, screw head or nut face and the base material or washer (the surface on which the fastener is rotating). Approximately 40 percent of the applied torque is used in overcoming thread friction. This leaves only about 10 percent of the applied torque to develop a useful clamp load (the force which holds a joint together). This means that friction can account for as much as 90 percent of the applied torque on a fastener.

TORQUE WRENCHES

▶ **See Figures 24, 25 and 26**

In most applications, a torque wrench can be used to assure proper installation of a fastener. Torque wrenches come in various designs and most automotive supply stores will carry a variety to suit your needs. A torque wrench should be used any time we supply a specific torque value for a fastener. A torque wrench can also be used if you are following the general guidelines in the

TCCS1015

Fig. 24 Various styles of torque wrenches are usually available at your local automotive supply store

	Mark	Class		Mark	Class
Hexagon head bolt	Bolt head No. 4— 5— 6— 7— 8— 9— 10— 11—	4T 5T 6T 7T 8T 9T 10T 11T	Stud bolt	No mark	4T
	No mark	4T			
Hexagon flange bolt w/ washer hexagon bolt	No mark	4T		Grooved	6T
Hexagon head bolt	Two protruding lines	5T			
Hexagon flange bolt w/ washer hexagon bolt	Two protruding lines	6T	Welded bolt		4T
Hexagon head bolt	Three protruding lines	7T			
Hexagon head bolt	Four protruding lines	8T			

TCCS1240

Fig. 25 Determining bolt strength of metric fasteners—NOTE: this is a typical bolt marking system, but there is not a worldwide standard

Class	Diameter mm	Pitch mm	Specified torque					
			Hexagon head bolt			Hexagon flange bolt		
			N·m	kgf·cm	ft·lbf	N·m	kgf·cm	ft·lbf
4T	6	1	5	55	48 in.·lbf	6	60	52 in.·lbf
	8	1.25	12.5	130	9	14	145	10
	10	1.25	26	260	19	29	290	21
	12	1.25	47	480	35	53	540	39
	14	1.5	74	760	55	84	850	61
	16	1.5	115	1,150	83	—	—	—
5T	6	1	6.5	65	56 in.·lbf	7.5	75	65 in.·lbf
	8	1.25	15.5	160	12	17.5	175	13
	10	1.25	32	330	24	36	360	26
	12	1.25	59	600	43	65	670	48
	14	1.5	91	930	67	100	1,050	76
	16	1.5	140	1,400	101	—	—	—
6T	6	1	8	80	69 in.·lbf	9	90	78 in.·lbf
	8	1.25	19	195	14	21	210	15
	10	1.25	39	400	29	44	440	32
	12	1.25	71	730	53	80	810	59
	14	1.5	110	1,100	80	125	1,250	90
	16	1.5	170	1,750	127	—	—	—
7T	6	1	10.5	110	8	12	120	9
	8	1.25	25	260	19	28	290	21
	10	1.25	52	530	38	58	590	43
	12	1.25	95	970	70	105	1,050	76
	14	1.5	145	1,500	108	165	1,700	123
	16	1.5	230	2,300	166	—	—	—
8T	8	1.25	29	300	22	33	330	24
	10	1.25	61	620	45	68	690	50
	12	1.25	110	1,100	80	120	1,250	90
9T	8	1.25	34	340	25	37	380	27
	10	1.25	70	710	51	78	790	57
	12	1.25	125	1,300	94	140	1,450	105
10T	8	1.25	38	390	28	42	430	31
	10	1.25	78	800	58	88	890	64
	12	1.25	140	1,450	105	155	1,600	116
11T	8	1.25	42	430	31	47	480	35
	10	1.25	87	890	64	97	990	72
	12	1.25	155	1,600	116	175	1,800	130

TCCS1241

Fig. 26 Typical bolt torques for metric fasteners—WARNING: use only as a guide

accompanying charts. Keep in mind that because there is no worldwide standardization of fasteners, the charts are a general guideline and should be used with caution. Again, the general rule of "if you are using the right tool for the job, you should not have to strain to tighten a fastener" applies here.

Beam Type

▶ See Figure 27

The beam type torque wrench is one of the most popular types. It consists of a pointer attached to the head that runs the length of the flexible beam (shaft) to a scale located near the handle. As the wrench is pulled, the beam bends and the pointer indicates the torque using the scale.

TCCS1039

Fig. 27 Example of a beam type torque wrench

Click (Breakaway) Type

▶ See Figure 28

Another popular design of torque wrench is the click type. To use the click type wrench you pre-adjust it to a torque setting. Once the torque is reached, the wrench has a reflex signaling feature that causes a momentary breakaway of the torque wrench body, sending an impulse to the operator's hand.

Pivot Head Type

▶ See Figures 28 and 29

Some torque wrenches (usually of the click type) may be equipped with a pivot head which can allow it to be used in areas of limited access. BUT, it must be used properly. To hold a pivot head wrench, grasp the handle lightly, and as you pull on the handle, it should be floated on the pivot point. If the handle comes in contact with the yoke extension during the process of pulling, there is a very good chance the torque readings will be inaccurate because this could alter the wrench loading point. The design of the handle is usually such as to make it inconvenient to deliberately misuse the wrench.

➡ It should be mentioned that the use of any U-joint, wobble or extension will have an effect on the torque readings, no matter what type of wrench you are using. For the most accurate readings, install the socket directly on the wrench driver. If necessary, straight extensions (which hold a socket directly under the wrench driver) will have the least effect on the torque reading. Avoid any extension that alters the length of the wrench from the handle to the head/driving point (such as a crow's foot). U-joint or wobble extensions can greatly affect the readings; avoid their use at all times.

Fig. 28 A click type or breakaway torque wrench—note that this one has a pivoting head

Rigid Case (Direct Reading)

▶ See Figure 30

A rigid case or direct reading torque wrench is equipped with a dial indicator to show torque values. One advantage of these wrenches is that they can be held at any position on the wrench without affecting accuracy. These wrenches are often preferred because they tend to be compact, easy to read and have a great degree of accuracy.

TORQUE ANGLE METERS

▶ See Figure 31

Because the frictional characteristics of each fastener or threaded hole will vary, clamp loads which are based strictly on torque will vary as well. In most applications, this variance is not significant enough to cause worry. But, in certain applications, a manufacturer's engineers may determine that more precise clamp loads are necessary (such is the case with many aluminum cylinder heads). In these cases, a torque angle method of installation would be specified. When installing fasteners which are torque angle tightened, a predetermined seating torque and standard torque wrench are usually used first to remove any compliance from the joint. The fastener is then tightened the specified additional portion of a turn measured in degrees. A torque angle gauge (mechanical protractor) is used for these applications.

Standard and Metric Measurements

▶ See Figure 32

Throughout this manual, specifications are given to help you determine the condition of various components on your vehicle, or to assist you in their installation. Some of the most common measurements include length (in. or cm/mm), torque (ft. lbs., inch lbs. or Nm) and pressure (psi, in. Hg, kPa or mm Hg). In most cases, we strive to provide the proper measurement as determined by the manufacturer's engineers.

Though, in some cases, that value may not be conveniently measured with what is available in your toolbox. Luckily, many of the measuring devices which are available today will have two scales so the Standard or Metric measurements may easily be taken. If any of the various measuring tools which are available to you do not contain the same scale as listed in the specifications, use the accompanying conversion factors to determine the proper value.

The conversion factor chart is used by taking the given specification and multiplying it by the necessary conversion factor. For instance, looking at the first line, if you have a measurement in inches such as "free-play should be 2 in." but your ruler reads only in millimeters, multiply 2 in. by the conversion factor of 25.4 to get the metric equivalent of 50.8mm. Likewise, if the specification was given only in a Metric measurement, for example in Newton Meters (Nm), then look at the center column first. If the measurement is 100 Nm, multiply it by the conversion factor of 0.738 to get 73.8 ft. lbs.

Fig. 30 The rigid case (direct reading) torque wrench uses a dial indicator to show torque

Fig. 31 Some specifications require the use of a torque angle meter (mechanical protractor)

Fig. 29 Torque wrenches with pivoting heads must be grasped and used properly to prevent an incorrect reading

CONVERSION FACTORS

LENGTH–DISTANCE

Inches (in.)	x 25.4	= Millimeters (mm)	x .0394	= Inches
Feet (ft.)	x .305	= Meters (m)	x 3.281	= Feet
Miles	x 1.609	= Kilometers (km)	x .0621	= Miles

VOLUME

Cubic Inches (in3)	x 16.387	= Cubic Centimeters	x .061	= in3
IMP Pints (IMP pt.)	x .568	= Liters (L)	x 1.76	= IMP pt.
IMP Quarts (IMP qt.)	x 1.137	= Liters (L)	x .88	= IMP qt.
IMP Gallons (IMP gal.)	x 4.546	= Liters (L)	x .22	= IMP gal.
IMP Quarts (IMP qt.)	x 1.201	= US Quarts (US qt.)	x .833	= IMP qt.
IMP Gallons (IMP gal.)	x 1.201	= US Gallons (US gal.)	x .833	= IMP gal.
Fl. Ounces	x 29.573	= Milliliters	x .034	= Ounces
US Pints (US pt.)	x .473	= Liters (L)	x 2.113	= Pints
US Quarts (US qt.)	x .946	= Liters (L)	x 1.057	= Quarts
US Gallons (US gal.)	x 3.785	= Liters (L)	x .264	= Gallons

MASS–WEIGHT

Ounces (oz.)	x 28.35	= Grams (g)	x .035	= Ounces
Pounds (lb.)	x .454	= Kilograms (kg)	x 2.205	= Pounds

PRESSURE

Pounds Per Sq. In. (psi)	x 6.895	= Kilopascals (kPa)	x .145	= psi
Inches of Mercury (Hg)	x .4912	= psi	x 2.036	= Hg
Inches of Mercury (Hg)	x 3.377	= Kilopascals (kPa)	x .2961	= Hg
Inches of Water (H_2O)	x .07355	= Inches of Mercury	x 13.783	= H_2O
Inches of Water (H_2O)	x .03613	= psi	x 27.684	= H_2O
Inches of Water (H_2O)	x .248	= Kilopascals (kPa)	x 4.026	= H_2O

TORQUE

Pounds–Force Inches (in–lb)	x .113	= Newton Meters (N·m)	x 8.85	= in–lb
Pounds–Force Feet (ft–lb)	x 1.356	= Newton Meters (N·m)	x .738	= ft–lb

VELOCITY

Miles Per Hour (MPH)	x 1.609	= Kilometers Per Hour (KPH)	x .621	= MPH

POWER

Horsepower (Hp)	x .745	= Kilowatts	x 1.34	= Horsepower

FUEL CONSUMPTION*

Miles Per Gallon IMP (MPG)	x .354	= Kilometers Per Liter (Km/L)
Kilometers Per Liter (Km/L)	x 2.352	= IMP MPG
Miles Per Gallon US (MPG)	x .425	= Kilometers Per Liter (Km/L)
Kilometers Per Liter (Km/L)	x 2.352	= US MPG

*It is common to covert from miles per gallon (mpg) to liters/100 kilometers (1/100 km), where mpg (IMP) x 1/100 km = 282 and mpg (US) x 1/100 km = 235.

TEMPERATURE

Degree Fahrenheit (°F)	= (°C x 1.8) + 32
Degree Celsius (°C)	= (°F – 32) x .56

TCCS1044

Fig. 32 Standard and metric conversion factors chart

SERIAL NUMBER IDENTIFICATION

Vehicle

♦ See Figures 33 and 34

The Vehicle Identification Number (VIN) is a seventeen digit sequence stamped on a plate attached to the left front of the instrument panel, visible through the windshield.

Engine

♦ See Figures 35 thru 43

Engine identification can take place using various methods. The VIN, described earlier in this section, contains a code identifying the engine which was originally installed in the vehicle. In most cases, this should be sufficient

87951100

Fig. 33 The VIN plate is visible through the windshield

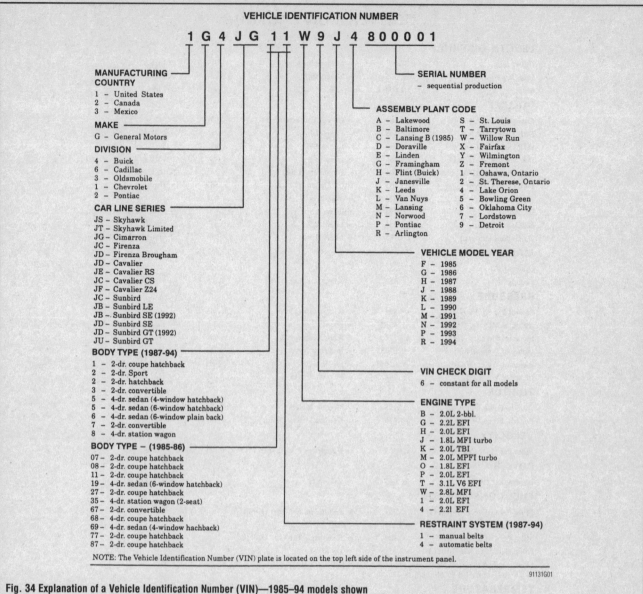

VEHICLE IDENTIFICATION NUMBER

1 G 4 J G 11 W 9 J 4 800001

MANUFACTURING COUNTRY
1 – United States
2 – Canada
3 – Mexico

MAKE
G – General Motors

DIVISION
4 – Buick
6 – Cadillac
3 – Oldsmobile
1 – Chevrolet
2 – Pontiac

CAR LINE SERIES
JS – Skyhawk
JT – Skyhawk Limited
JG – Cimarron
JC – Firenza
JD – Firenza Brougham
JD – Cavalier
JE – Cavalier RS
JC – Cavalier CS
JF – Cavalier Z24
JC – Sunbird
JB – Sunbird LE
JB – Sunbird SE (1992)
JD – Sunbird SE
JD – Sunbird GT (1992)
JU – Sunbird GT

BODY TYPE (1987-94)
1 – 2-dr. coupe hatchback
2 – 2-dr. Sport
2 – 2-dr. hatchback
3 – 2-dr. convertible
5 – 4-dr. sedan (4-window hatchback)
5 – 4-dr. sedan (6-window hatchback)
6 – 4-dr. sedan (6-window plain back)
7 – 2-dr. convertible
8 – 4-dr. station wagon

BODY TYPE – (1985-86)
07 – 2-dr. coupe hatchback
08 – 2-dr. coupe hatchback
11 – 2-dr. coupe hatchback
19 – 4-dr. sedan (6-window hatchback)
27 – 2-dr. coupe hatchback
35 – 4-dr. station wagon (2-seat)
67 – 2-dr. convertible
68 – 4-dr. coupe hatchback
69 – 4-dr. sedan (4-window hachback)
77 – 2-dr. coupe hatchback
87 – 2-dr. coupe hatchback

SERIAL NUMBER
– sequential production

ASSEMBLY PLANT CODE
A – Lakewood   S – St. Louis
B – Baltimore   T – Tarrytown
C – Lansing B (1985) W – Willow Run
D – Doraville   X – Fairfax
E – Linden   Y – Wilmington
G – Framingham   Z – Fremont
H – Flint (Buick)   1 – Oshawa, Ontario
J – Janesville   2 – St. Therese, Ontario
K – Leeds   4 – Lake Orion
L – Van Nuys   5 – Bowling Green
M – Lansing   6 – Oklahoma City
N – Norwood   7 – Lordstown
P – Pontiac   9 – Detroit
R – Arlington

VEHICLE MODEL YEAR
F – 1985
G – 1986
H – 1987
J – 1988
K – 1989
L – 1990
M – 1991
N – 1992
P – 1993
R – 1994

VIN CHECK DIGIT
6 – constant for all models

ENGINE TYPE
B – 2.0L 2-bbl.
G – 2.2L EFI
H – 2.0L EFI
J – 1.8L MFI turbo
K – 2.0L TBI
M – 2.0L MPFI turbo
O – 1.8L EFI
P – 2.0L EFI
T – 3.1L V6 EFI
W – 2.8L MFI
1 – 2.0L EFI
4 – 2.2l EFI

RESTRAINT SYSTEM (1987-94)
1 – manual belts
4 – automatic belts

NOTE: The Vehicle Identification Number (VIN) plate is located on the top left side of the instrument panel.

91131G01

Fig. 34 Explanation of a Vehicle Identification Number (VIN)—1985–94 models shown

VEHICLE IDENTIFICATION CHART

Engine Code						Model Year	
Code	Liters	Cu. In. (cc)	Cyl.	Fuel Sys.	Eng. Mfg.	Code	Year
G (1982)	1.8	110 (1819)	4	2bbl	Chevrolet	C	1982
O	1.8	110 (1819)	4	TBI	Pontiac	D	1983
J	1.8	110 (1819)	4	MFI-Turbo	Pontiac	E	1984
B	2.0	121 (2000)	4	①	Chevrolet	F	1985
P	2.0	121 (2000)	4	TBI	Chevrolet	G	1986
1	2.0	121 (2000)	4	TFI	Chevrolet	H	1987
K	2.0	121 (2000)	4	TFI	GM-Brazil	J	1988
M	2.0	121 (2000)	4	MFI-Turbo	GM-Brazil	K	1989
H	2.0	121 (2000)	4	MFI	GM-Brazil	L	1990
G (1990-91)	2.2	134 (2180)	4	TBI	Chevrolet	M	1991
4	2.2	134 (2180)	4	TBI	Chevrolet	N	1992
W	2.8	173 (2835)	6	MFI	Chevrolet	P	1993
T	3.1	192 (3146)	6	MFI	Chevrolet	R	1994

NOTE: Some 1983-85 Canadian models with the 2.0L engine use a 2 bbl carburetor

① 1982: 2 bbl carburetor
1983 and later: TBI

2bbl: 2 barrel carburetor
TBI: Throttle Body fuel Injection
MFI: Multi-port Fuel Injection
BOC: Buick/Oldsmobile/Cadillac

91131C01

Fig. 35 The engine identification number is stamped on top of the water pump housing for the 1982 1.8L and 2.0L OHV engines

Fig. 36 For the 1.8L (VIN J), the identification number is stamped on the engine front cover

Fig. 37 The engine identification tag is located on the oil pan for the 2.0L (VIN P) engine

Fig. 38 2.0L (VIN K and M) engine identification tag location

Fig. 39 Engine code label and partial VIN location—2.0L (VIN H) engine

Fig. 40 2.2L engine date code and partial VIN location

Fig. 41 Location of the 2.8L engine identification number—1986 vehicle shown

Fig. 42 Engine date code and partial VIN location—3.1L engine

Fig. 43 3.1L engine identification tag locations

ENGINE IDENTIFICATION

Year	Model	Engine Displacement Liters (cc)	Engine Series (ID/VIN)	Fuel System	No. of Cylinders	Engine Type
1982	Cavalier	1.8L (1819)	G	2bbl	4	OHV
	2000/Sunbird	1.8L (1819)	G	2bbl	4	SOHC
	2000/Sunbird	1.8L (1819)	O	TBI	4	SOHC
	Skyhawk	1.8L (1819)	G	2bbl	4	SOHC
	Skyhawk	1.8L (1819)	O	TBI	4	SOHC
	Firenza	1.8L (1819)	G	2 bbl	4	OHV
	Firenza	1.8L (1819)	G	2 bbl	4	OHV
	Cimarron	2.0L (1998)	B	2 bbl	4	OHV
1983	Cavalier	2.0L (1998)	B	2bbl	4	OHV
	Cavalier	2.0L (1998)	P	TBI	4	OHV
	2000/Sunbird	1.8L (1819)	O	TBI	4	SOHC
	2000/Sunbird	2.0L (1998)	B	2bbl	4	OHV
	2000/Sunbird	2.0L (1998)	P	TBI	4	OHV
	Skyhawk	1.8L (1819)	O	TBI	4	SOHC
	Skyhawk	2.0L (1998)	B	2bbl	4	OHV
	Skyhawk	2.0L (1998)	P	TBI	4	OHV
	Firenza	1.8L (1819)	O	TBI	4	SOHC
	Firenza	2.0L (1998)	B	2bbl	4	OHV
	Firenza	2.0L (1998)	P	TBI	4	OHV
	Cimarron	2.0L (1998)	B	TBI	4	OHV
1984	Cavalier	2.0L (1998)	B	TBI	4	OHV
	Cavalier	2.0L (1998)	P	TBI	4	OHV
	2000/Sunbird	1.8L (1819)	O	TBI	4	SOHC
	2000/Sunbird	1.8L (1819)	J	MFI-Turbo	4	SOHC
	2000/Sunbird	2.0L (1998)	B	2bbl	4	OHV
	2000/Sunbird	2.0L (1998)	P	TBI	4	OHV
	Skyhawk	1.8L (1819)	O	TBI	4	SOHC
	Skyhawk	1.8L (1819)	J	MFI-Turbo	4	SOHC
	Skyhawk	2.0L (1998)	B	2bbl	4	OHV
	Skyhawk	2.0L (1998)	P	TBI	4	OHV
	Firenza	1.8L (1819)	O	TBI	4	SOHC
	Firenza	2.0L (1998)	B	2bbl	4	OHV
	Firenza	2.0L (1998)	P	TBI	4	OHV
	Cimarron	2.0L (1998)	P	TBI	4	OHV
1985	Cavalier	2.0L (2000)	P	TBI	4	OHV
	Cavalier	2.8L (2835)	W	MFI	6	OHV
	Sunbird	1.8L (1819)	O	TBI	4	SOHC
	Sunbird	1.8L (1819)	J	MFI-Turbo	4	SOHC
	Skyhawk	1.8L (1819)	O	TBI	4	SOHC
	Skyhawk	1.8L (1819)	J	MFI-Turbo	4	SOHC
	Skyhawk	2.0L (2000)	P	TBI	4	OHV
	Firenza	1.8L (1819)	O	TBI	4	SOHC
	Firenza	2.0L (2000)	P	TBI	4	OHV
	Firenza	2.8L (2835)	W	MFI	6	OHV
	Cimarron	2.0L (1998)	P	TBI	4	OHV
	Cimarron	2.8L (2875)	W	MFI	6	OHV

91131C02

ENGINE IDENTIFICATION

Year	Model	Engine Displacement Liters (cc)	Engine Series (ID/VIN)	Fuel System	No. of Cylinders	Engine Type
1986	Cavalier	2.0L (2000)	P	TBI	4	OHV
	Cavalier	2.8L (2835)	W	MFI	6	OHV
	Sunbird	1.8L (1819)	O	TBI	4	SOHC
	Sunbird	1.8L (1819)	J	MFI-Turbo	4	SOHC
	Skyhawk	1.8L (1819)	O	TBI	4	SOHC
	Skyhawk	1.8L (1819)	J	MFI-Turbo	4	SOHC
	Skyhawk	2.0L (2000)	P	TBI	4	OHV
	Firenza	1.8L (1819)	O	TBI	4	SOHC
	Firenza	2.0L (2000)	P	TBI	4	OHV
	Firenza	2.8L (2835)	W	MFI	6	OHV
	Cimarron	2.0L (1998)	P	TBI	4	OHV
	Cimarron	2.8L (2875)	W	MFI	6	OHV
1987	Cavalier	2.0L (2000)	1	TBI	4	OHV
	Cavalier	2.8L (2835)	W	MFI	6	OHV
	Sunbird	2.0L (1998)	K	TBI	4	SOHC
	Sunbird	2.0L (1998)	M	MFI-Turbo	4	SOHC
	Skyhawk	2.0L (1983)	1	TBI	4	OHV
	Skyhawk	2.0L (1983)	K	TBI	4	SOHC
	Skyhawk	2.0L (1983)	M	MFI-Turbo	4	SOHC
	Firenza	2.0L (1983)	1	TBI	4	OHV
	Firenza	2.0L (1983)	K	MFI	4	SOHC
	Firenza	2.8L (2835)	W	MFI	6	OHV
	Cimarron	2.0L (2000)	1	TBI	4	OHV
	Cimarron	2.8L (2835)	W	MFI	6	OHV
1988	Cavalier	2.0L (2000)	1	TBI	4	OHV
	Cavalier	2.8L (2835)	W	MFI	6	OHV
	Sunbird	2.0L (1998)	K	MFI	4	SOHC
	Sunbird	2.0L (1998)	M	MFI-Turbo	4	SOHC
	Skyhawk	2.0L (1983)	K	TBI	4	SOHC
	Firenza	2.0L (1983)	1	TBI	4	OHV
	Firenza	2.0L (1983)	K	TBI	4	SOHC
	Cimarron	2.8L (2835)	W	MFI	6	OHV
1989	Cavalier	2.0L (2000)	1	TBI	4	OHV
	Cavalier	2.8L (2835)	W	MFI	6	OHV
	Sunbird	2.0L (1998)	K	MFI	4	SOHC
	Sunbird	2.0L (1998)	M	MFI-Turbo	4	SOHC
	Skyhawk	2.0L (1983)	K	TBI	4	SOHC
1990	Cavalier	2.0L (2000)	1	TBI	4	OHV
	Cavalier	2.2L (2180)	G	TBI	4	OHV
	Cavalier	3.1L (3130)	T	MFI	6	OHV
	Sunbird	2.0L (1998)	K	TBI	4	SOHC
	Sunbird	2.0L (1998)	M	MFI	4	SOHC
1991	Cavalier	2.2L (2180)	G	TBI	4	OHV
	Cavalier	3.1L (3130)	T	MFI	6	OHV
	Sunbird	2.0L (1998)	K	TBI	4	SOHC
	Sunbird	3.1L (3136)	T	MFI	6	OHV
1992	Cavalier	2.2L (2180)	4	TBI	4	OHV
	Cavalier	3.1L (3130)	T	MFI	6	OHV
	Sunbird	2.0L (1998)	H	TBI	4	SOHC
	Sunbird	3.1L (3136)	T	MFI	6	OHV

91131C03

ENGINE IDENTIFICATION

Year	Model	Engine Displacement Liters (cc)	Engine Series (ID/VIN)	Fuel System	No. of Cylinders	Engine Type
1993	Cavalier	2.2L (2180)	4	TBI	4	OHV
	Cavalier	3.1L (3130)	T	MFI	6	OHV
	Sunbird	2.0L (1998)	H	MFI	4	SOHC
	Sunbird	3.1L (3136)	T	MFI	6	OHV
1994	Cavalier	2.2L (2180)	4	TBI	4	OHV
	Cavalier	3.1L (3130)	T	MFI	6	OHV
	Sunbird	2.0L (1998)	H	MFI	4	SOHC
	Sunbird	3.1L (3136)	T	MFI	6	OHV

2 bbl: 2 barrel carburetor

TBI: Throttle Body fuel Injection

MFI: Multi-port Fuel Injection

OHV: Overhead valves

SOHC: Single Overhead Camshaft

91131C04

for determining the engine with which your car is currently equipped. But, some older vehicles may have had the engine replaced or changed by a previous owner. If this is the case, the first step in identification is to locate an engine serial number and code which is stamped on the block or located on adhesive labels that may be present on valve covers or other engine components.

Transaxle

The manual transaxle identification number is stamped on a pad on the forward side of the transaxle case, between the upper and middle transaxle-to-engine mounting bolts.

The automatic transaxle identification number is stamped on the oil flange pad to the right of the oil dipstick, at the rear of the transaxle. The automatic transaxle model code tag is on top of the case, next to the shift lever.

ROUTINE MAINTENANCE

♦ See Figures 44, 45 and 46

Proper maintenance and tune-up is the key to long and trouble-free vehicle life, and the work can yield its own rewards. Studies have shown that a properly tuned and maintained vehicle can achieve better gas mileage than an out-of-tune vehicle. As a conscientious owner and driver, set aside a Saturday morning, say once a month, to check or replace items which could cause major problems later. Keep your own personal log to jot down which services you performed, how much the parts cost you, the date, and the exact odometer reading at the time. Keep all receipts for such items as engine oil and filters, so that they may be referred to in case of related problems or to determine operating expenses. As a do-it-yourselfer, these receipts are the only proof you have that the required maintenance was performed. In the event of a warranty problem, these receipts will be invaluable.

The literature provided with your vehicle when it was originally delivered includes the factory recommended maintenance schedule. If you no longer have

3.1L V6 Engine *(CODE T)*
When you open the hood, you'll see:
1. Engine Coolant Surge Tank
2. Power Steering Fluid Reservoir
3. Automatic Transaxle Fluid Dipstick (if equipped)
4. Brake Fluid Reservoir
5. Hydraulic Clutch Fluid Reservoir (if equipped)
6. Battery
7. Windshield Washer Fluid Reservoir
8. Air Cleaner
9. Engine Oil Fill Cap
10. Engine Oil Dipstick

91131G03

Fig. 45 Underhood components locations—1994 Sunbird w/3.1L engine shown

3.1L V6 Engine *(CODE T)*
When you open the hood, you'll see:
1. Coolant Surge Tank
2. Power Steering Fluid Reservoir
3. Automatic Transaxle Fluid Dipstick (if equipped)
4. Brake Fluid Reservoir
5. Hydraulic Clutch Fluid Reservoir (if equipped)
6. Windshield Washer Fluid Reservoir
7. Battery
8. Air Cleaner
9. Engine Oil Fill Cap
10. Engine Oil Dipstick

91131G02

Fig. 44 Underhood components locations—1993 Cavalier w/3.1L engine shown

2.0L L4 Engine *(CODE H)*
When you open the hood, you'll see:
1. Engine Coolant Recovery Tank
2. Power Steering Fluid Reservoir
3. Automatic Transaxle Fluid Dipstick (if equipped)
4. Brake Fluid Reservoir
5. Hydraulic Clutch Fluid Reservoir (if equipped)
6. Windshield Washer Fluid Reservoir
7. Battery
8. Air Cleaner
9. Engine Oil Dipstick
10. Engine Oil Fill Cap
11. Radiator Pressure Cap

91131G04

Fig. 46 Engine date code and partial VIN location—2.0L (code H) and 2.2L (code 4) engines shown

UNDERHOOD COMPONENT LOCATIONS

1. Vehicle Emissions Control Information (VECI) label
2. Coolant overflow tank
3. EVAP canister
4. Accessory drive belt routing label
5. Engine vacuum schematic label
6. Radiator cap
7. Accessory drive belt
8. Spark plugs and wires
9. PCV valve
10. Power steering fluid reservoir
11. Engine oil dipstick and filler tube
12. Air cleaner filter canister
13. Automatic transmission fluid dipstick
14. Brake fluid reservoir
15. Upper radiator hose
16. Windshield washer fluid container
17. Battery

this literature, replacement copies are usually available from the dealer. A maintenance schedule is provided later in this section, in case you do not have the factory literature.

Air Cleaner

REMOVAL & INSTALLATION

▶ **See Figures 47, 48 and 49**

On many early model engines, the air cleaner is located in the center of the engine compartment, directly over the carburetor or throttle body. On some of the 1987 and later engines the air cleaner is more conveniently located toward the front of the engine compartment with an air duct connected to the throttle body. Depending upon the year of the vehicle and which engine it is equipped with, the air cleaner assembly lid may be retained by a wing nut, screws or different types of retaining clamps and/or fasteners.

1. Unscrew the wing nut or retaining screw(s), or unfasten the clamp(s), as applicable, securing the air cleaner lid, then lift off the housing lid.
2. Lift out the filter element and, if necessary, replace with a new one.
3. Before reinstalling the filter element, wipe out the housing with a damp cloth. Check the lid gasket to ensure that it has a tight seal.

To install:

4. Position the filter element in the air cleaner housing, the close the lid and tighten the wing nut, retaining screw(s) or clamps, as applicable.

Fuel Filter

✳✳ CAUTION

Before removing any fuel system component, always relieve pressure from the system. This procedure is outlined in Section 5. Never smoke when working around gasoline! Avoid all sources of sparks or ignition. Gasoline vapors are EXTREMELY volatile!

Fig. 47 Unfasten the air cleaner cover wing nuts

REMOVAL & INSTALLATION

✳✳ CAUTION

Filter replacement should not be attempted when the engine is HOT. Additionally, it is a good idea to place some absorbent rags under the fuel fittings to absorb any gasoline which will spill out when the lines are loosened.

Carbureted Engines

▶ **See Figure 50**

All models have a fuel filter located within the carburetor body. The fuel filter has a check valve to prevent fuel spillage in the event of an accident. When the filter is replaced, make sure the new one is of the same type. All filters are of the paper element type. Replace the filter every 15,000 miles (24,000 km).

1. Remove the air cleaner.
2. Place a few absorbent rags underneath the fuel line where it joins the carburetor.
3. Detach the fuel line connection at the fuel inlet filter nut. A backup wrench should be used to prevent the filter from loosening while trying to remove the line.
4. Carefully unscrew the fuel inlet filter nut from the carburetor. As the nut is removed, the filter will be pushed part way out by spring pressure.
5. Remove the filter and spring.

To install:

6. Install the new spring and filter with the hole in the filter toward the nut.
7. Position a new gasket on the inlet fitting nut, then install the nut into the carburetor. Tighten to 25 ft. lbs. (34 Nm).
8. Connect the fuel line, then tighten the connector to 18 ft. lbs. (24 Nm.) while holding the inlet nut with a backup wrench to prevent the filter nut from turning.
9. Install the air cleaner.
10. Start the engine and check for leaks.

Fuel Injected Engines

▶ **See Figures 51 and 52**

➡ **Most 1992–94 model vehicles are equipped with "Quick Connect" fuel fittings. For more information regarding these fittings, please refer to Section 5 of this manual.**

An inline filter can be found in the fuel feed line attached to the rear crossmember of the vehicle. To locate the filter, follow the fuel line back from the throttle body. Inline filters are often mounted to the frame rail underneath the vehicle. It may be necessary to raise and safely support the vehicle using jackstands in order to access the filter.

✳✳ CAUTION

Before disconnecting any component of the fuel system, refer to the fuel pressure release procedures found earlier in this section.

Fig. 48 Remove the air cleaner housing lid, then . . .

Fig. 49 . . . lift the air cleaner filter element from the housing

Fig. 50 The fuel filter on carbureted engines is located under the air cleaner, within the carburetor body

Fig. 51 Place a rag under the filter to catch any fuel which may spill out, then unfasten the fuel lines, using a back-up wrench

Fig. 52 Most fuel filters are retained by band clamps; you must loosen the retainers or completely remove the clamp and filter as an assembly

1. Properly relieve the fuel system pressure as outlined earlier in this section.
2. If necessary, raise and safely support the vehicle with jackstands.

→Always use a back-up wrench anytime the fuel filter is removed or installed.

3. Using a backup wrench (where possible) to prevent overtorquing the lines or fittings, loosen and disconnect the fuel lines from the filter. Be sure to position a rag in order to catch any remaining fuel which may escape when the fittings are loosened. Remove and discard any fuel line O-rings.
4. For 1992–94 vehicles, grasp the filter and nylon fuel connection line fitting. Twist the "quick-connect" fitting ¼ or a turn in each direction to loosen any dirt within the fitting. Use compressed air to blow out the dirt from the fittings at the end of the fuel filter.
5. If equipped, detach the quick-connect fitting by pushing inward toward the filter and grasping the plastic tab around the connector and pull apart. If additional assistance is required to disconnect the fitting, tool J 38778 or equivalent can be placed between the filter and the fitting release mechanism to carefully force the two apart. Be careful not to bend the special tool.
6. Remove the fuel filter from the retainer or mounting bolt. For most filters which are retained by band clamps, loosen the fastener(s) and remove the filter. For some filters, it may be necessary to completely remove the clamp and filter assembly.

To install:

7. Before installing a new filter, apply a few drops of clean engine oil to the male tube end of the filter. This will ensure proper attachment and prevent a fuel leak.
8. Position the filter and retaining bracket with the directional arrow facing away from the fuel tank, towards the throttle body.

→The filter has an arrow (fuel flow direction) on the side of the case, be sure to install it correctly in the system, the with arrow facing away from the fuel tank.

9. Install and tighten the filter/bracket retainer(s), as applicable.
10. If equipped with "quick-connect" fittings, push the connectors together to cause the retaining tabs/fingers to snap into place. Pull on both ends of the connection to be sure they are secure.
11. Using new O-rings, connect the fuel lines to the filter, then tighten, using a backup wrench to prevent damage, to 20–22 ft. lbs. (27–30 Nm).
12. If raised, carefully lower the vehicle.
13. Connect the negative battery cable and tighten the fuel filler cap, then start the engine and check for leaks.

PCV Valve

♦ See Figures 53 and 54

REMOVAL & INSTALLATION

♦ See Figures 55, 56 and 57

PCV Valve

The valve is located in a rubber grommet in the valve cover, connected to the air cleaner housing by a large diameter rubber hose. To replace the valve:

1. Pull the valve (with the hose attached) or the hose from the rubber grommet in the valve cover.
2. Remove the valve from the hose.
3. Install a new valve into the hose.
4. Press the valve or hose back into the rubber grommet in the valve cover.

| 1 | PCV VALVE | 3 | CRANKCASE VENT HOSE |
| 2 | AIR CLEANER | 4 | PCV VALVE HOSE |

Fig. 53 Positive Crankcase Ventilation air flow schematic

1 CHECK VALVE

Fig. 54 Cross-section of a PCV valve

Fig. 55 Pull the hose from the nipple in the valve or camshaft cover

Fig. 56 Remove the extension from the hose, to access the valve, then . . .

Fig. 57 . . . remove the PCV valve from the hose

PCV Filter

Some models have a PCV filter, located in the air cleaner housing. This filter must be replaced at every 50,000 miles (80,500 km), or sooner, upon inspection.

1. Remove the air cleaner housing lid.
2. Slide back the filter retaining clip and remove the old filter.
3. Install the new filter, replace the retaining clip and replace the housing lid.

Evaporative Canister

▶ **See Figures 58, 59 and 60**

This system is designed to limit gasoline vapor, which normally escapes from the fuel tank and the intake manifold, from discharging into the atmosphere. Vapor absorption is accomplished through the use of the charcoal canister. The canister absorbs fuel vapors and stores them until they can be remove and burned in the combustion process. Removal of the vapors from the canister to the engine is accomplished through: a canister mounted purge valve, the throttle valve position, a Thermostatic Vacuum Switch (TVS) or a computer controlled canister purge solenoid.

In addition to the canister, the fuel tank requires a non-vented gas cap. This cap does not allow fuel vapor to discharge into the atmosphere. All fuel vapor travels through a vent line (inserted high into the domed fuel tank) directly to the canister.

Check the evaporative emission control system every 15,000 miles (24,000 km). Check the fuel vapor lines and the vacuum hoses for proper connections and correct routing, as well as condition. Replace clogged, damaged or deteriorated parts as necessary.

For more details on the Evaporative Emissions Control (EEC) system, please refer to Section 4.

1	PURGE VALVE	4	VAPOR FROM
2	CONTROL VACUUM		FUEL TANK
	SIGNAL	5	AIR INLET / DRAIN
3	PCV TUBE		TUBE

Fig. 59 View of an evaporative canister—2.0L (VIN M) engine shown

1 Throttle body
2 Fuel tank
3 Canister
4 Vapor restriction
5 Purge control valve
6 Pressure/vacuum relief vented fuel filler cap

Fig. 58 Evaporative Emissions Control (EEC) system schematic

1 Canister purge
2 Vapor from fuel tank
3 Carbon
4 Air

Fig. 60 Evaporative canister—2.2L (VIN 4) shown

FUNCTIONAL TEST

1. Apply a short length of hose to the lower tube of the purge valve and attempt to blow through it. Little or no air should pass into the canister.

2. With a hand vacuum pump, apply a vacuum of 15 in. Hg (50 kPa) to the control valve tube (usually the upper tube). If the diaphragm does not hold vacuum for at least 20 seconds, the diaphragm is leaking and the canister must be replaced.

3. If the diaphragm holds vacuum, again try to blow through the hose connected to the lower tube while vacuum is still being applied. An increased flow of air should be observed. If not, the canister must be replaced.

Battery

PRECAUTIONS

Always use caution when working on or near the battery. Never allow a tool to bridge the gap between the negative and positive battery terminals. Also, be careful not to allow a tool to provide a ground between the positive cable/terminal and any metal component on the vehicle. Either of these conditions will cause a short circuit, leading to sparks and possible personal injury.

Do not smoke, have an open flame or create sparks near a battery; the gases contained in the battery are very explosive and, if ignited, could cause severe injury or death.

All batteries, regardless of type, should be carefully secured by a battery hold-down device. If this is not done, the battery terminals or casing may crack from stress applied to the battery during vehicle operation. A battery which is not secured may allow acid to leak out, making it discharge faster; such leaking corrosive acid can also eat away at components under the hood.

Always visually inspect the battery case for cracks, leakage and corrosion. A white corrosive substance on the battery case or on nearby components would indicate a leaking or cracked battery. If the battery is cracked, it should be replaced immediately.

GENERAL MAINTENANCE

◊ See Figure 61

A battery that is not sealed must be checked periodically for electrolyte level. You cannot add water to a sealed maintenance-free battery (though not all maintenance-free batteries are sealed); however, a sealed battery must also be checked for proper electrolyte level, as indicated by the color of the built-in hydrometer "eye."

Always keep the battery cables and terminals free of corrosion. Check these components about once a year. Refer to the removal, installation and cleaning procedures outlined in this section.

Keep the top of the battery clean, as a film of dirt can help completely discharge a battery that is not used for long periods. A solution of baking soda and water may be used for cleaning, but be careful to flush this off with clear water. DO NOT let any of the solution into the filler holes. Baking soda neutralizes battery acid and will de-activate a battery cell.

Batteries in vehicles which are not operated on a regular basis can fall victim

TCCA1G02

Fig. 61 A typical location for the built-in hydrometer on maintenance-free batteries

to parasitic loads (small current drains which are constantly drawing current from the battery). Normal parasitic loads may drain a battery on a vehicle that is in storage and not used for 6–8 weeks. Vehicles that have additional accessories such as a cellular phone, an alarm system or other devices that increase parasitic load may discharge a battery sooner. If the vehicle is to be stored for 6–8 weeks in a secure area and the alarm system, if present, is not necessary, the negative battery cable should be disconnected at the onset of storage to protect the battery charge.

Remember that constantly discharging and recharging will shorten battery life. Take care not to allow a battery to be needlessly discharged.

BATTERY FLUID

Check the battery electrolyte level at least once a month, or more often in hot weather or during periods of extended vehicle operation. On non-sealed batteries, the level can be checked either through the case on translucent batteries or by removing the cell caps on opaque-cased types. The electrolyte level in each cell should be kept filled to the split ring inside each cell, or the line marked on the outside of the case.

If the level is low, add only distilled water through the opening until the level is correct. Each cell is separate from the others, so each must be checked and filled individually. Distilled water should be used, because the chemicals and minerals found in most drinking water are harmful to the battery and could significantly shorten its life.

If water is added in freezing weather, the vehicle should be driven several miles to allow the water to mix with the electrolyte. Otherwise, the battery could freeze.

Although some maintenance-free batteries have removable cell caps for access to the electrolyte, the electrolyte condition and level on all sealed maintenance-free batteries must be checked using the built-in hydrometer "eye." The exact type of eye varies between battery manufacturers, but most apply a sticker to the battery itself explaining the possible readings. When in doubt, refer to the battery manufacturer's instructions to interpret battery condition using the built-in hydrometer.

➡**Although the readings from built-in hydrometers found in sealed batteries may vary, a green eye usually indicates a properly charged battery with sufficient fluid level. A dark eye is normally an indicator of a battery with sufficient fluid, but one which may be low in charge. And a light or yellow eye is usually an indication that electrolyte supply has dropped below the necessary level for battery (and hydrometer) operation. In this last case, sealed batteries with an insufficient electrolyte level must usually be discarded.**

Checking the Specific Gravity

◊ See Figures 62, 63 and 64

A hydrometer is required to check the specific gravity on all batteries that are not maintenance-free. On batteries that are maintenance-free, the specific gravity is checked by observing the built-in hydrometer "eye" on the top of the battery case. Check with your battery's manufacturer for proper interpretation of its built-in hydrometer readings.

✳✳ CAUTION

Battery electrolyte contains sulfuric acid. If you should splash any on your skin or in your eyes, flush the affected area with plenty of clear water. If it lands in your eyes, get medical help immediately.

The fluid (sulfuric acid solution) contained in the battery cells will tell you many things about the condition of the battery. Because the cell plates must be kept submerged below the fluid level in order to operate, maintaining the fluid level is extremely important. And, because the specific gravity of the acid is an indication of electrical charge, testing the fluid can be an aid in determining if the battery must be replaced. A battery in a vehicle with a properly operating charging system should require little maintenance, but careful, periodic inspection should reveal problems before they leave you stranded.

As stated earlier, the specific gravity of a battery's electrolyte level can be used as an indication of battery charge. At least once a year, check the specific gravity of the battery. It should be between 1.20 and 1.26 on the gravity scale. Most auto supply stores carry a variety of inexpensive battery testing hydrometers. These can be used on any non-sealed battery to test the specific gravity in each cell.

Fig. 62 On non-maintenance-free batteries, the fluid level can be checked through the case on translucent models; the cell caps must be removed on other models

Fig. 63 If the fluid level is low, add only distilled water through the opening until the level is correct

Fig. 64 Check the specific gravity of the battery's electrolyte with a hydrometer

The battery testing hydrometer has a squeeze bulb at one end and a nozzle at the other. Battery electrolyte is sucked into the hydrometer until the float is lifted from its seat. The specific gravity is then read by noting the position of the float. If gravity is low in one or more cells, the battery should be slowly charged and checked again to see if the gravity has come up. Generally, if after charging, the specific gravity between any two cells varies more than 50 points (0.50), the battery should be replaced, as it can no longer produce sufficient voltage to guarantee proper operation.

CABLES

▶ **See Figures 65 thru 75**

Once a year (or as necessary), the battery terminals and the cable clamps should be cleaned. Loosen the clamps and remove the cables, negative cable first. On batteries with posts on top, the use of a puller specially made for this purpose is recommended. These are inexpensive and available in most auto parts stores. Side terminal battery cables are secured with a small bolt.

Clean the cable clamps and the battery terminal with a wire brush, until all corrosion, grease, etc., is removed and the metal is shiny. It is especially important to clean the inside of the clamp thoroughly (an old knife is useful here), since a small deposit of foreign material or oxidation there will prevent a sound electrical connection and inhibit either starting or charging. Special tools are available for cleaning these parts, one type for conventional top post batteries and another type for side terminal batteries. It is also a good idea to apply some dielectric grease to the terminal, as this will aid in the prevention of corrosion.

After the clamps and terminals are clean, reinstall the cables, negative cable last; DO NOT hammer the clamps onto battery posts. Tighten the clamps securely, but do not distort them. Give the clamps and terminals a thin external coating of grease after installation, to retard corrosion.

Check the cables at the same time that the terminals are cleaned. If the cable insulation is cracked or broken, or if the ends are frayed, the cable should be replaced with a new cable of the same length and gauge.

Fig. 65 Maintenance is performed with household items and with special tools like this post cleaner

Fig. 66 The underside of this special battery tool has a wire brush to clean post terminals

Fig. 67 Place the tool over the battery posts and twist to clean until the metal is shiny

Fig. 68 A special tool is available to pull the clamp from the post

Fig. 69 The cable ends should be cleaned as well

Fig. 70 Loosen the battery cable retaining nut . . .

Fig. 71 . . . then disconnect the cable from the battery

Fig. 72 A wire brush may be used to clean any corrosion or foreign material from the cable

Fig. 73 The wire brush can also be used to remove any corrosion or dirt from the battery terminal

Fig. 74 The battery terminal can also be cleaned using a solution of baking soda and water

Fig. 75 Before connecting the cables, it's a good idea to coat the terminals with a small amount of dielectric grease

CHARGING

✳✳ CAUTION

The chemical reaction which takes place in all batteries generates explosive hydrogen gas. A spark can cause the battery to explode and splash acid. To avoid serious personal injury, be sure there is proper ventilation and take appropriate fire safety precautions when connecting, disconnecting, or charging a battery and when using jumper cables.

A battery should be charged at a slow rate to keep the plates inside from getting too hot. However, if some maintenance-free batteries are allowed to discharge until they are almost "dead," they may have to be charged at a high rate to bring them back to "life." Always follow the charger manufacturer's instructions on charging the battery.

REPLACEMENT

When it becomes necessary to replace the battery, select one with an amperage rating equal to or greater than the battery originally installed. Deterioration and just plain aging of the battery cables, starter motor, and associated wires makes the battery's job harder in successive years. The slow increase in electrical resistance over time makes it prudent to install a new battery with a greater capacity than the old.

Standard Drive Belts

INSPECTION & ADJUSTMENT

▶ See Figures 76 and 77

Every 12 months or 15,000 miles (24,000 km), check the water pump, alternator, power steering pump (if so equipped), and air conditioning compressor (if so equipped) drive belts for proper tension. Also look for signs of wear, fraying, separation, glazing and so on, and replace the belts as required.

Belt tension should be checked with a gauge made for the purpose. If a gauge is not available, tension can be checked with moderate thumb pressure applied to the belt at its longest span midway between pulleys. If the belt has a free span less than twelve inches, it should deflect approximately 1/8–1/4 in. (3–6mm). If the span is longer than twelve inches, deflection can range between 1/8–3/8 in. (3–9mm).

1. Loosen the driven accessory's pivot and adjustment bolts. The pivot bolts are the bolts that enable the accessory to move in the either direction for adjustment. The adjustment bolts are the bolts in the slotted brackets.

2. Move the accessory toward or away from the engine until the tension is correct. You can use a wooden hammer handle or a broomstick as a lever, but do not use anything metallic.

3. Tighten the bolts and recheck the tension. If new belts have been installed, run the engine for a few minutes, then recheck and readjust as necessary.

It is better to have belts too loose than too tight, because overtight belts will lead to bearing failure, particularly in the water pump and alternator. However, loose belts place an extremely high impact load on the driven component due to the whipping action of the belt.

REMOVAL & INSTALLATION

▶ See Figure 78

1. Loosen the accessory-to-mounting bracket bolt(s) and adjusting bolt.
2. Rotate the accessory to relieve belt tension.
3. Slip the drive belt from the accessory pulley and remove it from the engine.

➡ **If the engine uses more than one belt, it may be necessary to remove belts that are in front of the belt being removed**

To install:

4. Place the new belt over the crankshaft or drive pulley and stretch over the driven (accessory) pulley.

Fig. 76 Belt tension gauge for an engine with V-belts

	Tension
New Belt	650 N (Max.) 145 Lbs. (Max.)
Used Belt	300 N (Min.) 70 Lbs. (Min.)

Fig. 77 Many vehicles will have a decal illustrating the correct accessory belt routing

Fig. 78 If the engine uses more than one belt, it may be necessary to remove belts that are in front of the belt being removed

5. If removed, install the other belts in the same way.
6. Adjust the belts to the proper tension.
7. Tighten the adjusting and mounting bolts.

Serpentine Drive Belts

Models equipped with the V6 engine and most 1987–94 engines use a single (serpentine belt) to drive all engine accessories. The serpentine belt driven accessories are rigidly mounted with belt tension maintained by a spring loaded tensioner assembly. The belt tensioner has the ability to control belt tension over a fairly broad range of belt lengths. However, there are limits to the tensioner's ability to compensate for varying lengths of belts. Poor tension control and/or damage to the tensioner could result with the tensioner operating outside of its range.

INSPECTION & ADJUSTMENT

1. If fraying of the belt is noticed, check to make sure both the belt and the tensioner assembly are properly aligned and that the belt edges are not in contact with the flanges of the tensioner pulley.
2. If, while adjusting belt tension, tensioner runs out of travel, the belt is stretched beyond adjustment and should be replaced.
3. If a whining is heard around the tensioner or idler assemblies, check for possible bearing failure.

➡**Routine inspection of the belt may reveal cracks in the belt ribs. These cracks will not impair belt performance and therefore should not be considered a problem requiring belt replacement. However, the belt should be replaced if belt slip occurs or if sections of the belt ribs are missing.**

REMOVAL & INSTALLATION

To replace the belt push (rotate) the the belt tensioner and remove the belt. Use a 15mm socket on the 4-cyl. engines and a ¾ in. open end wrench on the V6 engines.

Timing Belt

SERVICING

Vehicles equipped with the 1.8L (VIN O and J) and the 2.0L (VIN K and M) engines are the only vehicles covered by this manual which utilize a timing belt. The timing belt should be inspected for cracks, wear or other damage and should be replaced every 60,000 miles (100,000 km).

For the timing belt removal and installation procedure, please refer to Section 3 of this manual.

Hoses

INSPECTION

▶ **See Figures 79, 80, 81 and 82**

Upper and lower radiator hoses, along with the heater hoses, should be checked for deterioration, leaks and loose hose clamps at least every 15,000 miles (24,000 km). It is also wise to check the hoses periodically in early spring and at the beginning of the fall or winter when you are performing other maintenance. A quick visual inspection could discover a weakened hose which might have left you stranded if it had remained unrepaired.

Whenever you are checking the hoses, make sure the engine and cooling system are cold. Visually inspect for cracking, rotting or collapsed hoses, and replace as necessary. Run your hand along the length of the hose. If a weak or swollen spot is noted when squeezing the hose wall, the hose should be replaced.

REMOVAL & INSTALLATION

1. Remove the radiator pressure cap.

Fig. 79 The cracks developing along this hose are a result of age-related hardening

Fig. 80 A hose clamp that is too tight can cause older hoses to separate and tear on either side of the clamp

Fig. 81 A soft spongy hose (identifiable by the swollen section) will eventually burst and should be replaced

Fig. 82 Hoses are likely to deteriorate from the inside if the cooling system is not periodically flushed

Fig. 83 CV-boots must be inspected periodically for damage

Fig. 84 A torn boot should be replaced immediately

✳✳ CAUTION

Never remove the pressure cap while the engine is running, or personal injury from scalding hot coolant or steam may result. If possible, wait until the engine has cooled to remove the pressure cap. If this is not possible, wrap a thick cloth around the pressure cap and turn it slowly to the stop. Step back while the pressure is released from the cooling system. When you are sure all the pressure has been released, use the cloth to turn and remove the cap.

2. Position a clean container under the radiator and/or engine draincock or plug, then open the drain and allow the cooling system to drain to an appropriate level. For some upper hoses, only a little coolant must be drained. To remove hoses positioned lower on the engine, such as a lower radiator hose, the entire cooling system must be emptied.

✳✳ CAUTION

When draining coolant, keep in mind that cats and dogs are attracted by ethylene glycol antifreeze, and are quite likely to drink any that is left in an uncovered container or in puddles on the ground. This will prove fatal in sufficient quantity. Always drain coolant into a sealable container. Coolant may be reused unless it is contaminated or several years old.

3. Loosen the hose clamps at each end of the hose requiring replacement. Clamps are usually either of the spring tension type (which require pliers to squeeze the tabs and loosen) or of the screw tension type (which require screw or hex drivers to loosen). Pull the clamps back on the hose away from the connection.

4. Twist, pull and slide the hose off the fitting, taking care not to damage the neck of the component from which the hose is being removed.

➡**If the hose is stuck at the connection, do not try to insert a screwdriver or other sharp tool under the hose end in an effort to free it, as the connection and/or hose may become damaged. Heater connections especially may be easily damaged by such a procedure. If the hose is to be replaced, use a single-edged razor blade to make a slice along the portion of the hose which is stuck on the connection, perpendicular to the end of the hose. Do not cut deep so as to prevent damaging the connection. The hose can then be peeled from the connection and discarded.**

5. Clean both hose mounting connections. Inspect the condition of the hose clamps and replace them, if necessary.

To install:

6. Dip the ends of the new hose into clean engine coolant to ease installation.

7. Slide the clamps over the replacement hose, then slide the hose ends over the connections into position.

8. Position and secure the clamps at least ¼ in. (6.35mm) from the ends of the hose. Make sure they are located beyond the raised bead of the connector.

9. Close the radiator or engine drains and properly refill the cooling system with the clean drained engine coolant or a suitable mixture of ethylene glycol coolant and water.

10. If available, install a pressure tester and check for leaks. If a pressure tester is not available, run the engine until normal operating temperature is reached (allowing the system to naturally pressurize), then check for leaks.

✳✳ CAUTION

If you are checking for leaks with the system at normal operating temperature, BE EXTREMELY CAREFUL not to touch any moving or hot engine parts. Once temperature has been reached, shut the engine OFF, and check for leaks around the hose fittings and connections which were removed earlier.

Upper and lower radiator hoses and all heater hoses should be checked for deterioration, leaks and loose hose clamps every 15,000 miles (24,000 km). To remove the hoses:

11. Drain the radiator as detailed later in this section.

12. Loosen the hose clamps at each end of the hose to be removed.

13. Working the hose back and forth, slide it off its connection and then install the new hose.

➡**If the hose is stuck, use a suitable razor cutting tool or knife, and carefully slit the hose enough to split it open along the connecting neck.**

14. Position the hose clamps at least ¼ in. from the end of the new hose and tighten them.

➡**Always make sure that the hose clamps are beyond the bead and placed in the center of the clamping surface before tightening them.**

CV-Boot

INSPECTION

▶ **See Figures 83 and 84**

The CV (Constant Velocity) boots should be checked for damage each time the oil is changed and any other time the vehicle is raised for service. These boots keep water, grime, dirt and other damaging matter from entering the CV-joints. Any of these could cause early CV-joint failure which can be expensive to repair. Heavy grease thrown around the inside of the front wheel(s) and on the brake caliper/drum can be an indication of a torn boot. Thoroughly check the boots for missing clamps and tears. If the boot is damaged, it should be replaced immediately. Please refer to Section 7 for procedures.

Spark Plugs

▶ **See Figure 85**

A typical spark plug consists of a metal shell surrounding a ceramic insulator. A metal electrode extends downward through the center of the insulator and protrudes a small distance. Located at the end of the plug and attached to the side of the outer metal shell is the side electrode. The side electrode bends in at a 90° angle so that its tip is just past and parallel to the tip of the center elec-

Fig. 85 Cross-section of a spark plug

trode. The distance between these two electrodes (measured in thousandths of an inch or hundredths of a millimeter) is called the spark plug gap.

The spark plug does not produce a spark, but instead provides a gap across which the current can arc. The coil produces anywhere from 20,000 to 50,000 volts (depending on the type and application) which travels through the wires to the spark plugs. The current passes along the center electrode and jumps the gap to the side electrode, and in doing so, ignites the air/fuel mixture in the combustion chamber.

SPARK PLUG HEAT RANGE

▶ See Figure 86

Spark plug heat range is the ability of the plug to dissipate heat. The longer the insulator (or the farther it extends into the engine), the hotter the plug will operate; the shorter the insulator (the closer the electrode is to the block's cooling passages) the cooler it will operate. A plug that absorbs little heat and remains too cool will quickly accumulate deposits of oil and carbon since it is not hot enough to burn them off. This leads to plug fouling and consequently to misfiring. A plug that absorbs too much heat will have no deposits but, due to the excessive heat, the electrodes will burn away quickly and might possibly lead to preignition or other ignition problems. Preignition takes place when plug tips get so hot that they glow sufficiently to ignite the air/fuel mixture before the actual spark occurs. This early ignition will usually cause a pinging during low speeds and heavy loads.

The general rule of thumb for choosing the correct heat range when picking a spark plug is: if most of your driving is long distance, high speed travel, use a colder plug; if most of your driving is stop and go, use a hotter plug. Original equipment plugs are generally a good compromise between the 2 styles and most people never have the need to change their plugs from the factory-recommended heat range.

REMOVAL & INSTALLATION

A set of spark plugs usually requires replacement after about 20,000–30,000 miles (32,000–48,000 km), depending on your style of driving. In normal oper-

ation plug gap increases about 0.001 in. (0.025mm) for every 2500 miles (4000 km). As the gap increases, the plug's voltage requirement also increases. It requires a greater voltage to jump the wider gap and about two to three times as much voltage to fire the plug at high speeds than at idle. The improved air/fuel ratio control of modern fuel injection combined with the higher voltage output of modern ignition systems will often allow an engine to run significantly longer on a set of standard spark plugs, but keep in mind that efficiency will drop as the gap widens (along with fuel economy and power).

When you're removing spark plugs, work on one at a time. Don't start by removing the plug wires all at once, because, unless you number them, they may become mixed up. Take a minute before you begin and number the wires with tape.

1. Disconnect the negative battery cable, and if the vehicle has been run recently, allow the engine to thoroughly cool.
2. Carefully twist the spark plug wire boot to loosen it, then pull upward and remove the boot from the plug. Be sure to pull on the boot and not on the wire, otherwise the connector located inside the boot may become separated.
3. Using compressed air, blow any water or debris from the spark plug well to assure that no harmful contaminants are allowed to enter the combustion chamber when the spark plug is removed. If compressed air is not available, use a rag or a brush to clean the area.

➡Remove the spark plugs when the engine is cold, if possible, to prevent damage to the threads. If removal of the plugs is difficult, apply a few drops of penetrating oil or silicone spray to the area around the base of the plug, and allow it a few minutes to work.

4. Using a spark plug socket that is equipped with a rubber insert to properly hold the plug, turn the spark plug counterclockwise to loosen and remove the spark plug from the bore.

✳✳ WARNING

Be sure not to use a flexible extension on the socket. Use of a flexible extension may allow a shear force to be applied to the plug. A shear force could break the plug off in the cylinder head, leading to costly and frustrating repairs.

To install:
5. Inspect the spark plug boot for tears or damage. If a damaged boot is found, the spark plug wire must be replaced.
6. Using a wire feeler gauge, check and adjust the spark plug gap. When using a gauge, the proper size should pass between the electrodes with a slight drag. The next larger size should not be able to pass while the next smaller size should pass freely.
7. Carefully thread the plug into the bore by hand. If resistance is felt before the plug is almost completely threaded, back the plug out and begin threading again. In small, hard to reach areas, an old spark plug wire and boot could be used as a threading tool. The boot will hold the plug while you twist the end of the wire and the wire is supple enough to twist before it would allow the plug to crossthread.

✳✳ WARNING

Do not use the spark plug socket to thread the plugs. Always carefully thread the plug by hand or using an old plug wire to prevent the possibility of crossthreading and damaging the cylinder head bore.

8. Carefully tighten the spark plug. If the plug you are installing is equipped with a crush washer, seat the plug, then tighten about ¼ turn to crush the washer. If you are installing a tapered seat plug, tighten the plug to specifications provided by the vehicle or plug manufacturer.
9. Apply a small amount of silicone dielectric compound to the end of the spark plug lead or inside the spark plug boot to prevent sticking, then install the boot to the spark plug and push until it clicks into place. The click may be felt or heard, then gently pull back on the boot to assure proper contact.

INSPECTION & GAPPING

▶ See Figures 87, 88, 89, 90 and 91

Check the plugs for deposits and wear. If they are not going to be replaced, clean the plugs thoroughly. Remember that any kind of deposit will decrease the

Fig. 86 Spark plug heat range

A normally worn spark plug should have light tan or gray deposits on the firing tip.

A carbon fouled plug, identified by soft, sooty, black deposits, may indicate an improperly tuned vehicle. Check the air cleaner, ignition components and engine control system.

This spark plug has been **left in the engine too long,** as evidenced by the extreme gap- Plugs with such an extreme gap can cause misfiring and stumbling accompanied by a noticeable lack of power.

An oil fouled spark plug indicates an engine with worn poston rings and/or bad valve seals allowing excessive oil to enter the chamber.

A physically damaged spark plug may be evidence of severe detonation in that cylinder. Watch that cylinder carefully between services, as a continued detonation will not only damage the plug, but could also damage the engine.

A bridged or almost bridged spark plug, identified by a build-up between the electrodes caused by excessive carbon or oil build-up on the plug.

TCCA1P40

Fig. 87 Inspect the spark plug to determine engine running conditions

TCCS1212
Fig. 88 A variety of tools and gauges are needed for spark plug service

TCCS2903
Fig. 89 Checking the spark plug gap with a feeler gauge

TCCS2904
Fig. 90 Adjusting the spark plug gap

Fig. 91 If the standard plug is in good condition, the electrode may be filed flat—WARNING: do not file platinum plugs

Fig. 92 Checking plug wire resistance through the distributor cap with an ohmmeter

Fig. 93 Checking individual plug wire resistance with a digital ohmmeter

efficiency of the plug. Plugs can be cleaned on a spark plug cleaning machine, which can sometimes be found in service stations, or you can do an acceptable job of cleaning with a stiff brush. If the plugs are cleaned, the electrodes must be filed flat. Use an ignition points file, not an emery board or the like, which will leave deposits. The electrodes must be filed perfectly flat with sharp edges; rounded edges reduce the spark plug voltage by as much as 50%.

Check spark plug gap before installation. The ground electrode (the L-shaped one connected to the body of the plug) must be parallel to the center electrode and the specified size wire gauge (please refer to the Tune-Up Specifications chart for details) must pass between the electrodes with a slight drag.

➡**NEVER adjust the gap on a used platinum type spark plug.**

Always check the gap on new plugs as they are not always set correctly at the factory. Do not use a flat feeler gauge when measuring the gap on a used plug, because the reading may be inaccurate. A round-wire type gapping tool is the best way to check the gap. The correct gauge should pass through the electrode gap with a slight drag. If you're in doubt, try one size smaller and one larger. The smaller gauge should go through easily, while the larger one shouldn't go through at all. Wire gapping tools usually have a bending tool attached. Use that to adjust the side electrode until the proper distance is obtained. Absolutely never attempt to bend the center electrode. Also, be careful not to bend the side electrode too far or too often as it may weaken and break off within the engine, requiring removal of the cylinder head to retrieve it.

Spark Plug Wires

TESTING

▶ **See Figures 92 and 93**

At every tune-up/inspection, visually check the spark plug cables for burns cuts, or breaks in the insulation. Check the boots and the nipples on the distributor cap and/or coil. Replace any damaged wiring.

Every 50,000 miles (80,000 Km) or 60 months, the resistance of the wires should be checked with an ohmmeter. Wires with excessive resistance will cause misfiring, and may make the engine difficult to start in damp weather.

To check resistance, remove the distributor cap, leaving the wires in place. Connect one lead of an ohmmeter to an electrode within the cap; connect the other lead to the corresponding spark plug terminal (remove it from the spark plug for this test). Replace any wire which shows a resistance over 30,000 ohms. Generally speaking, it is preferable that resistance be below 25,000 ohms, but 30,000 ohms must be considered the outer limit of acceptability. It should be remembered that resistance is also a function of length; the longer the wire, the greater the resistance. Thus, if the wires on your car are longer than the factory originals, resistance will be higher, quite possible outside these limits.

Wire length can therefore be used to determine appropriate resistance values:
- 0-15 in. (0–38cm)—3,000-10,000 ohms
- 15-25 in. (38–64cm)—4,000-15,000 ohms
- 25-35 in. (64–89cm)—6,000-20,000 ohms
- Wire over 35 in. (89cm)—25,000 ohms

REMOVAL & INSTALLATION

➡**If all of the wires must be disconnected from the spark plugs or from the distributor at the same time, be sure to tag the wires to assure proper reconnection.**

When installing a new set of spark plug wires, replace the wires one at a time so there will be no mix-up. Start by replacing the longest cable first. Install the boot firmly over the spark plug. Route the wire exactly the same as the original. Insert the nipple firmly onto the tower on the distributor cap, then install the cap cover and latches to secure the wires. Be sure to apply silicone dielectric compound to the spark plug wire boots and tower connectors prior to installation.

Distributor Cap and Rotor

REMOVAL & INSTALLATION

▶ **See Figures 94 thru 100**

1. Disconnect the negative battery cable.
2. If necessary, detach the wiring connector from the distributor.
3. Remove the retainer and spark plug wires from the cap. If there is no wire retainer, be sure to tag all of the wires before disconnecting them from the distributor cap. Tagging the wires will help preserve the proper firing order and greatly ease cap installation.
4. If retained by spring loaded locktabs, depress, twist and release the distributor cap-to-housing locktabs, then lift off the cap assembly. Most integral coil distributor caps will be retained by two or four spring loaded locktabs.
5. If retained by mounting screws, loosen the screws, then remove the cap from the distributor assembly.

➡**Although most rotors can only be installed in one direction, it is still wise to note the position of the rotor before remove to assure proper installation and ignition timing.**

6. Note the position of the rotor, unfasten the attaching screws, if applicable, then remove the rotor.
   To install:
7. Install the rotor in the position noted earlier, then secure using the retaining screws.
8. Position the distributor cap to the housing, then secure using the housing retainers.
9. Fasten the spark plugs and retainer to the cap. If no wire retainer is used, carefully connect the wires to the cap as tagged during removal.
10. Attach the wiring connector to the distributor, as applicable.
11. Connect the negative battery cable.

INSPECTION

Remove the distributor cap and inspect the inside for flashover, cracking of the carbon button, lack of spring tension on the carbon button, cracking of the cap, and burned, worn terminals. Also check for broken distributer cap towers. If any of these conditions are present, the distributor cap and/or cables should be replaced.

Fig. 94 Detach the coil wire—1988 2.0L Sunbird shown

Fig. 95 If necessary to remove any of the spark plug wires from the distributor cap, be sure to matchmark or tag them first

Fig. 96 Twist, then pull to remove the boot from the cap

Fig. 97 On some vehicles, it will help to matchmark the position of the distributor to the housing, as on the 1988 Sunbird

Fig. 98 Unfasten the mounting bolts or screws, then remove the distributor cap

Fig. 99 Matchmark the position of the rotor to ensure correct installation, then . . .

Fig. 100 . . . remove the rotor from the engine

When replacing the distributor cap, transfer cables from the original cap to the new cap one at a time. Ensure that each cable is installed into the corresponding tower of the new cap. Fully seat the wires into the towers. If necessary, refer to the appropriate engine firing order diagram.

Light scaling of the terminals can be cleaned with a sharp knife. If the terminals are heavily scaled, replace the distributor cap.

A cap that is greasy, dirty or has a powder-like substance on the inside should be cleaned with a solution of warm water and mild detergent. Scrub the cap with a soft brush. Thoroughly rinse the cap and dry it with a clean soft cloth.

Replace the rotor with a new one if it is cracked, or if the tip is excessively burned or heavily scaled. If the spring terminal does not have adequate tension, replace the rotor with a new one.

Ignition Timing

GENERAL INFORMATION

➡**Late model vehicles, both 4 cylinder and 6 cylinder engines, have Distributorless Ignition Systems (DIS). Because the reluctor wheel is an integral part of the crankshaft, and the crankshaft sensor is mounted in a fixed position, timing adjustment is not possible.**

Basic ignition timing is critical to the proper operation of the Electronic Spark Control (ESC) system. Always follow the Vehicle Emission Control Information (VECI) label procedures when adjusting ignition timing.

Some engines will incorporate a magnetic timing probe hole for use with special electronic timing equipment. Consult the manufacturer's instructions for the use of this electronic timing equipment.

Ignition timing is the measurement, in degrees of crankshaft rotation, of the point at which the spark plugs fire in each of the cylinders. It is measured in degrees before or after Top Dead Center (TDC) of the compression stroke.

Because it takes a fraction of a second for the spark plug to ignite the mixture in the cylinder, the spark plug must fire a little before the piston reaches TDC. Otherwise, the mixture will not completely ignited as the piston passes TDC and the full power of the explosion will not be used by the engine.

The timing measurement is given in degrees of crankshaft rotation before the piston reaches TDC (BTDC). If the setting for the ignition timing is 5° BTDC, the spark plug must fire 5° before each piston reaches TDC. This only holds true, however, when the engine is at idle speed.

As the engine speed increases, the pistons go faster. The spark plugs have to ignite the fuel even sooner if it is to be completely ignited when the piston reaches TDC.

If the ignition is set too far advanced (BTDC), the ignition and expansion of the fuel in the cylinder will occur too soon and tend to force the piston down while it is still traveling up. This causes engine ping. If the ignition spark is set too far retarded, after TDC (ATDC), the piston will have already passed TDC and started on its way down when the fuel is ignited. This will cause the piston to be forced down for only a portion of its travel. This will result in poor engine performance and lack of power.

Ignition timing for this engine should be accomplished using the averaging method in which the timing of each cylinder can be brought into closer agreement with the base timing specification.

The averaging method involves the use of a double notched crankshaft pulley. When timing the engine, the coil wire, instead of the Number 1 plug wire, should be used to trigger the timing light. The notch for the No. 1 cylinder is scribed across all three edges of the double sheave pulley. Another notch located 180° away from the No. 1 cylinder notch is scribed only across the center section of the pulley to make it distinguishable from the No. 1 cylinder notch.

Since the trigger signal for the timing light is picked up at the coil wire, each spark firing results in a flash from the timing light. A slight jiggling of the timing notch may be apparent since each cylinder firing is being displayed. Optimum timing of all cylinders is accomplished by centering the total apparent notch width about the correct timing specification.

There are three basic types of timing light available. The first is a simple neon bulb with two wire connections (one for the spark plug and one for the plug wire, connecting the light in series). This type of light is quite dim, and must be held closely to the marks to be seen, but it is quite inexpensive. The second type of light operates from the car's battery. Two alligator clips connect to the battery terminals, while a third wire connects to the spark plug with an adapter. This type of light is more expensive, but the xenon bulb provides a nice bright flash which can even be seen in sunlight. The third type replaces the battery source with 110 volt house current. Some timing lights have other functions built into them, such as dwell meters, tachometers, or remote starting switches. These are convenient, in that they reduce the tangle of wires under the hood, but may duplicate the functions of tools you already have.

Because your car has electronic ignition, you should use a timing light with an inductive pickup. This pickup simply clamps around the Number 1 spark plug wire (in this case, the coil wire), eliminating the adapter. It is not susceptible to crossfiring or false triggering, which may occur with a conventional light due to the greater voltages produced by HEI.

INSPECTION & ADJUSTMENT

1.8L and 2.0L OHV Engines

1982–86 VEHICLES

1. Refer to the instructions on the emission control sticker inside the engine compartment. follow all instructions on the label.
2. Locate the timing marks on the crankshaft pulley and the front of the engine.
3. Clean off the marks so that you can see them. Chalk or white paint will help to make them more visible.
4. Attach a tachometer to the engine as detailed previously.
5. Disconnect the 4-terminal EST connector at the distributor so that the engine will switch to the bypass timing mode (please refer to Section 4 for more information).
6. Attach a timing light as per the manufacturer's instructions. Clamp the inductive pick-up around the HIGH TENSION COIL WIRE (not the No. 1 spark plug wire) at the distributor. Before installing the pick-up on the wire, it will be necessary to peel back the protective plastic cover which encases the wire.
7. Loosen the distributor clamp bolt slightly so that the distributor may be rotated as necessary to adjust timing.
8. Check that all wires are clear of the fan and then start the engine. Allow the engine to reach normal operating temperature.
9. Aim the timing light at the marks. A slight jiggling of the notch on the pulley may appear due to the fact that each cylinder is being displayed as it fires. The apparent notch width cannot be reduced by a timing adjustment.
10. Center the total apparent notch width about the correct timing mark on the indicator by rotating the distributor housing. This will insure that the average cylinder timing is as close to specifications as possible. Once again, the apparent notch width cannot be reduced by timing adjustment.
11. Turn off the engine and tighten the distributor lock bolt. Start the engine and recheck the timing. Sometimes the distributor will move a little during the tightening process. If the ignition timing is within 1° of the correct setting, that is close enough; a tolerance of up to 2° is permitted by the manufacturer.
12. Turn off the engine and disconnect the timing light and the tachometer. Reconnect the 4-terminal EST connector.

2.0L (VIN 1) 2.2L, 2.8L and 3.1L Engines

1987–94 VEHICLES

The ignition timing on engines with distributorless ignitions, is controlled by the Electronic Control Module (ECM) or Powertrain Control Module (PCM), as applicable. No adjustments are possible.

2.0L (VIN K and M) Engines

1. Refer to the underhood emission control label and follow all of the timing instructions if they differ from below.
2. Warm the engine to normal operating temperature.
3. Place the transmission in N or P. Apply the parking brake and block wheels.
4. Air conditioning, cooling fan and choke must be OFF. Do not remove the air cleaner, except as noted.
5. Ground the ALCL connector under the dash by installing a jumper wire between the A and B terminals. The Check Engine light should begin flashing.
6. Connect an inductive timing light to the No. 1 spark plug wire lead and record timing.
7. Connect an inductive timing light to the No. 4 spark plug wire lead and record timing.
8. Add the 2 timing numbers and divide by 2 to obtain "average timing". For example: No. 1 timing = 4 degrees and No. 4 timing = 8 degrees; 4 + 8 = 12 / 2 = 6 degrees average timing. If a change is necessary, subtract the average timing from the timing specification to determine the amount of timing change to No. 1 cylinder. For example: if the timing specification is 8 degrees and the average timing is 6 degrees, advance the No. 1 cylinder 2 degrees to set the timing.
9. To correct the timing, loosen the distributor hold-down clamp, adjust the distributor and retighten the hold-down bolt.
10. Once the timing is properly set, remove the jumper wire from the ALCL connector.
11. If necessary to clear the ECM memory, disconnect the ECM harness from the positive battery pigtail for 10 seconds with the key in the OFF position.

Valve Lash

All engines in the vehicles covered by this manual are equipped with hydraulic valve lifters that do not require periodic valve lash adjustment. Proper adjustment is maintained automatically by hydraulic pressure in the valves.

Idle Speed and Mixture Adjustments

CARBURETED ENGINES

All carbureted vehicles are equipped with an Idle Speed Control (ISC) motor which is in turn controlled by the Electronic Control Module (ECM). All idle speeds are programmed into the ECM's memory and then relayed to the ISC motor as any given situation requires. Curb idle is pre-set at the factory and not routinely adjustable. Although curb idle is not to be adjusted under normal conditions, it can be adjusted, but only upon replacement of the ISC (for further details, refer to Section 5).

The idle mixture screws are concealed under staked-in plugs. Idle mixture is not considered to be a normal tune-up procedure, because of the sensitivity of emission control adjustments. Mixture adjustment requires not only the special tools with which to remove the concealing plugs, but also the addition of an artificial enrichment substance (generally propane) which must be introduced into the carburetor by means of a finely calibrated metering valve. These tools are not generally available and require a certain amount of expertise to use, therefore, mixture adjustments are purposely not covered in this book. If you suspect that your car's carburetor requires a mixture adjustment, we strongly recommend that the job be referred to a qualified service technician.

FUEL INJECTED ENGINES

The fuel injected vehicles are controlled by a computer which supplies the correct amount of fuel during all engine operating conditions; no adjustment is necessary.

TUNE-UP SPECIFICATIONS

Year	Engine ID/VIN	Engine Displacement Liters (cc)	Spark Plugs Gap (in.)	Ignition Timing (deg.) MT	AT	Fuel Pump (psi)	Idle Speed (rpm) MT	AT	Valve Clearance In.	Ex.
1982	G	1.8 (1819)	0.045 ①	12B	12B	4.5-6	②	②	HYD	HYD
	O	1.8 (1819)	0.060	8	8B	9-13	②	②	HYD	HYD
	B	2.0 (1998)	②	②	②	4.5-6	②	②	HYD	HYD
1983	O	1.8 (1819)	0.060	8	8B	9-13	②	②	HYD	HYD
	J	1.8 (1819)	0.035	②	②	30-40	②	②	HYD	HYD
	P	2.0 (1998)	0.035	②	②	12	②	②	HYD	HYD
	B	2.0 (1998)	0.035	-	12B	12	②	②	HYD	HYD
1984	O	1.8 (1819)	0.060	8	8B	9-13	②	②	HYD	HYD
	J	1.8 (1819)	0.035	②	②	30-40	②	②	HYD	HYD
	P	2.0 (1998)	0.035	②	②	12	②	②	HYD	HYD
1985	O	1.8 (1819)	0.060	8B	8B	9-13	③	③	HYD	HYD
	J	1.8 (1819)	0.035	②	②	26-32	③	③	HYD	HYD
	P	2.0 (1998)	0.035	NA	NA	12	NA	NA	HYD	HYD
	W	2.8 (2835)	0.045	NA	NA	9-13	NA	NA	HYD	HYD
1986	O	1.8 (1819)	0.060	8B	8B	9-13	③	③	HYD	HYD
	J	1.8 (1819)	0.035	②	②	26-32	③	③	HYD	HYD
	P	2.0 (1998)	0.035	NA	NA	12	NA	NA	HYD	HYD
	W	2.8 (2835)	0.045	NA	NA	9-13	NA	NA	HYD	HYD
1987	K	2.0 (1998)	0.045	8B	8B	9-13	③	③	HYD	HYD
	M	2.0 (1998)	0.035	8B	8B	41-47	③	③	HYD	HYD
	1	2.0 (1998)	0.035	②	②	10-12	③	③	HYD	HYD
	W	2.8 (2835)	0.045	②	②	9-13	③	③	HYD	HYD
1988	K	2.0 (1998)	0.045	8B	8B	9-13	③	③	HYD	HYD
	M	2.0 (1998)	0.035	8B	8B	25-30	③	③	HYD	HYD
	1	2.0 (1998)	0.035	②	②	10-12	③	③	HYD	HYD
	W	2.8 (2835)	0.045	②	②	9-13	③	③	HYD	HYD
1989	K	2.0 (1998)	0.045	8B	8B	9-13	③	③	HYD	HYD
	M	2.0 (1998)	0.035	8B	8B	25-30	③	③	HYD	HYD
	1	2.0 (1998)	0.035	②	②	10-12	③	③	HYD	HYD
	W	2.8 (2835)	0.045	②	②	9-13	③	③	HYD	HYD
1990	K	2.0 (1988)	0.045	8B	8B	9-13	③	③	HYD	HYD
	M	2.0 (1998)	0.035	8B	8B	35-38	③	③	HYD	HYD
	G	2.2 (2180)	0.035	②	②	9-13	③	③	HYD	HYD
	T	3.1 (3130)	0.045	②	②	34-47	③	③	HYD	HYD
1991	K	2.0 (1998)	0.045	②	②	9-13	600	500	HYD	HYD
	G	2.2 (2180)	0.035	②	②	9-13	②	②	HYD	HYD
	T	3.1 (3130)	0.045	②	②	41-47	③	③	HYD	HYD
1992	H	2.0 (1998)	0.045	②	②	41-47	600	600	HYD	HYD
	G	2.2 (2180)	0.035	②	②	9-13	③	③	HYD	HYD
	T	3.1 (3130)	0.045	②	②	41-47	③	③	HYD	HYD
1993	H	2.0 (1998)	0.045	②	②	41-47	③	③	HYD	HYD
	4	2.2 (2180)	0.045	②	②	41-47	③	③	HYD	HYD
	T	3.1 (3136)	0.045	②	②	41-47	675	675	HYD	HYD
1994	H	2.0 (1998)	0.045	②	②	41-47	③	③	HYD	HYD
	4	2.2 (2180)	0.045	②	②	41-47	③	③	HYD	HYD
	T	3.1 (3136)	0.045	②	②	41-47	③	③	HYD	HYD

NOTE: The Vehicle Emission Control Information label often reflects specification changes made during production. The label figures must be used if they differ from those in this chart.

B - Before top dead center

HYD - Hydraulic

NA - Not available

1 Certain models may use 0.035 in. gap. See the underhood specifications sticker to be sure

2 Refer to the Vehicles Emission Control Information label

3 Idle speed is maintained by the computer control module (ECM/PCM). There is no recommended adjustment procedure.

91131C06

Air Conditioning System

SYSTEM SERVICE & REPAIR

➡It is recommended that the A/C system be serviced by an EPA Section 609 certified automotive technician utilizing a refrigerant recovery/recycling machine.

The do-it-yourselfer should not service his/her own vehicle's A/C system for many reasons, including legal concerns, personal injury, environmental damage and cost. The following are some of the reasons why you may decide not to service your own vehicle's A/C system.

According to the U.S. Clean Air Act, it is a federal crime to service or repair (involving the refrigerant) a Motor Vehicle Air Conditioning (MVAC) system for money without being EPA certified. It is also illegal to vent R-12 and R-134a refrigerants into the atmosphere. Selling or distributing A/C system refrigerant (in a container which contains less than 20 pounds of refrigerant) to any person who is not EPA 609 certified is also not allowed by law.

State and/or local laws may be more strict than the federal regulations, so be sure to check with your state and/or local authorities for further information. For further federal information on the legality of servicing your A/C system, call the EPA Stratospheric Ozone Hotline.

➡Federal law dictates that a fine of up to $25,000 may be levied on people convicted of venting refrigerant into the atmosphere. Additionally, the EPA may pay up to $10,000 for information or services leading to a criminal conviction of the violation of these laws.

When servicing an A/C system you run the risk of handling or coming in contact with refrigerant, which may result in skin or eye irritation or frostbite. Although low in toxicity (due to chemical stability), inhalation of concentrated refrigerant fumes is dangerous and can result in death; cases of fatal cardiac arrhythmia have been reported in people accidentally subjected to high levels of refrigerant. Some early symptoms include loss of concentration and drowsiness.

➡Generally, the limit for exposure is lower for R-134a than it is for R-12. Exceptional care must be practiced when handling R-134a.

Also, refrigerants can decompose at high temperatures (near gas heaters or open flame), which may result in hydrofluoric acid, hydrochloric acid and phosgene (a fatal nerve gas).

R-12 refrigerant can damage the environment because it is a Chlorofluorocarbon (CFC), which has been proven to add to ozone layer depletion, leading to increasing levels of UV radiation. UV radiation has been linked with an increase in skin cancer, suppression of the human immune system, an increase in cataracts, damage to crops, damage to aquatic organisms, an increase in ground-level ozone, and increased global warming.

R-134a refrigerant is a greenhouse gas which, if allowed to vent into the atmosphere, will contribute to global warming (the Greenhouse Effect).

It is usually more economically feasible to have a certified MVAC automotive technician perform A/C system service on your vehicle. Some possible reasons for this are as follows:

• While it is illegal to service an A/C system without the proper equipment, the home mechanic would have to purchase an expensive refrigerant recovery/recycling machine to service his/her own vehicle.

• Since only a certified person may purchase refrigerant—according to the Clean Air Act, there are specific restrictions on selling or distributing A/C system refrigerant—it is legally impossible (unless certified) for the home mechanic to service his/her own vehicle. Procuring refrigerant in an illegal fashion exposes one to the risk of paying a $25,000 fine to the EPA.

R-12 Refrigerant Conversion

If your vehicle still uses R-12 refrigerant, one way to save A/C system costs down the road is to investigate the possibility of having your system converted to R-134a. The older R-12 systems can be easily converted to R-134a refrigerant by a certified automotive technician by installing a few new components and changing the system oil.

The cost of R-12 is steadily rising and will continue to increase, because it is no longer imported or manufactured in the United States. Therefore, it is often possible to have an R-12 system converted to R-134a and recharged for less than it would cost to just charge the system with R-12.

If you are interested in having your system converted, contact local automotive service stations for more details and information.

PREVENTIVE MAINTENANCE

◗ **See Figures 101 and 102**

Although the A/C system should not be serviced by the do-it-yourselfer, preventive maintenance can be practiced and A/C system inspections can be performed to help maintain the efficiency of the vehicle's A/C system. For preventive maintenance, perform the following:

• The easiest and most important preventive maintenance for your A/C system is to be sure that it is used on a regular basis. Running the system for five minutes each month (no matter what the season) will help ensure that the seals and all internal components remain lubricated.

➡Some newer vehicles automatically operate the A/C system compressor whenever the windshield defroster is activated. When running, the compressor lubricates the A/C system components; therefore, the A/C system would not need to be operated each month.

• In order to prevent heater core freeze-up during A/C operation, it is necessary to maintain proper antifreeze protection. Use a hand-held coolant tester (hydrometer) to periodically check the condition of the antifreeze in your engine's cooling system.

➡Antifreeze should not be used longer than the manufacturer specifies.

• For efficient operation of an air conditioned vehicle's cooling system, the radiator cap should have a holding pressure which meets manufacturer's specifications. A cap which fails to hold these pressures should be replaced.

TCCS1233

Fig. 101 A coolant tester can be used to determine the freezing and boiling levels of the coolant in your vehicle

GASKET

SEAL

TCCS1079

Fig. 102 To ensure efficient cooling system operation, inspect the radiator cap gasket and seal

• Any obstruction of or damage to the condenser configuration will restrict air flow which is essential to its efficient operation. It is, therefore, a good rule to keep this unit clean and in proper physical shape.

➡**Bug screens which are mounted in front of the condenser (unless they are original equipment) are regarded as obstructions.**

• The condensation drain tube expels any water which accumulates on the bottom of the evaporator housing into the engine compartment. If this tube is obstructed, the air conditioning performance can be restricted and condensation buildup can spill over onto the vehicle's floor.

SYSTEM INSPECTION

▶ **See Figure 103**

Although the A/C system should not be serviced by the do-it-yourselfer, preventive maintenance can be practiced and A/C system inspections can be performed to help maintain the efficiency of the vehicle's A/C system. For A/C system inspection, perform the following:

The easiest and often most important check for the air conditioning system consists of a visual inspection of the system components. Visually inspect the air conditioning system for refrigerant leaks, damaged compressor clutch, abnormal compressor drive belt tension and/or condition, plugged evaporator drain tube, blocked condenser fins, disconnected or broken wires, blown fuses, corroded connections and poor insulation.

A refrigerant leak will usually appear as an oily residue at the leakage point in the system. The oily residue soon picks up dust or dirt particles from the surrounding air and appears greasy. Through time, this will build up and appear to be a heavy dirt impregnated grease.

For a thorough visual and operational inspection, check the following:

• Check the surface of the radiator and condenser for dirt, leaves or other material which might block air flow.

• Check for kinks in hoses and lines. Check the system for leaks.

• Make sure the drive belt is properly tensioned. When the air conditioning is operating, make sure the drive belt is free of noise or slippage.

• Make sure the blower motor operates at all appropriate positions, then check for distribution of the air from all outlets with the blower on **HIGH** or **MAX**.

➡**Keep in mind that under conditions of high humidity, air discharged from the A/C vents may not feel as cold as expected, even if the system is working properly. This is because vaporized moisture in humid air retains heat more effectively than dry air, thereby making humid air more difficult to cool.**

• Make sure the air passage selection lever is operating correctly. Start the engine and warm it to normal operating temperature, then make sure the temperature selection lever is operating correctly.

Windshield Wipers

ELEMENT (REFILL) CARE & REPLACEMENT

▶ **See Figures 104 thru 113**

For maximum effectiveness and longest element life, the windshield and wiper blades should be kept clean. Dirt, tree sap, road tar and so on will cause streaking, smearing and blade deterioration if left on the glass. It is advisable to wash the windshield carefully with a commercial glass cleaner at least once a month. Wipe off the rubber blades with the wet rag afterwards. Do not attempt to move wipers across the windshield by hand; damage to the motor and drive mechanism will result.

To inspect and/or replace the wiper blade elements, place the wiper switch in the **LOW** speed position and the ignition switch in the **ACC** position. When the wiper blades are approximately vertical on the windshield, turn the ignition switch to **OFF**.

Examine the wiper blade elements. If they are found to be cracked, broken or torn, they should be replaced immediately. Replacement intervals will vary with usage, although ozone deterioration usually limits element life to about one year. If the wiper pattern is smeared or streaked, or if the blade chatters across

Fig. 103 Periodically remove any debris from the condenser and radiator fins

Fig. 104 Bosch® wiper blade and fit kit

Fig. 105 Lexor® wiper blade and fit kit

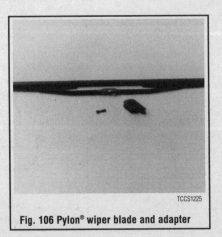

Fig. 106 Pylon® wiper blade and adapter

Fig. 107 Trico® wiper blade and fit kit

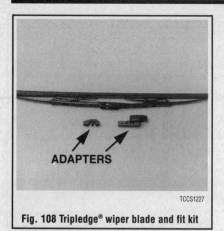

ADAPTERS

TCCS1227

Fig. 108 Tripledge® wiper blade and fit kit

TCCS1228

Fig. 109 To remove and install a Lexor® wiper blade refill, slip out the old insert and slide in a new one

TCCS1229

Fig. 110 On Pylon® inserts, the clip at the end has to be removed prior to sliding the insert off

TCCS1230

Fig. 111 On Trico® wiper blades, the tab at the end of the blade must be turned up . . .

TCCS1231

Fig. 112 . . . then the insert can be removed. After installing the replacement insert, bend the tab back

TCCS1232

Fig. 113 The Tripledge® wiper blade insert is removed and installed using a securing clip

the glass, the elements should be replaced. It is easiest and most sensible to replace the elements in pairs.

If your vehicle is equipped with aftermarket blades, there are several different types of refills and your vehicle might have any kind. Aftermarket blades and arms rarely use the exact same type blade or refill as the original equipment. Here are some typical aftermarket blades; not all may be available for your vehicle:

The Anco® type uses a release button that is pushed down to allow the refill to slide out of the yoke jaws. The new refill slides back into the frame and locks in place.

Some Trico® refills are removed by locating where the metal backing strip or the refill is wider. Insert a small screwdriver blade between the frame and metal backing strip. Press down to release the refill from the retaining tab.

Other types of Trico® refills have two metal tabs which are unlocked by squeezing them together. The rubber filler can then be withdrawn from the frame jaws. A new refill is installed by inserting the refill into the front frame jaws and sliding it rearward to engage the remaining frame jaws. There are usually four jaws; be certain when installing that the refill is engaged in all of them. At the end of its travel, the tabs will lock into place on the front jaws of the wiper blade frame.

Another type of refill is made from polycarbonate. The refill has a simple locking device at one end which flexes downward out of the groove into which the jaws of the holder fit, allowing easy release. By sliding the new refill through all the jaws and pushing through the slight resistance when it reaches the end of its travel, the refill will lock into position.

To replace the Tridon® refill, it is necessary to remove the wiper blade. This refill has a plastic backing strip with a notch about 1 in. (25mm) from the end. Hold the blade (frame) on a hard surface so that the frame is tightly bowed. Grip the tip of the backing strip and pull up while twisting counterclockwise. The backing strip will snap out of the retaining tabs. Do this for the remaining tabs until the refill is free of the blade. The length of these refills is molded into the end and they should be replaced with identical types.

Regardless of the type of refill used, be sure to follow the part manufacturer's instructions closely. Make sure that all of the frame jaws are engaged as the refill is pushed into place and locked. If the metal blade holder and frame are allowed to touch the glass during wiper operation, the glass will be scratched.

Tires and Wheels

Common sense and good driving habits will afford maximum tire life. Fast starts, sudden stops and hard cornering are hard on tires and will shorten their useful life span. Make sure that you don't overload the vehicle or run with incorrect pressure in the tires. Both of these practices will increase tread wear.

➡**For optimum tire life, keep the tires properly inflated, rotate them often and have the wheel alignment checked periodically.**

Inspect your tires frequently. Be especially careful to watch for bubbles in the tread or sidewall, deep cuts or underinflation. Replace any tires with bubbles in the sidewall. If cuts are so deep that they penetrate to the cords, discard the tire. Any cut in the sidewall of a radial tire renders it unsafe. Also look for uneven tread wear patterns that may indicate the front end is out of alignment or that the tires are out of balance.

TIRE ROTATION

◆ **See Figures 114 and 115**

Tires must be rotated periodically to equalize wear patterns that vary with a tire's position on the vehicle. Tires will also wear in an uneven way as the front steering/suspension system wears to the point where the alignment should be reset.

Rotating the tires will ensure maximum life for the tires as a set, so you will not have to discard a tire early due to wear on only part of the tread. Regular rotation is required to equalize wear.

When rotating "unidirectional tires," make sure that they always roll in the same direction. This means that a tire used on the left side of the vehicle must not be switched to the right side and vice-versa. Such tires should only be rotated front-to-rear or rear-to-front, while always remaining on the same side of the vehicle. These tires are marked on the sidewall as to the direction of rotation; observe the marks when reinstalling the tire(s).

Some styled or "mag" wheels may have different offsets front to rear. In these cases, the rear wheels must not be used up front and vice-versa. Furthermore, if

Fig. 114 Compact spare tires must NEVER be used in the rotation pattern

Fig. 115 Unidirectional tires are identifiable by sidewall arrows and/or the word "rotation"

Fig. 116 P-Metric tire coding

these wheels are equipped with unidirectional tires, they cannot be rotated unless the tire is remounted for the proper direction of rotation.

➡The compact or space-saver spare is strictly for emergency use. It must never be included in the tire rotation or placed on the vehicle for everyday use.

TIRE DESIGN

▶ See Figure 116

For maximum satisfaction, tires should be used in sets of four. Mixing of different types (radial, bias-belted, fiberglass belted) must be avoided. In most cases, the vehicle manufacturer has designated a type of tire on which the vehicle will perform best. Your first choice when replacing tires should be to use the same type of tire that the manufacturer recommends.

When radial tires are used, tire sizes and wheel diameters should be selected to maintain ground clearance and tire load capacity equivalent to the original specified tire. Radial tires should always be used in sets of four.

✳✳ CAUTION

Radial tires should never be used on only the front axle.

When selecting tires, pay attention to the original size as marked on the tire. Most tires are described using an industry size code sometimes referred to as P-Metric. This allows the exact identification of the tire specifications, regardless of the manufacturer. If selecting a different tire size or brand, remember to check the installed tire for any sign of interference with the body or suspension while the vehicle is stopping, turning sharply or heavily loaded.

Snow Tires

Good radial tires can produce a big advantage in slippery weather, but in snow, a street radial tire does not have sufficient tread to provide traction and control. The small grooves of a street tire quickly pack with snow and the tire behaves like a billiard ball on a marble floor. The more open, chunky tread of a snow tire will self-clean as the tire turns, providing much better grip on snowy surfaces.

To satisfy municipalities requiring snow tires during weather emergencies, most snow tires carry either an M + S designation after the tire size stamped on the sidewall, or the designation "all-season." In general, no change in tire size is necessary when buying snow tires.

Most manufacturers strongly recommend the use of 4 snow tires on their vehicles for reasons of stability. If snow tires are fitted only to the drive wheels, the opposite end of the vehicle may become very unstable when braking or turning on slippery surfaces. This instability can lead to unpleasant endings if the driver can't counteract the slide in time.

Note that snow tires, whether 2 or 4, will affect vehicle handling in all non-snow situations. The stiffer, heavier snow tires will noticeably change the turning and braking characteristics of the vehicle. Once the snow tires are installed, you must re-learn the behavior of the vehicle and drive accordingly.

➡Consider buying extra wheels on which to mount the snow tires. Once done, the "snow wheels" can be installed and removed as needed. This eliminates the potential damage to tires or wheels from seasonal

removal and installation. Even if your vehicle has styled wheels, see if inexpensive steel wheels are available. Although the look of the vehicle will change, the expensive wheels will be protected from salt, curb hits and pothole damage.

TIRE STORAGE

If they are mounted on wheels, store the tires at proper inflation pressure. All tires should be kept in a cool, dry place. If they are stored in the garage or basement, do not let them stand on a concrete floor; set them on strips of wood, a mat or a large stack of newspaper. Keeping them away from direct moisture is of paramount importance. Tires should not be stored upright, but in a flat position.

INFLATION & INSPECTION

▶ See Figures 117 thru 124

The importance of proper tire inflation cannot be overemphasized. A tire employs air as part of its structure. It is designed around the supporting strength of the air at a specified pressure. For this reason, improper inflation drastically reduces the tire's ability to perform as intended. A tire will lose some air in day-to-day use; having to add a few pounds of air periodically is not necessarily a sign of a leaking tire.

Two items should be a permanent fixture in every glove compartment: an accurate tire pressure gauge and a tread depth gauge. Check the tire pressure (including the spare) regularly with a pocket type gauge. Too often, the gauge on the end of the air hose at your corner garage is not accurate because it suffers too much abuse. Always check tire pressure when the tires are cold, as pressure increases with temperature. If you must move the vehicle to check the tire inflation, do not drive more than a mile before checking. A cold tire is generally one that has not been driven for more than three hours.

A plate or sticker is normally provided somewhere in the vehicle (door post, hood, tailgate or trunk lid) which shows the proper pressure for the tires. Never counteract excessive pressure build-up by bleeding off air pressure (letting some air out). This will cause the tire to run hotter and wear quicker.

✳✳ CAUTION

Never exceed the maximum tire pressure embossed on the tire! This is the pressure to be used when the tire is at maximum loading, but it is rarely the correct pressure for everyday driving. Consult the owner's manual or the tire pressure sticker for the correct tire pressure.

Once you've maintained the correct tire pressures for several weeks, you'll be familiar with the vehicle's braking and handling personality. Slight adjustments in tire pressures can fine-tune these characteristics, but never change the cold pressure specification by more than 2 psi. A slightly softer tire pressure will give a softer ride but also yield lower fuel mileage. A slightly harder tire will give crisper dry road handling but can cause skidding on wet surfaces. Unless you're fully attuned to the vehicle, stick to the recommended inflation pressures.

All tires made since 1968 have built-in tread wear indicator bars that show

Fig. 117 Tires should be checked frequently for any sign of puncture or damage

Fig. 118 Tires with deep cuts, or cuts which bulge, should be replaced immediately

- DRIVE WHEEL HEAVY ACCELERATION
- OVERINFLATION

- HARD CORNERING
- UNDERINFLATION
- LACK OF ROTATION

Fig. 119 Examples of inflation-related tire wear patterns

PROPERLY INFLATED IMPROPERLY INFLATED

RADIAL TIRE

Fig. 120 Radial tires have a characteristic sidewall bulge; don't try to measure pressure by looking at the tire. Use a quality air pressure gauge

up as ½ in. (13mm) wide smooth bands across the tire when ¹⁄₁₆ in. (1.5mm) of tread remains. The appearance of tread wear indicators means that the tires should be replaced. In fact, many states have laws prohibiting the use of tires with less than this amount of tread.

You can check your own tread depth with an inexpensive gauge or by using a Lincoln head penny. Slip the Lincoln penny (with Lincoln's head upside-down) into several tread grooves. If you can see the top of Lincoln's head in 2 adjacent grooves, the tire has less than ¹⁄₁₆ in. (1.5mm) tread left and should be replaced. You can measure snow tires in the same manner by using the "tails" side of the Lincoln penny. If you can see the top of the Lincoln memorial, it's time to replace the snow tire(s).

CARE OF SPECIAL WHEELS

If you have invested money in magnesium, aluminum alloy or sport wheels, special precautions should be taken to make sure your investment is not wasted and that your special wheels look good for the life of the vehicle.

Fig. 121 Common tire wear patterns and causes

Fig. 122 Tread wear indicators will appear when the tire is worn

Fig. 123 Accurate tread depth indicators are inexpensive and handy

Fig. 124 A penny works well for a quick check of tread depth

Special wheels are easily damaged and/or scratched. Occasionally check the rims for cracking, impact damage or air leaks. If any of these are found, replace the wheel. But in order to prevent this type of damage and the costly replacement of a special wheel, observe the following precautions:

• Use extra care not to damage the wheels during removal, installation, balancing, etc. After removal of the wheels from the vehicle, place them on a mat or other protective surface. If they are to be stored for any length of time, support them on strips of wood. Never store tires and wheels upright; the tread may develop flat spots.

• When driving, watch for hazards; it doesn't take much to crack a wheel.
• When washing, use a mild soap or non-abrasive dish detergent (keeping in mind that detergent tends to remove wax). Avoid cleansers with abrasives or the use of hard brushes. There are many cleaners and polishes for special wheels.
• If possible, remove the wheels during the winter. Salt and sand used for snow removal can severely damage the finish of a wheel.
• Make certain the recommended lug nut torque is never exceeded or the wheel may crack. Never use snow chains on special wheels; severe scratching will occur.

FLUIDS AND LUBRICANTS

Fluid Disposal

Used fluids such as engine oil, transmission fluid, antifreeze and brake fluid are hazardous wastes and must be disposed of properly. Before draining any fluids; consult with your local authorities; in many areas, waste oil, antifreeze, etc. is being accepted as a part of recycling programs. A number of service stations and auto parts stores are also accepting waste fluids for recycling.

Be sure of the recycling center's policies before draining any fluids, as many will not accept different fluids that have been mixed together.

Fuel and Engine Oil Recommendations

FUEL

→Some fuel additives contain chemicals that can damage the catalytic converter and/or oxygen sensor. Read all of the labels carefully before using any additive in the engine or fuel system.

All of the vehicles covered by this manual are designed to run on unleaded fuel. The use of a leaded fuel in a car requiring unleaded fuel will plug the catalytic converter and render it inoperative. It will also increase exhaust backpressure to the point where engine output will be severely reduced. The minimum octane rating of the the unleaded fuel being used must be at least 87, which usually means regular unleaded, but some high performance engines may require higher ratings. Fuel should be selected for the brand and octane which performs best with your engine. Judge a gasoline by its ability to prevent pinging, its engine starting capabilities (cold and hot) and general all weather performance.

As far as the octane rating is concerned, refer to the general engine specifications chart in Section 3 of this manual to find your engine and its compression ratio. If the compression ratio is 9.0:1 or lower, in most cases a regular unleaded grade of gasoline can be used. If the compression ratio is higher than 9.0:1 use a premium grade of unleaded fuel.

The use of a fuel too low in octane (a measure of anti-knock quality) will result in spark knock. Since many factors such as altitude, terrain, air temperature and humidity affect operating efficiency, knocking may result even though the recommended fuel is being used. If persistent knocking occurs, it may be necessary to switch to a higher grade of fuel. Continuous or heavy knocking may result in engine damage.

→Your engine's fuel requirement can change with time, mainly due to carbon build-up, which will in turn change the compression ratio. If you engine pings, knocks or diesels (runs with the ignition OFF) switch to a higher grade of fuel. Sometimes, just changing brands will cure the problem. If it becomes necessary to retard the timing from the specifications, don't change it more than a few degrees. Retarded timing will reduce power output and fuel mileage, in addition to making the engine run hotter.

ENGINE OIL

▶ See Figure 125

The SAE (Society of Automotive Engineers) grade number indicates the viscosity of the engine oil, and thus its ability to lubricate at a given temperature. The lower the SAE grade number, the lighter the oil; the lower the viscosity, the easier it is to crank the engine in cold weather. Oil viscosities should be chosen from those oils recommended for the lowest anticipated temperatures during the

oil change interval. With the proper viscosity, you will be assured of easy cold starting and sufficient engine protection.

Multi-viscosity oils (5W-30, 10W-30, etc..), offer the important advantage of being adaptable to temperature extremes. They allow easy starting at low temperatures, yet they give good protection at high speeds and engine temperatures. This is a decided advantage in changeable climates or in long distance touring.

The American Petroleum Institute (API) designation indicates the classification of engine oil used under certain given operating conditions. Only oils designated for use Service SH, or latest superceding oil grade, should be used. Oils of the SH type perform a variety of functions inside the engine in addition to the basic function as a lubricant. Through a balanced system of metallic detergents and polymeric dispersants, the oil prevents the formation of high and low temperature deposits, and also keeps sludge and dirt particles in suspension. Acids, particularly sulfuric acid, as well as other by products of combustion, are neutralized. Both the SAE grade number and the API designation can be found on the top of the oil can.

→Non-detergent or straight mineral oils must never be used. Oil viscosities should be chosen from those oils recommended for the lowest anticipated temperatures during the oil change interval.

Synthetic Oils

There are excellent synthetic and fuel-efficient oils available that, under the right circumstances, can help provide better fuel mileage and better engine protection. However, these advantages come at a price, which can be significantly more than the price per quart of conventional motor oils.

RECOMMENDED SAE VISCOSITY GRADE ENGINE OILS

FOR BEST FUEL ECONOMY AND COLD STARTING, SELECT THE LOWEST SAE VISCOSITY GRADE OIL FOR THE EXPECTED TEMPERATURE RANGE.

LOOK FOR ONE OF THESE LABELS

HOT WEATHER

COLD WEATHER

AMERICAN PETROLEUM INSTITUTE CERTIFIED FOR GASOLINE ENGINES

API SERVICE SH SAE 6W-30 ENERGY CONSERVING II

SAE 10W-30

SAE 6W-30 PREFERRED

IF NEITHER SAE 5W-30 NOR SAE 10W-30 GRADE OILS ARE AVAILABLE, SAE 30 GRADE MAY BE USED AT TEMPERATURES ABOVE 40 DEGREES F (4 DEGREES C).

DO NOT USE SAE 10W-40, SAE 20W-50 OR ANY OTHER GRADE OIL NOT RECOMMENDED

87951080

Fig. 125 Recommended SAE engine oil viscosity grades for gasoline engines

Before pouring any synthetic oils into your car's engine, you should consider the condition of the engine and the type of driving you do. It is also wise to check the vehicle manufacturer's position on synthetic oils.

Generally, it is best to avoid the use of synthetic oil in both brand new and older, high mileage engines. New engines require a proper break-in, and the synthetics are so slippery that they can impede this; most manufacturers recommend that you wait at least 5,000 miles (8,000 km) before switching to a synthetic oil. Conversely, older engines are looser and tend to lose more oil; synthetics will slip past worn parts more readily than regular oil. If your car already leaks oil, (due to worn parts or bad seals/gaskets), it may leak more with a synthetic inside.

Consider your type of driving. If most of your accumulated mileage is on the highway at higher, steadier speed, a synthetic oil will reduce friction and probably help deliver better fuel mileage. Under such ideal highway conditions, the oil change interval can be extended, as long as the oil filter can operate effectively for the extended life of the oil. If the filter can't do its job for this extended period, dirt and sludge will build up in your engine's crankcase, sump, oil pump and lines, no matter what type of oil is used. If using synthetic oil in this manner, you should continue to change the oil filter at the recommended intervals.

Cars used under harder, stop-and-go, short hop circumstances should always be serviced more frequently, and for these cars synthetic oil may not be a wise investment. Because of the necessary shorter change interval needed for this type of driving, you cannot take advantage of the long recommended change interval of most synthetic oils.

Engine

OIL LEVEL CHECK

▶ **See Figures 126; 127 and 128**

➡**On some of the vehicles covered by this manual, the oil fill cap contains the oil level indicator (dipstick).**

Every time you stop for fuel, check the engine oil making sure the engine has fully warmed and the vehicle is parked on a level surface. Because it takes some time for the oil to drain back to the oil pan, you should wait a few minutes before checking your oil. If you are doing this at a fuel stop, first fill the fuel tank, then open the hood and check the oil, but don't get so carried away as to forget to pay for the fuel. Most station attendants won't believe that you forgot.

1. Make sure the car is parked on level ground.
2. When checking the oil level, it is best for the engine to be at normal operating temperature, although checking the oil immediately after stopping will lead to a false reading. Wait a few minutes after turning off the engine to allow the oil to drain back into the crankcase.
3. Open the hood and locate the dipstick which will be in a guide tube mounted in the upper engine block. Pull the dipstick from its tube, wipe it clean (using a clean, lint free rag) and then reinsert it.
4. Pull the dipstick out again and, holding it horizontally, read the oil level. The oil should be between the FULL and ADD marks on the dipstick. The the oil is below the ADD mark, add oil of the proper viscosity through the capped opening in the top of the cylinder head cover or filler tube, as applicable. see the oil and fuel recommendations listed earlier in this section for the proper viscosity and rating of oil to use.

5. Insert the dipstick and check the oil level again after adding any oil. Approximately one quart of oil will raise the level from the ADD mark to the FULL mark. Be sure not to overfill the crankcase and waste the oil. Excess oil will generally be consumed at an accelerated rate.

✳✳ WARNING

DO NOT overfill the crankcase. It may result in oil-fouled spark plugs, oil leaks cause by oil seal failure or engine damage due to oil foaming.

OIL & FILTER CHANGE

▶ **See Figures 129, 130, 131, 132 and 133**

✳✳ CAUTION

The EPA warns that prolonged contact with used engine oil may cause a number of skin disorders, including cancer! You should make every effort to minimize your exposure to used engine oil. Protective gloves should be worn when changing the oil. Wash your hands and any other exposed skin areas as soon as possible after exposure to used engine oil. Soap and water, or waterless hand cleaner should be used.

If you purchased your J-car new, the engine oil and filter should be changed at the first 7,500 miles or 12 months (whichever comes first), and then at least every 7,500 miles or 12 months thereafter it the car is operated on a daily or semi-daily basis and most trips are for several miles (allowing the engine to properly warm up). If the car is driven under severe conditions, such as in extremely dusty weather, or when the car is used for trailer towing, prolonged high speed driving, or repeated short trips in freezing weather, it is suggested that the oil and filter be changed every 3,000 miles/4,800 km or 3 months.

Under certain circumstances, General Motors recommends changing both the oil and filter during the first oil change and then only replacing the filter at every other oil change thereafter. For the small price of an oil filter, it's cheap insurance to replace the filter at every oil change. One of the larger filter manufacturers points out in its advertisements that not changing the filter leaves as much as one quart of dirty oil in the engine. This claim is true and should be kept in mind when changing your oil.

Oil should always be changed after the engine has been running long enough to bring it up to normal operating temperature. Hot oil will flow easier and more contaminants will be removed along with the oil than if it were drained cold. The oil drain plug is located on the bottom of the oil pan (bottom of the engine).

You should have available a container that will hold a minimum of 6 quarts of liquid (to prevent spilling the oil even after it is drained), a wrench to fit the drain plug, a spout for pouring in new oil and a rag or two, which you will always need. If the filter is being replaced, you will also need a band wrench or a filter wrench that fits the end of the filter.

1. Drive the car until the engine is at normal operating temperature. A run to the parts store for oil and a filter should accomplish this. If the engine is not hot when the oil is changed, most of the acids and contaminants will remain inside the engine.

Fig. 126 Locate the dipstick, remove it from the guide tube, then . . .

Fig. 127 . . . wipe the dipstick clean and reinsert in the guide tube

1 Oil level indicator and
  fill tube cap
2 Bolt
3 Seal
4 Oil fill tube

Fig. 128 On some vehicles, such as this 2.2L (VIN 4) engine, the oil fill cap contains the oil dipstick

Fig. 129 Using a wrench, loosen the oil panel drain plug, then . . .

Fig. 130 . . . quickly withdraw the plug and allow it to drain into a pan

Fig. 131 Use a strap-type wrench to loosen the oil filter

2. Shut the engine **OFF**, make sure the parking brake is firmly set and the drive wheels are blocked.

3. Clearance may be sufficient to access the drain plug without raising the vehicle. If the car must be lifted, be sure to support it safely with jackstands and be sure to position the drain plug at a low point under the vehicle.

4. Slide a drain pan of at least 6 quarts capacity under the oil pan. Wipe the drain plug and surrounding area clean using an old rag.

➡ **Six quart plastic drain pan/containers are available, which can be capped, and taken later to a recycling station to dispose of the dirty oil. DO NOT pour the oil on or into the ground.**

5. Using a ratchet, short extension and socket or a box-wrench, loosen the drain plug from the engine oil pan. The drain plug is the bolt inserted at an angle into the lowest point of the oil pan. Turn the plug out by hand, using a rag to shield your fingers. By keeping an inward pressure on the plug as you unscrew it, oil won't escape past the threads and you can remove it without being burned by hot oil.

6. Quickly withdraw the plug and move your hands out of the way, but be careful not to drop the plug into the drain pan, as fishing it out can be an unpleasant mess. Allow the oil to drain completely in the pan, then wipe off the drain plug, removing any traces of metal particles. Pay particular attention to the threads.

7. Install and carefully tighten the drain plug. Be careful not to overtighten the drain plug, otherwise you'll be buying a new pan or a trick replacement plug for stripped threads.

➡ **Although some manufacturers have at times recommended changing the oil filter every other oil change, we recommend the filter be changed every time you change your oil. The added benefit of clean oil is quickly lost if the oil filter is clogged and the added protection to the heart of your engine far outweighs the few dollars saved by using an old filter.**

8. On some vehicles, the oil filter is at the back of the engine. It is impossible to reach from above, and almost as inaccessible from below, because of the location of the fender skirt. It may be easiest to remove the right front wheel and reach through the fender opening to get at the four cylinder oil filter. Use an oil filter strap wrench, or a wrench that fits like a cap over the oil filter, along with a rachet wrench, to loosen the oil filter; these are available at auto parts stores. Cover your hand with a rag and spin the filter off by hand. Keep in mind that it's holding about one quart of dirty, hot oil, so be careful.

9. Clean off the oil filter mounting surface with a clean rag. Be sure that the rag doesn't leave any lint which could clog an oil passage.

10. Apply a thin film of clean engine oil to the filter gasket. Screw the filter on by hand until the gasket makes contact. Then tighten it by hand an additional ½–¾ turn. Do not overtighten. No more, or you'll squash the gasket and the it may leak.

11. Remove the oil filler cap, after wiping the area clean, then refill the engine with the correct amount of fresh oil Please refer to the Capacities chart in this section. If you don't have an oil can spout, you will need a funnel. Be certain you do not overfill the engine, which can cause serious damage. Replace the cap.

12. Check the oil level on the dipstick. It is normal for the level to be a bit above the full mark. Start the engine and allow it to idle for a few minutes.

✦✦✦ WARNING

Do not run the engine above idle speed until it has built up oil pressure, indicated when the oil light goes out.

13. Check around the filter and drain plug for any leaks.

14. Shut off the engine, allow the oil to drain for a minute, and check the oil level.

After completing this job, you will have several quarts of filthy oil to dispose of. The best thing to do with it is to pour it into plastic jugs, such as milk or old antifreeze containers. Then, locate a service station or automotive parts store where you can pour it into their used oil tank for recycling.

✦✦✦ CAUTION

Improperly disposing of used motor oil not only pollutes the environment, it violates Federal law. Dispose of waste oil properly.

Manual Transaxle

FLUID RECOMMENDATIONS

All 4-speed manual transaxles use Dexron® III or IIE (or the latest superceding fluid grade) automatic transmission fluid, which is a thin, reddish fluid. All 5-speeds through 1987 use 5W-30 engine oil. 1988–94 5-speed manual transaxles use Synchromesh® transmission fluid, GM part no. 12345349.

➡ **Using the incorrect lubricant in your transaxle can lead to significant transaxle damage and a costly overhaul.**

LEVEL CHECK

▶ **See Figures 134, 135, 136 and 137**

The fluid level in the manual transaxle should be checked every 12 months or 7,500 miles (12,000 km), whichever comes first.

1. Park the car on a level surface. The transaxle should be cool to the touch. If it is hot, check the level later, when it has cooled.

2. Remove the dipstick from the transaxle.

3. Check the level with the marks located on the dipstick.

4. If lubricant is needed, add it through the filler tube until the level is correct. When the level is correct, reinstall the dipstick firmly.

➡ **The dipstick must be fully seated in the filler tube during vehicle operation or leakage will occur at the vent plug.**

DRAIN & REFILL

Under normal conditions, the manual transaxle fluid does not need to be changed. However, if the car is driven in deep water (as high as the transaxle casing) it is a good idea to replace the fluid. Little harm can come from a fluid change when you have just purchased a used vehicle, especially since the condition of the transaxle is usually not known.

If the fluid is to be drained, it is a good idea to warm the fluid first so it will flow better. This can be accomplished by 15–20 miles (24–32 km) of highway driving. Fluid which is warmed to normal operating temperature will flow faster, drain more completely and remove more contaminants from the housing.

Fig. 132 The oil filler cap is usually located on the camshaft carrier or valve cover—1988 2.0L Sunbird shown

Fig. 133 Fill the crankcase with the proper amount of engine oil, then check the oil level

Fig. 134 Location of the manual transaxle dipstick and filler tube—1984 5-speed shown, 4-speed similar

Fig. 135 Remove the dipstick from the transaxle

Fig. 136 Check the fluid level of the transaxle with the marks on the dipstick

Fig. 137 If the fluid level is low, add it through the filler tube until the level is correct. Make sure not to add too much fluid

1. Remove the filler plug (or dipstick) from the left side of the transaxle to provide a vent.
2. Raise and support the vehicle safely using jackstands.
3. The drain plug is located on the bottom of the transaxle case. Place a pan under the drain plug and remove it.

❈ CAUTION

The fluid will be HOT. Push up against the threads as you unscrew the plug to prevent leakage.

4. Allow the fluid to drain completely. Check the condition of the plug gasket and replace it if necessary. Clean off the plug and replace, tightening it until snug.
5. Fill the transaxle with fluid through the fill or dipstick tube. You will need the aid of a long neck funnel or a funnel and a hose to pour through.
6. Use the dipstick to gauge the level of the fluid.
7. Replace the filler plug or dipstick and dispose of the old fluid in the same manner as you would old engine oil.
Take a drive in the car, stop on a level surface, and check the oil level.

Automatic Transaxle

FLUID RECOMMENDATION

When adding to or refilling the automatic transaxle, always use Dexron® III, IIE or latest superceding equivalent transaxle fluid.

LEVEL CHECK

The fluid level in the automatic transaxle should be checked every 12 months or 7,500 miles (12,000 km), whichever comes first. Most of the automatic transaxles have a dipstick for fluid level checks.

Except 4T40E Automatic Transaxle

▶ See Figure 138

1. Drive the car until it is at normal operating temperature. The level should not be checked immediately after the car has been driven for a long time at high speed, or in city traffic in hot weather; in those cases, the transaxle should be given a half hour to cool down.
2. Stop the car, apply the parking brake, then shift slowly through all gear positions, ending in Park. Let the engine idle for about five minutes with the selector in Park. The car should be on a level surface.
3. With the engine still running, remove the dipstick, wipe it clean, then reinsert it, pushing it fully home.
4. Wait three seconds, then pull the dipstick out again and, holding it horizontally, read the fluid level. It should be within the cross-hatch area between "ADD" and "FULL".
5. Cautiously feel the end of the dipstick to determine the temperature. Note that on the J-cars the cool and warm level dimples are above the hot level area. If the fluid level is not in the correct area, more will have to be added.
6. Fluid is added through the dipstick tube. You will probably need the aid of a spout or a long-necked funnel. Be sure that whatever you pour through is perfectly clean and dry. Use an automatic transmission fluid marked DEXRON®III, IIE or equivalent. Add fluid slowly, and in small amounts, checking

Fig. 138 The transaxle fluid level is acceptable if it is anywhere within the crosshatch area on the dipstick. Do NOT add oil unless the fluid level is below the crosshatch area

the level frequently between additions. Do not overfill, which will cause foaming, fluid loss, slippage, and possible transaxle damage. It takes only one pint to raise the level from ADD to FULL when the transaxle is hot.

4T40E Automatic Transaxle

▶ See Figure 139

❈❈ CAUTION

Removal of the fluid level screw when the transaxle fluid is hot may cause injury. Use care to avoid contact of the transaxle fluid to exhaust pipe.

The fluid level screw is intended to be used for diagnosing a transaxle fluid leak or resetting the transaxle fluid level after service that involves a loss of fluid.

1. The fluid level should be checked when the transaxle is near room temperature or at 104°F (40°C). To acquire this, left the car idle for 3–5 minutes with all of the accessories off.
2. Apply the brake, then move the gear shift selector through all gear ranges, pausing three seconds in each range. Shift the lever into "Park".
3. Raise and safely support the vehicle.
4. Place a suitable drain pan under the check plug to catch any fluid that may drip out.
5. Remove the oil check plug. The oil level should be at the bottom of the oil check hole. Because the transaxle operates correctly over a range of fluid levels, fluid may or may not drain out of the screw hole when the screw is removed.
6. If fluid drains through the screw hole, the transaxle may have been over-filled. When fluid stops draining, then fluid level is correct and the check plug may be installed. If fluid does not drain through the oil check hole. Add fluid at the vent cap location in 1 pint increments until the oil level is at the bottom of the oil check hole.
7. Install the oil check plug/fluid level screw and tighten to 10 ft. lbs. (14 Nm).
8. Carefully lower the vehicle.

Fig. 139 Location of the fluid level screw and the fill/vent cap needed to check the fluid for the 4T40E automatic transaxle.

DRAIN & REFILL (INCLUDES PAN & FILTER SERVICE)

▶ See Figure 140

The fluid should be changed according to the schedule in the Maintenance Intervals chart. If the car is normally used in severe service, such as stop and start driving, trailer towing, or the like, the interval should be halved. If the car is driven under especially nasty conditions, such as in heavy city traffic where the temperature normally reaches 90°F (32°C), or in very hilly or mountainous areas, or in police, taxi, or delivery service, the fluid should be changed every 15,000 miles (24,000 km.).

The fluid must be hot before it is drained; a 20 minute drive should accomplish this.

1. To drain the automatic transaxle fluid, the fluid pan must be removed. Raise and safely support the vehicle. Place a drain pan underneath the transaxle pan, then remove the pan attaching bolts at the front and sides of the pan.
2. Loosen the rear pan attaching bolts approximately four turns each.

1. Transaxle assembly
2. Seal
3. Transaxle fluid strainer
4. Transaxle fluid pan
5. Transaxle fluid pan screw
6. Chip collector magnet
7. Transaxle fluid pan gasket

Fig. 140 When removing the transaxle pan and filter, always replace the gasket and O-ring with a new one before installation

3. Very carefully pry the pan loose. You can use a small prybar for this if you work CAREFULLY. Do not distort the pan flange, or score the mating surface of the transaxle case. You'll be very sorry later if you do. As the pan is pried loose, all of the fluid is going to come pouring out.
4. Remove the remaining bolts and remove the pan and gasket. Throw away the gasket.
5. Clean the pan with solvent and allow it to air dry. If you use a rag to wipe out the pan, you risk leaving bits of lint behind, which will clog the dinky hydraulic passages in the transaxle.
6. Remove and discard the filter and the O-ring seal.

To install:

7. Install a new filter and O-ring, locating the filter against the dipstick stop.
8. Position a new gasket on the pan, then install the pan. Tighten the bolts evenly and in rotation to 8 ft. lbs. (11 Nm.). Do not overtighten.
9. Add approximately 4 qts. (3.8 L) of DEXRON®III or IIE automatic transmission fluid to the transaxle through the dipstick tube. You will need a long necked funnel, or a funnel and tube to do this.
10. With the transaxle in Park, put on the parking brake, block the front wheels, start the engine and let it idle. DO NOT RACE THE ENGINE. DO NOT MOVE THE LEVER THROUGH ITS RANGES.
11. With the lever in Park, check the fluid level. If it's OK, take the car out for a short drive, park on a level surface, and check the level again, as outlined earlier in this section. Add more fluid if necessary. Be careful not to overfill, which will cause foaming and fluid loss.

➡If the drained fluid is discolored (brown or black), thick, or smells burnt, serious transmission troubles, probably due to overheating, should be suspected. Your car's transaxle should be inspected by a reliable transmission specialist to determine the problem.

Cooling System

▶ See Figures 141, 142 and 143

❈❈ CAUTION

Never remove the radiator cap under any conditions while the engine is running! Failure to follow these instructions could result in damage to the cooling system or engine and/or personal injury. To avoid having scalding hot coolant or steam blow out of the radiator, use extreme care when removing the radiator cap from a hot radiator. Wait until the engine has cooled, then wrap a thick cloth around the radiator cap and turn it slowly to the first stop. Step back while the pressure is released from the cooling system. When you are sure the pressure has been released, press down on the radiator cap (still have the cloth in position) turn and remove the radiator cap.

Fig. 141 Cutaway view of a typical cooling system flow

Dealing with the cooling system can be dangerous matter unless the proper precautions are observed. It is best to check the coolant level in the radiator when the engine is cold. The cooling system has, as one of its components, a coolant recovery tank. If the coolant level is at or near the FULL COLD line (engine cold) or the FULL HOT line (engine hot), the level is satisfactory. Always be certain that the filler caps on both the radiator and the recovery tank are closed tightly.

In the event that the coolant level must be checked when the engine is hot and the vehicle is not equipped with a coolant recovery tank, place a thick rag over the radiator cap and slowly turn the cap counterclockwise until it reaches the first detent. Allow all hot steam to escape. This will allow the pressure in the system to drop gradually, preventing an explosion of hot coolant. When the hissing noise stops, remove the cap the rest of the way.

If the coolant level is found to be low, add a 50/50 mixture of antifreeze and clean water. If not equipped with a recovery tank, coolant must be added through the radiator filler neck. On most models, which are equipped with a

Fig. 142 Coolant protection can easily be checked using a float-type hydrometer tester

recovery tank, coolant may be added either through the filler neck on the radiator or directly into the recovery tank.

** CAUTION

Never add coolant to a hot engine unless it is running. If it is not running you run the risk of cracking the engine block.

It is wise to pressure check the cooling system at least once per year. If the coolant level is chronically low or rusty, the system should be thoroughly checked for leaks.

At least once every two years or 30,000 miles (48,000 km), the engine cooling system should be inspected, flushed, and refilled with fresh coolant. If the coolant is left in the system too long, it loses its ability to prevent rust and corrosion. If the coolant has too much water, it won't protect against freezing.

The pressure cap should be examined for signs of age or deterioration. Fan belt and other drive belts should be inspected and adjusted to the proper tension. (See checking belt tension).

Hose clamps should be tightened, and soft or cracked hoses replaced. Damp spots, or accumulations of rust or dye near hoses, water pump or other areas, indicate possible leakage, which must be corrected before filling the system with fresh coolant.

FLUID RECOMMENDATIONS

Whenever adding or changing fluid, use a good quality ethylene glycol antifreeze (one that will not affect aluminum), mix it with clean water until a 50/50 antifreeze solution is attained.

LEVEL CHECK

▶ **See Figures 144 and 145**

On most late model vehicles, the fluid level may be checked by observing the fluid level marks of the recovery tank (see through plastic bottle). The level should be near the ADD or FULL COLD mark, as applicable, when the system is cold. At normal operating temperatures, the level should be above the ADD/FULL COLD mark or, if applicable, between the ADD/FULL COLD and the FULL HOT marks. Only add coolant to the recovery tank as necessary to bring the system up to a proper level.

** CAUTION

Should it be necessary to remove the radiator cap, made sure that the system has had time to cool, reducing the internal pressure.

On any vehicle that is not equipped with a coolant recovery or overflow tank, the level must be checked by removing the radiator cap. This should only be done when the cooling system has had time to sufficiently cool after the engine has been run. The coolant level should be within 2 in. (51mm) of the base of the radiator filler neck. If necessary, coolant can then be added directly to the radiator.

Fig. 143 If possible, a hand-held pressure tester should be used to check system integrity

Fig. 144 When the engine is cold, the coolant should be at the "Full Cold" mark on the recovery tank

Fig. 145 If necessary, add coolant to the tank until it is at the correct level

DRAIN & REFILL

▶ **See Figure 146**

> ✳✳ **CAUTION**
>
> **To avoid injuries from scalding fluid and steam, DO NOT remove the radiator cap while the engine and radiator are still HOT.**

1. Make sure the engine is cool and the vehicle is parked on a level surface, then remove the radiator neck cap and, if equipped, the recovery tank cap in order to relieve system pressure.
2. Position a large drain pan under the vehicle, then drain the existing coolant by opening the radiator drain valve (petcock). It is sometimes helpful to put a piece of vacuum hose ⅜ inches in diameter and about 12 in. (30 cm) long on the end of the radiator drain cock before opening the drain valve. This will help reduce some of the mess. It is also possible to drain the system by disconnecting the lower radiator hose from the bottom radiator outlet.

> ✳✳ **CAUTION**
>
> **When draining the coolant, keep in mind that cats and dogs are attracted by ethylene glycol antifreeze, and are quite likely to drink any that is left in an uncovered container or in puddles on the ground. This will prove fatal in sufficient quantity. Always drain the coolant into a sealable container. Coolant should be reused unless it is contaminated or several years old.**

3. Close the petcock or reconnect the lower hose. If you used it, don't forget to take the piece of vacuum hose off the valve.
4. If necessary, empty the coolant reservoir and flush it. This is most easily done by removing the reservoir tank from the vehicle.
5. Determine the capacity of your coolant system (see capacities specifications). Though the radiator filler neck, add a 50/50 mix of quality antifreeze (ethylene glycol) and water to provide the desired protection.
6. Leave the radiator pressure cap off, then start and run the engine until the thermostat heats up and opens, this will allow air to bleed from the system and provide room for additional coolant to be added to the radiator.
7. Add additional coolant to the radiator, as necessary, until the level is within 2 in. (51mm) of the radiator's filler neck base.
8. Stop the engine and check the coolant level.
9. Check the level of protection with an antifreeze tester, then install the radiator pressure cap.
10. If equipped with a coolant recovery/overflow tank, add coolant to the tank, as necessary, to achieve the proper level.
11. Start and run the engine to normal operating temperature, then check the system for leaks.

FLUSHING & CLEANING THE SYSTEM

The cooling system should be drained, thoroughly flushed and refilled at least every 30,000 miles (48,000 km) or 24 months. These operations should be done with the engine cold, especially if a backpressure flushing kit is being used. Completely draining and refilling the cooling system every two years will remove accumulated rust, scale and other deposits. Coolant in late model cars is a 50/50 mixture of ethylene glycol and water for year round use. Use a good quality antifreeze with water pump lubricants, rust inhibitors and other corrosion inhibitors along with acid neutralizers.

There are many products available for cooling system flushing. If a backpressure flushing kit is used, it is recommended that the thermostat be temporarily removed in order to allow free flow to the system with cold water. Always follow the kit or cleaner manufacturer's instructions and make sure the product is compatible with your vehicle.

1. Make sure the engine is cool and the vehicle is parked on a level surface, then remove the radiator neck cap and, if equipped, the recovery tank cap in order to relieve system pressure.
2. Position a large drain pan under the vehicle, then drain the existing coolant by opening the radiator drain valve (petcock). It is sometimes helpful to put a piece of vacuum hose ⅜ inches in diameter and about 12 in. (30 cm) long on the end of the radiator drain cock before opening the drain valve. This will help reduce some of the mess. It is also possible to drain the system by disconnecting the lower radiator hose from the bottom radiator outlet.

> ✳✳ **CAUTION**
>
> **When draining the coolant, keep in mind that cats and dogs are attracted by ethylene glycol antifreeze, and are quite likely to drink any that is left in an uncovered container or in puddles on the ground. This will prove fatal in sufficient quantity. Always drain the coolant into a sealable container. Coolant should be reused unless it is contaminated or several years old.**

3. Close the radiator/engine drains or reconnect the lower hose, as applicable. If you used it, don't forget to take the piece of vacuum hose off the valve.
4. Fill the system with water, then add a can of quality radiator flush.
5. Idle the engine until the upper radiator hose gets hot and the thermostat has opened. This will allow the solution to fully circulate through the system.
6. Drain the system again.
7. Repeat this process until the drained water is clear and free of scale.
8. Close all drains and connect all the hoses.
9. If equipped with a coolant recovery system, flush the reservoir with water and leave empty.
10. Determine the capacity of your coolant system (see capacities specifications). Add a 50/50 mix of quality antifreeze (ethylene glycol) and water to provide the desired protection.
11. Leave the radiator pressure cap off, then start and run the engine until the thermostat heats up and opens, this will allow air to bleed from the system and provide room for additional coolant to be added to the radiator.
12. Add additional coolant to the radiator, as necessary, until the level is within 2 in. (51mm) of the radiator's filler neck base.
13. Stop the engine and check the coolant level.
14. Check the level of protection with an antifreeze tester, then install the radiator pressure cap.
15. If equipped with a coolant recovery/overflow tank, add coolant to the tank, as necessary, to achieve the proper level.
16. Start and run the engine to normal operating temperature, then check the system for leaks.

Brake Master Cylinder

FLUID RECOMMENDATION

When adding fluid to the brake master cylinder, always use Delco Supreme fluid part no. 1052535 or equivalent DOT-3 brake fluid from a clean, sealed container.

> ✳✳ **CAUTION**
>
> **Brake fluid damages paint. It also absorbs moisture from the air; never leave a container or the master cylinder uncovered longer than necessary. All parts in contact with the brake fluid (master cylinder, hoses, plunger assemblies, etc.) must be kept clean, since any contamination of the brake fluid will adversely affect braking performance.**

VIEW A

1. Radiator drain valve
2. Radiator end tank
3. Radiator

87951091

Fig. 146 The radiator drain valve (petcock) is located on the bottom corner of the radiator

LEVEL CHECK

▶ **See Figures 147, 148, 149 and 150**

Once a month, the fluid level in the brake master cylinder should be checked.
1. Park the car on a level surface.
2. Clean off the master cylinder cover before removal.
3. On early models without a filler cap, the cover simply snaps onto the master cylinder body. Use your thumbs to press up on the two tabs on the side of the cover to unsnap it. Later model master cylinders have a fill cap.
4. Remove the cover or cap, being careful not to drop or tear the rubber diaphragm underneath. Be careful also not to drip any brake fluid on painted surfaces; the stuff eats paint.

➡Brake fluid absorbs moisture from the air, which reduces effectiveness, and will corrode brake parts once in the system. Never leave the master cylinder or the brake fluid container uncovered for any longer than necessary.

5. The fluid level should be about ¼ in. (6mm) below the lip of the master cylinder well on early models or the full mark on the inside on later models.
6. If fluid addition is necessary, use only extra heavy duty disc brake fluid meeting DOT 3 specifications. The fluid should be from a fresh, sealed container, because brake fluid deteriorates with age.
7. Replace the cover or cap, making sure that the diaphragm is correctly seated.

If the brake fluid level is constantly low, the system should be checked for leaks. However, it is normal for the fluid level to fall gradually as the disc brake pads wear; expect the fluid level to drop not more than ⅛ in. for every 10,000 miles (16,000 km) of wear.

Clutch Master Cylinder

➡The clutch master cylinder is mounted on the firewall next to the brake master cylinder.

FLUID RECOMMENDATIONS

Use only hydraulic clutch fluid part no. 12345347 or equivalent DOT-3 brake fluid.

LEVEL CHECK

▶ **See Figures 151, 152, 153 and 154**

The hydraulic clutch reservoir should be checked at least every 6 months. Fill to the line on the reservoir.

Power Steering Pump

FLUID RECOMMENDATIONS

Use GM Power Steering Fluid no. 1050017 or equivalent.

LEVEL CHECK

▶ **See Figures 155, 156, 157 and 158**

The power steering fluid should be checked at least every 6 months. Power steering fluid level is indicated either by marks on a see-through fluid reservoir or by marks on a fluid level indicator on the reservoir cap. There is a Cold and a Hot mark on the dipstick. To prevent possible overfilling, check the fluid level only when the fluid has warmed to operating temperatures and the engine is shut **OFF**. If necessary, add fluid to the power steering pump reservoir.

Steering Gear

The rack and pinion steering gear used on the J-cars is a sealed unit; no fluid level checks or additions are ever necessary.

Fig. 147 For 1982–86 vehicles, the proper brake fluid level is approximately ¼ in. below the lip of the master cylinder

Fig. 148 The fluid level full mark is located on the inside of the reservoir on 1987–94 models

Fig. 149 Clean off the master cylinder cover, then remove the cap

Fig. 150 If necessary, add fluid from a fresh, sealed container

Fig. 151 The hydraulic clutch reservoir is mounted on the firewall, next to the brake master cylinder

Fig. 152 Remove the clutch master cylinder cap, then . . .

Fig. 153 . . . remove the reservoir diaphragm

Fig. 154 If necessary, add fluid to the clutch master cylinder

Fig. 155 The power steering pump reservoir is usually mounted on the firewall

Fig. 156 Remove the power steering fluid dipstick from the reservoir, then . . .

Fig. 157 . . . check the level against the marks on the dipstick

Fig. 158 If the level is low, add fluid to the reservoir

Chassis Greasing

▶ See Figure 159

There are only two areas which require regular chassis greasing: the front suspension components and the steering linkage. These parts should be greased every 12 months or 7,500 miles (12,000 km) with an EP grease meeting G.M. specification 6031M.

If you choose to do this job yourself, you will need to purchase a hand operated grease gun, if you do not own one already, and a long flexible extension hose to reach the various grease fittings. You will also need a cartridge of the appropriate grease.

Press the fitting on the grease gun hose onto the grease fitting on the sus-

pension or steering linkage component. Pump a few shots of grease into the fitting, until the rubber boot on the joint begins to expand, indicating that the joint is full. Remove the gun from the fitting. Be careful not to overfill the joints, which will rupture the rubber boots, allowing the entry of dirt. You can keep the grease fittings clean by covering them with a small square of tin foil.

➡This is a good opportunity, while under the vehicle, to check for any tears or holes in the axle CV-joint boots, which may cause loss of or contamination of the axle grease. Damaged boots must be replaced as soon as possible or joint failure could result.

Body Lubrication

Every 12 months or 7,500 miles (12,000 km), the various linkages and hinges on the chassis and body should be lubricated, as follows:

TRANSAXLE SHIFT LINKAGE

Lubricate the manual transaxle shift linkage contact points with the EP grease used for chassis greasing, which should meet G.M. specification 6031M. The automatic transaxle linkage should be lubricated with clean engine oil.

HOOD LATCH & HINGES

Clean the latch surfaces and apply clean engine oil to the latch pilot bolts and the spring anchor. Use the engine oil to lubricate the hood hinges as well. Use a chassis grease to lubricate all the pivot points in the latch release mechanism.

DOOR HINGES

The gas tank filler door, car door, and rear hatch or trunk lid hinges should be wiped clean and lubricated with clean engine oil. Silicone spray also works well on these parts, but must be applied more often. Use engine oil to lubricate

Fig. 159 Lubrication fitting locations

the trunk or hatch lock mechanism and the lock bolt and striker. The door lock cylinders can be lubricated easily with a shot of silicone spray or one of the many dry penetrating lubricants commercially available.

PARKING BRAKE LINKAGE

➡**Do NOT lubricate the parking brake cables. Lubrication destroys the plastic coating on the cables.**

Use chassis grease on the parking brake cable guides where they contact the links, levers, and pulleys. The grease should be a water resistant one for durability under the car.

TRAILER TOWING

General Recommendations

Your car was primarily designed to carry passengers and cargo. It is important to remember that towing a trailer will place additional loads on your vehicle's engine, drivetrain, steering, braking and other systems. However, if you find it necessary to tow a trailer, using the proper equipment is a must.

Local laws may require specific equipment such as trailer brakes or fender mounted mirrors. Check your local laws.

❄❄ WARNING

Some early models equipped with the V6 engines were not recommended for trailer towing because of insufficient cooling system capacity. These vehicles could overheat. Check your owners manual or local GM dealer for any trailer towing warnings.

Trailer Weight

The weight of the trailer is the most important factor. A good weight-to-horsepower ratio is about 35:1, 35 lbs. of GCW (Gross Combined Weight) for every horsepower your engine develops. Multiply the engine's rated horsepower by 35 and subtract the weight of the car passengers and luggage. The result is the approximate ideal maximum weight you should tow, although a a numerically higher axle ratio can help compensate for heavier weight.

Hitch Weight

Figure the hitch weight to select a proper hitch. Hitch weight is usually 9–11% of the trailer gross weight and should be measured with the trailer loaded. Hitches fall into three types: those that mount on the frame and rear bumper or the bolt-on or weld-on distribution type used for larger trailers. Axle mounted or clamp-on bumper hitches should never be used.

Check the gross weight rating of your trailer. Tongue weight is usually figured as 10% of gross trailer weight. Therefore, a trailer with a maximum gross weight of 2,000 lb. will have a maximum tongue weight of 200 lb. Class I trailers fall into this category. Class II trailers are those with a gross weight rating of 2,000–3,500 lb., while Class III trailers fall into the 3,500–6,000 lb. category. Class IV trailers are those over 6,000 lb. and are for use with fifth wheel trucks, only.

When you've determined the hitch that you'll need, follow the manufacturer's installation instructions, exactly, especially when it comes to fastener torques. The hitch will subjected to a lot of stress and good hitches come with hardened bolts. Never substitute an inferior bolt for a hardened bolt.

ACCELERATOR LINKAGE

Lubricate the carburetor stud, carburetor lever, and the accelerator pedal lever at the support inside the car with clean engine oil.

Wheel Bearings

The J-body models are equipped with sealed hub and bearing assemblies. The hub and bearing assemblies are non-serviceable. If the assembly is damaged, the complete unit must be replaced. Refer to Section 8 for the hub and bearing removal and installation procedure.

Cooling

ENGINE

One of the most common, if not THE most common, problems associated with trailer towing is engine overheating.

If you have a standard cooling system, without an expansion tank, you'll definitely need to get an aftermarket expansion tank kit, preferably one with at least a 2 quart capacity. These kits are easily installed on the radiator's overflow hose, and come with a pressure cap designed for expansion tanks.

Aftermarket engine oil coolers are helpful for prolonging engine oil life and reducing overall engine temperatures. Both of these factors increase engine life.

While not absolutely necessary in towing Class I and some Class II trailers, they are recommended for heavier Class II and all Class III towing.

Engine oil cooler systems consist of an adapter, screwed on in place of the oil filter, a remote filter mounting and a multi-tube, finned heat exchanger, which is mounted in front of the radiator or air conditioning condenser.

TRANSMISSION

An automatic transmission is usually recommended for trailer towing. Modern automatics have proven reliable and, of course, easy to operate, in trailer towing.

The increased load of a trailer, however, causes an increase in the temperature of the automatic transmission fluid. Heat is the worst enemy of an automatic transmission. As the temperature of the fluid increases, the life of the fluid decreases.

It is essential, therefore, that you install an automatic transmission cooler.

The cooler, which consists of a multi-tube, finned heat exchanger, is usually installed in front of the radiator or air conditioning compressor, and hooked inline with the transmission cooler tank inlet line. Follow the cooler manufacturer's installation instructions.

Select a cooler of at least adequate capacity, based upon the combined gross weights of the car and trailer.

Cooler manufacturers recommend that you use an aftermarket cooler in addition to, and not instead of, the present cooling tank in your radiator. If you do want to use it in place of the radiator cooling tank, get a cooler at least two sizes larger than normally necessary.

➡**A transmission cooler can, sometimes, cause slow or harsh shifting in the transmission during cold weather, until the fluid has a chance to come up to normal operating temperature. Some coolers can be purchased with or retrofitted with a temperature bypass valve which will allow fluid flow through the cooler only when the fluid has reached operating temperature, or above.**

Handling A Trailer

Towing a trailer with ease and safety requires a certain amount of experience. It's a good idea to learn the feel of a trailer by practicing turning, stopping and backing in an open area such as an empty parking lot.

TOWING THE VEHICLE

The J-cars may not be pushed or towed to start, because doing so may cause the catalytic converter to explode. If the battery is weak, the engine may be jump started, using the procedure outlined in the following section.

Your J-car may be towed on all four wheels at speeds less than 35 mph (60 km/h) for distances up to 50 miles (80 km). The driveline and steering must be normally operable. If either one is damaged, the car may not be flat-towed. If the car is flat-towed (on all four wheels), the steering must be unlocked, the transaxle shifted to Neutral, and the parking brake released. Towing attachment must be made to the main structural members of the chassis, not to the bumpers or sheetmetal.

The car may be towed on its rear wheels by a wrecker; make sure that safety chains are used. J-cars with manual transaxles may be towed on their front wheels, for short distances and at low speeds. Be sure the transaxle is in Neutral. Cars with automatic transaxles should not be towed on their front wheels; transaxle damage may result. If it is impossible to tow the car on its rear wheels, place the front wheels on a dolly.

JUMP STARTING A DEAD BATTERY

▶ **See Figure 160**

Whenever a vehicle is jump started, precautions must be followed in order to prevent the possibility of personal injury. Remember that batteries contain a small amount of explosive hydrogen gas which is a by-product of battery charging. Sparks should always be avoided when working around batteries, especially when attaching jumper cables. To minimize the possibility of accidental sparks, follow the procedure carefully.

✳✳ CAUTION

NEVER hook the batteries up in a series circuit or the entire electrical system will go up in smoke, including the starter!

Vehicles equipped with a diesel engine may utilize two 12 volt batteries. If so, the batteries are connected in a parallel circuit (positive terminal to positive terminal, negative terminal to negative terminal). Hooking the batteries up in parallel circuit increases battery cranking power without increasing total battery voltage output. Output remains at 12 volts. On the other hand, hooking two 12 volt batteries up in a series circuit (positive terminal to negative terminal, positive terminal to negative terminal) increases total battery output to 24 volts (12 volts plus 12 volts).

Jump Starting Precautions

- Be sure that both batteries are of the same voltage. Vehicles covered by this manual and most vehicles on the road today utilize a 12 volt charging system.
- Be sure that both batteries are of the same polarity (have the same terminal, in most cases NEGATIVE grounded).
- Be sure that the vehicles are not touching or a short could occur.
- On serviceable batteries, be sure the vent cap holes are not obstructed.
- Do not smoke or allow sparks anywhere near the batteries.
- In cold weather, make sure the battery electrolyte is not frozen. This can occur more readily in a battery that has been in a state of discharge.
- Do not allow electrolyte to contact your skin or clothing.

Jump Starting Procedure

1. Make sure that the voltages of the 2 batteries are the same. Most batteries and charging systems are of the 12 volt variety.

2. Pull the jumping vehicle (with the good battery) into a position so the jumper cables can reach the dead battery and that vehicle's engine. Make sure that the vehicles do NOT touch.

3. Place the transmissions of both vehicles in **Neutral** (MT) or **P** (AT), as applicable, then firmly set their parking brakes.

➡**If necessary for safety reasons, the hazard lights on both vehicles may be operated throughout the entire procedure without significantly increasing the difficulty of jumping the dead battery.**

4. Turn all lights and accessories OFF on both vehicles. Make sure the ignition switches on both vehicles are turned to the **OFF** position.

5. Cover the battery cell caps with a rag, but do not cover the terminals.

6. Make sure the terminals on both batteries are clean and free of corrosion or proper electrical connection will be impeded. If necessary, clean the battery terminals before proceeding.

7. Identify the positive (+) and negative (–) terminals on both batteries.

8. Connect the first jumper cable to the positive (+) terminal of the dead battery, then connect the other end of that cable to the positive (+) terminal of the booster (good) battery.

9. Connect one end of the other jumper cable to the negative (–) terminal on the booster battery and the final cable clamp to an engine bolt head, alternator bracket or other solid, metallic point on the engine with the dead battery. Try to pick a ground on the engine that is positioned away from the battery in order to minimize the possibility of the 2 clamps touching should one loosen during the procedure. DO NOT connect this clamp to the negative (–) terminal of the bad battery.

✳✳ CAUTION

Be very careful to keep the jumper cables away from moving parts (cooling fan, belts, etc.) on both engines.

10. Check to make sure that the cables are routed away from any moving parts, then start the donor vehicle's engine. Run the engine at moderate speed for several minutes to allow the dead battery a chance to receive some initial charge.

11. With the donor vehicle's engine still running slightly above idle, try to start the vehicle with the dead battery. Crank the engine for no more than 10 seconds at a time and let the starter cool for at least 20 seconds between tries. If the vehicle does not start in 3 tries, it is likely that something else is also wrong or that the battery needs additional time to charge.

12. Once the vehicle is started, allow it to run at idle for a few seconds to make sure that it is operating properly.

13. Turn ON the headlights, heater blower and, if equipped, the rear defroster of both vehicles in order to reduce the severity of voltage spikes and subsequent risk of damage to the vehicles' electrical systems when the cables are disconnected. This step is especially important to any vehicle equipped with computer control modules.

14. Carefully disconnect the cables in the reverse order of connection. Start with the negative cable that is attached to the engine ground, then the negative cable on the donor battery. Disconnect the positive cable from the donor battery and finally, disconnect the positive cable from the formerly dead battery. Be careful when disconnecting the cables from the positive terminals not to allow the alligator clips to touch any metal on either vehicle or a short and sparks will occur.

MAKE CONNECTIONS IN NUMERICAL ORDER

DO NOT ALLOW VEHICLES TO TOUCH

① FIRST JUMPER CABLE

DISCHARGED BATTERY

SECOND JUMPER CABLE

MAKE LAST CONNECTION ON ENGINE, AWAY FROM BATTERY

BATTERY IN VEHICLE WITH CHARGED BATTERY

TCCS1080

Fig. 160 Connect the jumper cables to the batteries and engine in the order shown

JACKING

▶ See Figures 161, 162, 163, 164 and 165

The J-cars are supplied with a scissors jack for changing tires. This jack engages in notches behind the front wheel and forward of the rear wheel under the rocker flange. This jack is satisfactory for its intended purpose, changing tires. It should NOT, nor should any jack, be used to support the car while you crawl under it and work. To do so is to recklessly jeopardize your life. Whenever it is necessary to get under a car to perform service operation, always be sure that it is adequately supported using jackstands at the proper points. Always block the wheels when changing tires. Never crawl under the car when it is supported by only the scissors jack.

➡ Once the jackstands are in position and the vehicle's weight has been lowered onto them, shake the car a few times before crawling underneath to make sure the jackstands are securely supporting the weight.

The car may also be jacked at the rear axle between the spring seats, or at the front end at the engine cradle crossbar or lower control arm. The car must never be lifted by the rear lower control arms.

Service operations in this book often require that one end or both ends of the car be raised and safely supported. The ideal method, of course, would be to use a grease pit or hydraulic hoist. Since this is beyond both the resource and requirement of the do-it-yourselfer, a small hydraulic, screw or scissors jack will raise the vehicle sufficiently for almost all procedures in this guide. The rolling floor jack is probably the easiest and most convenient of these to use. But the vehicle must still be supported by at least two sturdy jackstands if you intend to work under the car at any time. An alternate method of raising the car would be drive-on ramps. When using ramps, be sure to block the wheels which remain on the ground. Spend a little extra time to make sure that your car is lifted and supported safely. Remember, the car you are laying under weighs at least 1 ton.

✷✷ CAUTION

Concrete blocks are not recommended for supporting a vehicle; they may crumble if the load is not evenly distributed. Boxes and milk crates of any description must not be used.

It is imperative that strict safety precautions be observed both while raising the car and in the subsequent support after the car is raised. If a jack is used to raise the car, the transaxle should be shifted to Park (automatic) or First (manual), the parking brake should be set, and the opposite wheel should be blocked. Jacking should only be attempted on a hard level surface.

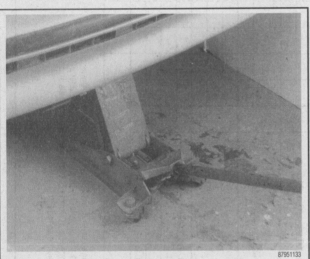

Fig. 161 A rolling floor jack is probably the easiest type of jack to use

Fig. 162 You can raise the front of the vehicle using a jack at the engine cradle crossbar

Fig. 163 After raising the front of the vehicle, ALWAYS support it using jackstands

Fig. 164 View of the proper locations for the jackstands on the front of the vehicle

Fig. 165 Proper jackstand location to support the rear end of the vehicle

MAINTENANCE INTERVALS CHART I of II

Follow Schedule I if the car is mainly operated under one or more of the following conditions:

- When most trips are less than 4 miles (6 kilometers).
- When most trips are less than 10 miles (16 kilometers) and outside temperatures remain below freezing.
- Idling and/or low-speed operation in stop-and-go traffic.
- Towing a trailer
- Operating in dusty areas.

Schedule I should also be followed if the car is used for delivery service, police, taxi or other commercial applications.

The services shown in this schedule up to 48,000 miles (80,000 km) are to be performed after 48,000 miles at the same intervals

ITEM NO.	TO BE SERVICED	WHEN TO PERFORM Miles (Kilometers) or Months, Whichever Occurs First	MILES (000) 3 / KM 5	6 / 10	9 / 15	12 / 20	15 / 25	18 / 30	21 / 35	24 / 40	27 / 45	30 / 50	33 / 55	36 / 60	39 / 65	42 / 70	45 / 75	48 / 80
1	Engine Oil & Filter Change*	Every 3,000 (5,000 km) or 3 mos.	•	•	•	•	•	•	•	•	•	•	•	•	•	•	•	•
2	Chassis Lubrication	Every other oil change		•		•		•		•		•		•		•		•
3	Carb. Choke & Hose Insp.* (If Equipped)††	At 6,000 mi. (10,000 km) and then every 30,000 mi. (50,000 km)		•								•						
4	Carb. or Throttle Body Mount Bolt Torque (Some Models)*			•														
5	Eng. Idle Speed Adj. (Some Models)*	At 6,000 mi. (10,000 km) only		•														
6	Tire & Wheel Insp. and Rotation	At 6,000 mi. (10,000 km) and then every 15,000 mi. (25,000 km)		•					•					•				
7	Vac. or Air Pump Drive Belt Insp.*	Every 30,000 mi. (50,000 km) or 24 mos.										•						
8	Cooling System Service*											•						
9	Wheel Brg. Repack (Rear-Wheel-Drive Cars Only)	See explanation for service interval																
10	Transmission/Transaxle Service																	
11	Spark Plug Service*	Every 30,000 mi. (50,000 km)										•						
12	Spark Plug Wire Insp. (Some Models)*											•						
13	PCV Valve Insp. (Some Models)* ††											•						
14	EGR System Insp.* ††	Every 30,000 mi. (50,000 km) or 36 mos.										•						
15	Air Cleaner & PCV Filter Rep.*											•						
16	Eng. Timing Check (Some Models)*											•						
17	Fuel Tank, Cap & Lines Insp.* ††	Every 30,000 (50,000 km)										•						
18	Thermostatically Controlled Air Cleaner Insp. (Some Models)*											•						

FOOTNOTES: * An Emission Control Service

†† The U.S. Environmental Protection Agency has determined that the failure to perform this maintenance item will not nullify the emission warranty or limit recall liability prior to the completion of vehicle useful life. General Motors, however, urges that all recommended maintenance services be performed at the indicated intervals and the maintenance be recorded in Section C of the owner's maintenance schedule.

87961510

MAINTENANCE INTERVALS CHART II of II

Follow Schedule II if, as a general rule, the car is driven on a daily basis for several miles (km) and none of the above conditions apply.

ITEM NO.	TO BE SERVICED	WHEN TO PERFORM Miles (Kilometers) or Months, Whichever Occurs First	The services shown in this schedule up to 45,000 miles (75,000 km) are to be performed after 45,000 miles at the same intervals					
		MILES (000)	7.5	15	22.5	30	37.5	45
		KILOMETERS (000)	12.5	25	37.5	50	62.5	75
1	Engine Oil & Filter Change*	Every 7,500 mi. (12,500 km) or 12 mos.	•	•	•	•	•	•
	Filter Change*	At first and every other oil change or 12 mos.	•		•		•	
2	Chassis Lubrication	Every 7,500 mi. (12,500 km) or 12 mos.	•	•	•	•	•	•
3	Carb. Choke & Hose Insp.* (If Equipped)††	At 7,500 mi. (12,500 km) and then at each 30,000 mi. (50,000 km) interval	•				•	
4	Carb. or Throttle Body Mount Bolt Torque (Some Models)*	At 7,500 mi. (12,500 km) only	•					
5	Eng. Idle Speed Adj. (Some Models)*	At 7,500 mi. (12,500 km) only	•					
6	Tire & Wheel Insp. and Rotation	At 7,500 mi. (12,500 km) and then every 15,000 mi. (25,000 km)	•		•		•	
7	Vac. or Air Pump Drive Belt Insp.*	Every 30,000 mi. (50,000 km) or 24 mos.				•		
8	Cooling System Service*	Every 30,000 mi. (50,000 km)				•		
9	Wheel Brg. Repack (Rear-Wheel-Drive Cars Only)	Every 30,000 mi. (50,000 km)				•		
10	Transmission/Transaxle Service	See explanation for service interval						
11	Spark Plug Service*	Every 30,000 mi. (50,000 km)				•		
12	Spark Plug Wire Insp. (Some Models)*	Every 30,000 mi. (50,000 km)				•		
13	PCV Valve Insp. (Some Models)*††					•		
14	EGR System Insp.*††	Every 30,000 mi. (50,000 km) or 36 mos.				•		
15	Air Cleaner & PCV Filter Rep.*					•		
16	Eng. Timing Check (Some Models)*	Every 30,000 (50,000 km)				•		
17	Fuel Tank, Cap & Lines Insp.*††					•		
18	Thermostatically Controlled Air Cleaner Insp. (Some Models)*					•		

FOOTNOTES: * An Emission Control Service

†† The U.S. Environmental Protection Agency has determined that the failure to perform this maintenance item will not nullify the emission warranty or limit recall liability prior to the completion of vehicle useful life. General Motors, however, urges that all recommended maintenance services be performed at the indicated intervals and the maintenance be recorded in Section C of the owner's maintenance schedule.

87961511

CAPACITIES

Year	Engine ID/VIN	Engine Displacement Liters (cc)	Engine Oil with Filter (qts.)	Transmission (pts.) 4-Spd	5-Spd	Auto.	Transfer Case (pts.)	Drive Axle Front (pts.)	Rear (pts.)	Fuel Tank (gal.)	Cooling System (qts.)
1982	G	1.8 (1819)	4.0	5.9	-	10.5	-	-	-	14.0	8.0
	O	1.8 (1819)	①	-	5.0	10.5	-	-	-	14.0	7.9
	B	2.0 (1998)	4.0	5.9	-	10.5	-	-	-	14.0	8.3
1983	O, J	1.8 (1819)	①	-	5.0	10.5	-	-	-	14.0	7.9
	B, P	2.0 (1998)	4.0	5.9	-	10.5	-	-	-	14.0	8.3
1984	O, J	1.8 (1819)	①	-	5.0	10.5	-	-	-	14.0	7.9
	P	2.0 (1998)	4.0	5.9	-	10.5	-	-	-	14.0 ②	8
1985	O	1.8 (1819)	4.5	6.0	4.0	8.0	-	-	-	13.6	③
	J	1.8 (1819)	4.5	6.0	4.0	8.0	-	-	-	13.6	③
	P	2.0 (1998)	4.5	5.9	-	10.5	-	-	-	14.0	8.3
	W	2.8 (2835)	4.0	6.0	-	8.0	-	-	-	14.0 ②	12.4
1986	O	1.8 (1819)	4.5	6.0	4.0	8.0	-	-	-	13.6	③
	J	1.8 (1819)	4.5	6.0	4.0	8.0	-	-	-	13.6	③
	P	2.0 (1998)	4.5	5.9	-	10.5	-	-	-	14.0	8.3
	W	2.8 (2835)	4.0	6.0	-	8.0	-	-	-	14.0	12.4
1987	K	2.0 (1998)	4.5	-	4.0	8.0	-	-	-	13.6	8.5
	M	2.0 (1998)	4.5	-	4.0	8.0	-	-	-	13.6	8.5
	1	2.0 (1998)	4.5	5.9	-	10.5	-	-	-	14.0	8.3
	W	2.8 (2835)	4.0	5.9	-	8.0	-	-	-	14.0 ②	12.4
1988	K	2.0 (1998)	4.0	-	6.0	8.0 ④	-	-	-	13.6	8.0
	M	2.0 (1998)	4.5	-	4.0	8.0 ④	-	-	-	13.6	8.5
	1	2.0 (1998)	4.5	-	4.0	10.5	-	-	-	14.0	8.3
	W	2.8 (2835)	4.0	-	4.0	8.0	-	-	-	14.0	12.4
1989	K	2.0 (1998)	4.5	-	4.0	8.0	-	-	-	13.6	8.5
	M	2.0 (1998)	4.5	-	4.0	8.0	-	-	-	13.6	8.5
	1	2.0 (1998)	4.5	-	4.0	10.5	-	-	-	14.0	8.3
	W	2.8 (2835)	4.0	-	4.0	8.0	-	-	-	14.0	12.4
1990	K	2.0 (1998)	4.5	-	4.0	8.0	-	-	-	13.6	8.5
	M	2.0 (1998)	4.5	-	4.0	8.0	-	-	-	13.6	8.5
	G	2.2 (2180)	4.5	-	4.0	8.0 ⑤	-	-	-	13.6	8.5
	T	3.1 (3130)	4.5	-	4.0	8.0 ⑤	-	-	-	13.6	11.0
1991	K	2.0 (1998)	4.5	-	4.0	8.0	-	-	-	13.6	11.7
	G	2.2 (2180)	4.5	-	4.0	8.0 ⑤	-	-	-	13.6	8.5
	T	3.1 (3130)	4.5	-	4.0	8.0 ⑤	-	-	-	13.6	11.0
1992	H	2.0 (1998)	4.5	-	4.0	8.0	-	-	-	15.2	11.7
	G	2.2 (2180)	4.5	-	4.0	8.0 ⑤	-	-	-	13.6	8.5
	T	3.1 (3130)	4.5	-	4.0	8.0 ⑤	-	-	-	13.6	11.0
1993	H	2.0 (1998)	4.5	-	4.0	8.0	-	-	-	13.6	11.7
	4	2.2 (2180)	4.5	-	4.0	8.0 ⑤	-	-	-	13.6	8.5
	T	3.1 (3130)	4.5	-	4.0	8.0 ⑤	-	-	-	13.6	11.0
1994	H	2.0 (1998)	4.5	-	4.0	8.0	-	-	-	15.2	10.7
	4	2.2 (2180)	4.5	-	4.0	8.0 ⑤	-	-	-	13.6	8.5
	T	3.1 (3136)	4.5	-	4.0	8.0	-	-	-	15.2	13.7

1 Add 3 quarts as necessary, check oil level at dipstick and add as necessary.
2 Cimarron - 16.0 gallons
3 With Turbo: 7.8 qts.
   Without Turbo: 7.9 qts.
4 With Isuzu transaxle: 3.30 pts.
5 10.0 pts. if equipped with O/D.

91131C07

ENGLISH TO METRIC CONVERSION: MASS (WEIGHT)

Current **mass** measurement is expressed in pounds and ounces (lbs. & ozs.). The metric unit of **mass** (or **weight**) is the kilogram (kg). Even although this table does not show conversion of masses (weights) larger than 15 lbs, it is **easy** to calculate larger units by following the data immediately below.

To convert ounces (oz.) to grams (g): multiply th number of ozs. by 28
To convert grams (g) to ounces (oz.): multiply the number of grams by .035

To convert pounds (lbs.) to kilograms (kg): multiply the number of lbs. by .45
To convert kilograms (kg) to pounds (lbs.): multiply the number of kilograms by 2.2

lbs	kg	lbs	kg	oz	kg	oz	kg
0.1	0.04	0.9	0.41	0.1	0.003	0.9	0.024
0.2	0.09	1	0.4	0.2	0.005	1	0.03
0.3	0.14	2	0.9	0.3	0.008	2	0.06
0.4	0.18	3	1.4	0.4	0.011	3	0.08
0.5	0.23	4	1.8	0.5	0.014	4	0.11
0.6	0.27	5	2.3	0.6	0.017	5	0.14
0.7	0.32	10	4.5	0.7	0.020	10	0.28
0.8	0.36	15	6.8	0.8	0.023	15	0.42

ENGLISH TO METRIC CONVERSION: TEMPERATURE

To convert Fahrenheit (°F) to Celsius (°C): take number of °F and subtract 32; multiply result by 5; divide result by 9

To convert Celsius (°C) to Fahrenheit (°F): take number of °C and multiply by 9; divide result by 5; add 32 to total

Fahrenheit (F)		Celsius (C)		Fahrenheit (F)		Celsius (C)		Fahrenheit (F)		Celsius (C)	
°F	°C	°C	°F	°F	°C	°C	°F	°F	°C	°C	°F
−40	−40	−38	−36.4	80	26.7	18	64.4	215	101.7	80	176
−35	−37.2	−36	−32.8	85	29.4	20	68	220	104.4	85	185
−30	−34.4	−34	−29.2	90	32.2	22	71.6	225	107.2	90	194
−25	−31.7	−32	−25.6	95	35.0	24	75.2	230	110.0	95	202
−20	−28.9	−30	−22	100	37.8	26	78.8	235	112.8	100	212
−15	−26.1	−28	−18.4	105	40.6	28	82.4	240	115.6	105	221
−10	−23.3	−26	−14.8	110	43.3	30	86	245	118.3	110	230
−5	−20.6	−24	−11.2	115	46.1	32	89.6	250	121.1	115	239
0	−17.8	−22	−7.6	120	48.9	34	93.2	255	123.9	120	248
1	−17.2	−20	−4	125	51.7	36	96.8	260	126.6	125	257
2	−16.7	−18	−0.4	130	54.4	38	100.4	265	129.4	130	266
3	−16.1	−16	3.2	135	57.2	40	104	270	132.2	135	275
4	−15.6	−14	6.8	140	60.0	42	107.6	275	135.0	140	284
5	−15.0	−12	10.4	145	62.8	44	112.2	280	137.8	145	293
10	−12.2	−10	14	150	65.6	46	114.8	285	140.6	150	302
15	−9.4	−8	17.6	155	68.3	48	118.4	290	143.3	155	311
20	−6.7	−6	21.2	160	71.1	50	122	295	146.1	160	320
25	−3.9	−4	24.8	165	73.9	52	125.6	300	148.9	165	329
30	−1.1	−2	28.4	170	76.7	54	129.2	305	151.7	170	338
35	1.7	0	32	175	79.4	56	132.8	310	154.4	175	347
40	4.4	2	35.6	180	82.2	58	136.4	315	157.2	180	356
45	7.2	4	39.2	185	85.0	60	140	320	160.0	185	365
50	10.0	6	42.8	190	87.8	62	143.6	325	162.8	190	374
55	12.8	8	46.4	195	90.6	64	147.2	330	165.6	195	383
60	15.6	10	50	200	93.3	66	150.8	335	168.3	200	392
65	18.3	12	53.6	205	96.1	68	154.4	340	171.1	205	401
70	21.1	14	57.2	210	98.9	70	158	345	173.9	210	410
75	23.9	16	60.8	212	100.0	75	167	350	176.7	215	414

TCCS1C01

ENGLISH TO METRIC CONVERSION: LENGTH

To convert inches (ins.) to millimeters (mm): multiply number of inches by 25.4

To convert millimeters (mm) to inches (ins.): multiply number of millimeters by .04

Inches	Decimals	Milli-meters	Inches to millimeters (inches)	Inches to millimeters (mm)	Inches	Decimals	Milli-meters	Inches to millimeters (inches)	Inches to millimeters (mm)
1/64	0.051625	0.3969	0.0001	0.00254	33/64	0.515625	13.0969	0.6	15.24
1/32	0.03125	0.7937	0.0002	0.00508	17/32	0.53125	13.4937	0.7	17.78
3/64	0.046875	1.1906	0.0003	0.00762	35/64	0.546875	13.8906	0.8	20.32
1/16	0.0625	1.5875	0.0004	0.01016	9/16	0.5625	14.2875	0.9	22.86
5/64	0.078125	1.9844	0.0005	0.01270	37/64	0.578125	14.6844	1	25.4
3/32	0.09375	2.3812	0.0006	0.01524	19/32	0.59375	15.0812	2	50.8
7/64	0.109375	2.7781	0.0007	0.01778	39/64	0.609375	15.4781	3	76.2
1/8	0.125	3.1750	0.0008	0.02032	5/8	0.625	15.8750	4	101.6
9/64	0.140625	3.5719	0.0009	0.02286	41/64	0.640625	16.2719	5	127.0
5/32	0.15625	3.9687	0.001	0.0254	21/32	0.65625	16.6687	6	152.4
11/64	0.171875	4.3656	0.002	0.0508	43/64	0.671875	17.0656	7	177.8
3/16	0.1875	4.7625	0.003	0.0762	11/16	0.6875	17.4625	8	203.2
13/64	0.203125	5.1594	0.004	0.1016	45/64	0.703125	17.8594	9	228.6
7/32	0.21875	5.5562	0.005	0.1270	23/32	0.71875	18.2562	10	254.0
15/64	0.234375	5.9531	0.006	0.1524	47/64	0.734375	18.6531	11	279.4
1/4	0.25	6.3500	0.007	0.1778	3/4	0.75	19.0500	12	304.8
17/64	0.265625	6.7469	0.008	0.2032	49/64	0.765625	19.4469	13	330.2
9/32	0.28125	7.1437	0.009	0.2286	25/32	0.78125	19.8437	14	355.6
19/64	0.296875	7.5406	0.01	0.254	51/64	0.796875	20.2406	15	381.0
5/16	0.3125	7.9375	0.02	0.508	13/16	0.8125	20.6375	16	406.4
21/64	0.328125	8.3344	0.03	0.762	53/64	0.828125	21.0344	17	431.8
11/32	0.34375	8.7312	0.04	1.016	27/32	0.84375	21.4312	18	457.2
23/64	0.359375	9.1281	0.05	1.270	55/64	0.859375	21.8281	19	482.6
3/8	0.375	9.5250	0.06	1.524	7/8	0.875	22.2250	20	508.0
25/64	0.390625	9.9219	0.07	1.778	57/64	0.890625	22.6219	21	533.4
13/32	0.40625	10.3187	0.08	2.032	29/32	0.90625	23.0187	22	558.8
27/64	0.421875	10.7156	0.09	2.286	59/64	0.921875	23.4156	23	584.2
7/16	0.4375	11.1125	0.1	2.54	15/16	0.9375	23.8125	24	609.6
29/64	0.453125	11.5094	0.2	5.08	61/64	0.953125	24.2094	25	635.0
15/32	0.46875	11.9062	0.3	7.62	31/32	0.96875	24.6062	26	660.4
31/64	0.484375	12.3031	0.4	10.16	63/64	0.984375	25.0031	27	690.6
1/2	0.5	12.7000	0.5	12.70					

ENGLISH TO METRIC CONVERSION: TORQUE

To convert foot-pounds (ft. lbs.) to Newton-meters: multiply the number of ft. lbs. by 1.3

To convert inch-pounds (in. lbs.) to Newton-meters: multiply the number of in. lbs. by .11

in lbs	N-m	in lbs	N-m	in lbs	N-m	in lbs	N-m	in lbs	N-m
0.1	0.01	1	0.11	10	1.13	19	2.15	28	3.16
0.2	0.02	2	0.23	11	1.24	20	2.26	29	3.28
0.3	0.03	3	0.34	12	1.36	21	2.37	30	3.39
0.4	0.04	4	0.45	13	1.47	22	2.49	31	3.50
0.5	0.06	5	0.56	14	1.58	23	2.60	32	3.62
0.6	0.07	6	0.68	15	1.70	24	2.71	33	3.73
0.7	0.08	7	0.78	16	1.81	25	2.82	34	3.84
0.8	0.09	8	0.90	17	1.92	26	2.94	35	3.95
0.9	0.10	9	1.02	18	2.03	27	3.05	36	4.0

TCCS1C02

ENGLISH TO METRIC CONVERSION: TORQUE

Torque is now expressed as either foot-pounds (ft./lbs.) or inch-pounds (in./lbs.). The metric measurement unit for torque is the Newton-meter (Nm). This unit—the Nm—will be used for all SI metric torque references, both the present ft./lbs. and in./lbs.

ft lbs	N-m	ft lbs	N-m	ft lbs	N-m	ft lbs	N-m
0.1	0.1	33	44.7	74	100.3	115	155.9
0.2	0.3	34	46.1	75	101.7	116	157.3
0.3	0.4	35	47.4	76	103.0	117	158.6
0.4	0.5	36	48.8	77	104.4	118	160.0
0.5	0.7	37	50.7	78	105.8	119	161.3
0.6	0.8	38	51.5	79	107.1	120	162.7
0.7	1.0	39	52.9	80	108.5	121	164.0
0.8	1.1	40	54.2	81	109.8	122	165.4
0.9	1.2	41	55.6	82	111.2	123	166.8
1	1.3	42	56.9	83	112.5	124	168.1
2	2.7	43	58.3	84	113.9	125	169.5
3	4.1	44	59.7	85	115.2	126	170.8
4	5.4	45	61.0	86	116.6	127	172.2
5	6.8	46	62.4	87	118.0	128	173.5
6	8.1	47	63.7	88	119.3	129	174.9
7	9.5	48	65.1	89	120.7	130	176.2
8	10.8	49	66.4	90	122.0	131	177.6
9	12.2	50	67.8	91	123.4	132	179.0
10	13.6	51	69.2	92	124.7	133	180.3
11	14.9	52	70.5	93	126.1	134	181.7
12	16.3	53	71.9	94	127.4	135	183.0
13	17.6	54	73.2	95	128.8	136	184.4
14	18.9	55	74.6	96	130.2	137	185.7
15	20.3	56	75.9	97	131.5	138	187.1
16	21.7	57	77.3	98	132.9	139	188.5
17	23.0	58	78.6	99	134.2	140	189.8
18	24.4	59	80.0	100	135.6	141	191.2
19	25.8	60	81.4	101	136.9	142	192.5
20	27.1	61	82.7	102	138.3	143	193.9
21	28.5	62	84.1	103	139.6	144	195.2
22	29.8	63	85.4	104	141.0	145	196.6
23	31.2	64	86.8	105	142.4	146	198.0
24	32.5	65	88.1	106	143.7	147	199.3
25	33.9	66	89.5	107	145.1	148	200.7
26	35.2	67	90.8	108	146.4	149	202.0
27	36.6	68	92.2	109	147.8	150	203.4
28	38.0	69	93.6	110	149.1	151	204.7
29	39.3	70	94.9	111	150.5	152	206.1
30	40.7	71	96.3	112	151.8	153	207.4
31	42.0	72	97.6	113	153.2	154	208.8
32	43.4	73	99.0	114	154.6	155	210.2

TCCS1C03

ENGLISH TO METRIC CONVERSION: FORCE

Force is presently measured in pounds (lbs.). This type of measurement is used to measure spring pressure, specifically how many pounds it takes to compress a spring. Our present force unit (the pound) will be replaced in SI metric measurements by the Newton (N). This term will eventually see use in specifications for electric motor brush spring pressures, valve spring pressures, etc.

To convert pounds (lbs.) to Newton (N): multiply the number of lbs. by 4.45

lbs	N	lbs	N	lbs	N	oz	N
0.01	0.04	21	93.4	59	262.4	1	0.3
0.02	0.09	22	97.9	60	266.9	2	0.6
0.03	0.13	23	102.3	61	271.3	3	0.8
0.04	0.18	24	106.8	62	275.8	4	1.1
0.05	0.22	25	111.2	63	280.2	5	1.4
0.06	0.27	26	115.6	64	284.6	6	1.7
0.07	0.31	27	120.1	65	289.1	7	2.0
0.08	0.36	28	124.6	66	293.6	8	2.2
0.09	0.40	29	129.0	67	298.0	9	2.5
0.1	0.4	30	133.4	68	302.5	10	2.8
0.2	0.9	31	137.9	69	306.9	11	3.1
0.3	1.3	32	142.3	70	311.4	12	3.3
0.4	1.8	33	146.8	71	315.8	13	3.6
0.5	2.2	34	151.2	72	320.3	14	3.9
0.6	2.7	35	155.7	73	324.7	15	4.2
0.7	3.1	36	160.1	74	329.2	16	4.4
0.8	3.6	37	164.6	75	333.6	17	4.7
0.9	4.0	38	169.0	76	338.1	18	5.0
1	4.4	39	173.5	77	342.5	19	5.3
2	8.9	40	177.9	78	347.0	20	5.6
3	13.4	41	182.4	79	351.4	21	5.8
4	17.8	42	186.8	80	355.9	22	6.1
5	22.2	43	191.3	81	360.3	23	6.4
6	26.7	44	195.7	82	364.8	24	6.7
7	31.1	45	200.2	83	369.2	25	7.0
8	35.6	46	204.6	84	373.6	26	7.2
9	40.0	47	209.1	85	378.1	27	7.5
10	44.5	48	213.5	86	382.6	28	7.8
11	48.9	49	218.0	87	387.0	29	8.1
12	53.4	50	224.4	88	391.4	30	8.3
13	57.8	51	226.9	89	395.9	31	8.6
14	62.3	52	231.3	90	400.3	32	8.9
15	66.7	53	235.8	91	404.8	33	9.2
16	71.2	54	240.2	92	409.2	34	9.4
17	75.6	55	244.6	93	413.7	35	9.7
18	80.1	56	249.1	94	418.1	36	10.0
19	84.5	57	253.6	95	422.6	37	10.3
20	89.0	58	258.0	96	427.0	38	10.6

TCCS1C04

ENGLISH TO METRIC CONVERSION: LIQUID CAPACITY

Liquid or fluid capacity is presently expressed as pints, quarts or gallons, or a combination of all of these. In the metric system the liter (l) will become the basic unit. Fractions of a liter would be expressed as deciliters, centiliters, or most frequently (and commonly) as milliliters.

To convert pints (pts.) to liters (l): multiply the number of pints by .47
To convert liters (l) to pints (pts.): multiply the number of liters by 2.1
To convert quarts (qts.) to liters (l): multiply the number of quarts by .95

To convert liters (l) to quarts (qts.): multiply the number of liters by 1.06
To convert gallons (gals.) to liters (l): multiply the number of gallons by 3.8
To convert liters (l) to gallons (gals.): multiply the number of liters by .26

gals	liters	qts	liters	pts	liters
0.1	0.38	0.1	0.10	0.1	0.05
0.2	0.76	0.2	0.19	0.2	0.10
0.3	1.1	0.3	0.28	0.3	0.14
0.4	1.5	0.4	0.38	0.4	0.19
0.5	1.9	0.5	0.47	0.5	0.24
0.6	2.3	0.6	0.57	0.6	0.28
0.7	2.6	0.7	0.66	0.7	0.33
0.8	3.0	0.8	0.76	0.8	0.38
0.9	3.4	0.9	0.85	0.9	0.43
1	3.8	1	1.0	1	0.5
2	7.6	2	1.9	2	1.0
3	11.4	3	2.8	3	1.4
4	15.1	4	3.8	4	1.9
5	18.9	5	4.7	5	2.4
6	22.7	6	5.7	6	2.8
7	26.5	7	6.6	7	3.3
8	30.3	8	7.6	8	3.8
9	34.1	9	8.5	9	4.3
10	37.8	10	9.5	10	4.7
11	41.6	11	10.4	11	5.2
12	45.4	12	11.4	12	5.7
13	49.2	13	12.3	13	6.2
14	53.0	14	13.2	14	6.6
15	56.8	15	14.2	15	7.1
16	60.6	16	15.1	16	7.6
17	64.3	17	16.1	17	8.0
18	68.1	18	17.0	18	8.5
19	71.9	19	18.0	19	9.0
20	75.7	20	18.9	20	9.5
21	79.5	21	19.9	21	9.9
22	83.2	22	20.8	22	10.4
23	87.0	23	21.8	23	10.9
24	90.8	24	22.7	24	11.4
25	94.6	25	23.6	25	11.8
26	98.4	26	24.6	26	12.3
27	102.2	27	25.5	27	12.8
28	106.0	28	26.5	28	13.2
29	110.0	29	27.4	29	13.7
30	113.5	30	28.4	30	14.2

ENGLISH TO METRIC CONVERSION: PRESSURE

The basic unit of pressure measurement used today is expressed as pounds per square inch (psi). The metric unit for psi will be the kilopascal (kPa). This will apply to either fluid pressure or air pressure, and will be frequently seen in tire pressure readings, oil pressure specifications, fuel pump pressure, etc.

To convert pounds per square inch (psi) to kilopascals (kPa): multiply the number of psi by 6.89

Psi	kPa	Psi	kPa	Psi	kPa	Psi	kPa
0.1	0.7	37	255.1	82	565.4	127	875.6
0.2	1.4	38	262.0	83	572.3	128	882.5
0.3	2.1	39	268.9	84	579.2	129	889.4
0.4	2.8	40	275.8	85	586.0	130	896.3
0.5	3.4	41	282.7	86	592.9	131	903.2
0.6	4.1	42	289.6	87	599.8	132	910.1
0.7	4.8	43	296.5	88	606.7	133	917.0
0.8	5.5	44	303.4	89	613.6	134	923.9
0.9	6.2	45	310.3	90	620.5	135	930.8
1	6.9	46	317.2	91	627.4	136	937.7
2	13.8	47	324.0	92	634.3	137	944.6
3	20.7	48	331.0	93	641.2	138	951.5
4	27.6	49	337.8	94	648.1	139	958.4
5	34.5	50	344.7	95	655.0	140	965.2
6	41.4	51	351.6	96	661.9	141	972.2
7	48.3	52	358.5	97	668.8	142	979.0
8	55.2	53	365.4	98	675.7	143	985.9
9	62.1	54	372.3	99	682.6	144	992.8
10	69.0	55	379.2	100	689.5	145	999.7
11	75.8	56	386.1	101	696.4	146	1006.6
12	82.7	57	393.0	102	703.3	147	1013.5
13	89.6	58	399.9	103	710.2	148	1020.4
14	96.5	59	406.8	104	717.0	149	1027.3
15	103.4	60	413.7	105	723.9	150	1034.2
16	110.3	61	420.6	106	730.8	151	1041.1
17	117.2	62	427.5	107	737.7	152	1048.0
18	124.1	63	434.4	108	744.6	153	1054.9
19	131.0	64	441.3	109	751.5	154	1061.8
20	137.9	65	448.2	110	758.4	155	1068.7
21	144.8	66	455.0	111	765.3	156	1075.6
22	151.7	67	461.9	112	772.2	157	1082.5
23	158.6	68	468.8	113	779.1	158	1089.4
24	165.5	69	475.7	114	786.0	159	1096.3
25	172.4	70	482.6	115	792.9	160	1103.2
26	179.3	71	489.5	116	799.8	161	1110.0
27	186.2	72	496.4	117	806.7	162	1116.9
28	193.0	73	503.3	118	813.6	163	1123.8
29	200.0	74	510.2	119	820.5	164	1130.7
30	206.8	75	517.1	120	827.4	165	1137.6
31	213.7	76	524.0	121	834.3	166	1144.5
32	220.6	77	530.9	122	841.2	167	1151.4
33	227.5	78	537.8	123	848.0	168	1158.3
34	234.4	79	544.7	124	854.9	169	1165.2
35	241.3	80	551.6	125	861.8	170	1172.1
36	248.2	81	558.5	126	868.7	171	1179.0

TCCS1C06

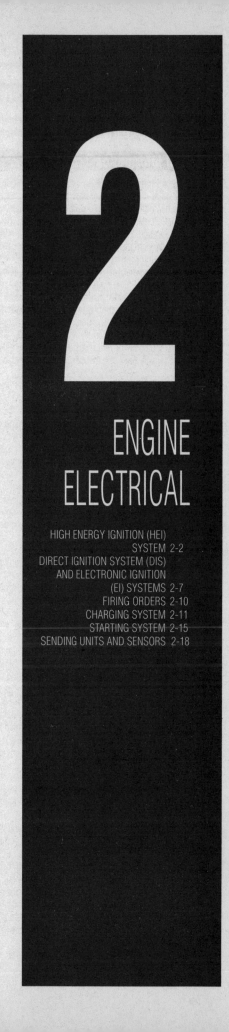

2

ENGINE ELECTRICAL

HIGH ENERGY IGNITION (HEI)
SYSTEM 2-2
DIRECT IGNITION SYSTEM (DIS)
AND ELECTRONIC IGNITION
(EI) SYSTEMS 2-7
FIRING ORDERS 2-10
CHARGING SYSTEM 2-11
STARTING SYSTEM 2-15
SENDING UNITS AND SENSORS 2-18

**HIGH ENERGY IGNITION (HEI)
SYSTEM 2-2**
GENERAL INFORMATION 2-2
HEI SYSTEM PRECAUTIONS 2-2
DIAGNOSIS AND TESTING 2-2
SECONDARY SPARK 2-3
PICK-UP COIL 2-3
IGNITION MODULE 2-3
HALL EFFECT SWITCH 2-3
ELECTRONIC SPARK TIMING (EST)
SYSTEM 2-3
ELECTRONIC SPARK CONTROL (ESC)
SYSTEM 2-4
IGNITION COIL 2-4
TESTING 2-4
REMOVAL & INSTALLATION 2-4
PICK-UP COIL 2-5
REMOVAL & INSTALLATION 2-5
IGNITION MODULE 2-6
REMOVAL & INSTALLATION 2-6
HALL EFFECT SWITCH 2-6
REMOVAL & INSTALLATION 2-6
DISTRIBUTOR 2-6
REMOVAL & INSTALLATION 2-6
INSTALLATION IF THE ENGINE WAS
DISTURBED 2-7
**DIRECT IGNITION SYSTEM (DIS)
AND ELECTRONIC IGNITION (EI)
SYSTEMS 2-7**
GENERAL INFORMATION 2-7
SYSTEM COMPONENTS 2-8
DIAGNOSIS AND TESTING 2-9
SYSTEM PERFORMANCE 2-9
EST PERFORMANCE 2-9
IGNITION COIL ASSEMBLY 2-9
REMOVAL & INSTALLATION 2-9
IGNITION MODULE 2-9
REMOVAL & INSTALLATION 2-9
CRANKSHAFT POSITION SENSOR 2-10
CAMSHAFT POSITION SENSOR 2-10
FIRING ORDERS 2-10
CHARGING SYSTEM 2-11
DESCRIPTION AND OPERATION 2-11
ALTERNATOR PRECAUTIONS 2-12
ALTERNATOR 2-12
DIAGNOSIS 2-12
REMOVAL & INSTALLATION 2-13
REGULATOR 2-14
REMOVAL & INSTALLATION 2-14
STARTING SYSTEM 2-15
DESCRIPTION AND OPERATION 2-15
STARTER 2-15
TESTING 2-15
REMOVAL & INSTALLATION 2-15
SOLENOID REPLACEMENT 2-18
**SENDING UNITS AND
SENSORS 2-18**
COOLANT TEMPERATURE SENDING
UNIT 2-18

REMOVAL & INSTALLATION 2-18
OIL PRESSURE SWITCH 2-18
REMOVAL & INSTALLATION 2-18
RADIATOR FAN TEMPERATURE
SWITCH 2-18
REMOVAL & INSTALLATION 2-18

HIGH ENERGY IGNITION (HEI) SYSTEM

➡For information on understanding electricity and troubleshooting electrical circuits, please refer to Section 6 of this manual.

General Information

The General Motors/Delco-Remy High Energy Ignition (HEI) system is a breakerless, pulse-triggered, transistor controlled, inductive discharge ignition system. It is used on all engines covered by this manual except for the 1987–89 2.0L (VIN 1), 2.2L (VIN G and 4), 1987 and later 2.8L (VIN W) engines and all 3.1L (VIN T) engines. The ignition coil is externally mounted on the engine, using a secondary circuit high tension wire to connect the coil to the distributor cap. Interconnecting primary wiring as part of the engine harness.

Depending upon what year your vehicle is, it may have one of three slightly different distributors. The first type has the pick-up coil mounted above the module. For the second type, the module has two outside terminal connections for the wiring harness. The third type of distributor which is used with the EST system is a tang driven unit. The unit is mounted horizontally to the valve cover housing and is driven by the camshaft, through a tang on the distributor shaft. All three have separately or remote mounted ignition coils. These distributors operated in basically the same manner but may be tested or removed in different ways.

The distributor contains the electronic ignition module, and the magnetic pick-up assembly which contains a permanent magnet, a pole piece with internal teeth, and a pick-up coil (not to be confused with the ignition coil).

The HEI distributor is equipped to aid in spark timing changes which is necessary to maintain emissions, economy and performance. This is achieved by the Electronic Spark Timing (EST) control system. On these vehicles, timing changes are electronically regulated through the computer control module.

In the HEI system, as in other electronic ignition systems, the breaker points have been replaced with an electronic switch, a transistor, which is located within the ignition module. This switching transistor performs the same function the points did in a conventional ignition system; it simply turns coil primary current on and off at the correct time. Essentially, the electronic and conventional ignition systems operate on the same principal.

The module which houses the switching transistor is controlled (turned on and off) by a magnetically generated impulse induced in the pick-up coil. When the teeth of the rotating timer align with the teeth of the pole piece, the induced voltage in the pick-up coil signals the electronic module to open the coil primary circuit. The primary current then decreases and a high voltage is induced in the ignition coil secondary windings which is then directed through the rotor and high voltage leads (spark plug wires) to fire the spark plugs.

In essence then, the pick-up coil module system simply replaces the conventional breaker points and condenser. The condenser found within the distributor is for radio suppression purposes only and has nothing to do with the ignition process. The module automatically controls the dwell period, increasing it with increasing engine speed. The HEI system features a longer spark duration which is instrumental in firing lean and Exhaust Gas Recirculation (EGR) diluted fuel/air mixtures. Since dwell is automatically controlled, it cannot be adjusted. The module itself is non-adustable and non-repairable and must be replaced if found defective.

All spark timing changes in the HEI (EST) distributors are done electronically by the Electronic Control Module (ECM), which monitors information from the various engine sensors, computes the desired spark timing and signals the distributor to change the timing accordingly. With this distributor, no vacuum or centrifugal advances are used.

A Hall Effect Switch is used on some of the distributors in the EST system. It is mounted above the pick-up coil in the distributor and takes the place of the reference terminal on the distributor module. The Hall Effect Switch provides a voltage signal to the ECM to tell it which cylinder will fire next.

Some of the engines covered by this manual are equipped with Electronic Spark Control (ESC). A knock sensor is mounted in the engine block. It is connected to the ESC module which is mounted to the cowl in the engine compartment. In response to engine knock, the sensor sends a signal to the ESC module. The module will then signal the ECM which will retard the spark timing in the distributor.

HEI SYSTEM PRECAUTIONS

Before proceeding with troubleshooting or HEI system service, please note the following precautions:

Timing Light Use

Inductive pick-up timing lights are the best kind to use with the HEI system. Timing lights which connect between the spark plug and the spark plug wire occasionally (not always) give false readings due to the high voltage of the HEI system which more easily leads to arcing.

Spark Plug Wires

The plug wires used with HEI systems are of a different construction than conventional wires. When replacing them, make sure you get the correct wires, since conventional point system wires won't carry the voltage. Also, handle them carefully to avoid cracking or splitting them and never pierce them.

Tachometer Use

Not all tachometers will operate or indicate correctly when used on a HEI system. While some tachometers may give a reading, this does not necessarily mean the reading is correct. In addition, some tachometers hook up differently from others. If you can't figure out whether or not your tachometer will work on your car, check with the tachometer manufacturer.

HEI System Testers

Instruments designed specifically for testing HEI systems are available from several tool manufacturers. Some of these will even test the module itself. However, most of the tests given in the following require only an ohmmeter and a voltmeter.

Diagnosis and Testing

Diagnosis and testing procedures in this section should be used in conjunction with those in Section 4 (Emission Controls) and Section 5 (Fuel System) of this manual. This will enable you to diagnose problems involving all components controlled by the computer control module.

➡An accurate diagnosis is the first step to problem solution and repair. For several of the following steps, a HEI spark tester, tool ST 125, to ground. Use of this tool is recommended, as there is more control of the high energy spark and less chance of being shocked. If a tachometer is connected to the TACH terminal on the distributor, disconnect it before proceeding with this test.

The symptoms of a defective components within the HEI system are exactly the same as those you would encounter in a conventional system. Some of these symptoms could be:

• Hard or no starting
• Rough idle
• Poor fuel economy
• Engine misses under load or while accelerating

If you suspect a problem in your ignition system, there are certain preliminary checks which you should carry out before you begin to check the electronic portions of the system. First, it is extremely important to make sure the vehicle battery is in a good state of charge. A defective or poorly charged battery will cause the various components of the ignition system to read incorrectly when they are being tested. Second, make sure all wiring connections are clean and tight, not only at the battery, but also at the distributor cap, ignition coil and at the computer control module.

The quickest and easiest test of the ignition system is to check the secondary ignition circuit first (check for spark). If the secondary circuit checks out properly, then the engine condition is probably not the fault of the ignition system. To check the secondary ignition circuit, perform a simple spark test. Remove one of the plug wires and insert a spark tester. If a normal spark occurs, then the problem is most likely not in the ignition system. Check for fuel system problems, or fouled spark plugs.

➡For further diagnosis, please refer to component testing found later in this section.

SECONDARY SPARK

1. Check for spark at the spark plugs by attaching the HEI spark tester, tool ST 125, to one of the plug wires, grounding the HEI spark tester on the engine and cranking the starter.
2. Check fuel system, plug wires, and spark plugs. If spark is present, the HEI system is good.
3. If no spark occurs from EST distributor, disconnect the 4 terminal EST connector and recheck for spark. If spark is present, EST system service check should be performed.

PICK-UP COIL

▶ See Figure 1

1. Remove the rotor and pick-up coil leads from the module.
2. Using an ohmmeter, attach one lead to the distributor base and the second lead to one of the pick-up coil terminals of the connector.
3. The reading should be infinite. If not, the pick-up coil is defective.
4. Attach both leads of the ohmmeter to the pick-up terminal ends of the connector.
5. The reading should be a steady value between 500–1500 ohms.
6. If the reading is not within the specifications, the pick-up coil is defective.

➡While testing, flex the leads to determine if wire breaks are present under the wiring insulation.

Fig. 1 When testing the pick-up coil, the reading should be a steady value from 500–1500 ohms. If not replace the pick-up coil

IGNITION MODULE

Because of the complexity of the internal circuitry of the HEI/EST module, it is recommended the module be tested with an accurate module tester.

HALL EFFECT SWITCH

▶ See Figure 2

1. Remove the switch connectors from the switch.
2. Connect a 12 volt battery and voltmeter to the switch. Note and follow the polarity markings.
3. With a knife blade inserted straight down and against the magnet, the voltmeter should read within 0.5 volts of battery voltage. If not, the switch is defective.
4. Without the knife blade inserted against the magnet, the voltmeter should read less than 0.5 volts. If not, the switch is defective.

Fig. 2 Testing the Hall Effect Switch; Note that not all distributors are equipped with this switch

ELECTRONIC SPARK TIMING (EST) SYSTEM

The HEI (EST) distributor uses a modified ignition module. This module has seven or eight terminals instead of the four used without EST. Different terminal arrangements are used, depending upon engine application.

To properly control ignition/combustion timing, the ECM (or PCM) needs to know the following information:
- Crankshaft position
- Engine speed (rpm)
- Engine load (manifold pressure or vacuum)
- Atmospheric (barometric) pressure
- Engine temperature
- Transmission gear position (certain models)

The EST system consists of the distributor module, ECM and its connecting wires. The distributor has four wires from the HEI module connected to a four terminal connector, which mates with a four wire connector from the ECM.

These circuits perform the following functions:
1. Distributor reference at terminal **B**. This provides the ECM with rpm and crankshaft position information.
2. Reference ground at terminal **D**. This wire is grounded in the distributor and makes sure the ground circuit has no voltage drop, which could affect performance. If this circuit is open, it could cause poor performance.
3. Bypass at terminal **C**. At approximately 400 rpm, the ECM applies 5 volts to this circuit to switch the spark timing control from the HEI module to the ECM. An open or grounded bypass circuit will set a Code 42 and the engine will run at base timing, plus a small amount of advance built into the HEI module.
4. EST at terminal **A**. This triggers the HEI module. The ECM does not know what the actual timing is, but it does know when it gets its reference signal. It then advances or retards the spark timing from that point. Therefore, if the base timing is set incorrectly, the entire spark curve will be incorrect.

An open circuit in the EST circuit will set a Code 42 and cause the engine to run on the HEI module timing. This will cause poor performance and poor fuel economy. A ground may set a Code 42, but the engine will not run.

The ECM uses information from the MAP or VAC and coolant sensors, in addition to rpm, in order to calculate spark advance as follows:
- Low MAP output voltage (high VAC sensor output voltage) would require MORE spark advance.
- Cold engine would require MORE spark advance.
- High MAP output voltage (low VAC sensor output voltage) would require LESS spark advance.
- Hot engine would require LESS spark advance.

Detonation could be caused by low MAP output (high VAC sensor output), or high resistance in the coolant sensor circuit.

Poor performance could be caused by high MAP output (low VAC sensor output) or low resistance in the coolant sensor circuit. Refer to the individual component tests in Section 4.

When the systems is operating on the HEI module with no voltage in the bypass line, the HEI module grounds the EST signal. The ECM expects to sense no voltage on the EST line during this condition. If it senses voltage, it sets Code 42 and will not go into the EST mode.

When the rpm for EST is reached (approximately 400 rpm), the ECM applies

5 volts to the bypass line and the EST should no longer be grounded in the HEI module, so the EST voltage should be varying.

If the bypass line is open, the HEI module will not switch to the EST mode, so the EST voltage will be low and Code 42 will be set.

If the EST line is grounded, the HEI module will switch to the EST, but because the line is grounded, there will be no EST signal and the engine will not operate. A Code 42 may or may not be set.

ELECTRONIC SPARK CONTROL (ESC) SYSTEM

The Electronic Spark Control (ESC) operates in conjunction with the Electronic Spark Timing (EST) system and modifies (retards) the spark advance when detonation occurs. The retard mode is held for approximately 20 seconds after which the spark control will again revert to the Electronic Spark Timing (EST) system. There are three basic components of the Electronic Spark Control (ESC) system.

The Electronic Spark Control (ESC) sensor detects the presence (or absence) and intensity of the detonation by the vibration characteristics of the engine. The output is an electrical signal that goes to the controller. A sensor failure would allow no spark retard.

The distributor is an HEI/EST unit with an electronic module, modified so it can respond to the ESC controller signal. This command is delayed when detonation is occurring, thus providing the level of spark retard required. The amount of spark retard is a function of the degree of detonation.

The Electronic Spark Control (ESC) controller processes the sensor signal into a command signal to the distributor, to adjust the spark timing. The process is continuous, so that the presence of detonation is monitored and controlled. The controller is a hard wired signal processor and amplifier which operates from 6-16 volts. Controller failure would be no ignition, no retard or full retard. The controller has no memory storage.

Should a Code 43 be set in the ECM memory, it would indicate that the ESC system retard signal has been sensed by the ECM for too long a period of time. When voltage at terminal **L** of the ECM is low, spark timing is retarded. Normal voltage in the non-retarded mode is approximately 7.5 volts or more.

Ignition Coil

TESTING

▶ **See Figure 3**

1. Detach the primary wiring connectors and secondary coil wire from the ignition coil.
2. Using an ohmmeter on the high scale, connect one lead to a grounding screw and the second lead to one of the primary coil terminals.
3. The reading should be infinite. If not, replace the ignition coil.
4. Using the low scale, place the ohmmeter leads on both the primary coil terminals.
5. The reading should be very low or zero. If not, replace the ignition coil.
6. Using the high scale, place one ohmmeter lead on the high tension output terminal and the other lead on a primary coil terminal.
7. The reading should NOT be infinite. If it is, replace the ignition coil.

Fig. 3 Connect the ohmmeter as shown to test the ignition coil

REMOVAL & INSTALLATION

1982–84 Vehicles

1. Disconnect the negative battery cable.
2. Raise and safely support the vehicle.
3. Disconnect the fuel pump outlet pipe from the carburetor, then detach the fuel pump inlet hose.
4. Remove the vacuum pipe bracket retaining nut at the coil, then move the pipe aside for access.
5. Unfasten the two fuel pump retaining nuts, then remove the fuel pump and gasket.
6. Remove the coil mounting bolts and stud.
7. Detach the electrical connectors, then remove the coil.
8. Installation is the reverse of the removal procedure.

1985–86 1.8L (VIN O) Engine

▶ **See Figure 4**

1. Disconnect the negative battery cable.
2. Remove the air cleaner assembly.
3. Unfasten the ignition coil mounts. There is usually one bolt and one stud.
4. Detach the coil electrical connectors, then remove the coil.
To install:
5. Position the coil, then attach the electrical connectors.
6. Secure the coil using the attaching bolt(s) and stud(s).
7. Install the air cleaner assembly.
8. Connect the negative battery cable.

Fig. 4 Ignition coil location and mounting—1986 1.8L (VIN O) shown

1985–86 2.0L (VIN P) Engine

EXCEPT FIRENZA

1. Disconnect the negative battery cable.
2. Raise and safely support the vehicle.
3. Label and detach the vacuum pipes from the vacuum pump, then remove the pump.
4. Unfasten the coil mounting bolts.
5. Detach the coil electrical connectors, then remove the ignition coil.
6. Installation is the reverse of the removal procedure.

FIRENZA

1. Disconnect the negative battery cable.
2. Raise and safely support the vehicle.
3. Remove the air cleaner hot air heat tube.
4. Unfasten the retaining bolt(s) and/or stud(s), then detach the electrical connectors and remove the ignition coil from the vehicle.
To install:
5. Position the coil in the vehicle, then attach the electrical connectors and secure using the bolts and nuts.
6. Carefully lower the vehicle.
7. Install the air cleaner hot air tube.
8. Connect the negative battery cable.

1985–86 2.8L (VIN W) Engine

▶ See Figure 5

1. Disconnect the negative battery cable.
2. Detach the two electrical connectors from the ignition coil.
3. Unfasten the 3 bolts and one screw securing the ignition coil to the bracket.
4. Disconnect the ignition coil lead from the distributor, then remove the coil.
5. Installation is the reverse of the removal procedure.

1	COIL
2	CYL. #1
3	CYL. #6
4	CYL. #5
5	CYL. #2
6	DISTRIBUTOR COIL LEAD
7	CYL. #3
8	CYL. #4

Fig. 5 View of the ignition coil in relation to the distributor and secondary wiring—1985 2.8L (VIN W) engine shown

1987–89 2.0L (VIN K & M) Engine

▶ See Figures 6, 7, 8 and 9

1. Disconnect the negative battery cable.
2. If necessary for access to the coil, remove the air cleaner assembly.
3. Detach the coil wire and electrical connectors.
4. Unfasten the coil mounts, there is usually one bolt and one stud, and remove the coil from the vehicle.

To install:
5. Position the coil in the vehicle, then attach the electrical connectors.
6. Secure the ignition coil using the retaining bolts and/or nuts.
7. If removed, install the air cleaner assembly.
8. Connect the negative battery cable.

Pick-Up Coil

REMOVAL & INSTALLATION

▶ See Figures 10 and 11

1. Disconnect the negative battery cable.
2. Remove the distributor from the vehicle. For details, please refer to the procedure later in this section. Remove the cap and rotor.
3. If the distributor has a Hall Effect Switch, remove the switch by removing the retaining screws. Matchmark the gear and shaft for installation purposes, then drive the roll pin from the gear and remove the shaft assembly.
4. Remove the thin "C" washer (waved retaining ring) or pry the retainer off (depending upon application), then lift the pick-up coil straight up to remove from the distributor.

To install:
5. Install the pickup coil and the thin "C" washer or retainer.
6. Assemble the shaft, gears parts and roll pin. Use the marks made during removal for alignment purposes.
7. If equipped, install the Hall Effect Switch.

Fig. 6 Disconnect the coil wire, then . . .

Fig. 7 . . . detach the coil electrical connectors

Fig. 8 Unfasten the ignition coil retaining fasteners, then . . .

Fig. 9 . . . remove the coil from the vehicle

Fig. 10 On the Type 1 and 3 distributors, you must remove the thin "C" washer to remove the pickup coil

Fig. 11 Carefully pry off the retainer, then remove the pick-up coil on the Type 2 distributors

8. Spin the distributor shaft to be sure the teeth do not touch. If the teeth make contact, loosen, then re-tighten the pickup coil teeth and Hall Effect Switch teeth (if used) to eliminate contact.

9. Install the rotor and cap, then install the distributor assembly. For details, please refer to the procedure located later in this section.

10. Connect the negative battery cable.

Ignition Module

REMOVAL & INSTALLATION

▶ **See Figure 12**

➡ **It is imperative that silicone lubricant be used under the module when it is installed, to prevent module failure due to overheating.**

1. Disconnect the negative battery cable.
2. Remove the distributor from the vehicle. For details, please refer to the procedure later in this section. Remove the cap and rotor.
3. If the distributor has a Hall Effect Switch, remove the switch by unfastening the retaining screws. Matchmark the gear and shaft for installation purposes, then drive the roll pin from the gear and remove the shaft assembly.
4. Remove the thin "C" washer (waved retaining ring) or pry the retainer off (depending upon application), then lift the pick-up coil straight up to remove from the distributor.
5. Detach the wiring connector(s) from the ignition module. Unfasten the two screws, then remove the module and copper shield (if used).

REMOVING MODULE
MODULE
APPLY SILICONE LUBRICANT

87952010

Fig. 12 Before installing the ignition module, apply a suitable silicone lubricant to the module for heat dissipation—type three distributor shown

To install:

6. Using a clean, dry rag, wipe the distributor base and module clean, the apply a thin coat of a suitable silicone lubricant between the module and the base for heat dissipation.
7. Position the module and copper shield (if used) to the base, then attach the wiring connectors to the module.
8. Install the pickup coil and the thin "C" washer or retainer.
9. Assemble the shaft, gears parts and roll pin. Use the marks made during removal for alignment purposes.
10. If equipped, install the Hall Effect Switch.
11. Spin the distributor shaft to be sure the teeth do not touch. If the teeth make contact, loosen, then re-tighten the pickup coil teeth and Hall Effect Switch teeth (if used) to eliminate contact.
12. Fasten the rotor and cap, then install the distributor assembly. For details, please refer to the procedure located later in this section.
13. Connect the negative battery cable.

Hall Effect Switch

The Hall Effect Switch, when used, is installed in the HEI distributor. The purpose of the switch is to sense engine speed and send the information to the Electronic Control Module (ECM). To remove the Hall Effect Switch, the distributor shaft must be removed from the distributor.

REMOVAL & INSTALLATION

1. Disconnect the negative battery cable.
2. Remove the distributor from the vehicle. For details, please refer to the procedure later in this section. Remove the cap and rotor.
3. Remove the switch by unfastening the retaining screws.
To install:
4. Position the switch, then securing using the retaining screws.
5. Fasten the rotor and cap, then install the distributor assembly. For details, please refer to the procedure located later in this section.
6. Connect the negative battery cable.

Distributor

REMOVAL & INSTALLATION

1.8L (VIN G) and 2.0L (VIN P) OHV Engines

1. Disconnect the negative battery cable.
2. Tag and disconnect all wires leading from the distributor cap.
3. Remove the air cleaner housing.
4. Remove the distributor cap.
5. Disconnect the AIR pipe-to-exhaust manifold hose at the air management valve.
6. Unscrew the rear engine lift bracket bolt and nut, lift it off the stud and then position the entire assembly out of the way to facilitate better access to the distributor.
7. Mark the position of the distributor, relative to the engine block and then scribe a mark on the distributor body indicating the initial position of the rotor.
8. Remove the hold-down nut and clamp from the base of the distributor. Remove the distributor from the engine. The drive gear on the distributor shaft is helical and the shaft will rotate slightly as the distributor is removed. Note and mark the position of the rotor at this second position. Do not crank the engine while the distributor is removed.
To install:

➡ **If the engine position was disturbed while the distributor was removed, refer to the appropriate installation procedure.**

9. To install the distributor, rotate the shaft until the rotor aligns with the second mark you made (when the shaft stopped moving). Lubricate the drive gear with clean engine oil and install the distributor into the engine. As the distributor is installed, the rotor should move to the first mark that you made. This will ensure proper timing. If the marks do not align properly, remove the distributor and try again.
10. Install the clamp and hold-down nut.

➡ **You may wish to use a magnet attached to an extension bar to position the clamp on the stud.**

11. Installation of the remaining components is in the reverse order of removal. Check the ignition timing.

1.8L (VIN O & J) and 2.0L (VIN K & M) OHC Engines

▶ **See Figures 13, 14 and 15**

1. Disconnect the negative battery cable.
2. Tag the spark plug wires, then remove the wires and coil.
3. Matchmark the position of the rotor, distributor body and cylinder head.
4. Detach the coil and EST electrical connectors from the distributor.
5. Unfasten the two distributor hold-down or retaining nuts, then remove the distributor.

Fig. 13 Unfasten the distributor-to-camshaft carrier retaining nuts—1988 2.0L (VIN K) Sunbird shown

87952104

Fig. 14 Remove the distributor from the engine—1988 2.0L (VIN K) engine shown

87952105

Fig. 15 On some vehicles, there is an O-ring on the base of the distributor which can be carefully removed and replaced, if necessary

87952106

➡️If the engine position was disturbed while the distributor was removed, refer to the appropriate installation procedure.

   6. Installation is the reverse of removal. Tighten the hold-down nuts to 13 ft. lbs. (18 Nm). Check the ignition timing.

1985–86 2.8L (VIN W) Engine

   1. Disconnect the negative battery cable.
   2. Unfasten the two screws securing the distributor cap, then remove the cap.
   3. Detach the two electrical connectors from the HEI module.
   4. Matchmark the position of the rotor and the distributor in the block, then remove the distributor hold-down screw and clamp.
   5. Rotate the distributor to disengage it from the drive gear, then pull it upward to remove it from the engine.

➡️If the engine position was disturbed while the distributor was removed, refer to the appropriate installation procedure.

   6. Installation is the reverse of the removal procedure. Check the ignition timing.

INSTALLATION IF THE ENGINE WAS DISTURBED

➡️If the engine was cranked while the distributor was removed, you will have to place the engine on TDC of the compression stroke for the No. 1 cylinder to obtain proper ignition timing.

   1. Remove the No. 1 spark plug.
   2. Place your thumb over the spark plug hole. Crank the engine slowly until compression is felt. It will be easier if you have someone rotate the engine by hand, using a wrench on the crankshaft pulley.
   3. Align the timing mark on the crankshaft pulley with the **0°** mark on the timing scale attached to the front of the engine. This places the engine at TDC of the compression stroke.
   4. Turn the distributor shaft until the rotor points to the No. 1 spark plug tower on the cap.
   5. Install the distributor into the engine. Be sure to align the distributor-to-engine block mark made earlier.
   6. Perform all necessary remaining service steps.

DIRECT IGNITION SYSTEM (DIS) AND ELECTRONIC IGNITION (EI) SYSTEMS

General Information

   The Direct Ignition System (DIS) or Electronic Ignition (EI) is used on the 1987–92 2.0L (VIN 1 and H), 2.2L (VIN G and 4), and all 1987 and later 2.8L (VIN W) and 3.1L (VIN T) engines.
   The DIS or EI system does not use the conventional distributor and ignition coil. The system consists of two (4-cylinder) or 3 (6-cylinder) separate ignition coils, an ignition module, DIS ignition module or Ignition Control Module (ICM) as applicable, crankshaft sensor or combination sensor, along with the related connecting wires and Electronic Spark Timing (EST) or Ignition Control (IC) portion of the computer control module (ECM/PCM).
   The distributorless system uses a "waste spark" method of spark distribution. Companion cylinders are paired and the spark occurs simultaneously in the cylinder with the piston coming up on the compression stroke and in the companion cylinder with the piston coming up on the exhaust stroke.
   Example of firing order and companion cylinders:

- 1-2-3-4-5-6; 1/4, 2/5, 3/6
- 1-6-5-4-3-2; 1/4, 6/3, 5/2
- 1-3-4-2; 1/4, 2/3

➡️Notice the companion cylinders in the V6 engine firing orders remain the same, but the cylinder firing order sequence differs.

   The cylinder on the exhaust stroke requires very little of the available voltage to arc, so the remaining high voltage is used by the cylinder in the firing position (TDC compression). This same process is repeated when the companion cylinders reverse roles.
   It is possible in an engine no-load condition, for one plug to fire, even though the spark plug lead from the same coil is disconnected from the other spark plug. The disconnected spark plug lead acts as one plate of a capacitor, with the engine being the other plate. These two capacitors plates are charged as a current surge (spark) jumps across the gap of the connected spark plug.
   These plates are then discharged as the secondary energy is dissipated in an oscillating current across the gap of the spark plug still connected. Because of the direction of current flow in the primary windings and thus in the secondary windings, one spark plug will fire from the center electrode to the side electrode, while the other will fire from the side electrode to the center electrode.
   These systems utilize the EST or IC signal from the computer control module, as do the convention distributor type ignition systems equipped with the EST system to control timing.
   In the Direct Ignition or Electronic Ignition system and while under 400 rpm, the DIS ignition module (Ignition Control Module) controls the spark timing through a module timing mode. Over 400 rpm, the ECM/PCM controls the spark timing through the EST/IC mode. To properly control the ignition timing, the computer control module relies on the following information from the various sensors:

- Engine load (manifold pressure or vacuum)
- Engine coolant temperature
- Atmospheric (barometric) pressure
- Engine temperature
- Manifold/Intake air temperature
- Crankshaft position
- Engine speed (rpm)
- Knock
- TP sensor

SYSTEM COMPONENTS

Crankshaft Position (CKP) Sensor

▶ See Figure 16

A magnetic crankshaft sensor (Hall Effect switch) is used which is remotely mounted on the opposite side of the engine from the DIS/IC module. The sensor protrudes in to the engine block, within about 0.050 in. (1.27mm) of the crankshaft reluctor.

The reluctor is a special wheel cast into the crankshaft with seven slots machined into it, six of which are equally spaced 60° apart. A seventh slot is spaced 10° from one of the other slots and serves as a generator of a "sync-pulse". As the reluctor rotates as part of the crankshaft, the slots change the magnetic field of the sensor, creating an induced voltage pulse.

The CKP sensor, ICM or DIS ignition module sends reference signals to the computer control module (ECM/PCM), based on the Crankshaft Position (CKP) sensor pulses, which are used to determine crankshaft position and engine speed. Reference pulses to the computer control module occur at a rate of 1 per each 180° of crankshaft rotation for vehicles through 1993, or 7 per 360° of crankshaft rotation for 1994 vehicles. This signal is called the 2X or 7X reference because it occurs 2 or 7 times per crankshaft revolution, depending on the year of your vehicle.

For 1994 vehicles, the 7X reference signal is necessary for the PCM to determine when to activate the fuel injectors.

The computer control module (ECM/PCM) activates the fuel injectors, based on the recognition of every other reference pulse, beginning at a crankshaft position 120° after piston Top Dead Center (TDC). By comparing the time between the pulses, the DIS module or Ignition Control Module (ICM) can recognize the pulse representing the seventh slot (sync-pulse) which starts the calculation of ignition coil sequencing. The second crankshaft pulse following the sync-pulse signals the DIS module to fire the No. 2–5 ignition coil, the fourth crankshaft pulse signals the module to fire No. 3–6 ignition coil and the sixth crankshaft pulse signals the module to fire the No. 1–4 ignition coil.

1	CRANKSHAFT RELUCTOR
2	CRANKSHAFT POSITION (CKP) SENSOR
3	IGNITION COIL ASSEMBLY

87952004

Fig. 16 View of the CKP sensor-to-crankshaft reluctor relationship

Ignition Coils

There are two separate coils for the four cylinder engines and three separate coils for the V6 engines, mounted to the coil/module assembly. Spark distribution is synchronized by a signal from the crankshaft sensor which the ignition module uses to trigger each coil at the proper time. Each coil provides the spark for two spark plugs simultaneously (waste spark distribution).

Two types of ignition coil assemblies are used, Type I and Type II. During the diagnosis of the systems, the correct type of ignition coil assembly must be identified and the diagnosis directed to that system.

The 2.0L (VIN H) engine is equipped with the Type 1 module/coil assembly. The Type I assembly has two twin tower ignition coils, combined into a single coil pack unit. This unit is mounted to the DIS module. If any of the coils are

faulty, the entire module must replaced. A separate current source through a fused circuit to the module terminal **P** is used to power the ignition coils.

All other engines are equipped with the Type II coil/module assembly. The Type II coil/module assembly has two or three (depending upon engine) separate coils that are mounted to the DIS or IC module. Each coil can be replaced separately. A fused low current source to the module terminal **M**, provides power for the sensors, ignition coils and internal module circuitry.

DIS Module/Ignition Control Module (ICM)

The DIS module or ICM, as it's called in later years, monitors the crankshaft sensor signal, then, based on these signals, sends a reference signal to the computer control module (ECM/PCM) so that correct spark and fuel injector control can be maintained during all driving conditions. During cranking, the module monitors the sync-pulse to begin the ignition firing sequence. Below 400 rpm, the module controls the spark advance by triggering each of the ignition coils at a predetermined interval, based on engine speed only. Above 400 rpm, the ECM controls the spark timing (EST) and compensates for all driving conditions. The module must receive a sync-pulse and then a crank signal, in that order, to enable the engine to start.

The DIS module or Ignition Control Module (ICM) is not repairable. When a module is replaced, the remaining DIS/ICM components must be transferred to the new module.

Direct Ignition Electronic Spark Timing (EST) Circuits

➡These circuits are applicable for vehicles through 1992 only.

The EST system is basically the same EST to ECM circuit used on the distributor type ignition systems with EST. This system includes the following circuits:

• DIS Reference (CKT 430)—The crankshaft sensor generates a signal to the ignition module, which results in a reference pulse being sent to the ECM. The ECM uses this signal to calculate crankshaft position and engine speed for injector pulse width.

• Reference Ground (CKT 453)—This wire is grounded through the module and insures that the ground circuit has no voltage drop between the ignition module and the ECM, which can affect performance.

• Bypass signal (CKT 424)—At approximately 400 rpm, the ECM applies 5 volts to this circuit to switch spark timing control from the DIS module to the ECM. An open or grounded by pass circuit will set a code 42 and result in the engine operating in a back-up ignition timing mode (module timing) at a calculated timing value. This may cause poor performance and reduced fuel economy.

• EST circuit (CKT 423)—The DIS module sends a reference signal to the ECM when the engine is cranking. While the engine is under 400 rpm, the DIS module controls the ignition timing. When the engine speed exceeds 400 rpm, the ECM applies 5 volts to the bypass line to switch the timing to the ECM control (EST). An open or ground in the EST circuit will result in the engine continuing to run, but in a back-up ignition timing mode (module timing mode) at a calculated timing value and the SERVICE ENGINE SOON light will not be on. If the EST fault is still present, the next time the engine is restarted, a code 42 will be set and the engine will operate in the module timing mode. This may cause poor performance and reduced fuel economy.

Ignition Control (IC)

➡These circuits are applicable for 1993–94 vehicles only.

This system uses the same circuits between the ICM and the PCM that distributor type systems use. This system includes the following circuits:

• 7X Reference (CKT 483)—The CKP sensor generates a signal to the ICM, resulting in a reference pulse which is sent to the PCM. The PCM uses this signal to determine crankshaft position, engine speed and injector pulse width. The engine will not start or run if this circuit is open or grounded.

• Reference low (CKT 453)—This wire is grounded through the module and insures that the ground circuit has no voltage drop between the ICM and the PCM which may affect engine performance.

• Ignition control 1 & 2 (CKTs 423 & 406)—The PCM sends the Ignition Control (IC) pulses to the ICM on these circuits. These signals are similar to the 7X reference pulse except that the PCM uses sensor inputs to determine the pulse timing to control spark advance. When the PCM receives the 7X signal, it will determine which pair of cylinders will be fired. (1–4 or 2–3). It will tell the ICM which cylinder pair will be fired via CKTs 423 or 406.

Diagnosis And Testing

SYSTEM PERFORMANCE

The computer control module uses information from the MAP and Coolant sensors, in addition to rpm to calculate spark advance as follows;

- Low MAP output voltage = More spark advance.
- Cold engine = More spark advance.
- High MAP output voltage = Less spark advance.
- Hot engine = Less spark advance.

Therefore, detonation could be caused by low MAP output or high resistance in the Engine Coolant Temperature (ECT) sensor circuit. Poor performance could be caused by high MAP output or low resistance in the coolant sensor circuit.

If the engine cranks but will not operate, or starts, then immediately stalls, diagnosis must be accomplished to determine if the failure is in the ignition system or the fuel system. Refer to the individual component tests.

EST PERFORMANCE

The ECM will set timing at a specified value when the diagnostic **TEST** terminal in the ALDL connector is grounded. To check for EST operation, run the engine at 1500 rpm with the terminal ungrounded. Then ground the **TEST** terminal. If the EST is operating, there should be a noticeable engine rpm change. A fault in the EST system will set a trouble code 42.

Ignition Coil Assembly

REMOVAL & INSTALLATION

2.2L (VIN G and 4) Engines

▶ See Figure 17

1. Disconnect the negative battery cable.
2. Raise and safely support the vehicle.
3. Detach the assembly electrical connectors.
4. Tag and disconnect the spark plug wires.
5. Unfasten the three ignition coil assembly-to-block bolts, then remove the assembly from the engine.

To install:

6. Position the ignition coil assembly to the engine. Install the mounting bolts, then tighten to 15–22 ft. lbs. (20–30 Nm).
7. Connect the spark plug wires to the proper coils, as tagged during removal.
8. Attach the coil electrical connectors.
9. Carefully lower the vehicle, then connect the negative battery cable.

2.0L (VIN 1 and H), 2.8L (VIN W) and 3.1L (VIN T) Engines

▶ See Figures 18 and 19

➥On 3.1L engines, an "Idle Learn" procedure must be performed which requires the use of a scan tool. You may wish to have the coil(s) replaced at a proper service facility.

1. Disconnect the negative battery cable.
2. Detach the electrical wires from the ignition coil assembly.
3. Tag and disconnect the spark plug wires from the assembly.
4. Unfasten the mounting bolts, then remove the assembly from the engine.

➥On the 2.8L and 3.1L engines, with the coil pack removed, each coil can be removed and the ignition module can be removed as well.

To install:

5. Position the ignition coil assembly on the engine. Install the mounting bolts, then tighten to 19 ft. lbs. (25 Nm) for the 2.8L and 3.1L engines. For the 2.0L (VIN 1) engine, tighten to 89 inch lbs. (10 Nm).
6. Attach the plug wires to the proper coils, as tagged during removal.
7. Fasten the ignition coil assembly wiring.
8. Connect the negative battery cable.

➥On the 3.1L engine, this test must be done before the engine is started and requires the use of a Tech 1®, or equivalent, scan tool.

9. If equipped with the 3.1L engine, perform the idle learn procedure to allow the ECM/PCM memory to be updated with the correct IAC valve pintle position and provide for a stable idle speed.

   a. Install an appropriate scan tool.
   b. Turn the ignition to the **ON** position, engine not running.
   c. Select **IAC SYSTEM**, then **IDLE LEARN** in the **MISC TEST** mode.
   d. Place the transaxle in park or neutral, as applicable.
   e. Proceed with idle learn as directed by the scan tool.

Ignition Module

REMOVAL & INSTALLATION

2.0L Engines

▶ See Figure 20

1. Disconnect the negative battery cable.
2. Detach the "DIS" electrical connectors.
3. Tag and disconnect the spark plug wires.
4. Unfasten the module-to-block bolts, then remove the module from the engine.
5. Installation is the reverse of the removal procedure.

1. Bracket
2. Ignition control module (ICM)
3. 2 - 3 ignition coil
4. 1 - 4 ignition coil
5. Screws (4) 40 in. lbs. (4.5 nm)

87952014

Fig. 17 Exploded view of the ignition coil assembly—2.2L (VIN 4) engine shown

1. Ignition coil assembly
2. Bolt (3)
3. Ignition cables

87952013

Fig. 18 On the 2.0L engine, if any part of the ignition coil is faulty, the entire coil assembly must be replaced

1. Bracket
2. Module
3. 1 - 4 coil
4. 6 - 3 coil
5. 5 - 2 coil
6. Bolts (3) - 19 ft. lbs. (25 m)

87952012

Fig. 19 When the DIS of Ignition Coil assembly is removed, you can remove each individual coil for replacement— 2.8L and 3.1L engines

1. "DIS" module
2. Bolt (3)
3. Ignition cables

87952200

Fig. 20 View of the ignition or DIS module location—2.0L engines

2.2L Engines

◆ See Figure 21

1. Disconnect the negative battery cable.
2. Raise and safely support the vehicle.
3. Remove the ignition coils from the module.
4. Remove the module from the assembly plate.
5. Installation is the reverse of the removal procedure.

1. Bracket
2. Ignition control module (ICM)
3. 2 - 3 ignition coil
4. 1 - 4 ignition coil
5. Screws (4)
   4.5 Nm (40 lb. in.)

87952201

Fig. 21 The ignition module or (ICM), is located under the coils

2.8L And 3.1L Engines

◆ See Figure 22

➡ On 3.1L engines, an "Idle Learn" procedure must be performed which requires the use of a scan tool. You may wish to have the coil(s) or ignition module replaced at a proper service facility.

1. Disconnect the negative battery cable.
2. Remove the ignition coil assembly from the engine, as outlined earlier in this section.
3. Remove the coils from the assembly.
4. Lift the module from the assembly plate.

To install:

5. Position the ignition module to the assembly plate.
6. Install the coils, then install the coil assembly to the engine.
7. Connect the negative battery cable.
8. If equipped with the 3.1L engine, perform the idle learn procedure to allow the ECM/PCM memory to be updated with the correct IAC valve pintle position and provide for a stable idle speed.

   a. Install an appropriate scan tool.
   b. Turn the ignition to the **ON** position, engine not running.
   c. Select **IAC SYSTEM**, then **IDLE LEARN** in the **MISC TEST** mode.
   d. Place the transaxle in park or neutral, as applicable.
   e. Proceed with idle learn as directed by the scan tool.

1. Bracket
2. Ignition control module
3. Shield
4. 1 - 4 coil
5. 6 - 3 coil
6. 5 - 2 coil
7. Screws (6)

87952203

Fig. 22 Location of the ignition module—1994 3.1L engine shown

Crankshaft Position Sensor

Refer to Section 4 under Electronic Engine Controls for removal, installation and testing of the crankshaft position sensor.

Camshaft Position Sensor

Refer to Section 4 under Electronic Engine Controls for removal, installation and testing of the camshaft position sensor.

FIRING ORDERS

◆ See Figures 23, 24, 25, 26 and 27

➡ To avoid confusion, remove and tag the spark plug wires one at a time, for replacement.

If a distributor is not keyed for installation with only one orientation, it could have been removed previously and rewired. The resultant wiring would hold the correct firing order, but could change the relative placement of the plug towers in relation to the engine. For this reason it is imperative that you label all wires before disconnecting any of them. Also, before removal, compare the current wiring with the accompanying illustrations. If the current wiring does not match, make notes in your book to reflect how your engine is wired.

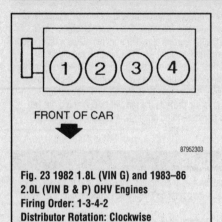

Fig. 23 1982 1.8L (VIN G) and 1983–86
2.0L (VIN B & P) OHV Engines
Firing Order: 1-3-4-2
Distributor Rotation: Clockwise

Fig. 24 1987–89 2.0L (VIN 1) and 1990–94
2.2L (VIN G & 4) OHV Engines
Firing Order: 1-3-4-2
Distributorless Ignition System

Fig. 25 1983–86 1.8L (VIN O & J) and
1987–91 2.0L (VIN K & M) OHC Engines
Firing Order: 1-3-4-2
Distributor Rotation: Clockwise

Fig. 26 1985–86 2.8L (VIN W) Engine
Firing Order: 1-2-3-4-5-6
Distributor Rotation: Clockwise

Fig. 27 1987–89 2.8L (VIN W) and 1990–94 3.1L (VIN M) Engines
Firing Order: 1-2-3-4-5-6
Distributorless Ignition System

CHARGING SYSTEM

Description and Operation

▶ See Figures 28, 29, 30 and 31

The automobile charging system provides electrical power for operation of the vehicle's ignition and starting systems and all the electrical accessories. The battery serves as an electrical surge of storage tank, storing (in chemical form) the energy originally produced by the engine driven generator. The system also provides a means of regulating generator output to protect the battery from being overcharged and to avoid excessive voltage to the accessories.

The storage battery is a chemical device incorporating parallel lead plates in a tank containing a sulfuric acid-water solution. Adjacent plates are slightly dissimilar, and the chemical reaction of the two dissimilar plates produces electrical energy when the battery is connected to a load such as the starter motor. The chemical reaction is reversible, so that when the generator is producing a voltage (electrical pressure) greater then that produced by the battery, electricity is forced into the battery, and the battery is returned to its fully charged state.

The vehicle's generator is driven mechanically, through V belts, by the engine crankshaft. It consists of two coils of fine wire, one stationary (the stator), and one movable (the rotor). The rotor may also be known as the armature and consists of fine wire wrapped around an iron core which is mounted on a shaft. The electricity which flows through the two coils of wire (provided initially by the battery in some cases) creates an intense magnetic field around both rotor and stator, and the interaction between the two fields creates voltage, allowing the generator to power the accessories and charge the battery.

Todays automobiles use alternating current generators or alternators because they are more efficient, can be rotated at higher speeds, and have fewer brush problems, In an alternator, the field rotates while all the current produced passes only through the stator windings. The brushes bear against continuous slip rings rather than a commutator. This causes the current produced to periodically reverse the direction of its flow. Diodes (electrical one-way switches) block the flow of current from traveling in the wrong direction. A series of

diodes is wired together to permit the alternating flow of the stator to be converted to a pulsating, but unidirectional flow of current from traveling in the wrong direction. A series of diodes is wires together to permit the alternating flow of the stator to be converted to a pulsating, but unidirectional flow at the alternator output. The alternator's field is wires in series with the voltage regulator.

The alternating current generator (alternator) supplies a continuous output of electrical energy at all engine speeds. The alternator generates electrical energy for the engine and all electrical components, and recharges the battery by supplying it with current. This unit consists of four main assemblies: two end frame assemblies, a rotor assembly, and a stator assembly. The rotor is supported in the drive end frame by a ball bearing and at the other end by a roller bearing.

Fig. 28 Sectional view of the SI model alternator

55 Bearing
57 Rotor
58 Stator
60 Rectifier bridge
64 Regulator
67 Double sealed ball bearing
68 Terminals
69 Internal fan

87952030

Fig. 29 Sectional view of the CS model alternator

87952033

Fig. 30 Schematic of the SI model alternator

87952031

Fig. 31 Schematic of the CS model alternator

These bearings are lubricated during manufacture and require no maintenance. There are six diodes in the end frame assembly. Diodes are electrical check valves that change the alternating current supplied from the stator windings to a direct current (DC), delivered to the output (BAT) terminal. Three diodes are negative and are mounted flush with the end frame; the other three are positive and are mounted into a strip called a heat sink. The positive diodes are easily identified as the ones within small cavities or depressions. A capacitor, or condenser, mounted on the end frame protects the rectifier bridge and diode trio from high voltages, and suppresses radio noise. This capacitor requires no maintenance.

Alternator Precautions

To prevent damage to the on-board computer, alternator and regulator, the following precautionary measures must be taken when working with the electrical system.

• Be absolutely sure of the polarity of a booster battery before making connections. Connect the cables positive to positive, and negative to negative. Connect positive cables first and then make the last connection to ground on the body of the booster vehicle so that arcing cannot ignite hydrogen gas that may have accumulated near the battery. Even momentary connection of a booster battery with the polarity reversed will damage alternator diodes.

• Disconnect both vehicle battery cables before attempting to charge a battery.

• Never ground the alternator or generator output or battery terminal. Be cautious when using metal tools around a battery to avoid creating a short circuit between the terminals.

• Never ground the field circuit between the alternator and regulator.

• Never run an alternator or generator without load unless the field circuit is disconnected.

• Never attempt to polarize an alternator.

• Keep the regulator cover in place when taking voltage and current limiter readings.

• Use insulated tools when adjusting the regulator.

• Whenever DC generator-to-regulator wires have been disconnected, the generator must be repolarized. To do this with an externally grounded, light duty generator, momentarily place a jumper wires between the battery terminal and the generator terminal of the regulator. With an internally grounded heavy duty unit, disconnect the wire to the regulator field terminal and touch the regulator battery terminal with it.

• When installing a battery, make sure that the positive and negative cables are not reversed.

• When jump-starting the car, be sure that like terminals are connected. This also applies to using a battery charger. Reversed polarity will burn out the alternator and regulator in a matter of seconds.

• Never operate the alternator with the battery disconnected or on an otherwise uncontrolled open circuit.

• Do not short across or ground any alternator or regulator terminals.

• Do not try to polarize the alternator.

• Do not apply full battery voltage to the field (brown) connector.

• Always disconnect the battery ground cable before disconnecting the alternator lead.

• Always disconnect the battery (negative cable first) when charging it.

• Never subject the alternator to excessive heat or dampness. If you are steam cleaning the engine, cover the alternator.

• Never use arc-welding equipment on the car with the alternator connected.

Alternator

DIAGNOSIS

SI Alternator

♦ See Figure 32

A charge indicator lamp is used in most cars to signal when there is a fault in the charging system. This lamp is located in the gauge package and is used in diagnosis. A voltmeter may be used instead of the charge indicator lamp in diagnosis.

Fig. 32 SI model alternator diagnosis and testing

CS-130 & CS-130D Alternator

1. Check the drive belt(s) for wear and tension. Check wiring for obvious damage.

2. Go to Step 7 for vehicles without a charge indicator lamp.

3. With the ignition switch **ON**, and the engine stopped, the lamp should be ON. If not, detach the wiring harness at the alternator and ground the "L" terminal lead.

4. If the lamp illuminates, replace the alternator. If the lamp does not illuminate, locate the open circuit between the grounding lead and the ignition switch. Check the lamp, it may be open.

5. With the ignition switch **ON** and the engine running at moderate speed, the lamp should be OFF. If not, stop the engine, then turn the switch **ON** and detach the wiring harness at the alternator.

6. If the lamp goes out, replace the alternator. If the lamp stays ON, check for a grounded "L" terminal wire in the harness.

7. Determine if the battery is undercharged or overcharged.

• An undercharged battery is evidenced by slow cranking or a dark hydrometer.

• An overcharged battery is evidenced by excessive spewing of electrolyte from the vents.

8. Detach the wiring harness connector from the alternator.

9. With the ignition switch **ON**, and the engine not running, connect a voltmeter from ground to the "L" terminal in the wiring harness, and to the "I" terminal, if used.

10. A zero reading indicated an open circuit between the terminal and the battery. Repair the circuit as necessary.

11. Engage the harness connector to the alternator and run the engine at moderate speed with all accessories OFF.

12. Measure the voltage across the battery. If above 16 volts, replace the alternator.

13. Connect an ammeter at the alternator output terminal, run the engine at moderate speed, turn ON all the accessories and load the battery with a carbon pile to obtain maximum amperage. Maintain voltage at 13 volts or above.

14. If the output is within 15 amps of the rated output of the alternator (stamped on the alternator case), the alternator is good. If the output is not within 15 amps, replace the alternator.

REMOVAL & INSTALLATION

▶ **See Figures 33 thru 39**

1. Disconnect the negative battery cable at the battery.

❋❋ CAUTION

Failure to disconnect the negative cable may result in injury from the positive battery lead at the alternator, and may short the alternator and regulator during the removal process.

2. Disconnect and label the two terminal plug and the battery leads from the rear of the alternator.

3. Loosen the alternator mounting bolts. Push the alternator inwards, then slip the drive belt off the pulley.

4. Remove the mounting bolts, then remove the alternator from the vehicle.

Fig. 33 Detach the connector(s) from the rear of the alternator

Fig. 34 Unfasten the lower rear mounting bolt

Fig. 35 Loosen the rear upper retainer

Fig. 36 Unfasten the front mounting bolt, then . . .

Fig. 38 Removal and installation of the alternator—1.8L and 2.0L OHC engines, except Turbo

1. Alternator
2. Spacer
3. Bracket
4. Bracket (front)
5. 45 N•m (34 lbs. ft.)
6. Bracket (rear)
7. 28 N•m (21 lbs. ft.)
8. 35 N•m (26 lbs. ft.)
9. 50 N•m (37 lbs. ft.)
10. Power steering pump

Fig. 37 . . . remove the alternator from the vehicle

To install:

5. Place the alternator in its brackets and install the mounting bolts. Do not tighten them yet.

6. Slip the belt back over the pulley. Pull outwards on the unit and adjust the belt tension (see Section 1). Tighten the mounting and adjusting bolts.

7. Attach the electrical leads to the alternator.

8. Connect the negative battery cable.

Regulator

REMOVAL & INSTALLATION

The alternators used in these vehicles have an internal regulator. A solid state regulator is mounted within the alternator. All regulator components are enclosed in a solid mold. The regulator is non-adjustable and requires no maintenance. The alternator is serviced as a complete unit and cannot be overhauled.

1. GENERATOR
2. 25 N•m (18 LBS. FT.)
3. BRACKET
4. 50 N•m (37 LBS. FT.)
5. BRACKET

Fig. 39 Alternator mounting for a 1987–89 2.8L and 1990–94 3.1L engine

STARTING SYSTEM

Description and Operation

The battery is the first link in the chain of mechanisms which work together to provide cranking of the automobile engine. In most modern cars, the battery is a lead-acid electrochemical device consisting of six 2 volt (2V) subsections connected in series so the unit is capable of producing approximately 12V of electrical pressure. Each subsection, or sell, consists of a series of positive and negative plates held a short distance apart in a solution of sulfuric acid and water. The two types of plates are of dissimilar metals. This causes a chemical reaction to be set up, and it is this reaction which produces current flow from the battery when its positive and negative terminals are connected to an electrical appliance such as a lamp or motor. The continued transfer of electrons would eventually convert the sulfuric acid in the electrolyte to water, and make the two plates identical in chemical composition. As electrical energy is removed from the battery, its voltage output tend to drop. Thus, measuring battery voltage and battery electrolyte composition are two ways of checking the ability of the unit to supply power. During the starting of the engine, electrical energy is removed from the battery. However, if the charging circuit is in good condition and the operating conditions are normal, the power removed from the battery will be replaced by the generator (or alternator) which will force electrons back through the battery, reversing the normal flow, and restoring the battery to its original chemical state.

The battery and starting motor are linked by very heavy electrical cables designed to minimize resistance to the flow of current. Generally, the major power supply cable that leaves the battery goes directly to the starter, while other electrical system needs are supplied by a smaller cable. During the starter operation, power flows from the battery to the starter and is grounded through the car's frame and the battery's negative ground strap.

The starting motor is a specially designed, direct current electric motor capable of producing a very great amount of power for its size. One thing that allows the motor to produce a great deal of power is its tremendous rotating speed. It drives the engine through a tiny pinion gear (attached to the starter's armature), which drives the very large flywheel ring gear at a greatly reduced speed. Another factor allowing it to produce so much power is that only intermittent operation is required of it. Thus, little allowance for air circulation is required, and the windings can be built into a very small space.

The starter solenoid is a magnetic device which employs the small current supplied by the starting switch circuit of the ignition switch. This magnetic action moves a plunger which mechanically engages the starter and electrically closes the heavy switch which connects it to the battery. The starting switch circuit consists of the starting switch contained within the ignition switch, a transmission neutral safety switch or clutch pedal switch, and the wiring necessary to connect these with the starter solenoid or relay.

A pinion, which is a small gear, is mounted to a one-way drive clutch. this clutch is splined to the starter armature shaft. When the ignition switch is moved to the start position, the solenoid plunger slides the pinion toward the flywheel ring gear via a collar and spring. If the teeth on the pinion and flywheel match properly, the pinion will engage the flywheel immediately. If the gear teeth butt one another, the spring will be compressed and will force the gears to mesh as soon as the starter turns far enough to allow them to do so. As the solenoid plunger reaches the end of its travel, it closes the contacts that connect the battery and starter and then the engine is cranked.

As soon as the engine starts, the flywheel ring gear begins turning fast enough to drive the pinion at an extremely high rate of speed. At this point, the one-way clutch begins allowing the pinion to spin faster that the starter shaft so that the starter will not operate at excessive speed. When the ignition switch is released from the starter position, the solenoid is de-energized, and a spring contained within the solenoid assembly pulls the gear out of mesh and interrupts the current flow to the starter.

Some starters employ a separate relay, mounted away from the starter, to switch the motor and solenoid current on and off. The relay thus replaces the solenoid electrical switch, but does not eliminate the need for a solenoid mounted on the starter used to mechanically engage the starter drive gears. The relay is used to reduce the amount of current the starting switch must carry.

Starter

TESTING

No-Load Test

▶ **See Figure 40**

Make the connections as shown in the illustration. Close the switch and compare the rpm, current and voltage readings with the specifications found in the chart located in this section.

• Current draw and no load speed within specifications indicates normal condition of the starter motor.

• Low free speed and high current draw indicates worn bearings, a bent armature shaft, a shorted armature or grounded armature fields.

• Failure to operate with high current draw indicates a direct ground in the terminal or fields, or frozen bearings.

• Failure to operate with no current draw indicates an open field circuit, open armature coils, broken brush springs, worn brushes or other causes which would prevent good contact between the communtator and the brushes.

• A low no load speed and low current draw indicates high internal resistance due to poor connections, defective leads or a dirty commutator.

• High free speed and current draw usually indicate shorted fields or a shorted armature.

Fig. 40 Proper connections for the starter no-load test

REMOVAL & INSTALLATION

1982–83 1.8L (VIN G & O) and 2.0L (VIN B) Engines

▶ **See Figure 41**

1. Disconnect the negative battery cable at the battery.
2. If necessary for access under the car, raise and safely support the vehicle.
3. From under the vehicle, label and disconnect the solenoid wires and battery cable.
4. Remove the rear motor support bracket.
5. If equipped, remove the A/C compressor support rod.
6. Working under the car, remove the two starter-to-engine bolts, and allow the starter to drop down. Note the location and number of any shims. Remove the starter.
7. Installation is the reverse of the removal procedure. Tighten the mounting bolts to 25–35 ft. lbs. (34–47 Nm). Check the starting system for proper operation.

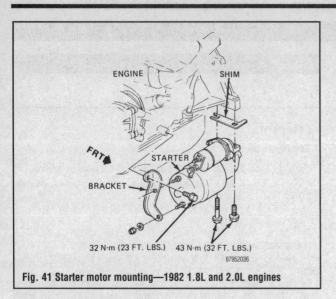

Fig. 41 Starter motor mounting—1982 1.8L and 2.0L engines

1984–86 1.8L and 2.0L Engines

EXCEPT 1.8L (VIN O) ENGINE

1. Disconnect the negative battery cable at the battery, then remove the engine harness bracket from the motor mount brace.
2. Remove the upper starter bolt.
3. Raise and safely support the vehicle.
4. Disconnect the fuel lines from the bracket, then loosen the fuel lines at the fuel regulator.
5. Remove the rear starter bracket.
6. Disconnect the cover and wiring to the solenoid and the negative battery cable grounding bolt.
7. Unfasten the lower starter bolt, then remove the starter from the vehicle.

To install:
8. Position the starter in the vehicle, then install the lower starter bolt.
9. Connect the wiring to the solenoid, then install the cover.
10. Install the rear starter bracket and the bolt for the negative grounding cable.
11. Fasten the fuel line support bracket, then connect the fuel lines.
12. Carefully lower the vehicle.
13. Fasten the upper starter bolt, then fasten the engine harness to the motor mount brace.
14. Connect the negative battery cable.

1.8L (VIN O) ENGINE

1. Disconnect the negative battery cable at the battery.
2. Remove the wiring harness clamp at the motor mount.
3. Unfasten the upper starter-to-engine block bolt.
4. Raise and safely support the vehicle.
5. If equipped with an automatic transaxle, disconnect the speedometer cable, then remove the transaxle rear strut.
6. Remove the throttle cable bracket.
7. Unfasten the rear starter brace bolts, then remove the brace.
8. Remove the lower starter-to-engine block bolt.
9. Detach the starter wiring, then remove the starter by nosing it down between the transaxle and sway bar. It may be necessary to pry the engine forward or detach the sway bar to remove the starter.

To install:
10. Position the starter, then install the lower mounting bolt.
11. Attach the starter wiring.
12. Install the throttle cable bracket.
13. If equipped with an automatic transaxle, install the transaxle rear strut and connect the speedometer cable.
14. Carefully lower the vehicle.
15. Install the upper starter-to-engine block bolt.
16. Fasten the wiring harness clamp at the motor mount, then connect the negative battery cable.

2.0L (VIN K & M) Engines

♦ See Figure 42

MANUAL TRANSAXLE

1. Disconnect the negative battery cable at the battery.
2. Remove the wire loom strap from the upper starter bolt.
3. Disconnect the shift and selector level cables at the external selector lever.
4. Remove the upper and lower transaxle control lever cable bracket and cables.
5. Remove the drive axle support brace.
6. Detach the starter electrical connectors, then remove the starter from the vehicle.

To install:
7. Position the starter in the vehicle, then attach the electrical connectors.
8. Install the drive axle support brace.
9. Install the upper and lower transaxle control lever cables and brackets.
10. Connect the shift and selector lever cable bracket and cable.
11. Fasten the wire loom strap to the upper starter bolt.
12. Connect the negative battery cable.

Fig. 42 When removing the starter, be sure to note the location of any shims that may have been used—2.0L (VIN K and M) engines

AUTOMATIC TRANSAXLE

1. Disconnect the negative battery cable at the battery.
2. Remove the blower motor. For details, please refer to the procedure located in Section 6 of this manual.
3. Label and detach the starter electrical connectors.
4. Remove the rear starter brace.
5. Disconnect the wire loom from the upper starter bolt.
6. Unfasten the upper starter bolt, then remove the transaxle strut.
7. Unfasten the lower starter bolt, then remove the starter from the vehicle through the blower motor opening.

To install:
8. Position the starter in the vehicle, then secure with the lower starter bolt.
9. Install the transaxle strut.
10. With the aid of an assistant, secure the upper starter bolt, then connect the wire loom to the upper bolt.
11. Install the rear starter brace.
12. Attach the starter electrical connectors.
13. Install the blower motor, as outlined in Section 6 of this manual.
14. Connect the negative battery cable.

2.0L (VIN H) Engine

♦ See Figure 43

1. Disconnect the negative battery cable at the battery.
2. Remove the upper starter bolt.
3. Raise and safely support the vehicle.

1 STARTER MOTOR SUPPORT
2 NUT – 3 N·m (27 LBS. IN.)
3 STARTER MOTOR
4 BOLT – 50 N·m (37 LBS. FT.)
5 BOLT – 27 N·m (20 LBS. FT.)

87952038

Fig. 43 Removing the starter on a 2.0L (VIN H) engine

4. For vehicles equipped with an automatic transaxle, detach the starter electrical connectors.

5. Disconnect the engine ground cable at the engine.

6. Remove the rear starter mount.

7. For vehicles equipped with a manual transaxle, detach the starter electrical connectors.

8. If equipped, unfasten the lower starter bolt, then remove the starter from the vehicle.

To install:

9. Position the starter in the vehicle, then secure using the lower retaining bolt.

10. If equipped with a manual transaxle, attach the starter electrical connectors at this time.

11. Install the rear starter mount.

12. For vehicles with an automatic transaxle, attach the starter electrical connectors at this time.

13. Connect the engine ground cable to the engine.

14. Carefully lower the vehicle.

15. Install the upper starter bolt.

16. Connect the negative battery cable.

2.0L (VIN 1) and 2.2L (VIN 4 & G) Engines

▶ **See Figure 44**

1. Disconnect the negative battery cable at the battery.

2. Raise and safely support the vehicle.

3. For vehicles equipped with a manual transaxle, remove the bending brace from around the starter.

1 STARTER ASSEMBLY
2 BOLT – 43 N·m (32 LBS. FT.)
3 BOLT – 32 N·m (24 LBS. FT.)
4 BRACKET, STARTER MOTOR
5 WASHER
6 NUT – 12 N·m (106 LBS. IN.)
7 BENDING BRACE (MANUAL TRANS ONLY)
8 BOLT – 47 N·m (20 LBS. FT.)

87952039

Fig. 44 Removal and installation of the starter—2.2L engine shown, 2.0L (VIN 1) similar

4. Unfasten the starter motor-to-engine bolts, then carefully lower the starter. Remember, the leads are still attached to the starter.

5. Remove the nuts/bolts that hold the starter bracket to the starter and engine.

6. Detach the electrical leads, then remove the starter from the vehicle.

To install:

7. Raise the starter into position, then connect the electrical leads. Tighten the "S" terminal to 22 inch lbs. (2.5 Nm) and the battery terminal to 106 inch lbs. (12 Nm).

8. Secure the starter using the retaining bolts. Tighten to 32 ft. lbs. (43 Nm). Install the nuts/bolts that hold the start bracket to the starter and the engine. Tighten the bracket-to-engine bolt to 24 ft. lbs. (32 Nm) and the brace-to-starter motor nut to 106 inch lbs. (12 Nm).

9. If equipped with a manual transaxle, install the bending brace.

10. Carefully lower the vehicle, then connect the negative battery cable.

2.8L (VIN W) and 3.1L (VIN T) Engines

▶ **See Figure 45**

➡ **On 3.1L engines, an "Idle Learn" procedure must be performed which requires the use of a scan tool. You may wish to have the starter replaced at a proper service facility.**

1. Disconnect the negative battery cable at the battery.

2. Raise and safely support the vehicle.

3. Remove the starter motor-to-engine bolts, then carefully lower the vehicle.

4. Detach the starter electrical leads, then remove the starter from the vehicle.

1 SHIM, STARTER MOTOR
2 STARTER MOTOR
3 BOLT – 43 N·m (32 LBS. FT.)

87952041

Fig. 45 Removing the starter—2.8L and 3.1L engines

To install:

5. Position the starter in the vehicle, then connect the electrical leads.

6. Raise and safely support the vehicle, then install the starter-to-engine bolts and tighten to 32 ft. lbs. (43 Nm).

7. Carefully lower the vehicle.

8. Connect the negative battery cable. Tighten the cable to 11 ft. lbs. (15 Nm). Be careful not to over-tighten.

➡ **On 3.1L engines, this test must be done before the engine is started and requires the use of a Tech 1® or equivalent scan tool.**

9. If equipped with the 3.1L engine, perform the idle learn procedure to allow the ECM/PCM memory to be updated with the correct IAC valve pintle position and provide for a stable idle speed.

    a. Install a suitable scan tool.

    b. Turn the ignition to the **ON** position, engine not running.

    c. Select **IAC SYSTEM**, then **IDLE LEARN** in the **MISC TEST** mode.

    d. Place the transaxle in park or neutral, as applicable.

    e. Proceed with idle learn as directed by the scan tool.

SOLENOID REPLACEMENT

▶ **See Figure 46**

Most vehicles covered by this manual are equipped with replaceable sole-noids. In all cases, the starter must first be removed from the vehicle for access.

1. Remove the starter and place it on a workbench.
2. If equipped, remove the heat shield.
3. Detach the field strap/lead from the solenoid.
4. Unfasten the solenoid-to-drive housing attaching screws, motor terminal bolt, and clamp (if equipped) then remove the solenoid by twisting.

To install:

5. Twist or place the solenoid in position.
6. Secure the solenoid using the retaining clamp, bolt and/or screws, as applicable.
7. Connect the field strap/lead to the solenoid.
8. Install the starter into the vehicle, as outlined earlier.

1	FRAME, COMMUTATOR END	11	LEVER, SHIFT
2	BRUSH AND HOLDER PKG.	12	SPRING, PLUNGER RETURN
3	BRUSH	13	SHAFT, SHIFT LEVER
4	HOLDER, BRUSH	14	WASHER, LOCK
5	HOUSING, DRIVE END	15	SCREW, BRUSH ATTACHING
6	FRAME AND FIELD ASSEMBLY	16	SCREW, FIELD LEAD TO SWITCH
7	SWITCH, SOLENOID	17	SCREW, SWITCH
8	ARMATURE	18	WASHER, BRAKE
9	DRIVE ASSEMBLY	19	BOLT, THRU
10	PLUNGER	20	BUSHING, COMMUTATOR END

21	BUSHING, DIVE END
22	COLLAR, PINION STOP
23	COLLAR, THRUST
24	GROMMET
25	PIN, PLUNGER
26	RING, PINION STOP RETAINER
27	RING, LEVER SHAFT RETAINER

87952042

Fig. 46 Exploded view of a late model starter assembly, including the solenoid

SENDING UNITS AND SENSORS

➡**This section describes the operating principles of sending units, warning lights and gauges. Sensors which provide information to the Electronic Control Module (ECM) are covered in Section 4 of this manual.**

Instrument panels contain a number of indicating devices (gauges and warning lights). These devices are composed of two separate components. One is the sending unit, mounted on the engine or other remote part of the vehicle, and the other is the actual gauge or light in the instrument panel.

Several types of sending units exist, however most can be characterized as being either a pressure type or a resistance type. Pressure type sending units convert liquid pressure into an electrical signal which is sent to the gauge. Resistance type sending units are most often used to measure temperature and use variable resistance to control the current flow back to the indicating device. Both types of sending units are connected in series by a wire to the battery (through the ignition switch). When the ignition is turned **ON**, current flows from the battery through the indicating device and on to the sending unit.

Coolant Temperature Sending Unit

The coolant temperature sending unit is usually located in the thermostat housing. This unit activates the coolant temperature gauge in the instrument cluster.

REMOVAL & INSTALLATION

1. Disconnect the negative battery cable.
2. Properly drain the cooling system to a level below the thermostat housing.
3. Detach the coolant temperature sending unit electrical connector.
4. Remove the sending unit from the thermostat housing.

To install:

5. Coat the sending unit with sealant, then install in the thermostat housing.
6. Attach the sending unit electrical connector.

7. Fill the cooling system to the proper level.
8. Connect the negative battery cable.

Oil Pressure Switch

REMOVAL & INSTALLATION

1. Disconnect the negative battery cable.
2. Drain the engine oil, as outlined in Section 1 of this manual.
3. Detach the oil pressure switch electrical connector.
4. Remove the switch from the cylinder block.

To install:

5. Coat the switch with sealant, then install in the cylinder block.
6. Attach the oil pressure switch electrical connector.
7. Fill the engine with oil.
8. Connect the negative battery cable.

Radiator Fan Temperature Switch

REMOVAL & INSTALLATION

1. Disconnect the negative battery cable.
2. Drain the cooling system to a level below the thermostat housing.
3. Detach the fan switch electrical connector.
4. Remove the switch from the thermostat housing.

To install:

5. Coat the switch with sealant, then install in the thermostat housing.
6. Attach the fan switch electrical connector.
7. Fill the cooling system to the proper level.
8. Connect the negative battery cable.

ENGINE MECHANICAL 3-2
ENGINE 3-7
   REMOVAL & INSTALLATION 3-7
ROCKER ARM (VALVE) COVER 3-13
   REMOVAL & INSTALLATION 3-13
CAMSHAFT CARRIER COVER 3-15
   REMOVAL & INSTALLATION 3-15
ROCKER ARMS AND PUSHRODS 3-16
   REMOVAL & INSTALLATION 3-16
THERMOSTAT 3-18
   REMOVAL & INSTALLATION 3-18
INTAKE MANIFOLD 3-20
   REMOVAL & INSTALLATION 3-20
EXHAUST MANIFOLD 3-25
   REMOVAL & INSTALLATION 3-25
TURBOCHARGER 3-29
   REMOVAL & INSTALLATION 3-29
RADIATOR 3-29
   REMOVAL & INSTALLATION 3-29
ELECTRIC COOLING FAN 3-31
   REMOVAL & INSTALLATION 3-31
WATER PUMP 3-31
   REMOVAL & INSTALLATION 3-31
CYLINDER HEAD 3-32
   REMOVAL & INSTALLATION 3-32
OIL PAN 3-38
   REMOVAL & INSTALLATION 3-38
OIL PUMP 3-41
   REMOVAL & INSTALLATION 3-41
TIMING BELT COVER 3-42
   REMOVAL & INSTALLATION 3-42
TIMING CHAIN FRONT COVER 3-43
   REMOVAL & INSTALLATION 3-43
TIMING CHAIN COVER OIL SEAL 3-44
   REPLACEMENT 3-44
TIMING CHAIN AND SPROCKETS 3-44
   REMOVAL & INSTALLATION 3-44
TIMING BELT 3-45
   REMOVAL & INSTALLATION 3-45
   INSPECTION 3-47
CAMSHAFT SPROCKET 3-47
   REMOVAL & INSTALLATION 3-47
CRANKSHAFT SPROCKET 3-48
   REMOVAL & INSTALLATION 3-48
CAMSHAFT 3-49
   REMOVAL & INSTALLATION 3-49
   BEARING REPLACEMENT 3-50
REAR MAIN SEAL 3-50
   REMOVAL & INSTALLATION 3-50
EXHAUST SYSTEM 3-52
INSPECTION 3-52
   REPLACEMENT 3-54
ENGINE RECONDITIONING 3-55
DETERMINING ENGINE CONDITION 3-55
   COMPRESSION TEST 3-55
   OIL PRESSURE TEST 3-56
BUY OR REBUILD? 3-56
ENGINE OVERHAUL TIPS 3-56
   TOOLS 3-56
   OVERHAUL TIPS 3-57

CLEANING 3-57
REPAIRING DAMAGED
   THREADS 3-57
ENGINE PREPARATION 3-58
CYLINDER HEAD 3-58
   DISASSEMBLY 3-59
   INSPECTION 3-62
   REFINISHING & REPAIRING 3-63
   ASSEMBLY 3-64
ENGINE BLOCK 3-65
   GENERAL INFORMATION 3-65
   DISASSEMBLY 3-65
   INSPECTION 3-66
   REFINISHING 3-68
   ASSEMBLY 3-68
ENGINE START-UP AND BREAK-IN 3-71
   STARTING THE ENGINE 3-71
   BREAKING IT IN 3-71
   KEEP IT MAINTAINED 3-71
SPECIFICATION CHARTS
   CAMSHAFT SPECIFICATIONS 3-2
   CRANKSHAFT AND CONNECTING ROD
     SPECIFICATIONS 3-3
   GENERAL ENGINE
     SPECIFICATIONS 3-2
   PISTON AND RING
     SPECIFICATIONS 3-5
   TORQUE SPECIFICATIONS 3-72
   VALVE SPECIFICATIONS 3-6

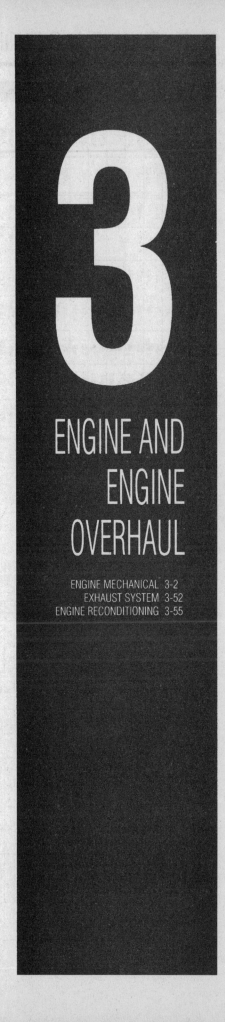

3

ENGINE AND ENGINE OVERHAUL

ENGINE MECHANICAL 3-2
EXHAUST SYSTEM 3-52
ENGINE RECONDITIONING 3-55

ENGINE MECHANICAL

CAMSHAFT SPECIFICATIONS
All measurements given in inches.

Year	Engine ID/VIN	Engine Displacement Liters (cc)	Journal Diameter 1	2	3	4	5	Elevation In.	Elevation Ex.	Bearing Clearance	Camshaft End-Play
1982	O	1.8 (1819)	1.8677-1.8696	1.8677-1.8696	1.8677-1.8696	1.8677-1.8696	1.8677-1.8696	0.2625	0.2625	0.0010-0.0039	NA
	B	1.8 (1819)	1.6714-1.6720	1.6812-1.6816	1.6812-1.6816	1.7009-1.7015	1.7108-1.7114	0.2409	0.2409	0.0010-0.0039	0.0160-0.0640
	O	2.0 (1998)	1.8677-1.8696	1.8677-1.8696	1.8677-1.8696	1.8677-1.8696	1.8677-1.8696	0.2600	0.2600	0.0010-0.0039	NA
1983	B	2.0 (1998)	1.6714-1.6720	1.6812-1.6816	1.6812-1.6816	1.7009-1.7015	1.7108-1.7114	0.2409	0.2409	0.0010-0.0039	0.0160-0.0640
	O	1.8 (1819)	1.8677-1.8696	1.8677-1.8696	1.8677-1.8696	1.8677-1.8696	1.8677-1.8696	0.2600	0.2600	0.0010-0.0039	0.0160-0.0640
	J	1.8 (1819)	1.6714-1.6720	1.6812-1.6816	1.6816	1.7009-1.7015	1.7108-1.7114	0.2409	0.2409	0.0010-0.0039	0.0160-0.0640
	P	2.0 (1998)	1.6720	1.6816	1.6816	1.7015	1.7114	0.2600	0.2600	0.0010-0.0039	NA
1984	B	2.0 (1998)	1.8677-1.8696	1.8677-1.8696	1.8677-1.8696	1.8677-1.8696	1.8677-1.8696	0.2600	0.2600	0.0010-0.0039	NA
	O	1.8 (1819)	1.8677-1.8696	1.8696	1.8696	1.8696	1.8696	0.2409	0.2409	0.0010-0.0039	0.0160-0.0640
1985	J	1.8 (1819)	1.6714-1.6720	1.6812-1.6816	1.6812-1.6816	1.7009-1.7015	1.7108-1.7114	0.2409	0.2409	0.0010-0.0039	0.0160-0.0640
	P	2.0 (1998)	1.6714-1.6720	1.6812-1.6816	1.6812-1.6816	1.7009-1.7015	1.7108-1.7114	0.2600	0.2600	0.0010-0.0039	0.0160-0.0640
	O	1.8 (1819)	1.8677-1.8696	1.8677-1.8696	1.8677-1.8696	1.8677-1.8696	1.8677-1.8696	0.2409	0.2409	0.0010-0.0039	NA
1986	J	1.8 (1819)	1.6714-1.6720	1.6812-1.6816	1.6812-1.6816	1.7009-1.7015	1.7108-1.7114	0.2409	0.2409	0.0010-0.0039	0.0016-0.0063
	P	2.0 (1998)	1.6714-1.6720	1.6812-1.6816	1.6812-1.6816	1.7009-1.7015	1.7108-1.7114	0.2600	0.2600	0.0010-0.0039	0.0016-0.0063
	W	2.8 (2835)	1.8677-1.8696	1.8677-1.8696	1.8677-1.8696	1.8677-1.8696	1.8677-1.8696	0.2625	0.2625	0.0010-0.0039	0.0016-0.0063
1987	O	1.8 (1819)	1.8696	1.8696	1.8696	1.8696	NA	0.2630	0.2730	0.0010-0.0040	NA
	J	1.8 (1819)	1.6714-1.6720	1.6810-1.6816	1.6911-1.6917	1.7009-1.7015	1.7108-1.7114	0.2409	0.2409	0.0008-0.0032	0.0016-0.0064
	K	2.0 (1998)	1.6714-1.6720	1.6810-1.6816	1.6911-1.6917	1.7009-1.7015	1.7108-1.7114	0.2409	0.2409	0.0008-0.0032	0.0016-0.0064
	M	2.0 (1998)	1.6714-1.6720	1.6810-1.6816	1.6911-1.6917	1.7009-1.7015	1.7108-1.7114	0.2409	0.2409	0.0008-0.0032	0.0016-0.0064
	1	2.0 (2000)	1.8677-1.8696	1.8677-1.8696	1.8677-1.8696	1.8677-1.8696	1.8677-1.8696	0.2625	0.2625	0.0010-0.0039	0.0016-0.0064
	W	2.8 (2835)	1.8696	1.8696	1.8696	1.8690	NA	0.2630	0.2730	0.0010-0.0040	NA

9113CC01

GENERAL ENGINE SPECIFICATIONS

Year	Engine ID/VIN	Engine Displacement Liters (cc)	Fuel System Type	Net Horsepower @ rpm	Net Torque @ rpm (ft. lbs.)	Bore x Stroke (in.)	Compression Ratio	Oil Pressure psi @ rpm
1982	G	1.8L (1819)	2bbl	88@5500	100@2800	3.50x2.91	9.0:1	45@2400
	O	1.8L (1819)	TBI	84@5200	102@2800	3.34x3.13	8.8:1	45@2400
1983	B	2.0L (1998)	2bbl	90@5100	111@2800	3.50x3.15	9.0:1	45@2400
	O	1.8L (1819)	TBI	84@5200	102@2800	3.34x3.13	8.8:1	45@2400
	J	1.8L (1819)	MFI-Turbo	150@5600	150@3000	3.34X3.13	8.0:1	65@2500
	P	2.0L (1998)	TBI	86@4900	100@3000	3.50x3.15	9.3:1	68@1200
1984	B	2.0L (1998)	TBI	90@5100	111@2800	3.50x3.15	9.3:1	45@2400
	O	1.8L (1819)	TBI	84@5200	102@2800	3.34x3.13	8.8:1	45@2400
	J	1.8L (1819)	MFI-Turbo	150@5600	150@3000	3.34x3.13	8.0:1	65@2500
	P	2.0L (1998)	TBI	86@4900	100@3000	3.50x3.15	9.3:1	68@1200
1985	O	1.8L (1819)	TBI	84@5200	102@2800	3.34x3.13	8.8:1	45@2400
	J	1.8L (1819)	MFI-Turbo	150@5600	150@3000	3.34x3.13	8.1:1	65@2500
	P	2.0L (1998)	TBI	86@4900	100@3000	3.50x3.15	9.3:1	68@1200
	W	2.8L (2835)	MFI	130@4800	155@3600	3.50x2.99	8.5:1	50-65@2500
1986	O	1.8L (1819)	TBI	84@5200	102@2800	3.34x3.13	8.8:1	45@2400
	J	1.8L (1819)	MFI-Turbo	150@5600	150@3000	3.34x3.13	8.1:1	65@2500
	W	2.0L (1998)	MFI	130@4800	155@3600	3.39x3.39	8.8:1	45@2400
	K	2.0L (1998)	TBI	102@5200	130@2800	3.39x3.39	8.0:1	63-77@1200
1987	M	2.0L (1998)	MFI-Turbo	160@5600	160@3600	3.39x3.39	8.0:1	50-65@1200
	W	2.8L (2835)	MFI	130@4800	155@3600	3.40x3.40	8.8:1	65@2500
	K	2.0L (1998)	TBI	102@5200	130@2800	3.50x3.15	8.0:1	63-77@1200
	1	2.0L (1998)	MFI	90@5600	108@3200	3.50x2.99	9.0:1	50-65@1200
1988	W	2.8L (2835)	MFI	125@4500	160@3600	3.50x2.99	8.9:1	45@2400
	K	2.0L (1998)	TBI	98@4800	118@3600	3.39x3.39	8.8:1	45@2400
1989	M	2.0L (1998)	MFI-Turbo	165@5500	165@4000	3.39x3.39	8.0:1	65@2500
	1	2.0L (1998)	TBI	90@5600	108@3200	3.50x3.15	9.0:1	63-77@1200
	W	2.8L (2835)	MFI	120@4800	108@3200	3.50x2.99	8.9:1	50-65@2400
1990	K	2.0L (1998)	TFI	98@4800	118@3600	3.39x3.39	8.8:1	65@2500
	M	2.0L (1998)	MFI-Turbo	165@5500	165@4000	3.39x3.39	8.0:1	63-77@1200
	G	3.1L (3130)	MFI	95@5200	120@3200	3.50x3.46	9.0:1	15@1100
1991	K	2.0L (1998)	TFI	96@4800	118@3600	3.39x3.39	8.8:1	45@2400
	G	3.1L (3130)	MFI	95@5200	120@3200	3.50x3.46	9.0:1	15@1100
1992	T	2.0L (1998)	MFI	140@4500	130@3200	3.39x3.39	8.5:1	45@2400
	H	2.2L (2180)	MFI	111@5200	125@3600	3.38x3.38	9.2:1	45@2400
	4	3.1L (3130)	MFI	95@5200	120@3200	3.50x3.46	9.0:1	63-77@1200
1993	T	2.0L (1998)	MFI	140@4500	124@3600	3.50x3.31	8.5:1	15@1100
	H	2.2L (2180)	MFI	110@5200	124@3200	3.50x3.46	9.2:1	30@2000
	4	3.1L (3130)	MFI	140@4200	185@3200	3.50x3.31	8.5:1	15@1100
1994	T	2.0L (1998)	MFI	110@5200	130@3200	3.38x3.38	9.2:1	30@2000
	H	2.2L (2180)	MFI	110@5200	124@3200	3.50x3.46	9.0:1	63-77@2000
	4	3.1L (3130)	MFI	140@4200	185@3200	3.50x3.31	8.5:1	15@1100

2bbl - 2 barrel carburetor
TBI - Throttle Body fuel injection
MFI - Multi-port Fuel Injection

9113CC00

CRANKSHAFT AND CONNECTING ROD SPECIFICATIONS
All measurements are given in inches.

Year	Engine ID/VIN	Engine Displacement Liters (cc)	Crankshaft				Connecting Rod		
			Main Brg. Journal Dia.	Main Brg. Oil Clearance	Shaft End-play	Thrust on No.	Journal Diameter	Oil Clearance	Side Clearance
1982	G	1.8 (1819)	2.4944-2.4954 [1]	0.0006-0.0018 [2]	0.0019-0.0071	4	1.9983-1.9993	0.0009-0.0031	0.0039-0.0240
	O	1.8 (1819)	NA	0.0006-0.0016	0.0027-0.0118	3	1.9278-1.9286	0.0007-0.0024	0.0027-0.0095
	B	2.0 (1998)	2.4944-2.4954 [1]	0.0006-0.0018 [2]	0.0019-0.0071	4	1.9983-1.9993	0.0009-0.0031	0.0039-0.0240
1983	O	1.8 (1819)	[3]	0.0006-0.0016	0.0027-0.0118	3	1.9278-1.9286	0.0007-0.0024	0.0027-0.0095
	J	1.8 (1819)	NA	0.0006-0.0016	0.0027-0.0118	3	1.9278-1.9286	0.0007-0.0024	0.0027-0.0095
	P	2.0 (1998)	2.4944-2.4954 [1]	0.0006-0.0018 [2]	0.0019-0.0071	4	1.9983-1.9993	0.0009-0.0031	0.0039-0.0240
	B	2.0 (1998)	2.4944-2.4954 [1]	0.0006-0.0018 [2]	0.0019-0.0071	4	1.9983-1.9993	0.0009-0.0031	0.0039-0.0240
1984	O	1.8 (1819)	[3]	0.0006-0.0016	0.0027-0.0118	3	1.9278-1.9286	0.0007-0.0024	0.0027-0.0095
	J	1.8 (1819)	[3]	0.0006-0.0016	0.0027-0.0118	3	1.9278-1.9286	0.0007-0.0024	0.0027-0.0095
	P	2.0 (1998)	2.4944-2.4954 [1]	0.0006-0.0018 [2]	0.0019-0.0071	4	1.9983-1.9993	0.0009-0.0031	0.0039-0.0240
1985	O	1.8 (1819)	[3]	0.0006-0.0016	0.0027-0.0118	3	1.9278-1.9286	0.0007-0.0024	0.0027-0.0095
	J	1.8 (1819)	[3]	0.0006-0.0016	0.0027-0.0118	3	1.9278-1.9286	0.0007-0.0024	0.0027-0.0095
	P	2.0 (2000)	2.4944-2.4954 [4]	0.0006-0.0018 [2]	0.0019-0.0071	4	1.9983-1.9993	0.0009-0.0031	0.0039-0.0240
	W	2.8 (2835)	2.4397-2.4946	0.0017-0.0030	0.0020-0.0067	3	1.9984-1.9994	0.0014-0.0036	0.0060-0.0170
1986	O	1.8 (1819)	[3]	0.0006-0.0016	0.0027-0.0118	3	1.9278-1.9286	0.0007-0.0024	0.0027-0.0095
	J	1.8 (1819)	[3]	0.0006-0.0016	0.0027-0.0118	3	1.9278-1.9286	0.0007-0.0024	0.0027-0.0095
	K	2.0 (1998)	[5]	0.0006-0.0016	0.0003-0.0012	3	1.9278-1.9286	0.0007-0.0024	0.0027-0.0095
1987	M	2.0 (1998)	[5]	0.0006-0.0016	0.0003-0.0012	3	1.9278-1.9286	0.0007-0.0024	0.0027-0.0095
	1	2.0 (2000)	2.4945-2.4954	0.0006-0.0019	0.0020-0.0080	4	1.9983-1.9994	0.0010-0.0031	0.0040-0.0150
	W	2.8 (2835)	2.4397-2.4946	0.0017-0.0030	0.0020-0.0067	3	1.9984-1.9994	0.0014-0.0036	0.0060-0.0170

9113C04

CAMSHAFT SPECIFICATIONS
All measurements given in inches.

Year	Engine ID/VIN	Engine Displacement Liters (cc)	Journal Diameter					Elevation		Bearing Clearance	Camshaft End-Play
			1	2	3	4	5	In.	Ex.		
1988	K	2.0 (1998)	1.6714-1.6720	1.6810-1.6816	1.6911-1.6917	1.7009-1.7015	1.7108-1.7114	0.2409	0.2409	0.0008-0.0032	0.0016-0.0064
	M	2.0 (1998)	1.6714-1.6720	1.6810-1.6816	1.6911-1.6917	1.7009-1.7015	1.7108-1.7114	0.2409	0.2409	0.0008-0.0032	0.0016-0.0064
	1	2.0 (2000)	1.8677-1.8696	1.8677-1.8696	1.8677-1.8696	1.8677-1.8696	1.8677-1.8696	0.2625	0.2625	0.0010-0.0032	0.0016-0.0064
	W	2.8 (2835)	1.8670-1.8810	1.8670-1.8810	1.8670-1.8810	1.8670-1.8810	NA	0.2530	0.2730	0.0010-0.0039	NA
1989	K	2.0 (1998)	1.6714-1.6720	1.6810-1.6816	1.6911-1.6917	1.7009-1.7015	1.7108-1.7114	0.2409	0.2409	0.0008-0.0032	0.0016-0.0064
	M	2.0 (1998)	1.6714-1.6720	1.6810-1.6816	1.6911-1.6917	1.7009-1.7015	1.7108-1.7114	0.2409	0.2409	0.0008-0.0032	0.0016-0.0064
	1	2.0 (2000)	1.8677-1.8696	1.8696	1.8696	1.8696	NA	0.2625	0.2625	0.0010-0.0032	0.0016-0.0064
	W	2.8 (2835)	1.8670-1.8810	1.8670-1.8810	1.8670-1.8810	1.8670-1.8810	1.8680-1.8810	0.2530	0.2730	0.0010-0.0040	NA
1990	K	2.0 (1998)	1.6706-1.6712	1.6812-1.6818	1.6911-1.6917	1.7009-1.7015	1.7100-1.7106	0.2366	0.2515	0.0011-0.0035	0.0016-0.0064
	M	2.0 (1998)	1.6706-1.6712	1.6812-1.6818	1.6911-1.6917	1.7009-1.7015	1.7100-1.7106	0.2366	0.2515	0.0011-0.0035	0.0016-0.0064
	G	2.2 (2180)	1.8670-1.8690	1.8670-1.8690	1.8670-1.8690	1.8670-1.8690	1.8670-1.8690	0.2590	0.2590	0.0010-0.0035	0.0064
	T	3.1 (3130)	1.8680-1.8810	1.8680-1.8810	1.8680-1.8810	1.8680-1.8810	NA	0.2630	0.2730	0.0010-0.0039	NA
1991	K	2.0 (1998)	1.6706-1.6712	1.6812-1.6818	1.6911-1.6917	1.7009-1.7015	1.7100-1.7106	0.2366	0.2515	0.0011-0.0035	0.0016-0.0064
	G	2.2 (2180)	1.8670-1.8690	1.8670-1.8690	1.8670-1.8690	1.8670-1.8690	1.8670-1.8690	0.2590	0.2590	0.0010-0.0035	NA
	T	3.1 (3130)	1.8680-1.8810	1.8680-1.8810	1.8680-1.8810	1.8680-1.8810	NA	0.2630	0.2730	0.0010-0.0039	NA
1992	H	2.0 (1998)	1.6706-1.6712	1.6812-1.6818	1.6911-1.6917	1.7009-1.7015	1.7100-1.7106	0.2626	0.2626	0.0011-0.0035	0.0016-0.0064
	4	2.2 (2180)	1.8670-1.8690	1.8670-1.8690	1.8670-1.8690	1.8670-1.8690	1.8670-1.8690	0.2590	0.2590	0.0010-0.0035	NA
	T	3.1 (3130)	1.8680-1.8810	1.8680-1.8810	1.8680-1.8810	1.8680-1.8810	NA	0.2630	0.2730	0.0010-0.0039	NA
1993	H	2.0 (1998)	1.6706-1.6712	1.6812-1.6818	1.6911-1.6917	1.7009-1.7015	1.7100-1.7106	0.2626	0.2626	0.0011-0.0035	0.0016-0.0064
	4	2.2 (2180)	1.8670-1.8690	1.8670-1.8690	1.8670-1.8690	1.8670-1.8690	1.8670-1.8690	0.2590	0.2590	0.0010-0.0035	NA
	T	3.1 (3130)	1.8680-1.8810	1.8680-1.8810	1.8680-1.8810	1.8680-1.8810	NA	0.2630	0.2730	0.0010-0.0039	NA
1994	H	2.0 (1998)	1.6706-1.6712	1.6812-1.6818	1.6911-1.6917	1.7009-1.7015	1.7100-1.7106	0.2626	0.2626	0.0011-0.0035	0.0016-0.0063
	4	2.2 (2180)	1.8670-1.8690	1.8670-1.8690	1.8670-1.8690	1.8670-1.8690	1.8670-1.8690	0.2590	0.2590	0.0010-0.0035	NA
	T	3.1 (3130)	1.8680-1.8810	1.8680-1.8810	1.8680-1.8810	1.8680-1.8810	NA	0.2630	0.2730	0.0010-0.0039	NA

NA - Not Available

91133CA2

CRANKSHAFT AND CONNECTING ROD SPECIFICATIONS
All measurements are given in inches.

Year	Engine ID/VIN	Engine Displacement Liters (cc)	Crankshaft Main Brg. Journal Dia.	Crankshaft Main Brg. Oil Clearance	Shaft End-play	Thrust on No.	Connecting Rod Journal Diameter	Connecting Rod Oil Clearance	Side Clearance
1994	H	2.0 (1998)	2.2828-2.2833	0.0006-0.0016	0.0028-0.0118	3	1.9279-1.9287	0.0007-0.0025	0.0028-0.0095
	4	2.2 (2180)	2.4945-2.4954	0.0006-0.0019	0.0020-0.0070	4	1.9983-1.994	0.0010-0.0030	0.0040-0.0150
	T	3.1 (3130)	2.6473-2.6483	0.0012-0.0030	0.0020-0.0080	3	1.9983-1.9994	0.0010-0.0040	0.0140-0.0270

NA - Not Available
① No. 5: 2.4936-2.4946
② No. 5: 0.0014-0.0027
③ Bearings are identified by color.
  Brown: 2.2830-2.2830
  Green: 2.2827-2.2830
④ No. 5: 2.4936-2.4946
⑤ Bearings are identified by color.
  Brown: 2.2830-2.2833
  Green: 2.2827-2.2830

91133C06

CRANKSHAFT AND CONNECTING ROD SPECIFICATIONS
All measurements are given in inches.

Year	Engine ID/VIN	Engine Displacement Liters (cc)	Crankshaft Main Brg. Journal Dia.	Crankshaft Main Brg. Oil Clearance	Shaft End-play	Thrust on No.	Connecting Rod Journal Diameter	Connecting Rod Oil Clearance	Side Clearance
1988	K	2.0 (1998)	⑤	0.0006-0.0016	0.0003-0.0012	3	1.9278-1.9286	0.0007-0.0024	0.0027-0.0095
	M	2.0 (1998)	⑤	0.0006-0.0016	0.0003-0.0012	3	1.9278-1.9286	0.0007-0.0024	0.0027-0.0095
	1	2.0 (2000)	2.4945-2.4954	0.0006-0.0019	0.0020-0.0080	4	1.9983-1.994	0.0010-0.0031	0.0040-0.0150
	W	2.8 (2835)	2.4397-2.4946	0.0017-0.0030	0.0020-0.0067	3	1.9984-1.994	0.0014-0.0036	0.0060-0.0170
1989	K	2.0 (1998)	⑤	0.0006-0.0016	0.0003-0.0012	3	1.9279-1.9287	0.0007-0.0024	0.0027-0.0095
	M	2.0 (1998)	⑤	0.0006-0.0016	0.0003-0.0012	3	1.9279-1.9287	0.0007-0.0024	0.0027-0.0095
	1	2.0 (2000)	2.4945-2.4954	0.0006-0.0019	0.0020-0.0080	4	1.9983-1.994	0.0010-0.0031	0.0040-0.0150
	W	2.8 (2835)	2.4397-2.4946	0.0017-0.0030	0.0020-0.0067	3	1.9984-1.994	0.0014-0.0060	0.0060-0.0170
1990	K	2.0 (1998)	2.2828-2.2833	0.0006-0.0016	0.0003-0.0012	3	1.9279-1.9287	0.0007-0.0024	0.0027-0.0095
	M	2.0 (1998)	2.2828-2.2833	0.0006-0.0016	0.0003-0.0012	3	1.9279-1.9287	0.0007-0.0024	0.0027-0.0095
	G	2.2 (2180)	2.4945-2.4954	0.0006-0.0019	0.0020-0.0070	4	1.9983-1.994	0.0010-0.0030	0.0040-0.0150
	T	3.1 (3130)	2.6473-2.6483	0.0012-0.0030	0.0020-0.0080	3	1.9983-1.9994	0.0010-0.0040	0.0140-0.0270
1991	K	2.0 (1998)	2.2828-2.2833	0.0006-0.0016	0.0028-0.0012	3	1.9279-1.9287	0.0007-0.0025	0.0028-0.0095
	G	2.2 (2180)	2.4945-2.4954	0.0006-0.0019	0.0020-0.0070	4	1.9983-1.994	0.0010-0.0030	0.0040-0.0150
	T	3.1 (3130)	2.6473-2.6483	0.0012-0.0030	0.0020-0.0080	3	1.9983-1.994	0.0010-0.0040	0.0140-0.0270
1992	H	2.0 (1998)	2.2828-2.2833	0.0006-0.0016	0.0028-0.0118	3	1.9279-1.9287	0.0007-0.0025	0.0028-0.0095
	4	2.2 (2180)	2.4945-2.4954	0.0006-0.0019	0.0020-0.0070	4	1.9983-1.994	0.0010-0.0030	0.0040-0.0150
	T	3.1 (3130)	2.6473-2.6483	0.0012-0.0030	0.0020-0.0080	3	1.9983-1.994	0.0010-0.0040	0.0140-0.0270
1993	H	2.0 (1998)	2.2828-2.2833	0.0006-0.0016	0.0028-0.0118	3	1.9279-1.9287	0.0007-0.0025	0.0028-0.0095
	4	2.2 (2180)	2.4945-2.4954	0.0006-0.0019	0.0020-0.0070	4	1.9983-1.994	0.0010-0.0030	0.0040-0.0150
	T	3.1 (3130)	2.6473-2.6483	0.0012-0.0030	0.0020-0.0080	3	1.9983-1.994	0.0010-0.0040	0.0140-0.0270

91133C05

PISTON AND RING SPECIFICATIONS
All measurements are given in inches.

Year	Engine ID/VIN	Engine Displacement Liters (cc)	Piston Clearance	Ring Gap Top Compression	Ring Gap Bottom Compression	Ring Gap Oil Control	Ring Side Clearance Top Compression	Ring Side Clearance Bottom Compression	Ring Side Clearance Oil Control
1988	M	2.0 (1998)	0.0012-0.0020	0.0098-0.0177	0.0118-0.0197	NA	0.0024-0.0036	0.0019-0.0032	NA
	1	2.0 (2000)	0.0010-0.0022	0.010-0.020	0.010-0.020	0.010-0.050	0.0010-0.0030	0.0010-0.0030	0.0080
	W	2.8 (2835)	0.0020-0.0030	0.010-0.020	0.010-0.020	0.020-0.055	0.0010-0.0030	0.0010-0.0030	0.0080
1989	K	2.0 (1998)	0.0004-0.0012	0.0098-0.0177	0.0118-0.0197	NA	0.0024-0.0036	0.0019-0.0032	NA
	M	2.0 (1998)	0.0012-0.0020	0.0098-0.0177	0.0118-0.0197	NA	0.0024-0.0036	0.0019-0.0032	NA
	1	2.0 (2000)	0.0098-0.0022	0.010-0.020	0.010-0.020	0.010-0.050	0.0010-0.0030	0.0010-0.0030	0.0080
	W	2.8 (2835)	0.0020-0.0030	0.010-0.020	0.010-0.020	0.020-0.055	0.0010-0.0030	0.0010-0.0030	0.0080
1990	K	2.0 (1998)	0.0004-0.0012	0.0098-0.0177	0.0118-0.0197	NA	0.0024-0.0036	0.0019-0.0032	NA
	M	2.0 (1998)	0.0012-0.0020	0.0098-0.0177	0.0118-0.0197	0.010-0.050	0.0024-0.0036	0.0019-0.0032	NA
	G	2.2 (2180)	0.0007-0.0017	0.010-0.020	0.010-0.020	0.010-0.050	0.0020-0.0030	0.0020-0.0030	0.0020-0.0082
	T	3.1 (3130)	0.0009-0.0022	0.010-0.020	0.020-0.020	0.010-0.030	0.0020-0.0030	0.0020-0.0030	0.0008
1991	K	2.0 (1998)	0.0004-0.0012	0.0098-0.0177	0.0118-0.0197	NA	0.0024-0.0036	0.0019-0.0032	NA
	G	2.2 (2180)	0.0007-0.0017	0.010-0.020	0.010-0.020	0.010-0.050	0.0020-0.0030	0.0020-0.0030	0.0020-0.0082
	T	3.1 (3130)	0.0009-0.0022	0.010-0.020	0.020-0.020	0.020-0.030	0.0020-0.0030	0.0020-0.0030	0.0020-0.0080
1992	H	2.0 (1998)	0.0004-0.0012	0.0098-0.0177	0.0188-0.0197	NA	0.0024-0.0036	0.0019-0.0032	NA
	4	2.2 (2180)	0.0007-0.0017	0.010-0.020	0.010-0.020	0.010-0.050	0.0020-0.0030	0.0020-0.0030	0.0020-0.0082
	T	3.1 (3130)	0.0009-0.0022	0.010-0.020	0.020-0.028	0.010-0.030	0.0020-0.0030	0.0020-0.0030	0.0020-0.0080
1993	H	2.0 (1998)	0.0004-0.0012	0.0098-0.0177	0.0118-0.0197	NA	0.0024-0.0036	0.0019-0.0032	NA
	4	2.2 (2180)	0.0007-0.0017	0.010-0.020	0.010-0.020	0.010-0.050	0.0020-0.0030	0.0020-0.0030	0.0020-0.0082
	T	3.1 (3130)	0.0009-0.0022	0.010-0.020	0.020-0.028	0.010-0.030	0.0020-0.0030	0.0020-0.0030	0.0020-0.0080
1994	H	2.0 (1998)	0.0004-0.0012	0.0098-0.0177	0.0118-0.0197	NA	0.0024-0.0036	0.0019-0.0032	NA
	4	2.2 (2180)	0.0007-0.0017	0.010-0.020	0.010-0.020	0.010-0.050	0.0020-0.0030	0.0020-0.0030	0.0020-0.0082
	T	3.1 (3130)	0.0009-0.0022	0.010-0.020	0.020-0.028	0.010-0.030	0.0020-0.0030	0.0020-0.0030	0.0020-0.0080

NA - Not Available

91133C08

PISTON AND RING SPECIFICATIONS
All measurements are given in inches.

Year	Engine ID/VIN	Engine Displacement Liters (cc)	Piston Clearance	Ring Gap Top Compression	Ring Gap Bottom Compression	Ring Gap Oil Control	Ring Side Clearance Top Compression	Ring Side Clearance Bottom Compression	Ring Side Clearance Oil Control
1982	G	1.8 (1819)	0.0008-0.0018	0.0098-0.0197	0.0098-0.0197	Snug	0.0012-0.0027	0.0012-0.0027	0.0078
	O	1.8 (1819)	0.0004-0.0012	0.0010-0.0020	0.0010-0.0020	0.0010-0.0020	0.0020-0.0030	0.0010-0.0024	Snug
	B	2.0 (1998)	0.0008-0.0018	0.0098-0.0197	0.0098-0.0197	Snug	0.0012-0.0027	0.0012-0.0027	0.0078
1983	O	1.8 (1819)	0.0004-0.0012	0.0010-0.0020	0.0010-0.0020	0.0010-0.0020	0.0020-0.0030	0.0010-0.0024	Snug
	J	1.8 (1819)	0.0004-0.0012	0.0010-0.0020	0.0010-0.0020	0.0010-0.0020	0.0020-0.0030	0.0010-0.0024	Snug
	P	2.0 (1998)	0.0008-0.0018	0.0098-0.0197	0.0098-0.0197	Snug	0.0012-0.0027	0.0012-0.0027	0.0078
	B	2.0 (1998)	0.0008-0.0018	0.0098-0.0197	0.0098-0.0197	Snug	0.0012-0.0027	0.0012-0.0027	0.0078
1984	O	1.8 (1819)	0.0004-0.0012	0.0010-0.0020	0.0010-0.0020	0.0010-0.0020	0.0020-0.0030	0.0010-0.0024	Snug
	J	1.8 (1819)	0.0004-0.0012	0.0010-0.0020	0.0010-0.0020	0.0010-0.0020	0.0020-0.0030	0.0010-0.0024	Snug
	P	2.0 (1998)	0.0007-0.0017	0.0098-0.0197	0.0098-0.0197	Snug	0.0012-0.0027	0.0012-0.0027	0.0078
1985	O	1.8 (1819)	0.0008	0.0120-0.0200	0.0120-0.0200	0.0160-0.0550	0.0020-0.0040	0.0010-0.0025	0.0047
	J	1.8 (1819)	0.0008	0.0120-0.0200	0.0120-0.0200	0.0160-0.0550	0.0020-0.0040	0.0010-0.0025	0.0047
	P	2.0 (2000)	0.0007-0.0017	0.010-0.020	0.010-0.020	Snug	0.0012-0.0027	0.0012-0.0027	0.0078
	W	2.8 (2835)	0.0012-0.0027	0.010-0.020	0.010-0.020	0.020-0.055	0.0012-0.0027	0.0016-0.0037	MAX
1986	O	1.8 (1819)	0.0008	0.0120-0.0200	0.0120-0.0200	0.0160-0.0550	0.0020-0.0040	0.0010-0.0025	0.0047
	J	1.8 (1819)	0.0008	0.0120-0.0200	0.0120-0.0200	0.0160-0.0550	0.0020-0.0040	0.0010-0.0025	0.0047
	P	2.0 (2000)	0.0007-0.0017	0.010-0.020	0.010-0.020	Snug	0.0012-0.0027	0.0012-0.0027	0.0078
	W	2.8 (2835)	0.0012-0.0027	0.010-0.020	0.010-0.020	0.020-0.055	0.0012-0.0027	0.0016-0.0037	MAX
1987	K	2.0 (1998)	0.0004-0.0012	0.0098-0.0177	0.0098-0.0197	NA	0.0024-0.0036	0.0019-0.0032	NA
	M	2.0 (1998)	0.0004-	0.0098-0.0177	0.0118-0.0197	NA	0.0024-0.0032	0.0019-0.0032	NA
	1	2.0 (2000)	0.0010-0.0022	0.010-0.020	0.025	0.055	0.0010-0.0030	0.0010-0.0030	0.0070
	W	2.8 (2835)	0.0020-0.0030	0.010-0.020	0.010-0.020	0.020-0.050	0.0010-0.0030	0.0010-0.0030	0.0080
1988	K	2.0 (1998)	0.0004-0.0012	0.0098-0.0177	0.0118-0.0197	NA	0.0024-0.0036	0.0019-0.0032	NA

NA - Not Available

91133C07

VALVE SPECIFICATIONS

Year	Engine ID/VIN	Engine Displacement Liters (cc)	Seat Angle (deg.)	Face Angle (deg.)	Spring Test Pressure (lbs. @ in.)	Spring Installed Height (in.)	Stem-to-Guide Clearance (in.) Intake	Stem-to-Guide Clearance (in.) Exhaust	Stem Diameter (in.) Intake	Stem Diameter (in.) Exhaust
1988	M	2.0 (1998)	45	46	74-82 @ 1.48	1.476	0.0006-0.0017	0.0012-0.0024	0.2753-0.2747	0.2755-0.2760
	1	2.0 (1998)	45	45	105 @ 1.48 ①	1.60	0.0011-0.0023	0.0014-0.0028	NA	NA
	W	2.8 (2835)	46	45	195 @ 1.18	1.57	0.0010-0.0027	0.0010-0.0027	0.3410-0.3416	0.3410-0.3416
1989	K	2.0 (1998)	46	45	63-71 @ 1.48	1.476	0.0006-0.0017	0.0012-0.0024	0.2753-0.2747	0.2755-0.2760
	M	2.0 (1998)	46	46	74-82 @ 1.48	1.476	0.0006-0.0017	0.0012-0.0024	0.2753-0.2747	0.2755-0.2760
	1	2.0 (1998)	45	45	105 @ 1.48 ①	1.60	0.0011-0.0023	0.0014-0.0028	NA	NA
	W	2.8 (2835)	46	45	195 @ 1.18	1.57	0.0010-0.0027	0.0010-0.0027	0.3410-0.3416	0.3410-0.3416
1990	K	2.0 (1998)	46	45	63-71 @ 1.476	1.476	0.0006-0.0017	0.0012-0.0024	0.2760-0.2753	0.2755-0.2747
	M	2.0 (1998)	46	45	74-82 @ 1.48	1.476	0.0006-0.0017	0.0012-0.0024	0.2760-0.2753	0.2755-0.2747
	G	2.2 (2180)	45	45	208-222 @ 1.22 ②	1.61 ③	0.0011-0.0026	0.0014-0.0030	NA	NA
	T	3.1 (3130)	46	45	90 @ ②	1.60 ③	0.0010-0.0027	0.0010-0.0027	NA	NA
1991	K	2.0 (1998)	45	46	63-71 @ 1.48	1.476	0.0006-0.0017	0.0012-0.0024	0.2760-0.2755	0.2753-0.2747
	G	2.2 (2180)	46	45	208-222 @ 1.22 ②	1.61 ③	0.0011-0.0026	0.0014-0.0030	NA	NA
	T	3.1 (3130)	46	45	90 @ ②	1.60 ③	0.0010-0.0027	0.0010-0.0027	NA	NA
1992	H	2.0 (1998)	45	46	63-71 @ 1.48	1.476	0.0006-0.0017	0.0012-0.0024	0.2760-0.2755	0.2753-0.2747
	4	2.2 (2180)	46	45	208-222 @ 1.22 ②	1.61 ③	0.0011-0.0026	0.0014-0.0030	NA	NA
	T	3.1 (3130)	46	45	90 @ ②	1.60 ③	0.0010-0.0027	0.0010-0.0027	NA	NA
1993	H	2.0 (1998)	46	45	90 @ 1.70 ②	1.693	0.0008-0.0021	0.0014-0.0030	0.2760-0.2753	0.2760-0.2755
	4	2.2 (2180)	46	45	225-233 @ 1.25 ②	1.64 ③	0.0011-0.0026	0.0014-0.0031	NA	NA
	T	3.1 (3130)	46	45	90 @ ②	1.60 ③	0.0010-0.0027	0.0010-0.0027	NA	NA
1994	H	2.0 (1998)	45	46	63-71 @ 1.48	1.476	0.0006-0.0017	0.0012-0.0024	0.2753-0.2747	0.2760-0.2755
	4	2.2 (2180)	46	45	225-233 @ 1.25 ②	1.64 ③	0.0011-0.0026	0.0014-0.0031	NA	NA
	T	3.1 (3130)	46	45	90 @ ②	1.60 ③	0.0010-0.0027	0.0010-0.0027	NA	NA

NA - Not Available
① With valve closed
② With valve open
③ With valve closed

91133CA0

VALVE SPECIFICATIONS

Year	Engine ID/VIN	Engine Displacement Liters (cc)	Seat Angle (deg.)	Face Angle (deg.)	Spring Test Pressure (lbs. @ in.)	Spring Installed Height (in.)	Stem-to-Guide Clearance (in.) Intake	Stem-to-Guide Clearance (in.) Exhaust	Stem Diameter (in.) Intake	Stem Diameter (in.) Exhaust
1982	G	1.8 (1819)	46	45	183 @ 1.33	1.60	0.0011-0.0026	0.0014-0.0031	0.3139-0.3144	0.3129-0.3136
1983	O	1.8 (1819)	46	46	NA	NA	0.0006-0.0016	0.0012-0.0024	NA	NA
	B	2.0 (1998)	46	45	183 @ 1.33	1.60	0.0011-0.0026	0.0014-0.0031	0.3139-0.3144	0.3129-0.3136
1984	O	1.8 (1819)	46	46	NA	NA	0.0006-0.0016	0.0012-0.0024	NA	NA
	J	1.8 (1819)	46	46	NA	NA	0.0006-0.0016	0.0012-0.0024	NA	NA
	P	2.0 (1998)	46	45	183 @ 1.33	1.60	0.0011-0.0026	0.0014-0.0031	0.3139-0.3144	0.3129-0.3136
	B	2.0 (1998)	46	45	183 @ 1.33	1.60	0.0011-0.0026	0.0014-0.0031	0.3139-0.3144	0.3129-0.3136
1985	O	1.8 (1819)	46	46	NA	NA	0.0006-0.0016	0.0012-0.0024	NA	NA
	J	1.8 (1819)	46	46	NA	NA	0.0006-0.0016	0.0012-0.0024	NA	NA
	P	2.0 (1998)	46	45	183 @ 1.33	1.60	0.0011-0.0026	0.0014-0.0031	0.3139-0.3144	0.3129-0.3136
	W	2.8 (2835)	46	45	78-88 @ 1.44	1.440	0.0006-0.0020	0.0010-0.0024	NA	NA
1986	O	1.8 (1819)	46	45	78-88 @ 1.44	1.440	0.0006-0.0020	0.0010-0.0024	NA	NA
	J	1.8 (1819)	46	45	78-88 @ 1.44	1.440	0.0006-0.0020	0.0010-0.0024	NA	NA
	P	2.0 (1998)	46	45	183 @ 1.33	1.60	0.0011-0.0026	0.0014-0.0031	0.3139-0.3144	0.3129-0.3136
	W	2.8 (2835)	46	45	195 @ 1.18	1.57	0.0010-0.0026	0.0010-0.0024	0.3410-0.3416	0.3410-0.3416
1987	O	1.8 (1819)	46	46	63-71 @ 1.48	1.476	0.0006-0.0017	0.0012-0.0024	0.2753-0.2747	0.2760-0.2755
	J	1.8 (1819)	46	46	74-82 @ 1.48	1.476	0.0006-0.0017	0.0012-0.0024	0.2753-0.2747	0.2760-0.2755
	P	2.0 (1998)	45	45	105 @ 1.48 ①	1.60	0.0011-0.0023	0.0014-0.0028	NA	NA
	W	2.8 (2835)	46	45	195 @ 1.18	1.57	0.0010-0.0027	0.0010-0.0027	0.3410-0.3416	0.3410-0.3416
	K	2.0 (1998)	46	45	63-71 @ 1.48	1.476	0.0006-0.0017	0.0012-0.0024	0.2753-0.2747	0.2760-0.2760
1988	M	2.0 (1998)	46	46	74-82 @ 1.48	1.476	0.0006-0.0017	0.0012-0.0024	0.2753-0.2747	0.2760-0.2755
	1	2.0 (1998)	45	45	105 @ 1.48 ①	1.60	0.0011-0.0023	0.0014-0.0028	NA	NA
	W	2.8 (2835)	46	45	195 @ 1.18	1.57	0.0010-0.0027	0.0010-0.0027	0.2765-0.2760	0.2765-0.2760
	K	2.0 (1998)	45	46	63-71 @ 1.48	1.476	0.0006-0.0017	0.0012-0.0024	0.2753-0.2747	0.2760-0.2760

91133C09

Engine

REMOVAL & INSTALLATION

❄❄ CAUTION

When draining the coolant, keep in mind that cats and dogs are attracted by ethylene glycol antifreeze, and are quite likely to drink any that is left in an uncovered container or in puddles on the ground. This will prove fatal in sufficient quantity. Always drain the coolant into a sealable container. Coolant should be reused unless it is contaminated or several years old.

1982–83 1.8L and 2.0L Engines

1. Disconnect the battery cables at the battery, negative cable first.
2. Remove the air cleaner. Drain the cooling system.
3. Remove the power steering pump (if so equipped) and position it out of the way. Leave the lines connected. Remove the windshield washer bottle and lay it aside.
4. If the car is equipped with A/C, remove the relay bracket at the bulkhead connector. Remove the bulkhead connector, then separate the wiring harness connections.
5. If equipped with cruise control, remove the servo bracket and position it out of the way.
6. Tag and disconnect all vacuum hoses and wires.
7. Unfasten the master cylinder attaching nuts at the vacuum booster, then lay it aside.
8. Detach the heater hose at the hot water pipe on the engine.
9. Remove the fan assembly. Remove the horn.
10. Disconnect the carburetor or TBI body linkage.
11. Raise the front of the car and support it with jackstands.
12. Properly relieve the fuel system pressure (see Section 1), then disconnect the fuel line and the heater hose at the intake manifold.
13. If equipped with A/C, remove the air conditioning brace.
14. Remove the exhaust pipe shield.
15. As outlined in Section 2 of this manual, remove the starter.
16. Disconnect the exhaust pipe at the manifold.
17. Remove the front tire and wheel assemblies.
18. Disconnect the stabilizer bar from the lower control arms. Remove the ball joints from the steering knuckle.
19. Remove the drive axles at the transaxle, then remove the transaxle strut.
20. If equipped with A/C, remove the inner fender shield. Remove the drive belt, tag and disconnect the wires, then remove the compressor. Do NOT disconnect any of the refrigerant lines.
21. Remove the rear engine mount, nuts and plate.
22. If equipped with an automatic transaxle, remove the oil filter.
23. Disconnect the speedometer cable.
24. Carefully lower the vehicle.
25. If equipped with an automatic transaxle, disconnect the oil cooler lines at the transaxle.
26. Remove the front engine mount nuts.
27. For vehicles equipped with a manual transaxle, disconnect the clutch cable at the transaxle. For automatic transaxle equipped vehicles, disconnect the detent cable at the transaxle.
28. Remove the transaxle mount.
29. Install a suitable engine lifting device, Lift the engine and transaxle assembly out of the car.

To install:

30. Install the engine mount alignment bolt (M6 x 1 x 65) to ensure proper powertrain alignment.
31. Lower the engine into the car, leaving the lifting device attached.
32. Install the transaxle bracket. Install the mount to the side frame and secure with NEW mount bolts.
33. With the weight not yet on the mounts, tighten the transaxle bolts. Tighten the right front mount nuts.
34. Lower the engine fully onto the mounts, remove the lifting device and then raise the front of the car.
35. Installation of the remaining components is in the reverse order of removal. Check the powertrain alignment bolt; if excessive force is required to remove the bolt, loosen the transaxle adjusting bolts and realign the powertrain. Adjust the drive belts and the clutch cable (if equipped with manual transaxle).
36. Connect the negative battery cable, then start the engine and check for proper operation, fluid levels, and/or leaks.

1984–86 1.8L (OHC) Engines

1. Disconnect the negative, then positive battery cables. Detach the engine ground wire.
2. Properly drain the cooling system into a suitable container.
3. Remove the air cleaner.
4. Disconnect the radiator hoses.
5. Label and detach the following wires:
 • Bulkhead (engine harness)
 • Brake master cylinder
 • A/C relay cluster switches (if equipped)
 • Windshield wiper motor
 • Cooling fan, relay and ground
 • ECM (pull the harness through the bulkhead
 • Temperature switch at the thermostat housing
6. Label and disconnect the fuel injection and MAP sensor and canister vacuum hoses.
7. Disconnect the throttle cable from the bracket and throttle body and the shift cable at the transaxle.
8. Detach the power steering hoses at the cut-off switch and the return hose at the pump.
9. Raise and safely support the vehicle.
10. Remove the speedometer cable and bracket.
11. Disconnect the exhaust pipe at the exhaust manifold and hangers, then position it aside.
12. Disconnect the hoses at the heater core, fuel lines and, if equipped with an automatic transaxle, the oil cooler lines.
13. Remove the front wheel and tire assemblies.
14. Remove the brake calipers. Be sure to support the calipers in the wheel opening with a piece of wire. Do NOT let the calipers hang by the brake line.
15. If equipped, disconnect the wires at the A/C compressor.
16. Using the proper equipment, evacuate the A/C system, then disconnect the lines from the compressor.
17. Remove the suspension supports. Remove the 2 center bolts on each side, then remove the bolt each end and loosen the remaining bolt.

❄❄ CAUTION

Be sure to properly support the vehicles, engine and transaxle weight during the following steps.

18. For vehicles equipped with an automatic transaxle, remove the rear transaxle lateral strut.
19. Remove the transaxle strut (front).
20. Support the front of the car with jackstands under the radiator core support.
21. Reposition the jack to the rear of the cowl with a 4 in. x 4 in. x 6 ft. (102mm x 102mm x 1.8m) piece of wood spanning the vehicle's width.
22. Raise the car enough to remove the jackstands. Position a dolly under the engine and transaxle with three 4 in. x 4 in. x 12 in. (102mm x 102mm x 30cm) wood blocks as a support. Carefully, lower the weight of the car onto the dolly.
23. Remove the remaining bolt at each end of the right and left front suspension supports.
24. Unfasten the one long mount-to-bracket bolt, then remove the transaxle mount.
25. Remove the front engine mount. There should be 2 mount-to-bracket retaining bolts.

➥**The lower strut bolt opening is a slot, rather than a round hole. This is to allow for camber adjustment. Be sure to carefully scribe the position of the strut on the hub to preserve camber adjustments.**

26. Unfasten the knuckle-to-strut bolts. There are 2 per side.
27. Raise the car, leaving the engine, transaxle and suspension on the dolly. Separate the engine and transaxle.

To install:

28. With the aid of an assistant, assemble the engine and transaxle, then position in the chassis.

29. Install the transaxle mount, and secure by tightening the long mount-to-bracket bolt.

30. Install the rear engine mount, then secure using the 2 mount-to-bracket-bolts. Install the front engine mount the same way.

31. Loosely bolt each end of the right and left front suspension supports.

32. Making sure to align with the marks made during removal, install the knuckle-to-strut bolts. There are two on each side; tighten to 133 ft. lbs. (180 Nm).

33. Raise the car, then remove the dolly. Using jackstands, remove the 6 ft. (1.8m) piece of wood, then move the hoist to the front of the vehicle.

34. Install the remaining bolts in the right and left front suspension supports, then tighten to 65 ft. lbs. (88 Nm).

35. Install the front and rear transaxle struts.

36. If equipped, connect the wiring at the A/C compressor.

37. Remove the wire supporting the brake calipers, then install the calipers.

38. Install the front wheel and tire assemblies.

39. Connect the following hoses:
- Oil cooler lines (if equipped with an automatic transaxle)
- Fuel lines
- Heater core hoses.

40. Fasten the exhaust pipe to the manifold and hangers.

41. Connect the speedometer cable, then install the bracket.

42. Carefully lower the vehicle.

43. If equipped, connect the power steering return hose at the pump and the cut-off switch.

44. Connect the shift cable at the transaxle and the throttle cable to the bracket and throttle body assembly.

45. Attach the vacuum hoses to the MAP sensor and canister and the throttle body assembly.

46. Connect the following wires, as tagged during removal:
- Temperature switch at the thermostat housing
- ECM wiring (feed the harness through the bulkhead)
- A/C relay cluster switches (if equipped)
- Windshield wiper motor
- Cooling fan, relay and ground
- Brake master cylinder
- Bulkhead (engine harness)

47. Connect the radiator hose(s).

48. Fill the cooling system with the proper type and quantity of suitable coolant.

49. If equipped, connect the A/C lines. Using the proper equipment, recharge the A/C system.

50. Connect the positive, then negative battery cables, then attach the engine ground wire.

1984–89 2.0L (OHV) Engines

1. Disconnect the negative, then the positive battery cables.

2. Properly drain the cooling system into a suitable container.

3. Remove the air cleaner assembly.

4. Disconnect the accelerator and T.V. cables at the throttle body.

5. Detach the ECM wiring harness at the throttle body.

6. Tag and disconnect all vacuum hoses, then remove the upper and lower radiator hoses and heater hoses at the engine.

7. Remove the exhaust heat shield.

8. For vehicles equipped with A/C, remove the adjustment bolt at the motor mount.

9. Disconnect the engine wiring harness at the bulkhead.

10. Remove the windshield washer bottle.

11. Remove the serpentine or alternator, power steering and A/C belts, as applicable.

12. If not done already, properly relieve the fuel system pressure. Disconnect the fuel lines.

13. Raise and safely support the vehicle.

14. If equipped with A/C, remove the A/C brace.

15. Remove the inner fender splash shield.

16. If equipped with A/C, remove the compressor, but do NOT disconnect the refrigerant lines.

17. Remove the flywheel splash shield.

18. Disconnect the starter wires.

19. Remove the front starter brace, then remove the starter as outlined in Section 2 of this manual.

20. Unfasten the torque converter bolts.

21. Remove the crankshaft pulley. Using tool J-24420 or equivalent, remove the crankshaft hub.

22. Remove the oil filter.

23. Unfasten and remove the engine-to-transaxle support bracket.

24. Remove the right rear motor mount.

25. Disconnect the exhaust pipe at the exhaust manifold, then disconnect the exhaust pipe at the center hanger and loosen the muffler hanger.

26. Remove the T.V. and shift cable bracket at the intake manifold.

27. Unfasten the 2 lower bellhousing bolts.

28. Carefully lower the vehicle.

29. Unfasten then remove the right front motor mount nuts.

30. Remove the alternator and adjusting brace.

31. Remove the brake master cylinder from the booster, then set aside, making sure it is suitably supported.

32. Install a suitable engine lifting device.

33. Remove the right front motor mount bracket.

34. Unfasten the remaining upper bellhousing bolts.

35. While lifting the engine, remove the power steering pump. Carefully lift the engine from the vehicle.

To install:

36. Position, then partially lower the engine assembly into the vehicle. Install the power steering pump, while lowering the engine.

37. Fasten the upper bellhousing bolts.

38. Install the right front motor mount bracket.

39. Remove the engine lifting device.

40. Fasten the master cylinder to the power brake booster.

41. Install the alternator and adjusting brace.

42. Install the right front motor mount nuts.

43. Raise and safely support the vehicle.

44. Install the remaining lower bellhousing bolts.

45. Install the T.V. and shift cable bracket.

46. Fasten the exhaust pipe at the center hanger, then tighten the muffler hanger. Connect the exhaust pipe at the exhaust manifold.

47. Install the right rear motor mount. If the rear engine mount bracket is removed, it will be necesary to perform the following steps to ensure proper engine mount bracket locations.
- a. Loosely install the engine mount bracket.
- b. Raise the engine and transaxle.
- c. Tighten the engine mount nuts and bolts.

48. Install the engine-to-support bracket.

49. Install the oil filter.

50. Using the correct tool, install the crankshaft hub and pulley.

51. Install the torque converter retaining bolts.

52. Install the front starter brace, then the starter.

53. Connect the starter wires.

54. Install the flywheel splash shield.

55. If equipped with A/C, install the compressor.

56. Install the inner fender splash shield.

57. If equipped with A/C, install the A/C brace.

58. Carefully lower the vehicle.

59. Connect the fuel lines.

60. Install the serpentine, alternator, power steering and/or A/C belts, as applicable.

61. Install the windshield washer bottle.

62. Connect the engine wiring harness at the bulkhead.

63. For vehicles equipped with A/C, install the adjustment bolt at the motor mount.

64. Install the exhaust heat shield.

65. Connect the vacuum hoses and the upper and lower radiator hoses and heater hoses at the engine.

66. Attach the ECM harness at the engine.

67. Connect the accelerator and T.V. cables at the throttle body.

68. Install the air cleaner assembly.

69. Fill the engine cooling system with the correct amount and type of coolant.

70. Connect the postive, followed by the negative battery cables.

71. Start the engine, then inspect for proper brake system operation, proper fluid levels and/or leakage.

2.0L (OHC) Engines

➡This procedure requires the use of a special tool.

1. Remove battery cables.
2. Drain cooling system.
3. Remove air cleaner.
4. Disconnect engine electrical harness at bulkhead.
5. Disconnect electrical connector at brake cylinder.
6. Remove throttle cable from bracket and E.F.I. assembly.
7. Remove vacuum hoses from E.F.I. assembly.
8. Remove power steering high pressure hose at cut-off switch.
9. Remove vacuum hoses at the MAP sensor and canister.
10. Disconnect air conditioning relay cluster switches.
11. Remove power steering return hose at pump.
12. Disconnect ECM wire connections and feed harness through bulkhead and lay harness over engine.
13. Remove upper and lower radiator hoses from engine.
14. Remove electrical connections from temperature switch at thermostat housing.
15. Disconnect transmission shift cable at transmission.
16. Hoist car.
17. Remove speedometer cable at transmission and bracket.
18. Disconnect exhaust pipe at exhaust manifold.
19. Remove exhaust pipe from converter.
20. Remove heater hoses from heater core.
21. Remove fuel lines at flex hoses.
22. Remove transmission cooler lines at flex hoses.
23. Remove left and right front wheels.
24. Remove right hand spoiler section and splash shield.
25. Remove right and left brake calipers and support with wire.
26. Remove right and left tie rod ends.
27. Disconnect electrical connections at air conditioning compressor.
28. Remove air conditioning compressor and mounting brackets, support air conditioning compressor with wire in wheel opening.
29. Remove front suspension support attachment bolts (6 bolts each side).
30. Lower car.
31. Support front of vehicle by placing two short jackstands under core support.
32. Position front post hoist to the rear of cowl.
33. Position a 4 in. (102mm) x 4 in. (102mm) x 6 ft. (2m) timber on front post hoist.
34. Raise vehicle enough to remove jackstands.
35. Position a 4-wheel dolly under engine and transaxle assembly.
36. Position three (3) 4 in. (102mm) x 4 in. (102mm) x 12 in. (305mm) blocks under engine and transaxle assembly only, letting support rails hang free.
37. Lower vehicle onto 4-wheel dolly slightly.
38. Remove rear transaxle mount attachment bolts (2).
39. Remove left front engine mount attachment bolts (3).
40. Remove two (2) engine support to body attachment bolts behind right-hand inner axle U-joint.
41. Remove one (1) attaching bolt and nut from right-hand chassis side rail to engine mount bracket.
42. Remove six (6) strut attachment nuts.
43. Raise vehicle letting engine, transaxle and suspension resting on 4-wheel dolly.

Reverse the removal procedure for engine installation with the following exceptions:

44. With one man's assistance, position engine and transaxle assembly in chassis.
45. Install transaxle and left front mounts to side rail bolts loosely.
46. Install a M6 x 1 x 65 alignment bolt in left front mount to prevent powertrain misalignment.
47. Tighten the transaxle mount bolts to 42 ft. lbs. and left front mount bolts to 18 ft. lbs.
48. Install right rear mount to body bolts and tighten to 38 ft. lbs. (52 Nm).
49. Install right rear mount to chassis side rail bolt and nut, then tighten to 38 ft. lbs. (52 Nm).

50. Place a floor jack under control arms, jack struts into position and install retaining nuts.
51. Raise vehicle.
52. Using a transmission jack or suitable lifting equipment, raise control arms and attach tie rod ends.

2.2L Engines

1990–93 VEHICLES

➡The following procedure is for the engine and transaxle assembly.

1. Disconnect the battery.
2. Drain the cooling system.
3. Relieve the fuel system pressure.
4. Disconnect the hood lamp wiring, if so equipped and remove the hood.
5. Disconnect the throttle body intake duct.
6. Remove the rear sight shields.
7. Disconnect the upper radiator hose.
8. Disconnect the brake booster vacuum hose.
9. Disconnect the alternator top brace and wiring.
10. Disconnect and tag the upper engine harness from the engine.
11. Discharge the A/C system as outlined in Section 1.
12. Disconnect the A/C compressor to condenser and accumulator lines.
13. Raise and support the vehicle safely.
14. Remove the left splash shield.
15. Disconnect the exhaust system.
16. Disconnect and tag the lower engine wiring.
17. Remove the flywheel inspection cover.
18. Remove the front wheels.
19. Disconnect the lower radiator hose.
20. Disconnect the heater hoses from the heater core.
21. Remove the brake calipers from the steering knuckle and wire up out of the way as outlined in Section 9.
22. Disconnect the tie rods from the struts.
23. Lower the vehicle.
24. Remove the clutch slave cylinder.
25. With the fuel system pressure released, place an absorbent shop towel around the connections and disconnect the fuel lines.
26. Disconnect the transaxle linkage at the transaxle.
27. Disconnect the accelerator cables from the TBI unit.
28. Disconnect the cruise control cables from the TBI unit.
29. Disconnect the throttle valve cables from the TBI, on vehicles equipped with an automatic transaxle.
30. Disconnect the automatic transaxle cooling lines.
31. Disconnect the power steering hoses from the power steering pump.
32. Remove the center suspension support bolts.
33. Align Engine/Transaxle Frame Handler tool No. J 36295 or equivalent under the suspension supports, engine and transaxle; lower vehicle to dolly and add support under the engine.
34. Safely support the rear of the vehicle.
35. Disconnect the upper transaxle mount.
36. Remove the upper strut bolts and nuts.
37. Disconnect the front engine mount.
38. Disconnect the rear engine mount.
39. Remove the 4 rear suspension support bolts.
40. Remove the 4 front suspension support bolts and wire the bolt holes together to prevent axle separation.
41. Raise the vehicle and remove the engine and transaxle assembly on tool No. J 36295 or equivalent.

To install:

42. Lower the vehicle and install the engine and transaxle assembly using tool No. J 36295 or equivalent.
43. Install the suspension supports bolts and tighten to 65 ft. lbs. for the front and rear suspension supports and 66 ft. lbs. for the center suspension support.
44. Install the transaxle mount but do not tighten.
45. Install the rear engine mount but do not tighten.
46. Install the front engine mount but do not tighten.
47. Tighten the manual transaxle mounting bolts as follows:
- Front transaxle strut to body bolts to 40 ft. lbs.
- Rear transaxle mount to body bolts to 23 ft. lbs.
48. Tighten the automatic transaxle mount bolts to 22 ft. lbs.

49. Tighten the front and rear engine mount bolts, please refer to the engine mount illustration.

➡**All engine mount bolts that have been removed must be cleaned and a new thread locking compound applied to the threads before reinstallation.**

50. Install the power steering hoses.
51. Connect the accelerator, cruise control and T.V. cables to the TBI.
52. Connect the transaxle cooling lines to the automatic transaxle.
53. Connect the transaxle linkage.
54. Reconnect the fuel lines.
55. Reconnect the clutch slave cylinder.
56. Raise and support the vehicle safely.
57. Install the tie rods.
58. Install the calipers to the steering knuckle.
59. Install the heater hoses to the heater core.
60. Install the lower radiator hose.
61. Install the A/C compressor.
62. Install the flywheel inspection cover.
63. Install the engine splash shield.
64. Install the front wheel and tighten the wheel stud nuts to 100 ft. lbs. (136 Nm).
65. Lower the vehicle.
66. Install the upper engine wiring.
67. Install the compressor to condenser and accumulator lines.
68. Install the brake booster vacuum hose.
69. Install the upper radiator hose.
70. Raise and support the vehicle safely.
71. Install the lower engine wiring.
72. Reconnect the exhaust system.
73. Lower the vehicle.
74. Connect the TBI wiring.
75. Install the air cleaner assembly.
76. Recharge the A/C system.
77. Check and adjust the wheel alignment.
78. Install the hood and connect the battery.

1994 VEHICLES

1. Properly relieve the fuel system pressure, then disconnect the negative battery cable.
2. Drain the cooling system into a suitable container.
3. Remove the air cleaner outlet duct.
4. Detach the upper radiator hose at the coolant outlet.
5. Disconnect the brake booster vacuum hose.
6. Tag and detach the following electrical connections:
• Idle Air Control (IAC)
• Alternator
• Throttle Position (TP) sensor
• Manifold Absolute Pressure (MAP) sensor
• EVAP emission solenoid
• Fuel injector harness
• Exhaust Gas Recirculation (EGR) valve
• Engine Coolant Temperature (ECT) sensor
• Transaxle Converter Clutch (TCC)
• Oxygen (O₂) sensor
• Park/Neutral position switch
• Engine grounds
7. Remove the serpentine drive belt.
8. Disconnect the transaxle shift control cable from the range select lever and bracket.
9. Detach the coolant surge tank hose, then remove the tank.
10. Disconnect the vacuum line near the master cylinder.
11. Install J 28467-A or equivalent engine support fixture.
12. Disconnect the lower radiator hose from the water pump.
13. Raise and safely support the vehicle.
14. Remove both front wheel and tire assemblies, then remove both splash shields.
15. Disconnect the exhaust pipe at the manifold and catalytic converter.
16. Remove the engine mount strut.
17. Disconnect the wheel speed sensor wire harness from the control arms.

18. Separate the ball joints from the steering knuckles. Using tool J 24319-01 or equivalent, separate the tie rod ends from the struts.
19. Detach the brake lines from the suspension supports.
20. If equipped, remove the A/C compressor and support with the lines attached.
21. Tag and detach the following electrical connectors:
• Electronic Ignition Module
• Vehicle Speed Sensors (VSS)
• Cooling Fan
• Starter
• A/C compressor
• Oil pressure and level sensors
• Engine grounds
22. Disconnect the power steering lines from the rack and pinion assembly. Detach the flexible coupling joint at the rack and pinion assembly.
23. Disconnect the accelerator control, cruise control (if equipped) and the T.V. cables from the accelerator control bracket.
24. Remove the suspension support assembly.
25. Disconnect the heater hoses at the front of the dash.
26. Remove both drive axles from the transaxle, then position them aside.
27. Disconnect the fuel lines.
28. Detach the cooler lines from the transaxle, then remove the transaxle mount.
29. Remove the engine mount assembly.
30. Place a suitable support under the vehicle. Carefully lower the vehicle so that it rests lightly on the support.
31. Remove the support fixture from the engine, then raise the vehicle, leaving the engine and transaxle assembly on the table.
32. Unfasten the retaining bolts, then separate the engine from the transaxle.
To install:
33. Position the engine to the transaxle, then install the retaining bolts. Tighten the bolts to 55 ft. lbs. (75 Nm).
34. Lower the vehicle onto the engine and transaxle assembly.
35. Install J 28467-A or equivalent engine support fixture onto the engine.
36. Install the engine mount assembly, then install the transaxle mount.
37. Attach the cooler lines to the transaxle.
38. Connect the fuel lines.
39. Install both drive axles into the transaxle.
40. Connect the heater hoses to the front of the cowl.
41. Install the suspension support assembly.
42. Connect the accelerator, cruise control, and T.V. cables to the accelerator control bracket.
43. Attach the flexible coupling joint to the rack and pinion assembly.
44. Connect the power steering lines to the rack and pinion assembly.
45. Attach the following electrical connectors as tagged during removal:
• Electronic Ignition Module
• Vehicle Speed Sensors (VSS)
• Cooling Fan
• Starter
• A/C compressor
• Oil pressure and level sensors
• Engine grounds
46. Install the A/C compressor, if equipped.
47. Connect the brake lines to the suspension support.
48. Fasten the tie rod ends to the struts, then connect the ball joints to the steering knuckles.
49. Connect the wheel speed sensor wire harness to the control arms.
50. Install the engine mount strut.
51. Fasten the exhaust pipe to the exhaust manifold and catalytic converter.
52. Install the splash shields and the wheel and tire assemblies.
53. Carefully lower the vehicle.
54. Connect the lower radiator hose to the water pump.
55. Remove the engine support fixture.
56. Attach the vacuum line, located near the master cylinder.
57. Install the coolant surge tank, then connect the tank's hose.
58. Connect the transaxle shift control cable.
59. Install the serpentine drive belt.
60. Attach the following electrical connectors, as tagged during removal:
• Idle Air Control (IAC)
• Alternator

- Throttle Position (TP) sensor
- Manifold Absolute Pressure (MAP) sensor
- EVAP emission solenoid
- Fuel injector harness
- Exhaust Gas Recirculation (EGR) valve
- Engine Coolant Temperature (ECT) sensor
- Transaxle Converter Clutch (TCC)
- Oxygen (O_2) sensor
- Park/Neutral position switch
- Engine grounds

61. Connect the brake booster vacuum hose.

62. Attach the upper radiator hose and the air cleaner outlet duct.

63. Fill the cooling system and crankcase with the correct type and amount of fluids.

64. Connect the negative battery cable, then start the engine. Check for proper operation, fluid levels and/or leaks.

2.8L and 3.1L Engines

1985–88 VEHICLES

1. Disconnect the negative battery cable. Drain the cooling system and remove the air cleaner assembly.

2. Remove the air flow sensor. Remove the exhaust crossover heat shield and remove the crossover pipe.

3. Remove the serpentine belt tensioner and belt.

4. Remove the power steering pump mounting bracket. Disconnect the heater pipe at the power steering pump mounting bracket.

5. Disconnect the radiator hoses from the engine.

6. Disconnect the accelerator and throttle valve cable at the throttle valve.

7. Remove the alternator. Tag and disconnect the wiring harness at the engine.

8. Relieve the fuel pressure (see Section 1) and disconnect the fuel hose. Disconnect the coolant bypass and the overflow hoses at the engine.

9. Tag and remove the vacuum hoses to the engine.

10. Raise the vehicle and support it safely.

11. Remove the inner fender splash shield. Remove the harmonic balancer.

12. Remove the flywheel cover. Remove the starter bolts. Tag and disconnect the electrical connections to the starter. Remove the starter.

13. Disconnect the wires at the oil sending unit.

14. Remove the air conditioning compressor and related brackets.

15. Disconnect the exhaust pipe at the rear of the exhaust manifold.

16. Remove the flex plate-to-torque converter bolts.

17. Remove the transaxle-to-engine bolts. Remove the engine-to-rear mount frame nuts.

18. Disconnect the shift cable bracket at the transaxle. Remove the lower bell housing bolts.

19. Lower the vehicle and disconnect the heater hoses at the engine.

20. Install a suitable engine lifting device. While supporting the engine and transaxle, remove the upper bell housing bolts.

21. Remove the front mounting bolts.

22. Remove the master cylinder from the booster.

23. Remove the engine assembly from the vehicle.

To install:

24. Install the engine and remove the engine lifting device.

25. Install the master cylinder to the booster.

26. Install the front mounting bolts.

27. Install the upper bell housing bolts.

28. Connect the heater hoses at the engine.

29. Connect the shift cable bracket at the transaxle. Install the lower bell housing bolts.

30. Install the transaxle-to-engine bolts. Install the engine-to-rear mount frame nuts.

31. Install the flex plate-to-torque converter bolts.

32. Connect the exhaust pipe at the rear of the exhaust manifold.

33. Install the air conditioning compressor and related brackets.

34. Connect the wires at the oil sending unit.

35. Install the flywheel cover. Install the starter bolts. Connect the electrical connections to the starter. Install the starter.

36. Install the inner fender splash shield. Install the harmonic balancer.

37. Lower the vehicle.

38. Install the vacuum hoses to the engine.

39. Connect the fuel hose. Connect the coolant bypass and the overflow hoses at the engine.

40. Install the alternator. Connect the wiring harness at the engine.

41. Connect the accelerator and throttle valve cable at the throttle valve.

42. Connect the radiator hoses to the engine.

43. Install the power steering pump mounting bracket. Connect the heater pipe at the power steering pump mounting bracket.

44. Install the serpentine belt tensioner and belt.

45. Install the air flow sensor. Install the exhaust crossover heat shield and crossover pipe.

46. Connect the negative battery cable. Fill the cooling system and install the air cleaner assembly.

1989–93 VEHICLES

1. Disconnect the negative battery cable. Properly drain the cooling system into a suitable container.

2. Remove the air cleaner and duct assembly.

3. Disconnect the exhaust manifold/crossover assembly.

4. Remove the serpentine belt tensioner and idler, if equipped.

5. Detach the radiator hoses from the engine.

6. Disconnect the cables from the bracket at the plenum.

7. Remove the alternator. Tag and disconnect the wiring harness at the engine.

8. Relieve the fuel pressure (see Section 1) and disconnect the fuel hose.

9. Disconnect the coolant bypass and the overflow hoses at the engine.

10. Support the engine using J 28467–A or equivalent engine support fixture.

11. Raise and safely support the vehicle.

12. Remove the inner fender splash shield.

13. Remove the flywheel cover.

14. Unfasten the starter bolts. Tag and detach the electrical connections to the starter, then remove the starter.

15. Remove the air conditioning compressor and related brackets.

16. Disconnect the exhaust pipe at the rear of the exhaust manifold.

17. Remove the flywheel-to-torque converter bolts.

18. Disconnect the engine mounts.

19. If equipped with a manual transaxle, disconnect the intermediate shaft bracket to the engine.

20. Disconnect the shift cable bracket at the transaxle. Remove the lower bell housing bolts.

21. Carefully lower the vehicle, then disconnect the heater hoses at the engine.

22. Install a suitable engine lifting device. While supporting the engine and transaxle, remove the J 28467–A engine support fixture.

23. Support the transaxle, then remove the transaxle bolts.

24. Remove the engine assembly from the vehicle.

To install:

25. Install J 28467–A engine support fixture, or equivalent.

26. Remove the engine lifting device.

27. Support the transaxle, then install the transaxle bolts.

28. Connect the heater hoses at the engine.

29. Raise and safely support the vehicle.

30. Fasten the lower bell housing bolts.

31. Install the shift cable bracket at the transaxle.

32. If equipped with a manual transaxle, connect the intermediate shaft bracket to the engine.

33. Reconnect the engine mounts, then tighten as follows:
- Front engine mount-to-bracket bolt to 50 ft. lbs. (68 Nm).
- Front engine mount-to-frame bolt (top) to 54 ft. lbs. (73 Nm).
- Front engine mount-to-frame bolt (bottom) to 61 ft. lbs. (83 Nm).
- Engine mount bracket-to-body lower bolt to 47 ft. lbs. (64 Nm).
- Engine mount bracket-to-body upper bolt to 74 ft. lbs. (100 Nm).
- Rear engine mount-to-engine bolt to 40 ft. lbs. (54 Nm).
- Rear engine bracket-to-body bolt to 45 ft. lbs. (61 Nm).

➡**All engine mount bolts that have been removed must be cleaned and a new thread locking compound applied to the threads before reinstallation.**

34. Install the flywheel-to-torque converter bolts.

35. Connect the exhaust pipe at the rear of the exhaust manifold.

36. Install the air conditioning compressor.

37. Install the starter.
38. Fasten the flywheel cover.
39. Install the inner fender splash shield.
40. Carefully lower the vehicle, then remove J 28467–A engine support fixture, or equivalent.
41. Connect the coolant bypass and the overflow hoses at the engine.
42. Reconnect the fuel lines.
43. Attach the wiring harness at the engine.
44. Install the alternator.
45. Connect the cables from the bracket at the plenum.
46. Fasten the radiator hoses.
47. Install the serpentine belt tensioner and idler, if equipped.
48. Refill the cooling system to the correct level with the proper type of coolant.
49. Install the air cleaner and duct assembly.
50. Connect the battery cable(s), then start the engine and check for proper operation and/or leaks.

1994 VEHICLES

➡ On these 3.1L engines, an "Idle Learn" procedure must be performed which requires the use of a scan tool.

1. Properly relieve the fuel system pressure.
2. Disconnect the negative, then positive battery cables, then remove the battery from the vehicle.
3. Remove the air cleaner assembly.
4. Properly drain the cooling system into an approved container.
5. For vehicles equipped with a manual transaxle, remove the left side sound insulator, then disconnect the push rod from the clutch pedal.
6. Disconnect the exhaust crossover pipe from the exhaust manifolds.
7. Remove the serpentine drive belt.
8. Disconnect the coolant bleed hose from the pipe. Disconnect the radiator hoses from the themostat housing and water pump. Remove the cooling fan assembly.
9. Disconnect the throttle, cruise control and T.V. cables from the throttle body.
10. Detach the power steering line from the bracket behind the alternator.
11. Remove the rear alternator brace, then the alternator.
12. Tag and detach the following electrical connections at the engine:
- Oxygen (O_2) sensor
- Engine Coolant Temperature (ECT) sensor
- EGR valve
- Manifold Absolute Pressure (MAP) sensor
- Idle Air Control (IAC) valve
- Throttle Position (TP) sensor
- Transaxle Converter Clutch (TCC)
- Park/Neutral Position switch (vehicles with an automatic transaxle only)
- Back-up Light switch (vehicles with a manual transaxle only)
- Ground connections
13. Disconnect the fuel lines.
14. Detach the coolant bypass hose at the engine.
15. Tag and disconnect all vacuum hoses from the engine.
16. Detach the power steering pressure and return lines.
17. Unfasten the clutch actuator cylinder quick disconnect fitting.
18. Disconnect the shift cables from the transaxle.
19. Unfasten the nuts from the top of the strut towers to allow tool J 28467-A, or equivalent, to be installed. Support the vehicles using tool J 28467-A or equivalent.
20. Remove the transaxle mount and bracket as an assembly.
21. Loosen the A/C accumulator bracket, then raise the accumulator a few inches to gain access to the upper front engine mount bolts. Remove the upper fasteners from the front engine mount.
22. Raise and safely support the vehicle.
23. Remove the front tire and wheel assemblies.
24. Remove the front air deflector and the right front splash shield.
25. If equipped, detach the front ABS wheel speed sensor connectors and harnesses from the suspension support.
26. Remove both front ball joints. For details, please refer to the procedure located in Section 8 of this manual.
27. Detach the engine mount strut from the transaxle bracket. Remove the front suspension support.
28. Remove the oil pressure switch from the engine.

➡ Make sure to use rags or shop towels between the A/C compressor and the radiator to prevent damage to the radiator cooling fins.

29. If equipped, remove the A/C compressor, leaving the lines attached, Support the compressor on the lower radiator tie-bar.
30. Disconnect the exhaust pipe at the rear of the manifold..
31. Detach the drive axles from the transaxles. Remove the strut mount bracket.
32. Tag and detach the following lower electrical connectors:
- Electronic Ignition system module
- Knock sensor
- Vehicle Speed Sensor (VSS)
- Connections at the starter
- Secondary ignition wires from the coils
33. As outlined in Section 2 of this manual, remove the starter.
34. Remove the flywheel housing or transaxle converter cover.
35. For vehicles equipped with a manual transaxle, remove the intermediate shaft bracket from the engine.
36. For vehicles equipped with an automatic transaxle, remove the shift cable bracket at the transaxle (press fit).
37. Disconnect the automatic transaxle cooler lines from the transaxle, if applicable.
38. Unfasten the lower engine mount bolts, then remove the rear engine mount.
39. Disconnect the heater hoses from the front of the dash.
40. Carefully lower the vehicle enough to place an engine/transaxle table under the vehicle.
41. Remove the engine and transaxle assembly from the vehicle.
42. Detach the transaxle selector cable bracket.
43. Unfasten the bolt, the remove the automatic transaxle fluid level indicator and fill tube assembly.
44. Remove the rear engine mount assembly from the engine, then remove the transaxle-to-engine bracket.
45. Unfasten the flywheel-to-torque converter bolts, then separate the engine from the transaxle.

To install:
46. Fasten the engine to the transaxle.
47. Install the flywheel-to-torque converter bolts.
48. Install the transaxle-to-engine bracket, then attach the rear engine mount assembly to the engine.
49. Position the automatic transaxle fluid level indicator and fill tube assembly and secure with the retaining bolt.
50. Install the transaxle selector cable bracket.
51. Carefully lower the vehicle enough to place an engine/transaxle table under the vehicle.
52. Position the engine and transaxle assembly into the vehicle.
53. Install the rear engine mount, then install the lower engine mount bolts.
54. Connect the heater hoses to the front of the dash.
55. Attach the automatic transaxle cooler lines to the transaxle, if applicable.
56. Install the shift cable bracket (press fit) to the automatic transaxle.
57. If equipped with a manual transaxle, fasten the intermediate shaft bracket to the engine.
58. Install the electronic ignition system coil and module assembly.
59. Fasten the flywheel housing or transaxle converter cover.
60. Install the starter, as outlined in Section 2 of this manual.
61. Attach the following electrical connectors, as tagged during removal:
- Electronic Ignition system module
- Knock sensor
- Vehicle Speed Sensor (VSS)
- Electrical connections at the starter
- Secondary ignition (spark plug) wires to the coils
62. Install the strut mount bracket.
63. Fasten the drive axles to the transaxle.
64. Attach the exhaust pipe to the rear of the manifold.
65. Remove the shop towels or rag from the lower radiator tie-bar, then install the A/C compressor.
66. Install the oil pressure switch.
67. Install the front suspension support, then install the engine mount strut-to-transaxle bracket.
68. As outlined in Section 8 of this manual, install both front ball joints.
69. If equipped, attach the front ABS wheel speed sensor connectors and harnesses to the suspension support.

70. Install the right front splash shield and the front air deflector.

71. Install both front tire and wheel assemblies, then carefully lower the vehicle.

72. Attach the upper fasteners to the front engine mount.

73. After carefully pushing the A/C accumulator back into place, tighten the accumulator bracket.

74. Install the transaxle mount and bracket as an assembly.

75. Remove tool J 28467-A or equivalent engine support fixture, then install the retaining nuts to the top of the strut towers.

76. Connect the transaxle shift cables.

77. For vehicles equipped with a manual transaxle, install the clutch actuator cylinder.

78. Connect the power steering pressure and return lines.

79. Attach all vacuum hoses, as tagged during removal.

80. Fasten the coolant bypass hose.

81. Connect the fuel lines.

82. Attach the following electrical connections, as tagged during removal:
• Ground connections
• Back-up Light switch (vehicles with a manual transaxle only)
• Park/Neutral Position switch (vehicles with an automatic transaxle only)
• Transaxle Converter Clutch (TCC)
• Throttle Position (TP) sensor
• Idle Air Control (IAC) valve
• Manifold Absolute Pressure (MAP) sensor
• EGR valve
• Engine Coolant Temperature (ECT) sensor
• Oxygen (O$_2$) sensor

83. Install the alternator, as outlined in Section 2 of this manual. Install the rear alternator brace.

84. Attach the power steering line.

85. Connect the throttle, cruise control (if equipped) and the T.V. cables to the throttle body.

86. Install the coolant fan assembly.

87. Attach the radiator hoses and the coolant bleed hose.

88. Install the serpentine belt.

89. Fasten the exhaust crossover pipe to the exhaust manifolds.

90. If equipped with a manual transaxle, fasten the push rod and left side sound insulator to the clutch pedal.

91. Install the air cleaner assembly, then install the battery. Connect the positive, then negative battery cables.

92. Fill the coolant, oil, transaxle and power steering fluids to the proper levels.

➡ On the 3.1L engine, a Tech 1® scan tool is needed to perform the "Idle Learn" procedure.

93. For the 3.1L engine perform the following "Idle Learn" procedure;
  a. Install a Tech 1® scan tool.
  b. Turn the ignition to the **ON** position, engine not running.
  c. Select **IAC SYSTEM**, then **IDLE LEARN** in the **MISC TEST** mode.
  d. Place the transaxle in park or neutral, as applicable.
  e. Proceed with idle learn as directed by the scan tool.

94. Bleed the power steering system.

95. Start the engine, then check for proper fluid levels and/or leaks.

Rocker Arm (Valve) Cover

REMOVAL & INSTALLATION

1.8L, 2.0L and 2.2L OHV Engines

1982–86 VEHICLES

▶ See Figure 1

1. Disconnect the negative battery cable.
2. Remove the air cleaner.
3. For the 2.0L engine, disconnect the canister purge line and the PCV valve.
4. For the 2.0L engine, tag and disconnect plug wires at the spark plugs, then pull the wires away from the rocker arm cover.
5. For the 1.8L engine, remove the distributor cap with the spark plug

NOTE: AT TIME OF INSTALLATION, FLANGES MUST BE FREE OF OIL. A 2.0-3.0 BEAD OF SEALANT MUST BE APPLIED TO FLANGES AND SEALANT MUST BE WET TO TOUCH WHEN BOLTS ARE TORQUED.

ROCKER ARM COVER

BALL — PUSH ROD RETAINER — ROCKER ARM — ROCKER ARM STUD — PUSH ROD

87953006

Fig. 1 Make sure to tighten the rocker arm cover bolts to specification when the RTV sealant is still wet

wires. Remove the spark plug wire clip from the rocker arm cover and lay the wires and cap aside.

6. For the 1.8L engine, tag and disconnect the vacuum hoses and pipes at the alternator bracket, at the front of the valve cover, at the deceleration valve and at the PCV valve. Detach the wires at the oxygen sensor, carburetor choke (if equipped) and the ground wire at the bracket.

7. Loosen the accelerator linkage bracket.

8. Remove the rocker arm cover bolts.

➡ When removing the rocker arm (valve) cover, be sure not to distort the sealing flange.

9. Remove the rocker arm cover. If the cover adheres to the cylinder head, lightly tap the end of the cover with a rubber mallet. If necessary, carefully pry until loose.

10. Clean the sealing surfaces of the cylinder head and the cover.

To install:

11. Place a ⅛ in. (3mm) wide bead of RTV sealant all around the rocker arm cover sealing surface.

➡ When going around the attaching bolt holes, always flow the RTV on the inboard side of the bolt holes.

12. Install the valve cover and tighten the bolts evenly to 8 ft. lbs. (10 Nm) while the sealant is still wet.

➡ Keep the sealant out of the bolt holes as this could cause a "hydraulic lock" condition which could damage the head casting.

13. The rest of installation is the reverse of the removal procedure.

14. Connect the negative battery cable, then start the engine and check for leaks.

1987–94 VEHICLES

▶ See Figure 2

1. Disconnect the negative battery cable.
2. Disconnect the air intake hose at the throttle body and air cleaner.

1 BOLT
2 ROCKER COVER
3 GASKET
4 ROCKER STUD
5 FLANGE, MUST BE FREE OF OIL UPON
   ROCKER COVER GASKET INSTALLATION.
6 PUSHROD
7 ROCKER ARM
8 BALL
9 NUT
10 SUPPORT, SPARK PLUG WIRE

87953007

Fig. 2 Rocker arm (valve) cover removal and installation—1994
2.2L (VIN 4) engine shown

3. For the 2.0L engine, detach the hose from the intake to the cover.
4. For the 2.2L engine, disconnect the PCV hose(s).
5. Unfasten the rocker arm cover bolts and remove the cover. Remove and discard the gasket.
6. Clean the sealing surfaces of the cylinder head and the cover using a suitable degreaser.

To install:
7. Install a new gasket, then reposition the cover and tighten the bolts evenly to 8 ft. lbs. (10 Nm).
8. For the 2.2L engine, connect the PCV hose(s).
9. For the 2.0L engine, attach the intake-to-cover hose.
10. Attach the air intake hose at the throttle body and air cleaner.
11. Connect the negative battery cable, then start the engine and check for leaks.

2.8L and 3.1L Engines

1985–86 VEHICLES (LEFT SIDE)

▸ See Figure 3

1. Disconnect the negative battery cable.
2. Detach the coil at the bracket.
3. Disconnect the PCV hose.
4. Tag and disconnect the spark plug wires at the plugs, then pull the wires away from the rocker arm cover.
5. If necessary for access, loosen the accelerator linkage bracket.

➡When removing the rocker arm cover, use extreme care not to distort the sealing flange or leakage will result.

6. Unfasten the retaining bolts, then remove the rocker arm cover. If the cover adheres to the cylinder head, lightly tap the end of the cover with a rubber mallet. If necessary, carefully pry until loose. Do not distort the sealing flange.
7. Clean the sealing surfaces of the head and the cover.

87953008

Fig. 3 Removing the rocker arm (valve) cover—1985 2.8L engine shown

To install:
8. Place a ⅛ in. (3mm) wide bead of RTV sealant at the intake manifold and the cylinder head split line.
9. Position the valve cover, then evenly tighten the bolts to 90 inch lbs. (10 Nm) while the sealant is still wet.
10. Install the remaining parts, then connect the negative battery cable. Start the engine and check for leaks.

1985–86 VEHICLES (RIGHT SIDE)

1. Disconnect the negative battery cable.
2. Remove the intake runners.

➡When removing the rocker arm cover, use extreme care not to distort the sealing flange or leakage will result.

3. Unfasten the rocker arm cover securing bolts, then remove the rocker arm cover. If the cover adheres to the cylinder head, lightly tap the end of the cover with a rubber mallet. If necessary, carefully pry until loose. Do not distort the sealing flange.

To install:
4. Clean the sealing surfaces of the head, intake manifold and the valve cover.
5. Place a ⅛ in. (3mm) wide bead of RTV sealant at the intake manifold and the cylinder head split line.
6. Position the valve cover, then install the retaining bolts. Tighten bolts evenly to 90 inch lbs. (10 Nm) while the sealant is still wet.
7. Install the remaining parts, then connect the negative battery cable. Start the engine and check for leaks.

1987–90 VEHICLES (LEFT SIDE)

1. Disconnect the negative battery cable.
2. Detach the bracket tube at the cover.
3. Remove the plug wire cover.
4. Disconnect the heater hose at the filler neck.

➡When removing the rocker arm cover, use extreme care not to distort the sealing flange or leakage will result.

5. Unfasten the cover retaining bolts, then remove the cover. If the cover adheres to the cylinder head, lightly tap the end of the cover with a soft rubber mallet or palm of the hand. Do not distort or scratch the sealing flange.
6. Remove and discard the gasket.

To install:
7. Clean the sealing surfaces of the head and the cover.
8. Install a new gasket and make sure it is seated properly in the rocker cover groove.
9. Apply a suitable RTV sealant in the notch.

10. Position the rocker arm cover, then install the retaining bolts. Tighten the bolts evenly to 6–9 ft. lbs. (8–12 Nm).

11. Install the remaining parts, then connect the negative battery cable. Start the engine and check for leaks.

1991–94 VEHICLES (LEFT SIDE)

▶ See Figure 4

➡ On 3.1L engines, an "Idle Learn" procedure must be performed which requires the use of a scan tool.

1. Disconnect the negative battery cable.
2. Detach the coolant bleed pipe from the thermostat housing.
3. Disconnect the vent tube from the rocker arm cover-to-air inlet.
4. Unfasten the retaining bolts, then remove the rocker arm cover. If the cover sticks to the cylinder head, remove by carefully bumping the end of the rocker arm cover with the palm of your hand or a soft rubber mallet. Remove and discard the gasket and bolt grommets.
5. Clean the sealing surfaces of the cylinder head and valve cover with a suitable degreaser.

To install:

6. Position a new gasket and bolt grommets, making sure it is properly seated in the valve cover groove. Apply part no. 1052917 or suitable sealer in the cylinder head notch. See the accompanying figure.
7. Position the rocker arm cover, then secure with the retaining bolts. Tighten the bolts to 89 inch lbs. (10 Nm).
8. Attach the vent tube to the rocker arm cover.
9. Fasten the coolant bleed tube to the thermostat housing.
10. Connect the negative battery cable.

➡ On the 3.1L engine, a Tech 1® scan tool is needed to perform the "Idle Learn" procedure.

11. For the 3.1L engine perform the following "Idle Learn" procedure;
  a. Install a Tech 1® scan tool.
  b. Turn the ignition to the **ON** position, engine not running.
  c. Select **IAC SYSTEM**, then **IDLE LEARN** in the **MISC TEST** mode.
  d. Place the transaxle in park or neutral, as applicable.
  e. Proceed with idle learn as directed by the scan tool.
12. Start the engine and check for leaks.

1987–94 VEHICLES (RIGHT SIDE)

▶ See Figure 4

➡ On 3.1L engines, an "Idle Learn" procedure must be performed which requires the use of a scan tool.

1. Disconnect the negative battery cable.
2. Unfasten the brake booster vacuum line at the bracket.
3. Disconnect the throttle cable and vacuum line bracket at the plenum.
4. Detach the power steering lines from the alternator bracket stud.
5. Unfasten the rear alternator brace.
6. Remove the serpentine belt.

7. As outlined in Section 2 of this manual, remove the alternator and lay it aside.
8. Tag and disconnect the rear bank spark plug wires from the plugs, then position them aside.
9. Remove the PCV valve.
10. Unfasten the rocker arm cover retaining bolts, then remove the cover. Remove and discard the gasket and bolt grommets.
11. If the cover adheres to the cylinder head, lightly tap the end of the cover with a soft rubber mallet or palm of the hand. Do not distort or scratch the sealing flange.

To install:

12. Clean the sealing surfaces of the head and the cover.
13. Install new bolt grommets, then install a new gasket making sure it is seated properly in the rocker arm cover groove.
14. Apply RTV sealant in the notch.
15. Position the cover, then secure using the retaining bolts. Tighten the bolts evenly to 89 inch lbs. (10 Nm).
16. Install the remaining parts, then connect the negative battery cable.

➡ On the 3.1L engine, a Tech 1® scan tool is needed to perform the "Idle Learn" procedure.

17. For the 3.1L engine perform the following "Idle Learn" procedure;
  a. Install a Tech 1® scan tool.
  b. Turn the ignition to the **ON** position, engine not running.
  c. Select **IAC SYSTEM**, then **IDLE LEARN** in the **MISC TEST** mode.
  d. Place the transaxle in park or neutral, as applicable.
  e. Proceed with idle learn as directed by the scan tool.
18. Start the engine and check for leaks.

Camshaft Carrier Cover

REMOVAL & INSTALLATION

1.8L and 2.0L SOHC Engines

▶ See Figures 5, 6, 7, 8 and 9

1. Disconnect the negative battery cable.
2. For non-turbo vehicles, remove the air cleaner.
3. Disconnect the breather hoses.
4. Detach the induction tube on turbo models.
5. Unfasten the retaining bolts, then remove the cover. Remove and discard the gasket.

To install:

6. Clean the sealing surfaces on the camshaft carrier and cover.
7. Reposition the cover with a new gasket and evenly tighten the retainer bolts to 62–84 inch lbs. (7–9.5 Nm).
8. Attach the induction tube, breather hoses, and/or air cleaner as applicable.
9. Connect the negative battery cable, then start the engine and inspect for leaks.

1 VALVE COVER AND GASKET
2 BOLT – 10 N·m (89 LBS. IN.)
3 CYLINDER HEAD
4 SEALER

87953009

Fig. 4 Apply a suitable sealer to the area shown—1994 3.1L engine shown

87953200

Fig. 5 Disconnect the PCV hose from the cover—1988 2.0L Sunbird shown

87953201

Fig. 6 Unfasten the camshaft carrier cover retaining bolts, then . . .

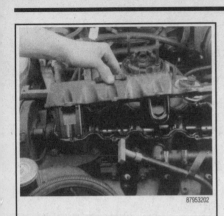

Fig. 7 . . . remove the cover

Fig. 8 When installing the camshaft cover, always use a new gasket—1994 2.0L engine shown

Fig. 9 Use a suitable scraper to CAREFULLY clean the gasket mating surfaces

Rocker Arms and Pushrods

REMOVAL & INSTALLATION

1.8L, 2.0L and 2.2L OHV Engines

1982–86 VEHICLES

▶ See Figure 10

1. Disconnect the negative battery cable.
2. Remove the air cleaner. As outlined earlier in this section, remove the rocker arm cover.

NOTE: AT TIME OF INSTALLATION, FLANGES MUST BE FREE OF OIL. A 2.0-3.0 BEAD OF SEALANT MUST BE APPLIED TO FLANGES AND SEALANT MUST BE WET TO TOUCH WHEN BOLTS ARE TORQUED.

ROCKER ARM COVER

BALL

PUSH ROD RETAINER

ROCKER ARM

ROCKER ARM STUD

PUSH ROD

Fig. 10 Removing the rocker arms and pushrods—1982 1.8L (OHV) engine shown

➡ Always place the components in a rack in order of assembly so they can easily be installed in the same locations, and with the same mating surface as when removed.

3. Unfasten the rocker arm nut and ball. Lift the rocker arm off the stud. Always keep the rocker arm assemblies together and install them on the same stud. Remove the pushrods.

To install:

4. Coat the bearing surfaces of the rocker arms and the rocker arm balls with Molykote® or its equivalent.
5. Install the pushrods making sure that they seat properly in the lifter.
6. Install the rocker arms, balls and nuts. Tighten the rocker arm nuts until all lash is eliminated.
7. Adjust the valves when the lifter is on the base circle of a camshaft lobe:

   a. Crank the engine until the mark on the crankshaft pulley lines up with the **O** mark on the timing tab. Make sure that the engine is in the No. 1 firing position. Place your fingers on the No. 1 rocker arms as the mark on the crank pulley comes near the **O** mark. If the valves are not moving, the engine is in the No. 1 firing position. If the valves move, the engine is in the No. 4 firing position; rotate the engine one complete revolution and it will be in the No. 1 position.

   b. When the engine is in the No. 1 firing position, adjust the following valves: Exhaust—1,3 Intake—1,2

   c. Back the adjusting nut out until lash can be felt at the pushrod, then turn the nut until all lash is removed (this can be determined by rotating the pushrod while turning the adjusting nut). When all lash has been removed, turn the nut in 1½ additional turns, this will center the lifter plunger.

   d. Crank the engine one complete revolution until the timing tab and the **O** mark are again in alignment. Now the engine is in the No. 4 firing position. Adjust the following valves: Exhaust—2,4 Intake—3,4

8. Installation of the remaining components is the reverse order of removal.

1987–89 VEHICLES

▶ See Figure 11

1. Disconnect the negative battery cable.
2. Remove the air cleaner. Remove the rocker arm cover. For details, please refer to the procedure located earlier in this section.

➡ Always place the components in a rack in order of assembly so they can easily be installed in the same locations, and with the same mating surface as when removed.

3. Unfasten the rocker arm nut(s) and ball(s). Lift the rocker arm off the stud. Always keep the rocker arm assemblies together and install them on the same stud. Remove the pushrods.

To install:

4. Coat the bearing surfaces of the rocker arms and the rocker arm balls with Molykote® or its equivalent.
5. Install the pushrods, making sure that they seat properly in the lifters.

| 1 | 8-12 N·m (6-9 FT. LBS.) |
| 2 | 15-25 N·m (11-18 FT. LBS.) |

87953017

Fig. 11 When removing the rocker arms and/or pushrods, always keep the assemblies together to ensure they are installed in the same locations that they were removed from

1	ROCKER ARM
2	THRUST PIECE
3	LASH ADJUSTER
4	VALVE STEM LOCK
5	VALVE SPRING CAP
6	VALVE SPRING
7	VALVE SEAL
8	EXHAUST ROTO CAP
9	INLET SPRING WASHER

87953018

Fig. 12 Exploded view of the valve train components—1989 2.0L shown

6. Install the rocker arms, then secure using the balls and nuts. Tighten the rocker arm nuts to 11–18 ft. lbs. (15–25 Nm).

7. As outlined earlier, install the rocker cover.

8. Connect the negative battery cable.

1.8L and 2.0L SOHC Engines

▶ See Figure 12

➥A special compressing tool is required for this procedure.

1. Disconnect the negative battery cable.

2. As outlined earlier, remove the camshaft carrier cover.

3. Using a valve train compressing fixture, tool J-33302 or equivalent, depress all the lifters at once.

4. Remove the rocker arms, placing them on the workbench in the same order that they were removed. Remove the thrust piece.

5. Remove the hydraulic valve lash compensators, keeping them in the order in which they were removed.

➥The valve lash compensators are not serviceable. If damaged or faulty, they must be replaced.

To install:

6. Compress the valve springs with tool J-33302 or equivalent.

7. Install the valve lash compensators into their original positions.

8. Install the thrust piece and rocker arms.

9. As outlined earlier, install the camshaft carrier cover.

10. Connect the negative battery cable.

2.8L and 3.1L Engines

1985–86 VEHICLES

▶ See Figures 13 and 14

1. Disconnect the negative battery cable.

2. As outlined earlier, remove the rocker arm (valve) covers.

3. Remove the rocker arm nuts, rocker arm balls, rocker arms and push

rods, then place in a rack so that they may be reinstalled in the same location.

To install:

4. Install the pushrods making sure that they seat properly in the lifter.

5. Coat the bearing surfaces of the rocker arms and the rocker arm balls with Molykote® or its equivalent.

6. Install the rocker arms, balls and nuts. Tighten the rocker arm nuts until all lash is eliminated.

7. Adjust the valves when the lifter is on the base circle of a camshaft lobe:

    a. Turn the engine until the mark on the crankshaft pulley lines up with the **O** mark on the timing tab. Make sure that the engine is in the No. 1 firing

87953019

Fig. 13 Assembled view of the valve mechanism—1986 2.8L engine shown

Fig. 14 On 1985–86 2.8L engines, the valves must be adjusted when removing the rocker arm assemblies

position. Place your fingers on the No. 1 rocker arms as the mark on the crank pulley comes near the **O** mark. If the valves are not moving, the engine is in the No. 1 firing position. If the valves move, the engine is in the No. 4 firing position; rotate the engine one complete revolution and it will be in the No. 1 position.

  b. When the engine is in the No. 1 firing position, adjust the following valves: Exhaust—1,2,3 Intake—1,5,6

  c. Back the adjusting nut out until lash can be felt at the pushrod, then turn the nut until all lash is removed (this can be determined by rotating the pushrod while turning the adjusting nut). When all lash has been removed, turn the nut in 1½ additional turns, this will center the lifter plunger.

  d. Turn the engine one complete revolution until the timing tab and the **O** mark are again in alignment. Now the engine is in the No. 4 firing position. Adjust the following valves: Exhaust—4,5,6 Intake—2,3,4

  8. Install the rocker arm (valve) cover, as outlined earlier.

  9. Connect the negative battery cable, then start the engine and check the timing. Adjust if necessary.

1987–94 VEHICLES

➟On 3.1L engines, an "Idle Learn" procedure must be performed which requires the use of a scan tool.

  1. Disconnect the negative battery cable.
  2. As outlined earlier, remove the rocker arm covers.
  3. Unfasten the rocker arm nuts. When removing the components, make sure to keep them separated so they can be installed in the same location.
  4. Remove the rocker arm pivot ball(s), rocker arms, push rod guides and push rods, then place them in a rack so that they may be reinstalled in the same location.

➟Intake pushrods are marked orange and are 6 in. (152.4mm) long. Exhaust pushrods are marked blue and are 6⅜ in. (161.9mm) long.

To install:

  5. Install the pushrods (correct length) making sure that they seat properly in the lifter.
  6. Coat the bearing surfaces of the rocker arms and the rocker arm balls with Molykote® or its equivalent.
  7. Install the pushrod guides, rocker arms, pivot balls and nuts.
  8. Tighten the rocker arm nuts to 14–20 ft. lbs. (19–27 Nm).
  9. Install the rocker arm covers.
  10. Connect the negative battery cable.

➟On the 3.1L engine, a Tech 1® scan tool is needed to perform the "Idle Learn" procedure.

  11. For the 3.1L engine perform the following "Idle Learn" procedure;
    a. Install a Tech 1® scan tool.
    b. Turn the ignition to the **ON** position, engine not running.
    c. Select **IAC SYSTEM**, then **IDLE LEARN** in the **MISC TEST** mode.

  d. Place the transaxle in park or neutral, as applicable.
  e. Proceed with idle learn as directed by the scan tool.

Thermostat

REMOVAL & INSTALLATION

  Poor heater output and slow warmup is often caused by a thermostat stuck in the open position; occasionally one sticks shut causing immediate overheating. Do not attempt to correct a chronic overheating condition by permanently removing the thermostat. Thermostat flow restriction is designed into the system; without it, localized overheating (due to coolant turbulence) may occur, causing expensive troubles.

✳✳ CAUTION

When draining the coolant, keep in mind that cats and dogs are attracted by ethylene glycol antifreeze, and are quite likely to drink any that is left in an uncovered container or in puddles on the ground. This will prove fatal in sufficient quantity. Always drain the coolant into a sealable container. Coolant should be reused unless it is contaminated or several years old.

1.8L and 2.0L OHV Engines

1982–86 VEHICLES

◗ See Figure 15

  The thermostat is located inside a housing on the back of the cylinder head. It is not necessary to remove the radiator hose from the thermostat housing when removing the thermostat.

  1. Disconnect the negative battery cable.
  2. Properly drain the cooling system into an approved container.
  3. Remove the air cleaner.
  4. On some models it may be necessary to disconnect the A.I.R. pipe at the upper check valve and the bracket at the water outlet.
  5. Disconnect the electrical lead.
  6. Remove the two retaining bolts from the thermostat housing and lift up the housing with the house attached. Lift out the thermostat. Clean the mating surfaces.

To install:

  7. Apply a ⅛ in. (3mm) bead of silicone sealer to the housing mating surface.
  8. Place the thermostat, with the power element down, in housing, then install the water outlet while the sealer is still wet. Tighten the housing retaining bolts to 6 ft. lbs. (8 Nm).
  9. Connect the electrical lead.

Fig. 15 Thermostat mounting—1985 2.0L engine shown

10. If applicable, attach the A.I.R. pipe at the check valve and bracket at the water outlet.

11. Install the air cleaner.

12. Fill the cooling system to the proper level, using the correct type of fluid.

13. Connect the negative battery cable, then start the engine and check for coolant leaks.

1987–89 VEHICLES

▶ See Figure 16

1. Disconnect the negative battery cable.
2. Properly drain the coolant until the level is below the thermostat.
3. If necessary for access, remove the air cleaner assembly.
4. Unfasten the coolant outlet-to-inlet manifold attaching bolt and nut.
5. Remove the coolant outlet, then remove the thermostat. Remove and discard the gasket, then clean the inlet manifold mating surfaces.

To install:

6. Position the thermostat in the inlet manifold.

➡ **When installing a thermostat, be sure to use a new gasket.**

7. Attach the coolant outlet to the inlet manifold. Coat the attaching bolt and nut with sealer, then tighten to 90 inch lbs. (10 Nm).
8. If removed, install the air cleaner assembly.
9. Refill the engine cooling system to the proper level.
10. Connect the negative battery cable, then start the engine and check for coolant leaks.

1.8L and 2.0L OHC Engines

▶ See Figures 17, 18, 19, 20 and 21

1. Remove the thermostat housing/radiator cap.
2. Grasp the handle of the thermostat and pull it from the housing.
3. Clean the thermostat housing and gasket. Replace the gasket if damaged.

To install:

4. Install the thermostat in the housing, carefully pushing it down as far as it will go to make sure it's properly seated.
5. Install the housing cap on the engine.

2.2L Engines

1987–91 VEHICLES

▶ See Figure 22

1. Disconnect the negative battery cable.
2. Drain the cooling system to a level below the thermostat housing.
3. Detach the upper radiator hose from the thermostat housing.
4. Unfasten the thermostat housing mounting nuts, then remove the housing.
5. Remove the thermostat. Clean all gasket surfaces completely.

To install:

6. Apply a thin bead of sealer around the gasket contact surface of the housing, then install a new gasket.
7. Position the thermostat in the housing.
8. Install the thermostat housing on the engine and tighten the mounting nuts to 89 inch lbs. (10 Nm).
9. Attach the upper radiator hose to the thermostat housing.
10. Refill the cooling system.
11. Connect the negative battery cable, then start the engine and check for leaks.

1992–94 VEHICLES

▶ See Figure 23

1. Disconnect the negative battery cable.
2. Properly drain and recover the coolant until the level is below the thermostat.

1. BOLT – 10 N·m (8 LBS. FT.)
2. THERMOSTAT AND HOUSING
3. GASKET

87953022

Fig. 16 Thermostat installation—1989 2.0L (OHV) engine shown

87953205

Fig. 17 Remove the radiator cap for access to the thermostat—1988 2.0L (VIN K) Sunbird shown

87953206

Fig. 18 Remove the thermostat by pulling it out by the handle

1 THERMOSTAT HOUSING CAP
2 THERMOSTAT
3 THERMOSTAT HOUSING ASM.
4 CYLINDER HEAD

87953026

Fig. 19 Removing the thermostat is simply a matter of removing the housing cap and pulling the thermostat up

1 - CAP
2 - THERMOSTAT
3 - HOUSING

87953027

Fig. 20 Location of the thermostat on the 2.0L (VIN K and M) engines

1 THERMOSTAT HOUSING CAP
2 THERMOSTAT
3 THERMOSTAT HOUSING ASM.
4 CYLINDER BLOCK

87953028

Fig. 21 Thermostat and housing mounting—1994 2.0L (VIN 1) engine shown

1. Water outlet stud
2. Engine coolant thermostat assembly
3. Water outlet
4. Water outlet nut

87953030

Fig. 22 Thermostat location and mounting—1987–91 2.2L engines

INSTALLED POSITION
SECTION A–A

VIEW A

1 THERMOSTAT
2 GASKET
3 BOLTS
4 OUTLET, RADIATOR

87953023

Fig. 23 After removing the coolant outlet, you can remove the thermostat—1994 2.2L engine shown

1 WATER OUTLET
2 THERMOSTAT
3 INLET MANIFOLD
4 BOLT/NUT –
 25 N·m (18 LBS. FT.)

87953025

Fig. 24 After unfastening the retaining bolts, remove the outlet and lift out the thermostat—3.1L engine shown

3. Unfasten the coolant outlet-to-inlet manifold attaching bolt and nut, then remove the outlet.

4. Remove the thermostat. Clean the inlet manifold and outlet mating surfaces.

To install:

5. Place the thermostat in the inlet manifold.

6. Attach the coolant outlet to the inlet manifold, using the bolt and nut. Tighten to 89 inch lbs. (10 Nm).

7. Refill the engine cooling system.

8. Connect the negative battery cable, then start the engine and check for coolant leaks.

2.8L and 3.1L Engines

♦ See Figure 24

1. Disconnect the negative battery cable.

2. Properly drain and recover the cooling system until the level is below the thermostat.

3. For the 3.1L engine, remove the air cleaner assembly.

4. Some models with cruise control have a vacuum modulator attached to the thermostat housing with a bracket. If your vehicle is equipped as such, remove the bracket from the housing.

5. Unfasten the coolant outlet-to-inlet manifold attaching bolt and nut, then remove the outlet and lift the thermostat out of the manifold. Clean the mating surfaces.

To install:

6. Position the thermostat in the inlet manifold.

7. Attach the coolant outlet to the inlet manifold. Coat the attaching nut and bolt with sealer, then tighten to 18 ft. lbs. (25 Nm).

8. If necessary, install the cruise control vacuum modulator bracket to the housing.

9. For the 3.1L engine, install the air cleaner assembly.

10. Refill the engine cooling system. On the 2.8L engine, use the vent plug on the thermostat housing.

11. Connect the negative battery cable. Start the engine, then check for coolant leaks and correct as required.

Intake Manifold

REMOVAL & INSTALLATION

❊❊ CAUTION

When draining the coolant, keep in mind that cats and dogs are attracted by ethylene glycol antifreeze, and are quite likely to drink any that is left in an uncovered container or in puddles on the ground. This will prove fatal in sufficient quantity. Always drain the coolant into a sealable container. Coolant should be reused unless it is contaminated or several years old.

1.8, 2.0L and 2.2L OHV Engines

1982–86 VEHICLES

♦ See Figure 25

1. Disconnect the negative battery cable.

2. Remove the air cleaner. Drain the cooling system.

3. Tag and disconnect all necessary vacuum lines and wires.

4. Remove the idler pulley.

5. If equipped, remove the A.I.R. drive belt. If equipped with power steering, remove the drive belt and then remove the pump with the lines attached. Position the pump out of the way.

6. If equipped, remove the A.I.R. bracket-to-intake manifold bolt. Remove the air pump pulley.

7. If equipped with power steering, remove the A.I.R. through-bolt and then the power steering adjusting bracket.

8. Loosen the lower bolt on the air pump mounting bracket so that the bracket will rotate.

❊❊ CAUTION

The fuel lines are pressurized (especially with fuel injection). Removal may cause fuel spray resulting in personal injury. Do not remove before bleeding the pressure from the fuel system. See Section 1 for the procedure.

9. Properly relieve the fuel system pressure.

10. Disconnect the fuel lines at the carburetor or TBI unit. Detach the carburetor or TBI linkage and then remove the carburetor or TBI unit.

INTAKE MANIFOLD

GASKET

87953029

Fig. 25 Removing the intake manifold—1982–86 OHV engines

11. Lift off the Early Fuel Evaporation (EFE) heater grid.

12. Remove the distributor. For details, please refer to Section 2 of this manual.

13. Unfasten the mounting bolts and nuts, then remove the intake manifold. Make sure to disconnect the heater hose and condenser from the bottom of the intake manifold before you lift it all the way out.

14. Clean the intake manifold-to-cylinder head mating surfaces. Be sure to clean all of old gasket material off.

To install:

15. Place a new gasket on the cylinder head, then position the manifold. Tighten the nuts and bolts to 20–25 ft. lbs. (27–34 Nm), working from the center position to the end position.

16. Installation of the remaining components is in the reverse order of removal. Adjust all necessary drive belts and check the ignition timing.

1987–91 VEHICLES

▶ See Figure 26

❊❊ CAUTION

Fuel injected vehicles maintain high fuel pressure within the fuel system, even after the engine has been shut off. Fuel system residual pressure must be properly relieved, prior to attempting this procedure; failure to do so can result in serious personal injury and/or property damage.

1. Disconnect the negative battery cable.

2. Remove the air cleaner. Properly drain the cooling system into an approved container.

3. Tag and disconnect all necessary vacuum lines and wires from the intake manifold and throttle body.

4. Disconnect and cap the fuel lines from the throttle body.

5. Detach the control cables from the throttle body lever.

6. Unfasten the throttle body mounting screws, then remove the throttle body from the intake manifold.

7. Remove the serpentine belt.

8. Unfasten the power steering pump-to-bracket bolts and support the pump out of the way. DO NOT disconnect the power steering hoses from the pump.

9. Raise and safely support the vehicle.

10. Remove the control cable bracket from the intake manifold.

11. Disconnect the heater (coolant) hose from the bottom of the intake manifold.

12. Unfasten the lower intake manifold bolts.

13. Carefully lower the vehicle.

14. Unfasten the intake manifold-to-cylinder head nuts/bolts, then remove the intake manifold.

15. Use a gasket scraper to carefully clean the gasket mating surfaces.

To install:

16. Position a new gasket, then install the intake manifold and tighten the manifold-to-cylinder head nuts/bolts (in the proper sequence) to 18 ft. lbs. (25 Nm).

17. Raise and safely support the vehicle.

18. Connect the heater hose to the underside of the intake manifold.

19. Install the control cable bracket to the intake manifold.

20. Carefully lower the vehicle.

21. Install the power steering pump in the mounting bracket, then tighten the mounting bolts.

22. Position the throttle body assembly on the intake manifold, then tighten the mounting bolts to 17 ft. lbs. (23 Nm).

23. Connect the control cables to the throttle body lever, then attach the fuel lines to the throttle body.

24. Attach the vacuum lines and wires, as tagged during removal.

25. Install the air cleaner assembly.

26. Connect the negative battery cable.

27. Properly fill the cooling system.

28. Pressurize the fuel system before starting the vehicle, and make sure there are no leaks.

29. Start the engine and check for oil and/or coolant leaks.

1992–94 VEHICLES

▶ See Figures 27 and 28

These vehicles use a two-piece intake manifold. The upper half, sometimes called a plenum, contains the throttle body and the control cable connections. The lower half has individual port runner to each intake port on the cylinder head. The lower half of the manifold bolts to the cylinder head and houses the fuel injectors. Note that these pieces are cast aluminum. Care should be exercised when working with any light allow component.

1. Properly relieve the fuel system pressure.

2. Disconnect the negative battery cable.

3. Remove the throttle body air intake duct.

4. Drain the cooling system into an approved container.

5. Identify, tag and disconnect all necessary vacuum lines.

6. Disconnect the control cables from the throttle body lever and remove the control cable bracket form the intake manifold.

7. Remove the serpentine belt.

8. Remove the power steering pump and lay it aside with the fluid lines attached.

9. Remove the transaxle fill tube.

10. Tag and disconnect the following electrical wires:

- Idle Air Control (IAC) valve
- Throttle Position (TP) sensor
- Manifold Absolute Pressure (MAP) sensor
- EVAP Emission solenoid
- Fuel injector harness
- Exhaust Gas Recirculation (EGR) valve

11. Remove the MAP sensor.

12. Unfasten the upper intake manifold mounting bolts, then remove the upper intake manifold.

13. Disconnect the fuel lines from the fuel rail.

14. Remove the EGR valve injector, then remove the EGR valve.

15. Remove the fuel injector retainer bracket, regulator and injectors.

16. Unfasten and remove the control cable bracket.

1. Fitting
2. Stud
3. Intake manifold
4. Gasket
5. Nut

20-30 N·m (15-22 FT. LBS.)

MANIFOLD OUTLINE

THIS FITTING MUST NOT BE POSITIONED OUTSIDE OF MANIFOLD OUTLINE

INLET MANIFOLD NUT TIGHTENING SEQUENCE

87953031

Fig. 26 When installing the intake manifold, you must use the correct tightening sequence, or leaks may occur

1	STUD
2	GASKET
3	INTAKE MANIFOLD
4	NUT
5	CLIP

INTAKE MANIFOLD NUT TIGHTENING SEQUENCE

87953032

Fig. 27 Lower intake manifold tightening sequence—1992–94 OHV vehicles

A	UPPER INTAKE MANIFOLD ASSEMBLY TIGHTENING SEQUENCE
1	BOLT
2	STUD
3	UPPER INTAKE MANIFOLD ASSEMBLY
4	GASKET
5	LOWER INTAKE MANIFOLD
6	EGR VALVE INJECTOR

Fig. 28 The upper manifold bolts to the lower one, but be sure to use the correct sequence when tightening

3. Properly drain the cooling system into an approved container.
4. Remove the alternator and bracket at the camshaft carrier.
5. Remove the power steering pump, then position it aside with the lines still attached.
6. Remove the ignition coil.
7. Disconnect the throttle cable from the intake manifold bracket.
8. Detach the throttle and TV cables from the throttle body.
9. Disconnect the wiring from the throttle body.
10. Detach the vacuum brake hose at the filter.
11. Disconnect the coolant hoses at the water pump and intake manifold and the inlet tube-to-water pump.
12. For access to the lower retaining nuts, detach the ECM electrical harness.
13. Unfasten the retaining nuts and washers, then remove the intake manifold. Clean the mating surfaces of the cylinder head and intake manifold.

To install:

14. Place a new gasket on the cylinder head, then position the intake manifold. Tighten intake manifold retaining nuts and washers evenly in sequence to 20–25 ft. lbs. (27–34 Nm) for 1982–86 and 16 ft. lbs. (22 Nm) for 1987–92. Start with the inner nuts and work outward.
15. Attach the ECM wiring harness.
16. Connect the coolant hoses at the water pump and intake manifold and the inlet tube-to-water pump.
17. Fasten the inlet and return fuel lines.
18. Connect the vacuum brake hose at the filter.
19. Attach the wiring at the throttle body.
20. Connect the throttle and TV cables to the throttle body. Attach the throttle cable to the intake manifold bracket.
21. Install the ignition coil.
22. Attach the power steering bracket to the intake manifold.
23. Install the power steering pump.
24. Attach the alternator and bracket to the camshaft carrier.
25. Fill the engine cooling system.
26. Install the air cleaner.
27. Connect the negative battery cable, then start the engine and check for leaks.

17. If necessary for access, raise and safely support the vehicle.
18. Unfasten the six intake manifold nuts, then remove the manifold.
19. Clean the gasket mounting surfaces.

To install:

20. Install a new gasket, then position the lower intake manifold. Tighten the lower intake manifold nuts in the proper sequence to 24 ft. lbs. (33 Nm).
21. Connect the control cables and cable bracket.
22. Install the EGR valve.
23. Attach the fuel lines to the fuel rail.
24. Install the fuel injectors, regulator and injector retainer bracket, then tighten the retaining bolts to 22 inch lbs. (3.5 Nm).
25. Install the EGR valve injector so that the port is facing directly towards the throttle body.
26. Install the upper intake manifold assembly. Tighten the upper intake manifold nuts in the proper sequence to 22 ft. lbs. (30 Nm).
27. Install the MAP sensor.
28. Attach the electrical connectors to the MAP sensor, EGR solenoid valve, Idle Air Control (IAC) valve, Throttle Position (TP) sensor, and the fuel injectors.
29. Install the transaxle fill tube.
30. Install the power steering pump, then install the serpentine belt.
31. Connect the vacuum lines, as tagged during removal.
32. Install the air intake duct.
33. Refill the coolant system.
34. Connect the negative battery cable, then start the engine and check for leaks.

1.8L and 2.0L OHC Engines

EXCEPT TURBO

▶ See Figure 29

1. Release the fuel pressure.
2. Disconnect the negative battery cable.

TURBO

▶ See Figures 30 and 31

1. Properly relieve the fuel system pressure.
2. Disconnect the negative battery cable.
3. Drain the cooling system into an approved container.
4. Unfasten the induction tube and hoses.
5. Detach the wiring to the throttle body, Manifold Absolute Pressure (MAP) sensor and the wastegate.
6. Disconnect the PCV hose, then detach the vacuum hose from the throttle body.
7. Detach the throttle cable and, if equipped, the cruise control cable.
8. Disconnect the wiring from the ignition coil.
9. Remove the manifold support bracket.
10. Unfasten the bolt attaching the rear alternator bracket to the alternator.
11. Remove the power steering adjusting bracket and the alternator front adjusting bracket.

Fig. 29 Intake manifold mounting—1.8L and 2.0L OHC engines; EXCEPT turbo

Fig. 30 Disconnect the turbo injection tube and hoses

1	INTAKE MANIFOLD
2	GASKET
3	NUT 24 N•M (17 LBS. FT.)

Fig. 31 Removing the intake manifold— 2.0L turbo engine

12. Disconnect the fuel lines from the fuel rail inlet and the regulator outlet.

13. Unfasten the retaining nuts and washers, then remove the intake manifold and gasket. If installing a new manifold, don't forget to transfer all necessary parts from the old manifold to the new one.

14. Clean the cylinder head and intake manifold mating surfaces so they are clean of old gasket material and other debris.

To install:

15. Place a new gasket on the cylinder head, then position the intake manifold. Tighten the retaining nuts and washers to 18 ft. lbs. (25 Nm).

16. Attach the fuel lines to the regulator outlet and fuel rail inlet.

➡Any time the rear power steering adjusting bracket is loosened or removed, proper adjusting bolt torque is essential for belt and pulley alignment. The rear adjusting bracket must be the last part secured to prevent distorting the accessory drive system to prevent the belt from coming off.

17. Install the power steering and alternator adjusting brackets.

18. Attach the wiring to the fuel injectors and ignition coil.

19. Connect the throttle cable and cruise control cable, if applicable.

20. Attach the vacuum hoses and PCV hose.

21. Connect the wiring to the throttle body, MAP sensor and wastegate.

22. Attach the induction tube and hoses.

23. Fill the engine cooling system.

24. Connect the negative battery cable, then start the engine and check for vacuum and/or fluid leaks and proper engine operation.

2.8L and 3.1L Engines

1985–88 VEHICLES

▶ **See Figure 32**

1. Properly relieve the fuel system pressure.
2. Disconnect the negative battery cable.
3. Detach the accelerator and TV cable bracket at the plenum.
4. Unfasten the throttle body at the plenum.

TORQUE TO
18 TO 34 N•M
(13-25 FT.LBS.)

INLET MANIFOLD BOLT/SCREW
& NUT TIGHTENING SEQUENCE

A NOTE APPLY A SMOOTH CONTINUOUS BEAD APPROX. 2.0-3.0 WIDE AND 3.0-5.0 THICK ON BOTH SURFACES. BEAD CONFIGURATION MUST INSURE COMPLETE SEALING OF WATER AND OIL. SURFACE MUST BE FREE OF OIL AND DIRT TO INSURE ADEQUATE SEAL.

87953037

Fig. 32 Intake manifold installation and retaining bolt torque sequence—1985 2.8L engine shown

5. Disconnect the EGR pipe from the EGR valve.

6. Remove the plenum assembly.

7. Detach the fuel inlet and outlet pipes at the fuel rail.

8. Disconnect the serpentine drive belt.

9. Remove the power steering pump mounting bracket.

10. Detach the heater pipe at the power steering pump bracket.

11. Tag and disconnect the wiring at the alternator, then remove the alternator.

12. Disconnect the wires from the cold start injector assembly. Remove the injector assembly from the intake manifold.

13. Disconnect the idle air vacuum hose at the throttle body. Detach the wires at the injectors.

14. Remove the fuel rail, breather tube and the fuel runners from the engine.

15. Tag and disconnect the coil wires.

16. Remove the rocker arm covers.

17. Drain the cooling system, the disconnect the radiator hose at the thermostat housing. Disconnect the heater hose from the thermostat housing and the thermostat wiring.

18. Remove the distributor.

19. Remove the thermostat assembly housing.

20. Unfasten the intake manifold bolts and remove the intake manifold from the engine.

To install:

21. The gaskets are marked for right and left side installation; do not interchange them. Clean the sealing surfaces of the engine block and intake manifold, and apply a 3/16 in. (5mm) wide bead of silicone sealer to each ridge.

22. Place the new gaskets onto the heads. The gaskets will have to be cut slightly to fit past the center pushrods. Do not cut any more material than necessary. Hold the gaskets in place by extending the ridge bead of sealer ¼ in. (6mm) onto the gasket ends.

23. Position the intake manifold. The area between the ridges and the manifold should be completely sealed.

24. Install the retaining bolts and nuts, and tighten in sequence to 23 ft. lbs. (31 Nm). Do not overtighten; the manifold is made from aluminum, and can be warped or cracked with excessive force.

25. The rest of installation is the reverse of removal. Adjust the ignition timing after installation, and check the coolant level after the engine has warmed up.

1989–93 VEHICLES

▶ **See Figure 33**

1. Properly relieve the fuel system pressure.
2. Disconnect the negative battery cable.
3. Detach the cables at the plenum.
4. Unfasten the brake vacuum pipe at the plenum.
5. Disconnect the throttle body and the EGR pipe from the EGR valve.
6. Remove the plenum assembly.
7. Disconnect the fuel line along the fuel rail.
8. Remove the serpentine drive belt.
9. Unfasten the alternator, then move it to one side. Loosen the alternator bracket.
10. Remove the power steering pump and move to one side.
11. Disconnect the idle air vacuum hose at the throttle body.
12. Detach the the wires at the fuel injectors.
13. Remove the fuel rail, breather tube and the fuel runners from the engine.
14. Tag and disconnect the plug wires at the manifold.
15. Remove the rocker arm covers; refer to the necessary service procedure located in this section.
16. Drain the cooling system, the disconnect the radiator hose at the thermostat housing. Disconnect the heater hose from the thermostat housing and tag and disconnect the thermostat wiring.
17. Unfasten the intake manifold bolts and remove the intake manifold from the engine.

➡Retain the Belleville washer in the same orientation on the 4 center bolts.

18. Loosen the rocker arms and remove the pushrods.

➡Intake pushrods are marked orange and are 6 in. (152.4mm) long. Exhaust pushrods are marked blue and are 6⅜ in. (161.9mm) long.

19. Remove and discard the intake manifold gasket.

1	TIGHTEN IN PROPER SEQUENCE TO 20 N·m (15 LB. FT.), THEN RETIGHTEN TO 33 N·m (24 LB. FT.)	2	INTAKE MANIFOLD
		3	GASKET
		4	CYLINDER HEAD
		5	SEALER

⑦ ④ ③ ⑥
⑧ ① ② ⑤

87953038

Fig. 33 Make sure to tighten the intake manifold retaining bolts in the proper sequence—1993 3.1L engine shown

FRT

TIGHTEN IN PROPER SEQUENCE TO 20 N·m (15 LBS. FT.) THEN RETIGHTEN TO 33 N·m (24 LBS. FT.)	2	INTAKE MANIFOLD
	3	GASKET
	4	CYLINDER HEAD
	5	SEALER

⑦ ④ ③ ⑥
⑧ ① ② ⑤

87953039

Fig. 34 When removing the intake manifold, be sure to keep the washers in the same orientation on the 4 center bolts

To install:

20. Clean the gasket material and grease from the mating surfaces.
21. Place a 0.08–0.12 in. (2–3mm) bead of RTV sealant on each ridge where the front and rear of the intake manifold contact the block.
22. Install the new intake manifold gasket.
23. Install the pushrods and make sure they are seated properly in the lifter.

➡Intake pushrods are marked orange and are 6 in. (152.4mm) long. Exhaust pushrods are marked blue and are 6⅜ in. (161.9mm) long.

24. Install the rocker arm nuts and tighten to 18 ft. lbs. (24 Nm).
25. Install the intake manifold and retaining bolts. Tighten the bolts to 15 ft. lbs. (20 Nm) in the proper sequence shown, then retighten in sequence to 24 ft. lbs. (33 Nm).
26. Install the heater pipe to the manifold.
27. Connect the coolant sensor and any other necessary wiring.
28. Fasten the upper radiator hose.
29. Install the rocker arm covers.
30. Connect the breather tube.
31. Install the fuel rail and attach the wires to the injectors.
32. Connect the idle air vacuum hose at the throttle body.
33. Install the alternator and bracket.
34. Install the power steering gear and pump.
35. Connect the power steering line at the alternator bracket.
36. Install the serpentine drive belt.
37. Connect the fuel lines to the fuel rail and to the bracket.
38. Install the plenum, plug harness and EGR valve.
39. Install the throttle body.
40. Attach the cables at the plenum.
41. Connect the negative battery cable and fill the cooling system.

1994 VEHICLES

▶ See Figure 34

➡On 3.1L engines, an "Idle Learn" procedure must be performed which requires the use of a scan tool.

1. Properly relieve the fuel system pressure.
2. Disconnect the negative battery cable.
3. Remove the battery and the air cleaner assembly.
4. Remove the serpentine belt.
5. Unfasten and remove the exhaust crossover pipe.
6. Disconnect the EGR transfer tube from the exhaust manifold.
7. Properly drain and recover the engine cooling system.
8. Remove the radiator surge or overflow tank.
9. Disconnect the brake vacuum pipe at the plenum.
10. Remove the throttle cable and the vacuum line bracket at the plenum.
11. Disconnect the power steering lines at the alternator bracket.
12. Unfasten the rear alternator brace, then remove the alternator.
13. Tag and disconnect the spark plug wires from the plug, then unroute them.
14. Remove the rear valve (rocker arm) cover. For details, please refer to the procedure located in this section.
15. Tag and disconnect, then unroute the following electrical connections:
- Throttle Position (TP) sensor
- Idle Air Control (IAC) sensor
- Exhaust Gas Recirculation (EGR) valve
- Engine Coolant Temperature (ECT) sensor
- Fuel injector wiring harness connector
16. Tag and disconnect the PCV hose and any other necessary vacuum lines.
17. Detach the cables at the throttle body.
18. Unfasten the throttle body heater hoses.
19. Remove the plenum.
20. Disconnect the fuel lines from the fuel rail and the fuel lines at the bracket.
21. Unfasten the power steering pump mounting bolts, then position the pump aside with the lines attached.
22. Disconnect the coolant bleed pipe from the thermostat housing.
23. Detach the heater pipe from the cylinder heads, thermostat housing and the water pump. Disconnect the upper radiator hose at the themostat housing.

24. Remove the thermostat housing.

25. As outlined earlier, remove the front valve (rocker arm) cover.

➡**When removing the manifold, make sure to retain the washers in the same orientation on the 4 center bolts.**

26. Unfasten the retaining bolts and/or nuts, then remove the intake manifold.

27. Loosen the rocker arms, then remove the pushrods.

➡**Intake pushrods are marked orange and are 6 in. (152.4mm) long. Exhaust pushrods are marked blue and are 6⅜ in. (161.9mm) long.**

28. Remove and discard the intake gasket, then clean the mating surfaces free of gasket material and old RTV sealant.

To install:

29. Place a 0.08–0.12 in. (2–3mm) bead of RTV sealant on each ridge where the front and rear of the intake manifold contact the block.

➡**Intake pushrods are marked orange and are 6 in. (152.4mm) long. Exhaust pushrods are marked blue and are 6⅜ in. (161.9mm) long.**

30. Position a new intake manifold gasket, then install the pushrods, making sure they seat in the lifters.

31. Tighten the rocker arm nuts to 18 ft. lbs. (25 Nm).

32. Position the intake manifold, then tighten the retaining bolts, in the proper sequence, in two steps; first to 15 ft. lbs. (20 Nm), then to 24 ft. lbs. (33 Nm).

33. Install the front valve (rocker arm) cover.

34. Attach the heater-pipe to the manifold.

35. Install the thermostat housing, then attach the upper radiator hose to the housing.

36. Connect the heater pipe to the cylinder heads, water pump and themostat housing.

37. Attach the coolant bleed pipe to the thermostat housing.

38. Install the power steering pump.

39. Attach the fuel lines to the fuel rail, the fasten fuel lines at the bracket.

40. Install the plenum.

41. Attach the throttle body heater hoses, then connect the cables to the throttle body.

42. Connect the PCV hose, and any other vacuum lines disconnected during removal.

43. Route and attach the following electrical connections, as tagged during removal:

- TP sensor
- IAC valve
- EGR valve
- ECT sensor
- Fuel injector wiring harness connector

44. Install the rear valve (rocker arm) cover.

45. Route and connect all spark plug wires, as tagged during removal.

46. Install the alternator and the alternator brace, then attach the power steering line to the brace.

47. Attach the throttle cable and vacuum lines bracket to the plenum.

48. Connect the brake vacuum pipe to the plenum.

49. Install the radiator surge or overflow tank.

50. Attach the EGR transfer tube to the exhaust manifold.

51. Connect the exhaust crossover to the exhaust manifolds.

52. Install the air cleaner assembly and the battery, then connect the negative battery cable.

➡**On the 3.1L engine, a Tech 1® scan tool is needed to perform the "Idle Learn" procedure.**

53. For the 3.1L engine perform the following "Idle Learn" procedure;
   a. Install a Tech 1® scan tool.
   b. Turn the ignition to the **ON** position, engine not running.
   c. Select **IAC SYSTEM**, then **IDLE LEARN** in the **MISC TEST** mode.
   d. Place the transaxle in park or neutral, as applicable.
   e. Proceed with idle learn as directed by the scan tool.

54. Fill the cooling system, then start the engine and check for leaks.

Exhaust Manifold

REMOVAL & INSTALLATION

1.8L, 2.0L and 2.2L OHV Engines

▶ See Figures 35 and 36

1. Disconnect the negative battery cable.

2. Detach the oxygen sensor wire.

3. Remove the serpentine belt or alternator drive belt.

4. Remove the alternator-to-bracket bolts, then support the alternator (with the wires attached) out of the way.

5. For 1982–84 vehicles equipped with the A.I.R. or pulse air system, disconnect the pipes and hoses.

6. Raise and support the vehicle safely.

7. Unfasten the exhaust pipe-to-exhaust manifold bolts, then carefully lower the vehicle.

8. If necessary for access to remove the manifold, remove the oil fill tube and disconnect the heater outlet hose assembly nut from the exhaust manifold.

9. Remove the exhaust manifold-to-cylinder head bolts.

10. Detach the exhaust manifold from the exhaust pipe flange.

11. Unfasten the retaining nuts, then remove the exhaust manifold from the vehicle. Remove and discard the gasket(s).

Fig. 35 Exploded view of the exhaust manifold mounting—OHV 1.8L engine shown

1. Stud
2. Gasket
3. Exhaust manifold
4. Nut

Fig. 36 When installing the exhaust manifold, always use a new gasket—OHV 2.2L engine shown

To install:

12. Using a gasket scraper, carefully clean the gasket mounting surfaces.

13. To install, use new gaskets and reverse the removal procedures. Tighten the exhaust manifold-to-cylinder head nuts to 3–12 ft. lbs. (4–16 Nm) and the bolts to 6–13 ft. lbs. (8–18 Nm).

14. Start the engine and check for exhaust leaks.

1.8L and 2.0L OHC Engines

EXCEPT TURBOCHARGER

◆ See Figure 37

1. Disconnect the negative battery cable.
2. Remove the air cleaner assembly.
3. Tag and disconnect the spark plug wires from the spark plugs, then remove the retainers.
4. Remove the oil dipstick tube and the breather.
5. Detach the Oxygen (O_2) sensor electrical connector.
6. Raise and safely support the vehicle.
7. Remove the exhaust pipe from the manifold, then support the pipe.
8. Unfasten the retaining nuts, then remove the exhaust manifold by lowering it from the bottom of the vehicle. Remove and discard the gasket. Clean the exhaust manifold and cylinder head gasket mating surfaces.

To install:

9. Use a new gasket, position the exhaust manifold, then secure using the retaining nuts. Tighten the nuts to 16 ft. lbs. (22 Nm), in the sequence shown in the accompanying figure.

10. Connect the exhaust pipe to the manifold. Tighten the retaining nuts to 16–19 ft. lbs. (22–26 Nm).

11. Carefully lower the vehicle.

12. Attach the (O_2) sensor electrical connector.

13. Install the breather and the oil dipstick tube.

14. Connect the spark plugs as tagged during remove, then install the retainers.

15. Install the air cleaner assembly.

16. Connect the negative battery cable.

Fig. 37 When installing the exhaust manifold, tighten runners #2 and #3 before #1 and #4—except 2.0L Turbo engines

TURBOCHARGER

◆ See Figures 38 and 39

1. Disconnect the negative battery cable.
2. Remove the turbo induction tube.
3. Label and detach the spark plug wires.
4. Remove the turbocharger. For details, please refer to the procedure located later in this section.
5. If applicable, detach the wiring from the oxygen sensor.
6. Unfasten the bolts and nuts retaining the exhaust manifold to the block and exhaust pipe, then remove the manifold. Remove and discard the gasket.

To install:

➡Before installing a new gasket on the 1.8L MFI Turbo engine (code J), check for the location of the stamped part number on the surface. This

Fig. 38 Removing the turbo induction tube is simply a matter of unfastening the clamps, then removing the tube from the engine

Fig. 39 Exhaust manifold mounting and retainer tightening sequence—2.0L engine

gasket should be installed with this number toward the manifold. The gasket appears to be the same in either direction but it is not. Installing the gasket backwards will result in a leak.

7. Install the exhaust manifold with a new gasket. Install the retainers, then tighten (in the sequence shown in the accompanying figure) the studs to 20 ft. lbs. (27 Nm,) and the nuts to 16 ft. lbs. (22 Nm).

8. Connect the exhaust pipe to the exhaust manifold and tighten the nuts to 19 ft. lbs. (25 Nm).

9. Attach the wire to the oxygen sensor, if applicable.

10. Install the turbocharger. For details, please refer to the procedure located later in this section.

11. Connect the spark plug wires as tagged during removal.

12. Install the turbo induction tube.

13. Connect the negative battery cable.

2.8L and 3.1L Engines

1985–86 VEHICLES (LEFT SIDE)

◆ See Figure 40

1. Disconnect the negative battery cable.
2. Remove the air cleaner assembly.
3. Remove the air flow sensor.
4. Unfasten, then remove the engine heat shield.
5. Detach the crossover pipe at the exhaust manifold.
6. Unfasten the exhaust manifold bolts, then remove the manifold.
7. Clean the surfaces of the cylinder head and manifold.

To install:

8. Place the manifold into position, then loosely install the manifold bolts just enough to hold the manifold.

9. Install the exhaust crossover pipe to the manifold.

Fig. 40 Exhaust manifold removal and installation—1985-86 2.8L engines

Fig. 41 Exhaust manifold removal and installation—1987 2.8L engine shown

Fig. 42 Removing the exhaust manifold—1993 3.1L engine shown

Fig. 43 The exhaust crossover pipe on the 3.1L engines is retained by two nuts

10. Tighten the manifold bolts evenly to 25 ft. lbs. (34 Nm).
11. Install the heat shield and the mass flow sensor.
12. Install the air cleaner and the negative battery cable.

1985-86 VEHICLES (RIGHT SIDE)

▶ See Figure 40

1. Disconnect the negative battery cable.
2. Remove the air cleaner assembly.
3. Remove the air flow sensor. Remove the heat shield.
4. Disconnect the crossover pipe at the manifold.
5. Detach the accelerator and Throttle Valve (TV) cable at the throttle lever and the plenum. Move aside to gain working clearance.
6. Disconnect the power steering line at the power steering pump.
7. Remove the EGR valve assembly.
8. Raise and safely support the vehicle.
9. Disconnect the exhaust pipe at the exhaust manifold.
10. Carefully lower the vehicle.
11. Unfasten the exhaust manifold bolts, then remove the manifold.
12. Clean the surfaces of the cylinder head and manifold.

To install:

13. Place the manifold into position and loosely install the retaining bolts just enough to hold the manifold.
14. Raise and safely support the vehicle.
15. Install the exhaust pipe at the manifold.
16. Carefully lower the vehicle.
17. Tighten the manifold bolts, evenly, to 25 ft. lbs. (34 Nm).
18. Install the EGR valve and related parts.
19. Connect the power steering line at the power steering pump.
20. Attach the accelerator and throttle valve cable at the throttle lever and the plenum.
21. Connect the crossover pipe at the manifold.
22. Install the heat shield and the mass air flow sensor.
23. Install the air cleaner assembly and connect the negative battery cable.

1987-93 VEHICLES (LEFT SIDE)

▶ See Figures 41, 42 and 43

1. Disconnect the negative battery cable.
2. Remove the air cleaner assembly.
3. Remove the air cleaner inlet hose and the mass air flow sensor, on models so equipped.
4. Properly drain the coolant, then remove the coolant by-pass pipe
5. Remove the heat shield.
6. Disconnect the exhaust crossover pipe at the manifold.
7. Unfasten the exhaust manifold bolts and remove the exhaust manifold or manifold/crossover assembly.

To install:

8. Clean the surfaces of the cylinder head and manifold.
9. Using a new gasket, place the manifold into position and loosely install the manifold bolts.
10. Attach the exhaust crossover pipe to the manifold.
11. Tighten the exhaust manifold bolts evenly to 18-21 ft. lbs. (24-28 Nm).
12. Install the heat shield. Tighten the nuts to 89 inch lbs. (10 Nm).
13. Connect the coolant pipe.
14. Install the air cleaner inlet hose and the air cleaner assembly
15. Fill the cooling system.
16. Connect the negative battery cable.

1987–93 VEHICLES (RIGHT SIDE)

▶ See Figures 41, 42 and 43

1. Disconnect the negative battery cable.
2. For 1993 vehicles, remove the air cleaner assembly.
3. Raise and safely support the vehicle.
4. Remove the heat shield.
5. Disconnect the exhaust pipe at the crossover.
6. Carefully lower the vehicle.
7. Remove the EGR valve or pipe.
8. Disconnect the oxygen sensor wire.
9. Unfasten the exhaust manifold bolts, then remove the manifold.
10. Clean the mating surfaces of the cylinder head and manifold. Discard the gasket.

To install:

11. Use a new manifold gasket, place the manifold into position and loosely install the manifold bolts.
12. Install the crossover at the manifold.
13. Tighten the manifold bolts evenly to 21–25 ft. lbs. (28–34 Nm).
14. Install the EGR valve or pipe and connect the oxygen sensor wire.
15. Raise and support the vehicle safely.
16. Connect the exhaust pipe to the crossover.
17. Install the engine heat shield.
18. Carefully lower the vehicle.
19. Connect the negative battery cable.

1994 VEHICLES (LEFT SIDE)

▶ See Figure 44

➡ On these 3.1L engines, and Idle Learn procedure must be performed which requires the use of a scan tool.

1. Disconnect the negative, then the positive battery cables.
2. Remove the battery.
3. Remove the air cleaner assembly.
4. Raise and safely support the vehicle.
5. Unfasten the lower cooling fan bolt and detach the electrical connector.
6. Carefully lower the vehicle.
7. Remove the cooling fan assembly.
8. Disconnect the exhaust crossover pipe.
9. Tag and disconnect the left side spark plug wires from the spark plugs and position aside.
10. Remove the exhaust manifold heat shield.
11. Unfasten the retaining bolts, then remove the exhaust manifold.
12. Clean the mating surfaces of the cylinder head and manifold. Discard the gasket.

To install:

13. Use a new manifold gasket, place the manifold into position and loosely install the manifold bolts.
14. Tighten the exhaust manifold bolts to 21 ft. lbs. (28 Nm).
15. Install the exhaust manifold heat shield. Tighten the retaining nuts to 89 inch lbs. (10 Nm).
16. Attach the spark plug wires to the plugs, as tagged during removal.
17. Fasten the exhaust crossover pipe to the manifolds.
18. Install the cooling fan, and secure with the upper retaining bolts.
19. Raise and safely support the vehicle.

20. Install the lower cooling fan assembly bolt and attach the electrical connector.
21. Carefully lower the vehicle.
22. Install the air cleaner assembly.
23. Install the battery, then connect the positive, then the negative battery cables.

➡ On the 3.1L engine, a Tech 1® scan tool is needed to perform the "Idle Learn" procedure.

24. For the 3.1L engine perform the following "Idle Learn" procedure;
   a. Install a Tech 1® scan tool.
   b. Turn the ignition to the **ON** position, engine not running.
   c. Select **IAC SYSTEM**, then **IDLE LEARN** in the **MISC TEST** mode.
   d. Place the transaxle in park or neutral, as applicable.
   e. Proceed with idle learn as directed by the scan tool.

1994 VEHICLES (RIGHT SIDE)

▶ See Figure 44

➡ On these 3.1L engines, and Idle Learn procedure must be performed which requires the use of a scan tool.

1. Disconnect the negative, then the positive battery cables.
2. Remove the battery.
3. Remove the air cleaner assembly.
4. Disconnect the exhaust crossover pipe from the manifolds.
5. Detach the Oxygen sensor electrical connector.
6. Disconnect the EGR pipe from the exhaust manifold.
7. For vehicles equipped with an automatic transaxle, remove the transaxle fluid level indicator and fill tube.
8. Raise and safely support the vehicle.
9. For vehicles equipped with an automatic transaxle, remove the suspension support crossmember brace.
10. For vehicles equipped with a manual transaxle, remove the heat shield. If equipped with an automatic transaxle, remove the nut but do not remove the heat shield from the vehicle at this time.
11. Disconnect the exhaust pipe from the exhaust manifold.
12. If equipped with an automatic transaxle, remove the exhaust manifold extension pipe.
13. Unfasten the retaining bolts, then remove the exhaust manifold from the vehicle. If equipped with an automatic transaxle, remove the heat shield with the exhaust manifold.
14. Clean the mating surfaces of the cylinder head and manifold. Discard the gasket.

To install:

15. Use a new manifold gasket, place the manifold (and heat shield, if automatic) into position and loosely install the manifold bolts.
16. Tighten the exhaust manifold bolts to 21 ft. lbs. (28 Nm).
17. If equipped with an automatic transaxle, install the exhaust manifold extension pipe.
18. If applicable, install the exhaust manifold heat shield, then tighten the nut to 89 inch lbs. (10 Nm).
19. Attach the exhaust pipe to the manifold.
20. If equipped with an automatic transaxle, install the suspension support crossmember brace.
21. Carefully lower the vehicle.
22. If equipped with an automatic transaxle, install the transaxle fluid level indicator and fill tube.
23. Attach the EGR pipe to the exhaust manifold.
24. Engage the Oxygen sensor connector.
25. Fasten the exhaust crossover to the manifolds.
26. Install the air cleaner assembly.
27. Install the battery, then connect the positive, then negative battery cables.

➡ On the 3.1L engine, a Tech 1® scan tool is needed to perform the "Idle Learn" procedure.

28. For the 3.1L engine perform the following "Idle Learn" procedure;
   a. Install a Tech 1® scan tool.
   b. Turn the ignition to the **ON** position, engine not running.
   c. Select **IAC SYSTEM**, then **IDLE LEARN** in the **MISC TEST** mode.
   d. Place the transaxle in park or neutral, as applicable.
   e. Proceed with idle learn as directed by the scan tool.

1. Cylinder head
2. Gasket
3. Manifold (left)
4. 28 Nm (21 lb. ft.)
5. 10 Nm (89 lb. ft.)
6. Heat shield
7. Manifold (right)

87953700

Fig. 44 View of the exhaust manifold mounting—1994 3.1L engine shown

Turbocharger

REMOVAL & INSTALLATION

▶ **See Figure 45**

1. Disconnect the negative battery cable. Raise the car and safely support it with jackstands.
2. Unfasten the lower fan retaining screw.
3. Disconnect the exhaust pipe.
4. Remove the rear air conditioning support bracket and loosen the remaining bolts.
5. Remove the turbo support bracket-to-engine bolt.
6. Disconnect the oil drain hose at the turbocharger.
7. Carefully lower the vehicle.
8. Disconnect the coolant recovery pipe, then move it to one side.
9. Detach the induction tube.
10. Remove the cooling fan.
11. Disconnect, then remove the oxygen sensor.
12. Unfasten the oil feed pipe at the union. Disconnect the water feed pipe.
13. Disconnect the air intake duct and vacuum hose at the actuator.
14. Unfasten the exhaust manifold retaining nuts and remove the exhaust manifold and turbocharger.

To install:

15. Install the exhaust manifold and turbocharger. Tighten the bolts evenly to 16 ft. lbs. (22 Nm).
16. Install the exhaust manifold retaining nuts.
17. Attach the air intake duct and vacuum hose at the actuator.
18. Connect the oil feed pipe at the union.
19. Attach the oxygen sensor.
20. Install the cooling fan.
21. Connect the induction tube.
22. Position and attach the coolant recovery pipe.
23. Raise and safely support the vehicle.

24. Fasten the rear turbo support bracket bolt to the engine.
25. Install the rear air conditioning support bracket.
26. Connect the oil drain hose at the turbocharger.
27. Fasten the lower fan screw.
28. Attach the exhaust pipe.
29. Connect the negative battery cable, then start the engine and check for intake and/or exhaust leaks.

Radiator

REMOVAL & INSTALLATION

▶ **See Figures 46 thru 55**

✳✳ CAUTION

When draining the coolant, keep in mind that cats and dogs are attracted by ethylene glycol antifreeze, and are quite likely to drink any that is left in an uncovered container or in puddles on the ground. This will prove fatal in sufficient quantity. Always drain the coolant into a sealable container. Coolant should be reused unless it is contaminated or several years old.

1. Disconnect the negative battery cable.
2. Properly drain and recover the cooling system into an approved container.
3. If necessary for access, remove the air cleaner cover and air cleaner.
4. Remove any necessary upper radiator/air duct shrouding.
5. Detach the forward lamp harness from the frame and unplug the fan connector.
6. Unfasten the fan frame-to-radiator support attaching bolts and then remove the fan assembly.
7. Scribe a line around the hood latch for installation purposes, then remove the latch from the radiator support.
8. If equipped, remove the radiator air inlet ducts.
9. Disconnect the upper and lower radiator hoses and the coolant recovery hose from the radiator.
10. Detach the transmission oil cooler lines from the radiator and wire them out of the way. If equipped with A/C, remove the 4 radiator to condenser bolts and the radiator tank to refrigerant line clamp bolt.
11. Unfasten the radiator-to-radiator support attaching bolts and clamps, then remove the radiator from the vehicle.

To install:

12. Place the radiator in the vehicle so that the bottom is positioned in the lower mounting pads. Tighten the attaching bolts and clamps.
13. If equipped with A/C, tighten the 4 radiator-to-condenser bolts and the condenser bolt-to-refrigerant line clamp bolt.

1	STUD
2	BOLT
3	GASKET
4	NUT 25 N•M (18 LBS. FT.)
5	STUD 25 N•M (18 LBS. FT.)
6	WASHER
7	NUT 25 N•M (18 LBS. FT.)
8	SUPPORT BRACKET
9	EXHAUST OUTLET ELBOW
10	BOLT 50 N•M (37 LBS. FT.)
11	ADAPTER PLATE

VIEW A

87953061

Fig. 45 View of the turbocharger mounting—1987 2.0L MFI-Turbo shown

87953207

Fig. 46 Unfasten the upper radiator shrouding/air duct retaining bolts, then . . .

Fig. 47 . . . remove the shrouding to expose the fan assembly

Fig. 48 Detach the radiator fan electrical connector

Fig. 49 Unfasten the fan-to-radiator support retaining bolts, then . . .

Fig. 50 . . . remove the fan assembly

Fig. 51 Disconnect the hoses from the radiator

Fig. 52 Unfasten the radiator-to-support retaining bolts, then . . .

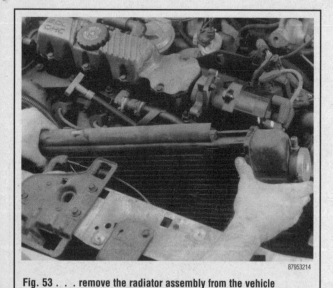

Fig. 53 . . . remove the radiator assembly from the vehicle

1 Nuts
2 Bracket
3 Insulator
4 Bolt/screw - 10 Nm (89 lbs. in.)

Fig. 54 The radiator is secured using brackets and retaining bolts and/or screws—1994 2.2L engine shown

14. Connect the transmission oil cooler lines, then tighten the bolts to 20 ft. lbs. (27 Nm).

15. Attach the upper and lower radiator hoses and the coolant recovery hose to the radiator.

16. Install the radiator air inlet ducts.

17. Install the fan, making sure the bottom leg of the frame fits into the rubber grommet (if used) at the lower radiator support. Install the retaining bolts and tighten them to 80 inch lbs. (9 Nm).

18. Fasten the fan connector, then attach the forward lamp harness to the fan frame. If used, be sure to connect the engine ground strap to the strut brace.

19. Install any necessary upper radiator shrouding.

1 FRONT END ASSEMBLY
2 RADIATOR WITH A/C CONDENSER
3 UPPER MOUNTING PANEL
4 BOLT - 10 N·m (89 LBS. IN.)
5 RETAINER
6 INSULATOR
7 CLIP

Fig. 55 Radiator mounting on a 1994 3.1L engine

20. Fill the coolant system, connect the negative battery cable, then check for coolant leaks.

Electric Cooling Fan

REMOVAL & INSTALLATION

✵✵ CAUTION

The electric cooling fan can start whether or not the engine is running.

4-Cylinder Engines

▶ See Figures 56 and 57

1. Disconnect the negative battery cable.
2. Remove the air cleaner duct.
3. Detach the wiring harness from the motor and the fan frame.
4. Remove the fan assembly from the radiator support.

To install:

5. Position the fan assembly to the radiator support. Tighten the fan assembly motor-to-fan to 29 inch lbs. (3.2 Nm) and fan-to-radiator support bolt to 80 inch lbs. (9 Nm).
6. Connect the fan electrical wiring harness.
7. Install the air cleaner duct.
8. Connect the negative battery cable.

Fig. 56 Early model cooling fans; with and without A/C—1982 vehicle shown

1 FAN ASSEMBLY
2 BOLT – 10 N·m (89 LBS. IN.)
3 NUT

87953066

Fig. 57 Coolant fan mounting—1994 vehicles shown

6-Cylinder Engines

1. Disconnect the negative battery cable. Drain engine coolant to level below the upper radiator hose.
2. Remove the air cleaner duct and the air cleaner assembly.
3. Scribe a latch position mark for reassembly purposes, then remove the main hood latch assembly.
4. Disconnect the upper radiator hose from the radiator and position aside.
5. On vehicles equipped with an automatic transaxle, disconnect, then position the transaxle cooler lines aside.
6. Detach the electrical wiring harness connector at the coolant fan, then remove the fan assembly from the radiator support.

To install:

7. Position the fan assembly onto the radiator support. Tighten the fan assembly motor-to-fan bolt to 29 inch lbs. (3.2 Nm) and fan-to-radiator support bolt to 80 inch lbs. (9 Nm).
8. Attach the fan electrical wiring harness.
9. For automatic transaxle equipped vehicles, connect the transaxle oil cooler lines to to the radiator.
10. Using the marks scribed during removal for alignment, install the main hood latch.
11. Install the air cleaner assembly and duct.
12. Properly refill the engine cooling system, then connect the negative battery cable.

Water Pump

REMOVAL & INSTALLATION

✵✵ CAUTION

When draining the coolant, keep in mind that cats and dogs are attracted by ethylene glycol antifreeze, and are quite likely to drink any that is left in an uncovered container or in puddles on the ground. This will prove fatal in sufficient quantity. Always drain the coolant into a sealable container. Coolant should be reused unless it is contaminated or several years old.

1.8L, 2.0L and 2.2L OHV Engines

▶ See Figures 58 and 59

1. Disconnect the negative battery cable.
2. Properly drain the cooling system into an approved container.
3. Remove all accessory drive belts or the serpentine belt.
4. Remove the alternator and bracket. For details, please refer to Section 2 of this manual.
5. Unscrew the water pump pulley mounting bolts and then pull off the pulley.
6. Unfasten the mounting bolts, then remove the water pump.
7. Using a putty knife, clean the gasket mounting surfaces.

To install:

8. Place a 1/8 in. (3mm) wide bead of RTV sealant on the water pump sealing surface or install a new gasket, on models so equipped. Install the pump and tighten the retaining bolts to 18 ft. lbs. (25 Nm).
9. Install the water pump pulley, then tighten the mounting bolts to 22 ft. lbs. (30 Nm).
10. As outlined in Section 2, install the alternator and bracket.
11. Install the drive belts or serpentine belt, as applicable.
12. Fill the cooling system to the proper level.
13. Connect the negative battery cable, then start the engine and check for leaks.

1.8L and 2.0L OHC Engines

▶ See Figure 60

1. Disconnect the negative battery cable.
2. Properly drain the engine cooling system into an approved container.
3. Remove the timing belt as described later in this section.
4. Remove the timing belt rear protective covers.
5. Disconnect the hose from the water pump.

Fig. 58 Water pump mounting—1982 1.8L OHV engine shown

1. BOLT — 25 N·m (18 LBS. FT.)

Fig. 59 Location and mounting of the water pump on the 2.0L and 2.2L OHV engines

1 28 Nm (21 lb. ft.) bolt
2 Water pump
3 Seal ring

Fig. 60 Water pump location on the 1.8L and 2.0L OHC engines

6. Unfasten the retaining bolt(s), then remove the water pump and seal ring. Inspect the ring for damage and replace if necessary. Clean the pump mating surfaces.

To install:

7. Install the seal ring and water pump. Do not fully tighten the retaining bolts. They will be tightened to specification during installation of the timing belt.

8. Connect the hose to the water pump.

9. Install the timing belt rear protective covers.

10. Install the timing belt and adjust it to specifications, as outlined later in this section. Tighten the water pump mounting bolts to 18–21 ft. lbs. (21–25 Nm).

11. Fill the engine cooling system to the proper level.

12. Connect the negative battery cable, then start the engine and check for leaks and make sure the coolant level is correct.

2.8L and 3.1L Engines

▶ See Figure 61

1. Disconnect battery negative cable.

2. Properly drain and recover the cooling system into an approved container.

3. Disconnect the serpentine belt at the water pump pulley.

4. On 1985–86 models, if equipped with A/C, disconnect the wires at the air conditioning pressure cycling switch and remove the cycling switch.

5. Unfasten the water pump pulley retaining bolts, then remove the pulley.

6. Unfasten the pump attaching bolts, then remove the water pump.

To install:

7. Clean the gasket mating surfaces.

8. Using a new gasket, install the water pump, then tighten the pump to block bolts to 18 ft. lbs. (24 Nm) for 2.8L engines and to 89 inch lbs. (10 Nm) for 3.1L engines.

9. Install the water pump pulley. Tighten the mounting bolt to 15 ft. lbs. (20 Nm).

10. On 1985–86 models, if equipped, install the air conditioning pressure cycling switch and connect the wires.

11. Install the serpentine belt.

12. Fill the cooling system to the proper level.

13. Connect the negative battery cable, then start the engine and check for leaks.

Cylinder Head

REMOVAL & INSTALLATION

1.8L, 2.0L and 2.2L OHV Engines

1982–86 VEHICLES

▶ See Figure 62

➡The engine should be overnight cold before removing the cylinder head.

1. Disconnect the negative battery cable.

2. Relieve the fuel system pressure.

3. Drain the cooling system into a clean container; the coolant can be reused if it is still good.

4. Remove the air cleaner assembly.

5. Raise and safely support the vehicle using jackstands.

6. Remove the exhaust shield, then disconnect the exhaust pipe.

1 COOLANT PUMP
2 GASKET
3 BOLT — 10 N·m (89 LBS. IN.)
4 LOCATOR (MUST BE VERTICAL)

Fig. 61 Water (coolant) pump mounting—2.8L and 3.1L engines

CYLINDER HEAD BOLT TIGHTENING SEQUENCE

Fig. 62 This sequence MUST be followed when installing the cylinder head bolts—1982–86 1.8L and 2.0L OHV engines

7. Disconnect the heater hose from the intake manifold.

8. Carefully lower the vehicle.

9. Unscrew the mounting bolts and remove the engine lift bracket (includes air management).

10. Remove (mark for correct installation) the distributor.

11. Disconnect the vacuum manifold at the alternator bracket.

12. Tag and detach the remaining vacuum lines at the intake manifold and thermostat.

13. Remove the air management pipe at the exhaust check valve.

14. Disconnect the accelerator linkage at the carburetor or T.B.I. unit, as applicable, and then remove the linkage bracket.

15. Tag and disconnect all necessary wires.

16. Detach the upper radiator hose at the thermostat.

17. Unfasten the bolt attaching the dipstick tube and hot water bracket.

18. Remove the idler pulley. Remove the A.I.R. and/or power steering pump drive belts.

19. For early model vehicles, unfasten the A.I.R. bracket-to-intake manifold bolt. If equipped with power steering, remove the air pump pulley, the A.I.R. through-bolt and the power steering adjusting bracket. Loosen the A.I.R. mounting bracket lower bolt so that the bracket will rotate.

20. If equipped with power steering, remove the power steering pump and lay aside with the lines still attached.

21. Disconnect and plug the fuel line(s) at the carburetor or TBI.

22. Remove the alternator with the wires attached and position aside. Remove the alternator brace from the head, then remove the upper mounting bracket.

23. Remove the rocker arm (valve) cover. Remove the rocker arms and pushrods.

24. Remove the cylinder head bolts in the reverse order given in the illustration. Remove the cylinder head with the carburetor or T.B.I. unit, intake and exhaust manifolds still attached.

To install:

25. To install, the gasket surfaces on both the head and the block must be clean of any foreign matter and free of any nicks or heavy scratches. Cylinder bolt threads in the block and the bolt must be clean.

26. Place a new cylinder head gasket in position over the dowel pins on the block. Carefully guide the cylinder head into position.

27. Coat the cylinder bolts with sealing compound and install them finger tight.

28. Using a torque wrench, tighten the cylinder head bolts as follows:

   a. 1982–85 vehicles: gradually tighten the bolts to 65–75 ft. lbs. (88–102 Nm) in the sequence shown in the illustration.

   b. 1986 vehicles: gradually tighten the bolts to 70–73 ft. lbs. (95–95 Nm) in the sequence shown in the illustration.

29. Install the rocker arms and pushrods and adjust the valve lash.

30. Install the cylinder head cover.

31. Install the alternator brace on the head, then fasten the upper mounting bracket.

32. Attach the wires, then install the alternator.

33. Connect the fuel line at the carburetor.

34. Install the A.I.R. bracket-to-intake manifold bolt. If equipped with power steering, install the air pump pulley, the A.I.R. through-bolt and the power steering adjusting bracket.

35. Install the idler pulley. Install the A.I.R. and/or power steering pump drive belts.

36. Install the bolt attaching the dipstick tube and hot water bracket.

37. Connect all wires, as tagged during removal.

38. Install the upper radiator hose at the thermostat.

39. Install the linkage bracket and connect the accelerator linkage at the carburetor or TBI.

40. Install the air management pipe at the exhaust check valve.

41. Connect the remaining vacuum lines at the intake manifold and thermostat.

42. Install the distributor.

43. Connect the vacuum manifold at the alternator bracket.

44. Install the engine lift bracket (includes air management).

45. Install the heater hose at the intake manifold.

46. Connect the exhaust pipe.

47. Install the exhaust shield.

48. Install the air cleaner.

49. Fill the cooling system.

50. Connect the negative battery cable, then start the engine and check for leaks.

1987–91 VEHICLES

♦ See Figures 63 and 64

➡The engine must be cold before removing the cylinder head. Always release the fuel pressure before starting repair.

1. Relieve the fuel system pressure.

2. Disconnect the negative battery cable.

3. Properly drain the cooling system into a suitable container.

4. Remove the TBI cover.

5. Raise and safely support the vehicle.

6. Remove the exhaust shield. Disconnect the exhaust pipe.

7. Detach the heater hose from the intake manifold.

8. Remove the accelerator and TV cable bracket.

9. Carefully lower the vehicle.

10. Tag and disconnect the remaining vacuum lines at the intake manifold.

11. Disconnect the accelerator linkage at the TBI unit.

12. Tag and detach all necessary wires.

13. Unfasten the upper radiator hose at the thermostat.

14. Remove the serpentine belt.

15. Remove the power steering pump and lay aside with the fluid lines attached.

16. Make sure the fuel system pressure is released, then disconnect and plug the fuel lines.

| 1 | 99-113 N·m (73-83 FT. LBS.) |
| 2 | 85-95 N·m (62-70 FT. LBS.) |

87953073

Fig. 63 Cylinder head bolt tightening sequence—1987–89 2.0L OHV engines

1. Long bolts
2. Short bolts
3. Stud
4. Numbers on gasket indicate torque sequence

87953074

Fig. 64 Cylinder head bolt tightening sequence—1990–91 2.2L OHV engines

17. Remove the alternator with the wires attached. Remove the rear alternator brace.

18. Remove the rocker arm (valve) cover. Remove the rocker arms and pushrods keeping all parts in order for correct installation.

19. Unfasten the cylinder head bolts. Remove the cylinder head with the TBI unit, intake and exhaust manifolds still attached.

To install:

20. The gasket surfaces on both the head and the block must be clean of any foreign matter and free of any nicks or heavy scratches. Bolt threads in the block and the bolts must be clean.

21. Place a new cylinder head gasket in position over the dowel pins on the block. Carefully guide the cylinder head into position.

22. Coat the cylinder bolts with sealing compound and install them finger tight.

23. For 1987–89 vehicles, tighten the long bolts to 73–83 ft lbs. (99–113 Nm) and the short bolts to 62–70 ft lbs. (85–95 Nm), in the sequence shown in the illustration.

24. For 1990–91 vehicles, tighten the bolts twice, in the sequence shown in the accompanying figure. For the first pass, tighten the long bolts to 23 ft. lbs. (32 Nm) and the short bolts and stud to 22 ft. lbs. (29 Nm). Make a second pass, tightening the long bolts to 78 ft. lbs. (106 Nm) and the short bolts to 66 ft. lbs. (90 Nm).

25. Install the pushrods and rocker arms, then install the rocker arm (valve) cover.

26. Install the alternator brace, connect the wires, then install the alternator.

27. Attach the fuel lines.

28. Install the power steering pump.

29. Install the serpentine belt.

30. Fasten the upper radiator hose at the thermostat.

31. Connect the wires as tagged during removal.

32. Attach the accelerator linkage at the throttle body.

33. Connect the vacuum lines at the intake manifold and thermostat.

34. Raise and safely support the vehicle.

35. Connect the heater hose to the intake manifold.

36. Install the accelerator and T.V. cable bracket.

37. Fasten the exhaust pipe, then carefully lower the vehicle.

38. Install the TBI cover.

39. Properly fill the cooling system, then connect the negative battery cable. Start the engine and check for leaks.

1992–94 VEHICLES

▶ See Figure 65

➡The engine must be cold before removing the cylinder head. Always release the fuel pressure before starting repair.

1. Properly relieve the fuel system pressure.

2. Disconnect the negative battery cable.

1 LONG BOLTS
2 SHORT BOLTS
3 STUD
4 NUMBERS ON GASKET INDICATE TORQUE SEQUENCE

CYLINDER HEAD BOLT TORQUE PROCEDURE
1 TIGHTEN BOLTS IN SEQUENCE (ITEM 4) TO:
  LONG BOLTS: 63 N·m (46 LBS. FT.)
  SHORT BOLTS: 58 N·m (43 LBS. FT.)
2 TIGHTEN ALL BOLTS AN ADDITIONAL ANGLE OF 90° IN SEQUENCE (ITEM 4) USING J 36660 OR EQUIVALENT

87953075

Fig. 65 Cylinder head bolt torque sequence for 1992–94 2.2L engines

3. Drain the cooling system into an approved container.

4. Label and disconnect the vacuum lines.

5. Tag and detach the following electrical connections:
- Idle Air Control (IAC) valve
- Throttle Position (TP) sensor
- Manifold Absolute Pressure (MAP) sensor
- EVAP emission solenoid
- Fuel injector harness
- Exhaust Gas Recirculation (EGR) valve

6. Disconnect the accelerator linkage, T.V. cable, cruise control cable (if equipped), and the splash shield at the throttle body.

7. Remove the coolant reservoir (overflow or surge tank).

8. Remove the serpentine belt.

9. Unfasten the alternator rear brace, then remove the alternator.

10. Disconnect the power steering lines, then remove the pump.

11. Remove the serpentine drive belt tensioner.

12. Tag and disconnect the spark plug wires from the plugs.

13. Detach the EVAP canister purge line from beneath the manifold.

14. Disconnect the upper radiator hose from the thermostat.

15. Unfasten the throttle body cables from the bracket.

16. Remove the transaxle fill tube and level indicator.

17. Disconnect the coolant inlet hose on the cylinder head.

18. Detach and plug the fuel lines.

19. Disconnect the heater hose from the cylinder head.

20. Remove the intake manifold brace (located on the power steering bracket).

21. Remove the rocker arm (valve) cover. Remove the rocker arms and pushrods keeping all parts in order for correct installation.

22. Remove the spark plug wire bracket and the engine lift bracket.

23. Raise and safely support the vehicle.

24. Disconnect the exhaust pipe from the manifold. You may have to remove the oil filter to access, so don't forget to drain the crankcase first!

25. Carefully lower the vehicle.

26. Unfasten the cylinder head bolts, then remove the head.

To install:

27. The gasket surfaces on both the head and the block must be clean of any foreign matter and free of any nicks or heavy scratches. Bolt threads in the block and the bolts must be clean.

28. Place a new cylinder head gasket in position over the dowel pins on the block. Carefully guide the cylinder head into position. Install the cylinder head bolts finger tight.

29. Tighten the bolts, in the sequence shown in the accompanying figure, as follows:
  a. Long bolts: tighten to 46 ft. lbs. (63 Nm).
  b. Short bolts: tighten to 43 ft. lbs. (58 Nm).
  c. Tighten all bolts, in sequence, an additional angle of 90° using tool J 36660 or equivalent.

30. Install the engine lift bracket and the spark plug wire bracket.

31. Install the pushrods and rocker arms, then install the rocker arm (valve) covers.

32. Fasten the intake manifold brace to the power steering bracket.

33. Unplug, then connect the fuel lines.

34. Connect the coolant inlet hose onto the cylinder head.

35. Attach the upper radiator hose to the thermostat housing.

36. Connect the EVAP emission canister purge line under the manifold.

37. Attach the throttle body cables and bracket.

38. Install the transaxle level indicator and fill tube, secure with the retaining bolt.

39. Connect the spark plug wires, as tagged during removal.

40. Install the serpentine drive belt tensioner.

41. Install the power steering pump, then connect the fluid lines.

42. Install the alternator and rear brace.

43. Fasten the serpentine drive belt.

44. Install the coolant recovery reservoir (overflow or surge tank).

45. Route and connect the vacuum lines, as tagged during removal.

46. Attach the following electrical connectors:
- Idle Air Control (IAC) valve
- Throttle Position (TP) sensor
- Manifold Absolute Pressure (MAP) sensor
- EVAP emission solenoid
- Fuel injector harness
- Exhaust Gas Recirculation (EGR) valve

47. Install the air cleaner assembly.
48. Raise and safely support the vehicle.
49. Attach the exhaust pipe at the manifold. If necessary, install an oil filter.
50. Connect the heater hose to the cylinder head.
51. Carefully lower the vehicle.
52. Refill the crankcase and the coolant.
53. Connect the negative battery cable, then bleed the power steering system. For details, please refer to Section 8 of this manual.
54. Start the engine and check for leaks.

1.8L and 2.0L OHC Engines

▶ See Figures 66 thru 76

1. Properly relieve the fuel system pressure.
2. Disconnect the negative battery cable.
3. Remove air cleaner or induction tube (turbo engines).
4. Drain cooling system.

5. Remove alternator and pivot bracket at camshaft carrier housing.
6. Remove power steering pump and bracket, then position aside.
7. Detach ignition coil electrical connections and remove coil.
8. Tag and disconnect spark plug wires and distributor cap and remove.
9. Remove throttle cable from bracket at intake manifold.
10. Disconnect throttle cable, downshift cable and T.V. cable from the throttle body assembly.
11. Detach the ECM connectors from throttle body assembly.
12. Remove vacuum brake hose at filter.
13. Disconnect inlet and return fuel lines at flex joints.

❋❋ CAUTION

The fuel lines are pressurized. Removal may cause fuel spray resulting in personal injury. Do not remove before bleeding the pressure from the fuel system. See Section 1 for the procedure.

Fig. 66 Remove the alternator and bracket from the camshaft carrier housing

Fig. 67 Unfasten the camshaft carrier/cylinder head bolt in sequence

Fig. 68 Camshaft carrier and cylinder head bolt loosening sequence—1.8L and 2.0L OHC engines

Fig. 69 Remove the retaining bolts, then . . .

Fig. 70 Remove the camshaft carrier/cylinder head, intake manifold and exhaust manifold as an assembly

Fig. 71 Remove and discard the cylinder head gasket

Fig. 72 Carefully use a suitable scraper to clean the gasket mating surfaces

Fig. 73 Apply a continuous bead of sealant to the camshaft carrier mating surface

Fig. 74 Tighten the cylinder head/camshaft carrier retaining bolts in sequence and to the proper torque specifications to avoid leakage, or other engine damage

Fig. 75 Camshaft carrier and cylinder head bolts tightening sequence—1.8L and 2.0L OHC engines

Fig. 76 Tighten all bolts an additional 60°, three times (in sequence)

14. Remove water pump bypass hose at intake manifold and water pump.
15. Disconnect ECM harness connectors at intake manifold.
16. Detach the heater hose from intake manifold.
17. Disconnect exhaust pipe at exhaust manifold. On turbo engines, disconnect the exhaust manifold at the turbo connection.
18. Disconnect breather hose at camshaft carrier.
19. Remove upper radiator hose.
20. Disconnect engine electrical harness and wires from thermostat housing.
21. Remove timing cover.
22. Remove timing probe holder.
23. Loosen water pump retaining bolts and remove timing belt.
24. Loosen camshaft carrier and cylinder head attaching bolts a little at a time, in the sequence shown in the accompanying figure.

➡**Camshaft carrier and cylinder head bolts should only be removed when engine is cold.**

25. Remove camshaft carrier assembly.
26. Remove cylinder head, intake manifold and exhaust manifold as an assembly. Remove and discard the gasket.
27. The gasket surfaces on both the head and the block must be clean of any foreign matter and free of any nicks or heavy scratches. Bolt threads in the block and the bolts must be clean.
To install:
28. Install a new cylinder head gasket in position on the block.
29. Apply a continuous bead of sealer to the cam carrier.
30. Install the cylinder head, reassembled with the intake and exhaust manifolds, if removed.
31. Position the camshaft carrier on the cylinder head and tighten the bolts, in the sequence in the accompanying figure, to the correct torque.
  a. Tighten all bolts in sequence to 18 ft. lbs. (25 Nm).
  b. Tighten all bolts an additional 180° in 3 steps of 60° each.
32. Install timing belt.
33. Install timing probe holder.

34. Install timing cover.
35. Connect engine electrical harness and wires at thermostat housing.
36. Install upper radiator hose.
37. Connect breather hose at camshaft carrier.
38. Connect exhaust pipe at exhaust manifold. On turbo engines, connect the exhaust manifold at the turbo connection.
39. Connect heater hose at intake manifold.
40. Attach the ECM harness connectors at intake manifold.
41. Install water pump bypass hose at intake manifold and water pump.
42. Connect inlet and return fuel lines at flex joints.
43. Install vacuum brake hose at filter.
44. Attach the ECM connectors at throttle body assembly.
45. Connect throttle cable, downshift cable and T.V. cable at throttle body assembly.
46. Install throttle cable at bracket on intake manifold.
47. Connect the spark plug wires as tagged during removal, then install the distributor cap.
48. Attach the ignition coil electrical connections, then install the coil.
49. Install power steering pump and bracket.
50. Install alternator and pivot bracket on camshaft carrier housing.
51. Fill cooling system.
52. Install air cleaner or induction tube (turbo engines).

2.8L and 3.1L Engines

1985–86 VEHICLES (LEFT SIDE)

▶ **See Figure 77**

1. Disconnect the negative battery cable.
2. Raise and safely support the vehicle.
3. Properly drain the cooling system, then carefully lower the vehicle.
4. Remove the intake and exhaust manifolds. For details, please refer to the procedures located earlier in this section.
5. Remove the oil level indicator tube.
6. Disconnect the wiring harness at the left head.
7. Remove the alternator bracket.
8. Loosen the rocker arm bolts until you are able to remove the pushrods, then remove the pushrods.
9. Unfasten the cylinder head retaining bolts, then remove the cylinder head.
To install:
10. Clean all gasket surfaces on the cylinder head, block and intake manifold and clean the bolt threads and bolts.
11. Place a new head gasket in position over the dowel pins with the words "This Side Up" facing upward.
12. Coat the cylinder head bolts with sealer and tighten them to 77 ft. lbs. (104 Nm) in the sequence shown in the accompany figure.

Fig. 77 Cylinder head bolt tightening sequence—1985–86 2.8L engines

13. Install the pushrods, making sure the lower ends are in the lifter seats, and loosely retain with the rocker arms.
14. Install the intake manifold and gaskets.
15. Install the exhaust manifold.
16. Attach the wiring harness.
17. Install the oil level indicator.
18. Install the alternator bracket.
19. Fill the cooling system.
20. Adjust the drive belt and the valve lash.
21. Connect the negative battery cable, then start the engine and check for leaks.

1985-86 VEHICLES (RIGHT SIDE)

▸ See Figure 77

1. Disconnect the negative battery cable.
2. Raise and safely support the vehicle.
3. Drain the cooling system, then lower the vehicle.
4. If equipped, remove the cruise control servo bracket.
5. Remove the intake and exhaust manifolds. For details, please refer to the procedure earlier in this section.
6. Tag and disconnect the spark plug wires, then remove the plugs.
7. Loosen the rocker arm bolts and remove the pushrods.
8. Unfasten the cylinder head bolts, then remove the cylinder head.

To install:

9. Clean all gasket surfaces on the cylinder head, block and intake manifold and clean the bolt threads and bolts.
10. Place a new head gasket in position over the dowel pins with the words "This Side Up" facing upward. Position the cylinder head.
11. Coat the cylinder head bolts with sealer, then tighten to 77 ft. lbs. (104 Nm), in the sequence shown in the accompanying figure.
12. Install the pushrods in the lifter seats and loosely retain with the rocker arms.
13. Install the intake manifold and gaskets.
14. If equipped, install the cruise control servo bracket.
15. Install the spark plugs, then connect the wires as tagged during removal.
16. Install the exhaust manifold.
17. Fill the cooling system.
18. Connect the negative battery cable, then start the vehicle and check for leaks.

1987-93 VEHICLES (LEFT SIDE)

▸ See Figure 78

1. Relieve the fuel system pressure and disconnect the negative battery cable.
2. Properly drain the cooling system.
3. Remove the rocker arm (valve) cover.

1 COAT THREADS WITH SEALER
  TIGHTEN IN PROPER SEQUENCE
  TO 45 N·m (33 LBS. FT.). TURN
  AN ADDITIONAL 90° WITH J 36660
2 CYLINDER HEAD
3 GASKET
4 CYLINDER BLOCK

TIGHTENING SEQUENCE

87953077

Fig. 78 Cylinder head bolt tightening sequence—1987–94 2.8L and 3.1L engines

4. Remove the intake manifold as outlined earlier in this section.
5. Disconnect the exhaust crossover at the right exhaust manifold.
6. Remove the oil level indicator tube bracket.
7. Loosen the rocker arms nuts enough to remove the pushrods, then remove the pushrods.
8. Starting with the outer bolts, remove the cylinder head bolts. Remove the cylinder head with the exhaust manifold.
9. Clean and inspect the surfaces of the cylinder head, block and intake manifold. Clean the threads in the block and the threads on the bolts.

To install:

10. Align the new gasket over the dowels on the block with the note "This Side Up" facing the cylinder head.
11. Position the cylinder head and exhaust manifold crossover assembly on the engine.
12. Coat the cylinder head bolts with a proper sealer and install the bolts hand tight.
13. Tighten the bolts, in the correct sequence, to 33 ft. lbs. (45 Nm), then rotate an additional 90° (¼ turn).
14. Install the pushrods in the same order they were removed.

➡ Intake pushrods are marked orange and are 6 in. (152.4mm) long. Exhaust pushrods are marked blue and are 6⅜ in. (161.9mm) long.

15. Install the rocker arms. The correct rocker arm torque is 14–20 ft. lbs. (19–27 Nm).
16. Install the intake manifold using a new gasket and following the correct sequence, tighten the bolts to the correct specification.
17. The remainder of the installation is the reverse of the removal.

1987-93 VEHICLES (RIGHT SIDE)

▸ See Figure 78

1. Disconnect the negative battery cable. Drain the cooling system.
2. Raise and safely support the vehicle.
3. Disconnect the exhaust manifold from the exhaust pipe.
4. Carefully lower the vehicle. Disconnect the exhaust manifold from the cylinder head and remove the manifold.
5. Remove the rocker cover, then remove the intake manifold. For details, please refer to the procedure located in this section.
6. Loosen the rocker arms enough so the pushrods can be removed. Note the position of the pushrods for assembly.
7. Starting with the outer bolts, unfasten the cylinder head bolts and remove the cylinder head.
8. Clean and inspect the surfaces of the cylinder head, engine block and intake manifold. Clean the threads in the engine block and the threads on the cylinder head bolts.

To install:

9. Align the new gasket on the dowels on the engine block with the note "This Side Up" facing the cylinder head.
10. Position the cylinder head on the engine. Coat the head bolts with a proper sealer. Install and tighten the bolts hand tight.
11. Tighten the bolts, in sequence, to 33 ft. lbs. (45 Nm), then rotate an additional 90° (¼ turn).
12. Install the pushrods in the same order as they were removed.

➡ Intake pushrods are marked orange and are 6 in. (152.4mm) long. Exhaust pushrods are marked blue and are 6⅜ in. (161.9mm) long.

13. Install the rocker arms. The correct rocker arm torque is 14–20 ft. lbs. (1987–88), 18 ft. lbs. (1989–92).
14. Install the intake manifold using a new gasket. Following the correct sequence, torque the bolts to the proper specification.
15. The remainder of the installation is the reverse of the removal.
16. Connect the negative battery cable, then start the engine and check for leaks.

1994 VEHICLES (LEFT SIDE)

▸ See Figure 78

➡ On these 3.1L engines, an "Idle Learn" procedure must be performed which requires the use of a scan tool.

1. Disconnect the negative battery cable.
2. Remove the battery and the air cleaner assembly.

3. Properly drain and recover the cooling system.
4. Detach the O_2 sensor connector.
5. Disconnect the exhaust crossover pipe from the exhaust manifold.
6. Remove the rocker arm covers, as outlined earlier in this section.
7. Remove the intake manifold and plenum.
8. Remove the exhaust crossover, then remove the left exhaust manifold.
9. Remove the oil level indicator.
10. Tag and disconnect the spark plug wires at the left cylinder head.
11. Loosen the rocker arms nuts enough to remove the pushrods, then remove the pushrods.

➡ **Intake pushrods are marked orange and are 6 in. (152.4mm) long. Exhaust pushrods are marked blue and are 6⅜ in. (161.9mm) long.**

12. Starting with the outer bolts, unfasten the cylinder head bolts and remove the cylinder head.
13. Clean and inspect the surfaces of the cylinder head, engine block and intake manifold. Clean the threads in the engine block and the threads on the cylinder head bolts.

To install:

14. Align the new gasket on the dowels on the engine block with the note "This Side Up" facing the cylinder head.
15. Position the cylinder head on the engine. Coat the head bolts with a proper sealer. Install and tighten the bolts hand tight.
16. Tighten the bolts, in sequence, to 33 ft. lbs. (45 Nm), then rotate an additional 90° (¼ turn).
17. Install the pushrods in the same order as they were removed. Make sure they seat properly in the lifters. Tighten the rocker arm nuts.

➡ **Intake pushrods are marked orange and are 6 in. (152.4mm) long. Exhaust pushrods are marked blue and are 6⅜ in. (161.9mm) long.**

18. Install the intake manifold and plenum.
19. Install the rocker arm covers.
20. Install the oil level indicator.
21. Install the left exhaust manifold.
22. Attach the O_2 sensor connector.
23. Connect the exhaust crossover pipe to the exhaust manifolds.
24. Install the battery and air cleaner assembly.
25. Fill the cooling system, then connect the negative battery cable.

➡ **On the 3.1L engine, a Tech 1® scan tool is needed to perform the "Idle Learn" procedure.**

26. For the 3.1L engine perform the following "Idle Learn" procedure;
   a. Install a Tech 1® scan tool.
   b. Turn the ignition to the **ON** position, engine not running.
   c. Select **IAC SYSTEM**, then **IDLE LEARN** in the **MISC TEST** mode.
   d. Place the transaxle in park or neutral, as applicable.
   e. Proceed with idle learn as directed by the scan tool.
27. Start the engine and check for leaks.

1994 VEHICLES (RIGHT SIDE)

♦ **See Figure 78**

➡ **On these 3.1L engines, an "Idle Learn" procedure must be performed which requires the use of a scan tool.**

1. Disconnect the negative battery cable.
2. Remove the air cleaner assembly.
3. Properly drain and recover the cooling system.
4. Detach the O_2 sensor connector.
5. Disconnect the exhaust crossover pipe from the exhaust manifold.
6. Remove the right exhaust manifold.
7. Remove the rocker arm covers, as outlined earlier in this section.
8. Remove the intake manifold and plenum.
9. Loosen the rocker arms nuts enough to remove the pushrods, then remove the pushrods.

➡ **Intake pushrods are marked orange and are 6 in. (152.4mm) long. Exhaust pushrods are marked blue and are 6⅜ in. (161.9mm) long.**

10. Starting with the outer bolts, unfasten the cylinder head bolts and remove the cylinder head.
11. Clean and inspect the surfaces of the cylinder head, engine block and

intake manifold. Clean the threads in the engine block and the threads on the cylinder head bolts.

To install:

12. Align the new gasket on the dowels on the engine block with the note "This Side Up" facing the cylinder head.
13. Position the cylinder head on the engine. Coat the head bolts with a proper sealer. Install and tighten the bolts hand tight.
14. Tighten the bolts, in sequence, to 33 ft. lbs. (45 Nm), then rotate an additional 90° (¼ turn).
15. Install the pushrods in the same order as they were removed. Make sure they seat properly in the lifters. Tighten the rocker arm nuts.

➡ **Intake pushrods are marked orange and are 6 in. (152.4mm) long. Exhaust pushrods are marked blue and are 6⅜ in. (161.9mm) long.**

16. Install the intake manifold and plenum.
17. Install the rocker arm covers.
18. Install the right exhaust manifold.
19. Attach the O_2 sensor connector.
20. Connect the exhaust crossover pipe to the exhaust manifolds.
21. Install the air cleaner assembly.
22. Fill the cooling system, then connect the negative battery cable.

➡ **On the 3.1L engine, a Tech 1® scan tool is needed to perform the "Idle Learn" procedure.**

23. For the 3.1L engine perform the following "Idle Learn" procedure;
   a. Install a Tech 1® scan tool.
   b. Turn the ignition to the **ON** position, engine not running.
   c. Select **IAC SYSTEM**, then **IDLE LEARN** in the **MISC TEST** mode.
   d. Place the transaxle in park or neutral, as applicable.
   e. Proceed with idle learn as directed by the scan tool.
24. Start the engine and check for leaks.

Oil Pan

✳✳ CAUTION

The EPA warns that prolonged contact with used engine oil may cause a number of skin disorders, including cancer! You should make every effort to minimize your exposure to used engine oil. Protective gloves should be worn when changing the oil. Wash your hands and any other exposed skin areas as soon as possible after exposure to used engine oil. Soap and water, or waterless hand cleaner should be used.

REMOVAL & INSTALLATION

1.8L, 2.0L and 2.2L OHV Engines

♦ **See Figure 79**

1. Disconnect the negative battery cable.
2. Drain the crankcase. Raise and support the front of the vehicle.
3. On 1982–86 models, remove the air conditioning brace at the starter and air conditioning bracket.
4. Unfasten the exhaust shield and disconnect the exhaust pipe at the manifold.
5. Remove the starter motor and position it out of the way.
6. Remove the flywheel cover.
7. On 1982–90 models, remove the 4 right support bolts. Lower the support slightly to gain clearance for oil pan removal.
8. On cars equipped with automatic transmission, remove the oil filter and extension.
9. Unfasten the oil pan bolts and remove the oil pan.

To install:

10. Prior to oil pan installation, check that the sealing surfaces on the pan, cylinder block and front cover are clean and free of oil. If installing the old pan, be sure that all old RTV has been removed.
11. Apply a ⅛ in. (3mm) bead of RTV sealant to the oil pan sealing surface. Use a new oil pan rear seal and apply a thin coat of RTV sealant to the ends of the gasket down to the ears and install the pan in place.

1 SEAL
2 BOLT, 10 N•m (89 LB. IN.)
3 OIL PAN
4 NUT, OIL PAN 10 N•m (89 LB. IN.)

87953089

VIEW A

Fig. 79 Oil pan installation—1995 2.2L OHV engine shown

12. On 1982–86 models, tighten the front bolts to 7–13 ft. lbs., the rear bolts to 11–18 ft. lbs., the stud to 5–7 ft. lbs., and all others to 4–9 ft. lbs. (5–12 Nm). On 1987–92 models tighten the bolts to 77 inch lbs. (8.6 Nm). On 1993–96 vehicles, tighten the bolts to 89 inch lbs. (10 Nm).

13. On cars equipped with an automatic transaxle, replace the oil filter adapter seal and replace the oil filter adapter.

14. Install the remaining components in the reverse order of removal.

1.8L and 2.0L OHC Engines

▶ **See Figures 80 thru 87**

1. Raise and support the car safely.
2. Remove right front wheel and tire assembly.
3. Remove right hand splash shield.
4. Position jackstands at jacking points.
5. Drain engine oil.
6. If necessary on some models, remove lower air conditioning bracket strut rod attachment bolt and swing aside.
7. Remove exhaust pipe-to-manifold attachment bolts. On turbo models, disconnect the exhaust pipe at the wastegate. Position the pipe out of the way.
8. Remove the flywheel dust cover by unfastening the four retaining bolts.
9. Unfasten the oil pan bolts, then remove the pan and scraper.

To install:

10. Clean the sealing surfaces, install the oil pan with a new gasket and apply RTV as shown in the illustration. Install the bolts to the oil pan with Loctite® on the threads. Tighten the pan bolts to 4 ft. lbs. (5 Nm).

11. Installation of the remaining components is the reverse of the removal procedure.

2.8L and 3.1L Engines

1985–88 VEHICLES

▶ **See Figure 88**

1. Disconnect the battery ground.
2. Raise and support the car on jackstands.
3. Drain the oil.

❊❊ CAUTION

The EPA warns that prolonged contact with used engine oil may cause a number of skin disorders, including cancer! You should

87953222

Fig. 80 Unfasten the exhaust pipe-to-manifold retaining bolts, then . . .

87953223

Fig. 81 Detach the exhaust pipe and position it out of the way

87953224

Fig. 82 Unfasten the flywheel dust cover retaining bolts, then . . .

87953225

Fig. 83 . . . remove the flywheel dust cover

87953226

Fig. 84 Unfasten the oil pan retaining bolts

87953227

Fig. 85 Carefully lower the oil pan

Fig. 86 Remove the oil pan assembly

Fig. 87 Clean the oil pan gasket mating surfaces

1 20-30 N·m (15-22 FT. LBS.)
ALL 8-12 N·m (6-9 FT. LBS.)

87953093

Fig. 88 Installing the oil pan—1988 2.8L engine shown

make every effort to minimize your exposure to used engine oil. Protective gloves should be worn when changing the oil. Wash your hands and any other exposed skin areas as soon as possible after exposure to used engine oil. Soap and water, or waterless hand cleaner should be used.

4. Remove the bellhousing cover.
5. Remove the starter.
6. Remove the oil pan bolts and remove the oil pan.

To install:

7. Installation is the reverse of removal. On 1985–86 models, the pan is installed using RTV gasket material in place of a gasket. Make sure that the sealing surfaces are free of old RTV material. Use a ⅛ in. (3mm) bead of RTV material on the pan sealing flange. On 1987–88 models the pan is installed using a gasket. Torque the M8 x 1.25 x 14.0 pan bolts to 15–30 ft. lbs. (20–41 Nm) and the M6 x 1 x 16.0 pan bolts to 6–15 ft. lbs. (8–20 Nm).

1989–94 VEHICLES

▶ See Figure 89

1. Disconnect the negative battery cable.
2. Remove the serpentine belt and the tensioner.
3. Support the engine with tool J–28467 or equivalent.
4. Raise and safely support the vehicle. Drain the engine oil.
5. Remove the starter shield and the flywheel cover. Remove the starter.
6. Remove the engine to frame mount retaining nuts.
7. Lower the vehicle.
8. Support the engine using tool J–28467–A or equivalent, then raise and support the vehicle safely.
9. Remove the right tire and wheel assembly. Remove the right inner fender splash shield.
10. Unfasten the oil pan retaining bolts and nuts and remove the oil pan.

To install:

11. Clean the gasket mating surfaces.
12. Install a new gasket on the oil pan. Apply silicon sealer to the portion of the pan that contacts the rear of the block.
13. Install the oil pan retaining nuts. Tighten the nuts to 71–89 inch lbs. (8–10 Nm).
14. Install the oil pan retaining bolts. Tighten the rear bolts to 18 ft. lbs. (25 Nm) and the remaining bolts to 71–89 inch lbs. (8–10 Nm).
15. Install the right inner fender splash shield.
16. Lower the vehicle and remove the engine support tool.
17. Raise and support the vehicle safely.
18. Install the engine to frame mounting nuts.
19. Install the starter and splash shield. Install the flywheel shield.
20. Lower the vehicle and fill the crankcase with oil, install the belt tensioner and belt and connect the negative battery cable. Run the engine to normal operating temperature and check for leaks.

1 8 Nm (71 lbs. in.) nut
2 8 Nm (71 lbs. in.) bolt
3 Oil pan
4 25 Nm (18 lbs. ft.) bolt
5 Apply sealer

87953094

Fig. 89 Installing the oil pan—1994 3.1L engines

Oil Pump

REMOVAL & INSTALLATION

1.8L, 2.0L and 2.2L OHV Engines

▶ **See Figure 90**

1. Disconnect the negative battery cable.
2. As outlined earlier, remove the engine oil pan.
3. Unfasten the pump to rear bearing cap bolt and remove the pump and extension shaft.
4. Remove the extension shaft and retainer.

To install:

5. Heat the retainer in hot water prior to assembling the extension shaft.
6. Install the extension to the oil pump, being careful not to crack the retainer.
7. Fasten pump to rear bearing cap bolt and torque is 26–38 ft. lbs. (35–51 Nm).
8. Install the oil pan.
9. Connect the negative battery cable.

Fig. 91 View of the oil pick-up tube and screen, after the pan is removed

1 BOLT, 43 N•m (32 LBS. FT.)
2 PUMP ASSEMBLY, OIL
3 RETAINER, OIL PUMP SHAFT
   THE RETAINER MUST BE HEATED AND SOAKED
   IN WATER PRIOR TO INSTALLATION. THE
   RETAINER MUST NOT HAVE ANY SPLITS IN IT
   AFTER INSTALLATION.
4 SHAFT, OIL PUMP DRIVE

Fig. 90 Oil pump mounting—1995 2.2L OHV engine shown

Fig. 92 Remove the oil pick-up tube, then . . .

1.8L and 2.0L OHC Engines

▶ **See Figures 91, 92, 93 and 94**

1. Remove the crankshaft sprocket.
2. Remove the timing belt rear covers.
3. Disconnect the oil pressure switch wires.
4. Remove the oil pan.
5. Remove the oil filter.
6. Unbolt and remove the oil pick-up tube and screen.
7. Unbolt and remove the oil pump.
8. On the 2.0L engine, pry out the front oil seal.

To install:

9. Installation is the reverse of removal. Use new gaskets in all instances. On the 2.0L engine, install a new front seal using tool J33083 Seal Installer. Tighten the oil pump bolts to 60 inch lbs. (6.7 Nm). Install the bolts to the oil pan with Loctite® on the threads. Tighten the pan bolts to 48 inch lbs. (5.4 Nm), and the oil pickup tube bolts to 60 inch lbs. (6.7 Nm).

Fig. 93 . . . remove the screen assembly

Fig. 94 Exploded view of the oil pump—
1989 2.0L engine shown

Fig. 95 Oil pump and drive assembly—
1994 3.1L engine shown

Fig. 96 Timing belt cover mounting—1.8L
OHC engines

2.8L and 3.1L Engines

▶ See Figure 95

1. Disconnect the negative battery cable. Drain the engine oil.
2. Remove the oil pan as described earlier.
3. Unbolt and remove the oil pump and pickup/drive shaft extension.

To install:

4. Position the oil pump and drive shaft extension. Engage the drive shaft extension into the drive gear.
5. Install the pump-to-rear bearing cap bolt. Tighten to 30 ft. lbs. (41 Nm).
6. Install the oil pan. Fill the crankcase with oil.
7. Connect the negative battery cable.

Timing Belt Cover

REMOVAL & INSTALLATION

1.8L OHC Engines

▶ See Figure 96

1. Disconnect the negative battery cable.
2. Unfasten the alternator pivot bolts.
3. Remove the power steering belt.
4. Unfasten the two upper timing belt cover bolts.
5. Disconnect the canister purge hose.
6. Raise the car and support it safely.
7. Remove the right front wheel and the splash shield.
8. Unfasten the two lower timing cover bolts.
9. Carefully lower the car, then remove the timing belt cover.
10. Reverse the above procedure to install.

2.0L OHC Engines

▶ See Figures 97, 98 and 99

1. Disconnect the negative battery cable.
2. Remove the serpentine belt. Unfasten the belt tensioner bolt, the tensioner arm will swing down, then remove the tensioner.
3. Either unsnap (upper first) or unfasten the cover bolts and nuts, then remove the cover.

To install:

4. Install the cover by snapping it in place, or secure with the retaining bolts and nut. Tighten to 89 inch lbs. (10 Nm).
5. Place the serpentine belt tensioner into position, then tighten the retaining bolt to 40 ft. lbs. (54 Nm). Install the serpentine belt.
6. Connect the negative battery cable.

Fig. 97 On vehicles through 1988, unsnap the top then the bottom of the timing belt cover, then . . .

Fig. 98 . . . remove the timing belt cover—1988 2.0L (VIN K) Sunbird shown

1. GROMMET
2. SLEEVE
3. BOLT 10 N·m (89 LB.IN.)
4. CAMSHAFT SPROCKET
5. WASHER
6. BOLT 45 N·m (33 LB.FT.)
7. TIMING BELT
8. FRONT COVER
9. BOLT 9 N·m (80 LB.IN.)

10. BOLT 155 N·m (114 LB.FT.)
11. WASHER
12. CRANKSHAFT SPROCKET
13. WASHER
14. REAR COVER
15. KEYWAY

16. STUD 48 N·m (35 LB.FT.)
17. BOLT 48 N·m (35 LB.FT.)
18. TENSIONER
19. ENGINE
20. CAMSHAFT

87953100

Fig. 99 Exploded view of the timing belt cover and related components—1989 2.0L OHC engine shown

Timing Chain Front Cover

REMOVAL & INSTALLATION

1.8L, 2.0L and 2.2L OHV Engines

▶ See Figure 100

➡ The following procedure requires the use of a special tool.

1. Remove the engine drive belts (1982–86 vehicles) or the serpentine belt and tensioner (1987–94 vehicles).

➡ Although not absolutely necessary, removal of the right front inner fender splash shield will facilitate access to the front cover.

2. Install engine support fixture J 28467-A, or equivalent.
3. Remove the engine mount assembly.
4. Remove the alternator rear brace, then remove the alternator.
5. Remove the power steering pump, then position it aside with the lines still attached.
6. Raise and safely support the vehicle.
7. Remove the oil pan.
8. Unscrew the center bolt from the crankshaft pulley and slide the pulley and hub from the crankshaft.

1 Bolt
2 Washer
3 Crankshaft pulley
4 Crankshaft pulley hub
5 Keyway

87953101

Fig. 100 Removing the timing chain front cover—2.2L engine shown

9. Unfasten the front cover-to-block bolts and then remove the front cover. If the front cover is difficult to remove, use a plastic mallet to carefully loosen the cover.

To install:

10. The surfaces of the block and front cover must be clean and free of oil. On 1982–86 models, apply a ⅛ in. (3mm) wide bead of RTV sealant to the cover. The sealant must be wet to the touch when the bolts are torqued down. On 1987–94 models a gasket is used. Torque the bolts to 6–9 ft. lbs. (8–12 Nm).

➡ When applying RTV sealant to the front cover, be sure to keep it out of the bolt holes.

11. Position the front cover on the block using a centering tool (J-23042) and tighten the screws.
12. Installation of the remaining components is in the reverse order of removal.

2.8L and 3.1L Engines

▶ See Figures 101 and 102

1. Disconnect the battery ground cable.
2. Drain the cooling system.
3. On 1985–86 models, disconnect the MAP sensor and the EGR solenoid.
4. On 1985–86 models, remove the coolant recovery tank.
5. Remove the serpentine belt adjustment pulley.
6. Remove the alternator and disconnect the electrical wires.
7. Remove the power steering pump bracket.
8. Disconnect the heater pipe at the power steering bracket.
9. Jack up the car and support it safely.
10. Remove the inner splash shield.
11. Remove the air conditioning compressor belt.
12. Remove the flywheel cover at the transaxle.
13. Remove the harmonic balancer with tool J-23523-1 or equivalent.

➡ The outer ring (weight) of the harmonic balancer is bonded to the hub with rubber. Breakage may occur if the balancer is hammered back onto the crankshaft. A press or special installation tool is necessary.

14. Remove the serpentine belt idler pulley.
15. Unfasten the pan-to-front cover bolts and remove the lower cover bolts.

1 FRONT COVER
2 GASKET
3 27 N·m (20 LB. FT.)
4 38 N·m (28 LB. FT.)
5 SEALER

87953104

Fig. 101 Timing chain front cover assembly mounting—1985–92 vehicles

1 FRONT COVER
2 STUD – 6 N·m (53 LBS. IN.)
3 GASKET
4 BOLT – 21 N·m (15 LBS. FT.)
5 BOLT – 45 N·m (35 LBS. FT.)
6 SEALER

87953105

Fig. 102 Timing chain front cover mounting and tightening specifications—1993–94 3.1L engines

16. Carefully lower the vehicle.

17. Disconnect the radiator hose at the water pump.

18. Remove the heater pipe at the goose neck.

19. Detach the bypass and overflow hoses.

20. Disconnect the canister purge hose.

21. Unfasten the upper front cover bolts and remove the front cover.

To install:

22. Clean all the gasket mounting surfaces on the front cover and block and place a new gasket to the front cover sealing surface. Apply a continuous ⅛ in. (3mm) wide bead of sealer (1052357 or equivalent) to the oil pan sealing surface of the front cover.

23. Place the front cover on the engine and install the upper front cover bolts.

24. Raise the vehicle and support it safely.

25. Install the lower cover bolts.

26. Install the oil pan to cover screws.

27. Install the serpentine belt idler pulley.

28. Install the harmonic balancer. (See the Harmonic Balancer Removal and Installation procedure.)

29. Install the flywheel cover on the transaxle.

30. Install the air conditioning compressor belt.

31. Install the inner splash shield.

32. Lower the vehicle and install the remainder of the parts in the reverse order of removal.

Timing Chain Cover Oil Seal

REPLACEMENT

1.8L, 2.0L, 2.8L and 3.1L OHV Engines

The oil seal can be replaced with the cover either on or off the engine. If the cover is on the engine, remove the crankshaft pulley and hub first. Pry out the seal using a suitable prying tool, being careful not to distort the seal mating surface. Install the new seal so that the open side or lip side is towards the engine. Press it into place with a seal driver made for the purpose. General Motors recommends a tool, J-35468 Seal Centering Tool. Install the hub if removed.

Timing Chain and Sprockets

REMOVAL & INSTALLATION

1.8L and 2.0L and 2.2L OHV Engines

▶ See Figures 103 and 104

1. Disconnect the negative battery cable.

2. Remove the front cover as previously detailed.

3. Place the No. 1 piston at TDC of the compression stroke so that the marks on the camshaft and crankshaft sprockets are in alignment (see illustration).

4. Loosen the timing chain tensioner nut as far as possible without actually removing it.

5. Remove the camshaft sprocket bolts and remove the sprocket and chain together. If the sprocket does not slide from the camshaft easily, a light blow with a soft mallet at the lower edge of the sprocket will dislodge it.

6. Use a gear puller (J-2288-8-20) and remove the crankshaft sprocket.

To install:

7. Press the crankshaft sprocket back onto the crankshaft.

8. Install the timing chain over the camshaft sprocket and then around the crankshaft sprocket. Make sure that the marks on the two sprockets are in alignment (see illustration). Lubricate the thrust surface with Molykote® or its equivalent.

9. Align the dowel in the camshaft with the dowel hole in the sprocket and then install the sprocket onto the camshaft. Use the mounting bolts to draw the sprocket onto the camshaft and then tighten to 66–68 ft. lbs.

10. Lubricate the timing chain with clean engine oil. Tighten the chain tensioner.

11. Installation of the remaining components is in the reverse order of removal.

2.8L and 3.1L Engines

▶ See Figures 105 and 106

1. Disconnect the negative battery cable.

2. Remove the front cover, as outlined earlier.

3. Place the No. 1 piston at TDC and the stamped timing marks on both sprockets are closest to one another and in line between the shaft centers (No. 4 firing position).

4. Take out the three bolts that hold the camshaft sprocket to the camshaft. This sprocket is a light press fit on the camshaft and will come off readily. If the sprocket does not come off easily, a light blow on the lower edge of the sprocket with a plastic mallet should dislodge the sprocket. The chain comes off with the camshaft sprocket. A gear puller will be required to remove the crankshaft sprocket.

To install:

5. Without disturbing the position of the engine, mount the new crank sprocket on the shaft, then mount the chain over the camshaft sprocket. Arrange the camshaft sprocket in such a way that the timing marks will line up between the shaft centers and the camshaft locating dowel will enter the dowel hole in the cam sprocket.

6. Place the cam sprocket, with its chain mounted over it, in position on the front of the camshaft and pull up with the three bolts that hold it to the camshaft. Torque the bolts to 18 ft. lbs. (25 Nm).

7. Lubricate the timing chain with oil.

8. After the sprockets are in place, turn the engine two full revolutions to make certain that the timing marks are in correct alignment between the shaft centers.

1 SPROCKET, CAMSHAFT
2 SPROCKET, CRANKSHAFT
3 TENSIONER, TIMING CHAIN
A LINE UP TIMING MARKS ON SPROCKETS WITH THE TABS ON THE TIMING CHAIN TENSIONER
B REMOVE PIN AFTER TIMING CHAIN IS INSTALLED

87953106

Fig. 103 Align the crankshaft sprocket and camshaft sprocket timing marks with the alignment tabs on the timing chain tensioner

A TIMING MARKS
1 BOLT, CAMSHAFT SPROCKET 130 N·m (96 LBS. FT.)
2 SPROCKET, CAMSHAFT
3 SPROCKET, CRANKSHAFT
4 PLATE, CAMSHAFT
5 BOLT, CAMSHAFT PLATE 12 N·m (106 LBS. IN.)
6 CAMSHAFT
7 CHAIN, TIMING
8 BLOCK, CYLINDER

87953107

Fig. 104 Removing the timing chain and sprockets from a 1994 2.2L OHV engine

#1 CYLINDER AT T.D.C.

#4 CYLINDER AT T.D.C.

87953112

Fig. 105 View of the alignment marks with the #1 and #4 cylinders at Top Dead Center (TDC)

Timing Belt

REMOVAL & INSTALLATION

1.8L and 2.0L OHC Engine

1983–88 VEHICLES

▶ See Figures 107 thru 116

➡The following procedure requires the use of a special adjustment tool J33039 and tension gauge J26486–A or their equivalents.

NOTE – ALIGN TIMING MARKS ON CAM AND CRANK SPROCKETS USING ALIGNMENT MARKS ON DAMPER STAMPING OR CAST ALIGNMENT MARKS ON CYL. AND CASE.

ALIGNMENT MARKS

1 TIMING CHAIN
2 CRANK SPROCKET
3 CAMSHAFT SPROCKET
4 DAMPER
5 28 N·m (21 LBS. FT.)
6 21 N·m (15 LBS. FT.)

87953113

Fig. 106 Exploded view of the timing chain and related components—2.8L and 3.1L engines

1. Remove the timing belt front cover, as outlined earlier in this section.
2. Raise and support the vehicle safely.
3. Remove the crankshaft pulley as follows:
   a. Remove the inner fender splash shield,
   b. Unfasten the retaining bolts, the remove the crankshaft pulley.
4. Carefully lower the vehicle until it is just above the floor.
5. If equipped, remove the coolant reservoir.
6. If necessary at this time, remove the lower portion of the timing belt cover.
7. Loosen the water pump retaining bolts and rotate the water pump to loosen the timing belt.
8. Remove the timing belt.

To install:

9. Position the timing belt over the sprockets.
10. Install the crankshaft pulley.
11. Check that the mark on the camshaft sprocket lines up with mark on the camshaft carrier, on the 1.8L engine and the mark on the camshaft sprocket must line up with the mark on the rear timing belt cover on the 2.0L engine. The timing mark on the crankshaft pulley should line up at 10° BTDC on the indicator scale.

✳✳ WARNING

Do not turn the camshaft. Use only the crankshaft nut to turn. Turning the nut on the camshaft directly can damage the camshaft bearings.

12. Rotate the water pump clockwise using Tool J-33039 until all slack is removed from the belt. Slightly tighten the water pump retaining bolts.
13. Install Tool J-26486 between the water pump and camshaft sprockets so that the pointer is midway between the sprockets.
14. If the tension is incorrect, loosen the water pump and rotate it using Tool J-33039 until the proper tension is obtained.
15. Fully tighten the water pump retaining bolts to 18 ft. lbs. (24 Nm), taking care not to further rotate the water pump.

87953236

Fig. 107 Remove the upper part of the timing belt cover by unsnapping it—1988 2.0L (VIN K) Sunbird shown

87953237

Fig. 108 Unfasten the retaining bolts, then . . .

87953238

Fig. 109 . . . remove the crankshaft pulley

87953242

Fig. 110 View of the lower part of the timing belt cover

87953243

Fig. 111 Unsnap the cover to remove it

87953117

Fig. 112 Exploded view of the timing belt and related components—1983–88 1.8L and 2.0L OHC engines

Fig. 113 The mark on the camshaft sprocket must line up with the mark on the rear timing belt cover—1988 2.0L (VIN K) Sunbird shown

Fig. 114 You must modify tool J-33039 to tighten the timing belt

Fig. 115 Adjusting the timing belt tension—1983–88 1.8L and 2.0L OHC engines

Fig. 116 Timing belt adjustment tool J-26486-A, used on the 1983–88 1.8L and 2.0L OHC engines

16. Install the timing probe holder. Tighten the nuts to 19 ft. lbs. (26 Nm).

17. If removed, install the coolant recovery reservoir.

18. Install the timing belt front cover, snap into place ot tighten the attaching bolts to 5 ft. lbs. (7 Nm), depending upon application.

19. Install and adjust the alternator and power steering belt. Refill the cooling system, if necessary.

1989–92 VEHICLES

▶ See Figure 117

1. Disconnect the negative battery cable.

2. Remove the serpentine belt and timing belt cover.

3. Loosen the water pump bolts and release tension with tool J–33039 or equivalent.

4. Raise and support the vehicle safely.

5. Remove the crankshaft pulley.

6. Carefully lower the vehicle, then remove the timing belt.

To install:

7. Turn the crankshaft and the camshaft gears clockwise to align the timing marks on the gears with the timing marks on the rear cover.

8. Install the timing belt, making sure the portion between the camshaft gear and crankcase gear is in tension.

9. Using tool J–33039 or equivalent, turn the water pump eccentric clockwise until the tensioner contacts the high torque stop. Tighten the water pump screws slightly.

10. Turn the engine by the crankshaft gear bolt 720° to fully seat the belt into the gear teeth.

11. Turn the water pump eccentric counterclockwise until the hole in the tensioner arm is aligned with the hole in the base.

1 GROMMET	11 WASHER
2 SLEEVE	12 CRANKSHAFT SPROCKET
3 BOLT; 10 N·M (89 LB–IN)	13 WASHER
4 CAMSHAFT SPROCKET	14 REAR COVER
5 WASHER	15 KEYWAY
6 BOLT; 45 N·M (22 LB–FT)	16 STUD; 48 N·M (35 LB–FT)
7 TIMING BELT	17 BOLT; 48 N·M (35 LB–FT)
8 FRONT COVER	18 TENSIONER
9 BOLT; 9 N·M (80 LB–IN)	19 ENGINE
10 BOLT; 155 N·M (114 LB–FT)	20 CAMSHAFT

Fig. 117 Exploded view of the timing belt assembly—1989–92 OHC engines

12. Tighten the water pump screws to 18 ft. lbs. (24 Nm), while checking that the tensioner holes remain as adjusted in the prior step.

13. Install the crankshaft pulley, timing belt cover and the serpentine drive belt.

1993–94 VEHICLES

▶ See Figure 118

1. Disconnect the negative battery cable, then partially drain and recover the cooling system.

2. Remove the coolant recovery reservoir.

3. If equipped, remove the A/C belt.

4. Remove the serpentine belt.

5. Disconnect the evaporative emission pipe assembly.

6. Remove the crankshaft pulley assembly.

7. As outlined earlier, remove the timing belt front cover.

8. Align the marks on the crankshaft sprocket with the marks on the rear timing belt cover by rotating the crankshaft.

9. Loosen the water pump retaining bolts, and release the tension with tool J 33039-A or equivalent.

10. Carefully lower the vehicle, then remove the timing belt.

To install:

11. Turn the crankshaft and camshaft gears clockwise to align the timing marks on the gears with the timing marks on the rear cover.

1	GROMMET	12	CRANKSHAFT SPROCKET
2	SLEEVE	13	WASHER
3	BOLT – 10 N·m (89 LBS. IN.)	14	REAR COVER
4	CAMSHAFT SPROCKET	15	KEYWAY
5	WASHER	16	STUD – 25 N·m (18 LBS. FT.)
6	BOLT – 45 N·m (22 LBS. FT.)	17	BOLT – 25 N·m (18 LBS. FT.)
7	TIMING BELT	18	TENSIONER
8	FRONT COVER	19	ENGINE
9	BOLT – 9 N·m (80 MLBS. IN.)	20	CAMSHAFT
10	BOLT – 155 N·m (144 LBS. FT.)	21	WASHER
11	WASHER	22	NUT

87953119

Fig. 118 Timing belt installation and tightening specifications—1993–94 2.0L OHC engines

12. Install the timing belt, making sure that the portion between the camshaft gear and crankshaft gear is in tension.

13. Using tool J 33039-A, or equivalent adjustment tool, turn the coolant pump eccentric clockwise until the tensioner arm contacts the high torque stop. Tighten the water pump screws slightly.

14. Turn the engine by the crankshaft gear bolt 720° clockwise to fully seat the belt into the gear teeth.

15. Turn the coolant pump eccentric counter clockwise until the hole in the tensioner arm is aligned with the hole in the base. This must be done with the engine at room temperature, approximately 68°F (20°C).

16. Tighten the water pump screws while checking that the tensioner holes remain as adjusted as in step 15.

17. As outlined earlier, install the timing belt cover.

18. Install the crankshaft pulley.

19. Connect the evaporative emission pipe assembly.

20. Install the serpentine drive belt and the A/C belt (if equipped).

21. Install the coolant recovery reservoir.

22. Properly fill the cooling system, then connect the negative battery cable.

INSPECTION

▶ **See Figures 119 thru 126**

Refer to the illustrations to check your belt for common wear problems.

Camshaft Sprocket

REMOVAL & INSTALLATION

OHC Engines

▶ **See Figures 127, 128 and 129**

1. Remove the camshaft carrier cover as previously outlined.

2. Remove the timing belt front cover.

3. Align the mark on camshaft sprocket with mark on or camshaft carrier or rear timing belt cover.

4. If equipped, remove the timing probe holder.

5. Loosen the water pump retaining bolts and remove the timing belt from the camshaft sprocket.

6. Hold the camshaft with an open-end wrench. For this purpose a hexagonal is provided in the camshaft. Unfasten the camshaft sprocket retaining bolt and washer, then remove the sprocket.

TCCS1243

Fig. 119 Check for premature parting of the belt

TCCS1244

Fig. 120 Check if the teeth are cracked or damaged

TCCS1245

Fig. 121 Look for noticeable cracks or wear on the belt face

TCCS1246

Fig. 122 You may only have damage on one side of the belt; if so, the guide could be the culprit

TCCS1247

Fig. 123 Foreign materials can get in between the teeth and cause damage

TCCS1300

Fig. 124 Inspect the timing belt for cracks, fraying, glazing or damage of any kind

Fig. 125 Damage on only one side of the timing belt may indicate a faulty guide

Fig. 126 ALWAYS replace the timing belt at the interval specified by the manufacturer

Fig. 127 Hold the camshaft with an open-end wrench and unfasten the camshaft sprocket retaining bolt and washer

To install:

7. Install the camshaft sprocket and align marks on camshaft sprocket and camshaft carrier.

8. Hold the camshaft with a hexagonal open-end wrench. Install the sprocket washer and retaining bolt. Tighten to 34 ft. lbs. (45 Nm).

9. Install the timing belt on sprockets and adjust as previously outlined.

10. Install timing probe holder, if so equipped, and tighten the nuts to 19 ft. lbs. (26 Nm).

11. Install timing belt front cover.

12. Install the camshaft carrier cover as previously outlined.

Fig. 128 Remove the retaining bolt and washer, then . . .

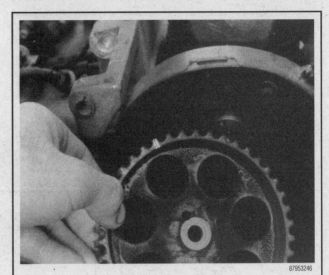

Fig. 129 . . . pull the sprocket from the camshaft

Crankshaft Sprocket

REMOVAL & INSTALLATION

OHC Engines

♦ See Figure 130

1. Remove the timing belt front cover.
2. As outlined earlier, remove the timing belt.
3. Unfasten the crankshaft sprocket-to-crankshaft attaching bolt and thrust washer, then remove the sprocket.

To install:

4. Position the sprocket over the key on end of crankshaft.
5. Install the thrust washer and the attaching bolt. Tighten to as follows:
- 1982–83 vehicles: 115 ft. lbs. (156 Nm)
- 1984–87 vehicles: 107 ft. lbs. plus a 45° rotation
- 1988 vehicles: 96 ft. lbs. (130 Nm) plus a 45° rotation
- 1989–94 vehicles: 114 ft. lbs. (154 Nm)
6. Install the timing belt and adjust as previously described.
7. Install the timing belt front cover.

Fig. 130 Unfasten the bolt and thrust washer, then remove the crankshaft sprocket

Camshaft

REMOVAL & INSTALLATION

1.8L, 2.0L and 2.2L OHV Engines

▶ See Figure 131

1. As outlined earlier, remove the engine and place it on a suitable engine stand.
2. Remove the cylinder head cover, pivot the rocker arms to the sides, and remove the pushrods, keeping them in order. Remove the valve lifters, keeping them in order. There are special tools which make lifter removal easier.
3. Remove the front cover.
4. If necessary, remove the oil pump drive.
5. If equipped, remove the distributor.
6. Remove the fuel pump and its pushrod.
7. Remove the timing chain and sprocket as described earlier in this section.
8. Carefully pull the camshaft from the block, being sure that the camshaft lobes do not contact the bearings.
To install:
9. To install, lubricate the camshaft journals with clean engine oil. Lubricate the lobes with Molykote® or the equivalent.

Fig. 131 After removing the timing chain, you can pull the camshaft from the engine. Be sure the camshaft lobes do NOT contact the bearings

10. Install the camshaft into the engine, being extremely careful not to contact the bearings with the cam lobes.
11. Install the timing chain and sprocket. Install the fuel pump and pushrod. Install the timing cover. Install the distributor.
12. Install the valve lifters. If a new camshaft has been installed, new lifters should be used to ensure durability of the cam lobes.
13. Install the pushrods and rocker arms and the intake manifold. Adjust the valve lash after installing the engine. Install the cylinder head cover.

1.8L and 2.0L OHC Engines

▶ See Figure 132

➡The following procedure requires the use of a special tool.

1. Disconnect the negative battery cable.
2. Remove camshaft carrier cover, as outlined earlier in this section.
3. Using valve train compressing Fixture J-33302, which holds the valves in place, compress valve springs and remove rocker arms.
4. As outlined earlier, remove the timing belt front cover and the timing belt.
5. Remove camshaft sprocket as previously outlined.
6. If equipped, remove the distributor.
7. Remove camshaft thrust plate from rear of camshaft carrier.
8. Slide camshaft rearward, then carefully remove it from the carrier.
To install:
9. Install a new camshaft carrier front oil seal using Tool J-33085.
10. Place camshaft in the carrier.

✳✳ WARNING

Take care not to damage the carrier front oil seal when installing the camshaft.

11. Install camshaft thrust plate retaining bolts. Tighten the bolts to 70 inch lbs. (7.8 Nm).
12. Check camshaft end play, which should be within 0.0006–0.0025 in. (0.016–0.064mm).
13. Install distributor.
14. Install camshaft sprocket as previously described.
15. Install timing belt as previously described.
16. Install timing belt front cover.
17. Using valve train compressing fixture J-33302, compress valve springs and replace rocker arms.
18. Install camshaft carrier cover as previously described.

Fig. 132 You must use a special tool to compress the valve springs

2.8L and 3.1L Engines

1. Remove the engine assembly as outlined earlier.
2. Remove intake manifold, valve lifters and timing chain cover as described in this section.
3. Remove fuel pump and pump pushrod.
4. Remove camshaft sprocket bolts, sprocket and timing chain. A light blow to the lower edge of a tight sprocket should free it (use a plastic mallet).
5. Remove the timing chain tensioner.
6. If applicable, remove the oil pump drive shaft extension.
7. Install two bolts in cam bolt holes and pull cam from block.

To install:

8. Lubricate the camshaft journals with engine oil and reverse removal procedure aligning the sprocket timing marks.

➡️If a new camshaft is being installed, coat the camshaft lobes with GM Engine Oil Supplement (E.O.S.), or equivalent.

BEARING REPLACEMENT

▶ **See Figure 133**

➡️It is recommended that this procedure be performed by a machine shop.

1. Remove the camshaft assembly, for details refer to the necessary service procedure.
2. To remove the camshaft bearings use a special tool (refer to the illustrations) select the proper pilot, nut and thrust washer.
3. Carefully pull out the camshaft bearings.
4. To install the camshaft bearings place the bearing onto the tool and index the oil holes of the bearing with the oil passages in the cylinder block. Pull bearing into proper place.

➡️Proper alignment of the oil holes is critical. Restriction of the oil flow will cause severe engine damage.

1	BACK-UP NUT	**5**	2 PIECE PULLER SCREW
2	EXPANDING COLLET	**6**	PULLING PLATE
3	BEARING	**7**	THRUST BEARING
4	EXPANDING MANDREL	**8**	PULLING NUT

87953127

Fig. 133 Removing and installation of the camshaft bearings

Rear Main Seal

REMOVAL & INSTALLATION

1.8L, 2.0L and 2.2L OHV Engines

1982–84 VEHICLES WITH TWO PIECE SEAL

▶ **See Figures 134 and 135**

1. Remove the oil pan and pump.
2. Remove the rear main bearing cap.
3. Gently pack the upper seal into the groove approximately ¼ in. (6mm) on each side.
4. Measure the amount the seal was driven in on one side and add ¹⁄₁₆ in. (0.8mm). Cut this length from the old lower cap seal. Be sure to get a sharp cut. Repeat for the other side.
5. Place the piece of cut seal into the groove and pack the seal into the block. Do this for each side.
6. Install a piece of Plastigage® or the equivalent on the bearing journal. Install the rear cap and tighten to 75 ft. lbs. Remove the cap and check the gauge for bearing clearance. If out of specification, the ends of the seal may be frayed or not flush, preventing the cap from proper seating. Correct as required.
7. Clean the journal, and apply a thin film of sealer to the mating surfaces of the cap and tighten to 70 ft. lbs. (95 Nm). Install the pan and pump.

➡️Some 1982 1.8L engines (Code G), experience a rear main seal oil leak. To correct this condition a new crankshaft part No. 14086053 and a one piece rear main seal kit part No. 14081761 has been released for service. The one piece seal kit contains an installation tool, rear main seal, and an instruction sheet.

1985–94 VEHICLES WITH ONE PIECE SEAL

▶ **See Figures 136 and 137**

1. Jack up the engine and support it safely.
2. Remove the transmission as outlined in Section 7.
3. Remove the flywheel.
4. Insert a suitable pry tool in through the dust lip and pry out the seal by moving the tool around the seal until it is removed.

➡️Use care not to damage the crankshaft seal surface with a pry tool.

To install:

5. Before installing, lubricate the seal bore to seal surface with engine oil.
6. Install the new seal using tool J-34686.
7. Slide the new seal over the mandrel until the dust lip bottoms squarely against the tool collar.
8. Align the dowel pin of the tool with the dowel pin hole in the crankshaft and attach the tool to the crankshaft. Tighten the attaching screws to 2–5 ft. lbs. (2.7–6.8 Nm).
9. Tighten the T-handle of the tool to push the seal into the bore. Continue until the tool collar is flush against the block.

COATED AREA INDICATED WITH #1052357 SEALER OR EQUIVALENT.

SEALER

87953128

Fig. 134 Apply sealer to the rear cap

CUT OFF SECTION OF OLD ROPE SEAL

USE BEARING CAP AS HOLDING FIXTURE

87953129

Fig. 135 Use the bearing cap to hold the old lower seal while you cut it

DUST LIP

87953130

Fig. 136 Removing the old seal—1985–94 OHV engines

Fig. 137 Installation of the one piece seal—1982–94 OHV engines

10. Loosen the T-handle completely. Remove the attaching screws and the tool.

➡️**Check to see that the seal is squarely seated in the bore.**

11. Install the flywheel and transmission.
12. Start the engine and check for leaks.

1.8L and 2.0 OHC Engines

▸ **See Figure 138**

➡️**The rear main bearing oil seal is a one piece unit and can be replaced without removing the oil pan or the crankshaft.**

1. Remove the transaxle assembly as outlined in Section 7.
2. Remove the flywheel retaining bolts and remove the flywheel.
3. If equipped with manual transaxle, remove the pressure plate and disc.
4. Pry out the rear main seal.
5. Clean the block and crankcase to seal mating surfaces.

To install:

6. Position the rear main seal to the block and press evenly into place using tool J33084 (1983–86) or tool J–36227 (1987–94 vehicles). Lubricate the outside of the seal to aid assembly.
7. Use new bolts and install the flywheel, then tighten the bolts to 44 ft. lbs. (60 Nm) on 1983–86 vehicles, or 48 ft. lbs. (65 Nm) plus a 30° turn on 1987–94 vehicles.
8. On automatic transaxle models, install the flexplate and tighten to 48 ft. lbs. (65 Nm).
9. Install the pressure plate and disc, if equipped with manual transaxle.
10. Install the transaxle assembly as outlined in Section 7.

2.8L and 3.1L Engines

▸ **See Figures 139, 140 and 141**

1. Support the engine with J-28467 engine support or equivalent.
2. Remove the transaxle as outlined in Section 7.

3. Remove the flywheel.
4. Insert a suitable pry tool in through the dust lip and pry out the seal by moving the tool around the seal until it is removed.

⁂ **WARNING**

Use care not to damage the crankshaft seal surface with a pry tool.

To install:

5. Before installing, lubricate the seal bore to seal surface with engine oil.
6. Install the new seal using tool J-34686.
7. Slide the new seal over the mandrel until the dust lip bottoms squarely against the tool collar.
8. Align the dowel pin of the tool with the dowel pin hole in the crankshaft and attach the tool to the crankshaft. Tighten the attaching screws to 2–5 ft. lbs. (2.7–6.8 Nm).
9. Tighten the T-handle of the tool to push the seal into the bore. Continue until the tool collar is flush against the block.
10. Loosen the T-handle completely. Remove the attaching screws and the tool.

➡️**Check to see that the seal is squarely seated in the bore.**

11. Install the flywheel and transaxle.
12. Start the engine and check for leaks.

1	ALIGNMENT HOLE
2	DUST LIP
3	DOWEL PIN
4	COLLAR
5	MANDRIL
6	ATTACHING SCREWS
7	SEAL

Fig. 141 Installing the rear main seal—1994 3.1L engine shown

Fig. 138 Installation of the one piece seal—1983–86 OHC engines

Fig. 139 When removing the rear main seal, be careful not to scratch the bore

Fig. 140 A special tool is needed to install the rear main seal

EXHAUST SYSTEM

▶ See Figures 142 thru 154

Inspection

▶ See Figures 155 thru 161

➡Safety glasses should be worn at all times when working on or near the exhaust system. Older exhaust systems will almost always be covered with loose rust particles which will shower you when disturbed. These particles are more than a nuisance and could injure your eye.

✳✳ CAUTION

DO NOT perform exhaust repairs or inspection with the engine or exhaust hot. Allow the system to cool completely before attempting any work. Exhaust systems are noted for sharp edges, flaking metal and rusted bolts. Gloves and eye protection are required. A healthy supply of penetrating oil and rags is highly recommended.

87953251

Fig. 142 Under-vehicle view of the exhaust components from the exhaust manifold leading to the catalytic converter

87953252

Fig. 143 View of the exhaust pipe running from the catalytic converter to the moffler and tailpipe

1 35 Nm (26 lbs. ft.) bolt
2 Exhaust seal
3 Spring

87953160

Fig. 144 Manifold attachment—2.2L with Federal Emissions or manual transaxle

VIEW A

1 Exhaust manifold
2 Gasket
3 Stud
4 Nut
5 Exhaust manifold pipe to manifold
6 Flex joint
7 Flange

87953161

Fig. 145 Manifold attachment—2.2L with California Emissions and automatic transaxle

1 Seal
2 25 Nm (18 lbs. ft.) stud
3 Spring
4 35 Nm (26 lbs. ft.) nut
5 Exhaust pipe

87953163

Fig. 146 Manifold attachment—3.1L engine

1 Crossover pipe
2 25 Nm (18 lbs. ft.) nut
3 Exhaust manifold

87953164

Fig. 147 Exhaust crossover pipe—3.1L engine

1 Seal
2 29 Nm (21 lbs. ft.) bolt
3 Exhaust intermediate pipe
4 Catalytic converter

87953165

Fig. 148 Converter attachment with flange

1 Catalytic converter
2 Gullotine clamp
  35 Nm (26 lbs. ft.)
3 Front exhaust pipe
4 Intermediate pipe

87953166

Fig. 149 Converter attachment without flange

1 Muffler heat shield
2 Fully driven, seated and not stripped screw

87953167

Fig. 150 Muffler heat shield mounting

1 Muffler strap
2 16 Nm (12 lbs. ft.) bolt
3 Muffler bracket

87953168

Fig. 151 Muffler assembly attachment

1 Cut line
2 Weld

87953169

Fig. 152 A proper muffler cut

1 Intermediate pipe hanger
2 27 Nm (20 lbs. ft.) bolt
3 Intermediate pipe

87953170

Fig. 153 Intermediate pipe hanger

1 CONVERTOR SHIELD
2 UNDERBODY
3 INTERMEDIATE EXHAUST PIPE
4 CONVERTER
5 ADJUST CLEARANCE TO PREVENT RATTLE
6 FUEL TANK
7 MUFFLER

87953174

Fig. 154 Exhaust system to body clearance specifications

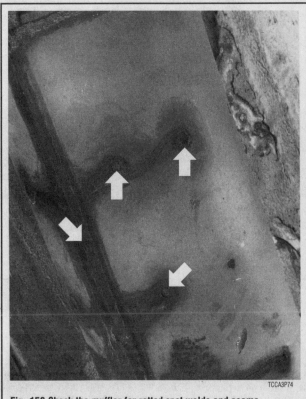

TCCA3P74

Fig. 156 Check the muffler for rotted spot welds and seams

TCCA3P73

Fig. 155 Cracks in the muffler are a guaranteed leak

TCCA3P77

Fig. 157 Make sure the exhaust components are not contacting the body or suspension

Fig. 158 Check for overstretched or torn exhaust hangers

Fig. 159 Example of a badly deteriorated exhaust pipe

Fig. 160 Inspect flanges for gaskets that have deteriorated and need replacement

Fig. 161 Some systems, like this one, use large O-rings (doughnuts) in between the flanges

Fig. 162 Nuts and bolts will be extremely difficult to remove when deteriorated with rust

Your vehicle must be raised and supported safely to inspect the exhaust system properly. By placing 4 safety stands under the vehicle for support should provide enough room for you to slide under the vehicle and inspect the system completely. Start the inspection at the exhaust manifold or turbocharger pipe where the header pipe is attached and work your way to the back of the vehicle. On dual exhaust systems, remember to inspect both sides of the vehicle. Check the complete exhaust system for open seams, holes loose connections, or other deterioration which could permit exhaust fumes to seep into the passenger compartment. Inspect all mounting brackets and hangers for deterioration, some models may have rubber O-rings that can be overstretched and non-supportive. These components will need to be replaced if found. It has always been a practice to use a pointed tool to poke up into the exhaust system where the deterioration spots are to see whether or not they crumble. Some models may have heat shield covering certain parts of the exhaust system , it will be necessary to remove these shields to have the exhaust visible for inspection also.

REPLACEMENT

▶ See Figure 162

There are basically two types of exhaust systems. One is the flange type where the component ends are attached with bolts and a gasket in-between. The other exhaust system is the slip joint type. These components slip into one another using clamps to retain them together.

✳✳ CAUTION

Allow the exhaust system to cool sufficiently before spraying a solvent exhaust fasteners. Some solvents are highly flammable and could ignite when sprayed on hot exhaust components.

Before removing any component of the exhaust system, ALWAYS squirt a liquid rust dissolving agent onto the fasteners for ease of removal. A lot of knuckle skin will be saved by following this rule. It may even be wise to spray the fasteners and allow them to sit overnight.

Flange Type

▶ See Figure 163

✳✳ CAUTION

Do NOT perform exhaust repairs or inspection with the engine or exhaust hot. Allow the system to cool completely before attempting any work. Exhaust systems are noted for sharp edges, flaking metal and rusted bolts. Gloves and eye protection are required. A healthy supply of penetrating oil and rags is highly recommended. Never spray liquid rust dissolving agent onto a hot exhaust component.

Before removing any component on a flange type system, ALWAYS squirt a liquid rust dissolving agent onto the fasteners for ease of removal. Start by unbolting the exhaust piece at both ends (if required). When unbolting the headpipe from the manifold, make sure that the bolts are free before trying to remove them. if you snap a stud in the exhaust manifold, the stud will have to be removed with a bolt extractor, which often means removal of the manifold itself. Next, disconnect the component from the mounting; slight twisting and turning may be required to remove the component completely from the vehicle. You may need to tap on the component with a rubber mallet to loosen the component. If all else fails, use a hacksaw to separate the parts. An oxy-acetylene cutting torch may be faster but the sparks are DANGEROUS near the fuel tank, and at the very least, accidents could happen, resulting in damage to the undercar parts, not to mention yourself.

Fig. 163 Example of a flange type exhaust system joint

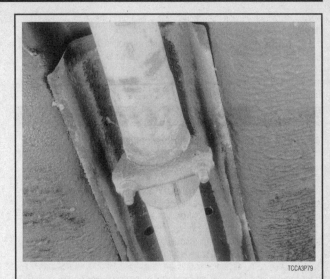

Fig. 164 Example of a common slip joint type system

Slip Joint Type

▶ See Figure 164

Before removing any component on the slip joint type exhaust system, ALWAYS squirt a liquid rust dissolving agent onto the fasteners for ease of removal. Start by unbolting the exhaust piece at both ends (if required). When unbolting the headpipe from the manifold, make sure that the bolts are free

before trying to remove them. if you snap a stud in the exhaust manifold, the stud will have to be removed with a bolt extractor, which often means removal of the manifold itself. Next, remove the mounting U-bolts from around the exhaust pipe you are extracting from the vehicle. Don't be surprised if the U-bolts break while removing the nuts. Loosen the exhaust pipe from any mounting brackets retaining it to the floor pan and separate the components.

ENGINE RECONDITIONING

Determining Engine Condition

Anything that generates heat and/or friction will eventually burn or wear out (for example, a light bulb generates heat, therefore its life span is limited). With this in mind, a running engine generates tremendous amounts of both; friction is encountered by the moving and rotating parts inside the engine and heat is created by friction and combustion of the fuel. However, the engine has systems designed to help reduce the effects of heat and friction and provide added longevity. The oiling system reduces the amount of friction encountered by the moving parts inside the engine, while the cooling system reduces heat created by friction and combustion. If either system is not maintained, a break-down will be inevitable. Therefore, you can see how regular maintenance can affect the service life of your vehicle. If you do not drain, flush and refill your cooling system at the proper intervals, deposits will begin to accumulate in the radiator, thereby reducing the amount of heat it can extract from the coolant. The same applies to your oil and filter; if it is not changed often enough it becomes laden with contaminates and is unable to properly lubricate the engine. This increases friction and wear.

There are a number of methods for evaluating the condition of your engine. A compression test can reveal the condition of your pistons, piston rings, cylinder bores, head gasket(s), valves and valve seats. An oil pressure test can warn you of possible engine bearing, or oil pump failures. Excessive oil consumption, evidence of oil in the engine air intake area and/or bluish smoke from the tailpipe may indicate worn piston rings, worn valve guides and/or valve seals. As a general rule, an engine that uses no more than one quart of oil every 1000 miles is in good condition. Engines that use one quart of oil or more in less than 1000 miles should first be checked for oil leaks. If any oil leaks are present, have them fixed before determining how much oil is consumed by the engine, especially if blue smoke is not visible at the tailpipe.

COMPRESSION TEST

▶ See Figure 165

A noticeable lack of engine power, excessive oil consumption and/or poor fuel mileage measured over an extended period are all indicators of internal engine wear. Worn piston rings, scored or worn cylinder bores, blown head gas-

kets, sticking or burnt valves, and worn valve seats are all possible culprits. A check of each cylinder's compression will help locate the problem.

➡A screw-in type compression gauge is more accurate than the type you simply hold against the spark plug hole. Although it takes slightly longer to use, it's worth the effort to obtain a more accurate reading.

1. Make sure that the proper amount and viscosity of engine oil is in the crankcase, then ensure the battery is fully charged.
2. Warm-up the engine to normal operating temperature, then shut the engine OFF.
3. Disable the ignition system.
4. Label and disconnect all of the spark plug wires from the plugs.

Fig. 165 A screw-in type compression gauge is more accurate and easier to use without an assistant

5. Thoroughly clean the cylinder head area around the spark plug ports, then remove the spark plugs.

6. Set the throttle plate to the fully open (wide-open throttle) position. You can block the accelerator linkage open for this, or you can have an assistant fully depress the accelerator pedal.

7. Install a screw-in type compression gauge into the No. 1 spark plug hole until the fitting is snug.

❊❊ WARNING

Be careful not to crossthread the spark plug hole.

8. According to the tool manufacturer's instructions, connect a remote starting switch to the starting circuit.

9. With the ignition switch in the **OFF** position, use the remote starting switch to crank the engine through at least five compression strokes (approximately 5 seconds of cranking) and record the highest reading on the gauge.

10. Repeat the test on each cylinder, cranking the engine approximately the same number of compression strokes and/or time as the first.

11. Compare the highest readings from each cylinder to that of the others. The indicated compression pressures are considered within specifications if the lowest reading cylinder is within 75 percent of the pressure recorded for the highest reading cylinder. For example, if your highest reading cylinder pressure was 150 psi (1034 kPa), then 75 percent of that would be 113 psi (779 kPa). So the lowest reading cylinder should be no less than 113 psi (779 kPa).

12. If a cylinder exhibits an unusually low compression reading, pour a tablespoon of clean engine oil into the cylinder through the spark plug hole and repeat the compression test. If the compression rises after adding oil, it means that the cylinder's piston rings and/or cylinder bore are damaged or worn. If the pressure remains low, the valves may not be seating properly (a valve job is needed), or the head gasket may be blown near that cylinder. If compression in any two adjacent cylinders is low, and if the addition of oil doesn't help raise compression, there is leakage past the head gasket. Oil and coolant in the combustion chamber, combined with blue or constant white smoke from the tailpipe, are symptoms of this problem. However, don't be alarmed by the normal white smoke emitted from the tailpipe during engine warm-up or from cold weather driving. There may be evidence of water droplets on the engine dipstick and/or oil droplets in the cooling system if a head gasket is blown.

OIL PRESSURE TEST

Check for proper oil pressure at the sending unit passage with an externally mounted mechanical oil pressure gauge (as opposed to relying on a factory installed dash-mounted gauge). A tachometer may also be needed, as some specifications may require running the engine at a specific rpm.

1. With the engine cold, locate and remove the oil pressure sending unit.

2. Following the manufacturer's instructions, connect a mechanical oil pressure gauge and, if necessary, a tachometer to the engine.

3. Start the engine and allow it to idle.

4. Check the oil pressure reading when cold and record the number. You may need to run the engine at a specified rpm, so check the specifications.

5. Run the engine until normal operating temperature is reached (upper radiator hose will feel warm).

6. Check the oil pressure reading again with the engine hot and record the number. Turn the engine **OFF**.

7. Compare your hot oil pressure reading to that given in the chart. If the reading is low, check the cold pressure reading against the chart. If the cold pressure is well above the specification, and the hot reading was lower than the specification, you may have the wrong viscosity oil in the engine. Change the oil, making sure to use the proper grade and quantity, then repeat the test.

Low oil pressure readings could be attributed to internal component wear, pump related problems, a low oil level, or oil viscosity that is too low. High oil pressure readings could be caused by an overfilled crankcase, too high of an oil viscosity or a faulty pressure relief valve.

Buy or Rebuild?

Now that you have determined that your engine is worn out, you must make some decisions. The question of whether or not an engine is worth rebuilding is largely a subjective matter and one of personal worth. Is the engine a popular one, or is it an obsolete model? Are parts available? Will it get acceptable gas mileage once it is rebuilt? Is the car it's being put into worth keeping? Would it be less expensive to buy a new engine, have your engine rebuilt by a pro, rebuild it yourself or buy a used engine from a salvage yard? Or would it be simpler and less expensive to buy another car? If you have considered all these matters and more, and have still decided to rebuild the engine, then it is time to decide how you will rebuild it.

➡**The editors at Chilton feel that most engine machining should be performed by a professional machine shop. Don't think of it as wasting money, rather, as an assurance that the job has been done right the first time. There are many expensive and specialized tools required to perform such tasks as boring and honing an engine block or having a valve job done on a cylinder head. Even inspecting the parts requires expensive micrometers and gauges to properly measure wear and clearances. Also, a machine shop can deliver to you clean, and ready to assemble parts, saving you time and aggravation. Your maximum savings will come from performing the removal, disassembly, assembly and installation of the engine and purchasing or renting only the tools required to perform the above tasks. Depending on the particular circumstances, you may save 40 to 60 percent of the cost doing these yourself.**

A complete rebuild or overhaul of an engine involves replacing all of the moving parts (pistons, rods, crankshaft, camshaft, etc.) with new ones and machining the non-moving wearing surfaces of the block and heads. Unfortunately, this may not be cost effective. For instance, your crankshaft may have been damaged or worn, but it can be machined undersize for a minimal fee.

So, as you can see, you can replace everything inside the engine, but, it is wiser to replace only those parts which are really needed, and, if possible, repair the more expensive ones. Later in this section, we will break the engine down into its two main components: the cylinder head and the engine block. We will discuss each component, and the recommended parts to replace during a rebuild on each.

Engine Overhaul Tips

Most engine overhaul procedures are fairly standard. In addition to specific parts replacement procedures and specifications for your individual engine, this section is also a guide to acceptable rebuilding procedures. Examples of standard rebuilding practice are given and should be used along with specific details concerning your particular engine.

Competent and accurate machine shop services will ensure maximum performance, reliability and engine life. In most instances it is more profitable for the do-it-yourself mechanic to remove, clean and inspect the component, buy the necessary parts and deliver these to a shop for actual machine work.

Much of the assembly work (crankshaft, bearings, piston rods, and other components) is well within the scope of the do-it-yourself mechanic's tools and abilities. You will have to decide for yourself the depth of involvement you desire in an engine repair or rebuild.

TOOLS

The tools required for an engine overhaul or parts replacement will depend on the depth of your involvement. With a few exceptions, they will be the tools found in a mechanic's tool kit (see Section 1 of this manual). More in-depth work will require some or all of the following:

- A dial indicator (reading in thousandths) mounted on a universal base
- Micrometers and telescope gauges
- Jaw and screw-type pullers
- Scraper
- Valve spring compressor
- Ring groove cleaner
- Piston ring expander and compressor
- Ridge reamer
- Cylinder hone or glaze breaker
- Plastigage®
- Engine stand

The use of most of these tools is illustrated in this section. Many can be rented for a one-time use from a local parts jobber or tool supply house specializing in automotive work.

Occasionally, the use of special tools is called for. See the information on Special Tools and the Safety Notice in the front of this book before substituting another tool.

OVERHAUL TIPS

Aluminum has become extremely popular for use in engines, due to its low weight. Observe the following precautions when handling aluminum parts:
• Never hot tank aluminum parts (the caustic hot tank solution will eat the aluminum.
• Remove all aluminum parts (identification tag, etc.) from engine parts prior to the tanking.
• Always coat threads lightly with engine oil or anti-seize compounds before installation, to prevent seizure.
• Never overtighten bolts or spark plugs especially in aluminum threads.

When assembling the engine, any parts that will be exposed to frictional contact must be prelubed to provide lubrication at initial start-up. Any product specifically formulated for this purpose can be used, but engine oil is not recommended as a prelube in most cases.

When semi-permanent (locked, but removable) installation of bolts or nuts is desired, threads should be cleaned and coated with Loctite® or another similar, commercial non-hardening sealant.

CLEANING

▶ See Figures 166 thru 169

Before the engine and its components are inspected, they must be thoroughly cleaned. You will need to remove any engine varnish, oil sludge and/or carbon deposits from all of the components to insure an accurate inspection. A crack in the engine block or cylinder head can easily become overlooked if hidden by a layer of sludge or carbon.

Most of the cleaning process can be carried out with common hand tools and readily available solvents or solutions. Carbon deposits can be chipped away using a hammer and a hard wooden chisel. Old gasket material and varnish or sludge can usually be removed using a scraper and/or cleaning solvent. Extremely stubborn deposits may require the use of a power drill with a wire brush. If using a wire brush, use extreme care around any critical machined surfaces (such as the gasket surfaces, bearing saddles, cylinder bores, etc.). Use of a wire brush is NOT RECOMMENDED on any aluminum components. Always

follow any safety recommendations given by the manufacturer of the tool and/or solvent. You should always wear eye protection during any cleaning process involving scraping, chipping or spraying of solvents.

An alternative to the mess and hassle of cleaning the parts yourself is to drop them off at a local garage or machine shop. They will, more than likely, have the necessary equipment to properly clean all of the parts for a nominal fee.

※ CAUTION

Always wear eye protection during any cleaning process involving scraping, chipping or spraying of solvents.

Remove any oil galley plugs, freeze plugs and/or pressed-in bearings and carefully wash and degrease all of the engine components including the fasteners and bolts. Small parts such as the valves, springs, etc., should be placed in a metal basket and allowed to soak. Use pipe cleaner type brushes, and clean all passageways in the components. Use a ring expander and remove the rings from the pistons. Clean the piston ring grooves with a special tool or a piece of broken ring. Scrape the carbon off of the top of the piston. You should never use a wire brush on the pistons. After preparing all of the piston assemblies in this manner, wash and degrease them again.

※ WARNING

Use extreme care when cleaning around the cylinder head valve seats. A mistake or slip may cost you a new seat.

When cleaning the cylinder head, remove carbon from the combustion chamber with the valves installed. This will avoid damaging the valve seats.

REPAIRING DAMAGED THREADS

▶ See Figures 170, 171, 172, 173 and 174

Several methods of repairing damaged threads are available. Heli-Coil® (shown here), Keenserts® and Microdot® are among the most widely used. All involve basically the same principle—drilling out stripped threads, tapping the

Fig. 166 Use a gasket scraper to remove the old gasket material from the mating surfaces

Fig. 167 Use a ring expander tool to remove the piston rings

Fig. 168 Clean the piston ring grooves using a ring groove cleaner tool, or . . .

Fig. 169 . . . use a piece of an old ring to clean the grooves. Be careful, the ring can be quite sharp

Fig. 170 Damaged bolt hole threads can be replaced with thread repair inserts

Fig. 171 Standard thread repair insert (left), and spark plug thread insert

Fig. 172 Drill out the damaged threads with the specified size bit. Be sure to drill completely through the hole or to the bottom of a blind hole

Fig. 173 Using the kit, tap the hole in order to receive the thread insert. Keep the tap well oiled and back it out frequently to avoid clogging the threads

Fig. 174 Screw the insert onto the installer tool until the tang engages the slot. Thread the insert into the hole until it is ¼–½ turn below the top surface, then remove the tool and break off the tang using a punch

hole and installing a prewound insert—making welding, plugging and oversize fasteners unnecessary.

Two types of thread repair inserts are usually supplied: a standard type for most inch coarse, inch fine, metric course and metric fine thread sizes and a spark lug type to fit most spark plug port sizes. Consult the individual tool manufacturer's catalog to determine exact applications. Typical thread repair kits will contain a selection of prewound threaded inserts, a tap (corresponding to the outside diameter threads of the insert) and an installation tool. Spark plug inserts usually differ because they require a tap equipped with pilot threads and a combined reamer/tap section. Most manufacturers also supply blister-packed thread repair inserts separately in addition to a master kit containing a variety of taps and inserts plus installation tools.

Before attempting to repair a threaded hole, remove any snapped, broken or damaged bolts or studs. Penetrating oil can be used to free frozen threads. The offending item can usually be removed with locking pliers or using a screw/stud extractor. After the hole is clear, the thread can be repaired, as shown in the series of accompanying illustrations and in the kit-manufacturer's instructions.

Engine Preparation

To properly rebuild an engine, you must first remove it from the vehicle, then disassemble and diagnose it. Ideally you should place your engine on an engine stand. This affords you the best access to the engine components. Follow the manufacturer's directions for using the stand with your particular engine. Remove the flywheel or flexplate before installing the engine to the stand.

Now that you have the engine on a stand, and assuming that you have drained the oil and coolant from the engine, it's time to strip it of all but the necessary components. Before you start disassembling the engine, you may want to take a moment to draw some pictures, or fabricate some labels or containers to mark the locations of various components and the bolts and/or studs which fasten them. Modern day engines use a lot of little brackets and clips which hold wiring harnesses and such, and these holders are often mounted on studs and/or bolts that can be easily mixed up. The manufacturer spent a lot of time and money designing your vehicle, and they wouldn't have wasted any of it by haphazardly placing brackets, clips or fasteners on the vehicle. If it's present when you disassemble it, put it back when you assemble, you will regret not remembering that little bracket which holds a wire harness out of the path of a rotating part.

You should begin by unbolting any accessories still attached to the engine, such as the water pump, power steering pump, alternator, etc. Then, unfasten any manifolds (intake or exhaust) which were not removed during the engine removal procedure. Finally, remove any covers remaining on the engine such as the rocker arm, front or timing cover and oil pan. Some front covers may require the vibration damper and/or crank pulley to be removed beforehand. The idea is to reduce the engine to the bare necessities (cylinder head(s), valve train, engine block, crankshaft, pistons and connecting rods), plus any other ëin block' components such as oil pumps, balance shafts and auxiliary shafts.

Finally, remove the cylinder head(s) from the engine block and carefully place on a bench. Disassembly instructions for each component follow later in this section.

Cylinder Head

There are two basic types of cylinder heads used on today's automobiles: the Overhead Valve (OHV) and the Overhead Camshaft (OHC). The latter can also be broken down into two subgroups: the Single Overhead Camshaft (SOHC) and the Dual Overhead Camshaft (DOHC). Generally, if there is only a single camshaft on a head, it is just referred to as an OHC head. Also, an engine with an OHV cylinder head is also known as a pushrod engine.

Most cylinder heads these days are made of an aluminum alloy due to its light weight, durability and heat transfer qualities. However, cast iron was the material of choice in the past, and is still used on many vehicles today. Whether made from aluminum or iron, all cylinder heads have valves and seats. Some use two valves per cylinder, while the more hi-tech engines will utilize a multi-valve configuration using 3, 4 and even 5 valves per cylinder. When the valve contacts the seat, it does so on precision machined surfaces, which seals the combustion chamber. All cylinder heads have a valve guide for each valve. The guide centers the valve to the seat and allows it to move up and down within it. The clearance between the valve and guide can be critical. Too much clearance and the engine may consume oil, lose vacuum and/or damage the seat. Too little, and the valve can stick in the guide causing the engine to run poorly if at all, and possibly causing severe damage. The last component all cylinder heads have are valve springs. The spring holds the valve against its seat. It also returns the valve to this position when the valve has been opened by the valve train or camshaft. The spring is fastened to the valve by a retainer and valve locks (sometimes called keepers). Aluminum heads will also have a valve spring shim to keep the spring from wearing away the aluminum.

An ideal method of rebuilding the cylinder head would involve replacing all of the valves, guides, seats, springs, etc. with new ones. However, depending on how the engine was maintained, often this is not necessary. A major cause of valve, guide and seat wear is an improperly tuned engine. An engine that is running too rich, will often wash the lubricating oil out of the guide with gasoline, causing it to wear rapidly. Conversely, an engine which is running too lean will place higher combustion temperatures on the valves and seats allowing them to wear or even burn. Springs fall victim to the driving habits of the individual. A driver who often runs the engine rpm to the redline will wear out or break the springs faster then one that stays well below it. Unfortunately, mileage takes it toll on all of the parts. Generally, the valves, guides, springs and seats in a cylinder head can be machined and re-used, saving you money. However, if a valve is burnt, it may be wise to replace all of the valves, since they were all operating in the same environment. The same goes for any other component on the cylinder head. Think of it as an insurance policy against future problems related to that component.

Unfortunately, the only way to find out which components need replacing, is to disassemble and carefully check each piece. After the cylinder head(s) are disassembled, thoroughly clean all of the components.

DISASSEMBLY

OHV Heads

▶ See Figures 175 thru 180

Before disassembling the cylinder head, you may want to fabricate some containers to hold the various parts, as some of them can be quite small (such as keepers) and easily lost. Also keeping yourself and the components organized will aid in assembly and reduce confusion. Where possible, try to maintain a components original location; this is especially important if there is not going to be any machine work performed on the components.

1. If you haven't already removed the rocker arms and/or shafts, do so now.
2. Position the head so that the springs are easily accessed.
3. Use a valve spring compressor tool, and relieve spring tension from the retainer.

➡Due to engine varnish, the retainer may stick to the valve locks. A gentle tap with a hammer may help to break it loose.

4. Remove the valve locks from the valve tip and/or retainer. A small magnet may help in removing the locks.
5. Lift the valve spring, tool and all, off of the valve stem.
6. If equipped, remove the valve seal. If the seal is difficult to remove with the valve in place, try removing the valve first, then the seal. Follow the steps below for valve removal.
7. Position the head to allow access for withdrawing the valve.

➡Cylinder heads that have seen a lot of miles and/or abuse may have mushroomed the valve lock grove and/or tip, causing difficulty in removal of the valve. If this has happened, use a metal file to carefully remove the high spots around the lock grooves and/or tip. Only file it enough to allow removal.

8. Remove the valve from the cylinder head.
9. If equipped, remove the valve spring shim. A small magnetic tool or screwdriver will aid in removal.
10. Repeat Steps 3 though 9 until all of the valves have been removed.

OHC Heads

▶ See Figures 181 and 182

Whether it is a single or dual overhead camshaft cylinder head, the disassembly procedure is relatively unchanged. One aspect to pay attention to is careful labeling of the parts on the dual camshaft cylinder head. There will be an intake camshaft and followers as well as an exhaust camshaft and followers and they must be labeled as such. In some cases, the components are identical and could easily be installed incorrectly. DO NOT MIX THEM UP! Determining which is which is very simple; the intake camshaft and components are on the same side of the head as was the intake manifold. Conversely, the exhaust camshaft and components are on the same side of the head as was the exhaust manifold.

CUP TYPE CAMSHAFT FOLLOWERS

▶ See Figures 183, 184 and 185

Most cylinder heads with cup type camshaft followers will have the valve spring, retainer and locks recessed within the follower's bore. You will need a C-clamp style valve spring compressor tool, an OHC spring removal tool (or equivalent) and a small magnet to disassemble the head.

1. If not already removed, remove the camshaft(s) and/or followers. Mark their positions for assembly.
2. Position the cylinder head to allow use of a C-clamp style valve spring compressor tool.

➡It is preferred to position the cylinder head gasket surface facing you with the valve springs facing the opposite direction and the head laying horizontal.

Fig. 175 When removing an OHV valve spring, use a compressor tool to relieve the tension from the retainer

Fig. 176 A small magnet will help in removal of the valve locks

Fig. 177 Be careful not to lose the small valve locks (keepers)

Fig. 178 Remove the valve seal from the valve stem—O-ring type seal shown

Fig. 179 Removing an umbrella/positive type seal

Fig. 180 Invert the cylinder head and withdraw the valve from the valve guide bore

Fig. 181 Exploded view of a valve, seal, spring, retainer and locks from an OHC cylinder head

Fig. 182 Example of a multi-valve cylinder head. Note how it has 2 intake and 2 exhaust valve ports

Fig. 183 C-clamp type spring compressor and an OHC spring removal tool (center) for cup type followers

Fig. 184 Most cup type follower cylinder heads retain the camshaft using bolt-on bearing caps

Fig. 185 Position the OHC spring tool in the follower bore, then compress the spring with a C-clamp type tool

3. With the OHC spring removal adapter tool positioned inside of the follower bore, compress the valve spring using the C-clamp style valve spring compressor.

4. Remove the valve locks. A small magnetic tool or screwdriver will aid in removal.

5. Release the compressor tool and remove the spring assembly.

6. Withdraw the valve from the cylinder head.

7. If equipped, remove the valve seal.

➡️Special valve seal removal tools are available. Regular or needlenose type pliers, if used with care, will work just as well. If using ordinary pliers, be sure not to damage the follower bore. The follower and its bore are machined to close tolerances and any damage to the bore will effect this relationship.

8. If equipped, remove the valve spring shim. A small magnetic tool or screwdriver will aid in removal.

9. Repeat Steps 3 through 8 until all of the valves have been removed.

ROCKER ARM TYPE CAMSHAFT FOLLOWERS

▶ See Figures 186 thru 194

Most cylinder heads with rocker arm-type camshaft followers are easily disassembled using a standard valve spring compressor. However, certain models may not have enough open space around the spring for the standard tool and may require you to use a C-clamp style compressor tool instead.

1. If not already removed, remove the rocker arms and/or shafts and the camshaft. If applicable, also remove the hydraulic lash adjusters. Mark their positions for assembly.

2. Position the cylinder head to allow access to the valve spring.

3. Use a valve spring compressor tool to relieve the spring tension from the retainer.

➡️Due to engine varnish, the retainer may stick to the valve locks. A gentle tap with a hammer may help to break it loose.

Fig. 186 Example of the shaft mounted rocker arms on some OHC heads

Fig. 187 Another example of the rocker arm type OHC head. This model uses a follower under the camshaft

Fig. 188 Before the camshaft can be removed, all of the followers must first be removed . . .

Fig. 189 . . . then the camshaft can be removed by sliding it out (shown), or unbolting a bearing cap (not shown)

Fig. 190 Compress the valve spring . . .

Fig. 191 . . . then remove the valve locks from the valve stem and spring retainer

Fig. 192 Remove the valve spring and retainer from the cylinder head

Fig. 193 Remove the valve seal from the guide. Some gentle prying or pliers may help to remove stubborn ones

Fig. 194 All aluminum and some cast iron heads will have these valve spring shims. Remove all of them as well

4. Remove the valve locks from the valve tip and/or retainer. A small magnet may help in removing the small locks.

5. Lift the valve spring, tool and all, off of the valve stem.

6. If equipped, remove the valve seal. If the seal is difficult to remove with the valve in place, try removing the valve first, then the seal. Follow the steps below for valve removal.

7. Position the head to allow access for withdrawing the valve.

➥Cylinder heads that have seen a lot of miles and/or abuse may have mushroomed the valve lock grove and/or tip, causing difficulty in removal of the valve. If this has happened, use a metal file to carefully remove the high spots around the lock grooves and/or tip. Only file it enough to allow removal.

8. Remove the valve from the cylinder head.

9. If equipped, remove the valve spring shim. A small magnetic tool or screwdriver will aid in removal.

10. Repeat Steps 3 though 9 until all of the valves have been removed.

INSPECTION

Now that all of the cylinder head components are clean, it's time to inspect them for wear and/or damage. To accurately inspect them, you will need some specialized tools:
- A 0–1 in. micrometer for the valves
- A dial indicator or inside diameter gauge for the valve guides
- A spring pressure test gauge

If you do not have access to the proper tools, you may want to bring the components to a shop that does.

Fig. 195 Valve stems may be rolled on a flat surface to check for bends

Valves

▶ See Figures 195 and 196

The first thing to inspect are the valve heads. Look closely at the head, margin and face for any cracks, excessive wear or burning. The margin is the best place to look for burning. It should have a squared edge with an even width all around the diameter. When a valve burns, the margin will look melted and the edges rounded. Also inspect the valve head for any signs of tulipping. This will show as a lifting of the edges or dishing in the center of the head and will usually not occur to all of the valves. All of the heads should look the same, any that seem dished more than others are probably bad. Next, inspect the valve lock grooves and valve tips. Check for any burrs around the lock grooves, especially if you had to file them to remove the valve. Valve tips should appear flat, although slight rounding with high mileage engines is normal. Slightly worn valve tips will need to be machined flat. Last, measure the valve stem diameter with the micrometer. Measure the area that rides within the guide, especially towards the tip where most of the wear occurs. Take several measurements along its length and compare them to each other. Wear should be even along the length with little to no taper. If no minimum diameter is given in the specifications, then the stem should not read more than 0.001 in. (0.025mm) below the unworn area of the valve stem. Any valves that fail these inspections should be replaced.

Springs, Retainers and Valve Locks

▶ See Figures 197 and 198

The first thing to check is the most obvious, broken springs. Next check the free length and squareness of each spring. If applicable, insure to distinguish between intake and exhaust springs. Use a ruler and/or carpenter's square to measure the length. A carpenter's square should be used to check the springs for squareness. If a spring pressure test gauge is available, check each springs rating and compare to the specifications chart. Check the readings against the specifications given. Any springs that fail these inspections should be replaced.

The spring retainers rarely need replacing, however they should still be checked as a precaution. Inspect the spring mating surface and the valve lock retention area for any signs of excessive wear. Also check for any signs of cracking. Replace any retainers that are questionable.

Valve locks should be inspected for excessive wear on the outside contact area as well as on the inner notched surface. Any locks which appear worn or broken and its respective valve should be replaced.

Cylinder Head

There are several things to check on the cylinder head: valve guides, seats, cylinder head surface flatness, cracks and physical damage.

VALVE GUIDES

▶ See Figure 199

Now that you know the valves are good, you can use them to check the guides, although a new valve, if available, is preferred. Before you measure anything, look at the guides carefully and inspect them for any cracks, chips or breakage. Also if the guide is a removable style (as in most aluminum heads),

Fig. 196 Use a micrometer to check the valve stem diameter

Fig. 197 Use a caliper to check the valve spring free-length

Fig. 198 Check the valve spring for squareness on a flat surface; a carpenter's square can be used

Fig. 199 A dial gauge may be used to check valve stem-to-guide clearance; read the gauge while moving the valve stem

Fig. 200 Check the head for flatness across the center of the head surface using a straightedge and feeler gauge

Fig. 201 Checks should also be made along both diagonals of the head surface

check them for any looseness or evidence of movement. All of the guides should appear to be at the same height from the spring seat. If any seem lower (or higher) from another, the guide has moved. Mount a dial indicator onto the spring side of the cylinder head. Lightly oil the valve stem and insert it into the cylinder head. Position the dial indicator against the valve stem near the tip and zero the gauge. Grasp the valve stem and wiggle towards and away from the dial indicator and observe the readings. Mount the dial indicator 90 degrees from the initial point and zero the gauge and again take a reading. Compare the two readings for a out of round condition. Check the readings against the specifications given. An Inside Diameter (I.D.) gauge designed for valve guides will give you an accurate valve guide bore measurement. If the I.D. gauge is used, compare the readings with the specifications given. Any guides that fail these inspections should be replaced or machined.

VALVE SEATS

A visual inspection of the valve seats should show a slightly worn and pitted surface where the valve face contacts the seat. Inspect the seat carefully for severe pitting or cracks. Also, a seat that is badly worn will be recessed into the cylinder head. A severely worn or recessed seat may need to be replaced. All cracked seats must be replaced. A seat concentricity gauge, if available, should be used to check the seat run-out. If run-out exceeds specifications the seat must be machined (if no specification is given use 0.002 in. or 0.051mm).

CYLINDER HEAD SURFACE FLATNESS

⬧ See Figures 200 and 201

After you have cleaned the gasket surface of the cylinder head of any old gasket material, check the head for flatness.

Place a straightedge across the gasket surface. Using feeler gauges, determine the clearance at the center of the straightedge and across the cylinder head at several points. Check along the centerline and diagonally on the head surface. If the warpage exceeds 0.003 in. (0.076mm) within a 6.0 in. (15.2cm) span, or 0.006 in. (0.152mm) over the total length of the head, the cylinder head must be resurfaced. After resurfacing the heads of a V-type engine, the intake manifold flange surface should be checked, and if necessary, milled proportionally to allow for the change in its mounting position.

CRACKS AND PHYSICAL DAMAGE

Generally, cracks are limited to the combustion chamber, however, it is not uncommon for the head to crack in a spark plug hole, port, outside of the head or in the valve spring/rocker arm area. The first area to inspect is always the hottest: the exhaust seat/port area.

A visual inspection should be performed, but just because you don't see a crack does not mean it is not there. Some more reliable methods for inspecting for cracks include Magnaflux®, a magnetic process or Zyglo®, a dye penetrant. Magnaflux® is used only on ferrous metal (cast iron) heads. Zyglo® uses a spray on fluorescent mixture along with a black light to reveal the cracks. It is strongly recommended to have your cylinder head checked professionally for cracks, especially if the engine was known to have overheated and/or leaked or consumed coolant. Contact a local shop for availability and pricing of these services.

Physical damage is usually very evident. For example, a broken mounting ear from dropping the head or a bent or broken stud and/or bolt. All of these defects should be fixed or, if unrepairable, the head should be replaced.

Camshaft and Followers

Inspect the camshaft(s) and followers as described earlier in this section.

REFINISHING & REPAIRING

Many of the procedures given for refinishing and repairing the cylinder head components must be performed by a machine shop. Certain steps, if the inspected part is not worn, can be performed yourself inexpensively. However, you spent a lot of time and effort so far, why risk trying to save a couple bucks if you might have to do it all over again?

Valves

Any valves that were not replaced should be refaced and the tips ground flat. Unless you have access to a valve grinding machine, this should be done by a machine shop. If the valves are in extremely good condition, as well as the valve seats and guides, they may be lapped in without performing machine work.

It is a recommended practice to lap the valves even after machine work has been performed and/or new valves have been purchased. This insures a positive seal between the valve and seat.

LAPPING THE VALVES

➡Before lapping the valves to the seats, read the rest of the cylinder head section to insure that any related parts are in acceptable enough condition to continue.

➡Before any valve seat machining and/or lapping can be performed, the guides must be within factory recommended specifications.

1. Invert the cylinder head.
2. Lightly lubricate the valve stems and insert them into the cylinder head in their numbered order.
3. Raise the valve from the seat and apply a small amount of fine lapping compound to the seat.
4. Moisten the suction head of a hand-lapping tool and attach it to the head of the valve.
5. Rotate the tool between the palms of both hands, changing the position of the valve on the valve seat and lifting the tool often to prevent grooving.
6. Lap the valve until a smooth, polished circle is evident on the valve and seat.
7. Remove the tool and the valve. Wipe away all traces of the grinding compound and store the valve to maintain its lapped location.

❊❊❊ WARNING

Do not get the valves out of order after they have been lapped. They must be put back with the same valve seat with which they were lapped.

Springs, Retainers and Valve Locks

There is no repair or refinishing possible with the springs, retainers and valve locks. If they are found to be worn or defective, they must be replaced with new (or known good) parts.

Cylinder Head

Most refinishing procedures dealing with the cylinder head must be performed by a machine shop. Read the sections below and review your inspection data to determine whether or not machining is necessary.

VALVE GUIDE

➡If any machining or replacements are made to the valve guides, the seats must be machined.

Unless the valve guides need machining or replacing, the only service to perform is to thoroughly clean them of any dirt or oil residue.

There are only two types of valve guides used on automobile engines: the replaceable-type (all aluminum heads) and the cast-in integral-type (most cast iron heads). There are four recommended methods for repairing worn guides.

- Knurling
- Inserts
- Reaming oversize
- Replacing

Knurling is a process in which metal is displaced and raised, thereby reducing clearance, giving a true center, and providing oil control. It is the least expensive way of repairing the valve guides. However, it is not necessarily the best, and in some cases, a knurled valve guide will not stand up for more than a short time. It requires a special knurlizer and precision reaming tools to obtain proper clearances. It would not be cost effective to purchase these tools, unless you plan on rebuilding several of the same cylinder head.

Installing a guide insert involves machining the guide to accept a bronze insert. One style is the coil-type which is installed into a threaded guide. Another is the thin-walled insert where the guide is reamed oversize to accept a split-sleeve insert. After the insert is installed, a special tool is then run through the guide to expand the insert, locking it to the guide. The insert is then reamed to the standard size for proper valve clearance.

Reaming for oversize valves restores normal clearances and provides a true valve seat. Most cast-in type guides can be reamed to accept an valve with an oversize stem. The cost factor for this can become quite high as you will need to purchase the reamer and new, oversize stem valves for all guides which were reamed. Oversizes are generally 0.003 to 0.030 in. (0.076 to 0.762mm), with 0.015 in. (0.381mm) being the most common.

To replace cast-in type valve guides, they must be drilled out, then reamed to accept replacement guides. This must be done on a fixture which will allow centering and leveling off of the original valve seat or guide, otherwise a serious guide-to-seat misalignment may occur making it impossible to properly machine the seat.

Replaceable-type guides are pressed into the cylinder head. A hammer and a stepped drift or punch may be used to install and remove the guides. Before removing the guides, measure the protrusion on the spring side of the head and record it for installation. Use the stepped drift to hammer out the old guide from the combustion chamber side of the head. When installing, determine whether or not the guide also seals a water jacket in the head, and if it does, use the recommended sealing agent. If there is no water jacket, grease the valve guide and its bore. Use the stepped drift, and hammer the new guide into the cylinder head from the spring side of the cylinder head. A stack of washers the same thickness as the measured protrusion may help the installation process.

VALVE SEATS

➡Before any valve seat machining can be performed, the guides must be within factory recommended specifications.

➡If any machining or replacements were made to the valve guides, the seats must be machined.

If the seats are in good condition, the valves can be lapped to the seats, and the cylinder head assembled. See the valves section for instructions on lapping.

If the valve seats are worn, cracked or damaged, they must be serviced by a machine shop. The valve seat must be perfectly centered to the valve guide, which requires very accurate machining.

CYLINDER HEAD SURFACE

If the cylinder head is warped, it must be machined flat. If the warpage is extremely severe, the head may need to be replaced. In some instances, it may be possible to straighten a warped head enough to allow machining. In either case, contact a professional machine shop for service.

➡Any OHC cylinder head that shows excessive warpage should have the camshaft bearing journals align bored after the cylinder head has been resurfaced.

✸✸ WARNING

Failure to align bore the camshaft bearing journals could result in severe engine damage including but not limited to: valve and piston damage, connecting rod damage, camshaft and/or crankshaft breakage.

CRACKS AND PHYSICAL DAMAGE

Certain cracks can be repaired in both cast iron and aluminum heads. For cast iron, a tapered threaded insert is installed along the length of the crack. Aluminum can also use the tapered inserts, however welding is the preferred method. Some physical damage can be repaired through brazing or welding. Contact a machine shop to get expert advice for your particular dilemma.

ASSEMBLY

The first step for any assembly job is to have a clean area in which to work. Next, thoroughly clean all of the parts and components that are to be assembled. Finally, place all of the components onto a suitable work space and, if necessary, arrange the parts to their respective positions.

OHV Engines

1. Lightly lubricate the valve stems and insert all of the valves into the cylinder head. If possible, maintain their original locations.
2. If equipped, install any valve spring shims which were removed.
3. If equipped, install the new valve seals, keeping the following in mind:
- If the valve seal presses over the guide, lightly lubricate the outer guide surfaces.
- If the seal is an O-ring type, it is installed just after compressing the spring but before the valve locks.
4. Place the valve spring and retainer over the stem.
5. Position the spring compressor tool and compress the spring.
6. Assemble the valve locks to the stem.
7. Relieve the spring pressure slowly and insure that neither valve lock becomes dislodged by the retainer.
8. Remove the spring compressor tool.
9. Repeat Steps 2 through 8 until all of the springs have been installed.

OHC Engines

▶ See Figure 202

CUP TYPE CAMSHAFT FOLLOWERS

To install the springs, retainers and valve locks on heads which have these components recessed into the camshaft follower's bore, you will need a small screwdriver-type tool, some clean white grease and a lot of patience. You will also need the C-clamp style spring compressor and the OHC tool used to disassemble the head.

1. Lightly lubricate the valve stems and insert all of the valves into the cylinder head. If possible, maintain their original locations.
2. If equipped, install any valve spring shims which were removed.
3. If equipped, install the new valve seals, keeping the following in mind:
- If the valve seal presses over the guide, lightly lubricate the outer guide surfaces.
- If the seal is an O-ring type, it is installed just after compressing the spring but before the valve locks.
4. Place the valve spring and retainer over the stem.
5. Position the spring compressor and the OHC tool, then compress the spring.
6. Using a small screwdriver as a spatula, fill the valve stem side of the lock with white grease. Use the excess grease on the screwdriver to fasten the lock to the driver.
7. Carefully install the valve lock, which is stuck to the end of the screwdriver, to the valve stem then press on it with the screwdriver until the grease squeezes out. The valve lock should now be stuck to the stem.

Fig. 202 Once assembled, check the valve clearance and correct as needed

8. Repeat Steps 6 and 7 for the remaining valve lock.

9. Relieve the spring pressure slowly and insure that neither valve lock becomes dislodged by the retainer.

10. Remove the spring compressor tool.

11. Repeat Steps 2 through 10 until all of the springs have been installed.

12. Install the followers, camshaft(s) and any other components that were removed for disassembly.

ROCKER ARM TYPE CAMSHAFT FOLLOWERS

1. Lightly lubricate the valve stems and insert all of the valves into the cylinder head. If possible, maintain their original locations.

2. If equipped, install any valve spring shims which were removed.

3. If equipped, install the new valve seals, keeping the following in mind:
- If the valve seal presses over the guide, lightly lubricate the outer guide surfaces.
- If the seal is an O-ring type, it is installed just after compressing the spring but before the valve locks.

4. Place the valve spring and retainer over the stem.

5. Position the spring compressor tool and compress the spring.

6. Assemble the valve locks to the stem.

7. Relieve the spring pressure slowly and insure that neither valve lock becomes dislodged by the retainer.

8. Remove the spring compressor tool.

9. Repeat Steps 2 through 8 until all of the springs have been installed.

10. Install the camshaft(s), rockers, shafts and any other components that were removed for disassembly.

Engine Block

GENERAL INFORMATION

A thorough overhaul or rebuild of an engine block would include replacing the pistons, rings, bearings, timing belt/chain assembly and oil pump. For OHV engines also include a new camshaft and lifters. The block would then have the cylinders bored and honed oversize (or if using removable cylinder sleeves, new sleeves installed) and the crankshaft would be cut undersize to provide new wearing surfaces and perfect clearances. However, your particular engine may not have everything worn out. What if only the piston rings have worn out and the clearances on everything else are still within factory specifications? Well, you could just replace the rings and put it back together, but this would be a very rare example. Chances are, if one component in your engine is worn, other components are sure to follow, and soon. At the very least, you should always replace the rings, bearings and oil pump. This is what is commonly called a "freshen up".

Cylinder Ridge Removal

Because the top piston ring does not travel to the very top of the cylinder, a ridge is built up between the end of the travel and the top of the cylinder bore.

Pushing the piston and connecting rod assembly past the ridge can be difficult, and damage to the piston ring lands could occur. If the ridge is not removed before installing a new piston or not removed at all, piston ring breakage and piston damage may occur.

➡It is always recommended that you remove any cylinder ridges before removing the piston and connecting rod assemblies. If you know that new pistons are going to be installed and the engine block will be bored oversize, you may be able to forego this step. However, some ridges may actually prevent the assemblies from being removed, necessitating its removal.

There are several different types of ridge reamers on the market, none of which are inexpensive. Unless a great deal of engine rebuilding is anticipated, borrow or rent a reamer.

1. Turn the crankshaft until the piston is at the bottom of its travel.
2. Cover the head of the piston with a rag.
3. Follow the tool manufacturers instructions and cut away the ridge, exercising extreme care to avoid cutting too deeply.
4. Remove the ridge reamer, the rag and as many of the cuttings as possible. Continue until all of the cylinder ridges have been removed.

DISASSEMBLY

♦ See Figures 203 and 204

The engine disassembly instructions following assume that you have the engine mounted on an engine stand. If not, it is easiest to disassemble the engine on a bench or the floor with it resting on the bell housing or transmission mounting surface. You must be able to access the connecting rod fasteners and turn the crankshaft during disassembly. Also, all engine covers (timing, front, side, oil pan, whatever) should have already been removed. Engines which are seized or locked up may not be able to be completely disassembled, and a core (salvage yard) engine should be purchased.

Pushrod Engines

If not done during the cylinder head removal, remove the pushrods and lifters, keeping them in order for assembly. Remove the timing gears and/or timing chain assembly, then remove the oil pump drive assembly and withdraw the camshaft from the engine block. Remove the oil pick-up and pump assembly. If equipped, remove any balance or auxiliary shafts. If necessary, remove the cylinder ridge from the top of the bore. See the cylinder ridge removal procedure earlier in this section.

Fig. 203 Place rubber hose over the connecting rod studs to protect the crankshaft and cylinder bores from damage

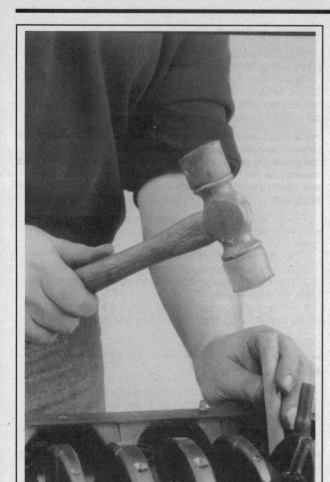

TCCS3804

Fig. 204 Carefully tap the piston out of the bore using a wooden dowel

OHC Engines

If not done during the cylinder head removal, remove the timing chain/belt and/or gear/sprocket assembly. Remove the oil pick-up and pump assembly and, if necessary, the pump drive. If equipped, remove any balance or auxiliary shafts. If necessary, remove the cylinder ridge from the top of the bore. See the cylinder ridge removal procedure earlier in this section.

All Engines

Rotate the engine over so that the crankshaft is exposed. Use a number punch or scribe and mark each connecting rod with its respective cylinder number. The cylinder closest to the front of the engine is always number 1. However, depending on the engine placement, the front of the engine could either be the flywheel or damper/pulley end. Generally the front of the engine faces the front of the vehicle. Use a number punch or scribe and also mark the main bearing caps from front to rear with the front most cap being number 1 (if there are five caps, mark them 1 through 5, front to rear).

❊❊ WARNING

Take special care when pushing the connecting rod up from the crankshaft because the sharp threads of the rod bolts/studs will score the crankshaft journal. Insure that special plastic caps are installed over them, or cut two pieces of rubber hose to do the same.

Again, rotate the engine, this time to position the number one cylinder bore (head surface) up. Turn the crankshaft until the number one piston is at the bottom of its travel, this should allow the maximum access to its connecting rod. Remove the number one connecting rods fasteners and cap and place two lengths of rubber hose over the rod bolts/studs to protect the crankshaft from damage. Using a sturdy wooden dowel and a hammer, push the connecting rod up about 1 in. (25mm) from the crankshaft and remove the upper bearing insert. Continue pushing or tapping the connecting rod up until the piston rings are out of the cylinder bore. Remove the piston and rod by hand, put the upper half of the bearing insert back into the rod, install the cap with its bearing insert installed, and hand-tighten the cap fasteners. If the parts are kept in order in this manner, they will not get lost and you will be able to tell which bearings came form what cylinder if any problems are discovered and diagnosis is necessary. Remove all the other piston assemblies in the same manner. On V-style engines, remove all of the pistons from one bank, then reposition the engine with the other cylinder bank head surface up, and remove that banks piston assemblies.

The only remaining component in the engine block should now be the crankshaft. Loosen the main bearing caps evenly until the fasteners can be turned by hand, then remove them and the caps. Remove the crankshaft from the engine block. Thoroughly clean all of the components.

INSPECTION

Now that the engine block and all of its components are clean, it's time to inspect them for wear and/or damage. To accurately inspect them, you will need some specialized tools:
• Two or three separate micrometers to measure the pistons and crankshaft journals
• A dial indicator
• Telescoping gauges for the cylinder bores
• A rod alignment fixture to check for bent connecting rods

If you do not have access to the proper tools, you may want to bring the components to a shop that does.

Generally, you shouldn't expect cracks in the engine block or its components unless it was known to leak, consume or mix engine fluids, it was severely overheated, or there was evidence of bad bearings and/or crankshaft damage. A visual inspection should be performed on all of the components, but just because you don't see a crack does not mean it is not there. Some more reliable methods for inspecting for cracks include Magnaflux®, a magnetic process or Zyglo®, a dye penetrant. Magnaflux® is used only on ferrous metal (cast iron). Zyglo® uses a spray on fluorescent mixture along with a black light to reveal the cracks. It is strongly recommended to have your engine block checked professionally for cracks, especially if the engine was known to have overheated and/or leaked or consumed coolant. Contact a local shop for availability and pricing of these services.

Engine Block

ENGINE BLOCK BEARING ALIGNMENT

Remove the main bearing caps and, if still installed, the main bearing inserts. Inspect all of the main bearing saddles and caps for damage, burrs or high spots. If damage is found, and it is caused from a spun main bearing, the block will need to be align-bored or, if severe enough, replacement. Any burrs or high spots should be carefully removed with a metal file.

Place a straightedge on the bearing saddles, in the engine block, along the centerline of the crankshaft. If any clearance exists between the straightedge and the saddles, the block must be align-bored.

Align-boring consists of machining the main bearing saddles and caps by means of a flycutter that runs through the bearing saddles.

DECK FLATNESS

The top of the engine block where the cylinder head mounts is called the deck. Insure that the deck surface is clean of dirt, carbon deposits and old gasket material. Place a straightedge across the surface of the deck along its centerline and, using feeler gauges, check the clearance along several points. Repeat the checking procedure with the straightedge placed along both diagonals of the deck surface. If the reading exceeds 0.003 in. (0.076mm) within a 6.0 in. (15.2cm) span, or 0.006 in. (0.152mm) over the total length of the deck, it must be machined.

CYLINDER BORES

▶ See Figure 205

The cylinder bores house the pistons and are slightly larger than the pistons themselves. A common piston-to-bore clearance is 0.0015–0.0025 in. (0.0381mm–0.0635mm). Inspect and measure the cylinder bores. The bore should be checked for out-of-roundness, taper and size. The results of this inspection will determine whether the cylinder can be used in its existing size and condition, or a rebore to the next oversize is required (or in the case of removable sleeves, have replacements installed).

The amount of cylinder wall wear is always greater at the top of the cylinder than at the bottom. This wear is known as taper. Any cylinder that has a taper of 0.0012 in. (0.305mm) or more, must be rebored. Measurements are taken at a number of positions in each cylinder: at the top, middle and bottom and at two points at each position; that is, at a point 90 degrees from the crankshaft centerline, as well as a point parallel to the crankshaft centerline. The measurements are made with either a special dial indicator or a telescopic gauge and micrometer. If the necessary precision tools to check the bore are not available, take the block to a machine shop and have them mike it. Also if you don't have the tools to check the cylinder bores, chances are you will not have the necessary devices to check the pistons, connecting rods and crankshaft. Take these components with you and save yourself an extra trip.

For our procedures, we will use a telescopic gauge and a micrometer. You will need one of each, with a measuring range which covers your cylinder bore size.

1. Position the telescopic gauge in the cylinder bore, loosen the gauges lock and allow it to expand.

➡**Your first two readings will be at the top of the cylinder bore, then proceed to the middle and finally the bottom, making a total of six measurements.**

2. Hold the gauge square in the bore, 90 degrees from the crankshaft centerline, and gently tighten the lock. Tilt the gauge back to remove it from the bore.

3. Measure the gauge with the micrometer and record the reading.

4. Again, hold the gauge square in the bore, this time parallel to the crankshaft centerline, and gently tighten the lock. Again, you will tilt the gauge back to remove it from the bore.

5. Measure the gauge with the micrometer and record this reading. The difference between these two readings is the out-of-round measurement of the cylinder.

6. Repeat steps 1 through 5, each time going to the next lower position, until you reach the bottom of the cylinder. Then go to the next cylinder, and continue until all of the cylinders have been measured.

The difference between these measurements will tell you all about the wear in your cylinders. The measurements which were taken 90 degrees from the crankshaft centerline will always reflect the most wear. That is because at this position is where the engine power presses the piston against the cylinder bore the hardest. This is known as thrust wear. Take your top, 90 degree measurement and compare it to your bottom, 90 degree measurement. The difference between them is the taper. When you measure your pistons, you will compare these readings to your piston sizes and determine piston-to-wall clearance.

Crankshaft

Inspect the crankshaft for visible signs of wear or damage. All of the journals should be perfectly round and smooth. Slight scores are normal for a used crankshaft, but you should hardly feel them with your fingernail. When measuring the crankshaft with a micrometer, you will take readings at the front and rear of each journal, then turn the micrometer 90 degrees and take two more readings, front and rear. The difference between the front-to-rear readings is the journal taper and the first-to-90 degree reading is the out-of-round measurement. Generally, there should be no taper or out-of-roundness found, however, up to 0.0005 in. (0.0127mm) for either can be overlooked. Also, the readings should fall within the factory specifications for journal diameters.

If the crankshaft journals fall within specifications, it is recommended that it be polished before being returned to service. Polishing the crankshaft insures that any minor burrs or high spots are smoothed, thereby reducing the chance of scoring the new bearings.

Pistons and Connecting Rods

PISTONS

▶ See Figure 206

The piston should be visually inspected for any signs of cracking or burning (caused by hot spots or detonation), and scuffing or excessive wear on the skirts. The wrist pin attaches the piston to the connecting rod. The piston should move freely on the wrist pin, both sliding and pivoting. Grasp the connecting rod securely, or mount it in a vise, and try to rock the piston back and forth along the centerline of the wrist pin. There should not be any excessive play evident between the piston and the pin. If there are C-clips retaining the pin in the piston then you have wrist pin bushings in the rods. There should not be any excessive play between the wrist pin and the rod bushing. Normal clearance for the wrist pin is approx. 0.001–0.002 in. (0.025mm–0.051mm).

Use a micrometer and measure the diameter of the piston, perpendicular to the wrist pin, on the skirt. Compare the reading to its original cylinder measurement obtained earlier. The difference between the two readings is the piston-to-wall clearance. If the clearance is within specifications, the piston may be used as is. If the piston is out of specification, but the bore is not, you will need a new piston. If both are out of specification, you will need the cylinder rebored and oversize pistons installed. Generally if two or more pistons/bores are out of specification, it is best to rebore the entire block and purchase a complete set of oversize pistons.

Fig. 205 Use a telescoping gauge to measure the cylinder bore diameter—take several readings within the same bore

TCCS3209

Fig. 206 Measure the piston's outer diameter, perpendicular to the wrist pin, with a micrometer

TCCS3210

CONNECTING ROD

You should have the connecting rod checked for straightness at a machine shop. If the connecting rod is bent, it will unevenly wear the bearing and piston, as well as place greater stress on these components. Any bent or twisted connecting rods must be replaced. If the rods are straight and the wrist pin clearance is within specifications, then only the bearing end of the rod need be checked. Place the connecting rod into a vice, with the bearing inserts in place, install the cap to the rod and torque the fasteners to specifications. Use a telescoping gauge and carefully measure the inside diameter of the bearings. Compare this reading to the rods original crankshaft journal diameter measurement. The difference is the oil clearance. If the oil clearance is not within specifications, install new bearings in the rod and take another measurement. If the clearance is still out of specifications, and the crankshaft is not, the rod will need to be reconditioned by a machine shop.

➡You can also use Plastigage® to check the bearing clearances. The assembling section has complete instructions on its use.

Camshaft

Inspect the camshaft and lifters/followers as described earlier in this section.

Bearings

All of the engine bearings should be visually inspected for wear and/or damage. The bearing should look evenly worn all around with no deep scores or pits. If the bearing is severely worn, scored, pitted or heat blued, then the bearing, and the components that use it, should be brought to a machine shop for inspection. Full-circle bearings (used on most camshafts, auxiliary shafts, balance shafts, etc.) require specialized tools for removal and installation, and should be brought to a machine shop for service.

Oil Pump

➡The oil pump is responsible for providing constant lubrication to the whole engine and so it is recommended that a new oil pump be installed when rebuilding the engine.

Completely disassemble the oil pump and thoroughly clean all of the components. Inspect the oil pump gears and housing for wear and/or damage. Insure that the pressure relief valve operates properly and there is no binding or sticking due to varnish or debris. If all of the parts are in proper working condition, lubricate the gears and relief valve, and assemble the pump.

REFINISHING

▶ See Figure 207

Almost all engine block refinishing must be performed by a machine shop. If the cylinders are not to be rebored, then the cylinder glaze can be removed with

Fig. 207 Use a ball type cylinder hone to remove any glaze and provide a new surface for seating the piston rings

a ball hone. When removing cylinder glaze with a ball hone, use a light or penetrating type oil to lubricate the hone. Do not allow the hone to run dry as this may cause excessive scoring of the cylinder bores and wear on the hone. If new pistons are required, they will need to be installed to the connecting rods. This should be performed by a machine shop as the pistons must be installed in the correct relationship to the rod or engine damage can occur.

Pistons and Connecting Rods

▶ See Figure 208

Only pistons with the wrist pin retained by C-clips are serviceable by the home-mechanic. Press fit pistons require special presses and/or heaters to remove/install the connecting rod and should only be performed by a machine shop.

All pistons will have a mark indicating the direction to the front of the engine and the must be installed into the engine in that manner. Usually it is a notch or arrow on the top of the piston, or it may be the letter F cast or stamped into the piston.

Fig. 208 Most pistons are marked to indicate positioning in the engine (usually a mark means the side facing the front)

C-CLIP TYPE PISTONS

1. Note the location of the forward mark on the piston and mark the connecting rod in relation.
2. Remove the C-clips from the piston and withdraw the wrist pin.

➡Varnish build-up or C-clip groove burrs may increase the difficulty of removing the wrist pin. If necessary, use a punch or drift to carefully tap the wrist pin out.

3. Insure that the wrist pin bushing in the connecting rod is usable, and lubricate it with assembly lube.
4. Remove the wrist pin from the new piston and lubricate the pin bores on the piston.
5. Align the forward marks on the piston and the connecting rod and install the wrist pin.
6. The new C-clips will have a flat and a rounded side to them. Install both C-clips with the flat side facing out.
7. Repeat all of the steps for each piston being replaced.

ASSEMBLY

Before you begin assembling the engine, first give yourself a clean, dirt free work area. Next, clean every engine component again. The key to a good assembly is cleanliness.

Mount the engine block into the engine stand and wash it one last time using water and detergent (dishwashing detergent works well). While washing it, scrub the cylinder bores with a soft bristle brush and thoroughly clean all of the oil passages. Completely dry the engine and spray the entire assembly down with an anti-rust solution such as WD-40® or similar product. Take a clean lint-free rag and wipe up any excess anti-rust solution from the bores, bearing saddles, etc. Repeat the final cleaning process on the crankshaft. Replace any freeze or oil galley plugs which were removed during disassembly.

Crankshaft

▶ See Figures 209, 210, 211 and 212

1. Remove the main bearing inserts from the block and bearing caps.
2. If the crankshaft main bearing journals have been refinished to a definite undersize, install the correct undersize bearing. Be sure that the bearing inserts and bearing bores are clean. Foreign material under inserts will distort bearing and cause failure.
3. Place the upper main bearing inserts in bores with tang in slot.

➡ The oil holes in the bearing inserts must be aligned with the oil holes in the cylinder block.

4. Install the lower main bearing inserts in bearing caps.
5. Clean the mating surfaces of block and rear main bearing cap.
6. Carefully lower the crankshaft into place. Be careful not to damage bearing surfaces.
7. Check the clearance of each main bearing by using the following procedure:

   a. Place a piece of Plastigage® or its equivalent, on bearing surface across full width of bearing cap and about ¼ in. off center.

Fig. 210 After the cap is removed again, use the scale supplied with the gauging material to check the clearance

Fig. 211 A dial gauge may be used to check crankshaft end-play

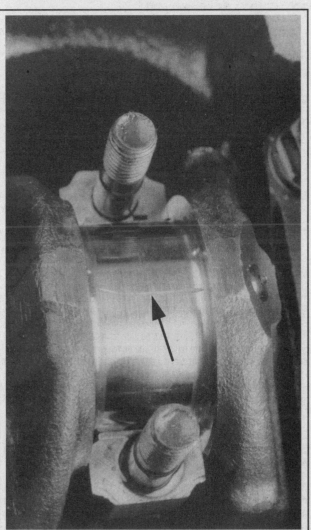

Fig. 209 Apply a strip of gauging material to the bearing journal, then install and torque the cap

Fig. 212 Carefully pry the crankshaft back and forth while reading the dial gauge for end-play

Fig. 213 Checking the piston ring-to-ring groove side clearance using the ring and a feeler gauge

Fig. 214 The notch on the side of the bearing cap matches the tang on the bearing insert

Fig. 215 Most rings are marked to show which side of the ring should face up when installed to the piston

Fig. 216 Install the piston and rod assembly into the block using a ring compressor and the handle of a hammer

b. Carefully pry the crankshaft toward the rear of the engine and hold it there while you zero the gauge.

c. Carefully pry the crankshaft toward the front of the engine and read the gauge.

d. Confirm that the reading is within specifications. If not, install a new thrust bearing and repeat the procedure. If the reading is still out of specifications with a new bearing, have a machine shop inspect the thrust surfaces of the crankshaft, and if possible, repair it.

15. Rotate the crankshaft so as to position the first rod journal to the bottom of its stroke.

Pistons and Connecting Rods

▶ See Figures 213, 214, 215 and 216

1. Before installing the piston/connecting rod assembly, oil the pistons, piston rings and the cylinder walls with light engine oil. Install connecting rod bolt protectors or rubber hose onto the connecting rod bolts/studs. Also perform the following:

a. Select the proper ring set for the size cylinder bore.

b. Position the ring in the bore in which it is going to be used.

c. Push the ring down into the bore area where normal ring wear is not encountered.

d. Use the head of the piston to position the ring in the bore so that the ring is square with the cylinder wall. Use caution to avoid damage to the ring or cylinder bore.

e. Measure the gap between the ends of the ring with a feeler gauge. Ring gap in a worn cylinder is normally greater than specification. If the ring gap is greater than the specified limits, try an oversize ring set.

f. Check the ring side clearance of the compression rings with a feeler gauge inserted between the ring and its lower land according to specification. The gauge should slide freely around the entire ring circumference without binding. Any wear that occurs will form a step at the inner portion of the lower land. If the lower lands have high steps, the piston should be replaced.

2. Unless new pistons are installed, be sure to install the pistons in the cylinders from which they were removed. The numbers on the connecting rod and bearing cap must be on the same side when installed in the cylinder bore. If a connecting rod is ever transposed from one engine or cylinder to another, new bearings should be fitted and the connecting rod should be numbered to correspond with the new cylinder number. The notch on the piston head goes toward the front of the engine.

3. Install all of the rod bearing inserts into the rods and caps.

4. Install the rings to the pistons. Install the oil control ring first, then the second compression ring and finally the top compression ring. Use a piston ring expander tool to aid in installation and to help reduce the chance of breakage.

5. Make sure the ring gaps are properly spaced around the circumference of the piston. Fit a piston ring compressor around the piston and slide the piston and connecting rod assembly down into the cylinder bore, pushing it in with the wooden hammer handle. Push the piston down until it is only slightly below the top of the cylinder bore. Guide the connecting rod onto the crankshaft bearing journal carefully, to avoid damaging the crankshaft.

6. Check the bearing clearance of all the rod bearings, fitting them to the crankshaft bearing journals. Follow the procedure in the crankshaft installation above.

b. Install cap and tighten bolts to specifications. Do not turn crankshaft while Plastigage® is in place.

c. Remove the cap. Using the supplied Plastigage® scale, check width of Plastigage® at widest point to get maximum clearance. Difference between readings is taper of journal.

d. If clearance exceeds specified limits, try a 0.001 in. or 0.002 in. undersize bearing in combination with the standard bearing. Bearing clearance must be within specified limits. If standard and 0.002 in. undersize bearing does not bring clearance within desired limits, refinish crankshaft journal, then install undersize bearings.

8. After the bearings have been fitted, apply a light coat of engine oil to the journals and bearings. Install the rear main bearing cap. Install all bearing caps except the thrust bearing cap. Be sure that main bearing caps are installed in original locations. Tighten the bearing cap bolts to specifications.

9. Install the rear main seal.

10. Install the thrust bearing cap with bolts finger-tight.

11. Pry the crankshaft forward against the thrust surface of upper half of bearing.

12. Hold the crankshaft forward and pry the thrust bearing cap to the rear. This aligns the thrust surfaces of both halves of the bearing.

13. Retain the forward pressure on the crankshaft. Tighten the cap bolts to specifications.

14. Measure the crankshaft end-play as follows:

a. Mount a dial gauge to the engine block and position the tip of gauge to read from the crankshaft end.

7. After the bearings have been fitted, apply a light coating of assembly oil to the journals and bearings.

8. Turn the crankshaft until the appropriate bearing journal is at the bottom of its stroke, then push the piston assembly all the way down until the connecting rod bearing seats on the crankshaft journal. Be careful not to allow the bearing cap screws to strike the crankshaft bearing journals and damage them.

9. After the piston and connecting rod assemblies have been installed, check the connecting rod side clearance on each crankshaft journal.

10. Prime and install the oil pump and the oil pump intake tube.

OHV Engines

CAMSHAFT, LIFTERS AND TIMING ASSEMBLY

1. Install the camshaft.
2. Install the lifters/followers into their bores.
3. Install the timing gears/chain assembly.

CYLINDER HEAD(S)

1. Install the cylinder head(s) using new gaskets.
2. Assemble the rest of the valve train (pushrods and rocker arms and/or shafts).

OHC Engines

CYLINDER HEAD(S)

1. Install the cylinder head(s) using new gaskets.
2. Install the timing sprockets/gears and the belt/chain assemblies.

Engine Covers and Components

Install the timing cover(s) and oil pan. Refer to your notes and drawings made prior to disassembly and install all of the components that were removed. Install the engine into the vehicle.

Engine Start-up and Break-in

STARTING THE ENGINE

Now that the engine is installed and every wire and hose is properly connected, go back and double check that all coolant and vacuum hoses are connected. Check that your oil drain plug is installed and properly tightened. If not already done, install a new oil filter onto the engine. Fill the crankcase with the proper amount and grade of engine oil. Fill the cooling system with a 50/50 mixture of coolant/water.

1. Connect the vehicle battery.
2. Start the engine. Keep your eye on your oil pressure indicator; if it does not indicate oil pressure within 10 seconds of starting, turn the vehicle off.

✳✳ WARNING

Damage to the engine can result if it is allowed to run with no oil pressure. Check the engine oil level to make sure that it is full. Check for any leaks and if found, repair the leaks before continuing. If there is still no indication of oil pressure, you may need to prime the system.

3. Confirm that there are no fluid leaks (oil or other).
4. Allow the engine to reach normal operating temperature (the upper radiator hose will be hot to the touch).
5. At this point you can perform any necessary checks or adjustments, such as checking the ignition timing.
6. Install any remaining components or body panels which were removed.

BREAKING IT IN

Make the first miles on the new engine, easy ones. Vary the speed but do not accelerate hard. Most importantly, do not lug the engine, and avoid sustained high speeds until at least 100 miles. Check the engine oil and coolant levels frequently. Expect the engine to use a little oil until the rings seat. Change the oil and filter at 500 miles, 1500 miles, then every 3000 miles past that.

KEEP IT MAINTAINED

Now that you have just gone through all of that hard work, keep yourself from doing it all over again by thoroughly maintaining it. Not that you may not have maintained it before, heck you could have had one to two hundred thousand miles on it before doing this. However, you may have bought the vehicle used, and the previous owner did not keep up on maintenance. Which is why you just went through all of that hard work. See?

TORQUE SPECIFICATIONS
All readings in ft. lbs.

Year	Engine ID/VIN	Engine Displacement Liters (cc)	Cylinder Head Bolts	Main Bearing Bolts	Rod Bearing Bolts	Crankshaft Damper Bolts	Flywheel Bolts	Manifold Intake	Manifold Exhaust	Spark Plugs	Lug Nut
1982	G	1.8 (1819)	65-75	63-74	34-40	66-84	45-55	20-25	22-28	15	100
	O	1.8 (1819)	①	57	39	20 ②	45	25	16	15	100
	B	2.0 (1998)	65-75 ①	63-74	34-43	66-89	45-63 ③	18-25	20-30	15	100
1983	O	1.8 (1819)	①	57	39	20 ②	45	25	16	15	100
	J	1.8 (1819)	①	57	39	20 ②	45	25	16	15	100
	P	2.0 (1998)	65-75	63-77	34-43	68-89	45-63 ③	18-25	20-30	15	100
	B	2.0 (1998)	65-75	63-77	34-43	68-89	45-63 ③	18-25	20-30	15	100
1984	O	1.8 (1819)	①	57	39	20 ②	45	25	16	15	100
	J	1.8 (1819)	①	57	39	20 ②	45	25	16	15	100
	P	2.0 (1998)	65-75	63-77	34-43	68-89	45-63 ③	18-25	20-30	15	100
1985	O	1.8 (1819)	①	57	39	115	45	25	16	15	100
	J	1.8 (1819)	①	57	39	115	45	25	16	15	100
	P	2.0 (1998)	65-75	63-77	34-43	68-89	⑨	18-25	20-30	15	100
	W	2.8 (2835)	70	68	37	75	45	23	23	15	100
1986	O	2.0 (1998)	①	57	39	115	45	25	16	15	100
	J	2.0 (1998)	①	57	39	115	45	25	16	15	100
	P	2.0 (1998)	65-75	63-77	34-43	68-89	⑨	18-25	20-30	15	100
	W	2.8 (2835)	70	68	37	75	45	23	23	15	100
1987	K	2.0 (1998)	①	④	⑤	114	⑥	16	16	15	100
	M	2.0 (1998)	①	④	⑤	114	⑥	16	16	15	100
	1	2.0 (1998)	⑩	63-77	34-43	66-89	⑨	15-22	6-13	20	80-100
	W	2.8 (2835)	70	68	37	75	45	23	23	15	100
1988	K	2.0 (1998)	①	④	⑤	114	48 ⑦	16	115 ⑧	15	100
	M	2.0 (1998)	①	④	⑤	114	48 ⑦	16	115 ⑧	15	100
	1	2.0 (1998)	⑩	63-77	34-43	66-89	⑨	15-22	6-13	20	80-100
	W	2.8 (2835)	70	68	37	75	45	23	23	15	100
1989	K	2.0 (1998)	①	④	⑤	114	48 ⑦	16	115 ⑧	15	100
	M	2.0 (1998)	①	④	⑤	114	48 ⑦	16	115 ⑧	15	100
	1	2.0 (1998)	⑩	63-77	34-43	66-89	⑨	15-22	6-13	20	80-100
	W	2.8 (2835)	70	68	37	75	45	23	23	15	100
1990	K	2.0 (1998)	①	④	⑤	114	48 ⑦	16	115 ⑧	15	100
	M	2.0 (1998)	①	④	⑤	114	48 ⑦	16	115 ⑧	15	100
	G	2.2 (2180)	⑪	77	38	85 ⑬	52-55	18	6-13	20	80-100
	T	3.1 (3130)	⑫	73	49	66-85	45-59	⑭	18	20	100
1991	K	2.0 (1998)	①	④	⑤	114	48 ⑦	16	115	15	100
	G	2.2 (2180)	⑪	77	38	85 ⑬	52-55	18	6-13	20	80-100
	T	3.1 (3130)	⑫	73	39	66-85	45-59	⑭	18	20	100
1992	H	2.0 (1998)	①	④	⑤	114	⑥	16	16	15	100
	4	2.2 (2180)	⑪	77	38	85 ⑬	52-55	18	6-13	20	80-100
	T	3.1 (3130)	⑫	73	39	66-85	45-59	⑭	18	20	100
1993	H	2.0 (1998)	①	④	⑤	114	⑥	16	16	15	Nut
	4	2.2 (2180)	⑪	77	38	85 ⑬	52-55	18	6-13	20	80-100
	T	3.1 (3130)	⑫	73	39	66-85	45-59	⑭	18	20	100
1994	H	2.0 (1998)	①	④	⑤	114	48	16	16	15	100
	4	2.2 (2180)	⑪	77	38	85 ⑬	52-55	18	6-13	20	100
	T	3.1 (3130)	⑫	73	39	66-85	45-59	⑭	18	20	100

NA - Not Available

① Step 1: 18 ft. lbs.
Step 2: Plus three turns of 60 degrees
Step 3: Plus 30-50 degrees after warm-up

② Crankshaft pulley-to-sprocket bolts

③ Automatic transaxle: 45-59 ft. lbs.

④ Step 1: 44 ft. lbs.
Step 2: Plus 40-50 degrees

⑤ Step 1: 26 ft. lbs.
Step 2: Plus 40-45 degrees

⑥ Step 1: 48 ft. lbs.
Step 2: Plus 30 degrees

⑦ Manual transaxle: Plus 30 degrees

⑧ Inch lbs.

⑨ Manual transaxle: 45-63 ft. lbs.
Automatic transaxle: 45-59 ft. lbs.

⑩ Short bolts: 62-70 ft. lbs.
Long bolts: 73-83 ft. lbs.

⑪ Step 1: 41 ft. lbs.
Step 2: Tighten an additional 45 degrees
Step 3: Repeat Step 2
Step 4: Long bolts - 1, 4-5, 8-9 an additional 45 degress
Step 5: Short bolts - 2-3, 6-7, 10 an additional 10 degrees

⑫ 33 ft. lbs. plus 90 degrees

⑬ Center bolt spec. shown; Pulley-to-hub bolts to 37 ft. lbs.

⑭ Step 1: 15 ft. lbs.
Step 2: 24 ft. lbs.

91133CA3

AIR POLLUTION 4-2
NATURAL POLLUTANTS 4-2
INDUSTRIAL POLLUTANTS 4-2
AUTOMOTIVE POLLUTANTS 4-2
   TEMPERATURE INVERSION 4-2
   HEAT TRANSFER 4-2
AUTOMOTIVE EMISSIONS 4-3
EXHAUST GASES 4-3
   HYDROCARBONS 4-3
   CARBON MONOXIDE 4-3
   NITROGEN 4-3
   OXIDES OF SULFUR 4-3
   PARTICULATE MATTER 4-3
CRANKCASE EMISSIONS 4-4
EVAPORATIVE EMISSIONS 4-4
EMISSION CONTROLS 4-4
CRANKCASE VENTILATION SYSTEM 4-4
   OPERATION 4-4
   TESTING 4-5
   REMOVAL & INSTALLATION 4-5
EVAPORATIVE EMISSION CONTROL
  SYSTEM 4-5
   OPERATION 4-5
   TESTING 4-6
   REMOVAL & INSTALLATION 4-6
EXHAUST GAS RECIRCULATION (EGR)
  SYSTEM 4-6
   OPERATION 4-6
   TESTING 4-8
   REMOVAL & INSTALLATION 4-8
**ELECTRONIC ENGINE
  CONTROLS 4-11**
GENERAL INFORMATION 4-11
ENGINE/POWERTRAIN CONTROL MOD-
  ULE (ECM/PCM) 4-11
   OPERATION 4-11
   REMOVAL & INSTALLATION 4-12
   FUNCTIONAL CHECK 4-12
OXYGEN (O₂) SENSOR 4-13
   OPERATION 4-13
   TESTING 4-13
   REMOVAL & INSTALLATION 4-13
IDLE AIR CONTROL (IAC) VALVE 4-13
   OPERATION 4-13
   REMOVAL & INSTALLATION 4-14
ENGINE COOLANT TEMPERATURE (ECT)
  SENSOR 4-14
   OPERATION 4-14
   TESTING 4-14
   REMOVAL & INSTALLATION 4-14
MANIFOLD AIR TEMPERATURE
  (MAT)/INTAKE AIR TEMPERATURE (IAT)
  SENSOR 4-15
   OPERATION 4-15
   TESTING 4-15
   REMOVAL & INSTALLATION 4-15
MANIFOLD ABSOLUTE PRESSURE (MAP)
  SENSOR 4-16
   OPERATION 4-16

TESTING 4-16
   REMOVAL & INSTALLATION 4-16
THROTTLE POSITION (TP) SENSOR 4-16
   OPERATION 4-16
   TESTING 4-16
   ADJUSTMENT 4-16
   REMOVAL & INSTALLATION 4-17
CAMSHAFT POSITION (CMP)
  SENSOR 4-17
   OPERATION 4-17
   REMOVAL & INSTALLATION 4-17
CRANKSHAFT POSITION (CKP)
  SENSOR 4-17
   OPERATION 4-17
   TESTING 4-17
   REMOVAL & INSTALLATION 4-17
KNOCK SENSOR (KS) 4-18
   OPERATION 4-18
   REMOVAL & INSTALLATION 4-18
TROUBLE CODES 4-18
GENERAL INFORMATION 4-18
   LEARNING ABILITY 4-19
   DASHBOARD WARNING LAMP 4-19
TOOLS AND EQUIPMENT 4-19
   SCAN TOOLS 4-19
   ELECTRICAL TOOLS 4-19
DIAGNOSIS AND TESTING 4-19
   TROUBLESHOOTING 4-19
READING CODES 4-20
CLEARING CODES 4-21
**COMPONENT LOCATION
  DIAGRAMS 4-23**
VACUUM DIAGRAMS 4-28

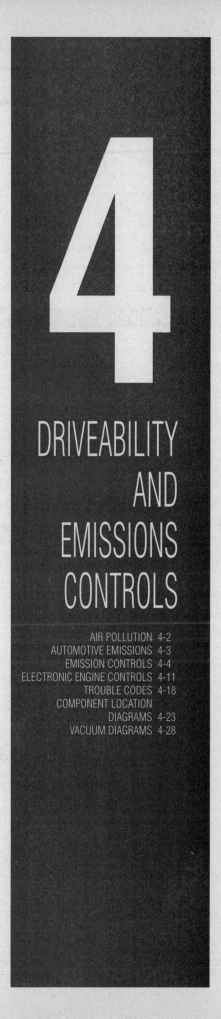

DRIVEABILITY
AND
EMISSIONS
CONTROLS

AIR POLLUTION 4-2
AUTOMOTIVE EMISSIONS 4-3
EMISSION CONTROLS 4-4
ELECTRONIC ENGINE CONTROLS 4-11
TROUBLE CODES 4-18
COMPONENT LOCATION
DIAGRAMS 4-23
VACUUM DIAGRAMS 4-28

AIR POLLUTION

The earth's atmosphere, at or near sea level, consists approximately of 78 percent nitrogen, 21 percent oxygen and 1 percent other gases. If it were possible to remain in this state, 100 percent clean air would result. However, many varied sources allow other gases and particulates to mix with the clean air, causing our atmosphere to become unclean or polluted.

Some of these pollutants are visible while others are invisible, with each having the capability of causing distress to the eyes, ears, throat, skin and respiratory system. Should these pollutants become concentrated in a specific area and under certain conditions, death could result due to the displacement or chemical change of the oxygen content in the air. These pollutants can also cause great damage to the environment and to the many man made objects that are exposed to the elements.

To better understand the causes of air pollution, the pollutants can be categorized into 3 separate types, natural, industrial and automotive.

Natural Pollutants

Natural pollution has been present on earth since before man appeared and continues to be a factor when discussing air pollution, although it causes only a small percentage of the overall pollution problem. It is the direct result of decaying organic matter, wind born smoke and particulates from such natural events as plain and forest fires (ignited by heat or lightning), volcanic ash, sand and dust which can spread over a large area of the countryside.

Such a phenomenon of natural pollution has been seen in the form of volcanic eruptions, with the resulting plume of smoke, steam and volcanic ash blotting out the sun's rays as it spreads and rises higher into the atmosphere. As it travels into the atmosphere the upper air currents catch and carry the smoke and ash, while condensing the steam back into water vapor. As the water vapor, smoke and ash travel on their journey, the smoke dissipates into the atmosphere while the ash and moisture settle back to earth in a trail hundreds of miles long. In some cases, lives are lost and millions of dollars of property damage result.

Industrial Pollutants

Industrial pollution is caused primarily by industrial processes, the burning of coal, oil and natural gas, which in turn produce smoke and fumes. Because the burning fuels contain large amounts of sulfur, the principal ingredients of smoke and fumes are sulfur dioxide and particulate matter. This type of pollutant occurs most severely during still, damp and cool weather, such as at night. Even in its less severe form, this pollutant is not confined to just cities. Because of air movements, the pollutants move for miles over the surrounding countryside, leaving in its path a barren and unhealthy environment for all living things.

Working with Federal, State and Local mandated regulations and by carefully monitoring emissions, big business has greatly reduced the amount of pollutant introduced from its industrial sources, striving to obtain an acceptable level. Because of the mandated industrial emission clean up, many land areas and streams in and around the cities that were formerly barren of vegetation and life, have now begun to move back in the direction of nature's intended balance.

Automotive Pollutants

The third major source of air pollution is automotive emissions. The emissions from the internal combustion engines were not an appreciable problem years ago because of the small number of registered vehicles and the nation's small highway system. However, during the early 1950's, the trend of the American people was to move from the cities to the surrounding suburbs. This caused an immediate problem in transportation because the majority of suburbs were not afforded mass transit conveniences. This lack of transportation created an attractive market for the automobile manufacturers, which resulted in a dramatic increase in the number of vehicles produced and sold, along with a marked increase in highway construction between cities and the suburbs. Multi-vehicle families emerged with a growing emphasis placed on an individual vehicle per family member. As the increase in vehicle ownership and usage occurred, so did pollutant levels in and around the cities, as suburbanites drove daily to their businesses and employment, returning at the end of the day to their homes in the suburbs.

It was noted that a smoke and fog type haze was being formed and at times, remained in suspension over the cities, taking time to dissipate. At first this

"smog," derived from the words "smoke" and "fog," was thought to result from industrial pollution but it was determined that automobile emissions shared the blame. It was discovered that when normal automobile emissions were exposed to sunlight for a period of time, complex chemical reactions would take place.

It is now known that smog is a photo chemical layer which develops when certain oxides of nitrogen (NOx) and unburned hydrocarbons (HC) from automobile emissions are exposed to sunlight. Pollution was more severe when smog would become stagnant over an area in which a warm layer of air settled over the top of the cooler air mass, trapping and holding the cooler mass at ground level. The trapped cooler air would keep the emissions from being dispersed and diluted through normal air flows. This type of air stagnation was given the name "Temperature Inversion."

TEMPERATURE INVERSION

In normal weather situations, surface air is warmed by heat radiating from the earth's surface and the sun's rays. This causes it to rise upward, into the atmosphere. Upon rising it will cool through a convection type heat exchange with the cooler upper air. As warm air rises, the surface pollutants are carried upward and dissipated into the atmosphere.

When a temperature inversion occurs, we find the higher air is no longer cooler, but is warmer than the surface air, causing the cooler surface air to become trapped. This warm air blanket can extend from above ground level to a few hundred or even a few thousand feet into the air. As the surface air is trapped, so are the pollutants, causing a severe smog condition. Should this stagnant air mass extend to a few thousand feet high, enough air movement with the inversion takes place to allow the smog layer to rise above ground level but the pollutants still cannot dissipate. This inversion can remain for days over an area, with the smog level only rising or lowering from ground level to a few hundred feet high. Meanwhile, the pollutant levels increase, causing eye irritation, respiratory problems, reduced visibility, plant damage and in some cases, even disease.

This inversion phenomenon was first noted in the Los Angeles, California area. The city lies in terrain resembling a basin and with certain weather conditions, a cold air mass is held in the basin while a warmer air mass covers it like a lid.

Because this type of condition was first documented as prevalent in the Los Angeles area, this type of trapped pollution was named Los Angeles Smog, although it occurs in other areas where a large concentration of automobiles are used and the air remains stagnant for any length of time.

HEAT TRANSFER

Consider the internal combustion engine as a machine in which raw materials must be placed so a finished product comes out. As in any machine operation, a certain amount of wasted material is formed. When we relate this to the internal combustion engine, we find that through the input of air and fuel, we obtain power during the combustion process to drive the vehicle. The by-product or waste of this power is, in part, heat and exhaust gases with which we must dispose.

The heat from the combustion process can rise to over 4000°F (2204°C). The dissipation of this heat is controlled by a ram air effect, the use of cooling fans to cause air flow and a liquid coolant solution surrounding the combustion area to transfer the heat of combustion through the cylinder walls and into the coolant. The coolant is then directed to a thin-finned, multi-tubed radiator, from which the excess heat is transferred to the atmosphere by 1 of the 3 heat transfer methods, conduction, convection or radiation.

The cooling of the combustion area is an important part in the control of exhaust emissions. To understand the behavior of the combustion and transfer of its heat, consider the air/fuel charge. It is ignited and the flame front burns progressively across the combustion chamber until the burning charge reaches the cylinder walls. Some of the fuel in contact with the walls is not hot enough to burn, thereby snuffing out or quenching the combustion process. This leaves unburned fuel in the combustion chamber. This unburned fuel is then forced out of the cylinder and into the exhaust system, along with the exhaust gases.

Many attempts have been made to minimize the amount of unburned fuel in the combustion chambers due to quenching, by increasing the coolant temperature and lessening the contact area of the coolant around the combustion area. However, design limitations within the combustion chambers prevent the complete burning of the air/fuel charge, so a certain amount of the unburned fuel is still expelled into the exhaust system, regardless of modifications to the engine.

AUTOMOTIVE EMISSIONS

Before emission controls were mandated on internal combustion engines, other sources of engine pollutants were discovered along with the exhaust emissions. It was determined that engine combustion exhaust produced approximately 60 percent of the total emission pollutants, fuel evaporation from the fuel tank and carburetor vents produced 20 percent, with the final 20 percent being produced through the crankcase as a by-product of the combustion process.

Exhaust Gases

The exhaust gases emitted into the atmosphere are a combination of burned and unburned fuel. To understand the exhaust emission and its composition, we must review some basic chemistry.

When the air/fuel mixture is introduced into the engine, we are mixing air, composed of nitrogen (78 percent), oxygen (21 percent) and other gases (1 percent) with the fuel, which is 100 percent hydrocarbons (HC), in a semi-controlled ratio. As the combustion process is accomplished, power is produced to move the vehicle while the heat of combustion is transferred to the cooling system. The exhaust gases are then composed of nitrogen, a diatomic gas (N_2), the same as was introduced in the engine, carbon dioxide (CO_2), the same gas that is used in beverage carbonation, and water vapor (H_2O). The nitrogen (N_2), for the most part, passes through the engine unchanged, while the oxygen (O_2) reacts (burns) with the hydrocarbons (HC) and produces the carbon dioxide (CO_2) and the water vapors (H_2O). If this chemical process would be the only process to take place, the exhaust emissions would be harmless. However, during the combustion process, other compounds are formed which are considered dangerous. These pollutants are hydrocarbons (HC), carbon monoxide (CO), oxides of nitrogen (NOx) oxides of sulfur (SOx) and engine particulates.

HYDROCARBONS

Hydrocarbons (HC) are essentially fuel which was not burned during the combustion process or which has escaped into the atmosphere through fuel evaporation. The main sources of incomplete combustion are rich air/fuel mixtures, low engine temperatures and improper spark timing. The main sources of hydrocarbon emission through fuel evaporation on most vehicles used to be the vehicle's fuel tank and carburetor float bowl.

To reduce combustion hydrocarbon emission, engine modifications were made to minimize dead space and surface area in the combustion chamber. In addition, the air/fuel mixture was made more lean through the improved control which feedback carburetion and fuel injection offers and by the addition of external controls to aid in further combustion of the hydrocarbons outside the engine. Two such methods were the addition of air injection systems, to inject fresh air into the exhaust manifolds and the installation of catalytic converters, units that are able to burn traces of hydrocarbons without affecting the internal combustion process or fuel economy.

To control hydrocarbon emissions through fuel evaporation, modifications were made to the fuel tank to allow storage of the fuel vapors during periods of engine shut-down. Modifications were also made to the air intake system so that at specific times during engine operation, these vapors may be purged and burned by blending them with the air/fuel mixture.

CARBON MONOXIDE

Carbon monoxide is formed when not enough oxygen is present during the combustion process to convert carbon (C) to carbon dioxide (CO_2). An increase in the carbon monoxide (CO) emission is normally accompanied by an increase in the hydrocarbon (HC) emission because of the lack of oxygen to completely burn all of the fuel mixture.

Carbon monoxide (CO) also increases the rate at which the photo chemical smog is formed by speeding up the conversion of nitric oxide (NO) to nitrogen dioxide (NO_2). To accomplish this, carbon monoxide (CO) combines with oxygen (O_2) and nitric oxide (NO) to produce carbon dioxide (CO_2) and nitrogen dioxide (NO_2). ($CO + O_2 + NO = CO_2 + NO_2$).

The dangers of carbon monoxide, which is an odorless and colorless toxic gas are many. When carbon monoxide is inhaled into the lungs and passed into the blood stream, oxygen is replaced by the carbon monoxide in the red blood cells, causing a reduction in the amount of oxygen supplied to the many parts of the body. This lack of oxygen causes headaches, lack of coordination, reduced mental alertness and, should the carbon monoxide concentration be high enough, death could result.

NITROGEN

Normally, nitrogen is an inert gas. When heated to approximately 2500°F (1371°C) through the combustion process, this gas becomes active and causes an increase in the nitric oxide (NO) emission.

Oxides of nitrogen (NOx) are composed of approximately 97–98 percent nitric oxide (NO). Nitric oxide is a colorless gas but when it is passed into the atmosphere, it combines with oxygen and forms nitrogen dioxide (NO_2). The nitrogen dioxide then combines with chemically active hydrocarbons (HC) and when in the presence of sunlight, causes the formation of photo-chemical smog.

Ozone

To further complicate matters, some of the nitrogen dioxide (NO_2) is broken apart by the sunlight to form nitric oxide and oxygen. (NO_2 + sunlight = NO + O). This single atom of oxygen then combines with diatomic (meaning 2 atoms) oxygen (O_2) to form ozone (O_3). Ozone is one of the smells associated with smog. It has a pungent and offensive odor, irritates the eyes and lung tissues, affects the growth of plant life and causes rapid deterioration of rubber products. Ozone can be formed by sunlight as well as electrical discharge into the air.

The most common discharge area on the automobile engine is the secondary ignition electrical system, especially when inferior quality spark plug cables are used. As the surge of high voltage is routed through the secondary cable, the circuit builds up an electrical field around the wire, which acts upon the oxygen in the surrounding air to form the ozone. The faint glow along the cable with the engine running that may be visible on a dark night, is called the "corona discharge." It is the result of the electrical field passing from a high along the cable, to a low in the surrounding air, which forms the ozone gas. The combination of corona and ozone has been a major cause of cable deterioration. Recently, different and better quality insulating materials have lengthened the life of the electrical cables.

. Although ozone at ground level can be harmful, ozone is beneficial to the earth's inhabitants. By having a concentrated ozone layer called the "ozonosphere," between 10 and 20 miles (16–32 km) up in the atmosphere, much of the ultra violet radiation from the sun's rays are absorbed and screened. If this ozone layer were not present, much of the earth's surface would be burned, dried and unfit for human life.

OXIDES OF SULFUR

Oxides of sulfur (SOx) were initially ignored in the exhaust system emissions, since the sulfur content of gasoline as a fuel is less than $\frac{1}{10}$ of 1 percent. Because of this small amount, it was felt that it contributed very little to the overall pollution problem. However, because of the difficulty in solving the sulfur emissions in industrial pollution and the introduction of catalytic converters to automobile exhaust systems, a change was mandated. The automobile exhaust system, when equipped with a catalytic converter, changes the sulfur dioxide (SO_2) into sulfur trioxide (SO_3).

When this combines with water vapors (H_2O), a sulfuric acid mist (H_2SO_4) is formed and is a very difficult pollutant to handle since it is extremely corrosive. This sulfuric acid mist that is formed, is the same mist that rises from the vents of an automobile battery when an active chemical reaction takes place within the battery cells.

When a large concentration of vehicles equipped with catalytic converters are operating in an area, this acid mist may rise and be distributed over a large ground area causing land, plant, crop, paint and building damage.

PARTICULATE MATTER

A certain amount of particulate matter is present in the burning of any fuel, with carbon constituting the largest percentage of the particulates. In gasoline, the remaining particulates are the burned remains of the various other compounds used in its manufacture. When a gasoline engine is in good internal condition, the particulate emissions are low but as the engine wears internally, the particulate emissions increase. By visually inspecting the tail pipe emissions, a determination can be made as to where an engine defect may exist. An engine with light gray or blue smoke emitting from the tail pipe normally indicates an increase in the oil consumption through burning due to internal engine wear. Black smoke would indicate a defective fuel delivery system, causing the engine to operate in a rich mode. Regardless of the color of the smoke, the internal part of the engine or the fuel delivery system should be repaired to prevent excess particulate emissions.

Diesel and turbine engines emit a darkened plume of smoke from the exhaust system because of the type of fuel used. Emission control regulations are mandated for this type of emission and more stringent measures are being used to prevent excess emission of the particulate matter. Electronic components are being introduced to control the injection of the fuel at precisely the proper time of piston travel, to achieve the optimum in fuel ignition and fuel usage. Other particulate after-burning components are being tested to achieve a cleaner emission.

Good grades of engine lubricating oils should be used, which meet the manufacturer's specification. Cut-rate oils can contribute to the particulate emission problem because of their low flash or ignition temperature point. Such oils burn prematurely during the combustion process causing emission of particulate matter.

The cooling system is an important factor in the reduction of particulate matter. The optimum combustion will occur, with the cooling system operating at a temperature specified by the manufacturer. The cooling system must be maintained in the same manner as the engine oiling system, as each system is required to perform properly in order for the engine to operate efficiently for a long time.

Crankcase Emissions

Crankcase emissions are made up of water, acids, unburned fuel, oil fumes and particulates. These emissions are classified as hydrocarbons (HC) and are formed by the small amount of unburned, compressed air/fuel mixture entering the crankcase from the combustion area (between the cylinder walls and piston rings) during the compression and power strokes. The head of the compression and combustion help to form the remaining crankcase emissions.

Since the first engines, crankcase emissions were allowed into the atmosphere through a road draft tube, mounted on the lower side of the engine block. Fresh air came in through an open oil filler cap or breather. The air passed through the crankcase mixing with blow-by gases. The motion of the vehicle and the air blowing past the open end of the road draft tube caused a low pressure area (vacuum) at the end of the tube. Crankcase emissions were simply drawn out of the road draft tube into the air.

To control the crankcase emission, the road draft tube was deleted. A hose and/or tubing was routed from the crankcase to the intake manifold so the blow-by emission could be burned with the air/fuel mixture. However, it was found that intake manifold vacuum, used to draw the crankcase emissions into the manifold, would vary in strength at the wrong time and not allow the proper emission flow. A regulating valve was needed to control the flow of air through the crankcase.

Testing, showed the removal of the blow-by gases from the crankcase as quickly as possible, was most important to the longevity of the engine. Should large accumulations of blow-by gases remain and condense, dilution of the engine oil would occur to form water, soots, resins, acids and lead salts, resulting in the formation of sludge and varnishes. This condensation of the blow-by gases occurs more frequently on vehicles used in numerous starting and stopping conditions, excessive idling and when the engine is not allowed to attain normal operating temperature through short runs.

Evaporative Emissions

Gasoline fuel is a major source of pollution, before and after it is burned in the automobile engine. From the time the fuel is refined, stored, pumped and transported, again stored until it is pumped into the fuel tank of the vehicle, the gasoline gives off unburned hydrocarbons (HC) into the atmosphere. Through the redesign of storage areas and venting systems, the pollution factor was diminished, but not eliminated, from the refinery standpoint. However, the automobile still remained the primary source of vaporized, unburned hydrocarbon (HC) emissions.

Fuel pumped from an underground storage tank is cool but when exposed to a warmer ambient temperature, will expand. Before controls were mandated, an owner might fill the fuel tank with fuel from an underground storage tank and park the vehicle for some time in warm area, such as a parking lot. As the fuel would warm, it would expand and should no provisions or area be provided for the expansion, the fuel would spill out of the filler neck and onto the ground, causing hydrocarbon (HC) pollution and creating a severe fire hazard. To correct this condition, the vehicle manufacturers added overflow plumbing and/or gasoline tanks with built in expansion areas or domes.

However, this did not control the fuel vapor emission from the fuel tank. It was determined that most of the fuel evaporation occurred when the vehicle was stationary and the engine not operating. Most vehicles carry 5–25 gallons (19–95 liters) of gasoline. Should a large concentration of vehicles be parked in one area, such as a large parking lot, excessive fuel vapor emissions would take place, increasing as the temperature increases.

To prevent the vapor emission from escaping into the atmosphere, the fuel systems were designed to trap the vapors while the vehicle is stationary, by sealing the system from the atmosphere. A storage system is used to collect and hold the fuel vapors from the carburetor (if equipped) and the fuel tank when the engine is not operating. When the engine is started, the storage system is then purged of the fuel vapors, which are drawn into the engine and burned with the air/fuel mixture.

EMISSION CONTROLS

There are three sources of automotive pollutants: crankcase fumes, exhaust gases, and gasoline evaporation. The pollutants formed from these substances fall into three categories: unburned hydrocarbons (HC), carbon monoxide (CO), and oxides of nitrogen (NOx). The equipment that is used to limit these pollutants is commonly called emission control equipment.

Crankcase Ventilation System

OPERATION

▶ **See Figures 1, 2 and 3**

A crankcase ventilation system is used on all vehicles to evacuate the crankcase vapors. There are 2 types of ventilation systems: Crankcase Ventilation (CV) and Positive Crankcase Ventilation (PCV). Both systems purge crankcase vapors and differ only in the use of fresh air.

The CV system, used on the 3.1L engine, introduces fresh air into the crankcase.

The PCV system and the CV system on the 3.1L engine, circulates fresh air from the air cleaner or intake duct through the crankcase, where it mixes with

CLEAN AIR
VOLATILE OIL FUMES
MIXTURE OF AIR AND FUMES

1. PCV valve
2. Air cleaner
3. Crankshaft vent hose
4. PCV valve hose

87954001

Fig. 1 The PCV system circulates crankcase vapors into the intake manifold for burning—1990 2.0L (VIN M) engine shown

Fig. 2 Cross-section of a PCV valve

⇨ CLEAN AIR
➡ VOLATILE OIL FUMES
---→ MIXTURE OF AIR AND FUMES

1. Crankcase ventilation valve
2. To throttle body
3. Crankcase vent hose
4. Crankcase ventilation valve hose
5. To intake manifold

87954003

Fig. 3 Crankcase Ventilation (CV) flow—3.1L engine shown

blow-by gases and then passes through the Positive Crankcase Ventilation (PCV) valve or constant bleed orifice into the intake manifold.

When manifold vacuum is high, such as at idle, the orifice or valve restricts the flow of blow-by gases into the intake manifold. If abnormal operating conditions occur, the system will allow excessive blow-by gases to back flow through the hose into the air cleaner. These blow-by gases will then be mixed with the intake air in the air cleaner instead of the manifold. The air cleaner has a small filter attached to the inside wall that connects to the breather hose to trap impurities flowing in either direction.

A plugged PCV valve, orifice or hose may cause rough idle, stalling or slow idle speed, oil leaks, oil in the air cleaner or sludge in the engine. A leak could cause rough idle, stalling or high idle speed. The condition of the grommets in the valve cover will also affect system and engine performance.

TESTING

PCV System

1. Run the engine at idle at normal operating temperature.
2. Remove the PCV valve or orifice from the grommet in the valve cover and place your thumb over the end to check if vacuum is present. If vacuum is not present, check for plugged hoses or manifold port. Repair or replace as necessary.
3. If the engine is equipped with a PCV valve, stop the engine and remove the valve. Shake and listen for the rattle of the check valve needle. If no rattle is heard, replace the valve.

CV System

1. Check the CV system for proper flow by looking for oil sludging or leaks.

2. If noted, check the smaller nipple of the oil/air separator by blowing through it or inserting a 0.06 in. (1.52mm) plug gauge into the orifice inside the nipple.
3. If the orifice is plugged, replace the CV oil/air separator assembly.

REMOVAL & INSTALLATION

Removal and installation of the PCV or CV valve is located in Section 1 of this manual.

Evaporative Emission Control System

OPERATION

▶ **See Figures 4 and 5**

The Evaporative Emission Control System (EECS) is designed to prevent fuel tank vapors from being emitted into the atmosphere. When the engine is not running, gasoline vapors from the tank are stored in in a charcoal canister, mounted under the hood. The charcoal canister absorbs the gasoline vapors and stores them until certain engine conditions are met and the vapors can be purged and burned by the engine. In some vehicles with fuel injection, any liquid fuel entering the canister goes into a reservoir in the bottom of the canister to protect the integrity of the carbon element in the canister above. A few different methods (depending upon application) are used to control the purge cycle of the charcoal canister.

1 Canister purge
2 Vapor from fuel tank
3 Carbon
4 Air

87954031

Fig. 4 Cross-sectional view of a typical EVAP canister

1 Throttle body
2 Fuel vapor canister
3 Fuel tank
4 Fuel vapor restriction
5 Pressure/vacuum relief vented fuel filler cap
6 Fuel tank pressure control valve
7 Fuel vapor purge solenoid assembly
8 Purge line
9 Air inlet

87954032

Fig. 5 Schematic of the evaporative emissions control system

In the first method, the charcoal canister purge cycle is controlled by throttle position without the use of a valve on the canister. A vacuum line connects the canister to a ported vacuum source on the throttle body. When the throttle is at any position above idle, a vacuum is created in the throttle body venturi. That vacuum acts on the canister causing fresh air to be drawn into the bottom of the canister and the fuel vapors to be carried into the throttle body at that vacuum port. The air/vapor flow volume is only what can be drawn through the vacuum port and is fairly constant.

For the second method, the flow volume is modulated with throttle position through a vacuum valve. The ported vacuum from the throttle body is used to open a diaphragm valve on top of the canister. When the valve is open, air and vapors are drawn into the intake manifold, usually through the same manifold port as the PCV system. With this method, the purge valve cycle is slaved to the throttle opening; more throttle opening, more purge air flow.

And third, the charcoal canister purge valve cycle is controlled by the computer control module through a solenoid valve mounted on or remotely from the canister. When the solenoid is activated, full manifold vacuum is applied to the top of the purge valve diaphragm to open the valve all the way. A high volume of fresh air is drawn into the canister and the gasoline vapors are purged quickly. The ECM activates the solenoid valve when the following conditions are met:

- The engine is at normal operating temperature.
- After the engine has been running for a specified period of time.
- Vehicle speed is above a predetermined speed.
- Throttle opening is above a predetermined value.

➡️**Remember that the fuel tank filler cap is an integral part of the system in that is was designed to seal in fuel vapors. If it is lost or damaged, make sure the replacement is or the correct size and fit so a proper seal can be obtained.**

A vent pipe allows fuel vapors to flow to the charcoal canister. On some vehicles, the tank is isolated from the charcoal canister by a tank pressure control valve, located either in the tank or in the vapor line near the canister. It is a combination roll-over, integral pressure and vacuum relief valve. When the vapor pressure in the tank exceeds 0.73 psi (5 kPa), the valve opens to allow vapors to vent to the canister. The valve also provides vacuum relief to protect against vacuum build-up in the fuel tank and roll-over spill protection.

Poor engine idle, stalling and poor driveability can be caused by an inoperative canister purge solenoid, a damaged canister or split, damaged or improperly connected hoses.

The most common symptom of problems in this system is fuel odors coming from under the hood. If there is not liquid fuel leak, check for a cracked or damaged vapor canister, inoperative or always open canister control valve, disconnected, mis-routed, kinked or damaged vapor pipe or canister hoses; or a damaged air cleaner or improperly seated air cleaner gasket.

TESTING

Charcoal Canister

1. Visually check the canister for cracks or damage.
2. If fuel is leaking from the bottom of the canister, replace the canister and check for proper hose routing.
3. Check the filter at the bottom of the canister. If dirty, replace the filter.

Tank Pressure Control Valve

1. Using a hand-held vacuum pump, apply a vacuum of 15 in. Hg (51 kPa) through the control vacuum signal tube to the purge valve diaphragm. If the diaphragm does not hold vacuum for at least 20 seconds, the diaphragm is leaking. Replace the control valve.
2. With the vacuum still applied to the control vacuum tube, attach a short piece of hose to the valve's tank tube side and blow into the hose. Air should pass through the valve. If it does not, replace the control valve.

Canister Purge Control Valve

1. Connect a clean length of hose to the fuel tank vapor line connection on the canister and attempt to blow through the purge control valve. It should be difficult or impossible to blow through the purge control valve. If air passes easily, the valve is stuck open and should be replaced.
2. Connect a hand-held vacuum pump to the top vacuum line fitting of the

purge control valve. Apply a vacuum of 15 in. Hg (51 kPa) to the purge valve diaphragm. If the diaphragm does not hold vacuum for at least 20 seconds, the diaphragm is leaking. Replace the control valve. If it is impossible to blow through the valve, it is stuck closed and must be replaced.

3. On vehicles with a solenoid activated purge control valve, unplug the connector and use jumper wires to supply 12 volts to the solenoid connections on the valve. With the vacuum still applied to the control vacuum tube, the purge control valve should open and it should be easy to blow through. If not, replace the valve.

REMOVAL & INSTALLATION

Charcoal Canister

➡️**On some models it may be necessary to remove the right side fender fascia and filler panels to gain access to the canister.**

1. Disconnect the negative battery cable.
2. Tag and disconnect the hoses from the canister.
3. Unfasten the charcoal canister retaining nuts/bolts and remove any retaining straps that may be securing the canister.
4. If necessary for access, and equipped with air conditioning, loosen the attachments holding the accumulator and pipe assembly.
5. Remove the canister from the vehicle.

➡️**Always replace any vapor hose(s) that may be showing signs of wear.**

6. Installation is the reverse of the removal procedure. Refer to the Vehicle Emission Control Information label, located in the engine compartment, for proper routing of the vacuum hoses.

Tank Pressure Control Valve

1. Tag and disconnect the hoses from the control valve.
2. Unfasten the mounting hardware.
3. Remove the control valve from the vehicle.
4. Installation is the reverse of the removal procedure. Refer to the Vehicle Emission Control Information label, located in the engine compartment, for proper routing of the vacuum hoses.

Canister Purge Control Solenoid Valve

1. Disconnect the negative battery cable.
2. Tag and detach the electrical connector(s), hose and line from the solenoid valve.
3. Unfasten the retainer (screw, bolts or locking tab), then remove the valve from the vehicle.
4. Installation is the reverse of the removal procedure.

Filter Replacement

1. Remove the vapor canister, as outlined earlier in this section.
2. Pull the filter out from the bottom of the canister.
3. Install a new filter and then replace the canister.

Exhaust Gas Recirculation (EGR) System

OPERATION

▶ **See Figures 6 thru 11**

The EGR system is used to reduce oxides of nitrogen (NOx) emission levels caused by high combustion chamber temperatures. This is accomplished by the use of an EGR valve which opens, under specific engine operating conditions, to admit a small amount of exhaust gas into the intake manifold, below the throttle plate. The exhaust gas mixes with the incoming air charge and displaces a portion of the oxygen in the air/fuel mixture entering the combustion chamber. The exhaust gas does not support combustion of the air/fuel mixture but it takes up volume, the net effect of which is to lower the temperature of the combustion process. This lower temperature also helps control detonation.

The EGR valve is mounted on the intake manifold and has an opening into the exhaust manifold. The EGR valve is opened by ported vacuum and allows

1. EGR valve   3. Intake air
2. Exhaust gas   4. Ported vacuum

87954004

Fig. 6 Exhaust Gas Recirculation (EGR) system flow

ASSEMBLY PLANT CODE

PART IDENTIFICATION NUMBER

DAY OF YEAR

SHIFT I.D.

YEAR

BUILD DATE CODE

TYPE OF VALVE:
P = POSITIVE BACKPRESSURE
N = NEGATIVE BACKPRESSURE
BLANK = PORTED VALVE

87954006

Fig. 7 Ported, negative and positive backpressure EGR valve identification

exhaust gases to flow into the intake manifold. If too much exhaust gas enters, combustion will not occur. Because of this, very little exhaust gas is allowed to pass through the valve. The EGR system will be activated once the engine reaches normal operating temperature and the EGR valve will open when engine operating conditions are above idle speed and below Wide Open Throttle (WOT). On California vehicles equipped with a Vehicle Speed Sensor (VSS), the EGR valve opens when the VSS signal is greater than 2 mph. The EGR system is deactivated on vehicles equipped with a Transmission Converter Clutch (TCC) when the TCC is engaged.

Too much EGR flow at idle, cruise, or during cold operation may result in the engine stalling after cold start, the engine stalling at idle after deceleration, vehicle surge during cruise and rough idle. If the EGR valve is always open, the vehicle may not idle. Too little or no EGR flow allows combustion temperatures to get too high which could result in spark knock (detonation), engine overheating and/or emission test failure.

There are 5 types of EGR valves used; The negative backpressure EGR valve, positive backpressure EGR valve, Ported EGR valve, Integrated Electronic EGR valve and the Digital EGR valve. The principle of all systems is the same; the only difference is in the method used to control how far the EGR valve opens.

Negative Backpressure EGR Valve

The negative backpressure EGR valve, used on the 2.0L (VIN P and K) and 2.2L engines, varies the amount of exhaust gas flow into the intake manifold depending on manifold vacuum and variations in exhaust backpressure. Like the ported EGR valve, the negative backpressure EGR valve uses a ported vacuum source. An air bleed valve, located inside the EGR valve assembly acts as a vacuum regulator. The bleed valve controls the amount of vacuum in the vacuum chamber by bleeding vacuum to outside air during the open phase of the cycle. The diaphragm on the valve has an internal air bleed hole which is held closed by a small spring when there is no exhaust backpressure. Engine vacuum opens the EGR valve against the pressure of a spring. When manifold vacuum combines with negative exhaust backpressure, the vacuum bleed hole opens and the EGR valve closes. This valve will open if vacuum is applied with the engine not running.

1. EGR valve   5. Diaphragm
2. Exhaust gas   6. Air bleed hole
3. Intake air   7. Small spring
4. Vacuum port   8. Large spring

87954005

Fig. 8 Cross-sectional view of a negative backpressure EGR valve

Positive Backpressure (EGR) Valve

The positive backpressure EGR valve is used on the 1.8L and 2.0L (VIN H) engines. A vacuum bleed valve, located in the EGR valve, acts as a vacuum regulator, controlling vacuum above the EGR valve diaphragm. Exhaust backpressure is passed through the hollow pintle shaft and exerted on the bleed valve. When sufficient backpressure is applied on the bleed valve, the valve will open, allowing vacuum above the diaphragm to vent to the atmosphere. This will result in the EGR valve closing.

1. EGR valve   5. Diaphragm
2. Exhaust gas   6. Vacuum bleed hole
3. Intake air   7. Small spring
4. Vacuum port   8. Large spring

87954007

Fig. 9 Positive backpressure EGR valve

Ported EGR Valve

The ported EGR valve, used on the 2.0L (VIN M), takes its name from the fact that it uses a ported vacuum source to open the EGR valve and modulate the EGR flow. The ported vacuum source is a small opening just above the throttle blade in the throttle body. When the throttle begins to open the air passing through the venturi, creates a low pressure which draws on the EGR valve diaphragm causing it to open. As the throttle blade opens further, the ported vacuum increases and opens the valve further.

The ECM controls EGR operation through an EGR control solenoid. Ported vacuum must flow through the EGR control solenoid to open the EGR valve. The ECM uses information received from the Coolant Temperature Sensor (CTS), Throttle Position Sensor (TPS) and the Mass Air Flow (MAF) sensor to determine when to allow EGR operation. When certain parameters are met, such as engine at normal operating temperature and the engine speed is above idle, the ECM signals the solenoid to open, allowing EGR operation.

1. Diaphragm
2. Pintle position sensor
3. Vacuum connection

87954008

Fig. 10 The 2.8L engine utilizes a integrated electronic EGR valve

1. Solenoid & mounting plate assembly
2. EGR base plate
3. EGR base gasket
4. Insulator gasket
5. EGR base
6. Armature assembly
7. Screw assembly

87954009

Fig. 11 Exploded view of the digital EGR valve which is used on the 3.1L engine

Integrated Electronic EGR Valve

The integrated electronic EGR valve, used on the 2.8L engines, functions like a ported EGR valve with a remote vacuum regulator, except the regulator and a pintle position sensor are sealed in the back plastic cover. The regulator and position sensor are not serviceable. There is a serviceable filter that provides clean fresh air to the regulator along side the vacuum tube.

This valve has a vacuum regulator to which the ECM provides variable current. This variable current produces the desired EGR flow using inputs from the Manifold Absolute Pressure (MAP) sensor, Engine Coolant Temperature (ECT) sensor and engine RPM.

Digital EGR Valve

The digital EGR valve, used on the 3.1L engine, is designed to accurately supply EGR to an engine, independent of intake manifold vacuum. The valve

controls EGR flow from the exhaust to the intake manifold through three orifices which increment in size to produce seven combinations. When a solenoid is energized, the armature, with attached shaft and swivel pintle is lifted, opening the orifice. The flow accuracy is dependent on metering orifice size only, which results in improved control.

The swivel pintle feature insures good sealing of exhaust gas, reducing the need of critical assembly alignment. In addition, the effects of EGR leakage on idle quality are reduced because the shaft and seals are exposed to exhaust pressure instead of manifold vacuum. The shafts are sealed from the exhaust chamber by floating seals held in place by the seal spring. These springs also hold the upper seals that seal the armature cavity in the solenoids. The solenoid coils are fastened together to maximize reliability and to seal the coils from the environment. The coils use a common power terminal with individual ground terminals.

The digital EGR valve is opened by the PCM quad-driver, grounding each respective solenoid circuit. This quad-driver activates the solenoid, raises the pintle, and allows exhaust gas flow into the intake manifold. The exhaust gas then moves with the air/fuel mixture into the combustion chamber. If too much exhaust gas enters, combustion will not occur. For this reason, very little exhaust gas is allowed to pass through the valve, with virtually none at idle.

TESTING

▶ **See Figures 12 thru 18**

Refer to the appropriate chart the test the EGR system.

REMOVAL & INSTALLATION

EGR Valve

▶ **See Figures 19 thru 24**

1. Disconnect the negative battery cable.
2. Remove the air cleaner assembly, as necessary, for access to the EGR valve.

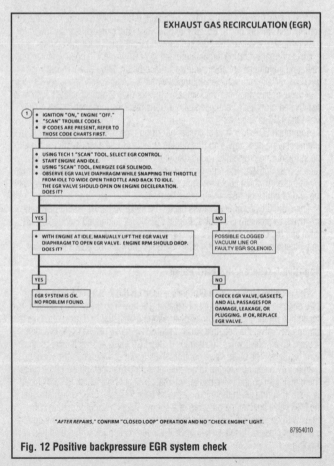

Fig. 12 Positive backpressure EGR system check

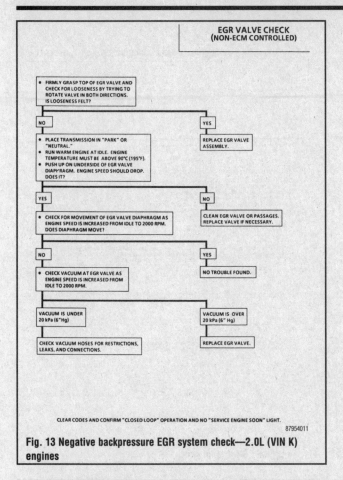

Fig. 13 Negative backpressure EGR system check—2.0L (VIN K) engines

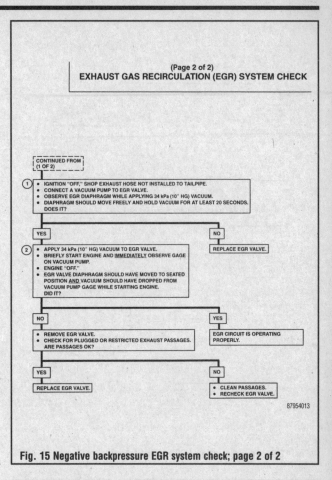

Fig. 15 Negative backpressure EGR system check; page 2 of 2

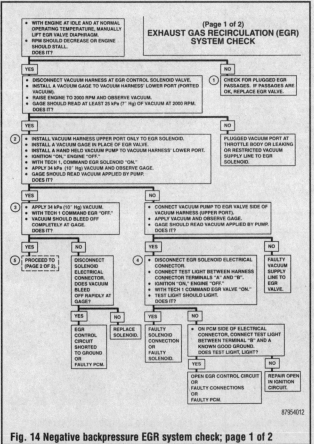

Fig. 14 Negative backpressure EGR system check; page 1 of 2

Fig. 16 Ported EGR system check

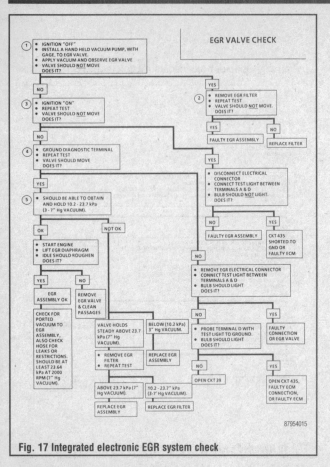

EGR VALVE CHECK

1. • IGNITION "OFF"
   • INSTALL A HAND HELD VACUUM PUMP, WITH GAGE, TO EGR VALVE.
   • APPLY VACUUM AND OBSERVE EGR VALVE
   • VALVE SHOULD NOT MOVE
   DOES IT?

NO

3. • IGNITION "ON"
   • REPEAT TEST
   • VALVE SHOULD NOT MOVE
   DOES IT?

NO

4. • GROUND DIAGNOSTIC TERMINAL
   • REPEAT TEST
   • VALVE SHOULD MOVE
   DOES IT?

YES

5. • SHOULD BE ABLE TO OBTAIN AND HOLD 10.2 - 23.7 kPa (3 - 7" Hg) VACUUM).

OK

• START ENGINE
• LIFT EGR DIAPHRAGM
• IDLE SHOULD ROUGHEN
DOES IT?

YES | NO

EGR ASSEMBLY OK

REMOVE EGR VALVE & CLEAN PASSAGES

CHECK FOR PORTED VACUUM TO EGR ASSEMBLY, ALSO CHECK HOSE FOR LEAKS OR RESTRICTIONS. SHOULD BE AT LEAST 23.64 kPa AT 2000 RPM (7" Hg VACUUM).

VALVE HOLDS STEADY ABOVE 23.7 kPa (7" Hg VACUUM).

• REMOVE EGR FILTER
• REPEAT TEST

ABOVE 23.7 kPa (7" Hg VACUUM).

REPLACE EGR ASSEMBLY

BELOW (10.2 kPa) 3" Hg VACUUM.

REPLACE EGR ASSEMBLY

10.2 - 23.7" kPa (3-7" Hg VACUUM).

REPLACE EGR FILTER

YES

2. • REMOVE EGR FILTER
   • REPEAT TEST
   • VALVE SHOULD NOT MOVE.
   DOES IT?

YES | NO

FAULTY EGR ASSEMBLY | REPLACE FILTER

YES

• DISCONNECT ELECTRICAL CONNECTOR
• CONNECT TEST LIGHT BETWEEN TERMINALS A & D
• BULB SHOULD NOT LIGHT.
DOES IT?

NO | YES

FAULTY EGR ASSEMBLY | CKT 435 SHORTED TO GND OR FAULTY ECM

NO

• REMOVE EGR ELECTRICAL CONNECTOR
• CONNECT TEST LIGHT BETWEEN TERMINALS A & D
• BULB SHOULD LIGHT
DOES IT?

NO | YES

• PROBE TERMINAL D WITH TEST LIGHT TO GROUND.
• BULB SHOULD LIGHT
DOES IT? | FAULTY CONNECTION OR EGR VALVE

NO | YES

OPEN CKT 39 | OPEN CKT 435, FAULTY ECM CONNECTION, OR FAULTY ECM

87954015

Fig. 17 Integrated electronic EGR system check

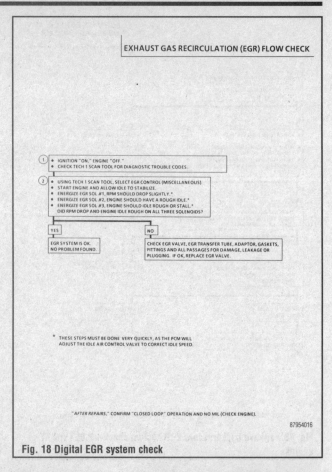

EXHAUST GAS RECIRCULATION (EGR) FLOW CHECK

1. • IGNITION "ON," ENGINE "OFF."
   • CHECK TECH 1 SCAN TOOL FOR DIAGNOSTIC TROUBLE CODES.

2. • USING TECH 1 SCAN TOOL, SELECT EGR CONTROL (MISCELLANEOUS).
   • START ENGINE AND ALLOW IDLE TO STABILIZE.
   • ENERGIZE EGR SOL #1, RPM SHOULD DROP SLIGHTLY.*
   • ENERGIZE EGR SOL #2, ENGINE SHOULD HAVE A ROUGH IDLE.*
   • ENERGIZE EGR SOL #3, ENGINE SHOULD IDLE ROUGH OR STALL.*
   DID RPM DROP AND ENGINE IDLE ROUGH ON ALL THREE SOLENOIDS?

YES | NO

EGR SYSTEM IS OK. NO PROBLEM FOUND. | CHECK EGR VALVE, EGR TRANSFER TUBE, ADAPTOR, GASKETS, FITTINGS AND ALL PASSAGES FOR DAMAGE, LEAKAGE OR PLUGGING. IF OK, REPLACE EGR VALVE.

* THESE STEPS MUST BE DONE VERY QUICKLY, AS THE PCM WILL ADJUST THE IDLE AIR CONTROL VALVE TO CORRECT IDLE SPEED.

"AFTER REPAIRS," CONFIRM "CLOSED LOOP" OPERATION AND NO MIL (CHECK ENGINE).

87954016

Fig. 18 Digital EGR system check

Fig. 19 To remove the air cleaner assembly for access to the EGR valve, detach the ducting, then . . .

Fig. 20 . . . remove the air cleaner assembly

Fig. 21 After removing the air cleaner assembly, disconnect the vacuum hose from the EGR valve

Fig. 22 Unfasten the retaining bolts, then . . .

Fig. 23 . . . remove the EGR valve from the vehicle

Fig. 24 Using a suitable tool, carefully clean the gasket mating surfaces

3. Disconnect the EGR vacuum hose or solenoid wire, as required.

4. Unfasten the EGR valve retaining bolts and remove the EGR valve from the manifold. Remove and discard the EGR valve gasket.

To install:

5. If reinstalling the old valve, inspect the EGR valve passages for excessive build-up of deposits, and clean as necessary.

➡**Loose particles should be completely removed to prevent them from being ingested into the engine.**

6. With a suitable scraper or wire wheel buff the deposits from the mounting surfaces.

7. Install the EGR valve to the intake manifold using a NEW gasket and tighten the bolts EVENLY.

8. Attach the vacuum hose or solenoid wire connector.

9. Install the air cleaner assembly, if removed.

10. Connect the negative battery cable.

EGR Control Solenoid

▶ **See Figure 25**

1. Disconnect the negative battery cable.

2. Detach the electrical connector at the solenoid.

3. Tag and disconnect the vacuum hose(s).

4. Unfasten the retaining nut(s), then remove the solenoid.

To install:

5. Position the solenoid, then secure with the retaining nuts. Tighten the nut(s) to 17 ft. lbs. (24 Nm).

6. Connect the vacuum hoses, as tagged during removal.

7. Attach the solenoid electrical connector.

8. Connect the negative battery cable.

1 EGR control solenoid assembly
2 Tube to EGR valve
3 Tube to throttle body
4 Electrical connector
5 Polyurethane foam filter
  (not serviceable)

87954018

Fig. 25 EGR control solenoid components—2.0L (VIN H) engine shown

ELECTRONIC ENGINE CONTROLS

General Information

The fuel injection system, described in detail in Section 5 of this manual, is operated along with the ignition system to obtain optimum performance and fuel economy while producing a minimum of exhaust emissions. The various sensors described in this section are used by the computer control module (ECM or PCM depending upon application) for feedback to determine proper engine operating conditions.

➡**Although most diagnosis may be conducted using a Digital Volt/Ohm Meter (DVOM), certain steps or procedures may require use of the TECH 1® diagnostic scan tool (a specialized tester) or an equivalent scan/testing tool. If the proper tester is not available, the vehicle should be taken to a reputable service station which has the appropriate equipment.**

When dealing with the electronic engine control system, keep in mind that the system is sensitive to improperly connected electrical and vacuum circuits. The condition and connection of all hoses and wires should always be the first step when attempting to diagnose a driveability problem. Worn or deteriorated hoses and damaged or corroded wires may well make a good component appear faulty.

➡**When troubleshooting the system, always check the electrical and vacuum connectors which may cause the problem before testing or replacing a component.**

For more information on troubleshooting the electronic engine control system, please refer to the information on trouble codes later in this section.

Engine/Powertrain Control Module (ECM/PCM)

OPERATION

The heart of the electronic control system which is found on all vehicles covered by this manual is a computer control module. The module gathers information from various sensors, then controls fuel supply and engine emission systems. Most vehicles are equipped with an Engine Control Module (ECM) which, as its name implies, controls the engine and related emissions systems. Some ECMs may also control the Torque Converter Clutch (TCC) on automatic transmission vehicles or the manual upshift light on manual transmission vehicles. Later model vehicles may be equipped with a Powertrain Control Module (PCM). This is similar to the original ECM, but is designed to control additional systems as well. The PCM may control the manual transmission shift lamp or the shift functions of the electronically controlled automatic transmission.

Regardless of the name, all computer control modules are serviced in a similar manner. Care must be taken when handling these expensive components in order to protect them from damage. Carefully follow all instructions included with the replacement part. Avoid touching pins or connectors to prevent damage from static electricity.

All of these computer control modules contain a Programmable Read Only Memory (PROM) chip, CALPAK or MEM-CAL that contains calibration information which is particular to the vehicle application. This chip is not supplied with a replacement module and must be transferred to the new module before installation. Some late model vehicles equipped with a 3.1L engine utilize both a PROM chip and an Erasable Programmable Read Only Memory (EPROM), which must be programmed with a scan tool after installation. On these models, it is recommended for this procedure to be performed at a properly equipped, reputable shop.

✳ WARNING

To prevent the possibility of permanent control module damage, the ignition switch MUST always be OFF when disconnecting power from or reconnecting power to the module. This includes unplugging the module connector, disconnecting the negative battery cable, removing the module fuse or even attempting to jump your dead battery using jumper cables.

REMOVAL & INSTALLATION

▶ **See Figures 26, 27, 28 and 29**

1. Turn the ignition switch **OFF**.
2. Disconnect the negative battery cable.
3. Remove the right side hush panel, glove box or interior access panel, as required for access to the control module.
4. Detach the electrical harness connectors from the computer control module.
5. Unfasten the module-to-bracket retaining screws, then remove the ECM or PCM as applicable.

1	POWERTRAIN CONTROL MODULE (PCM)
2	INSTRUMENT PANEL
3	I/P COMPARTMENT

87954035

Fig. 26 On most models, the ECM/PCM is located inside the vehicle

6. If replacement of the calibration unit is required, unfasten the access cover retaining screws, then remove the cover from the computer control module. Carefully remove the calibration unit from the ECM/PCM, as follows:
   a. If the ECM contains a PROM carrier, use the rocker type PROM removal tool.
   b. If the ECM contains a CAL-PAK, grasp the CAL-PAK carrier (at the narrow end only), using the removal tool. Remove the CAL-PAK carrier.
   c. If the ECM/PCM contains a MEM-CAL, EPROM or KS Module, push both retaining clips back away from the MEM-CAL/EPROM. At the same time, grasp it at both ends and lift it up out of the socket. Do not remove the cover of the MEM-CAL/EPROM/KS module.

➡ **Before replacement of a defective computer control module, first check the resistance of each ECM/PCM controlled solenoid. This can be done at the module connector, using an ohmmeter and the ECM or PCM connector wiring diagram. Any computer control module controlled device with low resistance will damage the replacement ECM/PCM due to high current flow through the internal circuits.**

To install:
7. Fit the replacement calibration unit into the socket.

➡ **The small notch of the carrier should be aligned with the small notch in the socket. Press on the ends of the carrier until it is firmly seated in the socket. Do not press on the calibration unit, only the carrier.**

8. Install the access cover, then secure using the retaining screws.
9. Position the computer control module in the vehicle, then install the module-to-bracket retaining screws.
10. Attach the module electrical harness connectors.
11. Install the right side hush panel, glove box or interior access panel as required.
12. Check that the ignition switch is **OFF**, then connect the negative battery cable.
13. If your vehicle has the 3.1L engine which is equipped with a PCM with EPROM, the EPROM must be reprogrammed using a scan tool and the latest available software. In all likelihood, the vehicle must be towed to a dealer or repair shop containing the suitable equipment for this service.
14. Enter the self-diagnostic system and check for trouble codes to be sure the module and calibration unit are properly installed. For details, refer to the procedure for checking trouble codes, later in this section.

FUNCTIONAL CHECK

1. Turn the ignition switch **ON**.
2. Enter diagnostics, by grounding the appropriate ALDL terminals. Refer to diagnostics procedures in this section.
3. Allow Code 12 to flash 4 times to verify that no other codes are present. This indicates the PROM or MEM-CAL is installed properly.
4. If trouble Codes 42, 43 or 51 are present or if the SERVICE ENGINE SOON light is on constantly with no codes, the PROM/MEM-CAL is not fully seated, installed backward, has bent pins or is defective.

1	ECM	3	ACCESS COVER
2	PROM		

87954037

Fig. 27 In order to remove the calibration unit, you must first remove the access cover from the control module—1992 vehicle shown

87954039

Fig. 28 Removing the PROM using the special rocker tool

PUSH

87954040

Fig. 29 To remove the EPROM from the PCM, push the retaining clips back away from the unit, grasping both ends, then lift it up out of the socket

➡Anytime the calibration unit is installed backward and the ignition switch is turned ON, the unit is destroyed.

5. If it is not fully seated, press firmly on the ends of the MEM-CAL.

Oxygen (O₂) Sensor

OPERATION

▶ See Figure 30

The oxygen sensor has the ability to produce a low voltage signal that feeds information on engine exhaust oxygen content to the control module.

The sensor is constructed from a zirconia/platinum electrolytic element. Zirconia is an electrolyte that conducts electricity under certain chemical conditions. The element is made up of a ceramic material which acts as an insulator when cold. At operating temperatures of approximately 600°F (315°C), the element becomes a semiconductor. A platinum coating on the outer surface of the element stimulates further combustion of the exhaust gases right at the surface and this helps to keep the element up to the desired temperature.

The oxygen sensor has an inner cavity which is filled with reference (atmospheric) air. The atmosphere has approximately 21 percent oxygen in it. In the circuit, this inner cavity is the positive terminal, while the outer surface (exposed to the exhaust stream) is the negative or ground terminal.

Due to the element's electrolytic properties, oxygen concentration differences between the reference air and exhaust gases produce small voltages. A rich exhaust (excess fuel) has almost no oxygen. So when there is a large difference in the amount of oxygen touching the inside and outside surfaces, more conduction occurs and the sensor puts out a voltage signal above 0.6 V (600 mV). The signal may vary as high as 0.9 V (999 mV).

With a lean exhaust (excessive oxygen), there is about 2 percent oxygen in the gases. The smaller difference in oxygen content causes less conduction and the sensor produces a smaller voltage somewhere below 0.3 V (300 mV). The signal could drop as low as 0.1 V (100 mV). Commonly, values outside this range will cause a trouble code to set for most control systems. When handling the oxygen sensor, follow these precautions:

• Careful handling of the oxygen sensor is essential.
• The electrical pigtail and connector are permanently attached and should not be removed from the oxygen sensor.
• The in-line electrical connector and louvered end of the oxygen sensor must be kept free of grease, dirt and other contaminants.
• Avoid using cleaning solvents of any type on the oxygen sensor.
• Do not drop or roughly handle the oxygen sensor.
• The oxygen sensor may be difficult to remove if the engine temperature is below 120°F (48°C). Excessive force may damage the threads in the exhaust manifold or exhaust pipe.

TESTING

➡This test requires the use of a scan tool.

1. Run the engine at normal operating temperature and connect a scan tool.
2. Disconnect the oxygen sensor. Jumper the purple wire to ground.

3. The scan tool should display O₂voltage below 0.2 volts (200 MV). If it does, then O₂ sensor or sensor connection is faulty and must be replaced. If not, proceed to the following step.
4. With the ignition ON and the engine off, check the voltage of the tan wire leading to the ECM/PCM using a Digital Voltmeter (DVM). The voltage should be 0.3–0.6 volts (300–600 MV).
    a. If the voltage reading is 0.3–0.6 volts, the ECM/PCM is faulty.
    b. If the voltage reading is over 0.6 volts, the wire is open, the connection is faulty or the computer control module is faulty.
    c. If the voltage reading is under 0.3 volts, the computer control module connections or computer control module is faulty.

REMOVAL & INSTALLATION

▶ See Figures 31 and 32

1. Disconnect the negative battery cable.
2. Detach the sensor electrical connector.
3. Carefully remove the Oxygen (O₂) sensor.
To install:

➡A special anti-seize compound is used on the O$BSB2sensor threads. This compound is made up of a liquid graphite and glass beads. The graphite will burn away, but the glass beads will remain, making the sensor easier to remove. New or service sensors will already have the compound applied to the threads. If a sensor is removed from the engine, and is to be reinstalled, the threads must have anti-seize compound applied prior to reinstallation.

4. If reinstalling the old sensor, coat the threads of the sensor with anti-seize compound 5613695 or equivalent.
5. Install the sensor and tighten it to 30 ft. lbs. (41 Nm).
6. Attach the sensor electrical connector.
7. Connect the negative battery cable.

Idle Air Control (IAC) Valve

OPERATION

▶ See Figure 33

Engine idle speeds are controlled by the computer control module (ECM/PCM) through the IAC valve mounted on the throttle body. The ECM or PCM sends voltage pulses to the IAC motor windings causing the IAC motor shaft and pintle to move in or out a given distance (number of steps) for each pulse (called counts). The movement of the pintle controls the airflow around the throttle plate, which in turn, controls engine idle speed. Idle air control valve pintle position counts can be observed using a scan tool. Zero (0) counts corresponds to a fully closed passage, while 140 counts or more correspond to full flow.

Idle speed can be categorized in 2 ways: actual (controlled) idle speed and minimum idle speed. Controlled idle speed is obtained by the ECM positioning the IAC valve pintle. Resulting idle speed is determined by total air flow (IAC

Fig. 30 The oxygen (O₂) sensor is threaded into the exhaust manifold

1 OXYGEN SENSOR (O2S)

87954046

Fig. 31 The oxygen sensor is usually mounted on the exhaust manifold—1988 2.0L (VIN K) engine shown

87954104

Fig. 32 A wrench may be used to remove the oxygen sensor

87954105

passage + PCV + throttle valve + calibrated vacuum leaks). Controlled idle speed is specified at normal operating conditions, which consists of engine coolant at normal operating temperature, air conditioning compressor OFF, manual transaxle in neutral or automatic transaxle in D.

Minimum idle air speed is set at the factory with a stop screw. This setting allows enough air flow by the throttle valves to cause the IAC valve pintle to be positioned a calibrated number of steps (counts) from the seat during normal controlled idle operation.

The idle speed is controlled by the computer control module through the IAC valve. No adjustment is required during routine maintenance. Tampering with the minimum idle speed adjustment is highly discouraged and may result in premature failure of the IAC valve.

REMOVAL & INSTALLATION

▶ **See Figure 34**

1. Disconnect the negative battery cable.
2. Detach the IAC valve electrical connector.
3. Unfasten the IAC valve retaining screws, then remove the valve.

❊❊ WARNING

If the IAC valve has been in service, DO NOT push or pull in the valve pintle. The force required to move the pintle may damage the threads on the worm drive. Do not soak the valve in any liquid cleaner or solvent, as damage may result.

4. Clean the IAC valve O-ring sealing surface, pintle valve seat and air passage. You can clean the valve using GM cleaner 1052626, GM X-66A or equivalent. Use clean shop towel or parts cleaning brush to remove any heavy deposits. If the air passage has heavy deposits, remove the throttle body for complete cleaning.
5. Inspect the O-ring for damage and replace, if necessary.
   To install:

➡ **If you're installing a new IAC valve, you must replace it with an identical part. IAC valve pintle shape and diameter are designed for the specific application.**

6. If you are installing a new IAC valve, measure the distance between the tip of the valve and the mounting flange. If it is greater than 1.10 in. (28mm), use finger pressure to slowly retract the pintle. The force required to retract the pintle of a NEW valve will not cause damage to the valve.
7. Lubricate the O-ring with clean engine oil, then position on the valve.
8. Install the IAC valve assembly, then secure using the attaching screws. Tighten the screws to 27 inch lbs. (30 Nm).

9. Attach the valve electrical connector.
10. Connect the negative battery cable.
11. Reset the IAC valve pintle position, as follows:
    a. Turn the ignition switch to the **ON** position (engine off).
    b. Turn the ignition **OFF** for ten seconds.
    c. Start the engine and check for proper idle operation.

Engine Coolant Temperature (ECT) Sensor

OPERATION

▶ **See Figure 35**

The Engine Coolant Temperature (ECT) sensor, sometimes referred to as the Coolant Temperature Sensor (CTS), is a thermistor (resistor which changes value based on temperature) mounted in the engine coolant stream. Low coolant temperatures produce a high resistance—100,000 ohms at −40°F (−40°C), while high temperatures cause low resistance—70 ohms at 266°F (130°C).

The control module provides a 5 volt reference signal to the sensor through a resistor in the module and measures the voltage. The voltage will be high when the engine is cold and low when the engine is hot. By measuring the voltage, the control module knows the engine coolant temperature. The engine coolant temperature affects most other systems controlled by the module.

TESTING

▶ **See Figure 36**

1. Disconnect the temperature sensor.
2. Connect an ohmmeter between the sensor terminals.
3. Measure the resistance with the engine off and cool. Then measure with the engine running and warmed up. Compare the resistance values obtained with the chart.
4. Replace the sensor if the readings are incorrect.

REMOVAL & INSTALLATION

▶ **See Figure 37**

1. Disconnect the negative battery cable.
2. Properly relieve the cooling system pressure, then drain to a level below the sensor.
3. Detach the ECT sensor electrical connector.
4. Carefully remove the sensor.

1	VALVE ASSEMBLY - IDLE AIR CONTROL (IAC)
2	BODY ASSEMBLY - THROTTLE
3	VALVE - THROTTLE
4	PINTLE - IAC VALVE
A	ELECTRICAL INPUT SIGNAL
B	AIR INLET

87954044

Fig. 33 Schematic of the IAC valve air flow

1	IAC VALVE O-RING
2	IAC VALVE ATTACHING SCREW ASSEMBLY
A	DISTANCE OF PINTLE EXTENSION
B	DIAMETER OF PINTLE

87954045

Fig. 34 Idle Air Control (IAC) valve components

1	HARNESS CONNECTOR
2	LOCKING TAB
3	SENSOR

87954042

Fig. 35 Engine Coolant Temperature (ECT) sensor and connector

DIAGNOSTIC AID

ENGINE COOLANT TEMPERATURE SENSOR

TEMPERATURE VS. RESISTANCE VALUES (APPROXIMATE)

°C	°F	OHMS
100	212	177
90	194	241
80	176	332
70	158	467
60	140	667
50	122	973
45	113	1188
40	104	1459
35	95	1802
30	86	2238
25	77	2796
20	68	3520
15	59	4450
10	50	5670
5	41	7280
0	32	9420
-5	23	12300
-10	14	16180
-15	5	21450
-20	-4	28680
-30	-22	52700
-40	-40	100700

87954057

Fig. 36 ECT sensor value chart

1 ENGINE COOLANT TEMPERATURE (ECT) SENSOR
2 ECT SENSOR ELECTRICAL CONNECTOR

87954043

Fig. 37 Location of the ECT sensor—2.2L engine shown

To install:

5. Coat the threads of the sensor with a suitable sealant. Install the sensor into the engine, tighten to 19 ft. lbs. (25 Nm).
6. Attach the ECT sensor electrical connector.
7. Refill the cooling system to the proper level.
8. Connect the negative battery cable.

Manifold Air Temperature (MAT)/Intake Air Temperature (IAT) Sensor

OPERATION

▶ See Figure 38

The MAT or IAT sensor (as equipped), is a thermistor (resistor which changes value based on temperature) mounted either in the air intake snorkel or the manifold (depending on the application). Low intake air temperatures produce a high resistance—100,000 ohms at -40°F (-40°C), while high temperatures cause low resistance—70 ohms at 266°F (130°C).

The control module provides a 5 volt reference signal to the sensor through a resistor in the module and measures the voltage. The voltage will be high when the air is cold and low when the air is hot. By measuring the voltage, the control module knows the intake/manifold air temperature.

The air temperature signal is used by the control module to delay EGR until the temperature reaches approximately 40°F (5°C). The control module also uses the signal to retard ignition timing during high air temperatures.

TESTING

▶ See Figure 39

1. Disconnect the MAT/IAT sensor.
2. Connect an ohmmeter between the sensor terminals.
3. Measure the resistance with the engine off and cool. Then measure with the engine running and warmed up. Compare the resistance values obtained with the chart.
4. Replace the sensor if the readings are incorrect.

REMOVAL & INSTALLATION

▶ See Figure 40

➡The MAT/IAT sensor is usually located in the air cleaner assembly or in the top of the intake manifold between the runners.

1. Disconnect the negative battery cable.
2. Detach the sensor electrical connector.
3. If necessary, remove the air cleaner assembly cover to gain access to the sensor.
4. Carefully remove the sensor and retainer (if equipped).
5. Installation is the reverse of the removal procedure.

1 Harness connector
2 Locking tab
3 Sensor

87954051

Fig. 38 View of the MAT/IAT sensor and electrical connector—1995 2.3L shown

DIAGNOSTIC AID

MAT SENSOR

TEMPERATURE TO RESISTANCE VALUES (APPROXIMATE)

°F	°C	OHMS
210	100	185
160	70	450
100	38	1,800
70	20	3,400
40	4	7,500
20	-7	13,500
0	-18	25,000
-40	-40	100,700

87954200

Fig. 39 MAT/IAT sensor value chart

87954107

Fig. 40 On the 1988 2.0L (VIN K) engine, the MAT sensor is mounted in the air cleaner assembly

Manifold Absolute Pressure (MAP) Sensor

OPERATION

▶ **See Figure 41**

The Manifold Absolute Pressure (MAP) sensor measures the changes in intake manifold pressure, which result from engine load and speed changes and converts this information to a voltage output. The MAP sensor reading is the opposite of a vacuum gauge reading: when manifold pressure is high, MAP sensor value is high and vacuum is low. A MAP sensor will produce a low output on engine coastdown with a closed throttle while a wide open throttle will produce a high output. The high output is produced because the pressure inside the manifold is the same as outside the manifold, so 100% of the outside air pressure is measured.

The MAP sensor is also used to measure barometric pressure under certain conditions, which allows the ECM to automatically adjust for different altitudes.

The MAP sensor changes the 5 volt signal supplied by the computer control module (ECM or PCM as applicable), which reads the change and uses the information to control fuel delivery and ignition timing.

TESTING

➡ **The test requires the use of a scan tool.**

1. If the engine idle is rough, unstable or incorrect, fix before using this test.
2. With the engine idling, hook up a scan tool. If the scan tool does not display a MAP of 4.0 or more volts, the trouble code is intermittent. Check all connections and make sure the sensor is mounted securely.
3. If the MAP is over 4.0 volts, turn the ignition **OFF**, then detach the MAP sensor connector and turn the ignition to the **ON** position. The scan tool should read a voltage of 1 volt or less.
   a. If the voltage reading is 1 volt or less, probe CKT 455 with a test light to 12 volts. If the test light lights, the MAP sensor hose is plugged or leak-

ing, or the MAP sensor is faulty. If the test light doesn't light, CKT 455 is open.
   b. If the voltage reading is more than 1 volt, CKT 432 is shorted to voltage, shorted to CKT 474 or the ECM/PCM is faulty.

REMOVAL & INSTALLATION

▶ **See Figures 42 and 43**

1. Disconnect the negative battery cable.
2. If necessary, unfasten the retainer clip from the engine bracket assembly-to-MAP sensor assembly.
3. Disconnect the vacuum line, then detach the electrical connector from the MAP sensor.
4. Remove the MAP sensor from the vehicle.

To install:

5. Attach the vacuum line and the electrical connector to the MAP sensor.
6. Fasten the MAP sensor assembly to the engine bracket.
7. Install the retaining clip.
8. Connect the negative battery cable.

Throttle Position (TP) Sensor

OPERATION

▶ **See Figure 44**

The TP sensor is mounted to the throttle body, opposite the throttle lever and is connected to the throttle shaft. Its function is to sense the current throttle valve position and relay that information to the ECM. Throttle position information allows the ECM to generate the required injector control signals. The TP sensor consists of a potentiometer which alters the flow of voltage according to the position of a wiper on the variable resistor windings, in proportion to the movement of the throttle shaft. As throttle angle is changed (the accelerator is pressed down), the output of the sensor changes.

At closed throttle, the output of the sensor is fairly low (0.5 V). As the throttle opens, the output voltage should rise towards 5 V. By monitoring the sensor output voltage, the control module can determine fuel delivery based on throttle angle.

TESTING

1. Remove air cleaner.
2. Disconnect TP sensor harness from the sensor.
3. Using three jumper wires, connect the TP sensor harness to then sensor.
4. With ignition **ON** and the engine stopped, use a digital voltmeter to measure voltage between the bottom and middle terminals.
5. Voltage should read 0.450–1.250 volts.

ADJUSTMENT

➡ **The TP sensor is not adjustable on most models. Adjustable TP sensors have elongated mounting holes to allow adjustment.**

1 Map sensor

87954048

Fig. 41 MAP sensor

87954106

Fig. 42 Be careful not to break the connector locktab

1 Retainer clip
2 Map sensor
3 Vacuum harness connector

87954050

Fig. 43 MAP sensor mounting—3.1L engine shown

1 Throttle position sensor (TP)
2 TP sensor attaching screw assembly

87954052

Fig. 44 The Throttle Position (TP) sensor is mounted to the throttle body

1. If necessary, remove the EGR valve and heat shield from engine.
2. Using three 6 in. (152mm) jumpers, connect the TP sensor harness to the TP sensor.
3. With ignition **ON**, engine stopped, use a digital voltmeter to measure voltage between the bottom and middle terminals.
4. Loosen the two TP sensor attaching screws and rotate the sensor to obtain a voltage reading of 0.450–1.250 volts.
5. With the ignition **OFF**, remove the jumpers and reconnect TP sensor harness to TP sensor.
6. Install the EGR valve and heat shield to engine, using new gasket as necessary.
7. Install the air cleaner gasket and air cleaner to throttle body unit.

REMOVAL & INSTALLATION

1. Disconnect the negative battery cable.
2. Detach the TP sensor electrical connector.
3. Unfasten the sensor attaching screws and retainer, then remove the TP sensor from the vehicle. If installing a new sensor, discard the screws. New ones are supplied in the service kit.
   To install:
4. With the throttle valve in the closed (idle) position, install the TP sensor on the throttle body assembly.

➠**When installing the TP sensor, always use new attaching screws.**

5. Secure the sensor using the retainers and two new attaching screws. Tighten the screws to 18 inch lbs. (2 Nm).
6. Attach the TP sensor electrical connector.
7. Connect the negative battery cable.

Camshaft Position (CMP) Sensor

OPERATION

The Camshaft Position (CMP) sensor is used to correlate crankshaft-to-camshaft position so that the PCM can determine which cylinder is ready to be fueled by the injector. The CMP sensor is also used to determine which cylinder is misfiring when when misfire is present. If the computer control module receives an intermittent signal from the CMP, then the "CMP Resync Counter" will increment. When the PCM cannot use the information from the CMP sensor, a Diagnostic Trouble Code (DTC) is set.

REMOVAL & INSTALLATION

1. Disconnect the negative battery cable.
2. Detach the sensor harness connector at the sensor.
3. Unfasten the retaining bolt, then remove the sensor from the camshaft housing. Inspect the sensor O-ring for wear, cracks or leakage and replace if necessary.
   To install:
4. Lubricate the O-ring with clean engine oil, then place on the sensor. Install the sensor into the camshaft housing.
5. Install the CMP sensor retaining bolt, then tighten to 88 inch lbs. (10 Nm).
6. Attach the sensor harness connector.
7. Connect the negative battery cable.

Crankshaft Position (CKP) Sensor

OPERATION

The Crankshaft Position (CKP) sensor (formerly named simply crankshaft sensor) is mounted remotely from the ignition module on an aluminum cover plate. Based on CKP sensor pulses, the sensor sends a reference signal to the computer control module, which is used to determine crankshaft position and engine speed.

TESTING

➠**This test requires the use of a Tech 1® or equivalent scan tool.**

1. Idle the engine for 5 minutes or until the Malfunction Indicator Light (MIL) turns on.
2. Install a scan tool. Does the scan tool display DTC 19?
3. If the scan tool displays the DTC, proceed as follows:
   a. With the engine running, wiggle the connections of the PCM and CKP sensor and related wires while listening for engine stumble.
   b. If the engine does not stumble, inspect the sensor, sensor wiring and connectors and replace as necessary.
   c. If the engine stumbles, repair the faulty circuit(s) or connector(s) and retest for the DTC.
4. If the scan tool does not display the specified DTC, proceed as follows:
5. Observe the scan tool 7X resync while operating all non-engine components on the vehicle. There should be no 7X resync during the operation of the components.
6. If there is no resync, with the engine running, wiggle the connections of the PCM and CKP sensor and related wires while listening for engine stumble.
   a. If the engine does not stumble, the DTC is intermittent.
   b. If the engine stumbles, repair the faulty circuit(s) or connector(s) and retest for the DTC.
7. If there is resync, repair the circuits of the fault components and retest for the DTC.

REMOVAL & INSTALLATION

Except 2.0L (VIN H) Engine

◗ See Figure 45

1. Disconnect the negative battery cable.
2. For the 2.2L (VIN G and 4), raise and safely support the vehicle.
3. Disconnect the sensor harness plug/connector.
4. Unfasten the sensor-to-block bolt/nut, then remove the sensor from the engine.
5. Inspect the sensor O-ring for damage and replace, if necessary. Be sure to lubricate the O-ring with clean engine oil prior to installation.
   To install:
6. Position the sensor in the block, then install the sensor retaining bolt/nut.
7. Tighten the sensor bolt to 71 inch lbs (8 Nm).
8. Attach the sensor harness plug/connector.
9. If raised, carefully lower the vehicle.
10. Connect the negative battery cable.

2.0L (VIN H) Engine

◗ See Figure 46

1. Disconnect the negative battery cable.
2. Raise and safely support the vehicle.
3. Remove the two lower power steering bracket nuts.

1. 1 - 4 coil	4. Crankshaft position (CKP)
2. 2 - 3 coil	sensor assembly
3. Ignition	5. Bracket
control	6. Nut
module (ICM)	

87952017

Fig. 45 Location of the CKP sensor and related components—2.2L (VIN 4) engine

1. Crankshaft position sensor bolt
   (hidden from view)
2. Crankshaft position sensor

87952016

Fig. 46 The CKP sensor mounting on the 2.0L (VIN H) engine

4. Carefully remove the vehicle, then remove the serpentine belt.

5. Unfasten the four bolts and two nuts, then remove the alternator from its mount, including removing the hinge and crankcase ventilation tube.

6. Remove the upper power steering brace by unfastening the 3 bolts.

7. Unfasten the retaining lower bracket bolts, then set the power steering pump assembly aside.

8. Unfasten the 4 bolts and 1 nut securing the timing belt cover, then remove the cover.

9. Detach the CKP sensor harness behind the engine and cut tie strap.

10. Feed the harness behind the timing plate, then remove the harness and CKP sensor.

To install:

11. Raise and safely support the vehicle.

12. Install the CKP sensor in the engine (1 bolts), then feed the harness through the A/C compressor mount.

13. Carefully lower the vehicle.

14. Feed the sensor wiring harness behind the timing plate.

15. Connect the harness at the rear of the engine, then install the tie strap.

16. Position the timing belt cover, then secure using the retainers.

17. Install the 2 top bolts for the lower power steering bracket.

18. Install the alternator, including the hinge and crankcase ventilation tube.

19. Raise and safely support the vehicle.

20. Secure the two lower power steering bracket nuts.

21. Carefully lower the vehicle.

22. Install the serpentine belt.

23. Attach the sensor-to-engine harness.

24. Connect the negative battery cable.

Knock Sensor (KS)

OPERATION

▶ **See Figure 47**

The Knock Sensor (KS) detects abnormal vibration (spark knocking) in the engine. The sensor is mounted in the engine block near the cylinders. The sensor produces an AC output voltage which increases with the severity of the knock. This signal voltage inputs to the ECM/PCM. The computer control module then adjusts the timing to reduce the knock. This allows the engine to use maximum spark advance to improve driveability and fuel economy.

REMOVAL & INSTALLATION

▶ **See Figure 48**

1. Disconnect the negative battery cable.

2. Raise and safely support the vehicle.

3. Detach the wiring harness connector from the Knock Sensor (KS).

4. Remove the knock sensor from the engine block.

To install:

5. Install the knock sensor into the engine block. Tighten to 12–16 ft. lbs. (16–22 Nm).

6. Attach the wiring harness connector to the sensor.

7. Carefully lower the vehicle.

8. Connect the negative battery cable.

KNOCK SENSOR

87954055

Fig. 47 View of the Knock Sensor (KS)

1   KNOCK SENSOR

87954056

Fig. 48 The knock sensor can be found mounted to the engine block—1992 3:1L engine shown

TROUBLE CODES

General Information

The computer control module (ECM/PCM) is required to maintain the exhaust emissions at acceptable levels. The module is a small, solid state computer which receives signals from many sources and sensors; it uses these data to make judgments about operating conditions and then control output signals to the fuel and emission systems to match the current requirements.

Inputs are received from many sources to form a complete picture of engine operating conditions. Some inputs are simply yes or no messages, such as that

from the Park/Neutral switch; the vehicle is either in gear or in Park/Neutral; there are no other choices. Other data is sent in quantitative input, such as engine RPM, coolant temperature and throttle position. The computer control module is pre-programmed to recognize acceptable ranges or combinations of signals and control the outputs to control emissions while providing good driveability and economy. The ECM/PCM also monitors some output circuits, making sure that the components function as commanded. For proper engine operation, it is essential that all input and output components function properly and communicate properly with the computer control module.

Since the control module is programmed to recognize the presence and value of electrical inputs, it will also note the lack of a signal or a radical change in values. It will, for example, react to the loss of signal from the vehicle speed sensor or note that engine coolant temperature has risen beyond acceptable (programmed) limits. Once a fault is recognized, a numeric code is assigned and held in memory. The dashboard warning lamp: CHECK ENGINE or SERVICE ENGINE SOON (SES) will illuminate to advise the operator that the system has detected a fault. This lamp is also known as the Malfunction Indicator Lamp (MIL).

More than one code may be stored. Although not every engine uses every code, possible codes range from 12 to over 100. Additionally, the same code may carry different meanings relative to each engine or engine family.

In the event of an computer control module failure, the system will default to a pre-programmed set of values. These are compromise values which allow the engine to operate, although possibly at reduced efficiency. This is variously known as the default, limp-in or back-up mode. Driveability is almost always affected when the ECM/PCM enters this mode.

LEARNING ABILITY

The computer control module can compensate for minor variations within the fuel system through the block learn and fuel integrator systems. The fuel integrator monitors the oxygen sensor output voltage, adding or subtracting fuel to drive the mixture rich or lean as needed to reach the ideal air fuel ratio of 14.7:1. The integrator values may be read with a scan tool; the display will range from 0–255 and should center on 128 if the oxygen sensor is seeing a 14.7:1 mixture.

The temporary nature of the integrator's control is expanded by the block learn function. The name is derived from the fact that the entire engine operating range (load vs. rpm) is divided into 16 sections or blocks. Within each memory block is stored the correct fuel delivery value for that combination of load and engine speed. Once the operating range enters a certain block, that stored value controls the fuel delivery unless the integrator steps in to change it. If changes are made by the integrator, the new value is memorized and stored within the block. As the block learn makes the correction, the integrator correction will be reduced until the integrator returns to 128; the block learn then controls the fuel delivery with the new value.

The next time the engine operates within the block's range, the new value will be used. The block learn data can also be read by a scan tool; the range is the same as the integrator and should also center on 128. In this way, the systems can compensate for engine wear, small air or vacuum leaks or reduced combustion.

Any time the battery is disconnected, the block learn values are lost and must be relearned by the ECM. This loss of corrected values may be noticed as a significant change in driveability. To reteach the system, make certain the engine is fully warmed up. Drive the vehicle at part throttle using moderate acceleration and idle until normal performance is felt.

DASHBOARD WARNING LAMP

The primary function of the dash warning lamp is to advise the operator and that a fault has been detected, and, in most cases, a code stored. Under normal conditions, the dash warning lamp will illuminate when the ignition is turned **ON**. Once the engine is started and running, the computer control module will perform a system check and extinguish the warning lamp if no fault is found.

Additionally, the dash warning lamp can be used to retrieve stored codes after the system is placed in the Diagnostic Mode. Codes are transmitted as a series of flashes with short or long pauses. When the system is placed in the Field Service Mode, the dash lamp will indicate open loop or closed loop function to the technician.

Tools and Equipment

SCAN TOOLS

Although stored Diagnostic Trouble Codes (DTC's) may be read with only the use of a small jumper wire, the use of a hand-held scan tool such as GM's TECH-1® or equivalent is recommended. There are many manufacturers of these tools; a purchaser must be certain that the tool is proper for the intended use. If you own a scan type tool, it probably came with comprehensive instructions on proper use. Be sure to follow the instructions that came with your unit if they differ from what is given here; this is a general guide with useful information included.

The scan tool allows any stored codes to be read from the ECM or PCM memory. The tool also allows the operator to view the data being sent to the computer control module while the engine is running. This ability has obvious diagnostic advantages; the use of the scan tool is frequently required for component testing. The scan tool makes collecting information easier; the data must be correctly interpreted by an operator familiar with the system.

An example of the usefulness of the scan tool may be seen in the case of a temperature sensor which has changed its electrical characteristics. The ECM is reacting to an apparently warmer engine (causing a driveability problem), but the sensor's voltage has not changed enough to set a fault code. Connecting the scan tool, the voltage signal being sent to the ECM may be viewed; comparison to normal values or a known good vehicle reveals the problem quickly.

The ECM is capable of communicating with a scan tool in 3 modes:

1. Normal or Open Mode. This mode is not applicable to all engines. When engaged, certain engine data can be observed on the scanner without affecting engine operating characteristics. The number of items readable in this mode varies with engine family. Most scan tools are designed to change automatically to the ALDL mode if this mode is not available.

2. ALDL Mode. Also referred to as the 10K or SPECIAL mode, the scanner will present all readable data as available. Certain operating characteristics of the engine are changed or controlled when this mode is engaged. The closed loop timers are bypassed, the spark (EST) is advanced and the PARK/NEUTRAL restriction is bypassed. If applicable, the IAC controls the engine speed to 950–1050 rpm, and, on some engines, the canister purge solenoid is energized.

3. Factory Test. Sometimes referred to as BACK-UP mode, this level of communication is primarily used during vehicle assembly and testing. This mode will confirm that the default or limp-in system is working properly within the computer control module. Other data obtainable in this mode has little use in diagnosis.

➡**A scan tool that is known to display faulty data should not be used for diagnosis. Although the fault may be believed to be in only one area, it can possibly affect many other areas during diagnosis, leading to errors and incorrect repair.**

To properly read system values with a scan tool, the following conditions must be met. All normal values given in the charts will be based on these conditions:
- Engine running at idle, throttle closed
- Engine warm, upper radiator hose hot
- Vehicle in park or neutral
- System operating in closed loop
- All accessories OFF

ELECTRICAL TOOLS

The most commonly required electrical diagnostic tool is the Digital Multimeter, allowing voltage, ohmage (resistance) and amperage to be read by one instrument. The multimeter must be a high-impedance unit, with 10 megohms of impedance in the voltmeter. This type of meter will not place an additional load on the circuit it is testing; this is extremely important in low voltage circuits. The multimeter must be of high quality in all respects. It should be handled carefully and protected from impact or damage. Replace batteries frequently in the unit.

Other necessary tools include an unpowered test light, a quality tachometer with an inductive (clip-on) pick up, and the proper tools for releasing GM's Metri-Pack, Weather Pack and Micro-Pack terminals as necessary. The Micro-Pack connectors are used at the computer control module electrical connector. A vacuum pump/gauge may also be required for checking sensors, solenoids and valves.

Diagnosis and Testing

TROUBLESHOOTING

Diagnosis of a driveablility and/or emissions problems requires attention to detail and following the diagnostic procedures in the correct order. Resist the temptation to perform any repairs before performing the preliminary diagnostic steps. In many cases this will shorten diagnostic time and often cure the problem without electronic testing.

The proper troubleshooting procedure for these vehicles is as follows:

Visual/Physical Underhood Inspection

This is possibly the most critical step of diagnosis. A detailed examination of connectors, wiring and vacuum hoses can often lead to a repair without further diagnosis. Performance of this step relies on the skill of the technician performing it; a careful inspector will check the undersides of hoses as well as the integrity of hard-to-reach hoses blocked by the air cleaner or other component. Wiring should be checked carefully for any sign of strain, burning, crimping, or terminal pull-out from a connector. Checking connectors at components or in harnesses is required; usually, pushing them together will reveal a loose fit.

Intermittents

If a fault occurs intermittently, such as a loose connector pin breaking contact as the vehicle hits a bump, the computer control module (ECM or PCM depending upon application) will note the fault as it occurs and energize the dash warning lamp. If the problem self-corrects, as with the terminal pin again making contact, the dash lamp will extinguish after 10 seconds but a code will remain stored in the computer control module's memory.

When an unexpected code appears during diagnostics, it may have been set during an intermittent failure that self-corrected; the codes are still useful in diagnosis and should not be discounted.

Circuit/Component Diagnosis and Repair

The fault codes and the scan tool data will lead to diagnosis and checking of a particular circuit. It is important to note that the fault code indicates a fault or loss of signal in an ECM-controlled system, not necessarily in the specific component.

Refer to the appropriate Diagnostic Code chart to determine the codes meaning. The component may then be tested following the appropriate component test procedures found in this section. If the component is OK, check the wiring for shorts or opens. Further diagnoses should be left to an experienced driveability technician.

If a code indicates the ECM to be faulty and the ECM is replaced, but does not correct the problem, one of the following may be the reason:

• There is a problem with the ECM terminal connections: The terminals may have to be removed from the connector in order to check them properly.

• The ECM or PROM is not correct for the application: The incorrect ECM or PROM may cause a malfunction and may or may not set a code.

• The problem is intermittent: This means that the problem is not present at the time the system is being checked. In this case, make a careful physical inspection of all portions of the system involved.

• Shorted solenoid, relay coil or harness: Solenoids and relays are turned "ON" and "OFF" by the ECM using internal electronic switches called "drivers." Each driver is part of a group of four called "Quad-Drivers." A shorted solenoid, relay coil or harness may cause an ECM to fail, and a replacement ECM to fail when it is installed. Use a short tester, J 34696, BT 8405, or equivalent, as a fast, accurate means of checking for a short circuit.

• The Programmable Read Only Memory (PROM) may be faulty: Although the PROM rarely fails, it operates as part of the ECM. Therefore, it could be the cause of the problem. Substitute a known good PROM.

• The replacement ECM may be faulty: After the ECM is replaced, the system should be rechecked for proper operation. If the diagnostic code again indicates the ECM is the problem, substitute a known good ECM. Although this is a rare condition, it could happen.

Reading Codes

▶ See Figures 49 thru 60

Listings of the Diagnostic Trouble Codes (DTC's) for the various engine control system covered in this manual are located in this section. Remember that a code only points to the faulty circuit NOT necessarily to a faulty component. Loose, damaged or corroded connections may contribute to a fault code on a circuit when the sensor or component is operating properly. Be sure that the components are faulty before replacing them, especially the expensive ones.

Keep in mind that most codes are only valid when the trouble is present. If the trouble is intermittent (often caused by loose or corroded terminals on cir-

cuit connections), it may lead to a dead end or "Intermittent code" ending in which the exact cause of the fault is still left undetermined. In these cases, check all related vacuum hoses and/or wiring for poor, worn or damaged connections. If bad connections are found, wiggle the connection in attempt to duplicate the fault condition so that troubleshooting may continue. Also, before replacing a computer control module, be ABSOLUTELY certain that the module is at fault. The price of module is usually quite significant and they are almost always NON-RETURNABLE components.

➡**After making repairs, clear the trouble codes and operate the vehicle to see if it will reset, indicating further problems.**

On 1982 models, a 5 terminal connector, located on the right side of the fuse panel, is used to activate the trouble code system in the ECM. This same connector is used at assembly and known as the Assembly Line Diagnostic Link (ALDL) or Assembly Line Communication Link (ALCL). A trouble code test terminal **D** is located in the 5 terminal connector and a ground terminal **E**, is located next to this terminal. With the ignition **ON**, car not running, jump the test terminal to ground.

On 1983–94 models, the ALDL connector or Data Link Connector (DLC), located under the dash, and sometimes covered with a plastic cover labeled DIAGNOSTIC CONNECTOR, can be activated by grounding test terminal **B**. The terminal is most easily grounded by connecting it to terminal **A** (internal ECM ground), the terminal to the right of terminal **B** on the top row of the ALDL connector. Once terminals **A** and **B** have been connected, the ignition switch must be moved to the **ON** position with the engine not running.

1. Turn the ignition switch **OFF**.

2. The Service Engine Soon or Check Engine light should be flashing. If it isn't, turn the ignition **OFF** and remove the jumper wire. Turn the ignition **ON** and confirm that light is now on. If it is not, replace the bulb and try again. If the bulb still will not light, or if it does not flash with the test terminal grounded, the system should be diagnosed by an experienced driveability technician. If the light is OK, proceed as follows.

3. The code(s) stored in memory may be read either through counting the flashes of the dashboard warning lamp or through the use of a hand-held scan tool. If using the scan tool, connect it correctly to the ALDL.

4. After the terminals are connected, turn the ignition switch to the **ON** position, but DO NOT start the engine. The dash warning lamp should begin to flash Code 12. The code will display as one flash, a pause and two flashes. Code 12 is not a fault code. It is used as a system acknowledgment or handshake code; its presence indicates that the ECM can communicate as requested. Code 12 is used to begin every diagnostic sequence. Some vehicles also use Code 12 after all diagnostic codes have been sent.

DTC	DESCRIPTION
13	Oxygen Sensor Circuit
14	Coolant Sensor
15	Coolant Sensor
21	Throttle Position Sensor
22	Throttle Position Sensor
23	MAT Sensor
24	Vehicle Speed Sensor
25	MAT Sensor
32	EGR System Failure
33	MAF Sensor
34	MAF Sensor
41	Cylinder Select
42	Electronic Spark Timing
44	Lean Exhaust Indication
45	Rich Exhaust Indication
51	PROM
52	CALPAK (Missing)
53	System Over Voltage
54	Fuel Pump Voltage Low
55	ECM

87954070

Fig. 49 Diagnostic Trouble Codes—1982–86 vehicles

5. After Code 12 has been transmitted 3 times, the fault codes, if any, will each be transmitted 3 times. The codes are stored and transmitted in numeric order from lowest to highest.

➡**The order of codes in the memory does not indicate the order of occurrence.**

6. If there are no codes stored, but a driveability or emissions problem is evident, the system should be diagnosed by an experienced driveability technician.

7. If one or more codes are stored, record them. Refer to the applicable Diagnostic Code chart in this section.

8. Switch the ignition **OFF** when finished with code retrieval or scan tool readings.

Clearing Codes

Stored fault codes may be erased from memory at any time by removing power from the ECM for at least 30 seconds. It may be necessary to clear stored codes during diagnosis to check for any recurrence during a test drive, but the stored codes must be written down when retrieved. The codes may still be required for subsequent troubleshooting. Whenever a repair is complete, the stored codes must be erased and the vehicle test driven to confirm correct operation and repair.

☼ WARNING

The ignition switch must be OFF any time power is disconnected or restored to the ECM. Severe damage may result if this precaution is not observed.

Depending on the electrical distribution of the particular vehicle, power to the ECM may be disconnected by removing the ECM fuse in the fusebox, disconnecting the in-line fuse holder near the positive battery terminal or disconnecting the ECM power lead at the battery terminal. Disconnecting the negative battery cable to clear codes is not recommended as this will also clear other memory data in the vehicle such as radio presets.

DTC	DESCRIPTION
13	Oxygen Sensor Circuit
14	Coolant Temperature Sensor
15	Coolant Temperature Sensor
21	Throttle Position Sensor Circuit
22	Throttle Position Sensor Circuit
23	MAT Sensor Circuit
24	Vehicle Speed Sensor (VSS) Circuit
25	MAT Sensor Circuit
33	MAP Sensor Circuit
34	MAP Sensor Circuit
35	Idle Speed Error
41	Cylinder Select Error (Faulty or Incorrect Mem-Cal)
42	Electronic Spark Timing Circuit
43	Electronic Spark Control Circuit
44	Oxygen Sensor Circuit (Lean)
45	Oxygen Sensor Circuit (Rich)
54	Fuel Pump Circuit
51	Mem-Cal Error
52	Calpak Error
53	System Over Voltage
61	Degraded Oxygen Sensor

87954073

Fig. 52 Diagnostic Trouble Codes—1988 vehicles, except Turbo

DTC	DESCRIPTION
13	Open Oxygen Sensor Circuit
14	Coolant Sensor Circuit
15	Coolant Sensor Circuit
21	Throttle Position Sensor
22	Throttle Position Sensor
23	MAT Sensor
24	Vehicle Speed Sensor
25	MAT Sensor
33	MAF Sensor
34	MAF Sensor
35	Idle Speed Error
41	Cylinder Select Error (Faulty or Incorrect Mem-Cal)
42	Electronic Spark Timing
43	Electronic Spark Control
44	Lean Exhaust Indication
45	Rich Exhaust Indication
54	Fuel Pump Circuit (Low Voltage)
51	Faulty MEM-CAL
53	System Over Voltage
55	ECM
61	Degraded Oxygen Sensor
63	MAP Sensor
64	MAP Sensor

87954071

Fig. 50 Diagnostic Trouble Codes—1987 vehicles, except Turbo

DTC	DESCRIPTION
13	Oxygen Sensor Circuit (Open Circuit)
14	Coolant Temperature Sensor Circuit (High Temperature Indicated)
15	Coolant Temperature Sensor Circuit (Low Temperature Indicated)
21	Throttle Position Sensor (TPS) Circuit (Signal Voltage High)
22	Throttle Position Sensor (TPS) Circuit (Signal Voltage Low)
23	Manifold Air Temperature (MAT) Sensor Circuit (Low Temperature Indicated)
24	Vehicle Speed Sensor (VSS) Circuit
25	Manifold Air Temperature (MAT) Sensor Circuit (High Temperature Indicated)
31	Turbo Wastegate Overboost
32	Exhaust Gas Recirculation (EGR) Circuit
33	Manifold Absolute Pressure (MAP) Sensor Circuit (Signal Voltage High)
34	Manifold Absolute Pressure (MAP) Sensor (Signal Voltage Low)
35	Idle Speed Error
42	Electronic Spark Timing (EST) Circuit
43	Electronic Spark Control (ESC) Circuit
44	Oxygen Sensor Circuit (Lean Exhaust Indicated)
45	Oxygen Sensor Circuit (Rich Exhaust Indicated)
51	Mem-Cal Error (Faulty or Incorrect Mem-Cal)

87954072

Fig. 51 Diagnostic Trouble Codes—1987 Turbo vehicles

DTC	DESCRIPTION
13	Oxygen Sensor Circuit (Open Circuit)
14	Coolant Temperature Sensor Circuit (High Temperature Indicated)
15	Coolant Temperature Sensor Circuit (Low Temperature Indicated)
21	Throttle Position Sensor (TPS) Circuit (Signal Voltage High)
22	Throttle Position Sensor (TPS) Circuit (Signal Voltage Low)
23	Manifold Air Temperature (MAT) Sensor Circuit (Low Temperature Indicated)
24	Vehicle Speed Sensor (VSS) Circuit
25	Manifold Air Temperature (MAT) Sensor Circuit (High Temperature Indicated)
31	Turbo Wastegate Overboost
32	Exhaust Gas Recirculation (EGR) Circuit
33	Manifold Absolute Pressure (MAP) Sensor Circuit (Signal Voltage High-Low Vacuum)
34	Manifold Absolute Pressure (MAP) Sensor Circuit (Signal Voltage Low-High Vacuum)
35	Idle Speed Error
42	Electronic Spark Timing (EST) Circuit
43	Electronic Spark Control (ESC) Circuit
44	Oxygen Sensor Circuit (Lean Exhaust Indicated)
45	Oxygen Sensor Circuit (Rich Exhaust Indicated)
51	PROM Error (Faulty or Incorrect PROM)

87954074

Fig. 53 Diagnostic Trouble Codes—1988 Turbo vehicles

DTC	DESCRIPTION
13	Oxygen Sensor Circuit (Open Circuit)
14	Coolant Temperature Sensor Circuit (High Temperature Indicated)
15	Coolant Temperature Sensor Circuit (Low Temperature Indicated)
21	Throttle Position Sensor (TPS) Circuit (Signal Voltage High)
22	Throttle Position Sensor (TPS) Circuit (Signal Voltage Low)
23	Manifold Air Temperature (MAT) Sensor Circuit (Low Temperature Indicated)
24	Vehicle Speed Sensor (VSS) Circuit
25	Manifold Air Temperature (MAT) Sensor Circuit (High Temperature Indicated)
32	Digital EGR Exhaust Gas Recirculation (EGR) Circuit (Electrical Diagnosis)
33	Manifold Absolute Pressure (MAP) Sensor Circuit (Signal Voltage High - Low Vacuum)
34	Manifold Absolute Pressure (MAP) Sensor Circuit (Signal Voltage Low - High Vacuum)
35	Idle Air Control (IAC)
41	Cylinder Select Error (Faulty or Incorrect Mem-Cal)
42	Electronic Spark Timing (EST) Circuit
43	Electronic Spark Control (ESC) Circuit
44	Oxygen Sensor Circuit (Lean Exhaust Indicated)
45	Oxygen Sensor Circuit (Rich Exhaust Indicated)
54	Fuel Pump Circuit (Low Voltage)
51	Mem-Cal Error (Faulty or Incorrect Mem-Cal)
52	Calpak Error (Faulty or Incorrect CalPak)
53	System Over Voltage
61	Degraded Oxygen Sensor
62	Transaxle Gear Switch Signal Circuits (Electrical Diagnosis)
66	A/C Pressure Sensor Circuit

87954075

Fig. 54 Diagnostic Trouble Codes—1989–90 vehicles, except Turbo

DTC	DESCRIPTION
13	Oxygen Sensor Circuit (Open Circuit)
14	Coolant Temperature Sensor Circuit (High Temperature Indicated)
15	Coolant Temperature Sensor Circuit (Low Temperature Indicated)
21	Throttle Position Sensor (TPS) Circuit (Signal Voltage High)
22	Throttle Position Sensor (TPS) Circuit (Signal Voltage Low)
23	Manifold Air Temperature (MAT) Sensor Circuit (Low Temperature Indicated)
24	Vehicle Speed Sensor (VSS) Circuit
25	Manifold Air Temperature (MAT) Sensor Circuit (High Temperature Indicated)
31	Turbo Wastegate Overboost
32	Exhaust Gas Recirculation (EGR) Circuit
33	Manifold Absolute Pressure (MAP) Sensor Circuit (Signal Voltage High-Low Vacuum)
34	Manifold Absolute Pressure (MAP) Sensor Circuit (Signal Voltage Low-High Vacuum)
35	Idle Speed Error
42	Electronic Spark Timing (EST) Circuit
43	Electronic Spark Control (ESC) Circuit
44	Oxygen Sensor Circuit (Lean Exhaust Indicated)
45	Oxygen Sensor Circuit (Rich Exhaust Indicated)
51	PROM Error (Faulty or Incorrect PROM)

87954076

Fig. 55 Diagnostic Trouble Codes—1989–90 Turbo vehicles

DTC	DESCRIPTION	ILLUMINATE "SES"
13	Oxygen Sensor (O2S) Circuit - open circuit	YES
14	Engine Coolant Temperature (ECT) Sensor Circuit - high temperature indicated	YES
15	Engine Coolant Temperature (ECT) Sensor Circuit - low temperature indicated	YES
21	Throttle Position (TP) Sensor Circuit - signal voltage high	YES
22	Throttle Position (TP) Sensor Circuit - signal voltage low	YES
23	Intake Air Temperature (IAT) Sensor Circuit - low temperature indicated	YES
24	Vehicle Speed Sensor (VSS) Circuit	YES
25	Intake Air Temperature (IAT) Sensor Circuit - high temperature indicated	YES
32	Exhaust Gas Recirculation (EGR) Circuit Electrical Diagnosis	YES
33	Manifold Absolute Pressure (MAP) Sensor Circuit Signal Voltage high-low vacuum	YES
34	Manifold Absolute Pressure (MAP) Sensor Circuit Signal Voltage low-high vacuum	YES
35	Idle Air Control (IAT) Circuit System Check - Tech 1	YES
41	Cylinder Select Error - faulty or incorrect PROM	YES
42	Ignition Control (IC) Circuit	YES
43	Knock Sensor (KS) Circuit	YES
44	Oxygen Sensor (O2S) Circuit - lean exhaust indicated	YES
45	Oxygen Sensor (O2S) Circuit - rich exhaust indicated	YES
54	Fuel Pump Circuit - low voltage	YES
51	PROM Error - faulty or incorrect MEM-CAL	YES
53	System Over Voltage	YES
61	Degraded Oxygen Sensor	YES
62	Transaxle Gear Switch Signal Circuit	YES
66	A/C Pressure Sensor Circuit	NO

If a DTC not listed above appears on Tech 1, ground DLC diagnostic terminal "B" and observe flashed DTC(s). If DTC does not reappear, Tech 1 data may be faulty. If DTC does reappear, check for incorrect or faulty PROM.

87954077

Fig. 56 Diagnostic Trouble Codes—1991 2.0L (VIN K), 1991–93 3.1L (VIN T) vehicles

ECM DIAGNOSTIC TROUBLE CODES (DTCs)

DTC	DESCRIPTION	ILLUMINATE MIL (CHECK ENGINE)
13	Oxygen Sensor (O2S) Circuit - open circuit	YES
14	Engine Coolant Temperature (ECT) Sensor Circuit - high/low temperature	YES
19	Crankshaft Position (CKP) Sensor Circuit - incorrect 58X signal - disconnected sensor	YES
21	Throttle Position (TP) Sensor Circuit - signal voltage high/low	YES
23	Intake Air Temperature (IAT) Sensor Circuit - high/low temperature	YES
24	Vehicle Speed Sensor (VSS) Circuit	YES
32	Exhaust Gas Recirculation (EGR) - system failure	YES
33	Manifold Absolute Pressure (MAP) Sensor Circuit - signal voltage high/low - low/high vacuum	YES
44	Oxygen Sensor (O2S) Circuit - lean exhaust indicated	YES
45	Oxygen Sensor (O2S) Circuit - rich exhaust indicated	YES
51	ECM failure (ECM failed or EPROM failure)	YES
66	A/C Refrigerant Pressure Sensor Circuit	NO

If a DTC not listed above appears on Tech 1, ground Data Link Terminal "B" and observe flashed DTCs. If DTC does not reappear, Tech 1 data may be faulty. If DTC does reappear, check for incorrect or faulty PROM.

87954078

Fig. 57 Diagnostic Trouble Codes—1992–94 2.0L (VIN H) Sunbird

ECM DIAGNOSTIC TROUBLE CODES

DTC	DESCRIPTION	ILLUMINATE MIL (CHECK ENGINE)
13	Oxygen Sensor (O2S) Circuit - open circuit	YES
14	Engine Coolant Temperature (ECT) Sensor Circuit - high/low temperature	YES
21	Throttle Position (TP) Sensor Circuit - Signal voltage high/low	YES
23	Intake Air Temperature (IAT) Sensor Circuit - high/low temperature	YES
24	Vehicle Speed Sensor (VSS) Circuit	YES
32	Exhaust Gas Recirculation (EGR) - System failure	YES
33	Manifold Absolute Pressure (MAP) Sensor Circuit - Signal voltage high/low - low/high vacuum	YES
42	Ignition Control (IC) Circuit	YES
44	Oxygen Sensor (O2S) Circuit - lean exhaust indicated	YES
45	Oxygen Sensor (O2S) Circuit - rich exhaust indicated	YES
51	EEPROM or ECM Failure	YES
66	A/C Refrigerant Pressure Sensor Circuit	NO

If a DTC not listed above appears on Tech 1, ground Data Link Terminal "B" and observe flashed DTC(S). If DTC does not reappear, Tech 1 data may be faulty. If DTC does reappear, replace ECM and program.

87954079

Fig. 58 Diagnostic Trouble Codes—1992–93 2.2L (VIN 4) Cavalier

PCM DIAGNOSTIC TROUBLE CODES

DTC	DESCRIPTION	ILLUMINATE MIL (SERVICE ENGINE SOON)
13	Oxygen Sensor (O2S) Circuit - open circuit	YES
14	Engine Coolant Temperature (ECT) Sensor Circuit - high temperature	YES
15	Engine Coolant Temperature (ECT) Sensor Circuit - low temperature	YES
19	Intermittent 7X Reference Signal	YES
21	Throttle Position (TP) Sensor Circuit - signal voltage high	YES
22	Throttle Position (TP) Sensor Circuit - signal voltage low	YES
23	Intake Air Temperature (IAT) Sensor Circuit - low temperature	YES
24	Vehicle Speed Sensor (VSS) Circuit	YES
25	Intake Air Temperature (IAT) Sensor Circuit - high temperature	YES
26	Quad-Driver Module (QDSM)	NO
27	Quad-Driver Module (QDM1)	YES
28	Quad-Driver Module (QDM2)	NO
32	Exhaust Gas Recirculation (EGR) Valve	YES
33	Manifold Absolute Pressure (MAP) Sensor Circuit - signal voltage high - low vacuum	YES
34	Manifold Absolute Pressure (MAP) Sensor Circuit - signal voltage low - high vacuum	YES
35	Improper Idle Speed (IAC)	YES
43	Electronic Spark Control (ESC) - knock sensor	YES
44	Oxygen Sensor (O2S) Circuit - lean exhaust indicated	YES
45	Oxygen Sensor (O2S) Circuit - rich exhaust indicated	YES
51	EPROM or PCM Failure	YES
53	Improper Ignition Voltage	YES
55	Lean in Power Enrichment	NO
66	A/C Refrigerant Pressure Sensor Circuit	NO

87954081

Fig. 59 Diagnostic Trouble Codes—1994 2.2L (VIN 4) Cavalier

PCM DIAGNOSTIC TROUBLE CODES

DTC	DESCRIPTION	ILLUMINATE MIL
13	Oxygen Sensor (O2S) Circuit (open circuit)	YES
14	Engine Coolant Temperature (ECT) Sensor (high temperature indicated)	YES
15	Engine Coolant Temperature (ECT) Sensor (low temperature indicated)	YES
21	Throttle Position (TP) Sensor (signal voltage high)	YES
22	Throttle Position (TP) Sensor (signal voltage low)	YES
23	Intake Air Temperature (IAT) Sensor - low temperature indicated	YES
24	Vehicle Speed (VSS) Sensor Circuit (no signal voltage)	YES
25	Intake Air Temperature (IAT) Sensor (high temperature indicated)	YES
32	Exhaust gas recirculation circuit	YES
33	Manifold Absolute Pressure (MAP) Sensor Circuit (signal voltage high - high MAP)	YES
34	Manifold Absolute Pressure (MAP) Sensor Circuit (sensor voltage low - low MAP)	YES
35	Idle Speed Error	YES
41	Cylinder Select Error	YES
42	Knock Sensor (KS) Circuit	YES
43	Ignition Control (IC) Circuit	YES
44	Oxygen Sensor (O2S) Circuit (lean exhaust indicated)	YES
45	Oxygen Sensor (O2S) Circuit (rich exhaust indicated)	YES
53	System Over Voltage	YES
54	Fuel Pump Circuit (low voltage)	YES
51	PROM Error (Faulty or Incorrect EPROM)	YES
55	PCM Error	YES
61	Degraded Oxygen (O2S) Sensor	YES
62	Transaxle Gear Switch Signal Circuit	NO
66	A/C Refrigerant Pressure Sensor Circuit (low pressure)	NO

If a DTC not listed above appears on Tech 1, ground DLC diagnostic terminal "B" and observe flashed DTC(s). If DTC does not reappear, refer to Tech 1 Operator's Guide. If DTC does reappear, check for incorrect or faulty EPROM.

87954082

Fig. 60 Diagnostic Trouble Codes—1994 3.1L (VIN T) Cavalier and Sunbird

COMPONENT LOCATION DIAGRAMS

'J' SERIES   RPO: LT2   VIN CODE: K   2.0L L4 TBI

87954059

COMPUTER HARNESS
- C1 Electronic Control Module (ECM)
- C2 ALDL diagnostic connector
- C3 "SERVICE ENGINE SOON" light
- C4 ECM power
- C5 ECM harness grounds
- C6 Fuse panel
- C8 Fuel pump test connector

NOT ECM CONNECTED
- N1 Crankcase vent valve (PCV)
- N17 Fuel vapor canister

CONTROLLED DEVICES
- 1 Fuel injector solenoid
- 2 Idle air control valve
- 3 Fuel pump relay
- 5 Trans. Conv. Clutch connector
- 8 Engine fan relay
- 13 A/C compressor relay

INFORMATION SENSORS
- A Manifold pressure (M.A.P.)
  - (Mounted On Air Cleaner)
- B Exhaust oxygen
- C Throttle position
- D Coolant temperature
- F Vehicle speed
- M P/N switch/neutral start
- S P/S pressure switch
- T Manifold Air Temperature
  - (Mounted On Air Cleaner)
- ⊚ Exhaust Gas Recirculation valve

'J' SERIES   RPO: LH8   VIN CODE: O   1.8L L4 TBI

87954058

COMPUTER HARNESS
- C1 Electronic Control Module (ECM)
- C2 ALCL diagnostic connector
- C3 "SERVICE ENGINE SOON" light
- C4 ECM power
- C5 ECM harness ground
- C6 Fuse panel
- C8 Fuel pump test connector

NOT ECM CONNECTED
- N1 Crankcase vent valve (PCV)
- N9 Exhaust Gas Recirculation valve
- N17 Fuel vapor canister

CONTROLLED DEVICES
- 1 Fuel injector solenoid
- 2 Idle air control valve
- 3 Fuel pump relay
- 5 Trans. Conv. Clutch connector
- 8 Engine fan relay
- 13 A/C compressor relay
- 14 A/C fan relay

INFORMATION SENSORS
- A Manifold pressure (M.A.P.)
- B Exhaust oxygen
- C Throttle position
- D Coolant temperature
- F Vehicle speed
- M P/N switch/neutral start
- S P/S pressure switch
- ⊚ Exhaust Gas Recirculation valve

'J' SERIES   RPO:LL8   VIN CODE: 1   2.0L L4 TBI

87954061

☐ **COMPUTER HARNESS**
C1 Electronic Control Module (ECM)
C2 ALDL Diagnostic Connector
C3 "Service Engine Soon" light
C4 ECM Power Fuse
C5 ECM Harness Grounds
C6 Fuse Panel
C8 Fuel Pump Test Connector

☐ **CONTROLLED DEVICES**
1 Fuel Injector Solenoid
2 Idle Air Control valve
3 Fuel Pump Relay
5 TCC Solenoid Connector
8 Cooling Fan Relay
13 A/C Compressor Relay
14 Direct Ignition System Assembly

◯ **INFORMATION SENSORS**
A Manifold Pressure (MAP)
B Exhaust Oxygen
C Throttle Position
D Coolant Temperature
F Vehicle Speed
M P/N Switch
S P/S Pressure Switch
T MAT Sensor

⬚ **NOT ECM CONNECTED**
N1 Crankcase Vent Valve (PCV)
N17 Fuel Vapor Canister

◎ Exhaust Gas Recirculation valve

'J' SERIES   RPO:LT3   VIN CODE: M   2.0L L4 PFI

87954060

☐ **COMPUTER HARNESS**
C1 Electronic Control Module (ECM)
C2 ALDL diagnostic connector
C3 "SERVICE ENGINE SOON" light
C4 ECM power (2)
C5 ECM harness grounds
C6 Fuse panel
C8 Fuel pump test connector

⬚ **NOT ECM CONNECTED**
N1 Crankcase vent valve (PCV) (inside PCV hose)
N17 Fuel vapor canister

☐ **CONTROLLED DEVICES**
1 Fuel injectors
2 Idle air control valve
3 Fuel pump relay
5 Trans. Converter Clutch connector
8 Low speed cooling fan relay
8a High Speed cooling fan relay
13 A/C compressor relay
16 Wastegate solenoid
17 EGR Relay (Below Manifold)

◯ **INFORMATION SENSORS**
A Manifold pressure (M.A.P.)
B Exhaust oxygen
C Throttle position
D Coolant temperature
F PM Generator
J ESC knock (Below Manifold)
M P/N switch/park neutral
S Power Steering Pressure Switch
T Manifold Air Temperature

"J" CARLINE   RPO: LM3   (VIN G)   2.2L L4 TBI

☐ COMPUTER HARNESS
- C1 Electronic Control Module (ECM)
- C2 ALDL Diagnostic Connector
- C3 "Service Engine Soon" light
- C4 ECM Power Fuse
- C5 ECM Harness Grounds
- C6 Fuse Panel
- C8 Fuel Pump Test Connector

NOT ECM CONNECTED
- N1 Crankcase Vent Valve (PCV)
- N17 Fuel Vapor Canister

☐ CONTROLLED DEVICES
- 1 Fuel Injector Solenoid
- 2 Idle Air Control (IAC) Valve
- 3 Fuel Pump Relay
- 5 Torque Converter Clutch (TCC) Solenoid Connector
- 8 Cooling Fan Relay
- 13 A/C Compressor Relay
- 14 Direct Ignition System (DIS) Assembly

◯ INFORMATION SENSORS
- A Manifold Absolute Pressure (MAP)
- B Oxygen (O_2) Sensor
- C Throttle Position Sensor (TPS)
- D Coolant Temperature Sensor (CTS)
- F Vehicle Speed Sensor (VSS)
- M Park/Neutral (P/N) Switch
- T Intake Air Temperature (IAT) Sensor (In Air Cleaner Assembly)

◎ Exhaust Gas Recirculation (EGR) Valve

87954063

"J" CARLINE   RPO: LE4   VIN CODE: H   2.0L L4 PORT

☐ COMPUTER HARNESS
- C1 Electronic Control Module (ECM)
- C2 ALDL Diagnostic Connector
- C3 "Check Engine" light
- C4 Power Feed Connector
- C5 ECM Harness Grounds
- C6 Fuse Panel
- C8 Fuel Pump Test Connector

NOT ECM CONNECTED
- N1 Crankcase Vent Valve (PCV)
- N17 Fuel Vapor Canister

☐ CONTROLLED DEVICES
- 1 Fuel Injector
- 2 Idle Air Control (IAC) Valve
- 3 Fuel Pump Relay*
- 5 TCC Solenoid
- 8 Cooling Fan Relay
- 13 A/C Compressor Relay*
- 14 Direct Ignition System (DIS) Coil Assy. (Under Intake Plenum)
- 16 Computer Controlled Purge (CCP) Solenoid
- 17 Exhaust Gas Recirculation (EGR) Solenoid

◎ Exhaust Gas Recirculation (EGR) Valve

◯ INFORMATION SENSORS
- A Manifold Absolute Pressure (MAP) Sensor
- B Oxygen (O_2) Sensor
- C Throttle Position Sensor (TPS)
- D Coolant Temperature Sensor (CTS)
- F_1 Vehicle Speed (Auto Trans.)
- F_2 Vehicle Speed (Manual Trans.)
- M Park/Neutral (P/N) Switch
- T Intake Air Temperature (IAT) Sensor (In Air Cleaner Assy.)
- U A/C Pressure Sensor
- Z Crankshaft Position Sensor

* Actual location may vary.

87954062

"J" CARLINE   RPO:LN2   VIN CODE: 4   2.2L L4 MFI

COMPUTER HARNESS
C1 Powertrain Control Module (PCM)
C2 Data Link Connector (DLC)
C3 Malfunction Indicator Lamp (MIL) "Check Engine"
C4 Power feed connector
C5 PCM harness grounds
C6 Fuse panel
C7 Cruise control module
C8 Fuel pump test connector

NOT PCM CONNECTED
N1 Crankcase vent valve
N17 Evaporative emission canister

CONTROLLED DEVICES
1 Fuel injector
2 Idle Air Control (IAC) valve
3 Fuel pump relay
5 Torque Converter Clutch (TCC) solenoid (backside of Engine block)
8 Cooling fan control relay
13 A/C compressor clutch control relay
14 Electronic ignition assembly (under intake manifold)
17 EGR control solenoid valve (located below MAP sensor)
18 Evaporative canister purge solenoid valve
19 Generator
◎ Exhaust Gas Recirculation (EGR) valve

FIRING ORDER 1-3-4-2

INFORMATION SENSORS
A Manifold Absolute Pressure (MAP) sensor
B Oxygen Sensor (O2S)
C Throttle Position (TP) sensor
D Engine Coolant Temperature (ECT) sensor
E Crankshaft position sensor
F1 Vehicle Speed Sensor (VSS) (auto trans.)
F2 Vehicle Speed Sensor (VSS) (manual trans.)
J Knock Sensor (KS)
M Trans range switch
T Intake Air Temperature (IAT) sensor (on air cleaner assembly)
U A/C refrigerant pressure sensor
W Oil level sensor
Z Coolant level sensor (in oil pan)

87954065

"J" CARLINE   RPO:LN2   VIN CODE: 4   2.2L L4 PORT

COMPUTER HARNESS
C1 Electronic Control Module (ECM)
C2 ALDL Diagnostic Connector
C3 "Check Engine" Light
C4 Power Feed Connector
C5 ECM Harness Grounds
C6 Fuse Panel
C8 Fuel Pump Test Connector

NOT ECM CONNECTED
N1 Crankcase Vent Valve (PCV)
N17 Fuel Vapor Canister

* Actual location may vary

CONTROLLED DEVICES
1 Fuel Injector
2 Idle Air Control (IAC) Valve
3 Fuel Pump Relay*
5 Torque Converter Clutch (TCC) Solenoid
8 Cooling Fan Relay
13 A/C Compressor Relay*
14 Direct Ignition System (DIS) Assembly (under intake manifold)
17 Exhaust Gas Recirculation (EGR) Solenoid
◎ Exhaust Gas Recirculation (EGR) valve

INFORMATION SENSORS
A Manifold Absolute Pressure (MAP) Sensor
B Oxygen (O2) Sensor
C Throttle Position Sensor (TPS)
D Coolant Temperature Sensor (CTS)
F1 Vehicle Speed (Auto Trans.)
F2 Vehicle Speed (Manual Trans.)
M Park/Neutral (P/N) Switch
T Intake Air Temperature (IAT) Sensor (On Air Cleaner Assembly)
U A/C Pressure Sensor

87954064

"J" CARLINE   RPO: LH0   VIN CODE: T   3.1L V6 PFI

87954069

COMPUTER HARNESS

- C1 Electronic Control Module (ECM)
- C2 ALDL diagnostic connector
- C3 "SERVICE ENGINE SOON" light
- C5 ECM harness ground
- C6 Fuse panel
- C8 Fuel pump test connector
- C9 Fuel pump/ECM fuse
- C10 ECM Power Feed

NOT ECM CONNECTED

- N1 Positive Crankcase Ventilation (PCV) valve
- N4 Engine temperature sensor gage and (telltale)
- N6 Fuel pump/oil pressure sensor gage and (telltale)
- N12 Fuel pressure connector

CONTROLLED DEVICES

- 1 Fuel injector
- 2 Idle Air Control (IAC) motor
- 3 Fuel pump prelay
- 5 Trans. Converter Clutch connector
- 6 Direct Ignition System (DIS)
- 8 Cooling fan relay
- 12 Exh. Gas Recirc. valve
- 13 A/C compressor relay
- 15 Fuel vapor canister solenoid

INFORMATION SENSORS

- A Manifold Air Pressure (MAP)
- B Exhaust oxygen (O₂)
- C Throttle Position Sensor (TPS)
- D Coolant Temperature Sensor (CTS)
- E Crank Shaft Sensor
- F Vehicle Speed Sensor (VSS)
- J Electronic Spark Control (ESC)
- K Intake Air Temperature (IAT)
- M P/N switch
- S P/S pressure switch
- U A/C pressure sensor

"J" SERIES   RPO: LB6   VIN CODE: W   2.8L V6 PFI

87954068

COMPUTER HARNESS

- C1 Electronic Control Module (ECM)
- C2 ALDL diagnostic connector
- C3 "SERVICE ENGINE SOON" light
- C5 ECM harness ground
- C6 Fuse panel
- C8 Fuel pump test connector
- C9 Fuel pump / ECM fuse

NOT ECM CONNECTED

- N1 Crankcase vent valve (PCV)
- N4 Engine temp. switch (telltale)
- N5 Engine temp. sensor (gage)
- N6 Oil press. switch (telltale)
- N7 Oil press. sensor (gage)
- N12 Fuel pressure connector

CONTROLLED DEVICES

- 1 Fuel injector
- 2 Idle air control motor
- 3 Fuel pump prelay
- 5 Trans. Converter Clutch connector
- 6 Direct Ignition System (DIS)
- 8 Engine fan relay
- 9. Air Control Solenoid (M/T only)
- 12 Exh. Gas Recirc. valve
- 13 A/C compressor relay
- 15 Fuel vapor canister solenoid

INFORMATION SENSORS

- A Manifold Pressure (MAP)
- B Exhaust oxygen
- C Throttle position
- D Coolant temperature
- E Crank Shaft Sensor
- F Vehicle speed
- J Knock (ESC)
- K MAT
- M P/N switch
- S P/S pressure switch
- U A/C pressure fan switch
- V A/C Low Press. switch (mounted in compressor)
- W A/C Hi Press. cut-out sw.

VACUUM DIAGRAMS

Following is a listing of vacuum diagrams for many of the engine and emissions package combinations covered by this manual. Because vacuum circuits will vary based on various engine and vehicle options, always refer first to the vehicle emission control information label. Should the label be missing, or should the vehicle be equipped with a different engine from the original equipment, refer to the diagrams below for the same or similar configuration.

Fig. 64 1983 2.0L (VIN P) engine with manual transaxle and without cruise control

Fig. 61 1983 2.0L (VIN P) engine with manual transaxle—Federal

Fig. 65 1984 1.8L (VIN O) engine without cruise control—California

Fig. 62 1983 2.0L (VIN P) engine with manual transaxle and cruise control

Fig. 66 1984 1.8L (VIN J) engine—Federal

Fig. 63 1983 2.0L (VIN P) engine with automatic transaxle and without cruise control

Fig. 67 1984 1.8L (VIN J) engine—California

Fig. 68 1984–86 2.0L (VIN P) engine—Federal

Fig. 69 1984–86 2.0L (VIN P) engine—California

Fig. 70 1984 1.8L (VIN O) engine—Federal

Fig. 71 1984 2.0L (VIN B) engine with 2bbl carburetor and manual transaxle—Canada

Fig. 72 1984 2.0L (VIN B) engine with 2bbl carburetor and automatic transaxle—Canada

Fig. 73 1987 2.0L OHC engine—Except Turbo

Fig. 74 1987 2.0L OHC Turbo engine

Fig. 75 1987 2.0L OHV engine

Fig. 76 1987 2.8L (VIN W) engine with manual transaxle

Fig. 80 1988 2.0L OHV engine

Fig. 77 1987 2.8L (VIN W) engine with manual transaxle

Fig. 81 1988 2.8L (VIN W) engine

Fig. 78 1988 2.0L OHC engine—Except Turbo

Fig. 82 1989 2.0L OHV engine

Fig. 79 1988 2.0L OHC Turbo engine

Fig. 83 1989 2.0L OHC engine—Except Turbo

Fig. 84 1988 2.0L OHC Turbo engine

Fig. 88 1990 2.0L OHC Turbo engine

Fig. 85 1989 2.8L (VIN W) engine

Fig. 89 1990 3.1L (VIN T) engine

Fig. 86 1990 2.2L OHV engine

Fig. 90 1991 2.2L OHV engine

Fig. 87 1990 2.0L OHC engine—Except Turbo

Fig. 91 1992 2.0L (VIN H) engine—Federal

Fig. 92 1992 2.2L (VIN 4) engine—Federal

Fig. 93 1992 2.2L (VIN 4) engine—California

Fig. 94 1992 3.1L (VIN T) engine—Federal

Fig. 95 1992 3.1L (VIN T) engine—California

Fig. 96 1993 2.0L (VIN H) engine—Federal

Fig. 97 1993 2.0L (VIN H) engine—California

Fig. 98 1993 2.2L (VIN 4) engine—Federal

Fig. 99 1993 2.2L (VIN 4) engine—California

Fig. 100 1993 3.1L (VIN T) engine—Federal

Fig. 104 1994 2.0L (VIN H) engine—Federal with manual transaxle

Fig. 101 1993 3.1L (VIN T) engine—California

Fig. 105 1994 2.0L (VIN H) engine—Federal and California

Fig. 102 1993 3.1L (VIN T) engine—California alternate

Fig. 106 1994 2.0L (VIN H) engine with automatic transaxle

Fig. 103 1993 3.1L (VIN T) engine—Federal alternate

Fig. 107 1994 2.2L (VIN 4) engine

Fig. 108 1994 2.2L (VIN 4) engine with manual transaxle

Fig. 111 1994 2.2L (VIN 4) engine—Federal

Fig. 109 1994 2.2L (VIN 4) engine with automatic transaxle

Fig. 112 1994 3.1L (VIN T) engine—Federal

Fig. 110 1994 2.2L (VIN 4) engine—California

Fig. 113 1994 3.1L (VIN T) engine—California

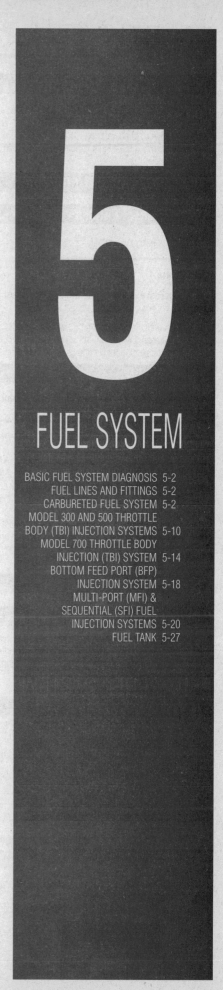

BASIC FUEL SYSTEM DIAGNOSIS 5-2
FUEL LINES AND FITTINGS 5-2
QUICK-CONNECT FITTINGS 5-2
  REMOVAL & INSTALLATION 5-2
CARBURETED FUEL SYSTEM 5-2
FUEL PRESSURE RELEASE 5-2
MECHANICAL FUEL PUMP 5-2
  REMOVAL & INSTALLATION 5-2
  TESTING 5-3
CARBURETOR 5-3
  MODEL IDENTIFICATION 5-3
  PRELIMINARY CHECKS 5-3
  ADJUSTMENTS 5-3
  REMOVAL & INSTALLATION 5-5
  OVERHAUL 5-6
MODEL 300 AND 500 THROTTLE
  BODY (TBI) INJECTION
  SYSTEMS 5-10
SYSTEM DESCRIPTION 5-10
RELIEVING FUEL SYSTEM
  PRESSURE 5-10
    EXCEPT 1985–86 2.0L (OHV)
     ENGINES 5-10
    1985–86 2.0L (OHV) 5-10
FUEL PUMP 5-11
  TESTING 5-11
  REMOVAL & INSTALLATION 5-11
THROTTLE BODY 5-11
  REMOVAL & INSTALLATION 5-11
FUEL INJECTOR 5-12
  REMOVAL & INSTALLATION 5-12
FUEL PRESSURE REGULATOR/
  COMPENSATOR 5-13
  REMOVAL & INSTALLATION 5-13
FUEL METER COVER 5-13
  REMOVAL & INSTALLATION 5-13
FUEL METER BODY 5-13
  REMOVAL & INSTALLATION 5-13
MODEL 700 THROTTLE BODY
  INJECTION (TBI) SYSTEM 5-14
SYSTEM DESCRIPTION 5-14
FUEL SYSTEM PRESSURE
  RELEASE 5-14
    2.0L AND 2.2L OHV ENGINES 5-14
    2.0L OHC ENGINE 5-15
FUEL PUMP 5-15
  TESTING 5-15
  REMOVAL & INSTALLATION 5-15
THROTTLE BODY 5-15
  REMOVAL & INSTALLATION 5-15
FUEL INJECTOR 5-16
  REMOVAL & INSTALLATION 5-16
FUEL PRESSURE REGULATOR 5-17
  REMOVAL & INSTALLATION 5-17
TUBE MODULE ASSEMBLY 5-18
  REMOVAL & INSTALLATION 5-18
BOTTOM FEED PORT (BFP)
  INJECTION SYSTEM 5-18
SYSTEM DESCRIPTION 5-18

FUEL SYSTEM PRESSURE RELIEF 5-18
  1992 VEHICLES 5-18
  1993–94 VEHICLES 5-19
BOTTOM FEED PORT FUEL
  INJECTORS 5-19
  REMOVAL & INSTALLATION 5-19
FUEL PRESSURE REGULATOR 5-20
  REMOVAL & INSTALLATION 5-20
MULTI-PORT (MFI) & SEQUENTIAL
  (SFI) FUEL INJECTION
  SYSTEMS 5-20
GENERAL INFORMATION 5-20
RELIEVING FUEL SYSTEM
  PRESSURE 5-21
    1.8L AND 2.0L OHC ENGINES 5-21
    1992 2.0L (VIN H) ENGINES 5-21
    2.8L AND 3.1L ENGINES 5-21
FUEL PUMP 5-21
  TESTING 5-21
  REMOVAL & INSTALLATION 5-21
THROTTLE BODY 5-22
  REMOVAL & INSTALLATION 5-22
FUEL INJECTORS 5-23
  REMOVAL & INSTALLATION 5-23
FUEL PRESSURE REGULATOR 5-24
  REMOVAL & INSTALLATION 5-24
FUEL RAIL ASSEMBLY 5-25
  REMOVAL & INSTALLATION 5-25
FUEL TANK 5-27
TANK ASSEMBLY 5-27
  REMOVAL & INSTALLATION 5-27
  MODULAR FUEL SENDER ASSEMBLY
    REPLACEMENT 5-28
SPECIFICATION CHART
  E2SE CARBURETOR 5-10

5

FUEL SYSTEM

BASIC FUEL SYSTEM DIAGNOSIS 5-2
FUEL LINES AND FITTINGS 5-2
CARBURETED FUEL SYSTEM 5-2
MODEL 300 AND 500 THROTTLE
BODY (TBI) INJECTION SYSTEMS 5-10
MODEL 700 THROTTLE BODY
INJECTION (TBI) SYSTEM 5-14
BOTTOM FEED PORT (BFP)
INJECTION SYSTEM 5-18
MULTI-PORT (MFI) &
SEQUENTIAL (SFI) FUEL
INJECTION SYSTEMS 5-20
FUEL TANK 5-27

BASIC FUEL SYSTEM DIAGNOSIS

When there is a problem starting or driving a vehicle, two of the most important checks involve the ignition and the fuel systems. The questions most mechanics attempt to answer first, "is there spark?" and "is there fuel?" will often lead to solving most basic problems. For ignition system diagnosis and testing, please refer to the information on engine electrical components and ignition systems found earlier in this manual. If the ignition system checks out (there is spark), then you must determine if the fuel system is operating properly (is there fuel?).

FUEL LINES AND FITTINGS

Quick-Connect Fittings

REMOVAL & INSTALLATION

▸ See Figure 1

➥This procedure requires Tool Set J37088–A fuel line quick-connect separator.

1. Grasp both sides of the fitting. Twist the female connector ¼ turn in each direction to loosen any dirt within the fittings. Using compressed air, blow out the dirt from the quick-connect fittings at the end of the fittings.

❊❊ CAUTION

Safety glasses MUST be worn when using compressed air to avoid eye injury due to flying dirt particles!

2. For plastic (hand releasable) fittings, squeeze the plastic retainer release tabs, then pull the connection apart.
3. For metal fittings, choose the correct tool from kit J37088–A for the size of the fitting to be disconnected. Insert the proper tool into the female connector, then push inward to release the locking tabs. Pull the connection apart.
4. If it is necessary to remove rust or burrs from the male tube end of a quick-connect fitting, use emery cloth in a radial motion with the tube end to prevent damage to the O-ring sealing surfaces. Using a clean shop towel, wipe off the male tube ends. Inspect all connectors for dirt and burrs. Clean and/or replace if required.

To install:
5. Apply a few drops of clean engine oil to the male tube end of the fitting.
6. Push the connectors together to cause the retaining tabs/fingers to snap into place.
7. Once installed, pull on both ends of each connection to make sure they are secure.

Fig. 1 Make sure you lubricate the male fitting before fastening the quick-connect fittings

CARBURETED FUEL SYSTEM

Fuel Pressure Release

To release the fuel pressure on the carbureted system, remove the fuel filler cap from the fuel tank in order to allow the fuel vapor to escape, the reinstall the cap. A rag should be placed around a fuel fitting before it is disconnected in order to catch any remaining fuel which may escape.

Mechanical Fuel Pump

A mechanical fuel pump is used on the 1982–84 carbureted engines. It is of the diaphragm-type and because of the design is serviced by replacement only. No adjustments or repairs are possible. The pump is operated by an eccentric on the camshaft.

REMOVAL & INSTALLATION

▸ See Figure 2

➥The fuel pump is located at the center rear of the engine.

1. Disconnect the negative cable at the battery. Raise and support the car.
2. Disconnect the inlet hose from the pump. Disconnect the vapor return hose, if equipped.
3. Loosen the fuel line at the carburetor, then disconnect the outlet pipe from the pump.
4. Unfasten the two mounting bolts and remove the pump from the engine.
To install:
5. Place a new gasket on the pump, then position the pump on the engine.

Fig. 2 Removal and installation of the fuel pump on a carbureted engine

Tighten the two mounting bolts alternately and evenly. Refer to the illustration for tightening specifications.
6. Install the pump outlet pipe. This is easier if the pipe is disconnected from the carburetor. Tighten the fitting while backing up the pump nut with another wrench. Install the pipe at the carburetor.
7. Install the inlet and vapor hoses. Lower the car, connect the negative battery cable, start the engine, and check for fuel leaks.

TESTING

To determine if the fuel pump is in good condition, tests for both pressure and volume should be performed. The tests are made with the pump installed, and the engine at normal operating temperature and idle speed. Never replace a fuel pump without first performing these simple tests.

Be sure that the fuel filter has been changed at the specified interval, If in doubt, install a new filter then test the system.

Pressure Test

1. Disconnect the fuel line at the carburetor and connect a fuel pump pressure gauge. Fill the carburetor float bowl with gasoline.
2. Start the engine and check the pressure with the engine at idle. If the pump has a vapor return hose, squeeze it off so that an accurate reading can be obtained. Pressure should not be below 4.5 psi (31 kPa).
3. If the pressure is incorrect, replace the pump. If it is ok, go on to the volume test.

Volume Test

1. Disconnect the pressure gauge. Run the fuel line into a graduated container.
2. Run the engine at idle until one pint of gasoline has been pumped. One pint should be delivered in 30 seconds or less. There is normally enough fuel in the carburetor float bowl to perform this test, but refill it if necessary.
3. If the delivery rate is below the minimum, check the lines for restrictions or leaks, then replace the pump.

Carburetor

The Rochester E2SE is used on all models. It is a two barrel, two stage carburetor of downdraft design used in conjunction with the Computer Command Control system of fuel control. The carburetor has special design features for optimum air/fuel mixture control during all ranges of engine operation.

MODEL IDENTIFICATION

▶ See Figure 3

General Motors Rochester carburetors are identified by their model code. The first number indicates the number of barrels, while one of the last letters indicates the type of choke used. These are V for the manifold mounted choke coil, C for the choke coil mounted in the carburetor body, and E for electric choke, also mounted on the carburetor. Model codes ending in A indicate an altitude-compensation carburetor.

PRELIMINARY CHECKS

The following should be observed before attempting any adjustments.
1. Thoroughly warm the engine. If the engine is cold, be sure that it reaches operating temperature.

Fig. 3 The carburetor identification number is stamped on the fuel bowl

2. Check the torque of all carburetor mounting nuts and assembly screws. Also check the intake manifold-to-cylinder head bolts. If air is leaking at any of these points, any attempts at adjustment will inevitably lead to frustration.
3. Check the manifold heat control valve (if used) to be sure that it is free.
4. Check and adjust the choke as necessary.
5. Adjust the idle speed and mixture. If the mixture screws are capped, don't adjust them unless all other causes of rough idle have been eliminated. If any adjustments are performed that might possibly change the idle speed or mixture, adjust the idle and mixture again when you are finished.

Before you make any carburetor adjustments make sure that the engine is in tune. Many problems which are thought to be carburetor-related can be traced to an engine which is simply out-of-tune. Any trouble in these areas will have symptoms like those of carburetor problems.

ADJUSTMENTS

Float Adjustment

▶ See Figure 4

1. Remove the air horn from the throttle body.
2. Use your fingers to hold the retainer in place, and to push the float down into light contact with the needle.
3. Measure the distance from the toe of the float (furthest from the hinge) to the top of the carburetor (gasket removed).
4. To adjust, remove the float and gently bend the arm to specification. After adjustment, check the float alignment in the chamber.

Accelerator Pump Adjustment

E2SE carburetors have a non-adjustable pump lever. Adjustment is neither necessary or possible.

Fast Idle Adjustment

▶ See Figure 5

1. Set the ignition timing and curb idle speed, and disconnect and plug hoses as directed on the emission control decal.
2. Place the fast idle screw on the highest step of the cam.
3. Start the engine and adjust the engine speed to specification with the fast idle screw.

Choke Coil Lever Adjustment

▶ See Figure 6

1. Remove the three retaining screws and remove the choke cover and coil. On models with a riveted choke cover, drill out the three rivets and remove the cover and choke coil.

➡ A choke stat cover retainer kit is required for reassembly.

2. Place the fast idle screw on the high step of the cam.
3. Close the choke by pushing in on the intermediate choke lever.
4. Insert a drill or gauge of the specified size into the hole in the choke housing. The choke lever in the housing should be up against the side of the gauge.
5. If the lever does not just touch the gauge, bend the intermediate choke rod to adjust.

Fast Idle Cam (Choke Rod) Adjustment

▶ See Figure 7

➡ A special angle gauge must be used.

1. Adjust the choke coil lever and fast idle first.
2. Rotate the degree scale until it is zeroed.
3. Close the choke and install the degree scale onto the choke plate. Center the leveling bubble.
4. Rotate the scale so that the specified degree is opposite the scale pointer.
5. Place the fast idle screw on the second step of the cam (against the high step). Close the choke by pushing in the intermediate lever.
6. Bend the fast idle cam rod at the U to adjust the angle to specifications.

Fig. 4 Adjusting the float on the E2SE carburetor

Fig. 7 Fast idle cam (choke rod) adjustment

Fig. 5 Fast idle adjustment

Fig. 6 Adjusting the choke coil lever

Air Valve Rod Adjustment

▶ **See Figure 8**

1. Seat the vacuum diaphragm with an outside vacuum source. Tape over the purge bleed hole if present.
2. Close the air valve.
3. Insert the specified gauge between the rod and the end of the slot in the plunger.
4. Bend the rod to adjust the clearance.

Primary Side Vacuum Break Adjustment

▶ **See Figure 9**

1. Follow Steps 1–4 of the Fast Idle Cam Adjustment.
2. Seat the choke vacuum diaphragm with an outside vacuum source.
3. Push in on the intermediate choke lever to close the choke valve, and hold closed during adjustment.
4. Adjust by using a ⅛ in. (3mm) hex wrench to turn the screw in the rear cover until the bubble is centered.
5. After adjusting, apply RTV silicone sealant over the screw to seal the setting.

Secondary Vacuum Break Adjustment

▶ **See Figure 10**

1. Follow Steps 1–4 of the Fast Idle Cam Adjustment.
2. Seat the choke vacuum diaphragm with an outside vacuum source.
3. Push in on the intermediate choke lever to close the choke valve, and hold closed during adjustment. Make sure the plunger spring is compressed and seated, if present.
4. Adjust by using a ⅛ in. (3mm) hex wrench to turn the screw in the rear cover until the bubble is centered.
5. After adjusting, apply RTV silicone sealant over the screw to seal the setting.

Choke Unloader Adjustment

▶ **See Figure 11**

1. Follow Steps 1–4 of the Fast Idle Cam Adjustment.
2. Hold the primary throttle wide open.
3. If the engine is warm, close the choke valve by pushing in on the intermediate choke lever.
4. Bend the unloader tang until the bubble is centered.

Fig. 8 Adjusting the air rod valve

Fig. 9 Adjusting the primary side vacuum break

Fig. 10 Secondary side vacuum break adjustment

Fig. 11 Choke unloader adjustment

Secondary Lockout Adjustment

▶ **See Figure 12**

1. Pull the choke wide open by pushing out on the intermediate choke lever.
2. Open the throttle until the end of the secondary actuating lever is opposite the toe of the lockout lever.
3. Gauge clearance between the lockout lever and secondary lever should be as specified.
4. To adjust, bend the lockout lever where it contacts the fast idle cam.

REMOVAL & INSTALLATION

▶ **See Figures 13 and 14**

1. Disconnect the negative battery cable.
2. Remove the air cleaner and gasket.
3. Disconnect the fuel pipe and all vacuum lines.
4. Tag and detach all electrical connections.
5. Disconnect the downshift cable.
6. If equipped with cruise control, disconnect the linkage.
7. Unscrew the carburetor mounting bolts, then remove the carburetor.

To install:

8. Before installing the carburetor, fill the float bowl with gasoline to reduce the battery strain and the possibility of backfiring when the engine is started again.

Fig. 12 Secondary lockout adjustment

Fig. 13 View of the Rochester E2SE carburetor components

Fig. 14 Exploded view of the carburetor mounting

9. Inspect the EFE heater for damage. Be sure that the throttle body and EFE mating surfaces are clean.

10. Install the carburetor and tighten the nuts alternately to the proper specifications. Refer to the accompanying figure.

11. Installation of the remaining components is the reverse of the removal procedure.

OVERHAUL

General Information

Efficient carburetion depends greatly on careful cleaning and inspection during overhaul, since dirt, gum, water, or varnish in or on the carburetor parts are often responsible for poor performance.

Overhaul your carburetor in a clean, dust-free area. Carefully disassemble the carburetor, referring often to the exploded views and directions packaged with the rebuilding kit. Keep all similar and look-alike parts segregated during disassembly and cleaning to avoid accidental interchange during assembly. Make a note of all jet sizes.

When the carburetor is disassembled, wash all parts (except diaphragms, electric choke units, pump plunger, and any other plastic, fiber, or rubber parts) in clean carburetor solvent. Do not leave parts in the solvent any longer than is necessary to sufficiently loosen the deposits. Excessive cleaning may remove the special finish from the float bowl and choke valve bodies, leaving these parts unfit for service. Rinse all parts in clean solvent and blow them dry with compressed air or allow them to air dry. Wipe clean all cork, plastic, and fiber parts with a clean, lint-free cloth.

Blow out all passages and jets with compressed air and be sure that there are no restrictions or blockages. Never use wire or similar tools to clean jets, fuel passages, or air bleeds. Clean all jets and valves separately to avoid accidental interchange.

Check all parts for wear or damage. If wear or damage is found, replace the defective parts. Especially check the following:

1. Check the float needle and seat for wear. If wear is found, replace the complete assembly.

2. Check the float hinge pin for wear and the float(s) for dents or distortion. Replace the float if fuel has leaked into it.

3. Check the throttle and choke shaft bores for wear or an out-of-round condition. Damage or wear to the throttle arm, shaft, or shaft bore will often require replacement of the throttle body. These parts require a close tolerance of fit; wear may allow air leakage, which could affect starting and idling.

➡️Throttle shafts and bushings are not included in overhaul kits. They may be purchased separately.

4. Inspect the idle mixture adjusting needles for burrs or grooves. Any such condition requires replacement of the needle, since you will not be able to obtain a satisfactory idle.

5. Test the accelerator pump check valves. They should pass air one way but not the other. Test for proper seating by blowing and sucking on the valve. Replace the valve check ball and spring as necessary. If the valve is satisfactory, wash the valve parts again to remove breath moisture.

6. Check the bowl cover for warped surfaces with a straightedge.

7. Closely inspect the accelerator pump plunger for wear and damage, replacing as necessary.

8. After the carburetor is assembled, check the choke valve for freedom of operation.

Carburetor overhaul kits are recommended for each overhaul. These kits contain all gaskets and new parts to replace those which deteriorate most rapidly. Failure to replace all parts supplied with the kit (especially gaskets) can result in poor performance later.

Some carburetor manufacturers supply overhaul kits for three basic types: minor repair; major repair; and gasket kits. Basically, they contain the following:

Minor Repair Kits:
- All gaskets
- Float needle valve
- All diagrams
- Spring for the pump diaphragm

Major Repair Kits:
- All jets and gaskets
- All diaphragms
- Float needle valve
- Pump ball valve
- Float
- Complete intermediate rod
- Intermediate pump lever
- Some cover hold-down screws and washers

Gasket Kits:
- All gaskets

After cleaning and checking all components, reassemble the carburetor, using new parts and referring to the exploded view. When reassembling, make sure that all screws and jets are tight in their seats, but do not overtighten as the tips will be distorted. Tighten all screws gradually, in rotation. Do not tighten needle valves into their seats; uneven jetting will result. Always use new gaskets. Be sure to adjust the float level when reassembling.

Disassembly

♦ See Figures 15 thru 27

1. Remove the carburetor from the vehicle. Refer to the necessary procedure located earlier in this section.

2. Mount the assembly in a holding fixture (special tool J–9787 or equiva-

lent). Without the use of the holding fixture, it is possible to damage the throttle valves.

3. Remove 3 attaching screws that hold the idle speed control/primary vacuum break to the carburetor.

4. Remove the idle speed control, vacuum break and bracket as an assembly.

5. Remove the secondary vacuum break and bracket assembly attaching screws from the throttle body. Then rotate the assembly to disengage the vacuum break link.

➡**Do not immerse the idle speed control or vacuum break units in any type of carburetor cleaner.**

6. To remove the air horn assembly, remove the clip from the hole in the pump rod. Remove the choke rod and plastic bushing from the choke lever. Remove the three mixture control solenoid screws, then lift the solenoid out of the air horn.

7. Remove the fast idle cam rod from the choke lever by rotating the rod to align the notch on the rod with the small slot in the lever.

8. To remove the float bowl assembly, remove the air horn gasket. Remove the pump plunger from the pump well. Remove the TP sensor and connector assembly from the float bowl. Remove the spring from the bottom of the TP sensor well in the bowl.

9. Remove the plastic filler block over the float valve. Remove the float assembly and float valve by pulling up on the hinge pin.

10. Remove the plastic filler block insert from the float bowl cavity.

11. Using a special removal tool or a wide-blade screwdriver that fully fits the slots on the top of the float valve seat and the extended metering jet, remove the float valve seat (with the gasket) and the extended metering jet from the float bowl. Do not remove or change the adjustment of the small calibration screw located deep inside the metering jet.

12. Remove the plastic retainer holding the pump discharge spring and check ball.

13. Remove the fuel inlet nut, gasket, check valve filter assembly and spring.

14. Unfasten the 4 throttle body-to-bowl attaching screws, then remove the throttle body assembly. Remove the throttle body-to-bowl insulator gasket.

Cleaning and Inspection

1. Thoroughly clean all metal parts and blow dry with compressed air. Make sure all fuel passages and metering parts are free of burrs and dirt. Do not pass drills or wires through the jets or passages

2. Inspect the upper and lower surfaces of the carburetor castings for damage.

3. Inspect the holes in the levers for excessive wear. Inspect the plastic bushings in the levers for damage, then replace as required.

Assembly

▶ **See Figures 28, 29 and 30**

1. To install the throttle body, hold the primary throttle lever wide open, install the lower end of the pump rod in the throttle lever by aligning the notch

Fig. 15 Primary vacuum break removal

Fig. 16 Secondary vacuum break removal

Fig. 17 Use pliers to remove the pump rod clip

Fig. 18 The intermediate choke rod linkage is secured by a retainer clip

Fig. 19 The mixture control solenoid is secured by screws

Fig. 20 Air horn removal

Fig. 21 Air horn components

Fig. 22 The Throttle Position (TP) sensor is positioned in the float bowl

Fig. 23 Float bowl components

Fig. 24 Bowl plastic insert removal

Fig. 25 Metering jet and float valve seat locations

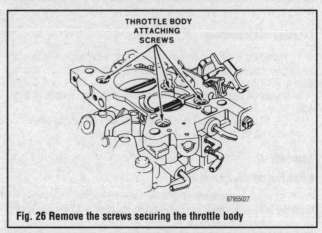

Fig. 26 Remove the screws securing the throttle body

Fig. 27 Idle mixture needle plug removal

on the rod with the slot in the elver. The end of the rod should point outward toward the throttle lever.

2. Install a new throttle body-to-bowl insulator gasket over the 2 locating dowels on the bowl.

3. Rotate the fast idle cam so that the steps face the fast idle screw on the throttle lever when properly installed, install the throttle body making certain it is properly located over the dowels on the float bowl. Install the screws and washers, then tighten them evenly to secure.

4. Place the carburetor assembly on a suitable holding fixture. Install the fuel inlet filter spring, check valve.filter assembly, new gasket and the inlet nut. Tighten the fuel filter inlet nut to 18 ft. lbs. (24 Nm).

➡**Tightening the fuel filter inlet nut beyond the specifications can damage the nylon gasket, causing a fuel leak.**

5. Install the choke housing on the throttle body, making sure the raised boss and locating lug on the rear housing fit into the recesses in the float bowl casting.

6. Install the intermediate choke shaft, lever and rod assembly in the float bowl by pushing the shaft through from the throttle lever side.

7. Install the choke coil lever inside the choke housing onto the flats on the intermediate choke shaft.

8. Instal the pump discharge steel check ball and spring in the passage next to the float chamber.

9. Insert the end of a new plastic retainer into the end of the spring, then install the retainer in the float bowl.

10. Using a special installation tool or a wide-bladed screwdriver that fully fits the slots on the top of the float valve and the extended metering jet, install the float valve seat (with gasket) and the extended metering jet. Tighten the seat and jet securely.

11. Place the plastic filler block insert into the blow cavity.

12. Install the float valve onto the float arm by sliding the float lever under the pull clip.

13. Install the float hinge pin into the float arm with the end of the loop of the pin facing the pump well. Install the float assembly by aligning the valve in the seat and float hinge pin into the locating channels in the float bowl. Adjust the float lever, as outlined earlier in this section.

14. Install the plastic filler block over the float valve, pressing downward until properly seated. Install the TP sensor return spring in the bottom of the well in the float bowl.

15. Install the TP sensor and electrical connector assembly.

16. Install the air horn gasket on the float bowl, locating gasket over the 2 dowel locating pins on the bowl. Install the pump return spring and plunger assembly in the pump well.

17. Rotate fast idle cam to the full Up position and tilt the air horn assembly to engage the lower end of fast idle cam rod in slot in the fast idle cam and install pump rod end into the pump lever; carefully lower the air horn assembly onto float bowl, guiding pump plunger stem through seal in air horn casting. DO NOT FORCE AIR HORN ASSEMBLY ONTO THE BOWL.

18. Fasten the 7 air horn to bowl attaching screws and lockwashers following proper installation location and tightening sequence. All air horn screws must be tightened EVENLY.

19. Install new retainer clip through hole in end of pump rod extending through pump lever, making sure clip is securely locked in place.

20. Install mixture control solenoid (spacer and rubber seal) on air horn, carefully aligning solenoid stem with recess in bottom of bowl.

21. Secure the plastic bushing in the hole in the choke lever, making sure the small end of the bushing faces the retaining clip when installed. Retain the rod with a new clip.

22. Install secondary side vacuum break assembly.

23. Install primary side vacuum break assembly (with idle speed control and bracket).

24. As outlined earlier in this section, install the carburetor.

Fig. 28 Exploded view of the choke assembly

Fig. 29 Air horn screw tightening sequences

Fig. 30 Be sure to properly position the mixture control solenoid seal and retainers

E2SE Carburetor Specifications

Carburetor Identification	Float Level (in.)	Fast Idle (rpm)	Choke Coil Lever (in.)	Fast Idle Cam (deg.)	Air Valve Rod (deg.)	Primary Vacuum Break (deg/in.)	Choke Setting (notches)	Secondary Vacuum Break (deg/in.)	Choke Unloader (deg/in.)	Secondary Lockout (in.)
17081600	5/16	①	.085	24	1	20/.110	①	27/.157	35/.220	.012
17081601	5/16	①	.085	24	1	20/.110	①	27/.157	35/.220	.012
17081607	5/16	①	.085	24	1	20/.110	①	27/.157	35/.220	.012
17081700	5/16	①	.085	24	1	20/.110	①	27/.157	35/.220	.012
17081701	5/16	①	.085	24	1	20/.110	①	27/.157	35/.220	.012

① See underhood emissions sticker

87955032

MODEL 300 AND 500 THROTTLE BODY (TBI) INJECTION SYSTEMS

System Description

The single bore, Model 300 throttle body unit used on the 1983–86 1.8L OHC engine and the Model 500 throttle body unit used on the 1982–86 2.0L OHV engine are similar systems.

In these throttle body systems, a single fuel injector mounted at the top of the throttle body sprays fuel down through the throttle valve and into the intake manifold. The throttle body resembles a carburetor in appearance but does away with much of the carburetor's complexity (choke system and linkage, power valves, accelerator pump, jets, fuel circuits, etc.), replacing these with the electrically operated fuel injector.

The injector is actually a solenoid which when activated lifts a pintle valve off its seat, allowing the pressurized (10 psi) fuel behind the valve to spray out. The nozzle of the injector is designed to atomize the fuel for complete air/fuel mixture.

The activating signal for the injector originates with the Electronic Control Module (ECM), which monitors engine temperature, throttle position, vehicle speed and several other engine-related conditions then continuously updates injector opening times in relation to the information given by these sensors.

The throttle body is also equipped with an idle air control valve. When the valve opens it allows air to bypass the throttle, which provides the additional air required to idle at elevated speed when the engine is cold. The idle air control motor also compensates for accessory loads and changing engine friction during break-in. The idle speed control valve is controlled by the ECM.

Fuel pressure for the system is provided by an in-tank fuel pump. The pump is a two-stage turbine designed powered by a DC motor. It is designed for smooth, quiet operation, high flow and fast priming. The design of the fuel inlet reduces the possibility of vapor lock under hot fuel conditions. The pump sends fuel forward through the fuel line to a stainless steel high-flow fuel filter mounted on the engine. From the filter the fuel moves to the throttle body. The fuel pump inlet is located in a reservoir in the fuel tank which insures a constant supply of fuel to the pump during hard cornering and on steep inclines. The fuel pump is controlled by a fuel pump relay, which in turn receives its signal from the ECM. A fuel pressure regulator inside the throttle body maintains fuel pressure at 10 psi and routes unused fuel back to the fuel tank through a fuel return line. On the dual throttle body system, a fuel pressure compensator is used on the second throttle body assembly to compensate for a momentary fuel pressure drop between the two units. This constant circulation of fuel through the throttle body prevents component overheating and vapor lock.

The electronic control module (ECM), also called a micro-computer, is the brain of the fuel injection system. After receiving input from various sensing elements in the system the ECM commands the fuel injector, idle air control motor, EST distributor, torque converter clutch and other engine actuators to operate in a pre-programmed manner to improve driveability and fuel economy while controlling emissions. The sensing elements update the computer every tenth of a second for general information and every 12.5 milliseconds for critical emissions and driveability information.

The ECM has limited system diagnostic capability. If certain system malfunctions occur, the diagnostic Check Engine light in the instrument panel will light, alerting the driver to the need for service.

Since both idle speed and mixture are controlled by the ECM on this system, no adjustments are possible or necessary.

Relieving Fuel System Pressure

✳✳ CAUTION

To reduce the risk of fire or personal injury, it is necessary to relieve the fuel system pressure before servicing the fuel system.

EXCEPT 1985–86 2.0L (OHV) ENGINES

1. Remove the fuel pump fuse from the fuse block.
2. Crank the engine. The engine will start and run until the fuel supply in the pipes is gone. Crank the engine again for 3 seconds making sure it is out of fuel.
3. Turn the ignition off and replace the fuse.

1985–86 2.0L (OHV)

The TBI injection systems used on the 1985–86 engines contain a constant bleed feature in the pressure regulator that relieves pressure any time the engine is turned off. Therefore, no special relieve procedure is required, however, a small amount of fuel may be released when the fuel line is disconnected.

✳✳ CAUTION

To reduce the chance of personal injury, cover the fuel line with cloth to collect the fuel and then place the cloth in an approved container.

Fuel Pump

TESTING

> ### ✱✱ CAUTION
>
> **To reduce the risk of fire and personal injury, it is necessary to relieve the fuel system pressure before servicing fuel system components (Refer to the appropriate procedure).**

1.8L and 2.0L OHV Engines

1. Remove the air cleaner. Plug the thermal vacuum port on the throttle body.
2. Remove the fuel line between the throttle body and filter.
3. Install a fuel pressure gauge between the throttle body and fuel filter. The gauge should be able to register at least 15 psi (30 kPa).
4. Start the car. The pressure reading should be 9–13 psi (18–26 kPa).
5. Depressurize the system and remove the gauge.
6. Assemble the system.

1.8L and 2.0L OHC Engines

1. Release the fuel system pressure.

> ### ✱✱ CAUTION
>
> **To reduce the risk of fire or personal injury, it is necessary to relieve the fuel system pressure before servicing the fuel system. Refer to Fuel System Pressure Release in the appropriate fuel injection system in this section.**

2. Obtain two sections of ⅜ in. steel tubing. Each should be about 10 in. (254mm) long. Double flare one end of each section.
3. Install a flare nut on each section. Connect each of the above sections of tubing into the flare nut-to-flare nut adapters that are included in J-29658 gauge.
4. Attach the pipe and the adapter assemblies to the J-29658 gauge.
5. Jack up the car and support it safely.
6. Disconnect the front fuel feed hose from the fuel pipe on the body.
7. Install a 10 in. (254mm) length of ⅜ in. fuel hose on the fuel pipe on the body. Attach the other end of the hose onto one of the sections of the pipe mentioned in Step 2. Secure the hose connections with clamps.
8. Start the engine and check for leaks.
9. Observe the fuel pressure reading. It should be 9–13 psi (18–26 kPa).
10. Depressurize the fuel system and remove the gauge with adapters. Reconnect the fuel feed hose to the pipe and torque the clamp to 15 inch lbs. (1.7 Nm).
11. Carefully lower the car, the start the engine and check for fuel leaks.

REMOVAL & INSTALLATION

▶ See Figure 31

1. Properly relieve the fuel system pressure, as outlined earlier in this section.
2. Disconnect the negative battery cable.
3. Raise and safely support the vehicle.
4. As outlined later in this section, remove the fuel tank.
5. Remove the fuel lever sending unit and pump assembly by turning the cam lock ring counterclockwise. Lift the assembly from the fuel tank and remove the fuel pump from the fuel level sending unit.
6. Pull the fuel pump up into the attaching hose or pulsator while pulling outward away from the bottom support. After the pump is clear of the bottom support, pull the pump assembly out of the rubber connector or pulsator for removal.

To install:

7. Position and push the pump into the attaching hose.
8. Install the fuel level sending unit and pump assembly into the tank assembly. Use new O-rings during reassembly.

Fig. 31 Vehicles equipped with the 300 and 500 throttle bodies have an in-tank fuel pump

> ### ✱✱ WARNING
>
> **Be careful not to fold over or twist the strainer when installing the sending unit as it will restrict fuel flow. Also, be careful the strainer does not block full travel of the float arm.**

9. Install the cam lock over the assembly and lock by turning clockwise.
10. Install the fuel tank.
11. Connect the negative battery cable, then start the engine and check the system for proper operation.

Throttle Body

REMOVAL & INSTALLATION

▶ See Figures 32 and 33

1. Disconnect the battery cables at the battery.
2. Remove the air cleaner assembly, noting the connection points of the vacuum lines.
3. Detach the electrical connectors at the injector, idle air control motor, and throttle position sensor.

Fig. 32 When removing the air cleaner assembly, make sure to tag any vacuum lines or electrical connections

Fig. 33 Exploded view of the throttle body mounting—1984 Model 500 throttle body shown

4. Tag and disconnect the vacuum lines from the TBI unit, noting the connection points. During installation, refer to the underhood emission control information decal for vacuum line routing information.

5. Disconnect the throttle and cruise control (if so equipped) cables at the TBI unit.

6. Unfasten the fuel return line.

7. Disconnect the fuel feed line.

8. Unfasten the retaining bolts, then remove the TBI unit.

To install:

9. Installation is the reverse of removal. Make sure to clean the gasket mating surfaces.

10. Tighten the TBI retaining bolts alternately and evenly to the following specifications:

- 1983–85 2.0L OHV engine: 26 ft. lbs. (35 Nm).
- 1986 2.0L OHV engine: 17 ft. lbs. (23 Nm).
- 1983–86 1.8L OHC engine: 17 ft. lbs. (23 Nm).

Fuel Injector

REMOVAL & INSTALLATION

▶ **See Figures 34 and 35**

1. Relieve the fuel system pressure.

2. Remove the air cleaner.

3. Detach the injector electrical connector by squeezing the two tabs together and pulling straight up.

✳✳ WARNING

Use care in removing to prevent damage to the electrical connector pins on top of the injector, injector fuel filter and nozzle. The fuel injector is only serviced as a complete assembly. Do not immerse it in any type of cleaner.

4. Remove the fuel meter cover, as outlined in this section.

5. With the fuel meter cover gasket in place to prevent damage to the throttle body, gently pry up on the injector evenly and carefully remove it, using a suitable prytool.

6. Remove the large O-ring and steel back-up washer from the top of the injector cavity in the fuel meter body, then remove the small O-ring at the bottom of the injector cavity. Discard the gaskets.

To install:

7. Lubricate a new, small O-ring with clean automatic transaxle fluid, then push the O-ring onto the nozzle end of the injector, pressing the ring up against the injector fuel filter.

8. Place the steel back-up washer in the recess of the fuel meter body.

Lubricate a new, large O-ring with clean automatic transaxle fluid, then install the O-ring directly above the back-up washer, pressing the O-ring down into the cavity recess. The O-ring is seated properly when it is flush with the fuel meter body casting surface.

✳✳ WARNING

Do not try to reverse this procedure and install backup washer and O-ring after injector is located in the cavity. This will prevent the O-ring from seating in the recess.

9. Install the injector by using a pushing/twisting motion to the center nozzle O-ring in the bottom of the injector cavity and aligning the raised lug on the injector base with the notch case into the fuel meter body. Push down on the injector, making sure it is fully seated in the cavity. The injector installation is correct with the lug seated in the notch and the electrical terminals parallel to the throttle shaft in the throttle body.

10. Install the fuel meter cover, as outlined later in this section.

11. Attach the fuel injector electrical connector.

12. Install the air cleaner assembly.

13. Connect the negative battery cable.

Fig. 34 Carefully remove the injector using a suitable prytool

Fig. 35 Installing the fuel injector in the throttle body

Fuel Pressure Regulator/Compensator

REMOVAL & INSTALLATION

▶ See Figures 36 and 37

1. Properly relieve the fuel system pressure, then disconnect the negative battery cable.
2. Remove air cleaner.
3. Detach the injector electrical connector by squeezing on the two tabs and pulling straight up.
4. Unfasten the five screws securing fuel meter cover to fuel meter body. Make sure to note the location of the two short screws during removal.

✳ CAUTION

Do not remove the four screws securing the pressure regulator to the fuel meter cover. The fuel pressure regulator includes a large spring under heavy tension which, if accidentally released, could cause personal injury. The fuel meter cover is only serviced as a complete assembly and includes the fuel pressure regulator preset and plugged at the factory.

Fig. 36 Note the location of the two short screws on the fuel meter cover/regulator assembly for installation purposes

Fig. 37 When removing the fuel pressure regulator, DO NOT remove the four regulator attaching screws

5. Remove the fuel pressure regulator.

✳ WARNING

DO NOT immerse the fuel meter cover (with pressure regulator) in any type of cleaner. Immersion in cleaner will damage the internal fuel pressure regulator diaphragms and gaskets.

To install:

6. Using new gaskets and dust seal, attach the fuel meter cover to the fuel meter body. The two short screws are located adjacent to the injector.
7. Attach the injector electrical connector by pushing straight down until it is seated firmly in place.
8. Install the air cleaner.
9. Connect the negative battery cable.

Fuel Meter Cover

REMOVAL & INSTALLATION

▶ See Figure 36

1. Properly relieve the fuel system pressure, then disconnect the negative battery cable.
2. Remove air cleaner.
3. Detach the injector electrical connector by squeezing on the two tabs and pulling straight up.
4. Unfasten the five screws and lockwashers securing the fuel meter cover to the fuel meter body.

✳ CAUTION

Do not remove the four screws securing the pressure regulator to the fuel meter cover. The fuel pressure regulator includes a large spring under heavy tension which, if accidentally released, could cause personal injury. The fuel meter cover is only serviced as a complete assembly and includes the fuel pressure regulator preset and plugged at the factory.

5. Lift off the fuel meter cover (including the fuel pressure regulator assembly).
6. Discard the fuel outlet passage gasket. Leave the fuel meter cover gasket in place on the fuel meter body.
7. Remove the sealing ring (dust seal) for the base of the fuel pressure regulator from the fuel meter body.

To install:

8. Install a new dust deal fuel the fuel pressure regulator, into the recess on the fuel meter body.
9. Position a new fuel return passage gasket on the fuel meter cover. Install a new fuel meter gasket on the fuel meter body.
10. Install the fuel meter cover, making sure the pressure regulator dust seal and cover gaskets are in place. Apply a suitable thread locking compound to the threads of the cover attaching screws. Install the attaching screws and lockwasher. The two short screws go next to the fuel injector. Tighten the screws to 28 inch lbs. (3 Nm).
11. Attach the injector electrical connector by pushing straight down until it is seated firmly in place.
12. Install the air cleaner.
13. Connect the negative battery cable.

Fuel Meter Body

REMOVAL & INSTALLATION

▶ See Figure 38

1. Properly relieve the fuel system pressure.
2. Disconnect the negative battery cable.
3. Remove the air cleaner assembly.
4. Remove the fuel inlet and outlet nuts and gaskets from fuel meter body.

5. Unfasten three screws and lockwashers, then remove the fuel meter body from the throttle body assembly.

➡**The air cleaner stud must have been removed previously.**

6. Remove and discard the fuel meter body insulator gasket.
To install:
7. Install a new fuel meter body insulator gasket. Place the throttle body assembly in a suitable holding fixture to avoid damaging the throttle valve.

➡**The gasket is installed correctly when the cut-out portions of the gasket match the openings in the throttle body assembly.**

8. Position the fuel meter body on the insulator gasket. Apply the thread locking compound, supplied in the service kit, to the threads on the three fuel meter body attaching screw, following the manufacturers directions.
9. Install the fuel meter body attaching screws and lockwasher, then tighten to 35 inch lbs. (4 Nm).
10. Install the fuel feed and return nut and new gaskets in the fuel meter body. Tighten the nut to 21 ft. lbs. (29 Nm).
11. The remainder of installation is the reverse of the removal procedure.

Fig. 38 The fuel meter body is secured by three screws

MODEL 700 THROTTLE BODY INJECTION (TBI) SYSTEM

System Description

▶ **See Figures 39 and 40**

➡**The Model 700 throttle body system is used on the 1987–91 2.0L OHC (non-turbo) and the 1987–91 2.0L and 2.2L OHV engines.**

The Throttle Body Injection (TBI) system is an electronic fuel metering system in which the amount of fuel delivered by the injector is determined by the Electronic Control Module (ECM). This small, on-board microcomputer monitors various engine and vehicle conditions to calculate the fuel delivery time (pulse width) of the injector. The fuel pulse may be modified by the ECM to account for special operating conditions, such as cranking, cold starting, altitude, acceleration, and deceleration.

The TBI system provides a means of fuel distribution for controlling exhaust emissions within legislated limits. The TBI system, by precisely controlling the air/fuel mixture under all operating conditions, provides as near as possible complete combustion.

In order to regulate the fuel delivery in such an efficient manner, the ECM receives electrical inputs from various sensors about engine operating conditions. An oxygen sensor in the main exhaust stream functions to provide feedback information to the ECM regarding oxygen content in the exhaust. The ECM uses this information from the oxygen sensor, and other sensors, in modifying fuel delivery to achieve, as near as possible, an ideal air/fuel ratio of 14.7:1.

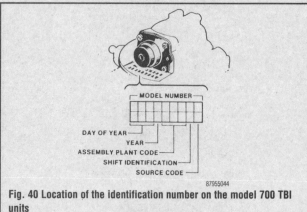

Fig. 40 Location of the identification number on the model 700 TBI units

This air/fuel ratio allows the 3-way catalytic converter to be more efficient in the conversion process of reducing exhaust emissions while, at the same time, providing acceptable levels of driveability and fuel economy.

The TBI unit is made up of 2 major casting assemblies: (1) a throttle body with a valve to control airflow and (2) a fuel body assembly with an integral pressure regulator and fuel injector to supply the required fuel. A device to control idle speed (IAC) and a device to provide information about throttle valve position (TPS) are included as part of the TBI unit.

Fuel System Pressure Release

✳✳ CAUTION

The fuel delivery pipe is under high pressure even after the engine is stopped. Direct removal of the fuel line, may result in dangerous fuel spray. Make sure to release the fuel pressure according to the following procedures:

2.0L AND 2.2L OHV ENGINES

1987 Vehicles

1. Release the fuel vapor pressure in the fuel tank by removing the fuel tank cap and reinstalling it.
2. Make sure the transaxle gear selector is in Park, for automatic transaxles, or Neutral, for manual transaxles, then set the parking brake and block the drive wheels.

1. FUEL INJECTOR
2. THROTTLE POSITION SENSOR (TPS)
3. THROTTLE BODY ASSEMBLY
4. TUBE MODULE ASSEMBLY
5. IDLE AIR CONTROL (IAC) VALVE
6. FUEL METER ASSEMBLY
7. PRESSURE REGULATOR COVER ASSEMBLY

Fig. 39 Model 700 TBI unit and integral components

3. Detach the fuel pump at the rear body connector and wait until the engine stops.

4. Start the engine and allow it to run a few seconds until it runs out of fuel.

5. Once the engine is stopped, crank it for 3 seconds to dissipate the fuel pressure in the lines.

1988–91 Vehicles

1. Disconnect the negative battery cable.

2. Release the fuel vapor pressure in the fuel tank by removing the fuel tank cap and reinstalling it.

3. The internal constant bleed feature of the TBI Models 700 on these vehicles, relieves the fuel pump system pressure when the engine is turned **OFF** and no further pressure relive procedure is required.

2.0L OHC ENGINE

1987–90 Vehicles

1. Release the fuel vapor pressure in the fuel tank by removing the fuel tank cap and reinstalling it.

2. Remove the fuel pump fuse from the fuse block.

3. Start the engine and allow it to run a few seconds until it runs out of fuel.

4. Once the engine is stopped, crank it for about 3 seconds to dissipate the fuel pressure in the lines.

5. If the fuel pressure can't be released in the above manner because the engine failed to run, disconnect the negative battery cable, cover the union bolt of the fuel line with an absorbent rag and loosen the union bolt slowly to release the fuel pressure gradually.

6. When the pressure is relieved and the necessary service is complete, return the fuse to the fuse block.

1991 Vehicles

1. Disconnect the negative battery cable.

2. Release the fuel vapor pressure in the fuel tank by removing the fuel tank cap and reinstalling it.

3. The internal constant bleed feature of this Model 700 TBI unit relieves the fuel pump system pressure when the engine is turned **OFF** and no further pressure relive procedure is required.

Fuel Pump

TESTING

1. Turn the ignition to the **OFF** position.

2. Make sure the fuel tank quantity is sufficient.

3. Install pressure gauge J 29658–B or BT–8205 or equivalent to the fuel line.

4. Apply battery voltage to the fuel pump test connector using a 10 amp fused jumper wire.

5. Note the fuel pressure which should be 9–13 psi. (18–26 kPa).

REMOVAL & INSTALLATION

▶ **See Figure 41**

1. Properly relieve the fuel system pressure.

2. Disconnect the negative battery cable.

3. Raise and safely support the vehicle.

4. Remove the fuel tank, as outlined later in this section.

5. Remove the fuel tank sending unit and pump assembly by turning the cam lock ring counterclockwise. Lift the assembly from the fuel tank, then remove the fuel pump from the fuel level sending unit.

6. Pull the fuel pump up into the attaching hose or pulsator while pulling outward away from the bottom support. After the pump is clear of the bottom support, pull the pump assembly out of the rubber connector or pulsator for removal.

7. Inspect the fuel pump attaching hose for any signs of deterioration, and replace as necessary. Also, make sure to check the rubber sound insulator at the bottom of pump and replace if required.

1. FUEL TANK METER ASSY.
2. PULSATOR
3. BUMPER
4. FUEL PUMP
5. SOUND ISOLATOR SLEEVE
6. SOUND INSULATOR
7. FILTER

87955041

Fig. 41 Exploded view of the sending unit and fuel pump assembly

To install:

8. Position, then push the fuel pump into the attaching hose.

9. Using a new O-ring, install the fuel level sending unit and pump assembly into the tank assembly.

※※ WARNING

Be careful not to fold over or twist the strainer when installing the sending unit as it will restrict fuel flow. Also, be careful the strainer does not block full travel of the float arm.

10. Position the cam lock over the assembly and lock by turning clockwise. Attach the electrical connector.

11. Install the fuel tank.

12. Connect the negative battery cable, then check the system for proper operation.

Throttle Body

REMOVAL & INSTALLATION

▶ **See Figures 42 thru 48**

1. Properly relieve the fuel system pressure.

2. Disconnect the negative battery cable.

3. Remove the air cleaner assembly and gasket.

4. Tag and detach the electrical connectors at the fuel injector, Idle Air Control (IAC) valve, and Throttle Position (TP) sensor.

5. Remove the grommet with the wires from the fuel meter body.

6. Tag and disconnect the vacuum lines at the rear of the throttle body.

7. Detach the throttle cable, transaxle control cable and cruise control cable (if so equipped) at the TBI unit.

8. Disconnect the fuel feed and return lines. Use tool J 29698-A, or equivalent back-up wrench, on the TBI fuel nuts to prevent them from turning. Remove and discard the fuel line O-rings.

9. Unfasten the retaining bolts and/or studs, then remove the TBI unit. Remove and discard the TBI flange gasket.

➡ **Stuff a clean rag in the manifold opening to avoid letting any dirt or other debris enter the engine.**

Fig. 42 Be sure to tag the connectors and hoses as you remove them, so they don't get mixed up during installation

Fig. 43 Always use a back-up wrench when disconnecting fuel lines to avoid distorting them

Fig. 44 Carefully remove, then discard the fuel line O-rings and replace with new ones for installation

Fig. 45 Unfasten the studs securing the throttle body, then . . .

Fig. 46 . . . remove the studs to allow for throttle body removal

Fig. 47 Lift the throttle body assembly from the intake manifold

Fig. 48 Remove and discard the throttle body flange gasket

10. Clean the gasket mating surfaces on the throttle body and intake manifold.

To install:

11. Position a new flange gasket, then install the TBI unit. Install the attaching bolts/studs and tighten to 12–16 ft. lbs. (17–22 Nm).

12. Place new O-rings on the fuel feed and return lines, then connect the fuel lines. Use tool J 29698-A or equivalent fuel line wrench, to prevent the lines from turning, and tighten the line nuts to 20 ft. lbs. (27 Nm).

13. Attach the vacuum lines at the rear of the TBI, as tagged during removal.

14. Connect the throttle, transaxle control, and cruise control cables.

15. Attach the electrical connectors, making sure they are fully seated and latched.

16. Tighten the fuel filler cap, if loosened during fuel pressure relief procedure.

17. Connect the negative battery cable, then with the engine **OFF**, check to see that the accelerator pedal is free by depressing, then releasing it. Turn the igni-

tion switch to the **ON** position for 2 seconds, then turn to the **OFF** position for 10 seconds. Again turn the switch to the **ON** position and check for fuel leaks.

18. Install the air cleaner assembly and gasket.

19. Reset the Idle Air Control (IAC) valve pintle position as follows:

a. Block the drive wheels and apply the parking brake.

b. Start the engine, and hold the engine speed above 2,000 rpm. Ground the diagnostic test terminal (ALDL) for 10 seconds, then remove the ground.

c. Turn the ignition **OFF**, then restart the engine and check for proper idle operation.

Fuel Injector

REMOVAL & INSTALLATION

▶ See Figures 49 thru 54

✳✳ WARNING

When removing the injectors, be careful not to damage the electrical connector pins (on top of the injector), the injector fuel filter and the nozzle. The fuel injector is serviced as a complete assembly ONLY. The injector is an electrical component and should not be immersed in any kind of cleaner.

1. Properly relieve the fuel system pressure, as outlined earlier in this section.

2. Remove the air cleaner.

3. Detach the fuel injector electrical connector.

4. Remove the injector retainer screw and retainer.

5. Using a smooth object such as a fulcrum, place the blade of a suitable prytool under the ridge opposite the connector end and carefully pry the injector out.

6. Remove and discard the upper and lower O-rings from the injector and in the fuel injector cavity.

7. Inspect the filter for evidence of dirt and/or contamination.

To install:

➡Be sure to replace the injector with an identical part. Injectors from other models can fit in the Model 700, but are calibrated for different flow rates. There is a part number located on the top of the injector

8. Lubricate the new upper and lower O-rings with clean engine oil and place them on the injector. Make sure the upper O-ring is in the groove and the lower one is flush up against the filter.

9. Install the fuel injector assembly as follows:

   a. Position the injector in the fuel meter body with the electrical connector facing the cut-out for the wire grommet.

   b. Push the injector down to seat it in the cavity.

➡Make sure the electrical connector end on the injector is facing in the general direction to the cut-out in the fuel meter body for the wire grommet.

10. Install the injector retainer, using appropriate thread locking compound on the retainer attaching screw. Tighten to 27 inch lbs. (3 Nm).

11. Tighten the fuel filler cap, if loosened during fuel pressure relief procedure.

12. Connect the negative battery cable, then with the engine **OFF**, check to see that the accelerator pedal is free by depressing, then releasing it. Turn the ignition switch to the **ON** position for 2 seconds, then turn to the **OFF** position for 10 seconds. Again turn the switch to the **ON** position and check for fuel leaks.

13. Install the air cleaner assembly and gasket.

Fuel Pressure Regulator

REMOVAL & INSTALLATION

▶ **See Figure 55**

1. Properly relieve the fuel system pressure.
2. Disconnect the negative battery cable.
3. Remove the air cleaner and gasket, then discard the gasket.
4. While keeping the pressure regulator compressed, unfasten the four pressure regulator attaching screws.

✷✷ CAUTION

The pressure regulator contains a large spring under heavy compression. Use care when removing the screws to prevent personal injury.

5. Remove the pressure regulator cover assembly.
6. Remove the spring seat and the pressure regulator diaphragm assembly.

➡To prevent leaks, the pressure regulator diaphragm assembly must be replaced whenever the cover is removed.

7. Inspect the pressure regulator valve seat for pitting, nicks or irregularities.

To install:

8. Install the pressure regulator diaphragm assembly, making sure it is seated in the groove in the fuel meter body.

9. Install the regulator spring seat and spring into the cover assembly.

Fig. 49 Detach the fuel injector electrical connector

Fig. 50 Unfasten the injector retaining screw

1 Fuel injector assembly
2 Fuel meter body
A Screwdriver blade
B Fulcrum

87955045

Fig. 51 Use a fulcrum to aid in prying the fuel injector out

Fig. 52 Remove and discard the injector O-rings and replace with new ones during installation

1 Injector retainer screw
2 Injector retainer
3 Fuel meter assembly
4 Fuel injector o-ring (lower)
5 Fuel injector o-ring (upper)
6 Fuel injector assembly

87955046

Fig. 53 Always replace the O-rings with new ones

1 Fuel injector (top view)
A Part number
B Build number
C Month
   1-9 (Jan-Sept)
   O, N, D (Oct, Nov, Dec)
D Day
E Year
* Indicates high dynamic range

87955047

Fig. 54 To ensure that you are using the correct part, check the fuel injector part number

1 Pressure regulator cover assembly
2 Pressure regulator attaching screw
3 Spring seat
4 Pressure regulator spring
5 Diaphragm assembly
6 Fuel meter assembly

87955048

Fig. 55 Exploded view of the pressure regulator assembly

10. Hold the cover in place to prevent the diaphragm from slipping out of the groove, install the cover assembly over the diaphragm.

11. While maintaining pressure on the regulator spring, install the four screw assemblies that have been coated with Loctite® 262, or equivalent thread locking compound. Tighten the screws to 21 inch lbs. (2.4 Nm).

12. Tighten the fuel filler cap, if loosened during fuel pressure relief procedure.

13. Connect the negative battery cable, then with the engine **OFF**, check to see that the accelerator pedal is free by depressing, then releasing it. Turn the ignition switch to the **ON** position for 2 seconds, then turn to the **OFF** position for 10 seconds. Again turn the switch to the **ON** position and check for fuel leaks.

14. Install the air cleaner assembly and gasket.

Tube Module Assembly

REMOVAL & INSTALLATION

▶ See Figure 56

1. Disconnect the negative battery cable.
2. Remove the air cleaner assembly.
3. Tag and disconnect the necessary vacuum hoses.
4. Unfasten the tube module attaching screws, then remove the module and gasket. Discard the gasket, then clean off the gasket mating surfaces.

To install:

5. Position a new tube module gasket, then install the tube module assembly. If there is no threadlocking material remaining on the tube module attaching screws, apply Loctite® 262, or equivalent. Tighten the screws to 27 inch lbs. (3 Nm).

6. Connect the vacuum lines as tagged during removal.
7. Install the air cleaner assembly.
8. Connect the negative battery cable.

1. Throttle body assembly
2. Tube module assembly gasket
3. Tube module assembly
4. Tube module screw

87955050

Fig. 56 The tube module assembly is mounted to the throttle body

BOTTOM FEED PORT (BFP) INJECTION SYSTEM

System Description

▶ See Figure 57

➡ The Bottom Feed Port (BFP) injection system is used on the 1992–94 2.2L OHV (VIN 4) engines.

The function of the fuel metering system is to deliver the correct amount of fuel to the engine under all operating conditions. In this system, fuel is delivered to the engine by individual bottom feed type multi-port fuel injectors mounted in the lower intake manifold near each cylinder.

The computer control module, ECM or PCM depending upon vehicle year, pulses the fuel injectors in pairs. Alternate pairs are pulsed every 180° of crankshaft revolution. This is called Alternating Synchronous Double Fire (ASDF) injection. The ECM or PCM uses two injector driver circuits, each controlling a pair of injectors. The current in each circuit is allowed to climb to a peak of 4 amps and then is reduced to 1 amp to hold the injector open. This happens very quickly.

The main control sensor of this system is the Oxygen (O_2) sensor, located in the exhaust manifold. This sensor indicates to the computer control module how much oxygen is in the exhaust gas, and the ECM/PCM changes the air/fuel ratio to the engine by controlling the fuel injectors. The best mixture to keep exhaust emissions to a minimum is 14.7:1 which allows the catalytic converter to operate most efficiently. Because of the constant measuring and adjusting of the air/fuel ratio, the fuel injection system is called a "Closed Loop" system.

Fuel System Pressure Relief

1992 VEHICLES

1. Loosen the full filler cap to relieve the tank vapor pressure. Leave the cap loose at this time.
2. Raise and support the vehicle safely.
3. Detach the fuel pump electrical connector.
4. Carefully lower the vehicle.
5. Start the engine and run until the fuel supply remaining in the fuel pipes is consumed. Engage the starter for 3 seconds to assure relief of any remaining pressure in the lines.

1 MANIFOLD ASM - UPPER
2 STUD - UPPER INLET MANIFOLD
3 HARNESS ASM - EGR VALVE AND
    FUEL PRESSURE REGULATOR VACUUM
4 SEAL - MAP SENSOR
5 SENSOR - MANIFOLD ABSOLUTE PRESSURE
    (MAP)
6 BOLT - MAP SENSOR ATTACHING
7 FITTING AND WASHER ASM
8 VALVE ASM - IDLE AIR CONTROL (IAC)
9 SCREW - IAC VALVE ATTACHING
10 O-RING - IAC VALVE
11 TUBE ASM - EGR TRANSPORT
12 BOLT - UPPER INLET MANIFOLD
13 GASKET - UPPER INLET MANIFOLD
14 FITTING - POWER BRAKE
15 O-RING- FUEL INJECTOR

16 INJECTOR ASM - (BOTTOM FEED) MFI FUEL
17 O-RING - LOWER
18 REGULATOR ASM - FUEL PRESSURE
19 SCREW - FUEL PRESSURE REGULATOR
    ATTACHING
20 O-RING - FUEL RETURN LINE
21 PIPE ASM - FUEL INJECTOR FUEL RETURN
22 SCREEN - FILTER (IF SO EQUIPPED)
23 O-RING - FUEL INLET FITTING
24 MANIFOLD ASM - LOWER
25 SCREW - INJECTOR RETAINER ATTACHING
26 SCREW - TP SENSOR ATTACHING
27 SENSOR - THROTTLE POSITION (TP)
28 RETAINER - INJECTOR
29 O-RING - FUEL FEED LINE
30 PIPE ASM - FUEL INJECTION FUEL FEED
31 NUT - FUEL FEED

87955055

Fig. 57 Exploded view of the BFP injection system components

6. Raise and support the vehicle safely.
7. Attach the fuel pump electrical connector.
8. Carefully lower the vehicle.
9. Tighten the fuel filler cap.
10. Disconnect the negative battery cable to avoid possible fuel discharge if an accidental attempt is made to start the engine.

1993–94 VEHICLES

1. Loosen the fuel filler cap to relieve tank pressure (do not tighten at this time).
2. Remove the fuel pump fuse from the fuse block.
3. Start the engine and run until the fuel supply remaining in the fuel pipes is consumed. Engage the starter for 3 seconds to assure relief of any remaining pressure.
4. Replace the fuel pump fuse in the fuse block.
5. Disconnect the negative battery cable to avoid possible fuel discharge if an accidental attempt is made to start the engine.

Bottom Feed Port Fuel Injectors

REMOVAL & INSTALLATION

▶ See Figure 58

✳✳ WARNING

Any time the injectors are removed for service, always remove the fuel pressure regulator to drain excess fuel, and prevent fuel from entering the engine cylinders. Flooded cylinders could result in engine damage.

1. Housing & solenoid   7. Spray tip
   assembly   8. Director
2. Pole piece   9. Housing - spray tip
3. Solenoid   10. Spring - core
4. Filter - fuel inlet   11. Screw & guide
5. Core assembly   assembly
6. Core seat   12. Solenoid body

87955056

Fig. 58 Cross-section view of a bottom feed fuel injector

1. Relieve the fuel system pressure as outlined earlier.
2. Disconnect the negative battery cable.
3. Remove the upper manifold assembly.

✳✳ CAUTION

To reduce the chance of personal injury, cover the fuel line connections with a shop towel, when disconnecting.

4. Disconnect the fuel return line retaining bracket nut and move the return line away from the regulator.
5. Remove the pressure regulator assembly.

✳✳ WARNING

Do not try to remove the injectors by lifting up on the injector retaining bracket while the injectors are still installed in the in the bracket slots or damage to the bracket and/or injectors could result. Do not attempt to remove the bracket without first removing the pressure regulator.

6. Remove the injector retainer bracket attaching screws and carefully slide the bracket off to clear the injector slots and regulator.
7. Detach the injector electrical connectors.
8. Remove the fuel injector(s), then remove and discard the O-ring seals.

✳✳ CAUTION

To reduce the risk fire and personal injury, make sure that the lower (small) O-ring of each injector does not remain in the lower manifold. If the O-ring is not removed with the injector, the replacement injector, with new O-rings, will not seat properly in the injector socket and could cause a fuel leak.

9. Cover the injector sockets to prevent dirt from entering the opening.

➡**Each injector is calibrated with a different flow rate so be sure to replace the injector with the identical part numbers.**

To install:
10. Lubricate the new injector O-ring seals with clean engine oil and install on the injector assembly.

11. Install the injector assembly into the lower manifold injector socket, with the electrical connectors facing inward.

12. Carefully position the injector retainer bracket so that the injector retaining slots and regulator are aligned with the bracket slots.

13. Attach the injector electrical connectors.

14. Install the pressure regulator assembly.

15. Install the injector retainer bracket retaining screws, coated with thread locking material and tighten to 31 inch lbs. (3.5 Nm).

16. Install the accelerator cable bracket with the attaching bolts/nuts finger-tight at this time.

✳✳ WARNING

The accelerator bracket must be aligned with the accelerator cam to prevent cable wear, which could result in cable breakage.

17. Align the accelerator bracket as follows:

   a. Place a steel rule across the bore of the throttle body, with one end in contact with the accelerator bracket.

   b. Adjust the accelerator bracket to obtain a 25/64 in. (9–11mm) gap between the bracket and the throttle body.

   c. Tighten the top bolt first and tighten all bolts/nuts to 18 ft. lbs. (25 Nm).

18. Tighten the fuel filer cap.

19. Connect the negative battery cable and turn the ignition **ON** for 2 seconds, **OFF** for 10 seconds, then **ON** and check for fuel leaks.

20. Install the air intake duct.

Fuel Pressure Regulator

REMOVAL & INSTALLATION

▶ See Figures 57 and 59

1. Relieve the fuel system pressure as outlined earlier.
2. Disconnect the negative battery cable.
3. Remove the vacuum hose from the regulator.
4. Place a rag under the connection and remove the fuel return pipe clamp.
5. Remove the fuel return pipe and O-ring from the regulator. Discard the O-ring.
6. Unfasten the pressure regulator bracket attaching screw, then remove the pressure regulator assembly and O-ring. Discard the O-ring.

1. Cover
2. Vacuum chamber
   (vacuum source tube not shown)
3. Seal - O-ring
4. Valve - fuel pressure regulator
5. Base assembly
6. Filter - screen (if equipped)
7. Diaphragm
8. Spring

87955057

Fig. 59 Cross-section view of the fuel pressure regulator assembly

To install:

7. Lubricate a new pressure regulator O-ring with clean engine oil, then install on the pressure regulator.

8. Install the pressure regulator assembly onto the manifold.

9. Install the pressure regulator bracket attaching screw coated with the appropriate thread locking material and tighten to 31 inch lbs. (3.5 Nm).

10. Connect the vacuum hose to the regulator.

11. Lubricate a new fuel return pipe O-ring with clean engine oil, then install on the end of the pipe.

12. Install the fuel return pipe to the pressure regulator and tighten the attaching nut to 22 inch lbs. (30 Nm).

13. Fasten the fuel return pipe clamp attaching nut to the lower manifold assembly.

14. Tighten the fuel filler cap.

15. Connect the negative battery cable and turn the ignition **ON** for 2 seconds, **OFF** for 10 seconds, then **ON** and check for fuel leaks.

MULTI-PORT (MFI) & SEQUENTIAL (SFI) FUEL INJECTION SYSTEMS

General Information

On 1985–94 2.8 and 3.1L engines, the multi-port fuel injection (MFI) system is available. The MFI system is controlled by a computer control module (ECM or PCM) which monitors engine operations and generates output signals to provide the correct air/fuel mixture, ignition timing and engine idle speed control. Input to the control unit is provided by an oxygen sensor, coolant temperature sensor, detonation sensor, hot film air mass sensor and throttle position sensor. The ECM/PCM also receives information concerning engine rpm, road speed, transmission gear position, power steering and air conditioning.

On 1.8L, 2.0L OHC and turbocharged engines, a sequential port fuel injection system (SFI) is used for more precise fuel control. With SFI, metered fuel is timed and injected sequentially through injectors into individual cylinder ports. Each cylinder receives one injection per working cycle (every two revolutions), just prior to the opening of the intake valve. The main difference between the two types of fuel injection systems is the manner in which fuel is injected. In the multiport system, all injectors work simultaneously, injecting half the fuel charge each engine revolution. The control units are different for SFI and MFI systems, but most other components are similar. In addition, the SFI system incorporates a new Computer Controlled Coil Ignition system that uses an electronic coil module that replaces the conventional distributor and coil used on most engines. An electronic spark control (ESC) is used to adjust the spark timing.

Both systems use Bosch injectors, one at each intake port, rather than the single injector found on the earlier throttle body system. The injectors are mounted on a fuel rail and are activated by a signal from the electronic control module. The injector is a solenoid-operated valve which remains open depending on the width of the electronic pulses (length of the signal) from the computer control module (ECM/PCM); the longer the open time, the more fuel is injected. In this manner, the air/fuel mixture can be precisely controlled for maximum performance with minimum emissions.

Fuel is pumped from the tank by a high pressure fuel pump, located inside the fuel tank. It is a positive displacement roller vane pump. The impeller serves as a vapor separator and pre-charges the high pressure assembly. A pressure regulator maintains 28–36 psi (28–50 psi on turbocharged engines) in the fuel line to the injectors and the excess fuel is fed back to the tank. On MFI systems, a fuel accumulator is used to dampen the hydraulic line hammer in the system created when all injectors open simultaneously.

The Mass Air Flow (MAF) sensor is used to measure the mass of air that is drawn into the engine cylinders. It is located just ahead of the air throttle in the intake system and consists of a heated film which measures the mass of air, rather than just the volume. A resistor is used to measure the temperature of the incoming air and the air mass sensor maintains the temperature of the film at 75° above ambient temperature. As the ambient (outside) air temperature rises, more energy is required to maintain the heated film at the higher temperature and the control unit uses this difference in required energy to calculate the mass of the incoming air. The control unit uses this information to determine the duration of fuel injection pulse, timing and EGR.

The throttle body incorporates an Idle Air Control (IAC) valve that provides for a bypass channel through which air can flow. It consists of an orifice and pintle which is controlled by the ECM through a stepper motor. The IAC provides air flow for idle and allows additional air during cold start until the engine reaches operating temperature. As the engine temperature rises, the opening through which air passes is slowly closed.

The throttle position sensor (TPS) provides the control unit with information on throttle position, in order to determine injector pulse width and hence correct mixture. The TPS is connected to the throttle shaft on the throttle body and consists of a potentiometer with one end connected to a 5 volt source from the ECM and the other to ground. A third wire is connected to the ECM to measure the voltage output from the TPS which changes as the throttle valve angle is changed (accelerator pedal moves). At the closed throttle position, the output is low (approximately 0.4 volts); as the throttle valve opens, the output increases to a maximum 5 volts at wide open throttle (WOT). The TPS can be misadjusted open, shorted, or loose and if it is out of adjustment, the idle quality or WOT performance may be poor. A loose TPS can cause intermittent bursts of fuel from the injectors and an unstable idle because the ECM thinks the throttle is moving. This should cause a trouble code to be set. Once a trouble

code is set, the ECM will use a preset value for TPS and some vehicle performance may return. A small amount of engine coolant is routed through the throttle assembly to prevent freezing inside the throttle bore during cold operation.

Relieving Fuel System Pressure

❊❊❊ CAUTION

To reduce the risk of fire or personal injury, it is necessary to relieve the fuel system pressure before servicing the fuel system.

1.8L AND 2.0L OHC ENGINES

1983–84 Vehicles

1. Remove the fuel pump fuse from the fuse block.
2. Crank the engine. The engine will run until it runs out of fuel. Crank the engine again for 3 seconds making sure it is out of fuel.
3. Turn the ignition **OFF** and replace the fuse.

1985–90 Vehicles

1. Disconnect the negative battery cable.
2. Disconnect the fuel filler cap.
3. Connect gauge J–34730–1 or equivalent, to the fuel pressure connection. Wrap a cloth around the fitting to absorb any fuel leakage.
4. Install the bleed hose into an approved container and open the valve to bleed system pressure.

1992 2.0L (VIN H) ENGINES

1. Remove the fuel pump fuse from the fuse block.
2. Crank the engine. The engine will run until it runs out of fuel. Crank the engine again for 3 seconds making sure it is out of fuel.
3. Turn the ignition **OFF** and replace the fuse.

2.8L AND 3.1L ENGINES

1. Disconnect the negative battery cable.
2. Loosen the fuel filler cap to relieve tank pressure.
3. Connect gauge J–34730–1, or equivalent, to the fuel pressure connection. Wrap a cloth around the fitting to absorb any fuel leakage.
4. Install the bleed hose into an approved container and open the valve to bleed system pressure.
5. Drain any fuel still in the gauge into an approved container.

Fuel Pump

TESTING

1.8L and 2.0L OHC Engines

1984–85 VEHICLES

1. Connect pressure gauge J-34370-1, or equivalent, to fuel pressure test point on the fuel rail. Wrap a rag around the pressure tap to absorb any leakage that may occur when installing the gauge.
2. Turn the ignition **OFF** for 10 seconds and the A/C **OFF**.
3. Turn the ignition **ON** and the fuel pump should run for about 2 seconds.
4. Note the fuel pressure after the pump stops. The pressure should be 30–40 psi (210–276 kPa) and hold steady.

1986 VEHICLES

1. Connect pressure gauge J-34370-1, or equivalent, to fuel pressure test point on the fuel rail. Wrap a rag around the pressure tap to absorb any leakage that may occur when installing the gauge.
2. Using a fused jumper, run the fuel pump by applying 12 volts to the fuel pump test terminal for several seconds.
3. Note the fuel pressure after the pump stops. The pressure should be 30–40 psi (210–276 kPa) and hold steady.

1987–90 VEHICLES

1. Connect pressure gauge J-34370-1, or equivalent, to fuel pressure test point on the fuel rail. Wrap a rag around the pressure tap to absorb any leakage that may occur when installing the gauge.
2. Disconnect the vacuum hose from the pressure regulator.
3. Turn the ignition **OFF** for 10 seconds and the A/C **OFF**.
4. Turn the ignition **ON** and the fuel pump should run for about 2 seconds.
5. Note the fuel pressure after the pump stops. The pressure should be 35–38 psi (241–262 kPa) and hold steady.

2.8L and 3.1L Engines

1. Connect pressure gauge J-34370-1, or equivalent, to fuel pressure test point on the fuel rail. Wrap a rag around the pressure tap to absorb any leakage that may occur when installing the gauge.
2. Turn the ignition **OFF** for 10 seconds and the A/C **OFF**.
3. Turn the ignition **ON** and the fuel pump should run for about 2 seconds.
4. Note the fuel pressure after the pump stops. The pressure should be 40.5–47 psi (279–324 kPa) and hold steady.

REMOVAL & INSTALLATION

1983–91 Vehicles

▶ See Figure 60

1. Release the fuel system pressure.

❊❊❊ CAUTION

To reduce the risk of fire or personal injury, it is necessary to relieve the fuel system pressure before servicing the fuel system. Refer to Fuel System Pressure Release procedure.

2. Disconnect the negative battery cable.
3. Raise and safely support the vehicle.
4. Drain and remove the fuel tank, as outlined later in this section.
5. Remove the fuel lever sending unit and pump assembly by turning the cam lock ring counterclockwise. Lift the assembly from the fuel tank and remove the fuel pump from the fuel level sending unit.
6. Pull the fuel pump up into the attaching hose or pulsator while pulling

1 Fuel tank meter assy.
2 Pulsator
3 Bumper
4 Fuel pump
5 Sound isolator sleeve
6 Sound insulator
7 Filter

87955075

Fig. 60 View of the fuel pump and related components—1983–91 vehicles

1. Gasket - flange
2. Throttle body assembly
3. Sensor - throttle position (TPS)
4. Screw assembly - TPS attaching
5. Tube module and seal assembly
6. Seal - tube module
7. Idle air control (IAC) valve assembly
8. O-ring - idle air control valve
9. Screw - IAC valve attaching

87955058

Fig. 61 View of the throttle body and integral components—1992 2.0L (VIN H) engine shown

outward away from the bottom support. After the pump is clear of the bottom support, pull the pump assembly out of the rubber connector or pulsator for removal.

To install:

7. Position and push the pump into the attaching hose.
8. Install the fuel level sending unit and pump assembly into the tank assembly. Use new O-ring during reassembly.

✳✳ WARNING

Be careful not to fold over or twist the strainer when installing the sending unit as it will restrict fuel flow. Also, be careful the strainer does not block full travel of the float arm.

9. Install the cam lock over the assembly and lock by turning clockwise.
10. Install the fuel tank.
11. Connect the negative battery cable.

1992–94 Vehicles

The electric fuel pumps on these vehicles are located as a part of the module sender assembly. For removal and installation information, please refer to the procedure located later in this section.

Throttle Body

REMOVAL & INSTALLATION

▶ See Figures 61 and 62

➡The TP sensor and IAC valve should NOT come into contact with any type of solvent or cleanser, as this may cause damage.

1. Properly relieve the fuel system pressure.
2. Disconnect the negative battery cable.
3. Remove the air cleaner cover and air duct.
4. Partially drain the coolant to allow the coolant hoses at the throttle body to be removed.
5. Disconnect the vacuum hose from the fuel pressure regulator.

1 Intake manifold
2 Gasket
3 Throttle body assembly
4 Stud end bolt
5 Bolt

87955060

Fig. 62 Exploded view of the throttle body mounting

6. Detach the electrical connectors from the TP sensor and IAC valve.
7. Disconnect the throttle, transaxle control and cruise control (if equipped) cables.
8. Unfasten the throttle body attaching bolts, then loosen the throttle body from the intake manifold.
9. Disconnect the coolant hoses from the throttle body.
10. Detach the vacuum hose from the bottom of the throttle body.
11. Remove the throttle body and gasket. Discard the gasket.

To install:

12. Connect the vacuum hose to the bottom of the throttle body.
13. Fasten the coolant hoses to the throttle body.
14. Position the throttle body, with a new gasket, against the manifold, then secure with the attaching bolts. Tighten the bolts to 11 ft. lbs. (15 Nm).
15. Fasten the throttle, cruise control and transaxle cables to the throttle body.
16. Attach the TP sensor and IAC valve electrical connectors.
17. Connect the vacuum hose to the fuel pressure regulator.
18. Refill the cooling system to the proper level.
19. Install the air duct and air cleaner cover.
20. Connect the the negative battery cable.

Fuel Injectors

REMOVAL & INSTALLATION

1.8L and 2.0L OHC Engines

▶ See Figures 63, 64 and 65

❊❊❊ WARNING

Use care in removing the fuel injectors to prevent damage to the electrical connector pins on the injector and the nozzle. The fuel injector is serviced as a complete assembly only and should not be immersed in any kind of cleaner.

1. Properly relieve fuel system pressure, as outlined earlier in this section.
2. Disconnect the negative battery cable.
3. Remove the throttle body from the intake manifold.
4. As outlined later in this section, remove the fuel rail.
5. Unfasten and discard the injector retaining clip, then remove the injector assembly. Remove and discard the O-rings from each end of the injector.

To install:

6. Lubricate new O-rings with clean engine oil, the install on the injector.
7. Position a new injector retaining clip on the injector.
8. Install the injector assembly into the fuel rail injector socket, with the electrical connector facing inward toward the manifold. Push the socket in far enough to engage the retainer clip with the groove on the rail.
9. Install the fuel rail assembly and throttle body.
10. Connect the negative battery cable.

1 Fuel rail and plug assembly
2 Fuel inlet fitting o-ring
3 Fuel inlet tube seal o-ring
4 Fuel inlet tube seal retainer
5 Fuel outlet fitting o-ring
6 Fuel inlet retainer attaching
7 MPFI injector assembly
8 Injector o-ring
9 Injector retainer clip
10 Retainer and spacer assembly
11 Pressure regulator assembly
12 Regulator attaching screw

87955063

Fig. 63 Exploded view of the fuel injector, retaining clip and O-rings

87955061

Fig. 64 Removing the fuel injector retaining clip

87955062

Fig. 65 Push the fuel injector into the socket, making sure it is fully seated

2.8L and 3.1L Engines

1985–86 VEHICLES

▶ See Figure 66

Each port injector is located and held in position by a retainer clip that must be rotated to release and/or lock the injector in place.

1. Disconnect the negative battery cable.
2. Properly relieve the fuel system pressure.
3. Remove the plenum and the fuel rail.
4. Rotate the injector retaining clip(s) the the unlocked position.
5. Remove the port injectors. Remove and discard the injector O-rings.

To install:

6. Install new O-ring seals and lubricate with engine oil.
7. Position the injectors to the fuel rail and pressure regulator assembly.
8. Rotate the injector retaining clips to the locking position.
9. Install the fuel rail and the plenum.
10. Connect the negative battery cable.

25 N·m (18 FT. LBS.)

25 N·m (18 FT. LBS.)

1 Intake manifold
2 Fuel rail assembly
3 Gasket
4 Plenum

87955064

Fig. 66 Fuel rail, injectors and manifold—1985–86 2.8L vehicles

▶ **See Figures 67, 68 and 69**

1. Disconnect the negative battery cable.
2. Properly relieve the fuel system pressure.
3. Remove the intake manifold plenum.
4. As outlined later in this section, remove the fuel rail.
5. Unfasten and discard the injector retaining clip, then remove the fuel

1 Fuel inlet line o-ring	12 Left hand fuel rail and plug assembly
2 Fuel return line o-ring	13 Right hand fuel rail and plug assembly
3 Fuel pressure connection assembly	14 Pressure regulator assembly
4 Fuel pressure connection seal	15 Base to rail connector
5 Fuel pressure connection cap	16 Connector o-ring seal
6 Fuel inlet fitting	17 Fuel return o-ring seal
7 Fuel outlet fitting	18 Pressure regulator mounting bracket
8 Fuel fitting gasket	19 Pressure regulator bracket attaching
9 Fuel injector assembly	screw assembly
10 Injector o-ring seal	20 Rail mounting bracket
11 Injector retainer clip	21 Bracket attaching screw assembly

87955066

Fig. 67 Exploded view of the fuel rail, injectors, retaining clip and O-rings

1 Plenum
2 Bolt (9)
3 Fuel rail assembly
4 Gasket
5 Bolt (4)

87955065

Fig. 68 You must remove the plenum and fuel rail for access to the injectors

1 Fuel injector assembly
2 Injector retainer clip
A Machined slots in rail

87955067

Fig. 69 Push the fuel injector into the socket, making sure it is fully seated

injector assembly. Remove and discard the O-rings from each end of the injector.

To install:

6. Lubricate new O-rings with clean engine oil, the install on the injector.
7. Position a new injector retaining clip on the injector. Place the open end of the clip facing the injector electrical connector.
8. Install the injector assembly into the fuel rail injector socket, with the electrical connector facing outward. Push it in far enough to engage the retainer clip with the machined slots on the rail.
9. Install the fuel rail assembly and throttle body.
10. Connect the negative battery cable.

➡ **This test must be done before the engine is started and requires the use of a Tech 1® scan tool.**

11. If equipped with the 3.1L engine, perform the idle learn procedure to allow the ECM/PCM memory to be updated with the correct IAC valve pintle position and provide for a stable idle speed.
    a. Install a Tech 1® scan tool.
    b. Turn the ignition to the **ON** position, engine not running.
    c. Select **IAC SYSTEM**, then **IDLE LEARN** in the **MISC TEST** mode.
    d. Place the transaxle in park or neutral, as applicable.
    e. Proceed with idle learn as directed by the scan tool.

Fuel Pressure Regulator

REMOVAL & INSTALLATION

✳ CAUTION

To reduce the risk of fire or personal injury, it is necessary to relieve the fuel system pressure before servicing the fuel system.

1.8L and 2.0L OHC Engines

EXCEPT 2.0L (VIN H) ENGINES

1. Relieve fuel system pressure.
2. Remove pressure regulator from fuel rail. Place a rag around the base of the regulator to catch any spilled fuel.
3. Installation is the reverse of removal procedure.

2.0L (VIN H) ENGINES

▶ **See Figure 70**

1. Properly relieve the fuel system pressure.
2. Disconnect the negative battery cable.

3. Remove the air duct and air cleaner cover.

4. Disconnect the vacuum hose from the pressure regulator.

5. Using a back-up wrench, remove the fuel return pipe at the pressure regulator.

6. Unfasten the pressure regulator attaching screw, then remove the regulator from the fuel rail, twisting it back and forth while pulling it apart.

To install:

7. If there is not enough thread locking material on the threads of the retaining screw, apply Loctite® 262 or equivalent to the threads.

8. The remainder of installation is the reverse of the removal procedure.

1 Vacuum tube
2 O-ring seal
3 Base assembly
4 Fuel outlet fitting
5 Fuel inlet fitting o-ring
6 Diaphragm
7 Pressure regulator spring
8 Pressure regulator cover

87955068

Fig. 70 Cross-sectional view of the fuel pressure regulator

2.8L and 3.1L Engines

1985–86 VEHICLES

The pressure regulator is factory adjusted and is not serviceable. Do not attempt to remove the regulator from the fuel rail.

1987–94 VEHICLES

▶ See Figure 71

1. Disconnect the negative battery cable.

2. Properly relieve the fuel system pressure.

3. Remove the intake manifold plenum and the fuel rail, as outlined in this section.

4. Unfasten and remove the fuel inlet and outlet fittings and gaskets.

5. Unfasten the pressure regulator bracket attaching screws and mounting bracket.

6. Remove the right and left hand fuel rail assemblies from the pressure regulator assembly.

7. Remove the base-to-rail connectors from the regulator or rails.

8. Disassemble connector O-rings from the base to rail connectors.

9. Remove the fuel return O-ring from the fuel rails. Discard all O-rings.

To install:

10. Lubricate new fuel return O-rings with engine oil and install on the fuel rails.

11. Lubricate new connector O-rings with engine oil and install to the base to rail connectors.

12. Install the base-to-rail connectors in the regulator assembly.

13. Fasten the right and left hand fuel rail assemblies to the pressure regulator assembly.

14. Install the pressure regulator mounting bracket with the attaching screws. Tighten the screws to 28 inch lbs. (3 Nm).

15. Connect new fuel inlet and outlet fitting gaskets and tighten the fittings to 20 inch lbs. (2.2 Nm).

16. Install the fuel rail and intake manifold plenum.

17. Connect the negative battery cable.

1 Fuel inlet line o-ring
2 Fuel return line o-ring
3 Fuel pressure connection assembly
4 Fuel pressure connection seal
5 Fuel pressure connection cap
6 Fuel inlet fitting
7 Fuel outlet fitting
8 Fuel fitting gasket
9 Fuel injector assembly
10 Injector o-ring seal
11 Injector retainer clip
12 Left hand fuel rail and plug assembly
13 Right hand fuel rail and plug assembly
14 Pressure regulator assembly
15 Base to rail connector
16 Connector o-ring seal
17 Fuel return o-ring seal
18 Pressure regulator mounting bracket
19 Pressure regulator bracket attaching screw assembly
20 Rail mounting bracket
21 Bracket attaching screw assembly

87955070

Fig. 71 Location of the fuel pressure regulator—1994 3.1L engine shown

➡**This test must be done before the engine is started and requires the use of a Tech 1® scan tool.**

18. If equipped with the 3.1L engine, perform the idle learn procedure to allow the ECM/PCM memory to be updated with the correct IAC valve pintle position and provide for a stable idle speed.

    a. Install a Tech 1® scan tool.

    b. Turn the ignition to the **ON** position, engine not running.

    c. Select **IAC SYSTEM**, then **IDLE LEARN** in the **MISC TEST** mode.

    d. Place the transaxle in park or neutral, as applicable.

    e. Proceed with idle learn as directed by the scan tool.

Fuel Rail Assembly

REMOVAL & INSTALLATION

1.8L and 2.0L OHC Engines

▶ See Figure 72

1. Properly relieve the fuel system pressure.

2. Disconnect the negative battery cable.

3. Remove the throttle body from the intake manifold.

4. Disconnect the PCV and breather hoses from the camshaft cover.

5. Tag and detach the electrical connectors and vacuum hoses from the canister purge solenoid, EGR valve and solenoid and the MAP sensor.

6. Remove the MAP sensor from the bracket.

7. Detach the fuel injector electrical connectors.

8. Unfasten the fuel inlet pipe retainer attaching screw, then remove the retainer and the pump. Remove and discard the O-ring seal located under the seal retainer at the fuel rail.

9. Disconnect the fuel return pipe at the pressure regulator, using a back-up wrench to prevent it from turning.

10. Unfasten the fuel rail attaching bolts, then remove the fuel rail.

➡**If an injector becomes separated from the rail and remains in the cylinder head, both injector O-ring seals and the retainer clip must be replaced.**

To install:

11. Position the fuel rail assembly, then install the retaining bolts. Tighten the bolts to 19 ft. lbs. (26 Nm).

1 Intake manifold
2 Throttle body gasket
3 Throttle body bolts
4 Throttle body
5 Fuel rail bolts
6 Fuel rail assembly

87955071

Fig. 72 The fuel rail is mounted on the intake manifold

12. Install a new fuel inlet pipe O-ring seal, coated with clean engine oil, under the seal retainer at the fuel rail. Tighten the retaining screw to 53 inch lbs. (6 Nm).

13. Connect the fuel return pipe. Tighten the fuel return pipe fitting to 14.8 ft. lbs. (20 Nm). Make sure to use a back-up wrench on the pressure regulator fitting to prevent it from turning.

14. Attach the injector electrical connectors.

15. Fasten the MAP sensor to the bracket. Tighten the screws to 27 inch lbs. (3 Nm).

16. Install the canister purge solenoid and bracket and the EGR solenoid and bracket. Tighten the bracket retaining screws to 37 ft. lbs. (50 Nm).

17. Connect the canister purge solenoid and the EGR solenoid and valve vacuum hoses and electrical connectors.

18. Fasten the PCV and breather hoses to the camshaft cover.

19. Install the throttle body, as outlined earlier in this section.

20. Tighten the fuel filler cap.

21. Connect the negative battery cable, then with the engine **OFF**, check to see that the accelerator pedal is free by depressing, then releasing it. Turn the ignition switch to the **ON** position for 2 seconds, then turn to the **OFF** position for 10 seconds. Again turn the switch to the **ON** position and check for fuel leaks.

2.8L and 3.1L Engines

1985–86 VEHICLES

▸ See Figure 73

1. Disconnect the negative battery cable.
2. Relieve fuel system pressure.
3. Remove the intake manifold plenum, as follows:
   a. Disconnect the vacuum lines.
   b. Remove the EGR-to-plenum nuts.
   c. Unfasten the two throttle body bolts.
   d. Remove the throttle cable to bracket bolts.
   e. Unfasten the plenum bolts and remove the plenum and gasket.
4. Remove the cold start valve and tube assembly.
5. Remove the retaining nut from the stud for the fuel lines at the head.
6. Unfasten the fuel lines at the rail.
7. Disconnect the vacuum line at the regulator.
8. Remove the rail retaining bolts.
9. Disconnect the injector electrical connectors.
10. Remove the fuel rail assembly.
To install:
11. Use new injector O-rings which have been lubricated with engine clean oil.
12. The remainder of installation is the reverse of the removal procedure.
13. Connect the negative battery cable. Turn the ignition to the **ON** position

1 Fuel inlet line o-ring
2 Fuel return line o-ring
3 Fuel rail and pressure regulator assembly
4 Fuel pressure connection assembly
5 Fuel pressure connection assembly seal
6 Fuel pressure connection cap
7 Fuel block
8 Fuel block seal
9 Fuel block attaching screw assembly
10 Port injector
11 O-ring injector seal
12 Injector retainer clip
13 Cold start valve
14 Tube and body assembly
15 Valve o-ring seal
16 Body o-ring seal
17 Tube o-ring seal
18 Cold start fitting

87955073

Fig. 73 Exploded view of the fuel rail assembly—1985–86 2.8L engines

for two seconds, then turn it to the **OFF** position for ten seconds. Turn again to the **ON** position and check for fuel leaks.

1987–94 VEHICLES

▸ See Figure 74

1. Disconnect the negative battery cable.
2. Properly relieve fuel system pressure.
3. Remove the intake manifold plenum, as follows:
   a. Disconnect the vacuum lines.
   b. Remove the EGR-to-plenum nuts.
   c. Unfasten the two throttle body bolts.
   d. Remove the throttle cable to bracket bolts.
   e. Unfasten the ignition wire plastic shield bolts.
   f. Remove the plenum bolts and remove the plenum and gasket.
4. Remove the fuel line bracket bolt.
5. Disconnect the fuel lines at the rail.

✴✴ CAUTION

Wrap a cloth around the fuel lines to collect fuel, then place the fuel in an approved container.

6. Remove the fuel line O-rings.
7. Disconnect the vacuum line at the pressure regulator.
8. Unfasten the four rail retaining bolts.
9. Detach the injector electrical connectors.
10. Remove the fuel rail assembly.
11. Remove the O-ring seal from each of the spray tip end of the injector.

1 Plenum
2 Bolt (9)
3 Fuel rail assembly
4 Gasket
5 Bolt (4)

87955074

Fig. 74 Exploded view of the intake manifold plenum and fuel rail—1987–94 2.8L and 3.1L engines

FUEL TANK

Tank Assembly

REMOVAL & INSTALLATION

1982–91 Vehicles

▶ **See Figure 75**

1. Disconnect the negative cable at the battery.
2. Raise and safely support the vehicles.
3. Drain the tank. There is no drain plug, so drain as follows:

1 Underbody supports
2 Nut
3 Body asm.
4 33 Nm (25 lbs. ft.) bolt
5 Fuel tank asm.
6 12 Nm (106 lbs. in.) nut
7 Left strap asm.
8 Bolt
9 Right strap asm.

87955076

Fig. 75 View of the fuel tank mounting—1991 vehicle shown

To install:

12. Lubricate new the O-ring seals, with clean engine oil and install to each of the spray tip ends of the injector.
13. Position the fuel rail assembly in the intake manifold and tilt the rail assembly and install the injectors.
14. Install the fuel rail attaching bolts and tighten to 19 ft. lbs. (26 Nm).
15. Attach the injector electrical connectors.
16. Connect the vacuum line at the pressure regulator.
17. Install new O-rings on the inlet and return fuel lines.
18. Tighten the fuel filler cap.
19. Connect the negative battery cable.
20. Using a back-up wrench, install the fuel inlet and outlet fittings.
21. Connect the negative battery cable. Turn the ignition to the **ON** position for two seconds, then turn it to the **OFF** position for ten seconds. Turn again to the **ON** position and check for fuel leaks.
22. Reversing the removal procedure, install the intake manifold plenum.

➡**This test must be done before the engine is started and requires the use of a Tech 1® scan tool.**

23. If equipped with the 3.1L engine, perform the idle learn procedure to allow the ECM/PCM memory to be updated with the correct IAC valve pintle position and provide for a stable idle speed.
   a. Install a Tech 1® scan tool.
   b. Turn the ignition to the **ON** position, engine not running.
   c. Select **IAC SYSTEM**, then **IDLE LEARN** in the **MISC TEST** mode.
   d. Place the transaxle in park or neutral, as applicable.
   e. Proceed with idle learn as directed by the scan tool.

   a. If available, use a hand-operated pump device to drain as much fuel through the filler tube as possible.
   b. If a hand-operated pump cannot be used or to complete the draining process, the remaining fuel in the tank must be siphoned through the main (not return) fuel feed line (the line to the fuel pump), because of the restrictor in the filler neck.
4. Detach the tank meter assembly harness connector form the body harness connector.
5. If used, remove the ground wire retaining screw from the underbody.
6. Disconnect the hoses from the tank meter assembly and the hoses at the tank from the filler and vent pipes.
7. If necessary, unplug the level sending unit electrical connector.
8. Support the tank, then unfasten the two tank support straps and lower and remove the tank. Installation is the reverse of removal.
9. Using tool J 24187 or equivalent, remove the fuel tank meter assembly and seal/gasket. Remove the sound insulators.
10. Installation is the reverse of the removal procedure.

1992–94 Vehicles

▶ **See Figure 76**

1. Disconnect the negative battery cable.
2. Drain the fuel tank by using a hand-operated pump device to drain as much fuel through the filler tube as possible.
3. Raise and safely support the vehicle.
4. Detach the fuel sender electrical connector.
5. Unfasten the muffler hanger bolts.
6. Remove the exhaust rubber hangers, then allow the exhaust system to rest on the rear axle.
7. Disconnect the hoses from the fuel tank sender. Grasp the filter and one nylon fuel connection line fitting. Twist the quick-connect fitting ¼ turn in each direction to loosen any dirt within the fitting. Repeat for the other fitting. Using compressed air, blow out the dirt from the quick-connect fittings at the end of the fuel filter.
8. Detach the quick-connect fittings by pulling the release tabs back on the fuel line quick connector and pulling apart. If difficulty is encountered, tool J 38778 or equivalent can be used to separate the fitting.
9. Disconnect the hoses at the tank from the filler, vent and vapor pipes.
10. With the help of an assistant, support the fuel tank, then disconnect the

1 Underbody supports
2 Nut
3 Body asm.
4 33 Nm (25 lbs. ft.) bolt
5 Fuel tank asm.
6 Left strap asm.
7 Right strap asm.

FIGURE 1

87955077

Fig. 76 View of fuel tank mounting—1992–94 vehicles

two tank retaining straps and lower the tank from the vehicle.

11. Remove the sound insulators.

12. Remove the modular fuel sender, as outlined later in this section.

13. Inspect all connectors for dirt and burrs. Clean or replace, as required. Inspect the fuel line O-rings for cuts, nicks, swelling and/or distortion and replace as necessary.

To install:

14. Install the fuel sender assembly to the tank, as outlined later in this section.

15. Install the sound insulators.

16. With the help of an assistant, raise the fuel tank to the vehicle, then fasten the retaining straps. Tighten the retaining bolts to 24 ft. lbs. (33 Nm).

17. Connect the hoses to the filler, vent and vapor pipes.

18. Attach the nylon fuel feed and return connecting line quick-connect fittings to the fuel sender, as follows:

a. Apply a few drops of clean engine oil to the male connector tube ends.

b. Push the connectors together to cause the retaining tabs/fingers to snap into place.

c. Once installed, pull on both ends of each connection to be sure they are secure.

19. Install the exhaust rubber hangers.

20. Install the muffler hanger bolts, then tighten to 11 ft. lbs. (15 Nm).

21. Attach the fuel tank sender electrical connector.

22. Carefully lower the vehicle.

23. Refill the fuel tank, then connect the negative battery cable.

24. Turn the ignition to the **ON** position for two seconds, then turn it to the **OFF** position for ten seconds. Turn again to the **ON** position and check for fuel leaks.

MODULAR FUEL SENDER ASSEMBLY REPLACEMENT

♦ See Figure 77

→Always replace fuel sender assembly O-ring when reinstalling the fuel sender assembly

1. Properly relieve fuel system pressure.

2. If not done already, disconnect the negative battery cable.

3. Drain fuel from the fuel tank assembly, as outlined in the fuel tank removal procedure.

4. Remove the fuel tank, as outlined earlier in this section.

✳✳ CAUTION

The modular fuel sender assembly may spring up from its position.

5. While holding down the modular fuel sender assembly down, remove the snap ring from the designated slots in the retainer.

→When removing the fuel sender from the fuel tank, be aware that the reservoir bucket is full of fuel. It must be tipped slightly during removal to avoid damage to the float. Carefully discard the reservoir fuel into an approved container.

6. Remove and discard the fuel sender O-ring.

To install:

7. Install a new O-ring on fuel sender-to-tank assembly.

8. Align tab on front of sender with the slot on front of the retainer snapring.

9. Slowly apply pressure to the top of the spring loaded sender, until it aligns flush with retainer on tank assembly.

10. Insert the snapring into the designated slots. Be sure that the snapring is fully seated in the retainer.

11. Install fuel tank, the carefully lower the vehicle and refill the gas tank.

12. Connect the negative battery cable, then turn the ignition to the **ON** position for two seconds, then turn it to the **OFF** position for ten seconds. Turn again to the **ON** position and check for fuel leaks.

1 Snap ring
2 Tab cover
3 Modular unit
4 Above cover wire harness
5 Fuel tank
6 Tank isolation strips (3)
7 Rubber isolator

87955078

Fig. 77 The module fuel sender assembly is mounted in the fuel tank

UNDERSTANDING AND TROUBLESHOOTING ELECTRICAL SYSTEMS 6-2
BASIC ELECTRICAL THEORY 6-2
  HOW DOES ELECTRICITY WORK: THE WATER ANALOGY 6-2
  OHM'S LAW 6-2
ELECTRICAL COMPONENTS 6-2
  POWER SOURCE 6-2
  GROUND 6-3
  PROTECTIVE DEVICES 6-3
  SWITCHES & RELAYS 6-3
  LOAD 6-3
  WIRING & HARNESSES 6-3
  CONNECTORS 6-4
TEST EQUIPMENT 6-4
  JUMPER WIRES 6-4
  TEST LIGHTS 6-5
  MULTIMETERS 6-5
TROUBLESHOOTING ELECTRICAL SYSTEMS 6-5
TESTING 6-6
  OPEN CIRCUITS 6-6
  SHORT CIRCUITS 6-6
  VOLTAGE 6-6
  VOLTAGE DROP 6-6
  RESISTANCE 6-6
WIRE AND CONNECTOR REPAIR 6-7
BATTERY CABLES 6-7
DISCONNECTING THE CABLES 6-7
SUPPLEMENTAL INFLATABLE RESTRAINT (SIR) SYSTEM 6-7
GENERAL INFORMATION 6-7
  SYSTEM OPERATION 6-7
  SYSTEM COMPONENTS 6-8
  SERVICE PRECAUTIONS 6-8
  DISABLING THE SYSTEM 6-9
  ENABLING THE SYSTEM 6-9
HEATING AND AIR CONDITIONING 6-9
BLOWER MOTOR 6-9
  REMOVAL & INSTALLATION 6-9
HEATER CORE 6-11
  REMOVAL & INSTALLATION 6-11
AIR CONDITIONING COMPONENTS 6-11
  REMOVAL & INSTALLATION 6-11
BLOWER SWITCH 6-11
  REMOVAL & INSTALLATION 6-11
TEMPERATURE CONTROL CABLE 6-12
  REMOVAL & INSTALLATION 6-12
  ADJUSTMENT 6-12
CONTROL PANEL 6-12
  REMOVAL & INSTALLATION 6-12
CRUISE CONTROL 6-13
GENERAL DESCRIPTION 6-13
ENTERTAINMENT SYSTEMS 6-14
RADIO RECEIVER/TAPE PLAYER/CD PLAYER 6-14
  REMOVAL & INSTALLATION 6-14

SPEAKERS 6-15
  REMOVAL & INSTALLATION 6-15
WINDSHIELD WIPERS AND WASHERS 6-16
WINDSHIELD WIPER BLADE AND ARM 6-16
  REMOVAL & INSTALLATION 6-16
  ADJUSTMENT 6-16
WINDSHIELD WIPER MOTOR 6-17
  REMOVAL & INSTALLATION 6-17
REAR WINDOW WIPER MOTOR 6-18
  REMOVAL & INSTALLATION 6-18
WIPER LINKAGE 6-18
  REMOVAL & INSTALLATION 6-18
WINDSHIELD WASHER FLUID RESERVOIR & PUMP 6-18
  REMOVAL & INSTALLATION 6-18
INSTRUMENTS AND SWITCHES 6-19
INSTRUMENT CLUSTER 6-19
  REMOVAL & INSTALLATION 6-19
SPEEDOMETER, TACHOMETER AND GAUGES 6-20
  REMOVAL & INSTALLATION 6-20
SPEEDOMETER CABLE 6-20
  REMOVAL & INSTALLATION 6-20
WINDSHIELD WIPER SWITCH 6-21
  REMOVAL & INSTALLATION 6-21
HEADLIGHT SWITCH 6-21
  REMOVAL & INSTALLATION 6-21
IGNITION SWITCH 6-22
LIGHTING 6-22
HEADLIGHTS 6-22
  REMOVAL & INSTALLATION 6-22
  HEADLIGHT AIMING 6-23
SIGNAL AND MARKER LIGHTS 6-25
  REMOVAL & INSTALLATION 6-25
FOG LAMPS 6-26
  REMOVAL & INSTALLATION 6-26
TRAILER WIRING 6-27
CIRCUIT PROTECTION 6-27
FUSES 6-27
  REPLACEMENT 6-28
FUSIBLE LINKS 6-28
  REPLACEMENT 6-28
CIRCUIT BREAKERS 6-28
  REPLACEMENT 6-28
FLASHERS 6-29
  REPLACEMENT 6-29
WIRING DIAGRAMS 6-31
TROUBLESHOOTING CHART
  CRUISE CONTROL 6-14
  FUSE PANELS 6-29

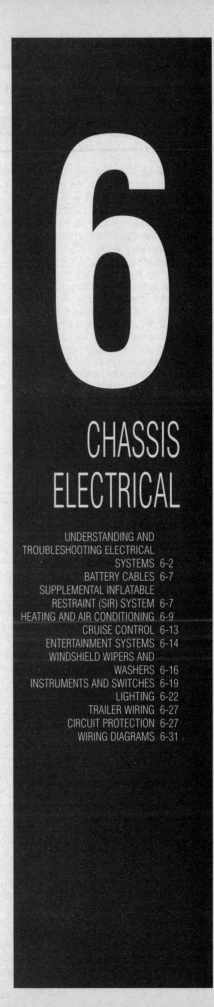

6

CHASSIS ELECTRICAL

UNDERSTANDING AND TROUBLESHOOTING ELECTRICAL SYSTEMS 6-2
BATTERY CABLES 6-7
SUPPLEMENTAL INFLATABLE RESTRAINT (SIR) SYSTEM 6-7
HEATING AND AIR CONDITIONING 6-9
CRUISE CONTROL 6-13
ENTERTAINMENT SYSTEMS 6-14
WINDSHIELD WIPERS AND WASHERS 6-16
INSTRUMENTS AND SWITCHES 6-19
LIGHTING 6-22
TRAILER WIRING 6-27
CIRCUIT PROTECTION 6-27
WIRING DIAGRAMS 6-31

UNDERSTANDING AND TROUBLESHOOTING ELECTRICAL SYSTEMS

Basic Electrical Theory

▶ **See Figure 1**

For any 12 volt, negative ground, electrical system to operate, the electricity must travel in a complete circuit. This simply means that current (power) from the positive (+) terminal of the battery must eventually return to the negative (-) terminal of the battery. Along the way, this current will travel through wires, fuses, switches and components. If, for any reason, the flow of current through the circuit is interrupted, the component fed by that circuit will cease to function properly.

Perhaps the easiest way to visualize a circuit is to think of connecting a light bulb (with two wires attached to it) to the battery—one wire attached to the negative (-) terminal of the battery and the other wire to the positive (+) terminal. With the two wires touching the battery terminals, the circuit would be complete and the light bulb would illuminate. Electricity would follow a path from the battery to the bulb and back to the battery. It's easy to see that with longer wires on our light bulb, it could be mounted anywhere. Further, one wire could be fitted with a switch so that the light could be turned on and off.

The normal automotive circuit differs from this simple example in two ways. First, instead of having a return wire from the bulb to the battery, the current travels through the frame of the vehicle. Since the negative (-) battery cable is attached to the frame (made of electrically conductive metal), the frame of the vehicle can serve as a ground wire to complete the circuit. Secondly, most automotive circuits contain multiple components which receive power from a single circuit. This lessens the amount of wire needed to power components on the vehicle.

Fig. 1 This example illustrates a simple circuit. When the switch is closed, power from the positive (+) battery terminal flows through the fuse and the switch, and then to the light bulb. The light illuminates and the circuit is completed through the ground wire back to the negative (-) battery terminal. In reality, the two ground points shown in the illustration are attached to the metal frame of the vehicle, which completes the circuit back to the battery

HOW DOES ELECTRICITY WORK: THE WATER ANALOGY

Electricity is the flow of electrons—the subatomic particles that constitute the outer shell of an atom. Electrons spin in an orbit around the center core of an atom. The center core is comprised of protons (positive charge) and neutrons (neutral charge). Electrons have a negative charge and balance out the positive charge of the protons. When an outside force causes the number of electrons to unbalance the charge of the protons, the electrons will split off the atom and look for another atom to balance out. If this imbalance is kept up, electrons will continue to move and an electrical flow will exist.

Many people have been taught electrical theory using an analogy with water. In a comparison with water flowing through a pipe, the electrons would be the water and the wire is the pipe.

The flow of electricity can be measured much like the flow of water through a pipe. The unit of measurement used is amperes, frequently abbreviated as amps (a). You can compare amperage to the volume of water flowing through a pipe. When connected to a circuit, an ammeter will measure the actual amount of current flowing through the circuit. When relatively few electrons flow through a circuit, the amperage is low. When many electrons flow, the amperage is high.

Water pressure is measured in units such as pounds per square inch (psi); The electrical pressure is measured in units called volts (v). When a voltmeter is connected to a circuit, it is measuring the electrical pressure.

The actual flow of electricity depends not only on voltage and amperage, but also on the resistance of the circuit. The higher the resistance, the higher the force necessary to push the current through the circuit. The standard unit for measuring resistance is an ohm. Resistance in a circuit varies depending on the amount and type of components used in the circuit. The main factors which determine resistance are:

• Material—some materials have more resistance than others. Those with high resistance are said to be insulators. Rubber materials (or rubber-like plastics) are some of the most common insulators used in vehicles as they have a very high resistance to electricity. Very low resistance materials are said to be conductors. Copper wire is among the best conductors. Silver is actually a superior conductor to copper and is used in some relay contacts, but its high cost prohibits its use as common wiring. Most automotive wiring is made of copper.

• Size—the larger the wire size being used, the less resistance the wire will have. This is why components which use large amounts of electricity usually have large wires supplying current to them.

• Length—for a given thickness of wire, the longer the wire, the greater the resistance. The shorter the wire, the less the resistance. When determining the proper wire for a circuit, both size and length must be considered to design a circuit that can handle the current needs of the component.

• Temperature—with many materials, the higher the temperature, the greater the resistance (positive temperature coefficient). Some materials exhibit the opposite trait of lower resistance with higher temperatures (negative temperature coefficient). These principles are used in many of the sensors on the engine.

OHM'S LAW

There is a direct relationship between current, voltage and resistance. The relationship between current, voltage and resistance can be summed up by a statement known as Ohm's law.

Voltage (E) is equal to amperage (I) times resistance (R): $E = I \times R$

Other forms of the formula are $R = E/I$ and $I = E/R$

In each of these formulas, E is the voltage in volts, I is the current in amps and R is the resistance in ohms. The basic point to remember is that as the resistance of a circuit goes up, the amount of current that flows in the circuit will go down, if voltage remains the same.

The amount of work that the electricity can perform is expressed as power. The unit of power is the watt (w). The relationship between power, voltage and current is expressed as:

Power (w) is equal to amperage (I) times voltage (E): $W = I \times E$

This is only true for direct current (DC) circuits; The alternating current formula is a tad different, but since the electrical circuits in most vehicles are DC type, we need not get into AC circuit theory.

Electrical Components

POWER SOURCE

Power is supplied to the vehicle by two devices: The battery and the alternator. The battery supplies electrical power during starting or during periods when the current demand of the vehicle's electrical system exceeds the output capacity of the alternator. The alternator supplies electrical current when the engine is running. Just not does the alternator supply the current needs of the vehicle, but it recharges the battery.

The Battery

In most modern vehicles, the battery is a lead/acid electrochemical device consisting of six 2 volt subsections (cells) connected in series, so that the unit is capable of producing approximately 12 volts of electrical pressure. Each subsection consists of a series of positive and negative plates held a short distance apart in a solution of sulfuric acid and water.

The two types of plates are of dissimilar metals. This sets up a chemical reaction, and it is this reaction which produces current flow from the battery when its positive and negative terminals are connected to an electrical load. The power removed from the battery is replaced by the alternator, restoring the battery to its original chemical state.

The Alternator

On some vehicles there isn't an alternator, but a generator. The difference is that an alternator supplies alternating current which is then changed to direct current for use on the vehicle, while a generator produces direct current. Alternators tend to be more efficient and that is why they are used.

Alternators and generators are devices that consist of coils of wires wound together making big electromagnets. One group of coils spins within another set and the interaction of the magnetic fields causes a current to flow. This current is then drawn off the coils and fed into the vehicles electrical system.

GROUND

Two types of grounds are used in automotive electric circuits. Direct ground components are grounded to the frame through their mounting points. All other components use some sort of ground wire which is attached to the frame or chassis of the vehicle. The electrical current runs through the chassis of the vehicle and returns to the battery through the ground (-) cable; if you look, you'll see that the battery ground cable connects between the battery and the frame or chassis of the vehicle.

➡It should be noted that a good percentage of electrical problems can be traced to bad grounds.

PROTECTIVE DEVICES

▶ See Figure 2

It is possible for large surges of current to pass through the electrical system of your vehicle. If this surge of current were to reach the load in the circuit, the surge could burn it out or severely damage it. It can also overload the wiring, causing the harness to get hot and melt the insulation. To prevent this, fuses, circuit breakers and/or fusible links are connected into the supply wires of the electrical system. These items are nothing more than a built-in weak spot in the system. When an abnormal amount of current flows through the system, these protective devices work as follows to protect the circuit:

• Fuse—when an excessive electrical current passes through a fuse, the fuse "blows" (the conductor melts) and opens the circuit, preventing the passage of current.

• Circuit Breaker—a circuit breaker is basically a self-repairing fuse. It will open the circuit in the same fashion as a fuse, but when the surge subsides, the circuit breaker can be reset and does not need replacement.

• Fusible Link—a fusible link (fuse link or main link) is a short length of special, high temperature insulated wire that acts as a fuse. When an excessive electrical current passes through a fusible link, the thin gauge wire inside the link melts, creating an intentional open to protect the circuit. To repair the circuit, the link must be replaced. Some newer type fusible links are housed in plug-in modules, which are simply replaced like a fuse, while older type fusible links must be cut and spliced if they melt. Since this link is very early in the electrical path, it's the first place to look if nothing on the vehicle works, yet the battery seems to be charged and is properly connected.

✳✳ CAUTION

Always replace fuses, circuit breakers and fusible links with identically rated components. Under no circumstances should a component of higher or lower amperage rating be substituted.

SWITCHES & RELAYS

▶ See Figures 3 and 4

Switches are used in electrical circuits to control the passage of current. The most common use is to open and close circuits between the battery and the various electric devices in the system. Switches are rated according to the amount of amperage they can handle. If a sufficient amperage rated switch is not used in a circuit, the switch could overload and cause damage.

Some electrical components which require a large amount of current to operate use a special switch called a relay. Since these circuits carry a large amount of current, the thickness of the wire in the circuit is also greater. If this large wire were connected from the load to the control switch, the switch would have to carry the high amperage load and the fairing or dash would be twice as large to accommodate the increased size of the wiring harness. To prevent these problems, a relay is used.

Relays are composed of a coil and a set of contacts. When the coil has a current passed though it, a magnetic field is formed and this field causes the contacts to move together, completing the circuit. Most relays are normally open, preventing current from passing through the circuit, but they can take any electrical form depending on the job they are intended to do. Relays can be considered "remote control switches." They allow a smaller current to operate devices that require higher amperages. When a small current operates the coil, a larger current is allowed to pass by the contacts. Some common circuits which may use relays are the horn, headlights, starter, electric fuel pump and other high draw ciruits.

LOAD

Every electrical circuit must include a "load" (something to use the electricity coming from the source). Without this load, the battery would attempt to deliver its entire power supply from one pole to another. This is called a "short circuit." All this electricity would take a short cut to ground and cause a great amount of damage to other components in the circuit by developing a tremendous amount of heat. This condition could develop sufficient heat to melt the insulation on all the surrounding wires and reduce a multiple wire cable to a lump of plastic and copper.

WIRING & HARNESSES

The average vehicle contains meters and meters of wiring, with hundreds of individual connections. To protect the many wires from damage and to keep them from becoming a confusing tangle, they are organized into bundles, enclosed in plastic or taped together and called wiring harnesses. Different harnesses serve different parts of the vehicle. Individual wires are color coded to help trace them through a harness where sections are hidden from view.

A. Relay   C. Fuse
B. Fusible link   D. Flasher

TCCA6P02

Fig. 3 The underhood fuse and relay panel usually contains fuses, relays, flashers and fusible links

TCCA6P01

Fig. 2 Most vehicles use one or more fuse panels. This one is located on the driver's side kick panel

TCCA6G02

Fig. 4 Relays are composed of a coil and a switch. These two components are linked together so that when one operates, the other operates at the same time. The large wires in the circuit are connected from the battery to one side of the relay switch (B+) and from the opposite side of the relay switch to the load (component). Smaller wires are connected from the relay coil to the control switch for the circuit and from the opposite side of the relay coil to ground

Automotive wiring or circuit conductors can be either single strand wire, multi-strand wire or printed circuitry. Single strand wire has a solid metal core and is usually used inside such components as alternators, motors, relays and other devices. Multi-strand wire has a core made of many small strands of wire twisted together into a single conductor. Most of the wiring in an automotive electrical system is made up of multi-strand wire, either as a single conductor or grouped together in a harness. All wiring is color coded on the insulator, either as a solid color or as a colored wire with an identification stripe. A printed circuit is a thin film of copper or other conductor that is printed on an insulator backing. Occasionally, a printed circuit is sandwiched between two sheets of plastic for more protection and flexibility. A complete printed circuit, consisting of conductors, insulating material and connectors for lamps or other components is called a printed circuit board. Printed circuitry is used in place of individual wires or harnesses in places where space is limited, such as behind instrument panels.

Since automotive electrical systems are very sensitive to changes in resistance, the selection of properly sized wires is critical when systems are repaired. A loose or corroded connection or a replacement wire that is too small for the circuit will add extra resistance and an additional voltage drop to the circuit.

The wire gauge number is an expression of the cross-section area of the conductor. Vehicles from countries that use the metric system will typically describe the wire size as its cross-sectional area in square millimeters. In this method, the larger the wire, the greater the number. Another common system for expressing wire size is the American Wire Gauge (AWG) system. As gauge number increases, area decreases and the wire becomes smaller. An 18 gauge wire is smaller than a 4 gauge wire. A wire with a higher gauge number will carry less current than a wire with a lower gauge number. Gauge wire size refers to the size of the strands of the conductor, not the size of the complete wire with insulator. It is possible, therefore, to have two wires of the same gauge with different diameters because one may have thicker insulation than the other.

It is essential to understand how a circuit works before trying to figure out why it doesn't. An electrical schematic shows the electrical current paths when a circuit is operating properly. Schematics break the entire electrical system down into individual circuits. In a schematic, usually no attempt is made to represent wiring and components as they physically appear on the vehicle; switches and other components are shown as simply as possible. Face views of harness connectors show the cavity or terminal locations in all multi-pin connectors to help locate test points.

CONNECTORS

▶ See Figures 5 and 6

Three types of connectors are commonly used in automotive applications—weatherproof, molded and hard shell.

• Weatherproof—these connectors are most commonly used where the connector is exposed to the elements. Terminals are protected against moisture and dirt by sealing rings which provide a weathertight seal. All repairs require the use of a special terminal and the tool required to service it. Unlike standard blade type terminals, these weatherproof terminals cannot be straightened once they are bent. Make certain that the connectors are properly seated and all of the sealing rings are in place when connecting leads.

• Molded—these connectors require complete replacement of the connector if found to be defective. This means splicing a new connector assembly into the harness. All splices should be soldered to insure proper contact. Use care when probing the connections or replacing terminals in them, as it is possible to create a

Fig. 5 Hard shell (left) and weatherproof (right) connectors have replaceable terminals

Fig. 6 Weatherproof connectors are most commonly used in the engine compartment or where the connector is exposed to the elements

short circuit between opposite terminals. If this happens to the wrong terminal pair, it is possible to damage certain components. Always use jumper wires between connectors for circuit checking and NEVER probe through weatherproof seals.

• Hard Shell—unlike molded connectors, the terminal contacts in hard-shell connectors can be replaced. Replacement usually involves the use of a special terminal removal tool that depresses the locking tangs (barbs) on the connector terminal and allows the connector to be removed from the rear of the shell. The connector shell should be replaced if it shows any evidence of burning, melting, cracks, or breaks. Replace individual terminals that are burnt, corroded, distorted or loose.

Test Equipment

Pinpointing the exact cause of trouble in an electrical circuit is most times accomplished by the use of special test equipment. The following describes different types of commonly used test equipment and briefly explains how to use them in diagnosis. In addition to the information covered below, the tool manufacturer's instructions booklet (provided with the tester) should be read and clearly understood before attempting any test procedures.

JUMPER WIRES

✳✳ CAUTION

Never use jumper wires made from a thinner gauge wire than the circuit being tested. If the jumper wire is of too small a gauge, it may overheat and possibly melt. Never use jumpers to bypass high resistance loads in a circuit. Bypassing resistances, in effect, creates a short circuit. This may, in turn, cause damage and fire. Jumper wires should only be used to bypass lengths of wire or to simulate switches.

Jumper wires are simple, yet extremely valuable, pieces of test equipment. They are basically test wires which are used to bypass sections of a circuit. Although jumper wires can be purchased, they are usually fabricated from lengths of standard automotive wire and whatever type of connector (alligator clip, spade connector or pin connector) that is required for the particular application being tested. In cramped, hard-to-reach areas, it is advisable to have insulated boots over the jumper wire terminals in order to prevent accidental grounding. It is also advisable to include a standard automotive fuse in any jumper wire. This is commonly referred to as a "fused jumper". By inserting an in-line fuse holder between a set of test leads, a fused jumper wire can be used for bypassing open circuits. Use a 5 amp fuse to provide protection against voltage spikes.

Jumper wires are used primarily to locate open electrical circuits, on either the ground (-) side of the circuit or on the power (+) side. If an electrical component fails to operate, connect the jumper wire between the component and a good ground. If the component operates only with the jumper installed, the ground circuit is open. If the ground circuit is good, but the component does not operate, the circuit between the power feed and component may be open. By moving the jumper wire successively back from the component toward the power source, you can isolate the area of the circuit where the open is located. When the component stops functioning, or the power is cut off, the open is in the segment of wire between the jumper and the point previously tested.

You can sometimes connect the jumper wire directly from the battery to the "hot" terminal of the component, but first make sure the component uses 12 volts in operation. Some electrical components, such as fuel injectors or sensors, are designed to operate on about 4 to 5 volts, and running 12 volts directly to these components will cause damage.

TEST LIGHTS

▶ **See Figure 7**

The test light is used to check circuits and components while electrical current is flowing through them. It is used for voltage and ground tests. To use a 12 volt test light, connect the ground clip to a good ground and probe wherever necessary with the pick. The test light will illuminate when voltage is detected. This does not necessarily mean that 12 volts (or any particular amount of voltage) is present; it only means that some voltage is present. It is advisable before using the test light to touch its ground clip and probe across the battery posts or terminals to make sure the light is operating properly.

✳✳ WARNING

Do not use a test light to probe electronic ignition, spark plug or coil wires. Never use a pick-type test light to probe wiring on computer controlled systems unless specifically instructed to do so. Any wire insulation that is pierced by the test light probe should be taped and sealed with silicone after testing.

Like the jumper wire, the 12 volt test light is used to isolate opens in circuits. But, whereas the jumper wire is used to bypass the open to operate the load, the 12 volt test light is used to locate the presence of voltage in a circuit. If the test light illuminates, there is power up to that point in the circuit; if the test light does not illuminate, there is an open circuit (no power). Move the test light in successive steps back toward the power source until the light in the handle illuminates. The open is between the probe and a point which was previously probed.

The self-powered test light is similar in design to the 12 volt test light, but contains a 1.5 volt penlight battery in the handle. It is most often used in place of a multimeter to check for open or short circuits when power is isolated from the circuit (continuity test).

The battery in a self-powered test light does not provide much current. A weak battery may not provide enough power to illuminate the test light even when a complete circuit is made (especially if there is high resistance in the circuit). Always make sure that the test battery is strong. To check the battery, briefly touch the ground clip to the probe; if the light glows brightly, the battery is strong enough for testing.

➡**A self-powered test light should not be used on any computer controlled system or component. The small amount of electricity transmitted by the test light is enough to damage many electronic automotive components.**

Fig. 7 A 12 volt test light is used to detect the presence of voltage in a circuit

TCCS2006

MULTIMETERS

Multimeters are an extremely useful tool for troubleshooting electrical problems. They can be purchased in either analog or digital form and have a price range to suit any budget. A multimeter is a voltmeter, ammeter and ohmmeter (along with other features) combined into one instrument. It is often used when testing solid state circuits because of its high input impedance (usually 10 megaohms or more). A brief description of the multimeter main test functions follows:

• Voltmeter—the voltmeter is used to measure voltage at any point in a circuit, or to measure the voltage drop across any part of a circuit. Voltmeters usually have various scales and a selector switch to allow the reading of different voltage ranges. The voltmeter has a positive and a negative lead. To avoid damage to the meter, always connect the negative lead to the negative (-) side of the circuit (to ground or nearest the ground side of the circuit) and connect the positive lead to the positive (+) side of the circuit (to the power source or the nearest power source). Note that the negative voltmeter lead will always be black and that the positive voltmeter will always be some color other than black (usually red).

• Ohmmeter—the ohmmeter is designed to read resistance (measured in ohms) in a circuit or component. Most ohmmeters will have a selector switch which permits the measurement of different ranges of resistance (usually the selector switch allows the multiplication of the meter reading by 10, 100, 1,000 and 10,000). Some ohmmeters are "auto-ranging" which means the meter itself will determine which scale to use. Since the meters are powered by an internal battery, the ohmmeter can be used like a self-powered test light. When the ohmmeter is connected, current from the ohmmeter flows through the circuit or component being tested. Since the ohmmeter's internal resistance and voltage are known values, the amount of current flow through the meter depends on the resistance of the circuit or component being tested. The ohmmeter can also be used to perform a continuity test for suspected open circuits. In using the meter for making continuity checks, do not be concerned with the actual resistance readings. Zero resistance, or any ohm reading, indicates continuity in the circuit. Infinite resistance indicates an opening in the circuit. A high resistance reading where there should be none indicates a problem in the circuit. Checks for short circuits are made in the same manner as checks for open circuits, except that the circuit must be isolated from both power and normal ground. Infinite resistance indicates no continuity, while zero resistance indicates a dead short.

✳✳ WARNING

Never use an ohmmeter to check the resistance of a component or wire while there is voltage applied to the circuit.

• Ammeter—an ammeter measures the amount of current flowing through a circuit in units called amperes or amps. At normal operating voltage, most circuits have a characteristic amount of amperes, called "current draw" which can be measured using an ammeter. By referring to a specified current draw rating, then measuring the amperes and comparing the two values, one can determine what is happening within the circuit to aid in diagnosis. An open circuit, for example, will not allow any current to flow, so the ammeter reading will be zero. A damaged component or circuit will have an increased current draw, so the reading will be high. The ammeter is always connected in series with the circuit being tested. All of the current that normally flows through the circuit must also flow through the ammeter; if there is any other path for the current to follow, the ammeter reading will not be accurate. The ammeter itself has very little resistance to current flow and, therefore, will not affect the circuit, but it will measure current draw only when the circuit is closed and electricity is flowing. Excessive current draw can blow fuses and drain the battery, while a reduced current draw can cause motors to run slowly, lights to dim and other components to not operate properly.

Troubleshooting Electrical Systems

When diagnosing a specific problem, organized troubleshooting is a must. The complexity of a modern automotive vehicle demands that you approach any problem in a logical, organized manner. There are certain troubleshooting techniques, however, which are standard:

• Establish when the problem occurs. Does the problem appear only under certain conditions? Were there any noises, odors or other unusual symptoms? Isolate the problem area. To do this, make some simple tests and observations, then eliminate the systems that are working properly. Check for obvious problems, such as broken wires and loose or dirty connections. Always check the obvious before assuming something complicated is the cause.

• Test for problems systematically to determine the cause once the problem area is isolated. Are all the components functioning properly? Is there power going to electrical switches and motors. Performing careful, systematic checks will often turn up most causes on the first inspection, without wasting time checking components that have little or no relationship to the problem.

• Test all repairs after the work is done to make sure that the problem is fixed. Some causes can be traced to more than one component, so a careful verification of repair work is important in order to pick up additional malfunctions that may cause a problem to reappear or a different problem to arise. A blown fuse, for example, is a simple problem that may require more than another fuse to repair. If you don't look for a problem that caused a fuse to blow, a shorted wire (for example) may go undetected.

Experience has shown that most problems tend to be the result of a fairly simple and obvious cause, such as loose or corroded connectors, bad grounds or damaged wire insulation which causes a short. This makes careful visual inspection of components during testing essential to quick and accurate troubleshooting.

Testing

OPEN CIRCUITS

▶ See Figure 8

This test already assumes the existence of an open in the circuit and it is used to help locate the open portion.
1. Isolate the circuit from power and ground.
2. Connect the self-powered test light or ohmmeter ground clip to the ground side of the circuit and probe sections of the circuit sequentially.
3. If the light is out or there is infinite resistance, the open is between the probe and the circuit ground.
4. If the light is on or the meter shows continuity, the open is between the probe and the end of the circuit toward the power source.

SHORT CIRCUITS

➡Never use a self-powered test light to perform checks for opens or shorts when power is applied to the circuit under test. The test light can be damaged by outside power.

1. Isolate the circuit from power and ground.
2. Connect the self-powered test light or ohmmeter ground clip to a good ground and probe any easy-to-reach point in the circuit.
3. If the light comes on or there is continuity, there is a short somewhere in the circuit.
4. To isolate the short, probe a test point at either end of the isolated circuit (the light should be on or the meter should indicate continuity).
5. Leave the test light probe engaged and sequentially open connectors or switches, remove parts, etc. until the light goes out or continuity is broken.
6. When the light goes out, the short is between the last two circuit components which were opened.

VOLTAGE

This test determines voltage available from the battery and should be the first step in any electrical troubleshooting procedure after visual inspection. Many electrical problems, especially on computer controlled systems, can be caused by a low state of charge in the battery. Excessive corrosion at the battery cable terminals can cause poor contact that will prevent proper charging and full battery current flow.
1. Set the voltmeter selector switch to the 20V position.
2. Connect the multimeter negative lead to the battery's negative (-) post or terminal and the positive lead to the battery's positive (+) post or terminal.
3. Turn the ignition switch ON to provide a load.
4. A well charged battery should register over 12 volts. If the meter reads below 11.5 volts, the battery power may be insufficient to operate the electrical system properly.

VOLTAGE DROP

▶ See Figure 9

When current flows through a load, the voltage beyond the load drops. This voltage drop is due to the resistance created by the load and also by small resistances created by corrosion at the connectors and damaged insulation on the wires. The maximum allowable voltage drop under load is critical, especially if there is more than one load in the circuit, since all voltage drops are cumulative.
1. Set the voltmeter selector switch to the 20 volt position.
2. Connect the multimeter negative lead to a good ground.
3. Operate the circuit and check the voltage prior to the first component (load).
4. There should be little or no voltage drop in the circuit prior to the first component. If a voltage drop exists, the wire or connectors in the circuit are suspect.
5. While operating the first component in the circuit, probe the ground side of the component with the positive meter lead and observe the voltage readings. A small voltage drop should be noticed. This voltage drop is caused by the resistance of the component.
6. Repeat the test for each component (load) down the circuit.
7. If a large voltage drop is noticed, the preceding component, wire or connector is suspect.

RESISTANCE

▶ See Figures 10 and 11

✷✷✷ WARNING

Never use an ohmmeter with power applied to the circuit. The ohmmeter is designed to operate on its own power supply. The normal 12 volt electrical system voltage could damage the meter!

1. Isolate the circuit from the vehicle's power source.
2. Ensure that the ignition key is OFF when disconnecting any components or the battery.

Fig. 8 The infinite reading on this multimeter indicates that the circuit is open

Fig. 9 This voltage drop test revealed high resistance (low voltage) in the circuit

Fig. 10 Checking the resistance of a coolant temperature sensor with an ohmmeter. Reading is 1.04 kilohms

Fig. 11 Spark plug wires can be checked for excessive resistance using an ohmmeter

3. Where necessary, also isolate at least one side of the circuit to be checked, in order to avoid reading parallel resistances. Parallel circuit resistances will always give a lower reading than the actual resistance of either of the branches.

4. Connect the meter leads to both sides of the circuit (wire or component) and read the actual measured ohms on the meter scale. Make sure the selector switch is set to the proper ohm scale for the circuit being tested, to avoid misreading the ohmmeter test value.

Wire and Connector Repair

Almost anyone can replace damaged wires, as long as the proper tools and parts are available. Wire and terminals are available to fit almost any need. Even the specialized weatherproof, molded and hard shell connectors are now available from aftermarket suppliers.

Be sure the ends of all the wires are fitted with the proper terminal hardware and connectors. Wrapping a wire around a stud is never a permanent solution and will only cause trouble later. Replace wires one at a time to avoid confusion. Always route wires exactly the same as the factory.

➡️**If connector repair is necessary, only attempt it if you have the proper tools. Weatherproof and hard shell connectors require special tools to release the pins inside the connector. Attempting to repair these connectors with conventional hand tools will damage them.**

BATTERY CABLES

Disconnecting the Cables

When working on any electrical component on the vehicle, it is always a good idea to disconnect the negative (-) battery cable. This will prevent potential damage to many sensitive electrical components such as the Engine Control Module (ECM), radio, alternator, etc.

➡️**Any time you disengage the battery cables, it is recommended that you disconnect the negative (-) battery cable first. This will prevent your accidentally grounding the positive (+) terminal to the body of the vehicle when disconnecting it, thereby preventing damage to the above mentioned components.**

Before you disconnect the cable(s), first turn the ignition to the **OFF** position. This will prevent a draw on the battery which could cause arcing (electricity trying to ground itself to the body of a vehicle, just like a spark plug jumping the gap) and, of course, damaging some components such as the alternator diodes.

When the battery cable(s) are reconnected (negative cable last), be sure to check that your lights, windshield wipers and other electrically operated safety components are all working correctly. If your vehicle contains an Electronically Tuned Radio (ETR), don't forget to also reset your radio stations. Ditto for the clock.

SUPPLEMENTAL INFLATABLE RESTRAINT (SIR) SYSTEM

General Information

▶ See Figure 12

The Supplemental Inflatable Restraint (SIR) system offers protection in addition to that provided by the seat belt by deploying an air bag from the center of the steering wheel or dash panel. The air bag deploys when the vehicle is involved in a frontal crash of sufficient force up to 30° off the centerline of the

vehicle. To further absorb the crash energy, there is also a knee bolster located beneath the instrument panel in the driver's area and the steering wheel is collapsible.

The system has an energy reserve, which can store a large enough electrical charge to deploy the air bag(s) for up to ten minutes after the battery has been disconnected or damaged. The system **MUST** be disabled before any service is performed on or around SIR components or SIR wiring.

SYSTEM OPERATION

The SIR system contains a deployment loop for each air bag and a Diagnostic Energy Reserve Module (DERM). The deployment loop supplies current through the inflator module which will cause air bag deployment in the event of a frontal collision of sufficient force. The DERM supplies the necessary power, even if the battery has been damaged.

The deployment loop is made up of the arming sensors, coil assembly, inflator module and the discriminating sensors. The inflator module is only supplied sufficient current when the arming sensor and at least one of the two discriminating sensors close simultaneously. The function of the DERM is to supply the deployment loop a 36 Volt Loop Reserve (36VLR) to assure sufficient voltage to deploy the air bag if ignition voltage is lost in a frontal crash.

The DERM, in conjunction with the sensor resistors, makes it possible to detect circuit and component malfunctions within the deployment loop. If the voltages monitored by the DERM fall outside expected limits, the DERM will indicate a malfunction by storing a diagnostic trouble code and illuminating the AIR BAG lamp.

Fig. 12 SIR system "deployment window"

SYSTEM COMPONENTS

▶ **See Figure 13**

Diagnostic Energy Reserve Module (DERM)

The DERM is designed to perform five main functions: energy reserve, malfunction detection, malfunction recording, driver notification and frontal crash recording.

The DERM maintains a reserve voltage supply to provide deployment energy for a few seconds when the vehicle voltage is low or lost in a frontal crash. The DERM performs diagnostic monitoring of the SIR system and records malfunctions in the form of diagnostic trouble codes, which can be obtained from a hand scan tool and/or on-board diagnostics. The DERM warns the driver of SIR system malfunctions by controlling the AIR BAG warning lamp and records SIR system status during a frontal crash.

AIR BAG Warning Lamp

The AIR BAG warning/indicator lamp is used to verify lamp and DERM operation by flashing 7 times when the ignition is first turned **ON**. It is also used to warn the driver of an SIR system malfunction.

Discriminating Sensors

Vehicles equipped with driver's side air bag only, have two discriminating sensors. The forward discriminating sensor is located in front of the radiator. The passenger compartment discriminating sensor is located behind the right side of the instrument panel.

The discriminating sensor consists of a sensing element, diagnostic resistor and normally open switch contacts. The sensing element closes the switch contact when vehicle velocity changes are severe enough to warrant air bag deployment.

Dual Pole Arming Sensor

The dual pole arming sensor is contained in the same housing as the passenger compartment discriminating sensor and is referred to as the dual sensor.

1	HOOD LATCH SUPPORT BRACKET	7	DASH PANEL ASSEMBLY
2	FORWARD DISCRIMINATING SENSOR	8	DASH WIRING HARNESS
3	TIEBAR ASSEMBLY	9	DERM
4	PASSENGER COMPARTMENT DISCRIMINATING SENSOR	10	SIR WIRING HARNESS
5	GLOVE BOX LEAD	11	DUAL POLE ARMING SENSOR
6	PASSENGER INFLATOR MODULE	12	DRIVER INFLATOR MODULE

87956002

Fig. 13 SIR system components

The arming sensor is a switch located in the power side of the deployment loop. It is calibrated to close at low level velocity changes (lower than the discriminating sensors), assuring that the inflator module is connected directly to the 36VLR output of the DERM or Ignition 1 voltage when any discriminating sensor closes.

SIR Coil Assembly

▶ **See Figure 14**

The SIR coil assembly consists of two current carrying coils. They are attached to the steering column and allow rotation of the steering wheel while maintaining continuous deployment loop contact through the inflator module.

There is a shorting bar on the lower steering column connector that connects the SIR coil to the SIR wiring harness. The shorting bar shorts the circuit when the connector is disengaged. The circuit to the inflator module is shorted in this way to prevent unwanted air bag deployment when servicing the steering column or other SIR components.

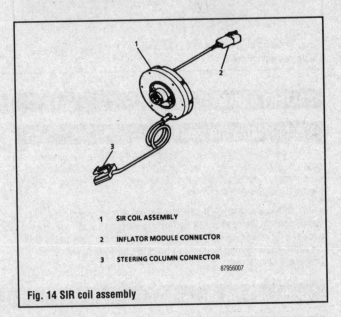

1	SIR COIL ASSEMBLY
2	INFLATOR MODULE CONNECTOR
3	STEERING COLUMN CONNECTOR

87956007

Fig. 14 SIR coil assembly

Inflator Module

The inflator module consists of an inflatable bag and an inflator (a canister of gas-generating material and an initiating device). When the vehicle is in a frontal crash of sufficient force to close the arming sensor and at least one discriminating sensor simultaneously, current flows through the deployment loop. Current passing through the initiator ignites the material in the inflator module, causing a reaction which produces a gas that rapidly inflates the air bag.

All vehicles are equipped with a driver's side inflator module located in the steering wheel and a passenger side inflator module located in the dash panel.

SERVICE PRECAUTIONS

▶ **See Figure 15**

- When performing service around the SIR system components or wiring, the SIR system **MUST** be disabled. Failure to do so could result in possible air bag deployment, personal injury or unneeded SIR system repairs.
- When carrying a live inflator module, make sure that the bag and trim cover are pointed away from you. Never carry the inflator module by the wires or connector on the underside of the module. In case of accidental deployment, the bag will then deploy with minimal chance of injury.
- When placing a live inflator module on a bench or other surface, always face the bag and trim cover up, away from the surface.

Fig. 15 When carrying a live inflator module, make sure that the bag and trim cover are pointed away from you. Never carry the inflator module by the wires or connector on the underside of the module

DISABLING THE SYSTEM

▶ **See Figure 16**

➡With the "AIR BAG" fuse removed and the ignition switch ON, the "AIR BAG" warning lamp will be on. The is normal and does not indicate any system malfunction.

1. Turn the steering wheel so that the vehicle's wheels are pointing straight ahead.
2. Turn the ignition switch to **LOCK**, remove the key, then disconnect the negative battery cable.
3. Remove the "AIR BAG" fuse from the fuse block.
4. Remove the steering column filler panel.
5. Disengage the Connector Position Assurance (CPA) and both yellow two way connectors and corresponding CPAs located near the base of the steering column.
6. Connect the negative battery cable.

ENABLING THE SYSTEM

▶ **See Figure 16**

1. Disconnect the negative battery cable.
2. Turn the ignition switch to **LOCK**, then remove the key.

REVERSE VIEW

1 TIEBAR ASSEMBLY
2 STEERING COLUMN BRANCH
3 PASSENGER SIDE CONNECTOR
   POSITION ASSURANCE (CPA)
4 DRIVER SIDE CONNECTOR
   POSITION ASSURANCE (CPA)
5 DRIVER SIDE SIR CONNECTOR
6 PASSENGER SIDE SIR CONNECTOR

87956011

Fig. 16 Location of the driver and passenger side SIR connectors

3. Engage both yellow SIR connectors and corresponding CPAs located near the base of the steering column.
4. Install the steering column filler panel.
5. Install the "AIR BAG" fuse to the fuse block.
6. Connect the negative battery cable.
7. Turn the ignition switch to **RUN** and make sure that the "AIR BAG" warning lamp flashes seven times and then shuts off. If the warning lamp does not shut off, make sure that the wiring is properly connected. If the light remains on, take the vehicle to a reputable repair facility for service.

HEATING AND AIR CONDITIONING

Blower Motor

REMOVAL & INSTALLATION

1982–91 Vehicles

▶ **See Figures 17, 18, 19, 20 and 21**

1. Disconnect the negative battery cable.
2. Detach the electrical connections at the blower motor and blower resistor.

➡On the 3.1L engine remove the tower to tower brace assembly.

3. On models through 1989, remove the plastic water shield from the right side of the cowl.
4. Unfasten the blower motor retaining screws and then pull the blower motor and cage out.
5. Hold the blower motor cage, then remove the cage retaining nut from the blower motor shaft.
6. Remove the blower motor and cage.

To install:
7. Install the cage on the new motor.
8. Check that the retaining nut is on tight, the motor rotates and the fan cage is not interfering with the motor.

Fig. 17 Unfasten the retaining nuts, then . . .

Fig. 18 . . . pull the motor and cage out

1. Heater case air inlet asm.
2. Stud dash panel
3. Locating studs dash panel
4. Heater core
5. Heater module asm.
6. Module cover

Fig. 19 Heater module and air inlet assembly—1982–87 vehicles without A/C

1. Heater & evaporator
2. Drain tube
3. Blower assembly

NOTICE: WHEN REMOVING THE HEATER & EVAPORATOR ASSEMBLY, PULL ASSEMBLY STRAIGHT TOWARD INTERIOR OF CAR UNTIL PLASTIC DRAIN TUBE CLEARS COWL. IF ASSEMBLY IS TILTED IN ANY DIRECTION BEFORE THE TUBE CLEARS THE COWL, THE TUBE MAY BREAK.

Fig. 20 Heater evaporator and blower assemblies and air inlet installation—1982–87 vehicles with A/C

9. Install the motor in the heater assembly (install tower to tower brace assembly if necessary) connect the wiring and check the motor operation in all speeds.

1992–94 Vehicles

♦ See Figure 22

EXCEPT 3.1L ENGINES

1. Disconnect the negative battery cable.
2. Tag and detach the electrical connector(s) at the blower motor.
3. Remove the blower motor cooling tube.
4. Unfasten the blower motor retaining screws, then remove the blower motor fan and motor assembly.

➡The blower motor and fan are serviced as an assembly.

1. HEATER MODULE ASSEMBLY
2. INLET AND BLOWER ASSEMBLY
3. 2.5 N·m (22 LBS. IN.)
4. SEAL
5. 3.4 N·m (30 LBS. IN.)
6. HEATER OUTLET
7. 1.4 N·m (12.5 LBS. IN.)

Fig. 21 Heater and blower assembly and related components—1988–89 vehicles

1. DASH PANEL ASSEMBLY
2. MODULE ASSEMBLY
3. GASKET
4. SCREW – 2 N.m (20 LBS. IN.)
   A INSTALL FIRST
   B INSTALL SECOND
   C INSTALL LAST (NO SEQUENCE)
5. NUT – 3 N.m (27 LBS. FT.)
6. BLOWER ASSEMBLY
7. GASKET – AIR INLET

Fig. 22 Blower case, air inlet and module assemblies—1994 vehicle shown

To install:
5. Place the blower motor and fan assembly in the correct position.
6. Install and tighten evenly the fan assembly retaining screws.
7. If equipped, connect blower motor cooling tube.
8. Attach the electrical connector(s).
9. Connect the negative battery cable, then check the blower motor operation in all speeds.

3.1L ENGINE

1. Disconnect the negative battery cable.
2. Remove the tower-to-tower brace.
3. Tag and detach the electrical connectors at the blower motor.
4. Disconnect the blower motor cooling tube.
5. Remove the alternator assembly, as outlined in Section 2 of this manual.
6. Unfasten the blower motor retaining screws, then remove the blower motor and fan assembly.

➡The blower motor and fan are serviced as an assembly.

To install:
7. Place the blower motor and fan assembly in the correct position.
8. Install and tighten evenly the fan assembly retaining screws.
9. Install the alternator assembly. Adjust the drive belt.
10. Connect blower motor cooling tube.
11. Attach the electrical connections, then install the tower-to-tower brace.
12. Connect the negative battery cable and check the blower motor operation in all speeds.

Heater Core

REMOVAL & INSTALLATION

✳✳ CAUTION

When draining the coolant, keep in mind that cats and dogs are attracted by ethylene glycol antifreeze, and are quite likely to drink any that is left in an uncovered container or in puddles on the ground. This will prove fatal in sufficient quantity. Always drain the coolant into a sealable container. Coolant should be reused unless it is contaminated or several years old.

1982–87 Vehicles

WITHOUT A/C

1. Disconnect the negative battery cable.
2. Properly drain the cooling system.
3. Disconnect the heater inlet and outlet hoses from the heater core.
4. Remove the heater outlet deflector.
5. Unfasten the retaining screws, then remove the heater core cover.
6. Detach the heater core retaining straps, then then remove the heater core.
7. Installation is the reverse of removal. Refill the cooling system. Check heater system for proper operation.

WITH A/C

1. Disconnect the negative battery cable and drain the cooling system.
2. Raise and support the front of the vehicle.
3. Disconnect the drain tube from the heater case.
4. Remove the heater hoses from the heater core.
5. Lower the car. Remove the right and left hush panels, the steering column trim cover, the heater outlet duct and the glove box.
6. Remove the heater core cover. Be sure to pull the cover straight to the rear so as not to damage the drain tube.
7. Remove the heater core clamps and then remove the core.
8. Reverse the above procedure to install, and fill the cooling system.

1988–94 Vehicles

▶ See Figures 23, 24 and 25

1. Disconnect the negative battery cable and drain the cooling system.
2. Raise and support the vehicle safely.
3. If equipped, remove the rear lateral transaxle strut mount.
4. Disconnect the drain tube from the heater case.
5. Detach the heater hoses from the heater core.
6. Carefully lower the vehicle.
7. Remove the right and left sound insulators.
8. Unfasten the steering column opening filler. Disconnect the heater outlet deflector (floor air outlet duct).
9. Remove the heater core cover.

10. Detach the heater core retaining straps (clamps), then remove the heater core.
To install:
11. Install the heater core and retaining straps (clamps).
12. Install the heater core cover.
13. Reconnect the heater outlet deflector (floor air outlet duct).
14. Install the right and left sound insulators. Install the steering column opening filler.
15. Raise and support the vehicle safely.
16. Connect the heater hoses (use new heater hose clamps if necessary) to the heater core.
17. Connect the drain tube to heater case.
18. Connect the rear lateral transaxle strut mount, if equipped.
19. Lower the vehicle.
20. Fill the cooling system and check for leaks. Check heater system for proper operation.

Air Conditioning Components

REMOVAL & INSTALLATION

Repair or service of air conditioning components is not covered by this manual, because of the risk of personal injury or death, and because of the legal ramifications of servicing these components without the proper EPA certification and experience. Cost, personal injury or death, environmental damage, and legal considerations (such as the fact that it is a federal crime to vent refrigerant into the atmosphere), dictate that the A/C components on your vehicle should be serviced only by a Motor Vehicle Air Conditioning (MVAC) trained, and EPA certified automotive technician.

➡If your vehicle's A/C system uses R-12 refrigerant and is in need of recharging, the A/C system can be converted over to R-134a refrigerant (less environmentally harmful and expensive). Refer to Section 1 for additional information on R-12 to R-134a conversions, and for additional considerations dealing with your vehicle's A/C system.

Blower Switch

REMOVAL & INSTALLATION

▶ See Figure 26

1. Disconnect the battery ground cable.
2. Remove the instrument panel (I/P) trim plate.
3. Unfasten the control assembly retaining screws, then pull the control assembly away from the instrument panel.
4. Remove the blower switch knob.
5. Detach the electrical connector.
6. Unfasten the blower switch retaining screws and remove the switch.
7. Installation is the reverse of the removal procedure. Check system for proper operation.

87956018

Fig. 23 Disconnect the floor air outlet duct

87956019

Fig. 24 Unfasten the retaining bolts, then remove the heater core cover

87956020

Fig. 25 Detach the retaining clamps or straps, then remove the heater core

1 CONSOLE ASSEMBLY
2 HEATER A/C CONTROL
3 SCREW – 1.5 N·m (13 LBS. IN.)
  A TIGHTEN 1st
  B TIGHTEN 2nd
  C TIGHTEN 3rd
  D TIGHTEN 4th

87956025

Fig. 26 Heater control assembly mounting—1994 vehicle shown

Temperature Control Cable

REMOVAL & INSTALLATION

▶ See Figure 27

1. Disconnect the negative battery cable.
2. Remove the right side sound insulator panel.
3. If necessary for access, remove the instrument panel (I/P) compartment.
4. Disconnect the cable at the module.
5. Remove the control panel trim plate and control panel assembly, as outlined later in this section.
6. Disconnect the cable from the control assembly, then remove the cable.
7. Installation is the reverse of the removal procedure. Adjust temperature control cable, as outlined later in this section.

ADJUSTMENT

▶ See Figure 28

If the temperature control lever fails to move to full COLD or HOT, or a large amount of lever spring back is noticed when moving to either of the full positions, the cable clip may need adjustment. Failure to grip clip in the correct manner will damage its ability to hold position on the cable. The temperature control cable must be replaced if clip retention fails.

VIEW A

VIEW B

1 TEMPERATURE CONTROL CABLE
2 CABLE RETAINER
3 HEATER CONTROL
4 MODE SLAVE LEVER
5 MODULE ASSEMBLY
6 DEFROST VACUUM ACTUATOR
7 SCREW – 4.2 mm (8 – 18)
  FULLY DRIVEN, SEATED AND
  NOT STRIPPED

87956022

Fig. 27 Temperature control cable routing—1994 vehicle shown

1 CLIP
2 PLIERS
3 TEMPERATURE CABLE

CORRECT CLIP GRIP FOR ADJUSTMENT

1 CLIP
2 PLIERS
3 TEMPERATURE CABLE

INCORRECT CLIP GRIP FOR ADJUSTMENT

87956023

Fig. 28 Temperature control cable clip adjustment

1. To adjust the clip, grip the clip (refer to the accompanying illustration for the correct manner to grip the cable) at module end of cable while pulling temperature control lever to the correct full position (COLD or HOT) and connect.
2. Verify correct adjustment by observing for little or no spring back of the temperature control lever and listening for temperature door "slam" when the control lever is moved to full positions quickly.

Control Panel

REMOVAL & INSTALLATION

▶ See Figure 29

1. Disconnect the battery ground cable.
2. Remove the instrument panel trim plate.
3. Remove the control assembly retaining screws and pull the control assembly away from the instrument panel.
4. Detach the electrical and vacuum connectors.
5. Disconnect the temperature control cable from the control assembly and remove assembly.

To install:

6. Connect the temperature control cable to the heater control.
7. Attach the vacuum and electrical connectors.
8. Install the control assembly and secure with the retaining screws.
9. Install the instrument panel trim plate.
10. Connect the negative battery cable.

87956024

Fig. 29 Remove the instrument panel trim plate for access to the temperature control panel

CRUISE CONTROL

General Description

▶ See Figures 30, 31, 32, 33 and 34

These models are equipped with an electronic/vacuum cruise control system which maintains a desired vehicle speed under normal driving conditions. The main components of the system are the mode control switches, controller (module), sevo unit, speed sensor, vacuum supply, electrical and vacuum release switches along with an electrical harness.

The cruise control release switch and stop lamp switch assemblies are used to disengage the system. Both switches are mounted on the brake pedal bracket. The system disengages electronically when the pedal is depressed.

The vehicle speed sensor (VSS) buffer assembly receives a signal form the VSS permanent magnet generator indicating the speed of the vehicle. The signal is then processed by the speed sensor and supplied to the ECM, cruise control module and speedometer. The VSS is usually mounted to the transaxle assembly.

The cruise control module location may be located in different areas on some models and engines. The module is usually mounted in the lower left front area near the kickpanel left of the steering wheel, under the steering wheel on the filler panel or above the glove box area to the right side of the vehicle. The module is not serviceable.

The cruise control engagement switch is part of the turn signal lever assembly and is not serviceable by itself. The switch is used to start or disengage the cruise control system. The turn signal lever and cruise control switch must be replaced as an assembly. Refer to the necessary service procedures in Section 8.

1 BRAKE PEDAL MOUNTING BRACKET
2 CRUISE CONTROL RELEASE VALVE (VACUUM) (MANUAL TRANSAXLE ONLY)
3 TORQUE CONVERTER CLUTCH TERMINALS
4 TCC AND CRUISE CONTROL RELEASE SWITCH/ VALVE (AUTOMATIC TRANSAXLE ONLY)
5 STOPLAMP SWITCH
6 CRUISE CONTROL RELEASE SWITCH TERMINALS
7 STOP LAMP SWITCH TERMINALS
8 BRAKE PEDAL ASM

87956046

Fig. 30 View of the brake pedal switches—1992 vehicle shown

1 Cruise control clutch switch
2 Clutch pedal asm.
3 Clutch pedal bracket
4 Retainer

87956047

Fig. 31 Cruise control switch mounting on the clutch pedal—1992 vehicle shown

1 Vehicle speed sensor
2 Seal
3 Retainer
4 Bolt

87956045

Fig. 32 View of the VSS mounting—manual transaxle shown

1 Left I/P trim plate
2 Cruise control module
3 Screws
4 Insulator pad

87956048

Fig. 33 Cruise control mounting—1994 vehicle shown

1 24 Nm (18 lbs. ft.)
2 Servo assembly
3 Bracket
4 12 Nm (108 lbs. in.)

87956051

Fig. 34 Cruise control servo mounting—1992 vehicle shown

CRUISE CONTROL TROUBLESHOOTING

Problem	Possible Cause
Will not hold proper speed	Incorrect cable adjustment
	Binding throttle linkage
	Leaking vacuum servo diaphragm
	Leaking vacuum tank
	Faulty vacuum or vent valve
	Faulty stepper motor
	Faulty transducer
	Faulty speed sensor
	Faulty cruise control module
Cruise intermittently cuts out	Clutch or brake switch adjustment too tight
	Short or open in the cruise control circuit
	Faulty transducer
	Faulty cruise control module
Vehicle surges	Kinked speedometer cable or casing
	Binding throttle linkage
	Faulty speed sensor
	Faulty cruise control module
Cruise control inoperative	Blown fuse
	Short or open in the cruise control circuit
	Faulty brake or clutch switch
	Leaking vacuum circuit
	Faulty cruise control switch
	Faulty stepper motor
	Faulty transducer
	Faulty speed sensor
	Faulty cruise control module

Note: Use this chart as a guide. Not all systems will use the components listed.

TCCA6C01

ENTERTAINMENT SYSTEMS

Radio Receiver/Tape Player/CD Player

REMOVAL & INSTALLATION

1982–87 Vehicles

▶ See Figure 35

✳✳✳ WARNING

Do not operate the radio with the speaker leads disconnected. Operating the radio without an electrical load will damage the output transistors.

1. Disconnect the negative battery cable.
2. Remove the instrument panel trim plate.
3. Check the right side of the radio to determine whether a nut or a stud is used for side retention.
4. If a nut is used, remove the hush panel and then loosen the nut from below on cars without air conditioning. On cars with air conditioning, remove the hush panel, the A/C duct and the A/C control head for access to the nut. Do not remove the nut; loosen it just enough to pull the radio out. If a rubber stud is used, go on to Step 5.
5. Unfasten the two radio bracket-to-instrument panel attaching screws. Pull the radio forward far enough to disconnect the wiring and antenna and then remove the radio.
6. Installation is the reverse of removal.

1	RADIO
2	SCREW ON SIDE OF RADIO FITS HERE
3	RETAINER
4	GRILLE
5	SPEAKER
6	FRT SPEAKER ASSEMBLY
7	FRT. SPEAKER ASSEMBLY
8	REAR SPEAKER WIRE
9	ANTENNA (SEE SEC. 9)
10	REAR SPEAKERS
11	FRONT SPEAKERS
12	I.P. HARNESS
13	RECEIVER ASM.
14	I.P. HARNESS

87956052

Fig. 35 Exploded view of the radio mounting—1987 vehicle shown

1988–94 Vehicles, Except Sunbird

▶ See Figure 36

1. Disconnect the negative battery cable.
2. Remove the instrument panel cluster or console trim plate.
3. Unfasten the radio-to-instrument panel attaching screws or nuts located at either the top of bottom of the radio.
4. Pull the radio out far enough to disconnect the wiring harness and antenna and remove the radio.

1 Retailer
2 Console assembly
3 AM - FM radio/cassette tape
  deck or compact disk player
4 Radio to console bracket
5 1.4 Nm (12 lbs.in.) screw
6 3 Nm (27 lbs.in.) nut
7 On stud threaded clip

Fig. 36 Radio assembly removal—1993 Cavalier shown

To install:

5. Reposition the radio and connect the wiring harness and antenna.
6. Fasten the radio retaining screws or nuts.
7. Install the instrument panel cluster or console trim plate.
8. Connect the negative battery cable.

1993–94 Sunbird

RADIO CONTROL ASSEMBLY

▶ See Figure 37

1. Disconnect the negative battery cable.
2. Detach the steering column opening filler panel.
3. Remove the instrument panel cluster or console trim plate.
4. Unfasten the radio-to-instrument panel attaching screws or nuts located at the top of the radio control assembly.
5. Pull the radio out far enough to disconnect the wiring harness and antenna and remove the radio.

To install:

6. Reposition the radio and connect the wiring harness and antenna.
7. Fasten the radio retaining screws or nuts.
8. Install the instrument panel cluster or console trim plate.
9. Fasten the steering column opening filler panel.
10. Connect the negative battery cable.

1 INSTRUMENT PANEL ASM.
2 BOLT/SCREW – FULLY DRIVEN, SEATED
  AND NOT STRIPPED
3 RADIO CONTROL ASM.

Fig. 37 On the Sunbird, the retaining screws are located at the top of the radio assembly

RADIO RECEIVER

▶ See Figure 38

1. Disconnect the negative battery cable.
2. Remove the right sound insulator.
3. Unfasten the nut from the bottom of the receiver securing the receiver to the HVAC duct.
4. Detach the electrical connector, then remove the receiver.
5. Installation is the reverse of the removal procedure.

1 INSTRUMENT PANEL ASM.
2 RADIO CONTROL ASM.
3 TO RECEIVER ASM.
4 AIR DISTRIBUTOR ASM.
5 RETAINER
6 STUD
7 RADIO RECEIVER
8 NUT – 9 N·m (6 LBS. FT.)
9 COMPACT DISK LEAD
10 LEAD FROM COMPACT DISK PLAYER OR CASSETTE PLAYER
11 TO RADIO CONTROL ASM.
12 TAPE PLAYER/COMPACT DISK PLAYER WIRING HARNESS
13 COMPACT DISC PLAYER OR CASSETTE
   TAPE DECK CONNECTOR

VIEW A

Fig. 38 Radio receiver mounting—1988–92 Sunbird

TAPE OR CD PLAYER

▶ See Figure 39

1. Disconnect the negative battery cable.
2. Remove the accessory trim plate.
3. Detach the two console housing side trim plates.
4. Unfasten the two nuts on the side of the deck, then pull the deck out, detach the electrical connectors and antenna lead and remove the deck.

To install:

5. Position the deck, attach the electrical connectors and antenna lead, then secure with the two retaining screws.
6. Attach the two console housing side trim plates.
7. Install the accessory trim plate.
8. Connect the negative battery cable.

1 NUT
2 RETAINER
3 COMPACT DISC HARNESS
4 COMPACT DISC ASSEMBLY
5 BOLT

Fig. 39 Removing the tape or CD player—1994 Sunbird shown

Speakers

REMOVAL & INSTALLATION

Front Dash Mounted

▶ See Figures 40 and 41

1. Disconnect the negative battery cable.
2. Carefully pry gently upwards on the speaker grille with a suitable prytool and remove the grille.
3. Unfasten the two screws retaining the speaker to instrument panel and pull the speaker partially out, to access the wiring.
4. Detach the wiring connector, then remove the speaker from the vehicle.
5. Installation is the reverse of the removal procedure, ensuring that the speaker grille cover snaps snugly into place.

Fig. 40 A tool like this can be very help for removing the speaker retaining screws when space is too cramped for a screwdriver

Fig. 41 Lift the speaker, detach the connector and remove the speaker from the vehicle

1	SPEAKER
2	RETAINING TABS
5	SPEAKER MOUNT BRACKET
6	SPRING HOOK
7	RETAINING SLOTS
8	SPRING HOOK RETAINER
9	REAR SPEAKER WIRE HARNESS CONNECTOR

Fig. 42 2 and 4-door model rear speaker mounting—1994 vehicle shown

Front Door Mounted

1. Disconnect the negative battery cable.
2. Remove the door trim panel for access to the speaker.
3. Unfasten the retaining screws, then pull speaker out, detach the connector and remove the speaker from the vehicle.
4. Installation is the reverse of the removal procedure.

Rear Mounted 2 and 4-Door Models

▶ See Figure 42

1. Disconnect the negative battery cable.
2. Open the deck (trunk) lid.
3. Unfasten the speaker cover retaining screws and remove the cover.
4. Detach the wiring harness connector.
5. Unfasten the spring hook from the spring retainer.
6. Disconnect the speaker retaining tabs from the retaining slots, then remove the speaker.
7. Installation is the reverse of the removal procedure.

Rear Mounted Station Wagon

▶ See Figure 43

1. Disconnect the negative battery cable.
2. Remove the lift gate trim finishing panel.

1	SPEAKER WIRE HARNESS CONNECTOR
2	SPEAKER GASKET (2)
3	RETAINING SCREWS (8)
4	SPEAKER (2)

Fig. 43 View of the rear speaker mounting on a station wagon—1994 vehicle shown

3. Unfasten the speaker retaining screws.
4. Detach the wiring harness connector, then remove the speakers.
5. Installation is the reverse of the removal procedure.

WINDSHIELD WIPERS AND WASHERS

Windshield Wiper Blade and Arm

REMOVAL & INSTALLATION

1982–92 Vehicles

▶ See Figure 44

➡Removal of the wiper arms requires the use of a special tool, G.M. J8966 or its equivalent. Equivalent versions of this tool are usually available in auto parts stores.

1. Insert tool J8966, or equivalent, under the wiper arm and lever the arm off the shaft.
2. Disconnect the washer hose from the arm (if so equipped). Remove the arm.
3. If necessary, replace the blade refill as outlined in Section 1 of this manual.
4. Installation is the reverse of removal.
   The proper park position is at the top of the blackout line on the glass. If the wiper arms and blades were in the proper position prior to removal, adjustment should not be required.

1993–94 Vehicles

▶ See Figure 45

1. Pull out the retaining latch with suitable prytool, then work the wiper arm assembly off the transmission driveshaft.
2. If necessary, replace the blade refill as outlined in Section 1 of this manual.
   To install:
3. If removed, install the blade refill.
4. Position the wiper arm assembly on the transmission driveshaft so that the blade assembly is as near as possible to the top edge of the blackout line on the windshield with the wiper motor in the park position.
5. Seat the wiper arm assembly firmly on the driveshaft, then press in the retaining latch.

ADJUSTMENT

The only adjustment for the wiper arms is to remove an arm from the transmission shaft, rotate the arm the required distance and direction and then install the arm back in position so it is in line with the blackout line on the glass. The wiper motor must be in the park position.

Fig. 44 Using the special tool to separate the wiper arm from the shaft

1	WIPER ARM
2	J8966 OR EQUIVALENT
3	WIPER BLADE ASSEMBLY
4	BLADE RETAINER
5	SCREWDRIVER
6	BLADE ELEMENT
7	ELEMENT RETAINER

87956067

A   Arm retaining latch
B   Transmission drive shaft
C   Blade retaining latch
D   Claw set (6)
E   Element vertebra
1   Wiper arm assembly
2   Wiper blade assembly
3   Blade superstructure
4   Blade element

87956071

Fig. 45 Wiper arm, blade and element components

The correct blade-out wipe position on the driver's side is 9/16–1¾ in. (15–45mm) from the tip of the blade to the left windshield pillar molding (driver's side). The correct blade-down wipe position on the passenger side of the car is in line with the blackout line at the bottom of the glass.

Windshield Wiper Motor

REMOVAL & INSTALLATION

▶ **See Figures 46 and 47**

1.   Remove the wiper arm and blade assemblies.
2.   Disconnect the negative battery cable.
3.   Remove the shroud top vent grille.
4.   For vehicles through 1991, loosen (but do not remove) the drive link-to-crank arm attaching nuts and detach the drive link from the motor crank arm.
5.   Tag and disconnect all electrical leads from the wiper motor.
6.   Using tool J 39232 or equivalent, remove the transmission drive link from the wiper motor crank arm.
7.   For vehicles through 1991, unscrew the mounting bolts, rotate the motor up and outward and remove it.
8.   For 1992 vehicles, unfasten the three screws, then remove the wiper motor assembly, guiding the crank arm through the hole.

To install:

9.   Guide the crank arm through the opening in the body and then tighten the mounting bolts to 4–6 ft. lbs. (5–8 Nm) and the screws to 80 inch lbs. (9 Nm).
10.   Install the drive link to the crank arm with the motor in the park position.
11.   Installation of the remaining components is the reverse of removal.

Fig. 46 Detach the electrical connector from the wiper motor—1988 Sunbird shown

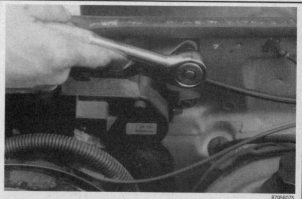

Fig. 47 Unfasten the mounting bolts, then rotate the motor up and out to remove it—1988 Sunbird shown

Rear Window Wiper Motor

REMOVAL & INSTALLATION

1. Turn the ignition switch **OFF**.
2. Pull the wiper arm from the pivot shaft.
3. Remove the pivot shaft nut and spacers.
4. Open the tailgate and remove the inner trim panel.
5. Remove the license plate housing.
6. Detach the license plate light wiring.
7. Disconnect the wiper motor wiring.
8. Remove the linkage arm locking clip, pry off the arm and remove the linkage.
9. Unfasten the motor and bracket attaching screws and remove the motor.
10. Installation is the reverse of removal.

Wiper Linkage

REMOVAL & INSTALLATION

▶ See Figure 48

1. Remove the wiper arms.
2. Remove the shroud top vent grille.
3. Loosen (but do not remove) the drive link-to-crank arm attaching nuts.

4. Unscrew the linkage-to-cowl panel retaining screws and remove the linkage.
5. Installation is the reverse of removal. Tighten the attaching screws and nuts to 64 inch lbs. (7 Nm).

Windshield Washer Fluid Reservoir & Pump

REMOVAL & INSTALLATION

1982–92 Vehicles

▶ See Figures 49, 50 and 51

1. Disconnect the negative battery cable.
2. Drain washer fluid from the washer reservoir.
3. Detach the electrical connection and washer hoses.
4. Remove the washer reservoir by unfastening the retainers and lifting the reservoir out of the vehicle.
5. Remove the washer pump from the washer reservoir.
6. Installation is the reverse of removal. Make sure washer pump is pushed all the way into the washer reservoir gasket.

1993–94 Vehicles

▶ See Figure 52

1. Disconnect the negative battery cable.
2. Drain the washer fluid from the reservoir.

Fig. 48 Removing the windshield wiper linkage

Fig. 49 Detach the windshield washer pump electrical connector, then . . .

Fig. 50 . . . lift the pump from the reservoir and disconnect the hose

1	WIRING HARNESS
2	WASHER PUMP
3	WASHER HOSES
4	GASKET
5	WASHER RESERVOIR

Fig. 51 Windshield washer reservoir and pump assembly—1992 vehicle shown

1 Solvent container
2 5 Nm (44 lb.in.) screw (2)
3 Mounting bracket
4 Washer pump
5 Washer hose

Fig. 52 View of the pump mounting in the washer reservoir—1994 vehicle shown

3. Detach the washer hose and the electrical connector from the washer pump.
4. Unfasten the screw from the mounting tab at the neck of the reservoir.
5. Remove the screw from the tab at the bottom of the container.
6. Extend the outer retaining clip of the mounting bracket outward and pull the container downward out of the mounting bracket.
7. Remove the pump from the reservoir.

To install:

8. Position the washer pump in the reservoir container. Make sure the pump is pushed all the way into the container seal.

9. Insert the neck of the container into the engine compartment., then extend the outer retaining clip of the mounting bracket outward and push the container upward into engagement with both bracket retaining clips.
10. Fasten the two screws in the lower and upper container mounting tabs. Tighten the screws to 44 inch lbs. (5 Nm).
11. Attach the washer hose and the electrical connector.
12. Fill the reservoir with windshield washer solvent, then connect the negative battery cable.

INSTRUMENTS AND SWITCHES

Instrument Cluster

REMOVAL & INSTALLATION

Cavalier

1982–90 VEHICLES

▶ **See Figures 53, 54, 55 and 56**

1. Disconnect the negative battery cable.
2. Remove the speedometer cluster trim plate.
3. Unfasten the speedometer cluster attaching screws.
4. Loosen the two steering column retaining bolts, then lower the steering column. Pull the cluster away from the instrument panel and disconnect the speedometer cable.
5. Disconnect the vehicle speed sensor connector from the cluster. Tag and detach all other electrical connectors as required.
6. Remove the cluster housing from the vehicle.
7. Installation is the reverse of the removal procedure.

1991–94 VEHICLES

▶ **See Figure 57**

1. Disconnect the negative battery cable.
2. Unfasten the 4 screws from the steering column opening filler and remove the steering column opening filler.
3. Pull down slightly on the steering column collar to gain access and remove the 2 screws from the bottom of the cluster extension and remove the extension.
4. Detach the electrical connectors from the instrument panel dimmer and interior lamp control switches.
5. Unfasten the 2 screws from the top of the cluster and pull the cluster rearward to remove.

To install:

6. Reposition the cluster and install the 2 screws to the top of the cluster.
7. Attach the electrical connectors to the instrument panel dimmer and interior lamp control switches.
8. Reposition the cluster extension and install the 2 screws to the bottom of the cluster extension.
9. Install the steering column opening filler and secure with the 4 retaining screws.
10. Connect the negative battery cable.

1 Instrument panel
2 Instrument cluster
3 1.4 Nm (12 lbs. in.) screw

87956087

Fig. 53 Base instrument panel cluster installation—1982–90 Cavalier

87956086

Fig. 54 Instrument cluster mounting— 1990 Cavalier Z24 shown

ELECTRONIC INSTRUMENT CLUSTER

87956088

Fig. 55 Electronic instrument panel cluster mounting—1985–90 Cavalier shown

1 Socket
2 Bulb
3 Cluster asm.
4 Trim plate
5 Bracket
6 Screw
7 Lens

87956089

Fig. 56 Disassembled view of the gauge instrument panel cluster— 1988–90 Cavalier

1 Instrument panel
2 2 Nm (19 lbs.in.) screw
3 I/P cluster assembly
4 I/P lamp dimmer switch connector
5 I/P cluster extension
6 Interior lamp switch connector

87956090

Fig. 57 Instrument cluster and extension mounting—1994 Cavalier shown

Cimarron

1. Disconnect the negative battery cable.
2. Remove the speedometer cluster trim plate.
3. Unfasten the speedometer cluster attaching screws.
4. Lower the steering column. Pull the cluster away from the instrument panel and disconnect the speedometer cable.
5. Disconnect the vehicle speed sensor connector from the cluster. Detach all other electrical connectors as required.
6. Remove the cluster housing from the vehicle.
7. Installation is the reverse of the removal procedure.

Sunbird

1982–88 VEHICLES

1. Disconnect the negative battery cable.
2. Remove the speedometer cluster trim plate.
3. Unfasten the speedometer cluster attaching screws.
4. Lower the steering column. Pull the cluster away from the instrument panel and disconnect the speedometer cable.
5. Disconnect the vehicle speed sensor connector from the cluster. Tag and detach all other electrical connectors as required.
6. Remove the cluster housing from the vehicle.
7. Installation is the reverse of the removal procedure.

1989–94 VEHICLES

♦ See Figure 58

1. Disconnect the negative battery cable.
2. Remove the speedometer cluster trim plate.
3. Unfasten the 4 speedometer cluster attaching screws.
4. Remove the steering column opening filler cover which is retained by spring clips.
5. Pull the cluster away from the instrument panel and disconnect the speedometer cable.
6. Detach all other electrical connectors as required.
7. Remove the instrument cluster from the vehicle.
8. Installation is the reverse of the removal procedure.

1 Instrument panel asm.
2 I/P cluster asm.
3 1.4 Nm (12 lbs.in.) screw

87956093

Fig. 58 Instrument panel cluster installation—1989–94 Sunbird

Skyhawk and Firenza

1. Disconnect the negative battery cable.
2. Remove the steering column trim cover. Remove the left and right hand trim cover.
3. Remove the cluster trim cover.
4. Remove the screws attaching the lens and bezel to the cluster carrier.
5. Lower the steering wheel column by removing the 2 upper steering column attaching bolts.
6. Unfasten the screws attaching the cluster housing to the cluster carrier. Pull the cluster out slightly from the instrument panel and disconnect the speedometer cable. Detach all other connectors.
7. Remove the cluster housing from the vehicle.
8. Installation is the reverse of the removal procedure.

REMOVAL & INSTALLATION

The gauges can be removed from the cluster assembly by:
1. Removing the lens.
2. Removing the printed circuit board from the back of the cluster.
3. Removing the gauge attaching screws.
4. Installation is the reverse of removal.

Speedometer Cable

REMOVAL & INSTALLATION

♦ See Figures 59 and 60

1. Reach behind the instrument cluster and push the speedometer cable casing toward the speedometer while depressing the retaining spring on the back of the instrument cluster case. Once the retaining spring has released, hold it in while pulling outward on the casing to disconnect the casing from the speedometer.

➡Removal of the steering column trim plate and/or the speedometer cluster may provide better access to the cable.

2. Remove the cable casing sealing plug from the dash panel. Then, pull the casing down from behind the dash and remove the cable.
3. If the cable is broken and cannot be entirely removed from the top, support the car securely, and then unscrew the cable casing connector at the transaxle. Pull the bottom part of the cable out, and then screw the connector back onto the transaxle.
4. Lubricate the new cable. Insert it into the casing until it bottoms. Push inward while rotating it until the square portion at the bottom engages with the coupling in the transaxle, permitting the cable to move in another inch or so.

1. Dash panel
2. Cluster asm.
3. Trans
4. Dash panel
5. Cluster asm.
6. Transducer
7. Transmission

EXCEPT CRUISE CONTROL

WITH CRUISE CONTROL

87956102

Fig. 59 Speedometer cable routing—1982–87 vehicles shown

FERRULE-PILOTS AND SPEEDO NECK AND PROTECTS TIP

BRAID LINER AND CASING

RETAINING SPRING PUSH TO DISENGAGE

TIP

87956103

Fig. 60 Cable disengagement at the speedometer

Then, reconnect the cable casing to the speedometer and install the sealing plug into the dash panel.

Windshield Wiper Switch

REMOVAL & INSTALLATION

Except 1989–94 Sunbird And Dash Mounted Type Switches

The wiper switch is located inside the steering column cover. To gain access to the switch the steering wheel, turn signal switch and ignition lock will have to be removed. Refer to Section 8 for these procedures.

1989–94 Sunbird

▶ See Figure 61

1. Disconnect the negative battery cable.
2. Remove the right side trim plate from the the instrument panel.
3. Unfasten the wiper switch housing attaching screw.
4. Unplug the wiring and remove the switch.

To install:

5. Attach the switch wiring harness connector.
6. Reposition the switch to the to the instrument panel and secure with the attaching screw.
7. Install the right side trim plate to the instrument panel.
8. Connect the negative battery cable.

Dash Mounted Type Switch

▶ See Figure 62

1. Disconnect the negative battery cable.
2. Pull out the right pad trim plate.
3. Unfasten the 2 screws securing the switch to the trim plate.
4. Unplug the electrical connection and remove the switch.

Fig. 61 View of the front and rear windshield wiper/washer and defogger switch—vehicles equipped with a dash mounted switch

To install:

5. Connect the switch electrical connector.
6. Install the 2 screws securing the switch to the trim plate.
7. Install the right pad trim plate.
8. Connect the negative battery cable.

Headlight Switch

REMOVAL & INSTALLATION

1982–90 All Cavalier

EXCEPT 1985–87 CAVALIER TYPE 10, 1988 RS/ Z24, 1989–90 Z24

▶ See Figure 63

1. Disconnect the negative battery cable.
2. Pull the knob out fully, remove the knob from the rod by depressing the retaining clip from the underside the knob.
3. Remove the trimplate.
4. Remove the switch by removing the nut, rotating the switch 180°, then tilting forward and and pulling out. Disconnect the wire harness.
5. Installation is the reverse of the removal procedure.

1985–87 CAVALIER TYPE 10, 1988 RS/Z24 AND 1989–90 Z24

▶ See Figure 64

1. Disconnect the negative battery cable.
2. Pull out the left pad trim plate.
3. Unfasten the 2 screws securing the switch to the trim plate.
4. Detach the headlight switch electrical connection and remove the switch.

To install:

5. Attach the switch electrical connector.
6. Fasten the 2 screws securing the switch to the trim plate.
7. Install the left pad trim plate.
8. Connect the negative battery cable.

1991–94 Cavalier

On these models the headlamp/parking lamp switch is a rotating switch, located on the left steering column lever, or multi-function lever, along with the cruise control and turn signal switch. Please refer to the Turn Signal Switch removal procedure in Section 8.

1982–88 J2000, 2000 and Sunbird and Cimarron

1. Disconnect the negative battery cable.
2. Pull the knob out fully, remove the knob from the rod by depressing the retaining clip from the underside the knob.
3. Remove the trimplate.
4. Remove the switch by removing the nut, rotating the switch 180°, then tilting forward and and pulling out. Disconnect the wire harness.
5. Installation is the reverse of the removal procedure.

Fig. 62 View of the windshield wiper and rear defogger switch removal—1989–94 Sunbird

Fig. 63 Headlamp switch installation—1982–90 Cavalier with base instrument panel

Fig. 64 Headlamp switch removal and installation—1985–87 Cavalier Type 10, 1988 RS and Z24 and 1989–90 Z24

Firenza, Skyhawk and 1989–94 Sunbird

▶ **See Figures 65, 66 and 67**

1. Disconnect the negative battery cable.
2. Pull out the left pad trim plate.
3. Unfasten the screws securing the switch to the trim plate.
4. Detach the switch electrical connection and remove the switch.
To install:
5. Attach the switch electrical connector.

6. Fasten the screws securing the switch to the trim plate.
7. Install the left pad trim plate.
8. Connect the negative battery cable.

Ignition Switch

The ignition switch removal and installation procedure is given in Section 8, under steering, because the steering wheel must be removed for access to the ignition switch.

Fig. 65 Headlamp switch removal and installation—1982–85 Firenza and Skyhawk

1. Plate
2. Headlamp switch
3. Dimmer switch
4. Fully driven, seated and not stripped

Fig. 66 Removing the headlamp switch—1986–88 Firenza and 1986–89 Skyhawk

1 Instrument panel assembly
2 Fully driven, seated and not stripped bolt/screw
3 Headlamp/foglamp switch assembly
4 Fully driven, seated and not stripped screw
5 Headlamp switch panel housing

Fig. 67 Exploded view of the headlamp switch assembly—1989–94 Sunbird shown

LIGHTING

Headlights

REMOVAL & INSTALLATION

Sealed Beam

▶ **See Figures 68 thru 76**

1. Disconnect the negative battery cable.
2. If equipped with retractable headlights, raise the headlamp door using the manual knob.
3. Remove the headlamp trim panel (grille panel or bezel) attaching screws.

➡**The trim panel retaining screws on the Cavalier are under the hood, on top of the front support. To avoid turning the vertical or horizontal aiming screws, refer to the illustration before removing the headlight retainer.**

4. Unfasten the four headlamp retaining screws. These are the screws which hold the retaining ring for the bulb to the front of the car. Do not touch

the two headlamp aiming screws, at the top and side of the retaining ring, or the headlamp aim will have to be readjusted.

5. Pull the bulb and ring forward and separate them. Unplug the electrical connector from the rear of the bulb.
To install:
6. Plug the new bulb into the electrical connector.
7. Install the bulb into the retaining ring and install the ring and bulb.
8. If equipped, install the headlamp door.
9. Install the trim panel (grill trim or bezel).
10. Connect the negative battery cable.

Composite

Most of the later model vehicles covered by this manual are equipped with composite headlight assemblies. Due to space constraints, no access may be provided to withdraw the bulbs, so the replacement usually requires removal of the composite assembly.

➡**The composite headlight assemblies use Halogen bulbs which contain a gas under pressure. Improper handling of the bulb could cause it to shatter into flying glass fragments. To help avoid personal injury, follow the precautions closely.**

Fig. 68 Raise the headlamp door using the manual knob

Fig. 69 Unfasten the bezel retaining screws, then . . .

Fig. 70 . . . remove the bezel from the headlamps

Fig. 71 Unfasten the headlamp retaining ring screws

Fig. 72 Do not confuse the headlight aiming screws with the retainer attaching screws

Fig. 73 Pull the retaining ring then the bulb forward, then . . .

Fig. 74 . . . unplug the connector and remove the headlamp

1—ACTUATOR ASM
2—BOLT/SCREW
3—NUT
4—NUT
5—DOOR ASM
6—BOLT/SCREW
7—BEZEL R&L
8—BOLT/SCREW
9—TO FWD LAMP
    WIRING ASM.

Fig. 76 View of the headlamp assembly—1987 Sunbird with retractable headlamps shown

1. Bracket
2. Nut
3. Torx screws
4. Bezel assembly
5. Adjuster assembly
6. Park/turn light
7. Outer headlight
   (low beam)
8. Springs
9. Inner headlight
   (hi beam)
10. Foglight

Fig. 75 Exploded view of the headlamp, foglamp and bezel—1987 Sunbird shown

Whenever handling a Halogen bulb, ALWAYS follow these precautions:
• Turn the headlight switch OFF and allow the bulb to cool before changing it. Leave the switch OFF until the change is complete.
• ALWAYS wear eye protection when changing a halogen bulb.
• Handle the bulb only by its base. Avoid touching the glass.
• DO NOT drop or scratch the bulb.
• Keep dirt and moisture off the bulb.
• Place the used bulb in the new bulb's carton and dispose of it properly.
1. Raise the hood and locate the bulb mounting location at the rear of the composite headlamp body.
2. Disconnect the negative battery cable.
3. If necessary for access, remove the splash shield or side marker lamp(s).
4. If there is enough room to access the plastic base, press in and turn the base ¼ turn counterclockwise and remove from the metal retaining ring by gently pulling back and away from the headlight. Remove the electrical connector from the bulb by raising the locktab and pulling the connector down and away from the bulb's plastic base.

5. If you can't access the bulb from the engine compartment, unfasten the thumb screws, and/or other retainers, then pull the composite headlight assembly forward slightly and disengage the wiring connector. Press in and turn the base ¼ turn counterclockwise and remove the bulb from the metal retaining ring by gently pulling back and away from the headlight.
To install:
6. Attach the electrical connector on the new bulb's plastic base making sure that the locktab is in place.
7. Install the bulb by inserting the smallest tab located on top of the plastic base into the corresponding notch in the metal retaining ring. Turn clockwise ¼ turn until it stops. The small plastic tab should be at the top of the metal ring.
8. Install the composite headlight assembly, then secure with the retainers.
9. Connect the negative battery cable, then check for proper headlight operation.

HEADLIGHT AIMING

▶ See Figures 77 thru 80

The headlights must be properly aimed to provide the best, safest road illumination. The lights should be checked for proper aim and adjusted as necessary. Certain state and local authorities have requirements for headlight aiming; these should be checked before adjustment is made.

✳✳ CAUTION

About once a year, when the headlights are replaced or any time front end work is performed on your vehicle, the headlight should be accurately aimed by a reputable repair shop using the proper equipment. Headlights not properly aimed can make it virtually impossible to see and may blind other drivers on the road, possibly causing an accident. Note that the following procedure is a temporary fix, until you can take your vehicle to a repair shop for a proper adjustment.

100. Vertical Adjusting Screw
101. Horizontal Adjusting Screw

85386087

Fig. 77 Headlight adjustment screw locations for most sealed beam headlight adjusting plates

91066P04

Fig. 78 Use a Torx screw driver for the adjustment

Headlight adjustment may be temporarily made using a wall, as described below, or on the rear of another vehicle. When adjusted, the lights should not glare in oncoming car or truck windshields, nor should they illuminate the passenger compartment of vehicles driving in front of you. These adjustments are rough and should always be fine-tuned by a repair shop which is equipped with headlight aiming tools. Improper adjustments may be both dangerous and illegal.

For most of the vehicles covered by this manual, horizontal and vertical aiming of each sealed beam unit is provided by two adjusting screws which move the retaining ring and adjusting plate against the tension of a coil spring. There is no adjustment for focus; this is done during headlight manufacturing.

➡Because the composite headlight assembly is bolted into position, no adjustment should be necessary or possible. Some applications, however, may be bolted to an adjuster plate or may be retained by adjusting screws. If so, follow this procedure when adjusting the lights, BUT always have the adjustment checked by a reputable shop.

Before removing the headlight bulb or disturbing the headlamp in any way, note the current settings in order to ease headlight adjustment upon reassembly. If the high or low beam setting of the old lamp still works, this can be done using the wall of a garage or a building:

1. Park the vehicle on a level surface, with the fuel tank about ½ full and with the vehicle empty of all extra cargo (unless normally carried). The vehicle should be facing a wall which is no less than 6 feet (1.8m) high and 12 feet (3.7m) wide. The front of the vehicle should be about 25 feet from the wall.

2. If aiming is to be performed outdoors, it is advisable to wait until dusk in order to properly see the headlight beams on the wall. If done in a garage, darken the area around the wall as much as possible by closing shades or hanging cloth over the windows.

3. Turn the headlights **ON** and mark the wall at the center of each light's low beam, then switch on the brights and mark the center of each light's high beam. A short length of masking tape which is visible from the front of the vehicle may be used. Although marking all four positions is advisable, marking one position from each light should be sufficient.

4. If neither beam on one side is working, and if another like-sized vehicle is available, park the second one in the exact spot where the vehicle was and mark the beams using the same-side light. Then switch the vehicles so the one to be aimed is back in the original spot. It must be parked no closer to or farther away from the wall than the second vehicle.

5. Perform any necessary repairs, but make sure the vehicle is not moved, or is returned to the exact spot from which the lights were marked. Turn the headlights **ON** and adjust the beams to match the marks on the wall.

6. Have the headlight adjustment checked as soon as possible by a reputable repair shop.

Signal and Marker Lights

REMOVAL & INSTALLATION

Front Turn Signal and Parking Lights

♦ See Figure 81

Bulbs at the front of the car can normally be replaced from beneath the car or from under the hood. Some bulbs may require removal of the outer lens. Remove the socket from the lamp housing by twisting, then replace the bulb and reinstall the socket.

TCCA6GZ4

Fig. 79 Low-beam headlight pattern alignment

TCCA6GZ

Fig. 80 High-beam headlight pattern alignment

1. Disconnect the negative battery cable.
2. On early model vehicles, unfasten the retaining screws, then remove the bezel and light housing from the front fascia of the vehicle. Remove the bulb.
3. On later model vehicles, remove the lamp assembly, unfasten the socket from the lamp housing by turning it counterclockwise, then remove the lamp from the socket by pressing in and turning counterclockwise.

To install:
4. Install the replacement lamp into the socket, matching the directional alignment pins on the base of the bulb with the complementary slots in the socket. This will assure that the proper filament is energized at the right time; i.e.: the turn signal filament and not the parking lamp filament is energized when the turn signal is turned on.
5. If you can get to the bulb from the engine compartment, push the lamp into the socket and turn clockwise. Install the socket to the lamp housing by turning clockwise.
6. If the bulb can't be accessed from the engine compartment, after the bulb is installed, fasten the housing and bezel to the front fascia of the vehicle.
7. Connect the negative battery cable.
8. Check operation of the parking lamp and turn signal.

Front Side Marker Lights

▶ **See Figure 82**

1. Disconnect the negative battery cable.
2. If equipped, manually crank up the head lamp door with the hood open.
3. If necessary, remove the headlamp assembly for access to the side marker light retaining screws.
4. Unfasten the side marker housing attaching screws.

[1] PARK AND TURN LAMP ASM.
[2] BOLT/SCREW — FULLY DRIVEN, SEATED AND NOT STRIPPED
[3] FRONT FASCIA

87956124

Fig. 81 Removing the turn signal/parking light lamp assembly— 1992 Sunbird shown

5. Lower the housing far enough to remove the socket from the housing by turning 45° counterclockwise.
6. Remove the bulb and socket assembly from the housing, then detach the bulb from the socket.

To install:
7. Position the bulb into the socket making sure it is secure.
8. Install the socket to the lamp housing.
9. Secure the socket to the lamp housing by turning 45° clockwise.
10. Install the side marker housing, then fasten using the attaching screws.
11. If necessary, install the headlight assembly.
12. Connect the negative battery cable.
13. If equipped, lower the headlamp door by turning the head lamps on and off.

Rear Stop And Turn Signal Lamps

▶ **See Figures 83 and 84**

Various methods are employed to remove and install the components of the tail lamp assemblies. Tail lamp bulbs can be replaced by removing the screws which retain the lamp assemblies to the rear end panel and then removing the lamp assemblies. On some models it will be necessary to remove the wing nut inside the rear compartment which retains the tail lamp to the body.

1. Disconnect the negative battery cable.
2. Open the trunk.
3. Remove the nuts or other retainers from the rear trim, then remove the trim.
4. From inside the trunk, unfasten the wing nuts or other retainers securing the tail lamp housing, then pull the tail lamp assembly out so the bulb sockets can be accessed.
5. Depending upon vehicle application, remove the lamp socket either by rotating it counterclockwise (approximately ¼ turn) until the plastic tabs disengage, or by squeezing the metal tangs while pulling the socket from the light assembly.
6. Remove the bulb from the socket using the appropriate method. Bulbs with blade-type bases pull straight out, while those with round bases and protruding pins (bayonet-type bulbs) must be depressed, then rotated counterclockwise (approximately ⅛ turn) before pulling out.

To install:
7. Secure the bulb in the socket using the appropriate method. Bulbs with blade-type bases push straight in, while those with round bases and protruding pins (bayonet-type bulbs) must be inserted, then depressed and rotated clockwise (approximately ⅛ turn).
8. Install the lamp socket using the appropriate method. Depending on the type of socket, either engage the plastic tabs, and rotate the socket clockwise (approximately ¼ turn), or push on the socket until the metal tangs engage.
9. Install the housing cover nuts/retainers.
10. Install the rear trim.
11. Connect the negative battery cable, then check the operation of the rear lights.

[1] HOUSING,SIDEMARKER, TURN SIGNAL AND PARK LAMP
[2] SCREW - FULLY DRIVEN, SEATED AND NOT STRIPPED
[3] PANEL FRONT END

87956127

Fig. 82 Side marker lamp mounting—1992 Pontiac Sunbird SE and GT shown

87956128

Fig. 83 After removing the retainers, pull the tail lamp assembly down . . .

87956129

Fig. 84 . . . then remove the bulb from the socket

High-mount Stop Light

VEHICLES WITHOUT LUGGAGE RACK

▶ See Figures 85 and 86

1. Remove the two mounting screws.
2. Unfasten the electrical connector.
3. Remove the two cover screws and remove the bulb.
4. Installation is the reverse of the removal procedure.

STATION WAGONS

▶ See Figure 87

1. Remove the four mounting screws.
2. Detach the electrical connector.
3. Remove the two cover screws and remove the bulb.
4. Installation is the reverse of the removal procedure.

VEHICLES WITH LUGGAGE RACK OR WING/SPOILER

▶ See Figure 88

1. Remove the two cover screws and remove the bulb.
2. Installation is the reverse of the removal procedure.

Dome Light

▶ See Figures 89 and 90

1. Pull the dome light lens or carefully pry the lens from the housing with a suitable prytool.
2. Remove the bulb from the housing.
3. Installation is the reverse of the removal procedure.

License Plate Lights

▶ See Figures 91, 92 and 93

1. On some vehicles, you may have to open the trunk and unfasten the lamp assembly retaining screw.

1. CENTER STOP LAMP
2. RETAINING SCREWS (4)
3. WIRE HARNESS CONNECTOR
4. LAMP MOUNT BRACKET
5. RETAINING SCREWS (2)

87956131

Fig. 87 View of the high-mount stop lamp replacement—Station wagons

1. RAIL, LUGGAGE RACK
2. HOUSING, CHMSL
3. LENS, CHMSL
4. SCREW - FULLY DRIVEN, SEATED AND NOT STRIPPED
5. BULB

87956132

Fig. 88 High-mount stop lamp bulb replacement—vehicles with a luggage rack or wing/spoiler

2. If necessary, unfasten the retainer from the lamp assembly.
3. Installation is the reverse of the removal procedure.
4. Remove the socket and bulb assembly, then replace the bulb if necessary.

Fog Lamps

REMOVAL & INSTALLATION

1. Unfasten the two screws from the lens retainers.
2. Remove the two lens retainers.
3. Remove the lens/bulb housing.
4. Disconnect the bulb retainer clip.
5. Detach the electrical connector and remove the bulb.
6. Installation is the reverse of the removal procedure.

1. STOP LAMP ASSEMBLY
2. ATTACHING SCREW
3. MOUNTING BRACKET
4. WIRE HARNESS

CUTOUT IN SHELF TRIM

SHELF PANEL TRIM

87956130

Fig. 85 View of the high-mount stop lamp—4-door vehicle (without luggage rack)

1. SEAT TO BACK WINDOW TRIM PANEL
2. CENTER STOP LAMP
3. STOP LAMP COVER
4. RETAINING NUTS (2)
5. WIRE HARNESS CONNECTORS

87956134

Fig. 86 View of the high-mount stop lamp—2-door vehicle (without luggage rack)

Fig. 89 Pull the dome light lens from the housing . . .

Fig. 90 . . . then remove the bulb from the housing

Fig. 91 On this 1988 Sunbird you must unfasten the retainer from the license plate lamp assembly

Fig. 92 Once it is unbolted, remove the light bulb and socket assembly, then . . .

Fig. 93 . . . pull the bulb from the socket

TRAILER WIRING

Wiring the vehicle for towing is fairly easy. There are a number of good wiring kits available and these should be used, rather than trying to design your own.

All trailers will need brake lights and turn signals as well as tail lights and side marker lights. Most areas require extra marker lights for overwide trailers. Also, most areas have recently required back-up lights for trailers, and most trailer manufacturers have been building trailers with back-up lights for several years.

Additionally, some Class I, most Class II and just about all Class III and IV trailers will have electric brakes. Add to this number an accessories wire, to operate trailer internal equipment or to charge the trailer's battery, and you can have as many as seven wires in the harness.

Determine the equipment on your trailer and buy the wiring kit necessary. The kit will contain all the wires needed, plus a plug adapter set which includes the female plug, mounted on the bumper or hitch, and the male plug, wired into, or plugged into the trailer harness.

When installing the kit, follow the manufacturer's instructions. The color coding of the wires is usually standard throughout the industry. One point to note: some domestic vehicles, and most imported vehicles, have separate turn signals. On most domestic vehicles, the brake lights and rear turn signals operate with the same bulb. For those vehicles without separate turn signals, you can purchase an isolation unit so that the brake lights won't blink whenever the turn signals are operated.

One, final point, the best kits are those with a spring loaded cover on the vehicle mounted socket. This cover prevents dirt and moisture from corroding the terminals. Never let the vehicle socket hang loosely; always mount it securely to the bumper or hitch.

CIRCUIT PROTECTION

Fuses

Fuses protect all the major electrical systems in the car. In case of an electrical overload, the fuse melts, breaking the circuit and stopping the flow of electricity.

The fuse block on most models covered by this manual is located under the instrument panel to the left of the steering column. The fuse block should be visible from underneath the steering column, near the pedal bracket. If the panel is not visible, check for a removable compartment door or trim panel which may used on later models to hide the block.

If a fuse blows, the cause should be investigated and corrected before the installation of a new fuse. This, however, is easier to say than to do. Because each fuse protects a limited number of components, your job is narrowed down somewhat. Begin your investigation by looking for obvious fraying, loose connections, breaks in insulation, etc. Use the techniques outlined at the beginning of this sec-

tion. Electrical problems are almost always a real headache to solve, but if you are patient and persistent, and approach the problem logically (that is, don't start replacing electrical components randomly), you will eventually find the solution.

Each fuse block uses miniature fuses (normally plug-in blade terminal-type for these vehicles) which are designed for increased circuit protection and greater reliability. The compact plug-in or blade terminal design allows for fingertip removal and replacement.

Although most fuses are interchangeable in size, the amperage values are not. Should you install a fuse with too high a value, damaging current could be allowed to destroy the component you were attempting to protect by using a fuse in the first place. The plug-in type fuses have a volt number molded on them and are color coded for easy identification. Be sure to only replace a fuse with the proper amperage rated substitute.

A blown fuse can easily be checked by visual inspection or by continuity checking.

REPLACEMENT

▶ See Figures 94 and 95

1. Locate the fuse for the circuit in question.

➡When replacing the fuse, DO NOT use one with a higher amperage rating.

2. Check the fuse by pulling it from the fuse block and observing the element. If it is broken, install a replacement fuse the same amperage rating. If the fuse blows again, check the circuit for a short to ground or faulty device in the circuit protected by the fuse.

3. Continuity can also be checked with the fuse installed in the fuse block with the use of a test light connected across the 2 test points on the end of the fuse. If the test light lights, replace the fuse. Check the circuit for a short to ground or faulty device in the circuit protected by the fuse.

Fig. 94 The fuse block on most models is located under the instrument panel to the left of the steering column

Fig. 95 Visual examination will reveal a blown fuse, but it should not be replaced until repairs are made

Fusible Links

A fusible link is a protective device used in an electrical circuit. When the current increases beyond a certain amperage, the fusible metal of the wire link melts, thus breaking the electrical circuit and preventing further damage to other components and wiring. Whenever a fusible link is melted because of a short circuit, correct the cause before installing a new one. There are four different gauge sizes commonly used and they are usually color coded so that they may be easily installed in their original positions.

REPLACEMENT

▶ See Figure 96

1. Disconnect the negative battery cable, followed by the positive cable.
2. Locate the burned out link.
3. If both ends of the link are ring terminal connectors which are easily accessed:

Fig. 96 Fusible links may be repaired by soldering a new link into the wire

a. Measure the installed length necessary for the new link.
b. Unbolt and remove the link and connector pieces.
c. Obtain a suitable length of link, then strip the insulation off the harness wire back ½ in. (12.7mm) to allow soldering of the new connectors.
d. Position the new connector around the new link and crimp it securely. Then, solder the connection, using rosin core solder and sufficient heat to guarantee a good connection. Repeat for the remaining connection.

➡Whenever splicing a new wire, always bond the splice with rosin core solder, then cover with electrical tape. Use acid core solder may cause corrosion.

4. If the ends of the connector are not easily access, repair the length in the vehicle:
a. Strip away the melted insulation and cut the burned link ends from the wire.
b. Strip the wire back ½ in. (12.7mm) to allow soldering of the new link.
c. Using a new fusible link of appropriate gauge and length, solder it into the circuit.
5. Tape all exposed wiring with electrical tape and seal with silicone or use a heat shrink tube, if available, to weatherproof the repair.
6. If removed from the vehicle, install the link and secure the connectors.
7. Reconnect the positive, followed by the negative battery cables.

Circuit Breakers

REPLACEMENT

Circuit breakers differ from fuses in that they are reusable. Circuit breakers open when the flow of current exceeds specified value and will close after a few seconds when current flow returns to normal. Some of the circuits protected by circuit breakers include electric windows and power accessories. Circuits breakers are used in these applications due to the fact that they must operated at times under prolonged high current flow due to demand even though there is not malfunction in the circuit.

There are 2 types of circuit breakers. The first type opens when high current flow is detected. A few seconds after the excessive current flow has been removed, the circuit breaker will close. If the high current flow is experienced again, the circuit will open again.

The second type is referred to as the Positive Temperature Coefficient (PTC) circuit breaker. When excessive current flow passes through the PTC circuit breaker, the circuit is not opened but its resistance increases. As the device heats ups with the increase in current flow, the resistance increases to the point where the circuit is effectively open. Unlike other circuit breakers, the PTC circuit breaker will not reset until the circuit is opened, removing voltage from the terminals. Once the voltage is removed, the circuit breaker will re-close within a few seconds.

Replace the circuit breaker by unplugging the old one and plugging in the new one. Confirm proper circuit operation.

Flashers

REPLACEMENT

The hazard flasher is located forward of the console on all J-Body vehicles. The turn signal flasher is located behind the instrument panel, on the left side of the steering column bracket. Replace the flasher by unplugging the old one and plugging in the new one. Confirm proper flasher operation.

1985-90 FUSE PANEL

#6 20A

Fuse	Amps	Protected Systems
1	3	Crank sensor
2	35	Power accessories
3	10	Radio, antenna, cruise control
4	5	Instrument lights
5	35	Power windows
6	20	Courtesy lights, cigarette lighter
7	25	Wiper
8	20	Gauges, chimes, indicators, defogger, trunk release
9	25	Ventilation system
10	20	Taillights
11	20	Foglights, radio (1990 sunbird)
12	20	Turn signals, back-up lights
13	20	Choke heater, coolant fan, alternator, foglights (1990 sunbird)
14	20	Stoplights, hazard flashers
15	10	ECM, fuel pump, oil pressure light
16	15	Computer command control module

91136C01

1991-94 FUSE PANEL (SUNBIRD)

Fuse	Amp	Protected Systems
1	10	Multiport fuel injection (1994), fuel pump
2	30 (circuit breaker)	Door locks, rear defogger
3	10	Radio, cruise power feed
4	5	Audible warning (1994), radio/audio system (1994), instrument panel lights, headlight remind (1991-92)
5	30 (circuit breaker)	Power window, daytime running, lights (Canada), convertible top (1994)
6	20	Courtesy lights, horn, cigarette lighter, trunk release, A/C, heater, power locks, rear compartment courtesy light, audible warning (1993-94), convertible top (1994), check oil light (1993), instrument panel (1994)
7	25	Windshield wiper/washer
8	10	Interior lights (1994), multiport fuel injection (1994), gauges/warning indicators, audible warning system, rear window defogger switch, automatic door locks (1994), A/C, heater, rear wiper/washer, seat belt warning, torque converter clutch, brake/transaxle shift interlock (1993-94), ABS (1994), multi-port fuel injection (1993)
9	25	Coolant fan (1994), starter and charging system (1994), heater & air conditioning, ABS, DRL module (1993-94)
10	15	Parking lights, side marker lights, license plate lights
11	10	Radio memory, digital clock
12	20	Exterior lights (1994), turn signal flasher, back-up lights
13	15	Foglights, headlights (1994), headlights with fog lights (1994), headlights with daytime running lights (1994)
14	15 (1992-94) — (1991)	Interior lights (1994), cigarette lighter, glove box light / Not used
15	20	Exterior lights (1994), stoplights, hazard flasher
16	10	ECM, MFI (1994)

91136C03

1991-94 FUSE PANEL (CAVALIER)

Fuse	Amp	Protected Systems
1	5	Instrument lights
2	10	ECM, fuel injectors (1993-94)
3	15 (1992-94) — (1991)	Cigarette lighter, glove box light (1993), interior lights (1994) / Not used (1991)
4	10	Radio power
5	10	Gauges, audio warning, cluster telltales, TCC, rear defogger relay, HVAL (1994), brake/transaxle shift interlock (1993-94), multi-port fuel injection (1993-94)
6	15	Headlights (1994), parking lights, turn lights
7	25	Coolant fan (1994), HVAC, heater & A/C power, ABS, DRL module (1993-94), starter & charging system (1994)
8	25	Wiper/washer
9	10	Fuel pump, injectors
10	10	Radio memory digital clock (1993-94)
11	20	Interior lights, glove box light horn, power locks, audible warning (1993-94), remote liftgate release (1993-94), check oil light (1993-94), instrument panel (1994), convertible top (1994)
12	30	Power window breaker, DRL breaker (Canada), convertible top (1994)
13	10	Cruise control
14	15	Exterior lights (1994), back-up lights, turn signal
15	20	Brake transaxle shift interlock (1994), stoplights, hazard flashers
16	20	Headlights (1994), flash-to-pass (not in Canada)
17	30 (circuit breaker)	Power locks & defogger circuit breaker
18	20 (circuit breaker)	Daytime running lights (1994), headlight circuit breaker
19	10 (1994)	Automatic door locks (1994)

91136C02

INDEX OF WIRING DIAGRAMS

DIAGRAM 1   Sample Diagram: How To Read & Interpret Wiring Diagrams
DIAGRAM 2   Wiring Diagram Symbols
DIAGRAM 3   1982-86 1.8L (VIN O) J-Body Engine Schematic
DIAGRAM 4   1982 2.0L (VIN B) J-Body Engine Schematic
DIAGRAM 5   1983 2.0L (VIN P) J-Body Wirinig Schematic
DIAGRAM 6   1984 1.8L (VIN J) J-Body Engine Schematic
DIAGRAM 7   1984-86 2.0L (VIN P) J-Body Engine Schematic
DIAGRAM 8   1985-86 1.8L (VIN J) J-Body Engine Schematic
DIAGRAM 9   1985-86 2.8L (VIN W) J-Body Engine Schematic
DIAGRAM 10   1987 2.0L (VIN 1) J-Body Engine Schematic
DIAGRAM 11   1987 2.0L (VIN K) J-Body Engine Schematic
DIAGRAM 12   1987 2.8L (VIN W) J-Body Engine Schematic
DIAGRAM 13   1987-89 2.0L (VIN M) J-Body Engine Schematic
DIAGRAM 14   1988-89 2.0L (VIN 1) J-Body Engine Schematic
DIAGRAM 15   1988-89 2.8L (VIN W) J-Body Engine Schematic
DIAGRAM 16   1988-89 2.0L (VIN K) J-Body Engine Schematic
DIAGRAM 17   1990 2.0L (VIN M) J-Body Engine Schematic
DIAGRAM 18   1990-91 2.0L (VIN K) J-Body Engine Schematic
DIAGRAM 19   1990-91 2.2L (VIN G) J-Body Engine Schematic
DIAGRAM 20   1992-94 2.0L (VIN H) J-Body Engine Schematic
DIAGRAM 21   1992-94 2.2L (VIN 4) J-Body Engine Schematic
DIAGRAM 22   1990-94 3.1L (VIN T) J-Body Engine Schematic
DIAGRAM 23   1982 J-Body Wiring Schematics
DIAGRAM 24   1982-83 J-body Wiring Schematics
DIAGRAM 25   1983 J-Body Wiring Schematics
DIAGRAM 26   1984 J-Body Wiring Schematics
DIAGRAM 27   1984-86 J-Body Wiring Schematics
DIAGRAM 28   1985-86 J-Body Wiring Schematics
DIAGRAM 29   1987-89 J-Body Wiring Schematics
DIAGRAM 30   1987-89 J-Body Wiring Schematics
DIAGRAM 31   1990-91 J-Body Wiring Schematics
DIAGRAM 32   1990-94 J-Body Wiring Schematics
DIAGRAM 33   1992-94 J-Body Wiring Schematics

91136W01

WIRING DIAGRAM SYMBOLS

IGNITION SWITCH
START · ACCY
RUN · LOCK
· OFF

KNOCK SENSOR

SOLENOID

SOLENOID

DIODE

CAPACITOR

SPLICES

GROUND

FUSE LINK

FUSE

CIRCUIT BREAKER

RELAY

RELAY

BATTERY

3 POSITION SWITCH

NORMALLY OPEN SWITCH

NORMALLY CLOSED SWITCH

NORMALLY CLOSED SWITCH

NORMALLY OPEN SWITCH

RESISTOR

RESISTOR

VARIABLE RESISTOR

VARIABLE RESISTOR

BULB

BULB

LED

MOTOR

CHOICE BRACKET

SPEED SENSOR

OXYGEN SENSOR

OXYGEN SENSOR

HEATING ELEMENT

HEATING ELEMENT

DIAGRAM 2

TCCA6W02V1

SAMPLE DIAGRAM: HOW TO READ & INTERPRET WIRING DIAGRAMS

WIRE COLOR ABBREVIATIONS

BLACK	B OR BLK
BROWN	BR OR BRN
RED	R OR RED
ORANGE	O OR ORG
YELLOW	Y OR YEL
GRAY	GY OR GRY
BLUE	BL OR BLU
VIOLET	V OR VIO
TAN	T OR TAN

PINK	PK OR PNK
PURPLE	P OR PPL
GREEN	G OR GRN
WHITE	W OR WHT
LIGHT BLUE	LBL OR LT BLU
LIGHT GREEN	LG OR LT GRN
DARK GREEN	DG OR DK GRN
DARK BLUE	DBL OR DK BLU
NO COLOR AVAILABLE	NCA

SPLICE or CONNECTOR

COMPONENT NAMES

MODEL OPTION BRACKET

CASE GROUND

CAPACITOR

POWER CONDITION

HOT AT ALL TIMES
FUSE S 30A

HOT IN RUN OR START
FUSE R 15A

HOT AT ALL TIMES
FUSE E 15A

IGNITION COIL

SPARK PLUGS

SPARK PLUGS

SPARK PLUGS

IGNITION CONTROL MODULE

SPARK OUTPUT CHECK CONN

ELECTRONIC AUTOMATIC TRANS AXLE (XA4S)

POWERTRAIN CONTROL MODULE

DATA LINK CONNECTOR

TO MIL

FUEL INJ.

PCM POWER RELAY

MASS AIR FLOW SENSOR

TO COOLING FANS

TO INSTRUMENT CLUSTER
DIGITAL ONLY

OCTANE ADJUST PLUG

TO TRANS RANGE SENSOR

TO FUEL PUMP RELAY

ENGINE COOLANT SENSOR

EVAP EMISSIONS CANISTER PURGE VALVE

IDLE AIR CONTROL VALVE

TERMINAL NUMBERS

HEATED OXYGEN SENSOR

HEATED OXYGEN SENSOR

OTHER SYSTEM REFERENCE

A/C AND HEATING SYSTEMS

TURBINE SHAFT SPEED SENSOR

GROUND

WIRE COLOR

DIAGRAM 1

TCCA6W01

1982 2.0L (VIN B) J-BODY ENGINE SCHEMATIC

DIAGRAM 4

1982-86 1.8L (VIN O) J-BODY ENGINE SCHEMATIC

DIAGRAM 3

1984 1.8L (VIN J) J-BODY ENGINE SCHEMATIC

1983 2.0L (VIN P) J-BODY ENGINE SCHEMATIC

DIAGRAM 6

DIAGRAM 5

1985-86 1.8L (VIN J) J-BODY ENGINE SCHEMATIC

DIAGRAM 8

1984-86 2.0L (VIN P) J-BODY ENGINE SCHEMATIC

DIAGRAM 7

1987 2.0L (VIN 1) J-BODY ENGINE SCHEMATIC

1985-86 2.8L (VIN W) J-BODY ENGINE SCHEMATIC

DIAGRAM 10

DIAGRAM 9

1987 2.8L (VIN W) J-BODY ENGINE SCHEMATIC

DIAGRAM 12

1987 2.0L (VIN K) J-BODY ENGINE SCHEMATIC

DIAGRAM 11

1988-89 2.0L (VIN 1) J-BODY ENGINE SCHEMATIC

1987-89 2.0L (VIN M) J-BODY ENGINE SCHEMATIC

DIAGRAM 14

DIAGRAM 13

1990-91 2.0L (VIN K) J-BODY ENGINE SCHEMATIC

DIAGRAM 18

1990 2.0L (VIN M) J-BODY ENGINE SCHEMATIC

DIAGRAM 17

1992-94 2.0L (VIN H) J-BODY ENGINE SCHEMATIC

DIAGRAM 20

1990-91 2.2L (VIN G) J-BODY ENGINE SCHEMATIC

DIAGRAM 19

1990-94 3.1L (VIN T) J-BODY ENGINE SCHEMATIC

DIAGRAM 22

1992-94 2.2L (VIN 4) J-BODY ENGINE SCHEMATIC

DIAGRAM 21

1982-83 J-BODY WIRING SCHEMATICS

DIAGRAM 24

1982 J-BODY WIRING SCHEMATICS

DIAGRAM 23

1984 J-BODY WIRING SCHEMATICS

1983 J-BODY WIRING SCHEMATICS

DIAGRAM 26

DIAGRAM 25

1985-86 J-BODY WIRING SCHEMATICS

DIAGRAM 28

1984-86 J-BODY WIRING SCHEMATICS

DIAGRAM 27

1987-89 J-BODY WIRING SCHEMATICS

DIAGRAM 30

1987-89 J-BODY WIRING SCHEMATICS

DIAGRAM 29

1990-94 J-BODY WIRING SCHEMATICS

DIAGRAM 32

1990-91 J-BODY WIRING SCHEMATICS

DIAGRAM 31

1992-94 J-BODY WIRING SCHEMATICS

DIAGRAM 33

91136T31

MANUAL TRANSAXLE 7-2
UNDERSTANDING THE MANUAL
 TRANSAXLE 7-2
ADJUSTMENTS 7-2
  LINKAGE 7-2
CLUTCH SWITCH 7-2
  REMOVAL & INSTALLATION 7-2
BACK-UP LIGHT SWITCH 7-3
  REMOVAL & INSTALLATION 7-3
TRANSAXLE 7-4
  REMOVAL & INSTALLATION 7-4
INTERMEDIATE SHAFT 7-8
  REMOVAL & INSTALLATION 7-8
HALFSHAFTS 7-10
  REMOVAL & INSTALLATION 7-10
  CV-JOINT OVERHAUL 7-12
CLUTCH 7-23
UNDERSTANDING THE CLUTCH 7-23
DRIVEN DISC AND PRESSURE
 PLATE/CLUTCH COVER AND
 DISC 7-23
  REMOVAL & INSTALLATION 7-23
  ADJUSTMENTS 7-24
CLUTCH HYDRAULIC SYSTEM 7-24
  REMOVAL & INSTALLATION 7-24
CLUTCH MASTER CYLINDER 7-25
  REMOVAL & INSTALLATION 7-25
ACTUATOR (SLAVE) CYLINDER 7-26
  REMOVAL & INSTALLATION 7-26
  HYDRAULIC SYSTEM
   BLEEDING 7-26
AUTOMATIC TRANSAXLE 7-27
UNDERSTANDING THE AUTOMATIC
 TRANSAXLE 7-27
  TORQUE CONVERTER 7-27
  PLANETARY GEARBOX 7-27
  SERVOS & ACCUMULATORS 7-27
  HYDRAULIC CONTROL
   SYSTEM 7-28
FLUID PAN AND FILTER 7-28
NEUTRAL START/BACK-UP LIGHT
 SWITCH 7-28
  REMOVAL & INSTALLATION 7-28
AUTOMATIC TRANSAXLE
 ASSEMBLY 7-29
  REMOVAL & INSTALLATION 7-29
  ADJUSTMENTS 7-32
HALFSHAFTS 7-32

7

DRIVE TRAIN

MANUAL TRANSAXLE 7-2
CLUTCH 7-23
AUTOMATIC TRANSAXLE 7-27

MANUAL TRANSAXLE

Understanding the Manual Transaxle

Because of the way an internal combustion engine breathes, it can produce torque, or twisting force, only within a narrow speed range. Most modern, overhead valve pushrod engines must turn at about 2500 rpm to produce their peak torque. By 4500 rpm they are producing so little torque that continued increases in engine speed produce no power increases. The torque peak on overhead camshaft engines is generally much higher, but much narrower.

The manual transaxle and clutch are employed to vary the relationship between engine speed and the speed of the wheels so that adequate engine power can be produced under all circumstances. The clutch allows engine torque to be applied to the transaxle input shaft gradually, due to mechanical slippage. Consequently, the vehicle may be started smoothly from a full stop. The transaxle changes the ratio between the rotating speeds of the engine and the wheels by the use of gears. The gear ratios allow full engine power to be applied to the wheels during acceleration at low speeds and at highway/passing speeds.

In a front wheel drive transaxle, power is usually transmitted from the input shaft to a mainshaft or output shaft located slightly beneath and to the side of the input shaft. The gears of the mainshaft mesh with gears on the input shaft, allowing power to be carried from one to the other. All forward gears are in constant mesh and are free from rotating with the shaft unless the synchronizer and clutch is engaged. Shifting from one gear to the next causes one of the gears to be freed from rotating with the shaft and locks another to it. Gears are locked and unlocked by internal dog clutches which slide between the center of the gear and the shaft. The forward gears employ synchronizers; friction members which smoothly bring gear and shaft to the same speed before the toothed dog clutches are engaged.

Adjustments

LINKAGE

No adjustments are possible on the 1988–94 manual transaxle shifting cables or linkage. If the transaxle is not engaging completely, check for stretched cables, broken shifter components or a faulty transaxle.

4-Speed

1982–87 VEHICLES

▶ See Figure 1

1. Disconnect the negative battery cable.
2. Place the transaxle in 1st gear, then loosen the shift cable attaching nuts **E** at the transaxle lever **D** and **F**.
3. Remove the console trim plate and remove the shifter boot and retainer.
4. With the shift lever in the 1st gear position (pulled to the left and held

against the stop) insert a yoke clip to hold the lever hard against the reverse lockout stop as shown in view **D**. Install a No. 22 (⁵⁄₃₂ in.) drill bit into the alignment hole at the side of the shifter assembly as shown in view **C**.
5. Remove the lash from the transaxle by rotating the upright select lever (lever D) while tightening the cable attaching pin nut **E**.
6. Tighten nut **E** on letter **F**.
7. Remove the drill bit and yoke at the shifter assembly, install the shifter boot and retainer and connect the negative battery cable.
8. Connect the negative battery cable.
9. Install the shifter boot and trim plate.
10. Road test the vehicle to check for good gate feel during shifting. Fine tune the adjustment as necessary.

5-Speed

1983–85 VEHICLES

▶ See Figure 2

1. Disconnect the negative battery cable.
2. Place the transaxle in 3rd gear. Remove the lock pin **H** and reinstall with the tapered end down. This will lock the transaxle in 3rd gear.
3. Loosen the shift cable attaching nuts **E** at the transaxle lever **G** and **F**.
4. Remove the console trim plate and remove the shifter boot. Remove the console.
5. Install a No. 22 (⁵⁄₃₂ in.) drill bit into the alignment hole at the side of the shifter assembly as shown in view **A**.
6. Align the hole in select lever (view B) with the slot in the shifter plate and install a ³⁄₁₆ in. drill bit.
7. Tighten nut **E** at levers **G** and **F**.
8. Remove the drill bits from the alignment holes at the shifter. Remove lockpin **H**.
9. Install the console, shifter boot and retainer and connect the negative battery cable.
10. Road test the vehicle to check for good gate feel during shifting. Fine tune the adjustment as necessary.

Fig. 2 Five speed manual transaxle shift cable adjustment—1983–85 vehicles

Clutch Switch

REMOVAL & INSTALLATION

▶ See Figure 3

1. Disconnect the negative battery cable.
2. Detach the instrument panel harness connector from the switch.
3. Unfasten the nuts retaining the switch to the harness bracket, then remove the switch.

Fig. 1 Four speed manual transaxle shift cable adjustment—1982–87 vehicles

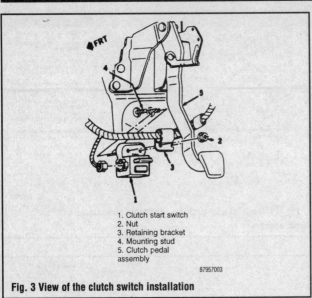

1. Clutch start switch
2. Nut
3. Retaining bracket
4. Mounting stud
5. Clutch pedal assembly

87957003

Fig. 3 View of the clutch switch installation

4. Installation is the reverse of the removal. Verify proper operation of the switch.

Back-up Light Switch

REMOVAL & INSTALLATION

1982–87 Vehicles

▶ See Figure 4

1. Disconnect the negative battery cable.
2. Remove the console, then replace the switch at the side of the shifter.
3. Installation is the reverse of the removal procedure.

1988–94 Vehicles

▶ See Figures 5, 6 and 7

1. Disconnect the negative battery cable.
2. Detach the back-up lamp connector.
3. Unscrew then remove the back-up lamp switch assembly.

1. Detent plate
2. Tang hole
3. Tang slot
4. "Neutral" notch
5. R
6. P
7. Transmission control shifter
8. Neutral start and back-up lamp switch
9. Carrier tang
10. Park brake switch
11. Transmission shifter
12. Retaining clip
13. Back-up lamp switch

Fig. 4 Back-up lamp switch removal and installation—1982–87 vehicles

87957004

1. Back-up switch assembly
2. Transaxle assembly

87957005

Fig. 5 Back-up lamp switch installation— HM-282 and 5TM40 5-speed manual transaxles

1. Back-up switch assembly
2. Transaxle assembly

87957006

Fig. 6 Back-up lamp switch location— Isuzu 5-speed manual transaxle

87957007

Fig. 7 Removal and installation of the back-up lamp switch—MK7/MT5 5-speed manual transaxles

To install:

4. Install the switch with pipe sealant and tighten to 80–84 inch lbs. (9–9.4 Nm).

5. Attach the switch electrical connector.

6. Connect the negative battery cable.

Transaxle

REMOVAL & INSTALLATION

1982–88 Vehicles

▶ **See Figures 8, 9, 10 and 11**

➡On 1982–84 models, whenever the transaxle mount is removed, the alignment bolt M6 x 1 x 65 must be installed in the right front engine mount to prevent powertrain misalignment

Fig. 8 Install a suitable engine support tool to take the pressure off the motor mounts

1. Thread onto strut attaching bolts above nuts - 3 per side

87957008

Fig. 9 View of the transaxle mounting points—1982–85 vehicles equipped with a 4-speed manual transaxle

87957009

FRONT SUSPENSION SUPPORT ATTACHING BOLT/SCREW SEQUENCE

1. INSTALL LOOSELY, THE CENTER SCREW INTO HOLE Ⓐ.
2. INSTALL LOOSELY, THE TIE BAR SCREW INTO THE SMALL SLOTTED OUTBOARD HOLE.
3. INSTALL AND TORQUE BOTH BOLTS IN THE REAR HOLES.
4. INSTALL AND TORQUE 2ND CENTER HOLE Ⓒ BOLT/SCREW.
5. TORQUE CENTER HOLE Ⓐ BOLT.
6. INSTALL OTHER TIE BAR BOLT (FRONT HOLE Ⓔ) AND TORQUE.
7. TORQUE 2ND BOLT/SCREW IN THE (FRONT HOLE Ⓑ).

87957010

Fig. 10 The front suspension support must be attached in this sequence

Fig. 11 Securing the front engine mount on 1982–84 vehicles

87957011

1. Disconnect the negative battery cable.

2. Install tool J-28467-A or equivalent, an engine holding bar/support fixture, so that one end is supported on the cowl tray over the wiper motor and the other end rests on the radiator support. Use padding and be careful not to damage the paint or body work with the bar. Attach a lifting hook to the engine lift ring and to the bar and raise the engine enough to take the pressure off the motor mounts.

➡If a lifting bar and hook is not available, a chain hoist can be used, however, during the procedure the vehicle must be raised, at which time the chain hoist must be adjusted to keep tension on the engine/transaxle assembly.

3. Remove the heater hose clamp at the transaxle mount bracket. On 4-cylinder engines, detach the electrical connector and remove the horn assembly.

4. Unfasten the transaxle mount attaching bolts. Discard the bolts attaching the mount to the side frame. Note that new bolts MUST be used during installation.

5. On 1982–84 models, disconnect the clutch cable from the clutch release lever. On 1985–87 models, disconnect the clutch slave cylinder from the transaxle support bracket and lay aside. Remove the transaxle mount bracket attaching bolts and nuts.

6. On 6-cylinder engines remove the following:

a. Remove the air intake duct from the air cleaner.

b. Unfasten the left fender brace.

c. Detach the M.A.T. sensor lead at the air cleaner.

d. Disconnect the mass air flow sensor lead.

e. Remove the PCV pipe retaining clamp from the air intake duct.

f. Unfasten the clamp retaining the air intake duct to the throttle body.

g. Remove the mass air flow sensor mounting bolt.

h. Unfasten the air cleaner bracket mounting bolts at the battery tray.

i. Remove the air cleaner, mass air flow sensor and air intake duct as an assembly.

j. Remove the heat shield at the crossover pipe and remove the crossover pipe.

7. Disconnect the shift cables and retaining clips at the transaxle. Detach the ground cables at the transaxle mounting stud.

8. Unfasten the four upper transaxle-to-engine mounting bolts.

9. Raise the and safely support vehicle and support it on stands. Remove the left front wheel and tire assembly.

10. Remove the left front inner splash shield. Remove the transaxle strut and bracket.

11. Unfasten the clutch housing cover bolts.

12. Detach the speedometer cable at the transaxle.

13. Disconnect the stabilizer bar at the left suspension support and control arm.

14. Disconnect the ball joint from the steering knuckle.

15. Unfasten the left suspension support attaching bolts and remove the support and control arm as an assembly.

16. Install boot protectors and disengage the drive axles at the transaxle. Remove the left side shaft from the transaxle.

17. Position a jack under the transaxle case, unfasten the lower two transaxle-to-engine mounting bolts and remove the transaxle by sliding it towards the driver's side, away from the engine. Carefully lower the jack, guiding the right shaft out the transaxle.

To install:

18. When installing the transaxle, guide the right drive axle into its bore as the transaxle is being raised. The right drive axle CANNOT be readily installed after the transaxle is connected to the engine.

19. Tighten the fasteners as follows:

a. Tighten the transaxle-to-engine mounting bolts to 55 ft. lbs. (75 Nm).

b. Tighten the suspension support-to-body attaching bolts to 59 ft. lbs. (80 Nm) on 1985–87 models and 65–67 ft. lbs. (88–91 Nm) on all other years.

c. Tighten the clutch housing cover bolts to 10 ft. lbs. (14 Nm).

d. Using new bolts, install and tighten the transaxle mount-to-side frame to 40 ft. lbs. (54 Nm). When installing the bolts attaching the mount-to-transaxle bracket on the 1982–84 models, check the alignment bolt at the engine mount. If excessive effort is required to remove the alignment bolt, realign the powertrain components and tighten the bolts to 40 ft. lbs. (54 Nm), and then remove the alignment bolt.

1989–91 Vehicles

EXCEPT ISUZU TRANSAXLE

▶ See Figures 12 and 13

1. Disconnect the negative battery cable.
2. Install an engine holding support fixture (bar), J–28467–A or equivalent.

➡ **If a lifting bar and hook is not available, a chain hoist can be used, however, during the procedure the vehicle must be raised, at which time the chain hoist must be adjusted to keep tension on the engine/transaxle assembly.**

3. Remove the left sound insulator.
4. Disconnect the clutch master cylinder pushrod from the clutch pedal.
5. Remove the air cleaner and air intake duct assembly.
6. Remove the clutch actuator cylinder from the transaxle support bracket and lay it aside.
7. Remove the transaxle mount through-bolt.
8. Raise and support the vehicle safely.
9. Remove the exhaust crossover bolts at the right hand manifold.
10. Carefully lower the vehicle.
11. Disconnect the transaxle mount bracket.
12. Detach the shift cables and linkage.
13. Remove the transaxle vent tube.
14. Unfasten the upper transaxle to engine bolts.
15. Raise and support the vehicle safely.
16. Remove the left front tire and wheel assembly.
17. Remove the left front inner splash shield.
18. Disconnect the transaxle strut and bracket.
19. Drain the transaxle.

1. Thread onto strut attaching bolts, above nuts - 3 per side.

Fig. 12 Installing a suitable engine support fixture—3.1L engine shown

VIEW A

1. Bolts
2. Transaxle assembly
3. Stud
4. Bracket
5. Engine assembly

Fig. 13 View of the engine-to-transaxle mounting—5TM40 manual transaxle shown

20. Unfasten the clutch housing cover bolts.

21. Detach the speedometer cable.

22. Disconnect the stabilizer shaft at the left suspension support and control arm.

23. Remove the left suspension support attaching bolts and swing the suspension support aside.

24. Install drive axle boot protector J–34754 or equivalent and remove the left drive axle from the transaxle.

25. Attach the transaxle case to a jack.

26. Unfasten the remaining transaxle to engine bolts.

27. Remove the transaxle by sliding it away from the engine and carefully lowering the jack while guiding the intermediate shaft out of the transaxle.

➡ **The engine may need to be lowered for transaxle-to-body clearance.**

To install:

28. Reposition the transaxle and guide the intermediate shaft into transaxle.

➡ **The intermediate shaft cannot be easily installed after the transaxle is connected to the engine.**

29. Install the transaxle to engine mounting bolts to 55 ft. lbs (75 Nm).

30. Install the left drive axle into its bore at the transaxle and seat the driveaxle at the transaxle.

31. Remove the drive axle boot protector.
32. Fasten the suspension support to body bolts and tighten to 65 ft. lbs. (88 Nm).
33. Install the stabilizer shaft at the left suspension support and control arm.
34. Attach the speedometer cable.
35. Install the clutch/flywheel housing cover bolts and tighten to 115 inch lbs. (13 Nm).
36. Fasten the strut bracket to the transaxle.
37. Install the strut.
38. Attach the inner splash shield.
39. Install the wheel and tire assembly and tighten the wheel nuts to 100 ft. lbs. (136 Nm).
40. Carefully lower the vehicle.
41. Install the upper engine to transaxle bolts and tighten to 55 ft. lbs. (75 Nm).
42. Install the transaxle vent tube.
43. Attach the shift cables.
44. Install the transaxle mount bracket.
45. Fasten the left exhaust crossover bolts.
46. Raise and support the vehicle safely.
47. Install the exhaust crossover bolts at the right hand manifold.
48. Carefully lower the vehicle.
49. Install the transaxle mount through-bolt.
50. Install the clutch actuator cylinder to the transaxle support bracket.
51. Install the air cleaner and air intake duct assembly.
52. Remove the engine holding support fixture (bar), J–28467–A or equivalent.
53. Connect the clutch master cylinder pushrod to the clutch pedal.
54. Install the left sound insulator.
55. Check the transaxle fluid level and add as necessary.
56. Connect the negative battery cable.

ISUZU TRANSAXLE

♦ See Figures 14 and 15

1. Disconnect the negative battery cable.
2. Install an engine holding support fixture (bar), J–28467–A or equivalent and raise the engine enough to take the pressure off the motor mounts.
3. Remove the left sound insulator.
4. Disconnect the clutch master cylinder pushrod from the clutch pedal.
5. Remove the clutch actuator cylinder from the transaxle support bracket and lay it aside.
6. Disconnect the wire harness at the mount bracket.
7. Unfasten the transaxle mount attaching bolts.
8. Remove the transaxle mount bracket attaching bolts and nuts.
9. Remove the shift cables and retaining clamp at the transaxle.
10. Detach the ground cables at the transaxle mounting studs.
11. Detach the back-up switch connector.
12. Raise and support the vehicle safely.
13. Drain the transaxle.
14. Remove the left front wheel assembly.
15. Detach the left front inner splash shield.
16. Disconnect the transaxle strut and bracket.
17. Remove the clutch housing cover bolts.

1. Thread onto strut attaching bolts above nuts - 3 per side

87957015

Fig. 14 Installing the engine support tool on the 1991 2.0L (VIN K) engine

VIEW A

1. Bolt
2. Transaxle assembly
3. Stud
4. Engine assembly

87957016

Fig. 15 Isuzu transaxle mounting—1991 2.0L (VIN K) engine shown

18. Detach the Vehicle Speed Sensor (VSS) at the transaxle.
19. Disconnect the stabilizer shaft at the left suspension support and control arm.
20. Remove the left suspension support attaching bolts and swing the suspension support aside.
21. Install drive axle boot protector J–34754 or equivalent, disconnect the drive axles and remove the left shaft from the transaxle.
22. Attach the transaxle case to a jack.
23. Remove the transaxle to engine bolts.
24. Remove the transaxle by sliding it away from the engine and carefully lowering the jack while guiding the right drive axle out of the transaxle.

To install:

25. Reposition the transaxle and guide the right drive axle into its bore as the transaxle is being raised.

➡**The right drive axle cannot be easily installed after the transaxle is connected to the engine.**

26. Install the transaxle to engine mounting bolts to 55 ft. lbs (75 Nm).
27. Install the left drive axle into its bore at the transaxle and seat both drive axles at the transaxle.
28. Remove the drive axle boot protector.
29. Install the suspension support to body bolts and tighten to 65 ft. lbs. (88 Nm).
30. Install the stabilizer shaft at the suspension support and control arm.
31. Install the vehicle speed sensor at the transaxle.
32. Install the flywheel/clutch housing cover bolts and tighten to 115 inch lbs. (13 Nm).
33. Install the strut bracket to the transaxle.
34. Install the strut.
35. Install the inner splash shield.
36. Install the wheel and tighten the wheel nuts to 100 ft. lbs. (140 Nm).
37. Lower the vehicle.
38. Install the ground cables at the transaxle mounting studs.
39. Install the back-up switch connector.
40. Install the actuator cylinder to the transaxle bracket aligning the pushrod into the pocket of the clutch release lever and install the retaining nuts and tighten evenly to prevent damage to the cylinder.
41. Install the transaxle mount bracket.
42. Install the transaxle mount to side frame and install the bolts.
43. Install the wiring harness at the transaxle mount bracket.
44. Install the bolt attaching the mount to the transaxle bracket and tighten to 88 ft. lbs. (120 Nm).
45. Remove the engine holding support fixture (bar), J–28467–A or equivalent.
46. Install the shift cables.
47. Check the transaxle fluid level and add as necessary.
48. Connect the negative battery cable.

1992–94 Vehicles

NVG-T550 TRANSAXLES

▶ See Figures 16 and 17

1. Disconnect the negative battery cable.
2. Remove the left sound insulator.
3. Disconnect the clutch master cylinder pushrod from the clutch pedal.
4. Remove the air cleaner assembly and the bracket.
5. Unfasten the exhaust crossover pipe.
6. Disconnect the hydraulic line from the clutch slave cylinder.
7. Remove the transaxle shift cables by snapping them off.
8. Remove the shift cable mount bracket.
9. Detach the back-up light switch connector.
10. Disconnect the transaxle vent tube from the transaxle.
11. Unfasten the top two transaxle-to-engine bolts.
12. Install engine support fixture J 28467-A, or equivalent, and raise the engine enough to remove the weight from the engine mounts.
13. Raise and support the vehicle safely, then drain the transaxle fluid.
14. Remove the front tire and wheel assemblies.
15. Remove the left side splash shield.
16. Unfasten the front air deflector.
17. Remove the right side splash shield.
18. Detach the ABS Wheel Speed Sensor (WSS) connectors from the WSS and harness from the left side suspension support.
19. Remove the left and right ball joint nuts.
20. Unfasten the left stabilizer link.
21. Remove the transaxle strut bracket from the transaxle bolts.
22. Remove the stabilizer bat and left side U-bolt.

1. A universal support fixture
2. Thread onto strut attaching bolts above nuts, 2 per side

87957018

Fig. 16 Installation of the engine support fixture on the 3.1L engine

1. Bolts 55 ft. lbs. (75 nm)
2. Transaxle assembly
3. Stud - 55 ft. lbs. (75 nm)
4. Bracket
5. Engine assembly

87957019

Fig. 17 Engine-to-transaxle mounting—NVG-550 manual transaxle shown

23. Unfasten the left suspension support attaching bolts.
24. Remove the intermediate shaft and housing.
25. Remove the left and drive drive axles (halfshafts), as outlined later in this section.
26. Unfasten the rear engine mount through-bolts.
27. Remove the rear engine mount bracket.
28. Detach the following electrical connectors:
- Vehicle Speed Sensor (VSS)
- Back-up light switch
29. Remove the starter motor.
30. Unfasten and remove the flywheel cover.
31. Lower the engine with engine support fixture J-28476-A, or equivalent, to ease removal of the transaxle, but be sure to count the number of turns for installation.
32. Detach the ground wires from the lower engine-to-transaxle bolts.
33. Install a transaxle jack, then unfasten the lower engine-to-transaxle bolts. Remove the transaxle.

To install:

34. Reposition the transaxle and install the lower transaxle bolts. tighten the bolts to 55 ft. lbs. (75 Nm).
35. Attach the ground wires to the lower engine-to-transaxle bolts.
36. Install the flywheel cover, then tighten the retaining bolts to 89 inch lbs. (10 Nm).
37. Install the starter motor.
38. Raise the engine with the support fixture to install the powertrain mounts.
39. Install the rear engine mount bracket, then install the rear engine mount and through-bolts.
40. Attach the VSS and back-up light switch electrical connectors.
41. Install the intermediate shaft and housing.
42. Fasten the right and left drive axles to the transaxle.
43. Install the left suspension support and attaching bolts.
44. Fasten the transaxle strut bracket and the bolt to the transaxle. Tighten the strut bracket bolts to 40 ft. lbs. (54 Nm).
45. Install the left side stabilizer U-bolt.
46. Install both ball joints and cotter pins.
47. Fasten the stabilizer link.
48. Attach the left side ABS WSS harness and attach both ABS wheel speed sensor connectors.
49. Fasten the right side splash shield, front air deflector and the left side splash shield.
50. Install both front wheel and tire assemblies.
51. Carefully lower the vehicle.
52. Install the upper transaxle mount and bracket, as an assembly. Tighten the mount nuts to 23 ft. lbs. (31 Nm) and the bolts to 38 ft. lbs. (52 Nm).
53. Remove the engine support fixture.
54. Attach the fluid line to the clutch slave cylinder.
55. Install the top two upper transaxle bolt, then tighten to 55 ft. lbs. (75 Nm).
56. Fasten the exhaust crossover pipe.
57. Attach the transaxle vent tube to the transaxle.
58. Fasten the back-up light switch and VSS electrical connectors.
59. Install the transaxle shift cable bracket, then snap on the shift cables.
60. Fasten the exhaust crossover pipe.
61. Install the air cleaner bracket and assembly.
62. Install the left sound insulator, then connect the clutch master cylinder pushrod to the clutch pedal.
63. Connect the negative battery cable.
64. Fill the transaxle with GM fluid 123455349, or equivalent.

ISUZU TRANSAXLE

▶ See Figures 18 and 19

1. Disconnect the negative battery cable.
2. Install an engine holding support fixture (bar), J–28467–A or equivalent and raise the engine enough to take the pressure off the motor mounts.
3. Remove the left sound insulator.
4. Disconnect the clutch master cylinder pushrod from the clutch pedal.
5. Remove the clutch actuator cylinder from the transaxle support bracket and lay it aside.
6. Disconnect the wire harness at the mount bracket.

1. A universal support fixture
2. Thread onto strut attaching bolts above nuts. 2 per side

87957021

Fig. 18 Installation of the engine support fixture—1994 2.0L engine shown

VIEW A

1. Bolt
2. Transaxle assembly
3. Stud
4. Engine assembly

87957023

Fig. 19 Isuzu transaxle mounting—1994 2.0L engine shown

7. Unfasten the transaxle mount attaching bolts.
8. Remove the transaxle mount bracket attaching bolts and nuts.
9. Remove the shift cables and retaining clamp at the transaxle.
10. Detach the ground cables at the transaxle mounting studs.
11. Detach the back-up switch connector.
12. Raise and support the vehicle safely.
13. Drain the transaxle.
14. Remove the left front wheel assembly.
15. Detach the left front inner splash shield.
16. Remove the transaxle front strut and bracket.
17. Unfasten the clutch housing cover bolts.
18. Detach the Vehicle Speed Sensor (VSS) electrical connector at the transaxle.
19. Unfasten the left and right drive axle nuts and the left and right ball joint nuts.
20. Unfasten the left and right stabilizer links.
21. Remove the drive axles (halfshafts).
22. Unfasten the left side U-bolt and remove it from the stabilizer bar.
23. Remove the left suspension support attaching bolts and swing the suspension support aside.
24. Attach the transaxle case to a suitable jack.
25. Unfasten the transaxle-to-engine bolts.
26. Remove the transaxle by sliding it away from the engine and carefully lowering the jack.
To install:
27. Reposition the transaxle, then install the transaxle to engine mounting bolts and tighten to 55 ft. lbs (75 Nm).
28. Install the flywheel housing cover, then tighten the retaining bolts to 89 inch lbs. (10 Nm).

29. Install the left suspension support and secure with the attaching bolts.
30. Fasten the left U-bolt to the stabilizer bar.
31. Install the left and right drive axles (halfshafts). Fasten the left and right drive axle, ball joint and stabilizer link nuts.
32. Attach the vehicle speed sensor connector at the transaxle.
33. Instal the front strut bracket to the transaxle. Tighten the bracket bolts to 38 ft. lbs. (52 Nm). Install the front strut. Tighten the mounting bolt and nut to 38 ft. lbs. (52 Nm).
34. Install the inner splash shield.
35. Install the wheel and tire assembly, then tighten the wheel nuts to 100 ft. lbs. (136 Nm).
36. Carefully lower the vehicle.
37. Fasten the ground cables at the transaxle mounting studs.
38. Attach the back-up switch connector.
39. Install the actuator cylinder to the transaxle bracket aligning the pushrod into the pocket of the clutch release lever and install the retaining nuts and tighten evenly to prevent damage to the cylinder.
40. Fasten the transaxle mount bracket. Tighten the bracket-to-transaxle mounting bolts to 55 ft. lbs. (75 Nm). Tighten the bracket-to-clutch cylinder support bolts to 38 ft. lbs. (52 Nm).
41. Install the transaxle mount-to-side frame and install the bolts. Tighten the mount nuts to 23 ft. lbs. (31 Nm) and the bolt to 38 ft. lbs. (52 Nm).
42. Attach the wiring harness at the transaxle mount bracket.
43. Install the bolt attaching the mount to the transaxle bracket and tighten to 83 ft. lbs. (113 Nm).
44. Remove the engine holding support fixture (bar), J–28467–A or equivalent.
45. Install the shift cables, clamp and nut. Tighten the nut to 89 inch lbs. (10 Nm).
46. Attach the clutch pushrod to the clutch pedal.
47. Install the left sound insulator.
48. Connect the negative battery cable.
49. Fill the transaxle with GM fluid 123455349, or equivalent.

Intermediate shaft

REMOVAL & INSTALLATION

2.8L and 3.1L Engines

1987 VEHICLES

♦ **See Figure 20**

1. Install engine support bar J–28467.
2. Raise and safely support the vehicle.
3. Remove the wheel and tire assembly.
4. Drain the transaxle.

1 Intermediate shaft assembly
2 Intermediate axle shaft
3 Bracket
4 Axle shaft retaining ring
5 Lip seal
6 Bolt 50 Nm (37 lbs. ft.)
7 Washer
8 Bolt 25 Nm (18 lbs. ft.)
9 Right drive axle
10 "O" ring seal

VIEW A

FRT

87957033

Fig. 20 Exploded view of the the intermediate shaft removal—1987 2.8L engine shown

5. Install the modified outer seal protector J–34754 or equivalent.
6. Remove the stabilizer shaft from the right control arm.
7. Separate the right ball joint from the steering knuckle.
8. Disconnect the drive axle (halfshaft) from the intermediate axle shaft.
9. Unfasten the two housing-to-bracket bolts.
10. Remove the bottom bracket-to-engine bolt and loosen the top bolt, then rotate the bracket out of the way.
11. Unfasten the 3 bolts holding the housing to the transaxle.
12. Carefully disengage the intermediate axle shaft from the transaxle, then remove the intermediate shaft assembly.

To install:
13. Place the intermediate shaft into position and lock the intermediate axle shaft into the transaxle.
14. Install the 3 bolts holding the housing to the transaxle and tighten to 18 ft. lbs. (24 Nm).
15. Rotate the bracket into position and install the bottom bolt, then tighten both bolts to 37 ft. lbs. (50 Nm).
16. Install the two housing to bracket bolts and tighten to 37 ft. lbs. (50 Nm).
17. Coat the splines with chassis grease.
18. Connect the drive axle to the intermediate axle shaft.
19. Fasten the right ball joint to the knuckle.
20. Install the stabilizer shaft to the right control arm.
21. Install the wheel and tire assembly.
22. Carefully the car, then fill the transaxle with the proper fluid.

1988–94 VEHICLES

▶ **See Figures 21, 22 and 23**

1. Install engine support bar J–28467 or equivalent.
2. Raise and safely support the vehicle.
3. Remove the right wheel and tire assembly.
4. Install the modified outer seal protector J–34754 or place shop towels underneath the outer joint to protect it from any sharp edges.
5. Remove the stabilizer shaft from the right control arm.
6. Remove the right ball joint from the knuckle.
7. For 1992–94 vehicles, remove the rear engine mount through-bolt.
8. Disconnect the drive axle from the intermediate axle shaft.
9. For 1988–91 vehicles, remove the rear engine mount.
10. Remove the bolt(s) retaining the intermediate shaft to the engine.
11. Carefully disengage the intermediate axle shaft from the transaxle and remove the intermediate shaft assembly.

To install:
12. Place the intermediate shaft assembly into position and lock the intermediate axle shaft into the transaxle.
13. Install the bolt retaining the intermediate shaft to the engine and tighten to 38 ft. lbs. (52 Nm).
14. For 1988–91 vehicles, install the rear engine mount.
15. Coat the intermediate axle shaft with chassis grease and install the intermediate axle shaft to the drive axle.

16. For 1992–94 vehicles, install the rear engine mount through-bolt.
17. Fasten the right ball joint to the knuckle.
18. Install the stabilizer shaft to the right control arm.
19. Remove the seal protector tool or shop towels, as applicable.
20. Install the wheel and tire assembly, then carefully lower the vehicle.
21. Remove the engine support bar holding fixture.
22. Fill the transaxle with the proper fluid.

2.0L (VIN M and H) Engines

1987 VEHICLES

▶ **See Figure 24**

1. Raise and safely support the vehicle.
2. Remove the wheel and tire assembly.
3. Remove the stabilizer shaft from the right control arm.
4. Using tool J 29330, or equivalent, separate the right ball joint from the knuckle.
5. Disconnect the drive axle from the intermediate axle shaft.
6. Detach the detonation sensor and connection.
7. Remove the power steering pump brace.
8. Unfasten the 3 intermediate shaft bracket bolts, then remove the intermediate shaft from the vehicle.

To install:
9. Install intermediate shaft, secure using the 3 bolts, then tighten the bolts to 35 ft. lbs. (47 Nm).
10. Install the power steering pump brace.
11. Install the detonation sensor.
12. Coat the splines of the intermediate shaft with chassis grease.
13. Attach the drive axle to the intermediate axle shaft.
14. Connect the right ball joint to the knuckle. Tighten to 45 ft. lbs. (60 Nm) and install a new cotter pin.
15. Install the stabilizer shaft to the right control arm.
16. Install the wheel and tire assembly.
17. Carefully lower the vehicles.

1988–90 VEHICLES

▶ **See Figure 25**

1. Raise and safely support the vehicle.
2. Remove the right wheel and tire assembly.
3. Drain the transaxle.
4. Install the modified outer seal protector J–34754.
5. Remove the stabilizer shaft from the right control arm.
6. Separate the right ball joint from the knuckle.
7. Disconnect the drive axle from the intermediate axle shaft.
8. Unfasten the bracket-to-engine bolts and the stud, then carefully disengage the intermediate axle shaft from the transaxle and remove the assembly.

1 Intermediate shaft
2 Right axle shaft
3 Engine mount bracket
4 Bolt 52 Nm (38 lbs. ft.)
5 Bolt 62 Nm (46 lbs. ft.)

87957034

Fig. 21 Intermediate shaft assembly removal—1988–90 2.8L and 3.1L engines

1 Engine
2 Bolt 52 Nm (38 lbs. ft.)
3 Intermediate shaft
4 Engine mount bracket
5 Transaxle

87957035

Fig. 22 Intermediate shaft assembly removal—1991–92 2.8L and 3.1L engines

1 Engine
2 50 Nm (37 lbs. ft.) bolt
3 Intermediate shaft
4 Transaxle

87957036

Fig. 23 View of the intermediate shaft— 1994 3.1L engine equipped with the NVT550 manual transaxle

1 Intermediate shaft
2 Right axle shaft
3 Bolt 47 Nm (35 lbs. ft.)

87957038

Fig. 24 Intermediate shaft removal and installation—1987 2.0L (VIN M) engine shown

1 Intermediate shaft
2 47 Nm (35 lbs. ft.) bolt
3 Support
4 Axle shaft
5 Transaxle
6 Engine

87957039

Fig. 25 Intermediate shaft removal and installation—1990 2.0L (VIN M) engine shown

1 Transaxle
2 Intermediate shaft support bracket
3 Bolt
4 Intermediate shaft

87957037

Fig. 26 View of the intermediate shaft—1994 2.0L engine equipped with the Isuzu manual transaxle

To install:

9. Place the intermediate shaft into position and lock the intermediate axle shaft into the transaxle.

10. Install the bracket to engine bolts and one stud and tighten to 35 ft. lbs. (47 Nm).

11. Coat the splines of the intermediate shaft with chassis grease.

12. Attach the drive axle to the intermediate axle shaft.

13. Fasten the right ball joint to the knuckle.

14. Install the stabilizer shaft to the right control arm.

15. Install the wheel and tire assembly.

16. Carefully lower the car and fill the transaxle with the proper fluid.

1991–94 VEHICLES

▶ See Figure 26

1. Install engine support bar J–28467 or equivalent.

2. Raise and safely support the vehicle.

3. Remove the right wheel and tire assembly.

4. Install the modified outer seal protector J–34754 or place shop towels underneath the outer joint to protect it from any sharp edges.

5. Remove the stabilizer shaft from the right control arm.

6. Remove the right ball joint from the knuckle.

7. Remove the rear engine mount through-bolt.

8. Disconnect the drive axle from the intermediate axle shaft.

9. Remove the bolt(s) retaining the intermediate shaft to the engine.

10. Carefully disengage the intermediate axle shaft from the transaxle and remove the intermediate shaft assembly.

To install:

11. Place the intermediate shaft assembly into position and lock the intermediate axle shaft into the transaxle.

12. Install the bolt retaining the intermediate shaft to the engine and tighten to 38 ft. lbs. (52 Nm).

13. Coat the intermediate axle shaft with chassis grease and install the intermediate axle shaft to the drive axle.

14. Install the rear engine mount through-bolt.

15. Fasten the right ball joint to the knuckle.

16. Install the stabilizer shaft to the right control arm.

17. Remove the seal protector tool or shop towels, as applicable.

18. Install the wheel and tire assembly, then carefully lower the vehicle.

19. Remove the engine support bar holding fixture.

20. Fill the transaxle with the proper fluid.

Halfshafts

Halfshafts are flexible assemblies consisting of an inner and outer Constant Velocity (CV) joint connected by an axle shaft.

These vehicles use unequal-length halfshafts. All halfshafts incorporate a male spline; the shafts interlock with the transaxle gears through the use of barrel-type snaprings. Four constant velocity joints are used, two on each shaft. The inner joints are of the double offset design; the outer joints are Rzeppa-type.

REMOVAL & INSTALLATION

1982–86 Vehicles

▶ See Figure 27

1. Remove the hub nut.

2. Raise and safely support the front of the car. Remove the wheel and tire assemblies.

3. Install an axle shaft boot seal protector, G.M. special tool No. J–28712 or the equivalent, onto the outer seal and install J–33162, or equivalent, on the inner seal.

4. Disconnect the brake hose clip from the MacPherson strut, but do not disconnect the hose from the caliper. Remove the brake caliper from the spindle, and hang the caliper out of the way by a length of wire. Do not allow the caliper to hang by the brake hose.

5. Mark the camber alignment cam bolt for reassembly. Remove the cam bolt and the upper attaching bolt from the strut and spindle.

6. Pull the steering knuckle assembly from the strut bracket.

7. Using G.M. special tool J–28468 or the equivalent, remove the axle shaft from the transaxle.

8. Using G.M. special tool J–28733 or the equivalent spindle remover, remove the axle shaft from the hub and bearing assembly.

9. If a new drive axle is to be installed, a new knuckle seal should be installed first.

To install:

10. Loosely install the drive axle into the transaxle and steering knuckle.

11. Loosely attach the steering knuckle to the suspension strut.

12. Install the brake caliper. Tighten the bolts to 30 ft. lbs. (40 Nm).

13. The drive axle is an interference fit in the steering knuckle. Press the

87957024

Fig. 27 A special tool is used to remove the halfshafts. A screwdriver may be used to help reinsert them

axle into place, then install the hub nut. When the shaft begins to turn with the hub, insert a drift through the caliper into one of the cooling slots in the rotor to keep it from turning. Tighten the hub nut to 70 ft. lbs. (100 Nm). to completely seat the shaft.

14. Load the hub assembly by lowering it onto a jackstand. Align the camber cam bolt marks made during removal, install the bolt and tighten to 140 ft. lbs. (190 Nm). Tighten the upper nut to the same value.

15. Install the axle shaft all the way into the transaxle using a screwdriver inserted into the groove provided on the inner retainer. Tap the screwdriver until the shaft seats in the transaxle.

16. Connect the brake hose clip to the strut.

17. Install the tire and wheel, the carefully lower the car and tighten the hub nut to 185 ft. lbs. (260 Nm).

1987–88 Vehicles

▶ **See Figures 28 and 29**

1. Raise and safely support the vehicle.
2. If necessary, remove the hub cap, then remove the tire and wheel assembly.
3. Insert a drift into the into the caliper and rotor to prevent the rotor from turning, then unfasten the shaft nut and washer.
4. Remove the caliper from the steering knuckle and suspend the caliper assembly with a wire.
5. Remove the rotor from the hub and bearing assembly.
6. Disconnect the stabilizer shaft from the control arm.
7. Remove the ball joint from the steering knuckle.
8. Remove the drive axle from the transaxle.
9. Remove the drive axle from the hub and bearing assembly using tool J–28733 or equivalent.

To install:

10. Install the drive axle into the hub and bearing assembly and the transaxle.
11. Install the lower ball joint to the steering knuckle.
12. Install the stabilizer shaft to the control arm.

13. Install the rotor to the hub and bearing assembly.
14. Install the caliper to the steering knuckle.
15. Install a washer and a new shaft nut.
16. Insert a drift into the into the caliper and rotor to prevent the rotor from turning and torque drive axle nut to 185 ft. lbs. (260 Nm).
17. Seat the drive axle into the transaxle by placing a screwdriver into the groove on the joint housing and tapping until seated.
18. Verify that the drive axle is seated into the transaxle by grasping on the housing and pulling outward.
19. Install the wheel assembly.
20. Lower the car.

1989–94 Vehicles

▶ **See Figures 30, 31 and 32**

1. Disconnect the negative battery cable.
2. Raise and safely support the vehicle.
3. Remove the tire and wheel assembly.
4. Install drive seal protector J-34754 on the outer joint, or place shop towels underneath the outer joint to protect from any sharp edges.
5. Insert a drift into the into the caliper and rotor to prevent the rotor from turning, then unfasten the shaft nut and washer.

➡**Use only the recommended tools for separating the ball joint from the steering knuckle or damage to the ball joint and seal may occur.**

6. Remove the lower ball joint cotter pin and nut and loosen the joint using tool J-38892, or equivalent. If removing the right axle, turn the wheel to the left, if removing the left axle, turn the wheel to the right.
7. If equipped with ABS, detach the ABS sensor wire.
8. Separate the joint, with a pry bar between the suspension support.
9. Disengage the axle from the hub and bearing using J 28733–A or equivalent.
10. Separate the hub and bearing assembly from the drive axle and move the strut and knuckle assembly rearward.

Fig. 28 Insert a drift into the caliper and rotor to prevent the rotor from turning while removing the shaft nut and washer

Fig. 29 Removing the halfshaft (drive axle) from the hub and bearing requires the use of a special tool

Fig. 30 Before removing the shaft nut and washer, insert a drift into the caliper and rotor to prevent the rotor from turning

A Turn forcing screw until axle splines are just loose

Fig. 31 The proper tool must be used to detach the axle from the hub and bearing

Fig. 32 Correct installation of the transaxle seal protector

11. Disconnect the inner joint from the transaxle using tool J–28468 or J–33008 attached to J–29794 and J–2619–01 or from the intermediate shaft (V6 and Turbo engines), if equipped.

To install:

➡Before installing the halfshaft (drive axle) assembly, cover all sharp edges in the area of the halfshaft with shop towels so the seal is not damaged during installation.

12. Install axle seal protector J–37292–A into the transaxle.

13. Insert the drive axle into the transaxle or intermediate shaft (V6 and Turbo engines), if equipped, by placing a suitable tool into the groove on the joint housing and tapping until seated.

✳ WARNING

Be careful not to damage the axle seal or dislodge the transaxle seal garter spring when installing the axle.

14. Verify that the drive axle is seated into the transaxle by grasping on the housing and pulling outward.

15. Install the drive axle into the hub and bearing assembly.

16. Fasten the lower ball joint to the knuckle. Tighten the ball joint-to-steering knuckle nut to 41–50 ft. lbs. (55–65 Nm) and install a new cotter pin.

17. Install the washer and new drive shaft nut.

18. Insert a drift into the caliper and rotor to prevent the rotor from turning and tighten the drive shaft nut to 185 ft. lbs. (260 Nm).

19. Remove both J–37292–B and J–34754 seal protectors.

20. Install the tire and wheel assembly.

21. Carefully lower the vehicle and connect the negative battery cable.

CV-JOINT OVERHAUL

1982–85 Double Off-Set and 1982–90 Tri-Pot Design

▶ **See Figures 33 thru 54**

For all overhaul procedures for the 1982–85 Double Off-Set type and 1982–90 Tri-Pot type drive axles, please refer to the accompanying figures.

1. C.V. joint outer race
2. C.V. joint cage
3. C.V. joint inner race
4. Space retaining ring
5. Ball (6)
6. Seal retainer
7. C.V. joint seal
8. Seal retaining clamp
9. Left hand axle shaft
10. Double-offset joint seal
11. Ball retaining ring
12. Ball (6)
13. Double-offset joint inner race
14. Double-offset joint cage
15. Double-offset joint outer race
16. Joint retaining ring
17. Double-offset joint outer race
18. Right hand axle shaft
19. Slinger

Fig. 33 Exploded view of the Double Off-Set design drive axle (halfshaft)—1982–84 Vehicles

1. Race, c.v. joint outer
2. Cage, c.v. joint
3. Race, c.v. joint inner
4. Ring, shaft retaining
5. Ball (6)
6. Retainer, seal
7. Seal, c.v. joint
8. Clamp, seal retaining
9. Shaft, axle (LH)
10. Seal, tri-pot joint
11. Spider, tri-pot joint
12. Roller, needle
13. Ball, tri-pot joint (3)
14. This no. not used
15. Housing assy, tri-pot (LH)
16. Housing assy, tri-pot (RH)
17. Shaft, axle (RH)
18. Ring, spacer
19. Ring, race retaining
20. Clamp, seal retaining
21. Retainer, needle
22. Ring, needle retainer
23. Ring, joint retaining

Fig. 34 Exploded view of the Tri-Pot design drive axle (halfshaft)—1982–84 Vehicles

Fig. 35 Double Off-Set CV-joint overhaul (part 1 of 2)—1982-84 Vehicles

Fig. 36 Double Off-Set CV-joint overhaul (part 2 of 2)—1982-84 Vehicles

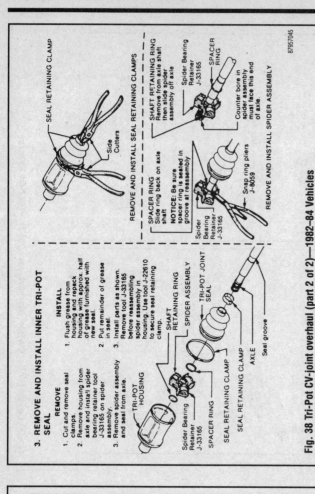

1. REMOVE AND INSTALL INNER TRI-POT SEAL.

REMOVE

1. Remove parts as shown

INSTALL

1. Flush grease from joint and repack joint with approx. half of grease provided
2. Put remainder of grease in seal
3. Install parts as shown. Use tool J-22610 to secure seal retaining clamp

3. REMOVE AND INSTALL INNER TRI-POT SEAL

REMOVE

1. Cut and remove seal clamps.
2. Remove housing from axle and install spider bearing retainer tool J-33165 on spider assembly.
3. Remove spider assembly and seal from axle.

INSTALL

1. Flush grease from housing and repack housing with approx. half of grease furnished with new seal.
2. Put remainder of grease in seal.
3. Install parts as shown. Remove tool J-33165 before reassembling spider assembly to housing. Use tool J-22610 to secure seal retaining clamp.

Fig. 38 Tri-Pot CV-joint overhaul (part 2 of 2)—1982–84 Vehicles

REMOVE AND INSTALL SEAL RETAINING CLAMPS

SHAFT RETAINING RING. Remove from axle shaft then slide spider assembly off axle

Counter bore in spider assembly must face this end of axle

SPACER RING. Slide ring back on axle shaft

NOTICE: Be sure spacer ring is seated in groove at reassembly

REMOVE AND INSTALL SPIDER ASSEMBLY

Fig. 39 Exploded view of the Double Off-Set halfshaft (drive axle)—1985 Vehicles

1. Race, c.v. joint outer	11. Ring, ball retaining
2. Cage, c.v. joint	12. Ball (6)
3. Race, c.v. joint inner	13. Race, D/O joint inner
4. Ring, race retaining	14. Cage, D/O joint
5. Ball (6)	15. Race, D/O joint outer
6. Retainer, seal	16. Ring, D/O joint retaining
7. Seal, cv joint	17. Race, D/O joint outer
8. Clamp, seal retaining	18. Shaft, axle (RH)
9. Shaft, axle (LH)	19. Ring, deflector
10. Seal, D/O joint	

AUTOMATIC TRANSMISSION (LH SIDE ONLY)

1. REMOVE AND INSTALL OUTER JOINT SEAL.

REMOVE

1. Remove parts as shown

INSTALL

1. Flush grease from joint and repack joint with approx. half of grease provided
2. Put remainder of grease in seal
3. Install parts as shown. Use tool J-22610 to secure seal retaining clamp

2. DISASSEMBLE AND ASSEMBLE OUTER JOINT ASSEMBLY.

REMOVE

1. Remove parts as shown

INSTALL

1. Put a light coat of recommended grease on ball grooves of inner and outer races
2. Install parts as shown

NOTICE: Be sure retaining ring side of inner race faces axle shaft

3. Pack joint with recommended grease.

Fig. 37 Tri-Pot CV-joint overhaul (part 1 of 2)—1982–84 Vehicles

1. REMOVE AND INSTALL DEFLECTOR RING

REMOVE
1. Use brass drift to remove damaged deflector ring.

INSTALL
1. Install deflector ring as shown below.

SHEET STEEL (3mm MIN THICKNESS) WITH 24mm DRILLED HOLE

M20 x 1.5 NUT

2½" PIPE COUPLING

DEFLECTOR RING

Install deflector ring

DEFLECTOR RING

DEFLECTOR RING

Fig. 40 Double Off-Set CV-joint overhaul (part 1 of 5)—1985 Vehicles

1. REMOVE AND INSTALL DEFLECTOR RING

REMOVE
1. For damaged deflector ring, remove parts as shown.

INSTALL
1. Install part as shown.

DEFLECTOR RING

DEFLECTOR RING

REMOVE AND INSTALL DEFLECTOR RING (RUBBER)

DEFLECTOR RING

Use brass drift to install, stretch ring and seal properly in groove

DEFLECTOR RING

DEFLECTOR RING

AXLE ASSEMBLY WITH STEEL DEFLECTOR RING

AXLE ASSEMBLY WITH RUBBER DEFLECTOR RING

REMOVE DEFLECTOR RING (STEEL)

SHEET STEEL (3mm MIN THICKNESS) WITH 24mm DRILLED HOLE

DEFLECTOR RING

2½" PIPE COUPLING

M20 x 1.5 NUT

INSTALL DEFLECTOR RING (STEEL)

Fig. 41 Double Off-Set CV-joint overhaul (part 2 of 5)—1985 Vehicles

Side cutter — Cut off clamp

SEAL RETAINING CLAMP

REMOVE CLAMP AND RETAINER

Snap ring pliers J-8059 Spread retaining ring ears apart and pull shaft out

RACE RETAINING RING

REMOVE JOINT ASSEMBLY

SEAL RETAINING CLAMPS

Drive Axle Boot Clamp Tool J-34773

Breaker Bar

Torque wrench Torque to 95 N·m (70 ft/lbs)Both clamps

Push assembly onto shaft until retaining ring is seated in groove

INSTALL JOINT ASSEMBLY

2. REMOVE AND INSTALL OUTER JOINT SEAL

REMOVE
1. Cut seal retaining clamps
2. Remove parts as shown.

INSTALL
1. Flush grease from joint and repack joint with approx. half of grease provided
2. Put remainder of grease in seal
3. Install parts as shown. Use tool J-34773 to secure seal retaining clamp. Torque to specifications.

CLAMP PROTECTOR
Used on some models

SEAL RETAINING CLAMP

DEFLECTOR RING

JOINT ASSEMBLY

AXLE SHAFT

OUTBOARD SEAL

Seal groove

RACE RETAINING RING

SEAL RETAINING CLAMP

Pry tabs 2 places both sides

Fig. 42 Double Off-Set CV-joint overhaul (part 3 of 5)—1985 Vehicles

RACE RETAINING RING

Snap ring pliers J-8059 Spread retaining ring ears apart and pull shaft out

SEAL RETAINING CLAMP

REMOVE JOINT ASSEMBLY

Push assembly onto shaft until seal is seated in groove

INSTALL JOINT ASSEMBLY

Drive axle boot clamp tool J-34773

Breaker Bar

Torque wrench torque to 95 N·m (70 ft/lbs) both clamps

INSTALL SEAL RETAINING CLAMP

4. REMOVE AND INSTALL INNER JOINT SEAL

REMOVE
1. Cut seal retaining clamps
2. Remove parts as shown.

INSTALL
1. Flush grease from joint. Repack joint with approx. half of grease provided
2. Put remainder of grease in seal
3. Install parts as shown. Use tool J-34773 to secure seal retaining clamp. Torque to specifications.

RETAINING RING

RACE RETAINING RING

SEAL

SEAL RETAINING CLAMP

AXLE SHAFT

Seal groove

SEAL

JOINT ASSEMBLY

SEAL RETAINING CLAMP

Fig. 43 Double Off-Set CV-joint overhaul (part 4 of 5)—1985 Vehicles

1. REMOVE AND INSTALL DEFLECTOR RING

REMOVE
1. Use brass drift to remove damaged deflector ring.

SHEET STEEL (3mm MIN THICKNESS) WITH 24mm DRILLED HOLE

M20 x 1.5 NUT

2½" PIPE COUPLING

DEFLECTOR RING

INSTALL
1. Install deflector ring as shown below.

Install deflector ring

DEFLECTOR RING

Fig. 46 Tri-Pot CV-joint overhaul (part 1 of 6)—1985–86 Vehicles

1. REMOVE AND INSTALL DEFLECTOR RING

REMOVE
1. For damaged deflector ring, remove parts as shown.

INSTALL
1. Install part as shown.

DEFLECTOR RING — To install, stretch ring and seal properly in groove

DEFLECTOR RING

Use brass drift to tap off deflector ring

REMOVE AND INSTALL DEFLECTOR RING (RUBBER)

DEFLECTOR RING

SHEET STEEL (3mm MIN THICKNESS) WITH 24mm DRILLED HOLE

M20 x 1.5 NUT

2½" PIPE COUPLING

DEFLECTOR RING

REMOVE DEFLECTOR RING (STEEL)

INSTALL DEFLECTOR RING (STEEL)

DEFLECTOR RING

AXLE ASSEMBLY WITH STEEL DEFLECTOR RING

DEFLECTOR RING

AXLE ASSEMBLY WITH RUBBER DEFLECTOR RING

Fig. 47 Tri-Pot CV-joint overhaul (part 2 of 6)—1985–86 Vehicles

5. DISASSEMBLE AND ASSEMBLE INNER JOINT

REMOVE
1. Remove parts as shown.

INSTALL
1. Install parts as shown.

NOTICE: Retaining ring side of inner race and small end of cage face axle shaft.

2. Pack joint with recommended grease.

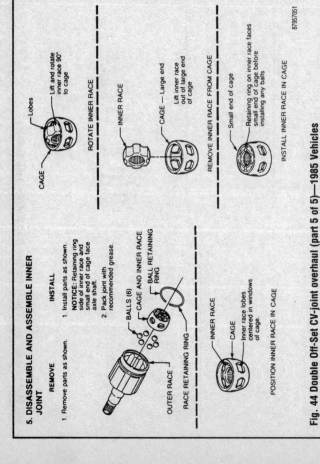

OUTER RACE

RACE RETAINING RING

BALLS (6)

CAGE AND INNER RACE

BALL RETAINING RING

INNER RACE

CAGE

Inner race lobes centered in windows of cage.

POSITION INNER RACE IN CAGE

Lobes

CAGE

Lift and rotate inner race 90° to cage

ROTATE INNER RACE

INNER RACE

CAGE — Large end

Lift inner race out of large end of cage

REMOVE INNER RACE FROM CAGE

Small end of cage

Retaining ring on inner race faces small end of cage before installing any balls

INSTALL INNER RACE IN CAGE

Fig. 44 Double Off-Set CV-joint overhaul (part 5 of 5)—1985 Vehicles

1. Outer race
2. Bearing cage
3. Inner race
4. Retaining ring
5. Bearings
6. Joint seal
7. Joint seal
8. Axle shaft
9. Joint seal
10. Joint seal
11. Needle roller
12. Joint spider
13. Joint ball
14. Ball and needle retainer
15. Housing assembly
16. Housing assembly
17. Axle shaft
18. Spacer ring
19. Retaining ring
20. Retaining clamp
21. Needle retainer
22. Retainer ring
23. Retaining ring
24. Housing
25. Retaining ring
26. Deflector ring
27. Bushing

A. Not used with A/T and 2.0L engine
B. Not used with A/T except 2.0L engine and all M/T

Fig. 45 Exploded view of the Tri-Pot halfshaft (drive axle)—1985–86 Vehicles

2. REMOVE AND INSTALL OUTER JOINT SEAL

REMOVE
1. Cut seal retaining clamps.
2. Remove parts as shown.

INSTALL
1. Flush grease from joint and repack joint with approx. half of grease provided
2. Put remainder of grease in seal.
3. Install parts as shown. Use tool J-34773 to secure seal retaining clamp. Torque to specifications.

Fig. 48 Tri-Pot CV-joint overhaul (part 3 of 6)—1985–86 Vehicles

3. DISASSEMBLE AND ASSEMBLE OUTER JOINT ASSEMBLY

REMOVE
1. Remove parts as shown.

INSTALL
1. Put a light coat of recommended grease on ball grooves of inner and outer races
2. Install parts as shown.

NOTICE: Be sure retaining ring side of inner race faces axle shaft.

3. Pack joint with recommended grease.

Fig. 49 Tri-Pot CV-joint overhaul (part 4 of 6)—1985–86 Vehicles

4. REMOVE AND INSTALL INNER TRI-POT SEAL

REMOVE
1. Cut seal retaining clamps.
2. Remove parts as shown.

INSTALL
1. Flush grease from housing and repack housing with approx. half of grease furnished with new seal
2. Put remainder of grease in seal.
3. Install parts as shown. Use tool J-34773 to secure seal retaining clamp. Torque to specifications.

Fig. 50 Tri-Pot CV-joint overhaul (part 5 of 6)—1985–86 Vehicles

5. DISASSEMBLE AND ASSEMBLE INNER JOINT

REMOVE
1. Remove parts as shown.

INSTALL
1. Install parts as shown.

NOTICE: Retaining ring side of inner race and small end of cage face axle shaft.

2. Pack joint with recommended grease.

Fig. 51 Tri-Pot CV-joint overhaul (part 6 of 6)—1985–86 Vehicles

2. REMOVE AND INSTALL OUTER JOINT SEAL

REMOVE

1. Cut seal retaining clamps.
2. Remove parts as shown.

INSTALL

1. Flush grease from joint and repack joint with approx. half of grease provided.
2. Put remainder of grease in seal.
3. Install parts as shown. Use tool J 35910 to secure seal retaining clamp. Torque to specifications.

1. REMOVE AND INSTALL DEFLECTOR RING

REMOVE

1. For damaged deflector ring, remove parts as shown.

INSTALL

1. Install part as shown.

Fig. 53 Tri-Pot CV-joint overhaul (part 1 of 2)—1987-90 Vehicles

Key No.	Part Name
1.	Race, c.v. joint outer
2.	Cage, c.v. joint
3.	Race, c.v. joint inner
4.	Ring, shaft retaining
5.	Ball (6)
7.	Seal, c.v. joint
8.	Clamp, seal retaining
9.	Shaft, axle (LH)
10.	Seal, tri-pot joint
11.	Spider, tri-pot joint
12.	Roller, needle
13.	Ball, tri-pot joint (3)
17.	Shaft, axle (RH)
18.	Ring, spacer
19.	Ring, race retaining
20.	Clamp, seal retaining
21.	Retainer, needle
22.	Ring, needle retainer
23.	Ring, joint retaining
24.	Housing, tri-pot (RH)
25.	Shaft assy., damper &
26.	Ring, deflector
27.	Bushing, triobal tri-pot

Fig. 52 Exploded view of the Tri-Pot halfshaft (drive axle)—1987-90 Vehicles

3. DISASSEMBLE AND ASSEMBLE OUTER JOINT ASSEMBLY

REMOVE

1. Remove parts as shown.

INSTALL

1. Put a light coat of recommended grease on ball grooves of inner and outer races.
2. Install parts as shown.

NOTICE: Be sure retaining ring side of inner race faces axle shaft.

3. Pack joint with recommended grease.

- BALLS (6)
- INNER RACE
- CAGE
- OUTER RACE

- OUTER RACE
- Remove ball
- INNER RACE
- CAGE
- Brass drift gently tap on cage until tilted enough to remove first ball. Remove other balls in similar manner.

DISASSEMBLE AND ASSEMBLE BALLS

Pivot cage and inner race at 90° to center line of outer race with cage windows aligned with lands of outer race, lift out cage and inner race.

- CAGE
- Land
- Land
- Windows
- OUTER RACE

DISASSEMBLE AND ASSEMBLE CAGE AND INNER RACE TO OUTER RACE

- Rotate up and out of cage
- INNER RACE
- CAGE
- Land
- Cage window

DISASSEMBLE AND ASSEMBLE INNER RACE AND CAGE

4. REMOVE AND INSTALL INNER TRI-POT SEAL

REMOVE

1. Cut seal retaining clamps with side cutters.
2. Remove parts as shown.

INSTALL

1. Flush grease from housing and repack housing with approx. half of grease furnished with new seal.
2. Put remainder of grease in seal.
3. Refer to manufacturer's seal installation dimension prior to crimping clamps. Use tool J 35910 or J 35566 to secure seal retaining clamps.

- SHAFT RETAINING RING
- SPIDER ASSEMBLY
- TRILOBAL TRI-POT BUSHING
- TRI-POT HOUSING
- SPACER RING
- SEAL RETAINING CLAMP
- TRI-POT JOINT SEAL
- AXLE
- Seal groove
- SEAL RETAINING CLAMP

- SEAL RETAINING CLAMP
- J 35566 Drive Axle Seal Clamp Tool (For Earless Clamp)
- Torque clamp to 136 N·m (100 ft/lbs)
- SEAL RETAINING CLAMPS
- Drive Axle Seal Clamp Tool J 35910
- Breaker Bar
- Torque clamp to 176 N·m (130 ft. lbs.)
- Torque wrench

INSTALL SEAL RETAINING CLAMP

- SPACER RING Slide ring back on axle shaft. **NOTICE:** Be sure spacer ring is seated in groove at reassembly
- SHAFT RETAINING RING Remove from axle shaft then slide spider assembly off axle
- SPIDER ASSEMBLY
- SPACER RING
- Snap ring pliers J 8059

REMOVE AND INSTALL SPIDER ASSEMBLY

Fig. 54 Tri-Pot CV-joint overhaul (part 2 of 2)—1987–90 Vehicles

87957061

1990–94 Cross-Groove and 1991–94 Tri-Pot Design

▶ **See Figures 55 and 56**

All 1990–94 models equipped with the Hydra-Matic® 5TM40 or NVT550 5-speed manual transaxles use the Cross-Groove type drive axle. All other models use the Tri-Pot type drive axle. The following overhaul procedures incorporate both designs, unless otherwise noted.

OUTER DEFLECTOR RING

▶ **See Figures 57 and 58**

1. Remove the halfshaft (drive axle).
2. Clamp the halfshaft in a soft jawed vise.

1 Deflector ring
2 C/V joint outer race
3 C/V joint cage
4 C/V joint inner race
5 Chrome alloy ball
6 Race retaining ring
7 Seal retaining clamp
8 Drive axle outboard seal
9 Seal retaining clamp
10 Axle shaft
11 Drive axle inboard seal
12 Ball retaining ring
13 C/G joint inner race
14 C/G joint cage
15 C/G joint outer race
16 Joint retaining ring

87957062

Fig. 55 Exploded view of the Cross-Groove halfshaft (drive axle)—1990–94 Vehicles

1 Retaining ring
2 Tri-pot housing asm.
3 Shaft retaining ring
4 Tri-pot joint spider
5 Needle retainer ring
6 Needle retainer
7 Tri-pot joint ball
8 Needle roller
9 Spacer ring
10 Seal retaining clamp
11 Trilobal tri-pot bushing
12 Tri-pot joint seal
13 Seal retaining clamp
14 Axle shaft
15 C/V joint seal
16 Seal retaining clamp
17 Race retaining ring
18 Ball
19 C/V joint inner race
20 C/V joint cage
21 C/V joint outer race
22 Deflector ring

87957063

Fig. 56 Exploded view of the Tri-Pot halfshaft (drive axle)—1991–94 Vehicles

3. Using a brass drift and a hammer, remove the deflecting ring from the CV-joint outer race.

To install:

4. Position and square up the deflecting ring at the press diameter of the CV-joint outer race.

5. Using a 3 in. pipe coupling, M24 x 1.5 nut, and a fabricated sheet metal sleeve, tighten the nut until the deflector bottoms against the shoulder of the CV outer joint.

OUTER JOINT SEAL

▶ **See Figures 59, 60 and 61**

1. Using a side cutter, remove the large seal retaining clamp from the CV-joint, then discard.
2. Remove the small seal retaining clamp on the axle shaft with a side cutter and discard.

Fig. 57 Using a hammer and a brass drift to remove the outer deflector ring

Fig. 58 Installing the CV-joint outer deflector ring

Fig. 59 Separating the CV-joint and axle

3. Separate the joint seal from the CV-joint race at large diameter and slide the seal away from the joint along the axle shaft.

4. Wipe the excess grease from the face of the CV-joint inner race.

5. Spread the ears on the race retaining ring with snapring pliers and remove the CV-joint from the axle shaft.

6. Remove the seal from the axle shaft.

7. Disassemble the joint and flush the grease prior to installing a new seal.

To install:

8. Install the small retaining clamp on the neck of the new seal, but do not crimp.

9. Slide the seal onto the axle shaft and position the neck of the seal in the seal groove on the axle shaft.

10. Crimp the seal retaining clamp with J 35910 seal clamp tool or equivalent, to 100 ft. lbs. (136 Nm).

11. Place approximately half of the grease provided in the seal kit, inside the seal and repack the CV-joint with the remaining grease.

12. Push the CV-joint onto the axle shaft until the retaining ring is seated in the groove on the axle shaft.

13. Slide the large diameter of the seal with the large seal retaining clamp in place over the outside of the CV-joint race and locate the lip of the seal in the groove on the race.

❊❊ WARNING

The seal must not be dimpled or out of shape in any way. If it is not shaped correctly, equalize pressure in the seal and reshape properly by hand.

14. Crimp the seal retaining clamp with J 35910 seal clamp tool or equivalent, to 130 ft. lbs. (176 Nm).

OUTER JOINT ASSEMBLY

▶ **See Figures 62, 63 and 64**

1. Remove the outer joint seal as outlined earlier.

2. Using a brass drift and a hammer, lightly tap on the inner race cage until it has tilted sufficiently to remove one of the balls. Remove the other balls in the same manner.

3. Pivot the cage 90 degrees and, with the cage ball windows aligned with the outer joint windows, lift out the cage and the inner race.

4. The inner race can be removed from the cage by pivoting it 90° and lifting out. Clean all parts thoroughly and inspect for wear.

To install:

5. To install, put a light coat of the grease provided in the rebuilding kit onto the ball grooves of the inner race and outer joint.

6. Install the parts in the reverse order of removal.

➡ **Make sure that the retaining ring side of the inner race faces the axle shaft.**

7. Install the outer seal as outlined earlier.

CROSS-GROOVE JOINT SEAL

▶ **See Figures 65, 66, 67 and 68**

1. Cut the seal retaining clamps with a side cutter.

2. Separate the seal from the C/G joint race at the large diameter and slide the seal away from the joint along the axle shaft.

3. Wipe the excess grease from the C/G joint inner race.

4. Spread the ears on the retaining ring with snapring pliers and remove the C/G joint from the axle shaft.

5. Remove the seal from the axle shaft.

6. Remove the seal from the shaft.

➡ **The cross-groove joint design uses precision grinding and selected dimensional component fits for proper assembly and operation. Due to its complexity, disassembly is not recommended.**

7. Flush the grease from the joint prior to installing a new seal.

To install:

8. Install the small retaining clamp on the neck of the new seal, but do not crimp.

9. Slide the seal onto the axle shaft and position the neck of the seal in the seal groove on the axle shaft.

10. Crimp the seal retaining clamp with J 35910 seal clamp tool or equivalent, to 100 ft. lbs. (136 Nm).

11. Place approximately half of the grease provided in the seal kit, inside the seal and repack the C/G joint with the remaining grease.

1 Drive axle outboard seal
2 Seal retaining clamp

87957067

Fig. 60 Seal retaining clamp installation

PUSH C/V JOINT ASSEMBLY ONTO AXLE SHAFT UNTIL RETAINING RING IS SEATED IN GROOVE ON AXLE SHAFT

87957068

Fig. 61 CV-joint-to-axle installation

GENTLY TAP ON CAGE UNTIL TILTED ENOUGH TO REMOVE FIRST BALL. REMOVE OTHER BALLS IN SIMILAR MANNER.

1 Ball
2 CV joint inner race
3 CV joint cage
4 CV joint outer race

87957069

Fig. 62 Removing the CV-joint balls

PIVOT CAGE AND INNER RACE AT 90° TO CENTER LINE OF OUTER RACE WITH CAGE WINDOWS ALIGNED WITH LANDS OF OUTER RACE. LIFT OUT CAGE AND INNER RACE.

1 CV joint cage
2 CV joint outer race

87957070

Fig. 63 Outer race and cage separation

1 C/V joint inner race
2 C/V joint cage
3 Rotate inner race up and out of cage
4 Cage window
5 Inner race land

87957071

Fig. 64 Inner race and cage separation

1 Axle shaft
2 Race retaining ring

87957072

Fig. 65 C/G joint and axle separation— 1990–94 vehicles with the Cross-Groove halfshaft

Fig. 66 Seal retaining clamp installation—
1990–94 vehicles with the Cross-Groove
halfshaft

1 Seal retaining clamp
2 Drive axle inboard seal
87957073

Fig. 67 C/G joint-to-axle installation—
1990–94 vehicles with the Cross-Groove
halfshaft

1 C/G joint outer race
2 Axle shaft
87957074

Fig. 68 C/G joint seal installation measurement—1990–94 vehicles with the
Cross-Groove halfshaft

1 C/G joint outer race
2 Drive axle inboard seal
3 Seal retaining clamp
87957075

12. Push the C/G joint onto the axle shaft until the retaining ring is seated in the groove on the axle shaft.

13. Slide the large diameter of the seal over the outside of the C/G joint and locate the lip of the seal in the groove on ball retainer.

※※ WARNING

The seal must not be dimpled or out of shape in any way. If it is not shaped correctly, equalize pressure in the seal and reshape properly by hand.

14. Crimp the seal retaining clamp with J 35910 seal clamp tool or equivalent, to 130 ft. lbs. (176 Nm).

INNER TRI-POT SEAL

▶ See Figures 69 thru 74

1. Remove the larger seal retaining clamp from the tri-pot joint with a side cutter and discard.

※※ WARNING

Do not cut through the seal and damage the sealing surface of the tri-pot outer housing and triobal bushing.

2. Remove the small seal retaining clamp from the axle shaft with a side cutter and discard.

3. Separate the seal from the trilobal tri-pot bushing at the large diameter and slide the seal away from the joint along the axle shaft.

4. Remove the tri-pot housing from the spider and shaft.

5. Spread the spacer ring with snapring pliers and slide the spacer ring and tri-pot spider back on the axle shaft.

6. Remove the shaft retaining ring from the groove on the axle shaft and slide the spider assembly off of the shaft.

7. Check the tri-pot balls and needle rollers for damage or wear.

➡Use care when handling the spider assembly as the tri-pot balls and rollers may separate from the spider trunnions.

Fig. 69 Spider assembly removal—
1991–94 Tri-Pot type axle

1 Shaft retaining ring
2 Spider assembly
3 Spacer
4 Axle shaft

A SLIDE SPACER RING AND SPIDER
ASSEMBLY BACK ON SHAFT.
REMOVE RETAINING RING AND SLIDE
SPIDER ASSEMBLY OFF OF SHAFT.
87957076

Fig. 70 Small seal retaining clamp installation—1991–94 Tri-Pot type axle

1 Spacer ring
2 Spider assembly
3 Axle shaft
87957077

Fig. 71 Spider assembly installation—
1991–94 Tri-Pot type axle

SLIDE SPACER RING INTO
GROOVE ON AXLE SHAFT

1 Torque wrench
2 Breaker bar
3 Seal retaining clamp
87957078

Fig. 72 Tri-Pot housing installation—
1991–94 Tri-Pot type axle

1 Axle shaft
2 Tri-pot housing assembly
87957079

Fig. 73 Seal installation measurement—
1991–94 Tri-Pot type axle

A 4.9" (125 MM)
1 Axle shaft
2 Tri-pot joint seal
3 Tri-pot housing assembly
87957080

Fig. 74 Large seal retaining clamp installation—1991–94 Tri-Pot type axle

1 Seal retaining clamp
87957081

8. Remove the trilobal tri-pot bushing from the tri-pot housing.

9. Remove the spacer ring and seal from the axle shaft.

10. Flush the grease from the tri-pot housing.

To install:

11. Install the small retaining clamp on the neck of the new seal, but do not crimp.

12. Slide the seal onto the axle shaft and position the neck of the seal in the seal groove on the axle shaft.

13. Crimp the seal retaining clamp with J 35910 seal clamp tool or equivalent, to 100 ft. lbs. (136 Nm).

14. Install the spacer ring on the axle shaft and beyond the 2nd groove.

15. Slide the tri-pot spider assembly against the spacer ring on the shaft.

➡ **Make sure the counterbored face of the tri-pot spider faces the end of the shaft.**

16. Install the shaft retaining ring in the groove of the axle shaft with the snapring pliers.

17. Slide the tri-pot spider towards the end of the shaft and reseat the spacer ring in the groove on the shaft.

18. Place approximately half of the grease provided in the seal kit, inside the seal and repack the tri-pot housing with the remaining grease.

19. Install the trilobal tri-pot bushing to the tri-pot housing.

20. Position the larger clamp on the seal.

21. Slide the tri-pot housing over the tri-pot spider.

22. Slide the large diameter of the seal, with the larger clamp in place, over the outside of the trilobal bushing and locate the lip of the seal in the bushing groove.

23. Position the tri-pot assembly at the proper vehicle dimension as shown.

✳✳ WARNING

The seal must not be dimpled or out of shape in any way. If it is not shaped correctly, equalize pressure by carefully inserting a thin flat blunt tool (with no sharp edges) between the large seal opening and the bushing and reshape properly by hand.

24. Crimp the seal retaining clamp with J 35566 seal clamp tool or equivalent.

CLUTCH

Understanding the Clutch

✳✳ CAUTION

The clutch driven disc may contain asbestos, which has been determined to be a cancer causing agent. Never clean clutch surfaces with compressed air! Avoid inhaling any dust from any clutch surface! When cleaning clutch surfaces, use a commercially available brake cleaning fluid.

The purpose of the clutch is to disconnect and connect engine power at the transaxle. A vehicle at rest requires a lot of engine torque to get all that weight moving. An internal combustion engine does not develop a high starting torque (unlike steam engines) so it must be allowed to operate without any load until it builds up enough torque to move the vehicle. Torque increases with engine rpm. The clutch allows the engine to build up torque by physically disconnecting the engine from the transaxle, relieving the engine of any load or resistance.

The transfer of engine power to the transaxle (the load) must be smooth and gradual; if it weren't, drive line components would wear out or break quickly. This gradual power transfer is made possible by gradually releasing the clutch pedal. The clutch disc and pressure plate are the connecting link between the engine and transaxle. When the clutch pedal is released, the disc and plate contact each other (the clutch is engaged) physically joining the engine and transaxle. When the pedal is pushed inward, the disc and plate separate (the clutch is disengaged) disconnecting the engine from the transaxle.

Most clutches utilize a single plate, dry friction disc with a diaphragm-style spring pressure plate. The clutch disc has a splined hub which attaches the disc to the input shaft. The disc has friction material where it contacts the flywheel and pressure plate. Torsion springs on the disc help absorb engine torque pulses. The pressure plate applies pressure to the clutch disc, holding it tight against the surface of the flywheel. The clutch operating mechanism consists of a release bearing, fork and cylinder assembly.

The release fork and actuating linkage transfer pedal motion to the release bearing. In the engaged position (pedal released) the diaphragm spring holds the pressure plate against the clutch disc, so engine torque is transmitted to the input shaft. When the clutch pedal is depressed, the release bearing pushes the diaphragm spring center toward the flywheel. The diaphragm spring pivots the fulcrum, relieving the load on the pressure plate. Steel spring straps riveted to the clutch cover lift the pressure plate from the clutch disc, disengaging the engine drive from the transaxle and enabling the gears to be changed.

The clutch is operating properly if:

1. It will stall the engine when released with the vehicle held stationary.

2. The shift lever can be moved freely between 1st and reverse gears when the vehicle is stationary and the clutch disengaged.

Driven Disc and Pressure Plate/Clutch Cover and Disc

REMOVAL & INSTALLATION

◀ **See Figures 75, 76 and 77**

1. Disconnect the negative battery cable.

2. If equipped with a cable clutch (1982–84 vehicles), disconnect the cable at the clutch release lever and transaxle, as outlined earlier in this section.

1 Flywheel	6 Flywheel "heavy side" identification
2 Clutch disc	7 Clutch cover "light side" identification
3 Clutch cover	8 Align identification marks on assembly
4 Washer	
5 Bolt	

87957086

Fig. 75 Exploded view of the clutch disc and cover assembly

TO DISCONNECT

1 MOVE RELEASE SLIDE IN
2 WHILE HOLDING RELEASE SLIDE IN, DISCONNECT LINES

87957085

Fig. 76 Disconnect the clutch actuator (slave) cylinder line—1995–96 vehicles

87957087

Fig. 77 You must follow the specified sequence when tightening the pressure plate retaining bolts

3. For 1985–94 vehicles remove the sound insulator from inside the vehicle. Disconnect the clutch master cylinder pushrod from the clutch pedal.

4. Remove the transaxle, as outlined earlier in this section.

5. Mark the pressure plate assembly and the flywheel so that they can be assembled in the same position. They were balanced as an assembly at the factory.

6. Loosen the attaching bolts one turn at a time until spring tension is relieved.

7. Support the pressure plate and remove the bolts. Remove the pressure plate and clutch disc. Do not disassemble the pressure plate assembly; replace it if defective.

8. Inspect the flywheel, clutch disc, pressure plate, throwout bearing and the clutch fork and pivot shaft assembly for wear. Replace the parts as required. If the flywheel shows any signs of overheating, or if it is badly grooved or scored, it should be refaced or replaced.

To install:

9. Clean the pressure plate and flywheel mating surfaces thoroughly.

10. Position the clutch disc and pressure plate into the installed position, and support with a dummy shaft or clutch aligning tool, tool J 29074 or equivalent. The clutch plate is assembled with the damper springs offset toward the transaxle. One side of the factory supplied clutch disc is stamped "Flywheel Side".

11. Install the pressure plate-to-flywheel bolts. Tighten them in the sequence shown in the accompanying figure, as follows: .

   a. Tighten bolts 1,2,3, then 4,5,6 in the sequence shown to 12 ft. lbs. (16 Nm).

   b. Tighten bolts 1,2,3, then 4,5,6 in the sequence shown to 15–22 ft. lbs. (22–30 Nm) plus an additional 30° turn.

   c. Remove the clutch alignment tool.

12. Lubricate the outside groove and the inside recess of the release bearing with high temperature grease. Wipe off any excess. Install the release bearing.

13. Install the transaxle, as outlined earlier in this section.

※※ WARNING

When adjusting the cruise control switch, do NOT exert an upward force on the clutch pedal pad of more than 20 lbs. (89 N) or damage to the master cylinder pushrod retaining ring may result.

14. For 1985–94 vehicles, attach the clutch master cylinder pushrod to the clutch pedal and secure with the retaining clip. If equipped with cruise control, check the switch adjustment at the clutch pedal bracket. Install the sound insulator.

15. If equipped with a cable clutch, attach the clutch cable at the transaxle and clutch release lever. Check the clutch operation by lifting the clutch pedal up to allow the mechanism to adjust the cable length. Depress the pedal slowly a few times to set the pawl into mesh with the quandrant teeth.

ADJUSTMENTS

All 1982–84 models have a self-adjusting clutch mechanism located on the clutch pedal, eliminating the need for periodic free play adjustments. The self-adjusting mechanism should be inspected periodically as follows:

1. Depress the clutch pedal and look for the pawl on the self-adjusting mechanism to firmly engage the teeth on the ratchet.

2. Release the clutch. The pawl should be lifted off of the teeth by the metal stop on the bracket.

On 1985 and later models, the hydraulic clutch system provides automatic clutch adjustment. No adjustment of clutch linkage or pedal position is required.

Clutch Hydraulic System

REMOVAL & INSTALLATION

▶ **See Figures 78, 79 and 80**

➡ **The clutch hydraulic system used on 1985–94 models is serviced as a complete unit (except 1994 3.1L). It has been bled of air and filled with fluid. Individual components of the system are not available separately.**

Fig. 78 View of the clutch hydraulic system—1985–87 vehicles

1. BOLT – 50 N·m (36 LBS. FT.)
2. LEVER
3. TRANSAXLE SUPPORT
4. CLUTCH MASTER AND ACTUATOR CYLINDER ASSEMBLY
5. NUT – 27 N·m (20 LBS. FT.)
6. ACTUATOR ROD
7. BUTTON
   BUTTON END OF STRAP MUST REMAIN BETWEEN LEVER AND ACTUATOR ROD AFTER ASSEMBLY. THE STRAPS WILL BREAK ON FIRST CLUTCH PEDAL APPLICATION.
8. RESTRICTOR
   PEDAL RESTRICTOR SHOULD NOT BE REMOVED FROM REPLACEMENT SYSTEM UNTIL AFTER ACTUATOR CYLINDER HAS BEEN ATTACHED TO TRANSAXLE SUPPORT.
9. NUT – 22 N·m (16 LBS. FT.)
10. CLUTCH PEDAL
11. MASTER CYLINDER PUSHROD – LUBRICATE BEFORE INSTALLING
12. NUT
13. BRACKET

Fig. 79 Clutch hydraulic system—1988–89 vehicles

1. Bolt—50 N·m (36 lbs. ft.)
2. Lever
3. Transaxle support
4. Clutch master and actuator cylinder assembly
5. Nut—22 N·m (16 lbs. ft.)
6. Actuator rod
7. Button
   Button end of strap must remain between lever and actuator rod after assembly. The straps will break on first clutch pedal application.
8. Restrictor
   Pedal restrictor should not be removed from replacement system until after actuator cylinder has been attached to transaxle support.
9. Nut—22 N·m (16 lbs. ft.)
10. Clutch pedal and bracket
11. Master cylinder pushrod—lubricate before installing
12. Nut

Fig. 80 Location of the clutch hydraulic system components—1990 vehicles

1.8L, 2.0L and 2.2L Engines

1. Disconnect the negative battery cable.
2. Remove the hush panel from inside the vehicle.
3. Disconnect the clutch master cylinder pushrod from the clutch pedal.
4. Unfasten the clutch master cylinder retaining nuts at the front of the dash.
5. Remove the slave cylinder or actuator retaining nuts at the transaxle.

6. Remove the hydraulic system as a unit from the vehicle.

To install:

7. Install the new slave cylinder or actuator to the transaxle support bracket aligning the pushrod into the pocket on the clutch fork outer lever. Tighten the retaining nuts evenly to prevent damage to the slave cylinder. Tighten to 14–20 ft. lbs. (19–27 Nm).

➡ **Do not remove the plastic pushrod retainer from the slave or actuator cylinder. The straps will break on the first clutch pedal application.**

8. Position the clutch master cylinder to the front of the dash. Install the retaining nuts and tighten the nuts evenly to prevent damage to the master cylinder. Tighten to 15–25 ft. lbs. (20–34 Nm).

9. Remove the pedal restrictor from the pushrod. Lube the pushrod bushing on the clutch pedal. Connect the pushrod to the clutch pedal and install the retaining clip.

10. If equipped with cruise control, check the switch adjustment at the pedal bracket.

✳✳ WARNING

When adjusting the cruise control switch, do not exert an upward force on the clutch pedal pad of more than 20 lbs. (89 N) or damage to the master cylinder pushrod retaining ring can result.

11. Install the hush panel.
12. Press the clutch pedal down several times. This will break the plastic retaining straps on the slave or actuator cylinder pushrod. Do not remove the plastic button on the end of the pushrod.
13. Connect the negative battery cable.

2.8L and 3.1L Engines

1. Remove the air intake duct from the air cleaner.
2. Disconnect the negative, then the positive battery cables.
3. Remove the left fender brace, then unfasten the battery hold-down clamp bolt and remove the battery.
4. Detach the MAT or IAT sensor lead from the air cleaner.
5. Unfasten the PCV pipe retaining clamp from the air intake duct.
6. Remove the clamp fastening the air intake duct to the throttle body.
7. Unfasten the MAF sensor mounting bolts, then unfasten the air cleaner bracket mounting bolts at the battery tray.
8. Remove the air cleaner, mass air flow sensor and the air intake duct as an assembly.
9. Detach the electrical lead at the washer bottle. Unfasten the attaching bolts, then remove the washer bottle from the vehicle.
10. If equipped with cruise control, remove the mounting bracket retaining nuts from the strut tower.
11. Remove the hush panel/sound insulator from inside the vehicle.
12. Disconnect the clutch master cylinder pushrod from the clutch pedal.
13. Unfasten the clutch master cylinder retaining nuts at the front of the dash, then remove the master cylinder.
14. For 1993 vehicles, unfasten the clutch actuator cylinder quick disconnect fitting from the master cylinder line.
15. For 1993, vehicles, remove the transaxle, as outlined earlier in this section, then remove the clutch actuator cylinder from the transaxle.
16. For vehicles through 1992, remove the slave or actuator cylinder retaining nuts at the transaxle, then remove the hydraulic system as a unit from the vehicle.

To install:

17. For vehicles through 1992, install the new slave or actuator cylinder to the transaxle support bracket aligning the pushrod into the pocket on the clutch fork outer lever. Tighten the retaining nuts evenly to prevent damage to the slave cylinder. Tighten to 14–20 ft. lbs. (19–27 Nm).

➡ **Do not remove the plastic pushrod retainer from the slave or actuator cylinder. The straps will break on the first clutch pedal application.**

18. For 1993 vehicles, install the clutch actuator cylinder to the transaxle, then install the transaxle assembly. Attach the quick connect fitting to the master cylinder line.

19. Position the clutch master cylinder to the front of the dash. Install the retaining nuts and tighten the nuts evenly to prevent damage to the master cylinder. Tighten to 15–25 ft. lbs. (20–34 Nm).

20. Remove the pedal restrictor from the pushrod. Lube the pushrod bushing on the clutch pedal. Connect the pushrod to the clutch pedal and install the retaining clip.

21. If equipped with cruise control, check the switch adjustment at the pedal bracket.

✳✳ WARNING

When adjusting the cruise control switch, do not exert an upward force on the clutch pedal pad of more than 20 lbs. (89 N) or damage to the master cylinder pushrod retaining ring can result.

22. Install the hush panel/sound insulator.
23. For 1993 vehicles, bleed the hydraulic system, as outlined later in this section.
24. For vehicles through 1992, press the clutch pedal down several times. This will break the plastic retaining straps on the slave or actuator cylinder pushrod. Do not remove the plastic button on the end of the pushrod.
25. Install the washer bottle, then attach the electrical connection.
26. Install the air cleaner, mass air flow sensor and the air intake duct as an assembly.
27. Fasten the air cleaner bracket mounting bolts, and the MAF sensor mounting bolt.
28. Install the clamp retaining the air intake duct to the throttle body.
29. Fasten the PCV pipe retaining clamp to the air intake duct.
30. Attach the MAF sensor lead, then connect the MAT or IAT sensor lead at the air cleaner.
31. Install the battery and the left fender brace.
32. Connect the positive, then the negative battery cables.
33. Attach the air intake duct to the air cleaner.

Clutch Master Cylinder

REMOVAL & INSTALLATION

▶ **See Figures 81 and 82**

➡ **For 1994 3.1L vehicles, the clutch master cylinder can be replaced as a separate assembly.**

1. Disconnect the negative battery cable.
2. Remove the sound insulator from inside the vehicle.
3. Disconnect the clutch master cylinder pushrod from the clutch pedal.
4. Unfasten the clutch master cylinder retaining nuts at the front of the cowl, then remove the remote reservoir.
5. Detach the master cylinder assembly from the actuator cylinder by disconnecting the hydraulic line, then remove the master cylinder from the vehicle.

To install:

6. Attach the master cylinder to the actuator cylinder by fastening the hydraulic line.

TO DISCONNECT

1 MOVE RELEASE SLIDE IN
2 WHILE HOLDING RELEASE SLIDE IN, DISCONNECT LINES

87957102

Fig. 81 Disconnecting the master cylinder-to-actuator cylinder hydraulic line

TO CONNECT

1 MOVE RELEASE SLIDE TO OUT
   POSITION (AS SHOWN)
2 WHILE HOLDING RELEASE SLIDE IN OUT POSITION,
   CONNECT LINES (CLICK SHOULD BE HEARD)

87957104

Fig. 82 Connecting the master cylinder-to-actuator cylinder hydraulic line

7. Install the remote fluid reservoir, then secure with the retaining nuts. Tighten the nuts evenly to 18 ft. lbs. (25 Nm).

8. Connect the pushrod to the clutch pedal. If equipped, adjust the cruise control switch, as outlined in Section 6 of this manual.

9. Install the sound insulator.

10. Bleed the hydraulic system, as outlined later in this section.

11. Connect the negative battery cable.

Actuator (Slave) Cylinder

REMOVAL & INSTALLATION

▶ **See Figures 81, 82 and 83**

➡**For 1994 3.1L vehicles, the clutch actuator cylinder can be replaced as a separate assembly.**

1. For the 3.1L engine, remove the air intake duct from the air cleaner.

2. Disconnect the negative battery cable.

3. Detach the master cylinder assembly from the actuator cylinder by disconnecting the hydraulic line.

4. Remove the transaxle assembly, as outlined earlier in this section.

5. Remove the clutch actuator cylinder from the transaxle.

To install:

6. Lubricate the inside diameter of the bearing with clutch bearing lubricant GM part no. 12345777 or equivalent.

7. Install the actuator cylinder in the transaxle, then install the transaxle assembly.

8. Connect the master cylinder-to-actuator hydraulic line.

9. Bleed the hydraulic system, as outlined later in this section.

10. If removed, install the air intake duct.

11. Connect the negative battery cable.

1. To clutch master cylinder
2. Clutch master and actuator cylinder assembly
3. Nut
4. Bolt—50 N·m (36 lbs. ft.)
5. Lever
6. Pushrod retainer (do not remove)
7. Nut
8. Transaxle support

87957097

Fig. 83 Clutch actuator cylinder mounting—Isuzu transaxle shown

HYDRAULIC SYSTEM BLEEDING

1988–89 Vehicles

1. Remove any dirt or grease around the clutch master cylinder reservoir cap so that dirt cannot enter the system, then remove the cap and diaphragm.

2. Fill the reservoir to the top step with with Delco Supreme II® GM part no. 1052535, or equivalent approved DOT 3 brake fluid.

3. Fully loosen, but do not remove, the bleeder screw which is located on the slave (actuator) cylinder, next to the inlet connection.

4. Fluid will now flow from the master cylinder to the slave cylinder.

➡**It is important that the reservoir remain filled throughout the procedure.**

5. Air bubbles should now appear at the bleeder screw.

6. Continue this procedure until a steady stream of fluid without any air bubbles is present, then tighten the bleeder screw to 17 inch lbs. (2 Nm).

7. Check the fluid level in the reservoir and refill to the proper mark.

8. Fasten the master cylinder reservoir cap.

9. The system is now fully bled. Check the clutch operation by starting the engine, pushing the clutch pedal to the floor, then wait ten seconds and place transaxle in reverse.

10. If any grinding of the gears is noted, air may still be present in the system. The entire bleeding procedure must be repeated.

➡**Never under any circumstances reuse fluid that has been in the system. The fluid may be contaminated with dirt and moisture.**

1990–94 Vehicles

WITH BLEED SCREW

1. Remove any dirt or grease around the clutch master cylinder reservoir cap so that dirt cannot enter the system, then remove the cap and diaphragm.

2. Fill the reservoir to the top step with with Delco Supreme II® GM part no. 1052535, Hydraulic Clutch fluid GM part no. 12345347, or equivalent approved DOT 3 brake fluid.

3. Fully loosen, but do not remove, the bleeder screw on the slave cylinder next to the inlet connection.

4. Fluid will now flow from the master cylinder to the slave cylinder.

➡**For efficient gravity fill, keep the reservoir filled throughout the procedure.**

5. When a steady stream of fluid without any air bubbles is present, tighten the bleeder screw to 17 inch lbs. (2 Nm).

6. Check the fluid level in the reservoir and refill to the proper mark, then install the master cylinder reservoir diaphragm and cap.

7. The system is now fully bled. Check the clutch operation by starting the engine, pushing the clutch pedal to the floor, then wait ten seconds and place transaxle in reverse.

8. If any grinding of the gears is noted, air may still be present in the system. The entire bleeding procedure must be repeated.

➡**Never under any circumstances reuse fluid that has been in the system. The fluid may be contaminated with dirt and moisture.**

WITHOUT BLEED SCREW

1. Remove the actuator (slave) cylinder from the transaxle, as outlined earlier in this section.

2. Loosen the master cylinder mounting attaching nuts to the end of the studs, but do not remove the master cylinder.

3. Remove any dirt or grease around the reservoir cap so dirt cannot enter the system, then remove the cap and diaphragm. Fill the reservoir with an approved DOT 3 brake fluid.

4. Depress the hydraulic actuator cylinder pushrod about 0.787 in. (20.0mm) into the slave cylinder bore and hold.

5. Install the diaphragm and cap on the reservoir while holding the slave cylinder pushrod in as described in the previous step.

6. Release the slave cylinder pushrod.

➡**The slave cylinder should be lower than the master cylinder.**

7. Hold the slave cylinder vertically with the pushrod end facing the ground.

8. Press the pushrod into the slave cylinder bore with short 0.390 in. (10.0mm) strokes.
9. Observe the reservoir for air bubbles. Continue until air bubbles no longer enter the reservoir.
10. Install the actuator (slave) cylinder to the transaxle.
11. Tighten the master cylinder attaching nuts to 15 ft. lbs. (20 Nm).

12. Check the fluid reservoir in the clutch master cylinder and add, if necessary. Install the diaphragm and cap to the reservoir.
13. To test the system, start the engine and push the clutch pedal to the floor. Wait 10 seconds and select reverse gear. There should be no gear clash. If clash is present, air may still be present in the system. Repeat bleeding procedure.

AUTOMATIC TRANSAXLE

Understanding the Automatic Transaxle

The automatic transaxle allows engine torque and power to be transmitted to the front wheels within a narrow range of engine operating speeds. It will allow the engine to turn fast enough to produce plenty of power and torque at very low speeds, while keeping it at a sensible rpm at high vehicle speeds (and it does this job without driver assistance). The transaxle uses a light fluid as the medium for the transmission of power. This fluid also works in the operation of various hydraulic control circuits and as a lubricant. Because the transaxle fluid performs all of these functions, trouble within the unit can easily travel from one part to another. For this reason, and because of the complexity and unusual operating principles of the transaxle, a very sound understanding of the basic principles of operation will simplify troubleshooting.

TORQUE CONVERTER

▶ See Figure 84

The torque converter replaces the conventional clutch. It has three functions:
1. It allows the engine to idle with the vehicle at a standstill, even with the transmission in gear.
2. It allows the transmission to shift from range-to-range smoothly, without requiring that the driver close the throttle during the shift.
3. It multiplies engine torque to an increasing extent as vehicle speed drops and throttle opening is increased. This has the effect of making the transmission more responsive and reduces the amount of shifting required.

The torque converter is a metal case which is shaped like a sphere that has been flattened on opposite sides. It is bolted to the rear end of the engine's crankshaft. Generally, the entire metal case rotates at engine speed and serves as the engine's flywheel.

The case contains three sets of blades. One set is attached directly to the case. This set forms the torus or pump. Another set is directly connected to the output shaft, and forms the turbine. The third set is mounted on a hub which, in turn, is mounted on a stationary shaft through a one-way clutch. This third set is known as the stator.

A pump, which is driven by the converter hub at engine speed, keeps the torque converter full of transmission fluid at all times. Fluid flows continuously through the unit to provide cooling.

Under low speed acceleration, the torque converter functions as follows:

The torus is turning faster than the turbine. It picks up fluid at the center of the converter and, through centrifugal force, slings it outward. Since the outer edge of the converter moves faster than the portions at the center, the fluid picks up speed.

The fluid then enters the outer edge of the turbine blades. It then travels back toward the center of the converter case along the turbine blades. In impinging upon the turbine blades, the fluid loses the energy picked up in the torus.

If the fluid was now returned directly into the torus, both halves of the converter would have to turn at approximately the same speed at all times, and torque input and output would both be the same.

In flowing through the torus and turbine, the fluid picks up two types of flow, or flow in two separate directions. It flows through the turbine blades, and it spins with the engine. The stator, whose blades are stationary when the vehicle is being accelerated at low speeds, converts one type of flow into another. Instead of allowing the fluid to flow straight back into the torus, the stator's curved blades turn the fluid almost 90° toward the direction of rotation of the engine. Thus the fluid does not flow as fast toward the torus, but is already spinning when the torus picks it up. This has the effect of allowing the torus to turn much faster than the turbine. This difference in speed may be compared to the difference in speed between the smaller and larger gears in any gear train. The result is that engine power output is higher, and engine torque is multiplied.

Fig. 84 The torque converter housing is rotated by the engine's crankshaft, and turns the impeller—The impeller then spins the turbine, which gives motion to the turbine shaft, driving the gears

As the speed of the turbine increases, the fluid spins faster and faster in the direction of engine rotation. As a result, the ability of the stator to redirect the fluid flow is reduced. Under cruising conditions, the stator is eventually forced to rotate on its one-way clutch in the direction of engine rotation. Under these conditions, the torque converter begins to behave almost like a solid shaft, with the torus and turbine speeds being almost equal.

PLANETARY GEARBOX

▶ See Figures 85, 86 and 87

The ability of the torque converter to multiply engine torque is limited. Also, the unit tends to be more efficient when the turbine is rotating at relatively high speeds. Therefore, a planetary gearbox is used to carry the power output of the turbine to the driveshaft.

Planetary gears function very similarly to conventional transmission gears. However, their construction is different in that three elements make up one gear system, and, in that all three elements are different from one another. The three elements are: an outer gear that is shaped like a hoop, with teeth cut into the inner surface; a sun gear, mounted on a shaft and located at the very center of the outer gear; and a set of three planet gears, held by pins in a ring-like planet carrier, meshing with both the sun gear and the outer gear. Either the outer gear or the sun gear may be held stationary, providing more than one possible torque multiplication factor for each set of gears. Also, if all three gears are forced to rotate at the same speed, the gearset forms, in effect, a solid shaft.

Most automatics use the planetary gears to provide various reductions ratios. Bands and clutches are used to hold various portions of the gearsets to the transmission case or to the shaft on which they are mounted. Shifting is accomplished, then, by changing the portion of each planetary gearset which is held to the transmission case or to the shaft.

SERVOS & ACCUMULATORS

▶ See Figure 88

The servos are hydraulic pistons and cylinders. They resemble the hydraulic actuators used on many other machines, such as bulldozers. Hydraulic fluid enters the cylinder, under pressure, and forces the piston to move to engage the band or clutches.

The accumulators are used to cushion the engagement of the servos. The transmission fluid must pass through the accumulator on the way to the servo.

Fig. 85 Planetary gears work in a similar fashion to manual transmission gears, but are composed of three parts

Fig. 86 Planetary gears in the maximum reduction (low) range. The ring gear is held and a lower gear ratio is obtained

Fig. 87 Planetary gears in the minimum reduction (drive) range. The ring gear is allowed to revolve, providing a higher gear ratio

Fig. 88 Servos, operated by pressure, are used to apply or release the bands, to either hold the ring gear or allow it to rotate

The accumulator housing contains a thin piston which is sprung away from the discharge passage of the accumulator. When fluid passes through the accumulator on the way to the servo, it must move the piston against spring pressure, and this action smooths out the action of the servo.

HYDRAULIC CONTROL SYSTEM

The hydraulic pressure used to operate the servos comes from the main transmission oil pump. This fluid is channeled to the various servos through the shift valves. There is generally a manual shift valve which is operated by the transmission selector lever and an automatic shift valve for each automatic upshift the transmission provides.

➡ **Many new transmissions are electronically controlled. On these models, electrical solenoids are used to better control the hydraulic fluid. Usually, the solenoids are regulated by an electronic control module.**

There are two pressures which affect the operation of these valves. One is the governor pressure which is effected by vehicle speed. The other is the modulator pressure which is effected by intake manifold vacuum or throttle position. Governor pressure rises with an increase in vehicle speed, and modulator pressure rises as the throttle is opened wider. By responding to these two pressures, the shift valves cause the upshift points to be delayed with increased throttle opening to make the best use of the engine's power output.

Most transmissions also make use of an auxiliary circuit for downshifting. This circuit may be actuated by the throttle linkage the vacuum line which actuates the modulator, by a cable or by a solenoid. It applies pressure to a special downshift surface on the shift valve or valves.

The transmission modulator also governs the line pressure, used to actuate the servos. In this way, the clutches and bands will be actuated with a force matching the torque output of the engine.

Fluid Pan and Filter

Pan removal, fluid and filter changes are covered in Section 1 of this manual.

Neutral Start/Back-up Light Switch

The automatic transaxle utilizes the neutral safety switch and back-up light switch as a combined unit. This switch is located under the console, next to the shifter on 1982–84 models and on top of the of the transaxle on 1985–94 models.

REMOVAL & INSTALLATION

1982–84 Vehicles

▶ **See Figure 89**

1. Disconnect the negative battery cable.
2. Remove the console assembly.
3. Detach the electrical connector.
4. Unfasten the retaining bolt/screw, then remove the switch from the side of the shifter.
5. Installation is the reverse of the removal procedure.

1	Switch assembly	6	"Neutral" notch
2	2 Nm (32.4 in. lb.)	7	Transmission control
3	Carrier tang		shifter
4	Tang hole	8	Detent plate
5	Tang slot		

Fig. 89 Neutral safety/back-up switch on 1982–84 vehicles is located under the console next to the shifter

1987–94 Vehicles

▶ **See Figure 90**

1. Disconnect the negative battery cable.
2. Remove the shift linkage.
3. Detach the electrical connector from the switch.
4. Unfasten the switch-to-transaxle screws/bolts, then remove the switch.

To install:

➡ **After switch adjustment, make sure that the engine will only start in "Park" or "Neutral". If the engine will start in any other gear, re-adjust the switch.**

1 24 Nm (18 lbs. ft.) bolt
2 Switch asm.
3 Trans. shaft
4 Service adjustment hole
5 3/32 inch drill bit or 2.34 dia. gage pin

87957109

Fig. 90 View of the neutral safety/back-up light switch—1992 vehicle shown

5. If installing the old switch, proceed as follows:
   a. Place the shift shaft/control lever in "Neutral".
   b. Align the flats of the shift shaft with the switch, then loosely install the mounting bolts.
   c. Insert a gauge pin in the service adjustment hole and rotate the switch until the pin drops to a depth of ⁹⁄₆₄ in. (9mm).
   d. Tighten the bolts to 18 ft. lbs. (24 Nm), then remove the gauge pin.
6. If installing a new switch, proceed as follows:
   a. Place the shift shaft/control lever in "Neutral".
   b. Align the flats of the shift shaft to the flats in the switch, then install the switch assembly. Tighten the bolts to 18 ft. lbs. (24 Nm).
   c. If the bolt holes do not align with the mounting boss on the transaxle, verify the transaxle is in the "Neutral" position, do not rotate the switch.
   d. If the shift has been rotated and the pin broken, the switch can be adjusted by following the procedure in Step 5.
7. Attach the electrical connector to the switch.
8. Install the shift linkage.
9. Connect the negative battery cable.
10. Start the engine and check the switch operation.

Automatic Transaxle Assembly

REMOVAL & INSTALLATION

1982–86 Vehicles

▶ See Figures 91 and 92

1. Disconnect the negative battery cable at the battery and where it attaches to the transaxle.
2. On the 1982–84 models, insert a ¼ in. x 2 in. bolt into the hole in the right front motor mount to prevent any mislocation during the transaxle removal.
3. On 4-cylinder engines, remove the air cleaner.
4. On V6 engines remove the following:
   a. Remove the air intake duct from the air cleaner.
   b. Remove the left fender brace.
   c. Disconnect the MAT sensor lead at the air cleaner.
   d. Disconnect the mass air flow sensor lead.
   e. Remove the PCV pipe retaining clamp from the air intake duct.
   f. Remove the clamp retaining the air intake duct to the throttle body.
   g. Remove the mass air flow sensor mounting bolt. Remove the air cleaner bracket mounting bolts at the battery tray.
   h. Remove the air cleaner, mass air flow sensor and air intake duct as an assembly.
   i. Remove the heat shield at the crossover pipe and remove the crossover pipe.
5. Disconnect the T.V. cable at the throttle body.
6. Unscrew the bolt securing the T.V. cable to the transaxle. Pull up on the cable cover at the transaxle until the cable can be seen. Disconnect the cable from the transaxle rod.
7. Remove the wiring harness retaining bolt at the top of the transaxle.

1. TOOL J-28467
2. THREAD ONTO STRUT ATTACHING BOLTS, ABOVE NUTS – 3 PER SIDE.

87957112

Fig. 91 Install a suitable engine support fixture—1986 2.8L engine shown

75 N·m (55 FT. LBS.)
STARTER
75 N·m (55 FT. LBS.)
FRONT OF CAR
TRANSAXLE ASSEMBLY
TRANSAXLE TO ENGINE

87957114

Fig. 92 Transaxle-to-engine mounting—1986 2.8L engine shown

8. Disconnect the hose from the air management valve and then pull the wiring harness up and out of the way.
9. Install an engine support bar as shown in the illustration. Raise the engine just enough to take the pressure off the motor mounts.

✷✷ CAUTION

The engine support bar must be located in the center of the cowl and the bolts must be tightened before attempting to support the engine.

10. Remove the transaxle mount and bracket assembly. It may be necessary to raise the engine slightly to aid in removal.
11. Disconnect the shift control linkage from the transaxle.
12. Unfasten and remove the top transaxle-to-engine mounting bolts. Loosen, but do not remove, the transaxle-to-engine bolt nearest to the starter.
13. Unlock the steering column. Raise and support the front of the car. Remove the front wheels.
14. Pull out the cotter pin and loosen the castellated ball joint nut until the ball joint separates from the control arm. Repeat on the other side of the car.
15. Disconnect the stabilizer bar from the left lower control arm.
16. Remove the six bolts that secure the left front suspension support assembly.
17. Install drive axle seal protectors and connect an axle shaft removal tool (J–28468) to a slide hammer (J–23907).

18. Position the tool behind the axle shaft cones and then pull the cones out and away from the transaxle. Remove the axle shafts and plug the transaxle bores to reduce fluid leakage.

19. Remove the nut that secures the transaxle control cable bracket to the transaxle, then remove the engine-to-transaxle stud.

20. Detach the speedometer cable at the transaxle.

21. Disconnect the transaxle strut (stabilizer) at the transaxle.

22. Unfasten the four retaining screws and remove the torque converter shield.

23. Scribe a mark for on the flywheel for reassembly and remove the three bolts securing the torque converter to the flex plate.

24. Disconnect and plug the oil cooler lines at the transaxle. Remove the starter.

25. Unfasten the screws that hold the brake and fuel line brackets to the left side of the underbody. This will allow the lines to be moved slightly for clearance during transaxle removal.

26. Remove the bolt that was loosened in Step 12.

27. Remove the transaxle from the vehicle.

To install:

28. Position the transaxle in the car.

29. Place a small amount of light grease on the torque converter pilot hub.

30. Make sure to properly seat the torque convertor in the oil pump.

31. Guide the right drive axle shaft into its bore as the transaxle is being raised. The right drive axle cannot be installed AFTER the transaxle is connected to the engine.

32. Lower the transaxle to the engine bolts and remove the transaxle jack.

33. Install the transaxle to engine support bracket.

34. Install the transaxle cooler lines.

35. Position the LH axle into the transaxle.

36. Install the torque converter-to-flywheel bolts and tighten to 46 ft. lbs. (62 Nm). Re-torque the first bolt after all three have been tightened.

37. Install the transaxle converter shield.

38. The remainder of the installation is the reverse of removal with the following precautions.

    a. Check the suspension alignment.

    b. Check the transaxle fluid level.

1987–94 Vehicles

▶ **See Figures 93, 94, 95 and 96**

1. Disconnect the negative battery cable.

2. For 1989–93 vehicles, drain the cooling system, then disconnect the heater core hoses.

3. Remove the air intake duct or air cleaner assembly.

4. For 6-cylinder engines only, disconnect the exhaust crossover pipe from the manifolds.

5. Disconnect the TV cable from the throttle lever and the transaxle and unroute.

6. Remove the fluid level indicator and the filler tube.

7. For 1987–88 vehicles, insert a a ¼ in. x 2 in. bolt into the hole in the right front motor mount to maintain drive line alignment.

8. Install J 28467-A or equivalent engine support fixture.

9. Unfasten the nut securing the wiring harness to the transaxle.

10. Remove the wiring harness-to-transaxle nut.

11. Label and detach the wires at the TCC connector and the neutral safety/back up light switch.

❋❋ WARNING

When servicing requires that the "T" latch type wiring connector be detached from the switch, be sure to reassemble the "T" latch and the connector. Failure to do so may result in intermittent loss of switch functions.

12. Disconnect the shift linkage from the transaxle.

13. Unfasten the top two transaxle-to-engine bolts.

14. Remove the left upper transaxle mount and bracket assembly.

15. Disconnect the rubber hose from the transaxle-to-vent pipe.

16. Unfasten the remaining upper engine-to-transaxle bolts.

17. Raise and safely support the vehicle.

18. Remove the front wheel and tire assemblies.

19. If equipped, remove both front ABS wheel speed sensors and the harness from the left suspension support.

1 Universal support fixture J 28467-A
2 Thread onto strut attaching bolts above nuts, 2 per side

87957120

Fig. 93 View of the correct installation of the engine support fixture on the 2.0L (VIN H) engine

20. Separate both ball joints from the control arms.
21. Remove the engine-to-transaxle brace.
22. Unfasten the left stabilizer link pin bolt and frame bushing clamp nuts.
23. Remove the left suspension support assembly and cross bar. Remove both drive axles (halfshafts) from the transaxle, then support them.
24. On the 2.0L (VIN H) engine, disconnect the exhaust pipe from the manifold.
25. Remove the starter motor, as outlined in Section 2 of this manual.
26. Disconnect the coolant inlet pipe from the transaxle and manifold.
27. Remove the transaxle converter cover.
28. On the 2.0L (VIN H) engine, remove the lower intake manifold brace.
29. Unfasten the torque converter-to-transaxle bolts, then matchmark the converter to the flywheel for assembly.
30. Disconnect and plug the transaxle cooler pipes. Remove the transaxle cable selector bracket.
31. Detach the Vehicle Speed Sensor (VSS) connector from the sensor.
32. Remove the transaxle-to-engine support bracket.
33. Position a suitable transaxle jack under the transaxle, then remove the transaxle mounting strut at the transaxle.
34. Unfasten the remaining engine-to-transaxle bolts, then remove the transaxle from the vehicle.

➡The transaxle cooler and lines should be flushed any time the transaxle is removed for overhaul or to replace the pump, case or converter.

To install:

35. Put a small amount of grease on the pilot hub of the converter and make sure the converter is properly engaged with the pump.
36. Position the transaxle in the vehicle. Install the lower engine-to-transaxle bolts, then tighten to 55 ft. lbs. (75 Nm) for all except the 3.1L engine. Remove the jack.
37. Fasten the transaxle mounting strut to the transaxle.

➡Install the transaxle-to-engine support bracket. It is important to center the bolt in the left rear transaxle mount slot to the body. This will minimize idle shake and harsh engagement.

POSITION 2 STUD — 96 N·m (71 LBS. FT.)
POSITION 3 STUD — 96 N·m (71 LBS. FT.)
POSITION 4 AND 6 — 96 N·m (71 LBS. FT.)
POSITION 5 BOLT — 96 N·m (71 LBS. FT.)
POSITION 8 BOLT — 56 N·m (41 LBS. FT.)

A Oil pan
B Spacer
C 56 Nm (41 lbs. ft.) nut
D 13 Nm (115 lbs. in.) stud

87957122

Fig. 95 View of the engine to transaxle mounting and torque specifications—1994 3.1L engine shown

1 75 Nm (55 lbs. ft.) stud
2 Adapter assembly
3 75 Nm (55 lbs. ft.) bolt
4 Transaxle assembly
5 Engine assembly

87957121

Fig. 94 Engine-to-transaxle mounting—1994 2.0L (VIN H) engine shown

1 Flywheel bolts
2 Transaxle assembly
3 Flywheel
4 Net slot

87957123

Fig. 96 Location of the flywheel net slot

38. Install the transaxle-to-engine support bracket.
39. Connect the transaxle cooler pipes.
40. Align the converter with the marks made previously on the flywheel. Hand start and tighten the net slot bolt first, then hand start and tighten the two remaining bolts. Tighten the converter bolts to 46 ft. lbs. (62 Nm).
41. For the 2.0L (VIN H) engine, install the lower intake manifold brace.
42. Fasten the transaxle selector bracket.
43. Connect the coolant inlet pipe to the transaxle and exhaust manifold studs.
44. Install the transaxle converter cover.
45. Install the starter assembly.
46. For the 2.0L (VIN H) engine, connect the exhaust pipe to the manifold.
47. Install the drive axles (halfshafts) to the transaxle.
48. Fasten the left suspension support assembly and the cross bar.
49. Install the left stabilizer shaft frame bushing clamp nuts and link pin bolt.
50. Install the engine-to-transaxle brace.
51. Fasten the right and left ball joints to the control arms.
52. Attach the VSS connector to the transaxle.
53. Connect the left side ABS harness and the WSS connector to the sensor.
54. Install the wheel and tire assemblies.
55. Carefully lower the vehicle.
56. Install the upper transaxle mount bolts, tighten to 55 ft. lbs. (75 Nm), except for the 3.1L engine. For the 3.1L engine, tighten to the specifications shown in the accompanying figure.
57. Fasten the left side transaxle mount.
58. Attach the shift linkage to the transaxle.
59. Fasten the wiring connectors at the TCC converter and the park/neutral switch.
60. Install the wiring harness and secure to the transaxle with the retaining nut.
61. For 1987–88 vehicles, remove the alignment bolt.
62. Remove the engine support fixture.
63. On the 3.1L engine, install the crossover pipe to the exhaust manifold.
64. Install the oil level indicator and fill tube.
65. Connect the TV cable at the transaxle and throttle lever.
66. Attach the rubber hose to the transaxle vent pipe.
67. Install the air inlet duct or air cleaner assembly.
68. Connect the negative battery cable, then check the transaxle fluid level and add if necessary.

ADJUSTMENTS

Shift Control Cable Adjustment

1. Place the shift lever in the **N**.

➥Neutral can be found by rotating the transaxle selector shaft clockwise from P through R to N.

2. Loosely attach the cable to the transaxle shift lever with a nut. Assemble the cable to the cable bracket and to the shift lever. Tighten the cable to transaxle shift lever nut.

➥The lever must be held out of P when torquing the nut.

Throttle Valve (TV) Cable Adjustment

Setting of the TV cable must be done by rotating the throttle lever at the carburetor or throttle body. Do not use the accelerator pedal to rotate the throttle lever.
1. With the engine off, depress and hold the reset tab at the engine end of the TV cable.
2. Move the slider until it stops against the fitting.
3. Release the rest tab.
4. Rotate the throttle lever to its full travel.
5. The slider must move (ratchet) toward the lever when the lever is rotated to its full travel position.
6. Recheck after the engine is hot and road test the vehicle.

Halfshafts

For halfshaft remove and installation and CV-joint overhaul, please refer to the procedures located under manual transaxle located in this section.

WHEELS 8-2
FRONT AND REAR WHEELS 8-2
  REMOVAL & INSTALLATION 8-2
  INSPECTION 8-3
WHEEL LUG STUDS 8-3
  REPLACEMENT 8-3
FRONT SUSPENSION 8-4
MACPHERSON STRUTS 8-5
  REMOVAL & INSTALLATION 8-5
  OVERHAUL 8-6
STRUT CARTRIDGE 8-8
  REMOVAL & INSTALLATION 8-8
LOWER BALL JOINT 8-8
  INSPECTION 8-8
  REMOVAL & INSTALLATION 8-8
STABILIZER SHAFT (SWAY BAR) 8-9
  REMOVAL & INSTALLATION 8-9
CONTROL ARM/SUSPENSION
  SUPPORT 8-10
  REMOVAL & INSTALLATION 8-10
  CONTROL ARM BUSHING
    REPLACEMENT 8-11
STEERING KNUCKLE 8-11
  REMOVAL & INSTALLATION 8-11
FRONT HUB AND BEARING 8-11
  REMOVAL & INSTALLATION 8-11
WHEEL ALIGNMENT 8-12
  CASTER 8-12
  CAMBER 8-12
  TOE 8-12
REAR SUSPENSION 8-13
COIL SPRINGS 8-14
  REMOVAL & INSTALLATION 8-14
SHOCK ABSORBERS 8-15
  REMOVAL & INSTALLATION 8-15
  TESTING 8-15
REAR AXLE/CONTROL ARM 8-15
  REMOVAL & INSTALLATION 8-16
STABILIZER BAR 8-16
  REMOVAL & INSTALLATION 8-16
REAR HUB AND BEARING 8-16
  REMOVAL & INSTALLATION 8-16
STEERING 8-17
STEERING WHEEL 8-17
  REMOVAL & INSTALLATION 8-17
TURN SIGNAL (COMBINATION)
  SWITCH 8-18
  REMOVAL & INSTALLATION 8-18
WINDSHIELD WIPER SWITCH 8-19
  REMOVAL & INSTALLATION 8-19
IGNITION SWITCH 8-19
  REMOVAL & INSTALLATION 8-19
IGNITION LOCK CYLINDER 8-21
  REMOVAL & INSTALLATION 8-21
STEERING COLUMN HOUSING
  STEERING SHAFT AND IGNITION
  SWITCH HOUSING JACKET
  BUSHING 8-22
    DISASSEMBLY 8-22

STEERING LINKAGE 8-22
  REMOVAL & INSTALLATION 8-22
RACK AND PINION UNIT 8-23
  REMOVAL & INSTALLATION 8-23
POWER STEERING PUMP 8-23
  REMOVAL & INSTALLATION 8-23
  SYSTEM BLEEDING 8-24
COMPONENT LOCATIONS
  FRONT SUSPENSION COMPONENT
    LOCATIONS 8-4
  REAR SUSPENSION COMPONENT
    LOCATIONS 8-13

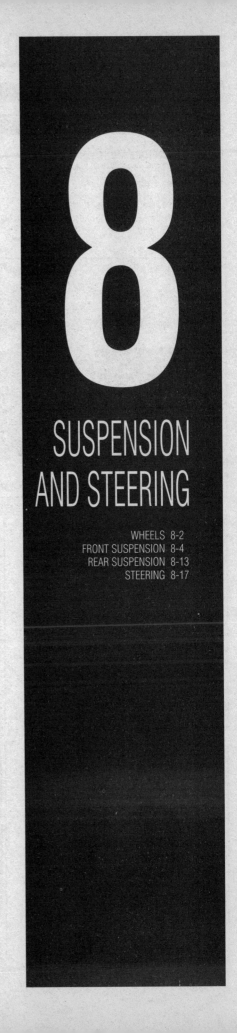

8

SUSPENSION AND STEERING

WHEELS 8-2
FRONT SUSPENSION 8-4
REAR SUSPENSION 8-13
STEERING 8-17

WHEELS

Front and Rear Wheels

REMOVAL & INSTALLATION

▶ **See Figures 1 thru 7**

1. Park the vehicle on a level surface.
2. Remove the jack, tire iron and, if necessary, the spare tire from their storage compartments.

Fig. 1 Place the jack at the proper lifting point on your vehicle

3. Check the owner's manual or refer to Section 1 of this manual for the jacking points on your vehicle. Then, place the jack in the proper position.
4. If equipped with lug nut trim caps, remove them by either unscrewing or pulling them off the lug nuts, as appropriate. Consult the owner's manual, if necessary.
5. If equipped with a wheel cover or hub cap, insert the tapered end of the tire iron in the groove and pry off the cover.
6. Apply the parking brake and block the diagonally opposite wheel with a wheel chock or two.

➡ **Wheel chocks may be purchased at your local auto parts store, or a block of wood cut into wedges may be used. If possible, keep one or two of the chocks in your tire storage compartment, in case any of the tires has to be removed on the side of the road.**

7. If equipped with an automatic transaxle, place the selector lever in **P** or Park; with a manual transaxle, place the shifter in Reverse.
8. With the tires still on the ground, use the tire iron/wrench to break the lug nuts loose.

➡ **If a nut is stuck, never use heat to loosen it or damage to the wheel and bearings may occur. If the nuts are seized, one or two heavy hammer blows directly on the end of the bolt usually loosens the rust. Be careful, as continued pounding will likely damage the brake drum or rotor.**

9. Using the jack, raise the vehicle until the tire is clear of the ground. Support the vehicle safely using jackstands.
10. Remove the lug nuts, then remove the tire and wheel assembly.
   To install:
11. Make sure the wheel and hub mating surfaces, as well as the wheel lug studs, are clean and free of all foreign material. Always remove rust from the

Fig. 2 Before jacking the vehicle, block the diagonally opposite wheel with one or, preferably, two chocks

Fig. 3 With the vehicle still on the ground, break the lug nuts loose using the wrench end of the tire iron

Fig. 4 After the lug nuts have been loosened, raise the vehicle using the jack until the tire is clear of the ground

Fig. 5 Remove the lug nuts from the studs

Fig. 6 Remove the wheel and tire assembly from the vehicle

Fig. 7 Typical wheel lug tightening sequence

wheel mounting surface and the brake rotor or drum. Failure to do so may cause the lug nuts to loosen in service.

12. Install the tire and wheel assembly and hand-tighten the lug nuts.

13. Using the tire wrench, tighten all the lug nuts, in a crisscross pattern, until they are snug.

14. Raise the vehicle and withdraw the jackstand, then lower the vehicle.

15. Using a torque wrench, tighten the lug nuts in a crisscross pattern to 100 ft. lbs. (140 Nm). Check your owner's manual or refer to Section 1 of this manual for the proper tightening sequence.

✳✳ WARNING

Do not overtighten the lug nuts, as this may cause the wheel studs to stretch or the brake disc (rotor) to warp.

16. If so equipped, install the wheel cover or hub cap. Make sure the valve stem protrudes through the proper opening before tapping the wheel cover into position.

17. If equipped, install the lug nut trim caps by pushing them or screwing them on, as applicable.

18. Remove the jack from under the vehicle, and place the jack and tire iron/wrench in their storage compartments. Remove the wheel chock(s).

19. If you have removed a flat or damaged tire, place it in the storage compartment of the vehicle and take it to your local repair station to have it fixed or replaced as soon as possible.

INSPECTION

Inspect the tires for lacerations, puncture marks, nails and other sharp objects. Repair or replace as necessary. Also check the tires for treadwear and air pressure as outlined in Section 1 of this manual.

Check the wheel assemblies for dents, cracks, rust and metal fatigue. Repair or replace as necessary.

Wheel Lug Studs

All models use metric wheel nuts and studs. The nut will have the word "metric" stamped on the face and the stud will have the letter "M" into the threaded end.

The thread size of the metric wheel nuts and wheel studs are M12 X 1.5, this signifies:

- M = Metric
- 12 = Diameter in millimeters
- 1.5 = Millimeters per thread

REPLACEMENT

➥Never try to reuse a wheel stud. Once a wheel stud has been removed, discard it and replace it with a new one.

Front Wheels

▶ **See Figures 8 and 9**

1. Remove the tire and wheel assembly.

2. As described later in this section, remove the hub and bearing assembly.

3. Using tool J 6627-A or equivalent wheel stud remover tool, remove and discard the wheel stud(s).

To install:

4. Insert the new stud from the rear of the hub.

5. Install flat washers and nut (flat side down), onto the wheel stud, then tighten until the wheel stud is fully seated.

6. Remove the nut and washers.

7. Install the hub and bearing assembly as outlined later in this section.

8. Install the tire and wheel assembly.

A HUB AND BEARING ASSEMBLY REMOVED FROM VEHICLE
B WHEEL NUT INSTALLED ON WHEEL STUD

87958002

Fig. 8 Once the hub and bearing is removed from the vehicle, use the proper tool to remove the wheel stud(s)

A HUB AND BEARING ASSEMBLY REMOVED FROM VEHICLE
B INSERT WASHER OVER WHEEL STUD
C TIGHTEN NUT TO DRAW WHEEL STUD INTO CORRECT POSITION

87958003

Fig. 9 Install washers and a nut on the wheel stud, then tighten until the stud is properly seated

Rear Wheels

▶ **See Figure 9**

1. Remove the tire and wheel assembly.

2. Remove the brake drum, then remove the hub and bearing assembly. For details, please refer to the procedure located later in this section.

3. Unfasten and remove the wheel stud(s) using tool J 6627-A or an equivalent wheel stud removal tool. DIscard the removed stud(s).

To install:

4. Insert the new stud from the rear of the hub.

5. Install 4 flat washers onto the stud.

6. Install the wheel nut with the flat side toward the washers.

7. Tighten the nut until the stud head is properly seated in the hub flange.

8. Remove the nut and washers.

9. Install the hub and bearing assembly and the brake drum.

10. Install the tire and wheel assembly.

FRONT SUSPENSION

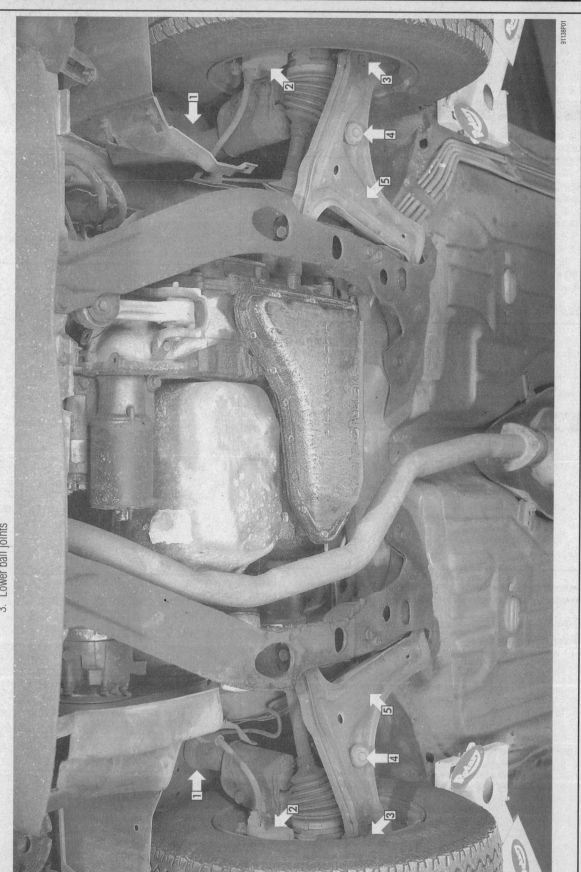

FRONT SUSPENSION COMPONENT LOCATIONS

1. Struts
2. Steering knuckle
3. Lower ball joints
4. Stabilizer bar links
5. Lower control arms

91138P01

The J-cars use MacPherson strut front suspension designs. A MacPherson strut combines the functions of a shock absorber and an upper suspension member (upper arm) into one unit. The strut is surrounded by a coil spring, which provides normal front suspension functions.

The strut bolts to the body shell at its upper end, and to the steering knuckle at the lower end. The strut pivots with the steering knuckle by means of a sealed mounting assembly at the upper end which contains a preloaded, non-adjustable bearing.

The steering knuckle is connected to the chassis at the lower end by a conventional lower control arm, and pivots in the arm in a preloaded ball joint of standard design. The knuckle is fastened to the ball joint stud by means of a castellated nut and cotter pin.

Advantages of the MacPherson strut design, aside from its relative simplicity, include reduced weight and friction, minimal intrusion into the engine and passenger compartments, and ease of service.

MacPherson Struts

The struts retain the springs under tremendous pressure even when removed from the car. For these reasons, several expensive special tools and substantial specialized knowledge are required to safely and effectively work on these parts. We recommend that if spring or shock absorber repair work is required, you remove the strut or struts involved and take them to a repair facility which is fully equipped and familiar with the car.

REMOVAL & INSTALLATION

▶ **See Figures 10 thru 16**

1. From inside the engine compartment, pry off the cover on the strut tower, if equipped, then unfasten the upper strut-to-body nuts and/or bolts.
2. Loosen the wheel lug nuts, then raise and safely support the vehicle.
3. Place jackstands under the front crossmember. Lower the vehicle slightly so the weight of the car rests on the jackstands and NOT the control arms.

4. Remove the wheel and tire assembly.
5. Before removing front suspension components, their positions should be marked so they may assemble correctly. Refer to the illustration.

❋❋ WARNING

Whenever working near the drive axles, use care to prevent damage from over extension of the drive shaft joints. When either end of the shaft is disconnected, over extension of the joint could result in separation of the internal components and possible joint failure.

1 Strut assembly
2 Knuckle
3 Bolt
4 180 Nm (133 lbs. ft.) nut
5 Suspension support
6 Cover
7 24 Nm (18 lbs. ft.) nut

87958006

Fig. 10 Exploded view of the strut assembly

Fig. 11 Unfasten the strut tower retaining nuts

Fig. 12 Remove and discard the tie rod end cotter pin

Fig. 13 Use a suitable tie rod end puller, then . . .

Fig. 14 . . . separate the tie rod end from the strut bracket

Fig. 15 Unfasten the strut-to-steering knuckle bolts, then carefully remove the strut assembly

A   SCRIBE KNUCKLE ALONG LOWER OUTBOARD STRUT RADIUS
B   SCRIBE STRUT FLANGE ON INBOARD SIDE ALONG CURVE OF KNUCKLE
C   SCRIBE ACROSS STRUT/KNUCKLE INTERFACE

87958004

Fig. 16 Scribe a matchmark as illustrated, for alignment purposes during installation

6. Install a drive axle joint protective cover (modified), such as J–34754 or equivalent.

7. If necessary, remove the brake line bracket.

8. Remove the cotter pin and nut, then press the tie rod out of the strut bracket using J 24319-01 or equivalent two-armed puller. Discard the cotter pin.

9. Unfasten and remove the strut-to-steering knuckle bolts and carefully lift out the strut.

➡ **The steering knuckle MUST be supported to prevent axle joint overextension.**

10. Remove the strut assembly from the vehicle. Be careful to avoid chipping or cracking the spring coating when handling the front suspension coil spring assembly.

To install:

11. Move the strut into position, then install the nuts and/or bolts connecting the strut assembly to the body.

➡ **On 1982–87 vehicles, make sure that the flat sides of the strut-to-knuckle bolt heads are horizontal, as shown in the accompanying figure, before tightening.**

12. Align the steering knuckle with the strut flange scribe mark made during removal, then install the bolts and nuts. For 1982 vehicles, tighten to 140 ft. lbs. (190 Nm). For 1983–94 vehicles, tighten to 133 ft. lbs. (180 Nm).

13. Position the tie rod end into the strut assembly, then secure with the tie rod end bolt and new cotter pin. Tighten the tie rod end bolt to 44 ft. lbs. (60 Nm).

14. Tighten the nuts and/or bolts attaching the top of the strut to the body to 18–20 ft. lbs. (25–27 Nm).

15. Install the brake line bracket.

16. Slightly raise the vehicle, then remove the jackstands from under the suspension supports.

17. Install the tire and wheel assembly.

18. Carefully lower the vehicle, then final tighten the lug nuts to 100 ft. lbs. (140 Nm).

OVERHAUL

✳✳ CAUTION

The coil springs are retained under considerable pressure. They can exert enough force to cause serious injury. Exercise extreme caution when disassembling the strut for coil spring removal. This procedure requires the use of a spring compressor and several other special tools. It cannot be performed without them. If you do not have access to these tools, DO NOT attempt to disassemble the strut!

1982–84 Vehicles

▶ **See Figure 17**

1. Remove the strut assembly from the vehicle, as outlined earlier in this section.

2. Clamp the spring compressor J 26584, or equivalent, in a vise. Position the strut assembly in the bottom adapter of the compressor and install the special tool J26584–86 (see illustration). Be sure that the adapter captures the strut and that the locating pins are engaged.

3. Rotate the strut assembly so that the top mounting assembly lip aligns with the compressor support notch. Insert two top adapters (J26584–88) between the top mounting assembly and the top spring seat. Position the adapters so that the split lines are in the 3 o'clock and 9 o'clock positions.

4. Using a 1 in. socket, turn the screw on top of the compressor clockwise until the top support flange contacts the adapters. Continue turning the screw until the coil spring is compressed approximately ½ in. (13mm) or 4 complete turns. Never bottom the spring or the strut damper rod.

5. Unscrew the nut from the strut damper shaft and then lift off the top mounting assembly.

6. Turn the compressor adjusting screw counterclockwise until the spring tension has been relieved. Remove the adapters and then remove the coil spring.

To install:

7. Clamp the strut compressor body J 26584 in a vise.

8. Position the strut assembly in the bottom adapter of the compressor and install the special tool J26584–86 (see illustration). Be sure that the adapter captures the strut and that the locating pins are engaged.

9. Position the spring on the strut. Make sure the spring is properly seated on the bottom of the spring plate.

10. Install the spring strut seat assembly on top of the spring.

11. Place BOTH J 26584–88 top adapters over the spring seat assemblies.

12. Turn the compressor forcing the screw until the compressor top support just contacts the top adapters (do not compress the spring at this time).

13. Install long extension with a socket to fit the hex on the damper shaft through the top of the spring seat. Use the extension to guide the components during reassembly.

✳✳ WARNING

NEVER place a hard tool such as pliers or screwdriver against the polished surface of the damper shaft. The shaft can be held up with your fingers or an extension in order to prevent it from receding into the strut assembly while the spring is being compressed.

14. Compress the screw by turning the screw clockwise until approximately 1½ in. (38mm) of damper shaft extends through the top spring plate.

Fig. 17 Strut disassembly—1982–84 vehicles

✳✳ WARNING

Do not compress the spring until it bottoms.

15. Remove the extension and socket, position the top mounting assembly over the damper shaft and install the nut. Tighten to 68 ft. lbs. (92 Nm).

16. Turn the forcing screw counterclockwise to back off support, remove the top adapters and bottom adapter and remove the strut assembly from the compressor.

17. Install the strut assembly in the vehicle, as outlined earlier in this section.

1985–94 Vehicles

▶ **See Figures 18, 19, 20 and 21**

1. Remove the strut assembly from the vehicle, as outlined earlier in this section.

2. Mount the strut compressor J–34013 in holding fixture J–3289–20.

3. Mount the strut assembly into the compressor. Note that the strut compressor has strut mounting holes drilled for specific car lines.

4. Compress the strut approximately ½ its height after initial contact with the top cap.

✳✳ WARNING

Never bottom the spring or dampener rod!

1 Strut assembly
2 Install locking pins through strut assembly
3 Tighten nuts until flush with strut compressor
4 Compressor forcing screw

87958008

Fig. 18 View of the strut assembly mounted in a compressor

87958009

Fig. 19 Use a socket and a wrench to remove the dampener shaft nut spring cap while compressing the spring

87958010

Fig. 20 Install the rod to guide the dampener shaft straight down through the spring cap while compressing the spring

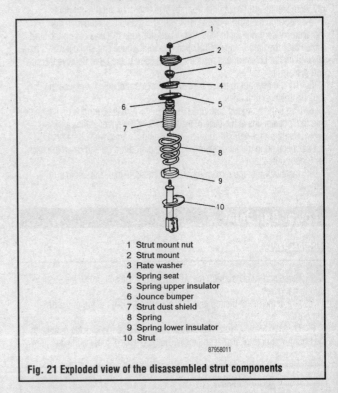

1 Strut mount nut
2 Strut mount
3 Rate washer
4 Spring seat
5 Spring upper insulator
6 Jounce bumper
7 Strut dust shield
8 Spring
9 Spring lower insulator
10 Strut

87958011

Fig. 21 Exploded view of the disassembled strut components

5. Remove the nut from the strut dampener shaft and place alignment/guiding rod J–34013–27 on top of the dampener shaft. Use the rod to guide the dampener shaft straight down through the spring cap while compressing the spring. Remove the components.

➡ **Be careful to avoid chipping or cracking the spring coating when handling the front suspension coil spring assembly.**

To install:

6. Install the bearing cap into the strut compressor if previously removed.

7. Mount the strut assembly in strut compressor, using bottom locking pin only. Extend the dampener shaft and install clamp J–34013–20 on the dampener shaft.

8. Install the spring over the dampener and swing the assembly up so the upper locking pin can be installed.

9. Install all shields, bumpers and insulators on the spring seat. Install the spring seat on top of the spring. Be sure the flat on the upper spring seat is facing in the proper direction. The spring seat flat should be facing the same direction as the centerline of the strut assembly spindle.

10. Install the guiding rod and turn the forcing screw while the guiding rod centers the assembly. When the threads on the dampener shaft are visible, remove the guiding rod and install the nut. Tighten the nut to 65 ft. lbs. (85 Nm). Use a crowsfoot line wrench while holding the dampener shaft with a socket.

11. Remove the clamp.

Strut Cartridge

REMOVAL & INSTALLATION

▶ See Figure 22

➡On 1982–87 models only, the internal piston rod, cylinder assembly and fluid can be replaced utilizing a service cartridge and nut. Internal threads are located inside the tube immediately below a cut line groove.

1. Remove the strut and the coil springs. Clamp the strut in a vise. Do not overtighten it as this will cause damage to the strut tube.

2. Locate the cut line groove just below the top edge of the strut tube. It is imperative that the groove be accurately located as any mislocation will cause inner thread damage. Using pipe cutters, cut around the groove until the tube is completely cut through.

3. Remove and discard the end cap, the cylinder and the piston rod assembly. Remove the strut assembly from the vise and pour out the old fluid.

4. Reclamp the strut in the vise. A flaring cup tool is included in the replacement cartridge kit to flare and deburr the edge that was cut on the strut tube. Place the flaring cup on the open edge of the tube and strike it with a mallet until its flat outer surface rests on the top edge of the tube. Remove the cup and discard it.

5. Try the new nut to make sure that it threads properly. If not, use the flaring cup again until it does.

6. Place the new strut cartridge into the tube. Turn the cartridge until it settles into the indentations at the base of the tube. Place the nut over the cartridge.

7. Using tool J–29778–A or equivalent, and a torque wrench, tighten the nut as specified in the kit directions. Pull the piston rod up and down to check for proper operation.

8. Installation of the remaining components is in the reverse order of removal.

Lower Ball Joint

INSPECTION

1. Raise and safely support the vehicles on jackstands. Allow the suspension to hang free.

2. Grasp the tire at the top and the bottom and move the top of the tire in and out.

3. Observe for any horizontal movement of the steering knuckle relative to the front lower control arm. If any movement is detected, replace the ball joint.

Fig. 22 On 1982–87 vehicles, it is possible to replace the strut cartridge

4. If the ball stud is disconnected from the steering knuckle and any looseness is detected, or if the ball stud can be twisted in its socket using finger pressure, replace the ball joint.

REMOVAL & INSTALLATION

1982–87 Vehicles

▶ See Figure 23

1. Loosen the wheel nuts, raise the car, and remove the wheel.

2. Use a ⅛ in. (3mm) drill bit to drill a hole through the center of each of the three ball joint rivets.

3. Use a ½ in. (13mm) drill bit to drill completely through the rivet.

4. Use a hammer and punch to remove the rivets. Drive them out from the bottom.

5. Use the special tool J29330 or a ball joint removal tool to separate the ball joint from the steering knuckle, as shown in the accompanying figure. Don't forget to remove and discard the cotter pin.

6. Disconnect the stabilizer bar from the lower control arm, then remove the ball joint.

To install:

7. Install the new ball joint into the control arm with the three bolts supplied as shown and tighten to 50 ft. lbs. (68 Nm).

8. Installation of the remaining components is in the reverse order of removal.

9. Tighten the castellated nut on the ball joint to 55 ft. lbs. (75 Nm) and use a new cotter pin.

10. Have a reputable repair shop check the toe setting and adjust, if necessary.

Fig. 23 Ball joint removal and installation—1982–87 vehicles

1988–94 Vehicles

▶ See Figures 24, 25, 26, 27 and 28

1. Raise and support the vehicle safely.

2. Place jack stands under the suspension support.

3. Lower the car slightly so the weight of the car rests on the suspension supports and not the control arms.

4. Remove the tire and wheel assembly.

✳✳ WARNING

Use care to prevent damage from over extension of the drive shaft joints. When either end of the shaft is disconnected, over extension of the joint could result in separation of the internal components

87958017

Fig. 24 Remove and discard the cotter pin from the ball joint

87958018

Fig. 25 Unfasten the ball joint retaining nut

87958019

Fig. 26 The recommended procedure for disconnecting the ball joint from the steering knuckle is to use a suitable ball joint separator

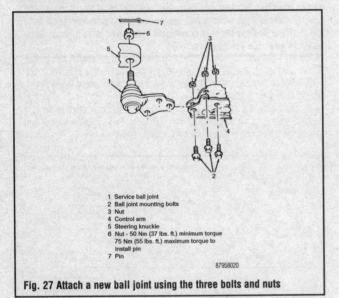

1 Service ball joint
2 Ball joint mounting bolts
3 Nut
4 Control arm
5 Steering knuckle
6 Nut - 50 Nm (37 lbs. ft.) minimum torque
   75 Nm (55 lbs. ft.) maximum torque to
   install pin
7 Pin

87958020

Fig. 27 Attach a new ball joint using the three bolts and nuts

1 Pin
2 Nut - 50 Nm (37 lbs. ft.)
   minimum torque 75 Nm (55 lbs. ft.)
   maximum torque to install pin
3 Ball joint

87958021

Fig. 28 Position the ball joint stud through the steering knuckle, then fasten the retaining nut and install a new cotter pin

and possible joint failure. The steering knuckle should be supported and drive axle joint protectors should be used.

5. Install a drive axle joint protective cover (modified), such as J–34754 or equivalent.

6. Remove the cotter pin from the ball joint castellated nut. Discard the pin.

7. Remove the castellated nut and disconnect the ball joint from the steering knuckle using ball joint separator J-34505, J-29330, or equivalent.

➡**Be sure to use on the recommended tool for separating the ball joint from the knuckle. Failure to use the proper tool may cause damage to the ball joint and seal.**

8. Drill out the three rivets retaining the ball joint to the lower control arm. Use a ⅛ in. (3mm) drill bit to make a pilot hole through the rivets. Finish drilling the rivets with a ½ in. (13mm) drill bit.

➡**Be careful not to damage the drive axle boot when drilling out the ball joint rivets.**

9. Loosen the stabilizer shaft bushing assembly nut.

10. Remove the ball joint from the steering knuckle and control arm.

To install:

11. Piston the ball joint in the control arm.

12. Install the three ball joint bolts and nuts as shown on the instructions sheet in the ball joint kit, then tighten the bolts to specifications.

13. Position the ball joint stud through the steering knuckle.

14. Install the ball joint nut. Tighten the stabilizer shaft bushing clamp nuts to 15–22 ft. lbs. (20–30 Nm).

15. Fasten the ball joint-to-steering knuckle nut to 55 ft. lbs. (75 Nm), plus a 60° rotation. Do NOT loosen the nut at any time during installation.

16. Install a new cotter pin to the ball joint castellated nut.

17. If installed, remove the boot protector.

18. Fasten the nut attaching the stabilizer link to the stabilizer shaft. Tighten to 22 ft. lbs. (30 Nm), then slightly raise the vehicle and remove the jackstands from under the suspension.

19. Install the front tire and wheel assembly and hand-tighten the lug nuts.

20. Carefully lower the vehicle, then tighten the wheel lug nuts to 103 ft. lbs. (140 Nm).

➡**The front end alignment should be checked and adjusted.**

Stabilizer Shaft (Sway Bar)

REMOVAL & INSTALLATION

▶ **See Figures 29, 30 and 31**

1. Raise and safely support the vehicle. Allow the front suspension to hang free.

2. For vehicles through 1991, remove the left front wheel and tire. For 1992–94 vehicles, remove both front wheel and tire assemblies.

3. Detach the stabilizer shaft from the control arms.

4. Unfasten the retaining clamps, then disconnect the stabilizer shaft from the support assemblies.

5. Remove the rear and center bolts from the suspension support assembly, then loosen, but do not remove, the front bolts.

6. Remove the stabilizer shaft with the insulators.

To install:

7. Position the stabilizer shaft with the insulators, into the vehicle.

Fig. 29 Stabilizer shaft removal and installation—1982–87 vehicles

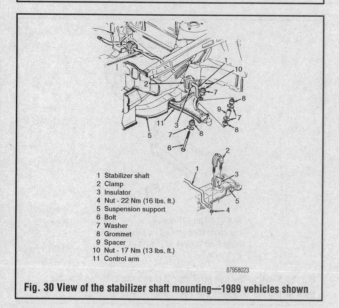

1 Stabilizer shaft
2 Clamp
3 Insulator
4 Nut - 22 Nm (16 lbs. ft.)
5 Suspension support
6 Bolt
7 Washer
8 Grommet
9 Spacer
10 Nut - 17 Nm (13 lbs. ft.)
11 Control arm

Fig. 30 View of the stabilizer shaft mounting—1989 vehicles shown

1 Stabilizer shaft
2 Clamp
3 Insulator
4 Nut - 17 Nm (12 lbs. ft.)
5 Bushing
6 Nut - 25 Nm (18 lbs. ft.)

Fig. 31 Stabilizer shaft removal and installation—1991–94 vehicles

8. Fasten the clamps attaching the stabilizer shaft to the suspension support assemblies and hand-tighten the retainers.

9. Move the suspension support assemblies into position and hand-tighten the bolts.

10. Install the nut attaching the stabilizer shaft to the stabilizer links.

11. Tighten the suspension support bolts, in sequence, as follows:
- Center bolts first, to 66 ft. lbs. (90 Nm)
- Front bolts second, to 65 ft. lbs. (88 Nm)
- Rear bolts third, to 65 ft. lbs. (88 Nm)

12. Tighten the stabilizer shaft-to-support assembly nuts to 16–22 ft. lbs. (22–30 Nm) and the stabilizer shaft to control arm nuts to 13–22 ft. lbs. (17–30 Nm).

13. Tighten the clamp nuts to 17 ft. lbs. (23 Nm).

14. Install the wheel and tire assemblies.

15. Carefully lower the vehicle.

Control Arm/Suspension Support

REMOVAL & INSTALLATION

♦ See Figures 32 and 33

1. Raise and safely support the vehicle. Place jackstands under the suspension supports, then lower the vehicle slightly so the weight of the vehicle rests on the suspension supports, and not on the control arms.

2. Remove the tire and wheel assembly.

3. Unfasten the nut attaching the stabilizer link to the stabilizer shaft, then unfasten the nuts attaching the stabilizer shaft clamps to the suspension support. Detach the stabilizer shaft from the control arm and/or support assembly.

✷✷ WARNING

Be careful to avoid over-extending the axle shaft joints. When either end of the shaft is disconnected, over-extension of the joint could result in separation of internal components and possible joint failure. Failure to observe this can result in interior joint or boot damage and possible joint failure.

4. Disconnect the ball joint from the steering knuckle using separator tool J-29330 or equivalent. For details, see the ball joint removal and installation procedure located in this section.

5. To remove the support assembly with the control arm attached, remove the bolts mounting the support assembly to the car. To remove the control arm only, remove the control arm to support assembly bolts.

Fig. 32 Control arm, suspension support and related components—1982–89 vehicles

1 Control arm
2 Suspension support
3 Bolt - 83 Nm (61 lbs. ft.)
4 Washer
5 Nut
6 Bolt - 90 Nm (66 lbs. ft.) tighten first
7 Bolt - 88 Nm (65 lbs. ft.) tighten second
8 Bolt - 88 Nm (65 lbs. ft.) tighten third

Fig. 33 Control arm and suspension support mounting—1988–86 vehicles

To install:

6. Move the control arm into position, then loosely install the bolts attaching the control arm to the suspension support.

7. Place the suspension support into position, guiding the ball joint into the steering knuckle, then loosely install the retaining bolts.

8. Fasten the nuts attaching the stabilizer shaft clamps to the suspension support. Tighten to 22 ft. lbs. (30 Nm).

9. Install the nuts attaching the ball joint to the steering knuckle. Tighten to the specifications located in the ball joint removal and installation procedure, then install a new cotter pin.

10. Install the stabilizer link-to-shaft nut, then tighten to 22 ft. lbs. (30 Nm).

11. Slightly raise the vehicle, then remove the jackstands from the under the suspension supports.

12. Install the tire and wheel assembly.

13. With the vehicle at ground height, tighten the suspension support bolts, as follows:
- Center bolts first, to 66 ft. lbs. (90 Nm)
- Front bolts second, to 65 ft. lbs. (88 Nm)
- Rear bolts third, to 65 ft. lbs. (88 Nm)

14. With the vehicle still at curb height, tighten the control arm retaining bolts to 61 ft. lbs. (83 Nm).

15. Have the front end wheel alignment checked.

CONTROL ARM BUSHING REPLACEMENT

▶ See Figure 34

1. Remove the lower control arm as outlined earlier in this section.
2. Install bushing removal tools J 29792 or equivalent.
3. Coat the threads of the tool with extreme pressure lubricant.
4. Remove the lower control arm bushings.

To install:

5. Install the bushing installation tools.
6. Coat the outer case of the bushing with a light coating of a suitable lubricant, then install the lower control arm bushings.
7. As outlined earlier, install the lower control arm.

Steering Knuckle

REMOVAL & INSTALLATION

1. Raise and safely support the vehicle with jackstands. Place the jackstands under the frame so that the front suspension hangs freely.
2. Remove the front tire and wheel assembly.
3. Remove the hub and bearing assembly, as outlined in this section.
4. Unfasten the bolts attaching the knuckle to the strut, then remove the steering knuckle.

To install:

5. Position the steering knuckle into the strut, then install the retaining bolts. Tighten the bolts to 133 ft. lbs. (180 Nm).
6. Install the hub and bearing assembly, as outlined in this section.
7. Install the wheel and tire assembly, then carefully lower the vehicle.
8. Have the wheel alignment checked by a reputable facility.

Front Hub and Bearing

REMOVAL & INSTALLATION

▶ See Figures 35, 36 and 37

➡**This procedure requires the use of a number of special tools.**

1. Raise and safely support the vehicle with jackstands. Place the jackstands under the frame so that the front suspension hangs freely.
2. Remove the front tire and wheel assembly.
3. If a silicone (gray) boot is used on the inboard axle joint, place boot seal protector J-33162 or equivalent. If a thermoplastic (black) boot is used, no seal protector is necessary.
4. Insert a drift punch through the rotor cooling vanes to lock the rotor in place and remove the hub nut and washer. Clean the drive axle threads of all dirt and grease. Discard the nut and washer.
5. Separate the ball joint from the steering knuckle as outlined in this section.
6. Attach a puller, G.M. part no. J-28733 or the equivalent, and remove the bearing. If corrosion is present, make sure the bearing is loose in the knuckle before using the puller.
7. Move the axle shaft inward and support at an angle near the normal drive angle.
8. Remove the brake caliper and rotor, as follows:
    a. Remove the caliper mounting bolts.
    b. Remove the caliper from the knuckle and suspend from a length of wire. Do not allow the caliper to hang from the brake hose. Pull the rotor from the knuckle.
9. Unfasten the three hub and bearing attaching bolts. If the old bearing is to be reused, match mark the bolts and holes for installation. If equipped, the brake rotor splash shield will have to come off, too.
10. Clean the mating surfaces of all dirt and corrosion. Check the knuckle bore and knuckle seal for damage. If a new bearing is to be installed, remove and discard the old knuckle seal and replace with a new one during installation.

To install:

11. Position the hub and bearing assembly and splash shield (if equipped) on the steering knuckle and install the retaining bolts. Tighten the bolts to 70 ft. lbs. (95 Nm).
12. Grease the lips of the new seal before installation; install with a seal driver made for the purpose, G.M. tool no. J-28671 or the equivalent.
13. Install the rotor and caliper. Be sure that the caliper hose isn't twisted. Install the caliper bolts and tighten to 21–38 ft. lbs. (28–51 Nm).
14. Position the axle shaft into the hub and bearing assembly.
15. Insert a drift in the rotor, then install a new hub nut and washer. Use a torque wrench to tighten the nut to 185 ft. lbs. (260 Nm).
16. Fasten the ball joint to the steering knuckle.
17. Remove the drift and the boot seal protector (if used).
18. Install the wheel and tire assembly, then carefully lower the vehicles.

Fig. 34 View of the front and rear lower control arm bushings

Fig. 35 Insert a drift into the rotor when removing the hub nut

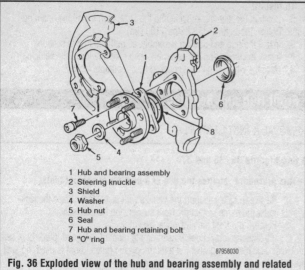

1 Hub and bearing assembly
2 Steering knuckle
3 Shield
4 Washer
5 Hub nut
6 Seal
7 Hub and bearing retaining bolt
8 "O" ring

87958030

Fig. 36 Exploded view of the hub and bearing assembly and related components—1989 vehicle shown

87958031

Fig. 37 Use a seal driver when installing the new seal into the steering knuckle

Wheel Alignment

If the tires are worn unevenly, if the vehicle is not stable on the highway or if the handling seems uneven in spirited driving, the wheel alignment should be checked. If an alignment problem is suspected, first check for improper tire inflation and other possible causes. These can be worn suspension or steering components, accident damage or even unmatched tires. If any worn or damaged components are found, they must be replaced before the wheels can be properly aligned. Wheel alignment requires very expensive equipment and involves minute adjustments which must be accurate; it should only be performed by a trained technician. Take your vehicle to a properly equipped shop.

Following is a description of the alignment angles which are adjustable on most vehicles and how they affect vehicle handling. Although these angles can apply to both the front and rear wheels, usually only the front suspension is adjustable.

CASTER

▶ See Figure 38

Looking at a vehicle from the side, caster angle describes the steering axis rather than a wheel angle. The steering knuckle is attached to a control arm or strut at the top and a control arm at the bottom. The wheel pivots around the line between these points to steer the vehicle. When the upper point is tilted back, this is described as positive caster. Having a positive caster tends to make the wheels self-centering, increasing directional stability. Excessive positive caster makes the wheels hard to steer, while an uneven caster will cause a pull to one side. Overloading the vehicle or sagging rear springs will affect caster, as will raising the rear of the vehicle. If the rear of the vehicle is lower than normal, the caster becomes more positive.

TCCA8G01

Fig. 38 Caster affects straight-line stability. Caster wheels used on shopping carts, for example, employ positive caster

CAMBER

▶ See Figure 39

Looking from the front of the vehicle, camber is the inward or outward tilt of the top of wheels. When the tops of the wheels are tilted in, this is negative camber; if they are tilted out, it is positive. In a turn, a slight amount of negative camber helps maximize contact of the tire with the road. However, too much negative camber compromises straight-line stability, increases bump steer and torque steer.

A A CYLINDER WILL ROLL STRAIGHT AHEAD
B A CONE WILL ROLL IN A CIRCLE TOWARD THE SMALL END
C TIRE CONTACTS THE ROAD SURFACE
D POSITIVE CAMBER ANGLE
E VERTICAL

TCCA8G02

Fig. 39 Camber influences tire contact with the road

TOE

▶ See Figure 40

Looking down at the wheels from above the vehicle, toe angle is the distance between the front of the wheels, relative to the distance between the back of the wheels. If the wheels are closer at the front, they are said to be toed-in or to have negative toe. A small amount of negative toe enhances directional stability and provides a smoother ride on the highway.

TCCA8G03

Fig. 40 With toe-in, the distance between the wheels is closer at the front than at the rear

REAR SUSPENSION

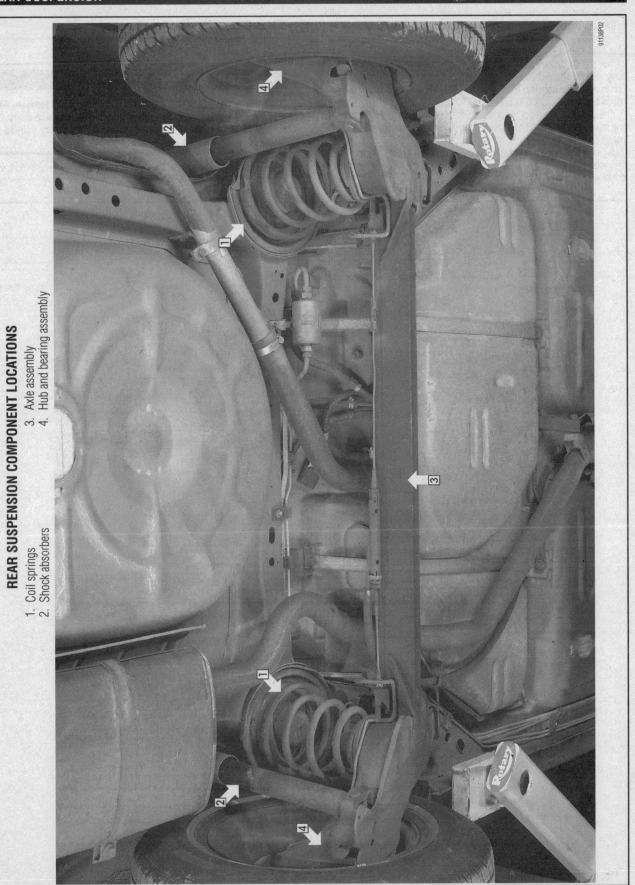

REAR SUSPENSION COMPONENT LOCATIONS

1. Coil springs
2. Shock absorbers
3. Axle assembly
4. Hub and bearing assembly

The J-cars have a semi-independent rear suspension system which consists of an axle with trailing arms and two coil springs, shock absorbers, upper spring insulators and spring compression bumpers. The axle assembly attaches to the body through a rubber bushing located at the front of each control arm. The brackets are integral with the underbody side rails. A stabilizer bar is available as an option.

Two coil springs are used, each being retained between a seat in the underbody and one on the control arm. A rubber cushion is used to isolate the coil spring upper end from the underbody seat, while the lower end sits on a combination bumper and spring insulator.

The double acting shock absorbers are filled with a calibrated amount of fluid and sealed during production. They are non-adjustable, non-refillable and cannot be disassembled.

A single unit hub and bearing assembly is bolted to both ends of the rear axle assembly; it is a sealed unit and must be replaced as one if found to be defective.

Coil Springs

REMOVAL & INSTALLATION

▶ See Figures 41 and 42

❋❋ CAUTION

The coil springs are under a considerable amount of tension. Be very careful when removing or installing them; they can exert enough force to cause very serious injuries. Make sure vehicle is safely supported on the proper type equipment.

1. Raise and safely support the vehicle. Remove the rear wheel and tire assemblies.

VIEW B

VIEW C

VIEW D

1	STABILIZER SHAFT	9	NUT	17	NUT - 83 N.m (61 LBS. FT.)
2	STABILIZER SHAFT INSULATOR	10	BOLT - 18 N.m (13 LBS. FT.)	18	SHOCK ABSORBER NUT
3	STABILIZER SHAFT CLAMP	11	AXLE	19	BOLT - 47 N.m (35 LBS. FT.)
4	UPPER SPACER	12	AXLE BUMPER	20	SHOCK ABSORBER
5	LOWER SPACER	13	SPRING	21	SHOCK ABSORBER UPPER MOUNT
6	BOLT	14	SPRING UPPER INSULATOR	22	RETAINER
7	NUT 22 N.m (16 LBS. FT.)	15	UNDERBODY	23	NUT - 29 N.m (21 LBS. FT.)
8	STABILIZER SHAFT CLAMP	16	WASHER	24	NUT - 17 N.m (13 LBS. FT.)
				25	SHOCK ABSORBER UPPER COVER

87958041

Fig. 41 View of the coil spring and shock mounting and related components—1991 vehicle shown

Fig. 42 Removing the spring and insulator—1994 vehicle shown

2. Using the proper equipment, support the weight of the rear axle. Unfasten the right and left brake line bracket attaching screws, then allow the brake line to hang free.

❋ WARNING

Do NOT suspend the rear axle by the brake hoses or damage to the hoses may result.

3. Unfasten both shock absorber lower attaching bolts from the axle.
4. Carefully lower the axle, then remove the coil spring(s) and/or insulator(s).
To install:
5. Position the spring(s) and insulator(s) in the seats, and raise the axle. The ends of the upper coil in the spring must be positioned in the spring seat and within 7/16 in. (15mm) of the spring stop.

➡**Before installing the springs, it may be necessary to install the upper insulators to the body with adhesive to keep them in position while raising the axle assembly.**

6. Install the shock absorber bolts. Tighten to 41 ft. lbs. (55 Nm). Install the brake line brackets. Tighten to 8 ft. lbs. (11 Nm).

Shock Absorbers

REMOVAL & INSTALLATION

♦ **See Figures 41 and 43**

1. Open the hatch or trunk lid, remove the upper shock absorber cover, then unfasten the upper shock absorber nut.
2. Raise and safely support the vehicle. Support the rear axle with adjustable jackstands.
3. Remove the lower attaching bolt and remove the shock.

Fig. 43 Shock absorber removal and installation—1994 vehicle shown

➡**If both shock absorbers are being replaced, remove the shocks one at a time as suspending rear axle at full length could result in damage to the brake lines/hoses.**

To install:
4. If new shock absorbers are being installed, repeatedly compress them while inverted and extend them in their normal upright position. This will purge them of air.
5. Connect the shock absorbers at the lower attachment and install the attaching bolt and nut hand-tight.
6. Lower the vehicle enough to guide the shock absorber upper stud through the body opening, then fasten the upper shock absorber attaching nut loosely. Tighten the lower shock absorber mounting bolt to 35 ft. lbs. (47 Nm).
7. Remove the axle support, then carefully lower the vehicle. Tighten the shock absorber upper nut to 21 ft. lbs. (29 Nm).
8. If equipped, install the retaining nut cover, then install the rear trim cover. Close the trunk or hatch lid.

TESTING

♦ **See Figure 44**

The purpose of the shock absorber is simply to limit the motion of the spring during compression and rebound cycles. If the vehicle is not equipped with these motion dampers, the up and down motion would multiply until the vehicle was alternately trying to leap off the ground and to pound itself into the pavement.

Contrary to popular rumor, the shocks do not affect the ride height of the vehicle. This is controlled by other suspension components such as springs and tires. Worn shock absorbers can affect handling; if the front of the vehicle is rising or falling excessively, the "footprint" of the tires changes on the pavement and steering is affected.

The simplest test of the shock absorber is simply push down on one corner of the unladen vehicle and release it. Observe the motion of the body as it is released. In most cases, it will come up beyond it original rest position, dip back below it and settle quickly to rest. This shows that the damper is controlling the spring action. Any tendency to excessive pitch (up-and-down) motion or failure to return to rest within 2-3 cycles is a sign of poor function within the shock absorber. Oil-filled shocks may have a light film of oil around the seal, resulting from normal breathing and air exchange. This should NOT be taken as a sign of failure, but any sign of thick or running oil definitely indicates failure. Gas filled shocks may also show some film at the shaft; if the gas has leaked out, the shock will have almost no resistance to motion.

While each shock absorber can be replaced individually, it is recommended that they be changed as a pair (both front or both rear) to maintain equal response on both sides of the vehicle. Chances are quite good that if one has failed, its mate is weak also.

Rear Axle/Control Arm

The control arms and axle are are one unit. The axle structure itself maintains the geometrical relationship of the wheels relative to the body. The axle assembly attaches to the underbody through a rubber bushing located at the front of each control arm. Each control arm bolts to underbody brackets.

Fig. 44 When fluid is seeping out of the shock absorber, it's time to replace it

REMOVAL & INSTALLATION

1982–91 Vehicles

1. Raise and safely support the vehicle. Support the vehicle with jackstands under the axle.
2. Remove the stabilizer shaft from the axle assembly.
3. Remove the wheel and tire assembly, then remove the brake drum.

✳✳ WARNING

Do not hammer on the brake drum as damage to the bearing could result!

4. Unfasten the shock absorber lower attaching bolts and paddle nuts at the axle, then disconnect the shocks from the control arm/axle.
5. Disconnect the parking brake cable and the rear ABS wiring connector and clip, if equipped, from the axle assembly.
6. Disconnect the brake line at the brackets from the axle assembly. This will ensure that the axle assembly is not suspended by the brake lines.
7. Lower the rear axle, then remove the coil springs and insulators.
8. Unfasten the control arm bolts from the underbody bracket and lower the axle from the underbody.
9. Remove the hub attaching bolts, then and remove the hub, bearing and backing plate assembly from the axle.

To install:
10. Install the hub, bearing and backing plate assembly. Hold the nuts and tighten the attaching bolts to 39 ft. lbs. (53 Nm).
11. Install the stabilizer shaft.
12. Place the axle assembly on a transmission jack and raise into position. Attach the control arm/axle to the underbody bracket with bolts and nuts. Tighten the retainers to 61 ft. lbs. (83 Nm) with the weight of the vehicle on the axle.
13. Install the brake line connections to the axle assembly. Tighten the brake line-to-axle screw to 11 ft. lbs. (15 Nm).
14. Attach the brake cable and the rear ABS wiring connector and clip, if equipped, to the rear axle assembly.
15. Position the coil springs and insulators in seats and raise the rear axle.
16. The end of the upper coil on the springs must be parallel to the axle assembly and seated in the pocket.
17. Install the shock absorber lower attachment bolts and paddle nuts to the rear axle and tighten the bolts to 41 ft. lbs. (56 Nm).
18. Install the parking brake cable to the guide hook and adjust as necessary.
19. Install the brake drums and the wheel and tire assemblies.
20. Bleed the brake system, as outlined in Section 9, then carefully lower the car.

1992–94 Vehicles

1. Raise and safely support the vehicle. Support the rear axle with jackstands.
2. Remove the rear tire and wheel assembly.
3. Disconnect the brake line at the brackets from the axle assembly. This will ensure that the axle assembly is not suspended by the brake lines.
4. Unfasten the lower shock mount bolt.
5. Lower the rear axle.
6. Disconnect the parking brake cable at the equalizer unit right wheel assembly.
7. If equipped, detach the rear ABS wiring connector and mount clip located near the fuel tank.
8. Disconnect the right and left brake lines.
9. Unfasten the control arm bolts and nuts, then remove the axle assembly.

To install:
10. Position the rear axle assembly and loosely install the attaching bolts.
11. Connect the right and left brake lines.
12. Attach the ABS wiring connector and mount clip.
13. Fasten the parking brake cable at the right rear wheel cable connector and cable equalizer.
14. Install the lower mount bolt. Tighten the control arm nuts to 44 ft. lbs. (80 Nm) plus a 120° rotation. Tighten the shock absorber lower attaching bolt and nut to 125 ft. lbs. (170 Nm).

15. Fasten the left and right side brake line bracket mount bolts to the body. Tighten the screws to 97 inch lbs. (11 Nm).
16. Install the tire and wheel assembly, then remove the jackstands from under the vehicle.
17. Carefully lower the vehicle, then bleed the brake system, as outlined in Section 9 of this manual.

Stabilizer Bar

REMOVAL & INSTALLATION

1. Raise the vehicle and support the body with jackstands.
2. Unfasten the nuts and bolts at both the axle and control arm attachments and remove the control arm and remove the bracket, insulator and stabilizer bar.

To install:
3. Install the U-bolts, upper clamp, spacer and insulators in the trailing axle. Position the stabilizer bar in the insulators and loosely install the lower clamp and nuts.
4. Attach the end of the stabilizer bar to the control arms, then tighten all nuts to 13 ft. lbs. (18 Nm).
5. Tighten the axle attaching nut to 10 ft. lbs. (14 Nm).
6. Carefully lower the vehicle.

Rear Hub and Bearing

REMOVAL & INSTALLATION

▶ See Figure 45

1. Loosen the wheel lug nuts. Raise and safely support the vehicle, then remove the wheel and tire assembly.
2. Remove the brake drum. Removal procedures are covered in Section 9 of this manual, if needed.

✳✳ WARNING

Do not hammer on the brake drum to remove; damage to the bearing will result.

3. If equipped, detach the rear ABS wheel speed sensor wire connector.
4. Unfasten the four hub and bearing retaining bolts and remove the assembly from the axle. The top rear attaching bolt will not clear the brake shoe when removing the hub and bearing assembly. Partially remove the hub and bearing assembly prior to removing this bolt.

To install:
5. If equipped, attach the rear ABS wheel speed sensor wire.
6. Position the top rear attaching bolt in the hub and bearing assembly, then install the assembly.
7. Tighten the hub and bearing-to-axle bolts to 39–44 ft. lbs. (52–60 Nm).
8. Install the brake drum.
9. Install the wheel and tire assembly, then carefully lower the vehicle and tighten the lug nut to 100 ft. lbs. (140 Nm).

1 Nut
2 Rear axle assembly
3 Backing plate
4 Hub and bearing assembly
5 Bolt

87958045

Fig. 45 Exploded view of the rear hub and bearing assembly

STEERING

Most J-cars are equipped with, as standard equipment, (except Cimarron), a Saginaw manual rack and pinion steering gear. The pinion is supported by and turns in a sealed ball bearing at the top and a pressed-in roller bearing at the bottom. The rack moves in bushings pressed into each end of the rack housing.

Wear compensation occurs through the action of an adjuster spring which forces the rack against the pinion teeth. This adjuster eliminates the need for periodic pinion preload adjustments. Preload is adjustable only at overhaul.

The inner tie rod assemblies are bolted to the front of the rack. A special bushing is used, allowing both rocking and rotating motion of the tie rods. Any service other than replacement of the outer tie rods or the boots requires removal of the unit from the car.

The power steering gear is an integral unit and shares most features with the manual gear. A rotary control valve directs the hydraulic fluid to either side of the rack piston. The integral rack piston is attached to the rack and converts the hydraulic pressure into left or right linear motion. A vane-type constant displacement pump with integral reservoir provides hydraulic pressure. No in-car adjustments are necessary or possible on the system, except for periodic belt tension checks and adjustments for the pump. See Section 1 for belt tension adjustments.

Steering Wheel

REMOVAL & INSTALLATION

▶ See Figures 46 thru 52

✳✲ CAUTION

Some models covered by this manual may be equipped with a Supplemental Restraint System (SRS), which uses an air bag. Whenever working near any of the SRS components, such as the impact sensors, the air bag module, steering column and instrument panel, disable the SRS, as described in Section 6.

1. If equipped, disable the SIR system. For details, please refer to the procedure located in Section 6 of this manual.
2. If not done already, disconnect the negative cable.
3. Unfasten the retaining screws or pull the pad/center cap from the steering wheel.
4. Detach the horn lead, then remove remove the retainer (if so equipped).
5. Unfasten the steering shaft nut.
6. There should be alignment marks already present on the wheel and shaft. If not, matchmark the steering wheel to the shaft.
7. Using a suitable steering wheel puller, remove the wheel from the vehi-

Fig. 46 Pull the horn pad from the steering wheel—1988 Sunbird shown

Fig. 47 Detach the horn electrical connector

Fig. 48 On some earlier model vehicles, you must remove a retaining circlip

Fig. 49 Unfasten the steering shaft nut

Fig. 50 If there are no factory alignment marks, matchmark the steering wheel to the shaft

Fig. 51 Use a suitable puller to remove the steering wheel from the vehicle

Fig. 52 When installing the steering wheel, make sure the align the matchmarks made during removal

cle. On some vehicles, a horn spring, eyelet and insulator are underneath; don't lose the parts.

To install:

8. If equipped, install the spring, eyelet and insulator into the tower on the column.

9. Install the wheel on the shaft, aligning the matchmarks. Install the shaft nut and tighten to 30 ft. lbs. (41 Nm).

10. Install the retainer.

11. Attach the horn lead, then install the pad or center cap.

12. If equipped, make sure to enable the SIR system as outlined in Section 6 of this manual.

13. Connect the negative battery cable.

Turn Signal (Combination) Switch

REMOVAL & INSTALLATION

1982–90 Vehicles

▶ **See Figures 53, 54 and 55**

1. Disconnect the negative battery cable.
2. Remove the steering wheel and the trim cover.
3. Pry the cover from the steering column.
4. Position a U-shaped lockplate compressing tool on the end of the steering shaft and compress the lock plate by turning the shaft nut clockwise. Pry the wire snapring out of the shaft groove.
5. Remove the tool and lift the lockplate off the shaft.
6. Slip the cancelling cam, upper bearing preload spring, and thrust washer off the shaft.
7. Remove the turn signal lever. Remove the hazard flasher button retaining screw and remove the button, spring and knob.
8. Pull the switch connector out of the mast jacket and tape the upper part to facilitate switch removal. Attach a long piece of wire to the turn signal switch connector. When installing the turn signal switch, feed this wire through the column first, and then use this wire to pull the switch connector into position. On tilt wheels, place the turn signal and shifter housing in low position and remove the harness cover.
9. Unfasten the three switch mounting screws. Remove the switch by pulling it straight up while guiding the wiring harness cover through the column.

To install:

10. Install the replacement switch by working the connector and cover down through the housing and under the bracket. On tilt models, the connector is worked down through the housing, under the bracket, and then the cover is installed on the harness.

11. Install the switch mounting screws and the connector on the mast jacket bracket. Install the column-to-dash trim plate.

12. Install the flasher knob and the turn signal lever.

13. With the turn signal lever in neutral and the flasher knob out, slide the thrust washer, upper bearing preload spring, and cancelling cam onto the shaft.

14. Position the lock plate on the shaft and press it down until a new snapring can be inserted in the shaft groove. Always use a new snapring when assembling.

15. Install the cover and the steering wheel.

16. Connect the negative battery cable.

1991–94 Sunbird

▶ **See Figure 56**

1. Disconnect the negative battery cable.
2. Remove the pad and horn lead, retainer and nut and remove the steering wheel from the column, using a suitable puller.
3. Unfasten the 2 lower column cover retaining screws.
4. Remove the 3 bottom retaining screws from lower column cover.
5. Separate the rose bud fastener (integral to wire harness) from the jacket assembly.
6. Remove the turn signal switch retaining screws.
7. Compress the locking tab and remove the 2 wire harness connector from the switch.
8. Depress the locking tab and remove the cruise connector from the wire harness, if so equipped.

To install:

9. Installation is the reverse of the removal procedure.

10. Tighten the cover and switch retaining screws to 49 inch lbs. (5.5 Nm) and the steering wheel retaining nut to 30 ft. lbs. (41 Nm).

11. Connect the negative battery cable.

1991–94 Cavalier

▶ **See Figure 57**

➡ **This procedure covers removal and installation of the headlamp, headlamp dimmer switch, turn signal and hazard switches, as well as the cruise control switch.**

1. If equipped, disable the SIR system. For details, please refer to the procedure located in Section 6 of this manual.

2. If not already done, disconnect the negative battery cable.

3. Unfasten the horn pad, then remove the steering wheel. For details, please refer to the procedure earlier in this section.

➡ **If necessary, using locking pliers with a piece of rubber (such as a spark plug boot) between the jaws to help prevent damage to the tilt lever during removal.**

4. If equipped, remove the tilt lever from the steering column by grasping the lever firmly and twisting counterclockwise, while pulling it from the column.

5. Remove the upper and lower steering column covers.

6. Remove the dampener assembly, then unfasten and remove the switch assembly from the vehicle.

To install:

7. Position and secure the switch assembly.

8. Install the dampener and the upper and lower steering column covers.

Fig. 53 Depress the lock plate and remove the snapring

Fig. 54 You must remove these parts for access to the turn signal switch

Fig. 55 Turn signal switch removal and installation—1982–90 vehicles

9. If equipped, attach the tilt lever to the column.
10. Install the steering wheel, then fasten the horn pad.
11. If equipped, enable the SIR system, as outlined in Section 6 of this manual.
12. Connect the negative battery cable.

1 Turn signal switch asm
2 Wiring protector
3 Support bolt
4 Strg col support bracket asm

87958057

Fig. 56 Removing the turn signal switch—1992 Sunbird shown

1 Headlamp/Turn signal/Cruise control
  Hazard switch
2 Windshield wiper/Washer switch
3 Tilt lever (If equipped)

87958058

Fig. 57 View of the steering column showing the turn signal and windshield wiper switch locations

Windshield Wiper Switch

REMOVAL & INSTALLATION

1991–94 Cavalier

▶ See Figure 57

1. If equipped, disable the SIR system. For details, please refer to the procedure located in Section 6 of this manual.
2. Disconnect the negative battery cable.
3. Remove the pad and horn lead, retainer and nut and remove the steering wheel from the column, using a suitable puller.
4. If equipped, remove the tilt lever from the steering column.
5. Remove the upper and lower steering column covers.
6. Remove the dampener assembly.
7. Remove the headlight switch assembly, then remove the windshield wiper switch assembly.
8. Installation is the reverse of the removal procedure.

Ignition Switch

REMOVAL & INSTALLATION

1982–91 Vehicles

▶ See Figures 58, 59 and 60

The switch is located on the steering column and is completely inaccessible without first lowering the steering column. The switch is actuated by a rod and rack assembly. A gear on the end of the lock cylinder engages the toothed upper end of the rod.

1. Lower the steering column; be sure to properly support it.
2. Put the switch in the **OFF-UNLOCKED** position. With the cylinder removed, the rod is in **OFF-UNLOCKED** position when it is in the next to the uppermost detent.
3. Unfasten the two switch screws and remove the switch assembly.

To install:

4. Before installing, move the new switch slider (standard columns with automatic transaxle) to the extreme left position. Move the switch slider (stan-

5. REMOVE AND INSTALL IGNITION AND DIMMER SWITCH

REMOVE

1. Remove parts as shown.

INSTALL

1. Install parts as shown
2. Position rod in slider hole and install ignition switch. Install lower stud and tighten to 4.0 N·m.
3. Install dimmer switch and depress switch slightly to insert 3/32″ drill. Force switch up to remove lash, then tighten screw, and nut to 4.0 N·m.
4. Place shifter in neutral and install shift lever.

SCREWS (2)
STUD   SCREW
IGN. SWITCH INHIBITOR HOUSING ASSEMBLY
IGNITION SWITCH ASSEMBLY
PARK LOCK
BOWL LOWER BEARING
RACK PRELOAD SPRING
UPPER SHIFT LEVER SPRING
SWITCH RACK & ACTUATOR ASSEMBLY
SPRING THRUST WASHER
NUT
SCREWS (KEY REL ONLY)
SHIFT BOWL SHROUD
GEAR SHIFT LEVER BOWL
SPRING AND BOLT ASSEMBLY
DIMMER SWITCH
DIMMER SWITCH ACTUATOR ROD
STEERING COLUMN JACKET

● KEY RELEASE
  Leave slider at extreme left
● PARK LOCK
  Move slider one detent to the right (off lock)
● ALL OTHER COLUMNS
  Move slider two detents to the right (off unlock)

MOVE SWITCH SLIDER TO EXTREME LEFT POSITION
INSTALL IGNITION SWITCH

DIMMER SWITCH
3/32″ Drill
DIMMER SWITCH ACTUATOR ROD
ADJUST DIMMER SWITCH

87958059

Fig. 58 Removal and installation of the ignition switch and related steering column components—1990 vehicle shown

1. RETAINER
2. HEXAGON JAM NUT
3. SHAFT LOCK COVER
4. RETAINING RING
5. STEERING SHAFT LOCK
6. TURN SIGNAL CANCELLING CAM ASM
7. UPPER BEARING SPRING
8. BINDING HEAD CROSS RECESS SCREW
9. ROUND WASHER HEAD SCREW
10. SWITCH ACTUATOR ARM ASM
11. TURN SIGNAL SWITCH ASM
12. HEX WASHER HEAD TAPPING SCREW
13. THRUST WASHER
14. BUZZER SWITCH ASM
15. BUZZER SWITCH RETAINING CLIP
16. LOCK RETAINING SCREW
17. STEERING COLUMN HOUSING
18. SWITCH ACTUATOR SECTOR
19. STEERING COLUMN LOCK CYLINDER SET
20. BEARING ASM
21. BEARING RETAINING BUSHING
22. UPPER BEARING RETAINER
23. PIVOT & SWITCH ASM
24. LOCK BOLT
25. RACK PRELOAD SPRING
26. SWITCH ACTUATOR RACK
27. SWITCH ACTUATOR ROD
28. SPRING THRUST WASHER
29. SWITCH ACTUATOR PIVOT PIN
30. WIRING PROTECTOR
31. FLOOR SHIFT BOWL
32. BINDING HD CROSS RECESS SCREW
33. DIMMER SWITCH ACTUATOR ROD
34. DIMMER SWITCH ASM
35. HEXAGON NUT
36. STEERING COLUMN JACKET ASM
37. ADAPTER & BEARING ASM
38. HEX WASHER HEAD TAPPING SCREW
39. BEARING RETAINER
40. LOWER BEARING SEAT
41. LOWER BEARING SPRING
42. LOWER SPRING RETAINER
43. STRG. COLUMN JACKET BUSHING
44. RETAINING RING
45. STEERING SHAFT ASM
46. IGN. SWITCH HOUSING ASM
47. WASHER HEAD SCREW
48. PAN HD SCREW
49. DIMR & IGN SW MOUNTING STUD
50. IGNITION SWITCH ASM

87958060

Fig. 59 Exploded view of a steering column including the ignition switch—1990 vehicle with standard column shown

1. RETAINER
2. HEXAGON JAM NUT
3. SHAFT LOCK COVER
4. RETAINING RING
5. SHAFT LOCK
6. TURN SIGNAL CANCELLING CAM ASSY
7. UPPER BEARING SPRING
8. BINDING HEAD CROSS RECESS SCREW
9. ROUND WASHER HEAD SCREW
10. SIGNAL SWITCH ARM ASSY
11. TURN SIGNAL SWITCH ASSY
12. UPPER BEARING INNER RACE SEAT
13. INNER RACE
14. PAN HEAD CROSS RECESS SCREW
15. BUZZER SWITCH ASSY
16. BUZZER SWITCH RETAINING CLIP
17. LOCK RETAINING SCREW
18. LOCK HOUSING COVER
19. STEERING COLUMN LOCK CYLINDER SET
20. DIMMER SWITCH ROD ACTUATOR
21. TILT LEVER OPENING SHIELD
22. BEARING ASSY
23. LOCK BOLT
24. LOCK BOLT SPRING
25. STEERING WHEEL LOCK SHOE
26. STEERING WHEEL LOCK SHOE
27. DRIVE SHAFT
28. DOWEL PIN
29. PIVOT PIN
30. SHOE SPRING
31. RELEASE LEVER SPRING
32. RELEASE LEVER PIN
33. SHOE RELEASE LEVER
34. BEARING ASSY
35. IGNITION SWITCH ACTUATOR ASSY
36. SWITCH ACTUATOR RACK
37. RACK PRELOAD SPRING
38. STEERING COLUMN HOUSING
39. SWITCH ACTUATOR SECTOR
40. HEX WASHER HEAD SCREW
41. SPRING GUIDE
42. WHEEL TILT SPRING
43. SPRING RETAINER
44. COLUMN HOUSING COVER END CAP
45. SWITCH ACTUATOR PIVOT PIN
46. PIVOT & SWITCH ASSY
47. PIN PRELOAD SPRING
48. IGNITION SWITCH ASSY
49. DIMMER & IGNITION SWITCH MOUNTING STUD
50. WASHER HEAD SCREW
51. SHROUD RETAINING PLATE
52. OVAL HEAD CROSS RECESS SCREW
53. DOWEL PIN
54. WIRING PROTECTOR
55. RACE & UPPER SHAFT ASSY
56. CENTERING SPHERE
57. JOINT PRELOAD SPRING
58. LOWER STEERING SHAFT ASSY
59. SUPPORT SCREW
60. STEERING COLUMN HOUSING SUPPORT
61. LOCK PLATE
62. RELEASE LEVER FINGER PAD
63. KEY RELEASE LEVER
64. KEY RELEASE SPRING
65. STEERING COLUMN HOUSING SHROUD
66. DIMMER SWITCH ROD
67. DIMMER SWITCH ASSY
68. HEXAGON NUT
69. STEERING COLUMN JACKET ASSY.
70. STEERING COLUMN JACKET BUSHING

87958061

Fig. 60 Exploded view of the steering column including the ignition switch—1990 vehicle with tilt column shown

dard columns with manual transaxle) to the extreme left position. Move the slider (adjustable columns with automatic transaxle) to the extreme right position and then move the slider one detent to the left (off lock). Move the slider (adjustable columns with manual transaxle) to the extreme right position.

5. Install the activating rod into the switch and assemble the switch on the column. Tighten the mounting screws. Use only the specified screws, since overlength screws could impair the collapsibility of the column.

6. Reinstall the steering column.

1992–94 Sunbird

▶ See Figure 61

1. Disconnect the negative battery cable.
2. Remove the pad and horn lead, retainer and nut and remove the steering wheel from the column, using a suitable puller.
3. Remove the tilt lever, if so equipped.
4. Unfasten the 2 lower column cover retaining screws.
5. Remove the 3 bottom retaining screws from lower column cover.
6. Unfasten the washer head screw and hex nut.
7. Remove the dimmer switch assembly from the rod. Remove the dimmer switch and ignition switch mounting stud.
8. Disconnect the ignition switch from the actuator assembly, by unfastening the two cross recess screws. Detach the electrical connector, then remove the switch.

To install:

➡Install the ignition switch to the jacket with the switch in the "OFF-LOCK" position. A new swtich will be pinned in the "OFF-LOCK" position. Don't forget to remove the plastic pin after the switch is attached to the column

1 Dimmer & ignition switch mounting stud
2 Dimmer switch asm
3 Ignition switch asm
4 Hex nut (#10-24)
5 Wash head screw (#10-24x.25)
6 Pan Head c/rec screw (#4-24x.25)
7 Dimmer switch actuator rod
8 Ignition switch inhibitor housing asm

87958062

Fig. 61 Location and mounting of the ignition switch—1994 Sunbird shown

9. Connect the ignition switch to the ignition switch actuator assembly and adjust as follows:
   a. Move the switch slider to the extreme left position.
   b. Move the switch slider one detent to the right "OFF-LOCK" position.
10. Install the ignition switch assembly and stud. Tighten the retaining screws to 30 inch lbs. (3.4 Nm).
11. Fasten the dimmer switch assembly to the rod.
12. Install the hex nut and washer head screw and tighten finger-tight.
13. Adjust the dimer switch as follows:
   a. Place a ³⁄₃₂ in. (2.4mm) drill bit in the hole in the switch to limit travel.
   b. Position the switch on the column and push against the dimmer switch rod to remove all lash.
   c. Remove the drill bit.
14. Attach the switch electrical connector.
15. Install the steering column, as outlined in this section.
16. Connect the negative battery cable.

1992–94 Cavalier

▶ See Figure 62

1. Disconnect the negative battery cable.
2. If equipped, disable the SIR system. For details, please refer to the procedure located in Section 6 of this manual.
3. Remove the steering column as outlined later in this section.
4. Disconnect the wire harness from the ignition switch.
5. Unfasten the retaining screws, then remove the switch.
To install:
6. Installation is the reverse of the removal procedure.
7. If equipped, enable the SIR system as outlined in Section 6 of this manual.

Ignition Lock Cylinder

REMOVAL & INSTALLATION

1982–90 Vehicles

▶ See Figures 63 and 64

1. Remove the steering wheel.
2. Turn the lock to the **RUN** position.
3. Remove the lock plate, turn signal switch or combination switch, and the key warning buzzer switch. The warning buzzer switch can be fished out with a bent paper clip.
4. Remove the lock cylinder retaining screw and lock cylinder.

✳✳ WARNING

If the screw is dropped on removal, it could fall into the column, requiring complete disassembly to retrieve the screw.

1 Ignition switch assembly
2 Tapping screw

87958063

Fig. 62 Ignition switch mounting—1995 vehicle shown

KEY WARNING SWITCH   PAPER CLIP

87958065

Fig. 63 You can use a bent paper clip to remove the key warning buzzer switch on 1982–90 vehicles

TO ASSEMBLE, ROTATE TO STOP WHILE HOLDING CYLINDER
LOCK CYLINDER
LOCK RETAINING SCREW
CLIP
KEY WARNING SWITCH
HOUSING

87958066

Fig. 64 Installing the lock cylinder on 1982–90 vehicles

To install:

5. Rotate the cylinder clockwise to align the cylinder key with the keyway in the housing.

6. Push the lock all the way in.

7. Install the screw, then tighten it (1.7 Nm) to 15 inch lbs.

8. The rest of installation is the reverse of removal. Turn the lock to **RUN** to install the key warning buzzer switch, which is simply pushed down into place.

Steering Column Housing Steering Shaft and Ignition Switch Housing Jacket Bushing

DISASSEMBLY

▶ **See Figures 65, 66 and 67**

1. Disconnect the negative battery cable and disable the SIR system, if equipped.

2. Remove the pad and horn lead, retainer and nut and remove the steering wheel from the column, using a suitable puller.

3. Remove the tilt lever, if so equipped.

4. Remove the 2 lower column cover retaining screws.

5. Remove the 3 bottom retaining screws from lower column cover.

6. Disconnect the park lock cable from the ignition switch and lock cylinder assembly by depressing the locking tab with a small screwdriver.

7. Disconnect the wire harness at the bulkhead.

8. Remove the steering column from the vehicle as outlined in this section.

9. Remove the steering column jacket bushing from from the lower end of the jacket assembly.

10. Separate the rose bud fastener (integral to wire harness) from the jacket assembly.

11. Remove the turn signal switch retaining screws.

12. Depress the locking tab and remove the 2 wire harness connector from the switch.

13. Depress the locking tab and remove the cruise connector from the wire harness, if so equipped.

14. Depress the locking tab and remove the harness connector from the wipe/wash switch.

15. Depress the locking tabs and remove the 2 wire harness connectors from the ignition switch.

16. Remove the ignition switch screws and remove the ignition switch from the housing.

➡ **The turn signal switch must be removed before compressing the cam plate and shaft spring to prevent damage to the switch.**

17. Compress the cam plate and shaft spring with tools J 23653–91 and J 23653–C or equivalent, and remove the retaining ring, orientation cam plate, cancelling cam assembly, upper steering shaft spring and thrust washer.

18. Place the lock cylinder in the **RUN** position.

19. Remove the steering shaft assembly from the lower end of the jacket assembly.

20. Remove the shear bolts, shear bolt washers and ignition switch housing as follows:

a. Drill of the head of the shear bolts with a ¼ in. (6mm) drill bit.

b. Separate the washers and switch housing from the column housing.

c. Remove the threaded ends of the shear bolts from the ignition switch housing with pliers.

d. Clean all metal shavings from the housing.

21. Remove the 4 hex head screws from the housing.

22. Separate the column housing from the jacket assembly.

To install:

➡ **Firmly seat all the fasteners in the following steps before tightening them to the specified torque.**

23. Install the column housing to the jacket assembly and torque to 47 inch lbs. (5.3 Nm).

24. Install the ignition switch housing to the column housing with shear bolt washers and shear bolts. Tighten the shear bolts until the bolt head separates from the body, approximately 8 ft. lbs. (11 Nm).

25. Place the lock cylinder in the **RUN** position.

26. Install the steering shaft assembly into the lower end of the jacket assembly until bottomed.

27. Place the lock cylinder in the **OFF** position and remove the key.

28. Rotate the steering shaft until the lock bolt engages and locks the steering shaft into position.

29. Install the thrust washer and upper steering shaft spring on the steering shaft.

30. Fasten the cancelling cam and orientation cam plate.

31. Install the retaining ring into the groove on the shaft.

32. Place the jacket bushing over the lower end of the steering shaft, into the lower end of the jacket assembly and snap into position.

33. Attach the 2 wire harness connectors to the ignition switch.

34. Fasten the wiper/wash switch retaining screws and tighten to 49 inch lbs. (5.5 Nm).

35. Install the turn signal switch retaining screws and tighten to 49 inch lbs. (5.5 Nm).

36. Install the steering column in the vehicle as outlined later in this section.

37. Connect the wire harness at the bulkhead.

38. Connect the park lock cable to the ignition switch and lock cylinder assembly.

39. Install the rose bud fastener (integral to wiring harness) to the jacket assembly.

40. Tighten the upper and lower cover screws to 49 inch lbs. (5.5 Nm) and the steering wheel retaining nut to 30 ft. lbs. (41 Nm).

Steering Linkage

REMOVAL & INSTALLATION

Tie Rod Ends

▶ **See Figure 68**

1. Loosen both pinch bolts at the outer tie rod.

2. Remove the tie rod end from the strut assembly using a suitable removal tool.

Fig. 65 Ignition switch connectors

Fig. 66 Park/lock cable removal and installation

Fig. 67 Shear bolt removal using a proper sized drill bit

Fig. 68 Tie rod end removal and installation

3. Unscrew the outer tie rod end from the tie rod adjuster, counting the number of revolutions required before they are disconnected.

To install:

4. Install the new tie rod end, screwing it on the same number of revolutions as counted in Step 3. When the tie rod end is installed, the tie rod adjuster must be centered between the tie rod and the tie rod end, with an equal number of threads exposed on both sides of the adjuster nut. Tighten the pinch bolts to 20 ft. lbs. (27 Nm)

5. Install the tie rod end to the strut assembly and tighten to 50 ft. lbs. If the cotter pin cannot be installed, tighten the nut up to ⅙ or a turn further. Never back off the nut to align the holes for the cotter pin.

6. Have the front end alignment checked or adjusted.

Rack and Pinion Unit

REMOVAL & INSTALLATION

▶ **See Figures 69 and 70**

1. Disconnect the negative battery cable and disable the SIR system, if equipped.

2. From the driver's side, remove the sound insulator.

3. From under the instrument panel, pull the seal assembly down from the steering column and remove the upper pinch bolt from the flexible coupling.

4. Remove the air cleaner and the windshield washer fluid reservoir, if necessary for easier access.

5. On power steering models: disconnect the pressure line from the steering gear and remove the screw securing the pressure line bracket to the cowl. Move the pressure line aside.

6. Raise and support the car on jackstands.

7. Remove both front wheel and tire assemblies.

8. Disconnect both tie rods from the struts.

9. Carefully lower the car.

10. Remove the right side rack mounting clamp.

11. Remove the left side rack mounting clamp.

12. Move the gear forward slightly. On power steering models, disconnect the fluid return pipe from the gear.

13. Remove the lower pinch bolt from the flexible coupling and separate the rack from the coupling.

14. Remove the dash seal from the rack assembly.

15. Raise and support the car on jackstands.

16. On some models it may be necessary to remove the splash shield from the inner, left fender.

17. Turn the left knuckle and hub assembly to the full left turn position and remove the rack and pinion assembly through the access hole on the left fender.

To install:

18. Installation is the reverse of removal while noting the following points:

1. Steering gear asm.
2. L.H. clamp (dark)
3. R.H. clamp (light)
4. Nut—30 N·m (22 lbs. ft.)—hand start all nuts, tighten left side clamp nuts first, then tighten right side nuts.
5. Stud—20 N·m (15 lbs. ft.) after second reuse of stud, thread locking kit no 1052624 must be used.
6. Nut 50 N·m (35 lbs. ft.)
   75 N·m (50 lbs. ft.) maximum to install cotter pin
7. Cotter pin

Fig. 69 Manual rack and pinion assembly

1. Steering gear assembly
2. L.H. clamp—horizontal slot at top
3. R.H. clamp—horizontal slot at top
4. Nut—30 N·m (22 lbs. ft.)—hand start all nuts. Tighten left side clamp nuts first, then tighten right side nuts.
5. Stud—20 N·m (15 lbs. ft.) after second reuse of stud, thread locking kit no. 1052624 must be used.
6. Nut—50 N·m (35 lbs. ft.)
   75 N·m (50 lbs. ft.) maximum to install cotter pin
7. Cotter pin

Fig. 70 Power rack and pinion assembly

a. If the mounting studs backed out during removal, it will be necessary to re-position them prior to rack installation. Double-nut the stud so that it can be torqued to 15 ft. lbs. (20 Nm).

b. It will be helpful to have an assistant inside the car to guide the flexible coupling onto the stub shaft and onto the steering column.

c. Observe the following torques:

• Coupling-to-stub shaft: 1982–86 vehicles: 37 ft. lbs. (50 Nm), 1987–94 vehicles: 29–30 ft. lbs. (39–41 Nm)

• Coupling-to-column: 30 ft. lbs. (41 Nm)

• Mounting clamps: 1982–86 vehicles: 28 ft. lb. (38 Nm), 1987–94 vehicles: 22 ft. lbs. (30 Nm)

• Tie rod nuts: 35–37 ft. lbs. (47–50 Nm)

Power Steering Pump

REMOVAL & INSTALLATION

▶ **See Figures 71, 72, 73 and 74**

1. Disconnect the negative battery cable.

2. Detach the vent hole at the carburetor if so equipped.

1. OUTLET HOSE
2. INLET HOSE
3. INLET PIPE
4. 27 N·m (20 LBS. FT.)
5. CLAMP 1.7 N·m (15 LBS. IN.)
6. RESERVOIR
7. POWER STEERING PUMP
8. IDLE SPEED POWER STEERING PRESSURE SWITCH
9. RETAINER
10. STEERING GEAR
11. SCREW - 8 N·m (71 LBS. IN.)

87958076

Fig. 71 Power steering fluid line routing—1.8L and 2.0L engines

1 POWER STEERING PUMP
2 PULLEY
3 BOLTS - 34 N·m (25 LBS. FT.)
4 POWER STEERING PUMP BRACKET
5 ENGINE MOUNT BRACKET
6 BOLTS - 52 N·m (38 LBS. FT.)
7 BRACE
8 TENSIONER

87958078

Fig. 73 Power steering pump mounting—2.2L engine shown

1. POWER STEERING PUMP
2. PULLEY
3. BOLT - 27 N·m (20 LBS. FT.)

87958077

Fig. 72 View of the power steering pump mounting—1.8L and 2.0L engines

1 POWER STEERING PUMP
2 BOLTS - 25 N.m (18 LBS. FT.)
3 PULLEY
4 FRONT COVER ASSEMBLY

87958080

Fig. 74 Power steering pump removal and installation—3.1L engine

3. Loosen the adjusting bolt and pivot bolt on the pump or release tension on drive belt tensioner assembly, then remove the pump's drive belt.

4. Unfasten the pump-to-bracket or mounting bolts (through the access hole in the pulley as necessary) and remove the adjusting bolt if so equipped.

5. Remove the high pressure fitting from the pump.

6. Disconnect the reservoir-to-pump hose from the pump.

7. Remove the power steering pump from the vehicle. If installing a new pump, transfer the pulley to the new pump.

8. Installation is in the reverse order of removal. Adjust the belt tension and bleed the system, as outlined in this section.

SYSTEM BLEEDING

1. Raise the front of the vehicle and support safely. This will minimize steering effort. Fill the power steering pump reservoir with the appropriate type of power steering fluid.

2. With the engine off, keep the reservoir full as an assistant turns the steering wheel from lock-to-lock several times. Stop with the steering system at one lock.

3. Start the engine and allow it to idle. Turn the wheel from lock-to-lock several times. Note the amount of air bubbles in the fluid. Repeat the procedure until no more air bubbles appear.

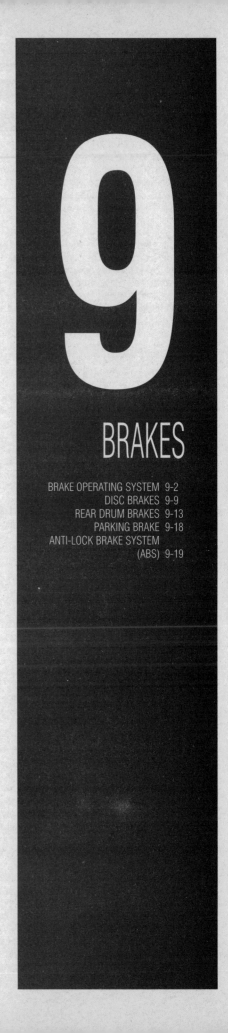

BRAKE OPERATING SYSTEM 9-2
BASIC OPERATING PRINCIPLES 9-2
  DISC BRAKES 9-2
  DRUM BRAKES 9-2
  POWER BOOSTERS 9-3
BRAKE LIGHT SWITCH 9-5
  REMOVAL & INSTALLATION 9-5
MASTER CYLINDER 9-5
  REMOVAL & INSTALLATION 9-5
POWER BRAKE BOOSTER 9-5
  REMOVAL & INSTALLATION 9-5
PROPORTIONING VALVES AND FAILURE
  WARNING SWITCH 9-6
  REMOVAL & INSTALLATION 9-6
BRAKE HOSES AND PIPES 9-7
  REMOVAL & INSTALLATION 9-7
BLEEDING THE BRAKE SYSTEM 9-8
  MANUAL BLEEDING 9-8
  PRESSURE BLEEDING 9-9
DISC BRAKES 9-9
BRAKE PADS 9-9
  REMOVAL & INSTALLATION 9-9
  INSPECTION 9-10
BRAKE CALIPER 9-10
  REMOVAL & INSTALLATION 9-11
  OVERHAUL 9-12
BRAKE DISC (ROTOR) 9-12
  REMOVAL & INSTALLATION 9-12
  INSPECTION 9-13
REAR DRUM BRAKES 9-13
BRAKE DRUMS 9-13
  REMOVAL & INSTALLATION 9-13
  INSPECTION 9-14
BRAKE SHOES 9-14
  INSPECTION 9-14
  REMOVAL & INSTALLATION 9-14
  ADJUSTMENT 9-15
WHEEL CYLINDERS 9-16
  REMOVAL & INSTALLATION 9-16
  OVERHAUL 9-17
PARKING BRAKE 9-18
CABLES 9-18
  REMOVAL & INSTALLATION 9-18
  ADJUSTMENT 9-19
**ANTI-LOCK BRAKE SYSTEM
  (ABS) 9-19**
DESCRIPTION AND OPERATION 9-19
  BASIC KNOWLEDGE REQUIRED 9-19
  ONBOARD DIAGNOSTICS 9-20
  ENHANCED DIAGNOSTICS 9-20
DIAGNOSTIC PROCEDURES 9-20
  DISPLAYING CODES 9-22
  CLEARING CODES 9-22
  INTERMITTENT FAILURES 9-23
  INTERMITTENTS AND POOR
    CONNECTIONS 9-23
ABS SERVICE 9-23
  PRECAUTIONS 9-23
ELECTRICAL CONNECTORS 9-23

ABS HYDRAULIC MODULATOR
  ASSEMBLY BLEEDER VALVES 9-24
  REMOVAL & INSTALLATION 9-24
FLUID LEVEL SENSOR 9-24
  REMOVAL & INSTALLATION 9-24
ENABLE RELAY 9-24
  REMOVAL & INSTALLATION 9-24
ABS LAMP DRIVER MODULE 9-24
  REMOVAL & INSTALLATION 9-24
ABS HYDRAULIC MODULATOR/MASTER
  CYLINDER ASSEMBLY 9-24
  REMOVAL & INSTALLATION 9-24
ABS CONTROL MODULE 9-25
  REMOVAL & INSTALLATION 9-25
SPEED SENSORS 9-25
  REMOVAL & INSTALLATION 9-25
ABS HYDRAULIC MODULATOR
  SOLENOID 9-26
  REMOVAL & INSTALLATION 9-26
FILLING AND BLEEDING 9-26
  SYSTEM FILLING 9-26
  BLEEDING THE ABS HYDRAULIC
    SYSTEM 9-26
SPECIFICATIONS CHART
  BRAKE SPECIFICATIONS 9-28
TROUBLESHOOTING CHART
  TROUBLESHOOTING THE BRAKE
    SYSTEM 9-3

BRAKE OPERATING SYSTEM 9-2
DISC BRAKES 9-9
REAR DRUM BRAKES 9-13
PARKING BRAKE 9-18
ANTI-LOCK BRAKE SYSTEM
(ABS) 9-19

9

BRAKES

BRAKE OPERATING SYSTEM

Basic Operating Principles

Hydraulic systems are used to actuate the brakes of all modern automobiles. The system transports the power required to force the frictional surfaces of the braking system together from the pedal to the individual brake units at each wheel. A hydraulic system is used for two reasons.

First, fluid under pressure can be carried to all parts of an automobile by small pipes and flexible hoses without taking up a significant amount of room or posing routing problems.

Second, a great mechanical advantage can be given to the brake pedal end of the system, and the foot pressure required to actuate the brakes can be reduced by making the surface area of the master cylinder pistons smaller than that of any of the pistons in the wheel cylinders or calipers.

The master cylinder consists of a fluid reservoir along with a double cylinder and piston assembly. Double type master cylinders are designed to separate the front and rear braking systems hydraulically in case of a leak. The master cylinder coverts mechanical motion from the pedal into hydraulic pressure within the lines. This pressure is translated back into mechanical motion at the wheels by either the wheel cylinder (drum brakes) or the caliper (disc brakes).

Steel lines carry the brake fluid to a point on the vehicle's frame near each of the vehicle's wheels. The fluid is then carried to the calipers and wheel cylinders by flexible tubes in order to allow for suspension and steering movements.

In drum brake systems, each wheel cylinder contains two pistons, one at either end, which push outward in opposite directions and force the brake shoe into contact with the drum.

In disc brake systems, the cylinders are part of the calipers. At least one cylinder in each caliper is used to force the brake pads against the disc.

All pistons employ some type of seal, usually made of rubber, to minimize fluid leakage. A rubber dust boot seals the outer end of the cylinder against dust and dirt. The boot fits around the outer end of the piston on disc brake calipers, and around the brake actuating rod on wheel cylinders.

The hydraulic system operates as follows: When at rest, the entire system, from the piston(s) in the master cylinder to those in the wheel cylinders or calipers, is full of brake fluid. Upon application of the brake pedal, fluid trapped in front of the master cylinder piston(s) is forced through the lines to the wheel cylinders. Here, it forces the pistons outward, in the case of drum brakes, and inward toward the disc, in the case of disc brakes. The motion of the pistons is opposed by return springs mounted outside the cylinders in drum brakes, and by spring seals, in disc brakes.

Upon release of the brake pedal, a spring located inside the master cylinder immediately returns the master cylinder pistons to the normal position. The pistons contain check valves and the master cylinder has compensating ports drilled in it. These are uncovered as the pistons reach their normal position. The piston check valves allow fluid to flow toward the wheel cylinders or calipers as the pistons withdraw. Then, as the return springs force the brake pads or shoes into the released position, the excess fluid reservoir through the compensating ports. It is during the time the pedal is in the released position that any fluid that has leaked out of the system will be replaced through the compensating ports.

Dual circuit master cylinders employ two pistons, located one behind the other, in the same cylinder. The primary piston is actuated directly by mechanical linkage from the brake pedal through the power booster. The secondary piston is actuated by fluid trapped between the two pistons. If a leak develops in front of the secondary piston, it moves forward until it bottoms against the front of the master cylinder, and the fluid trapped between the pistons will operate the rear brakes. If the rear brakes develop a leak, the primary piston will move forward until direct contact with the secondary piston takes place, and it will force the secondary piston to actuate the front brakes. In either case, the brake pedal moves farther when the brakes are applied, and less braking power is available.

All dual circuit systems use a switch to warn the driver when only half of the brake system is operational. This switch is usually located in a valve body which is mounted on the firewall or the frame below the master cylinder. A hydraulic piston receives pressure from both circuits, each circuit's pressure being applied to one end of the piston. When the pressures are in balance, the piston remains stationary. When one circuit has a leak, however, the greater pressure in that circuit during application of the brakes will push the piston to one side, closing the switch and activating the brake warning light.

In disc brake systems, this valve body also contains a metering valve and, in some cases, a proportioning valve. The metering valve keeps pressure from traveling to the disc brakes on the front wheels until the brake shoes on the rear wheels have contacted the drums, ensuring that the front brakes will never be used alone. The proportioning valve controls the pressure to the rear brakes to lessen the chance of rear wheel lock-up during very hard braking.

Warning lights may be tested by depressing the brake pedal and holding it while opening one of the wheel cylinder bleeder screws. If this does not cause the light to go on, substitute a new lamp, make continuity checks, and, finally, replace the switch as necessary.

The hydraulic system may be checked for leaks by applying pressure to the pedal gradually and steadily. If the pedal sinks very slowly to the floor, the system has a leak. This is not to be confused with a springy or spongy feel due to the compression of air within the lines. If the system leaks, there will be a gradual change in the position of the pedal with a constant pressure.

Check for leaks along all lines and at wheel cylinders. If no external leaks are apparent, the problem is inside the master cylinder.

DISC BRAKES

Instead of the traditional expanding brakes that press outward against a circular drum, disc brake systems utilize a disc (rotor) with brake pads positioned on either side of it. An easily-seen analogy is the hand brake arrangement on a bicycle. The pads squeeze onto the rim of the bike wheel, slowing its motion. Automobile disc brakes use the identical principle but apply the braking effort to a separate disc instead of the wheel.

The disc (rotor) is a casting, usually equipped with cooling fins between the two braking surfaces. This enables air to circulate between the braking surfaces making them less sensitive to heat buildup and more resistant to fade. Dirt and water do not drastically affect braking action since contaminants are thrown off by the centrifugal action of the rotor or scraped off the by the pads. Also, the equal clamping action of the two brake pads tends to ensure uniform, straight line stops. Disc brakes are inherently self-adjusting. There are three general types of disc brake:

1. A fixed caliper.
2. A floating caliper.
3. A sliding caliper.

The fixed caliper design uses two pistons mounted on either side of the rotor (in each side of the caliper). The caliper is mounted rigidly and does not move.

The sliding and floating designs are quite similar. In fact, these two types are often lumped together. In both designs, the pad on the inside of the rotor is moved into contact with the rotor by hydraulic force. The caliper, which is not held in a fixed position, moves slightly, bringing the outside pad into contact with the rotor. There are various methods of attaching floating calipers. Some pivot at the bottom or top, and some slide on mounting bolts. In any event, the end result is the same.

DRUM BRAKES

Drum brakes employ two brake shoes mounted on a stationary backing plate. These shoes are positioned inside a circular drum which rotates with the wheel assembly. The shoes are held in place by springs. This allows them to slide toward the drums (when they are applied) while keeping the linings and drums in alignment. The shoes are actuated by a wheel cylinder which is mounted at the top of the backing plate. When the brakes are applied, hydraulic pressure forces the wheel cylinder's actuating links outward. Since these links bear directly against the top of the brake shoes, the tops of the shoes are then forced against the inner side of the drum. This action forces the bottoms of the two shoes to contact the brake drum by rotating the entire assembly slightly (known as servo action). When pressure within the wheel cylinder is relaxed, return springs pull the shoes back away from the drum.

Most modern drum brakes are designed to self-adjust themselves during application when the vehicle is moving in reverse. This motion causes both shoes to rotate very slightly with the drum, rocking an adjusting lever, thereby causing rotation of the adjusting screw. Some drum brake systems are designed to self-adjust during application whenever the brakes are applied. This on-board adjustment system reduces the need for maintenance adjustments and keeps both the brake function and pedal feel satisfactory.

POWER BOOSTERS

Virtually all modern vehicles use a vacuum assisted power brake system to multiply the braking force and reduce pedal effort. Since vacuum is always available when the engine is operating, the system is simple and efficient. A vacuum diaphragm is located on the front of the master cylinder and assists the driver in applying the brakes, reducing both the effort and travel he must put into moving the brake pedal.

The vacuum diaphragm housing is normally connected to the intake manifold by a vacuum hose. A check valve is placed at the point where the hose enters the diaphragm housing, so that during periods of low manifold vacuum brakes assist will not be lost.

Depressing the brake pedal closes off the vacuum source and allows atmospheric pressure to enter on one side of the diaphragm. This causes the master cylinder pistons to move and apply the brakes. When the brake pedal is released, vacuum is applied to both sides of the diaphragm and springs return the diaphragm and master cylinder pistons to the released position.

If the vacuum supply fails, the brake pedal rod will contact the end of the master cylinder actuator rod and the system will apply the brakes without any power assistance. The driver will notice that much higher pedal effort is needed to stop the car and that the pedal feels harder than usual.

Vacuum Leak Test

1. Operate the engine at idle without touching the brake pedal for at least one minute.
2. Turn off the engine and wait one minute.
3. Test for the presence of assist vacuum by depressing the brake pedal and releasing it several times. If vacuum is present in the system, light application will produce less and less pedal travel. If there is no vacuum, air is leaking into the system.

System Operation Test

1. With the engine OFF, pump the brake pedal until the supply vacuum is entirely gone.
2. Put light, steady pressure on the brake pedal.
3. Start the engine and let it idle. If the system is operating correctly, the brake pedal should fall toward the floor if the constant pressure is maintained.

Power brake systems may be tested for hydraulic leaks just as ordinary systems are tested.

Troubleshooting the Brake System

Problem	Cause	Solution
Low brake pedal (excessive pedal travel required for braking action.)	• Excessive clearance between rear linings and drums caused by inoperative automatic adjusters	• Make 10 to 15 alternate forward and reverse brake stops to adjust brakes. If brake pedal does not come up, repair or replace adjuster parts as necessary.
	• Worn rear brakelining	• Inspect and replace lining if worn beyond minimum thickness specification
	• Bent, distorted brakeshoes, front or rear	• Replace brakeshoes in axle sets
	• Air in hydraulic system	• Remove air from system. Refer to Brake Bleeding.
Low brake pedal (pedal may go to floor with steady pressure applied.)	• Fluid leak in hydraulic system	• Fill master cylinder to fill line; have helper apply brakes and check calipers, wheel cylinders, differential valve tubes, hoses and fittings for leaks. Repair or replace as necessary.
	• Air in hydraulic system	• Remove air from system. Refer to Brake Bleeding.
	• Incorrect or non-recommended brake fluid (fluid evaporates at below normal temp).	• Flush hydraulic system with clean brake fluid. Refill with correct-type fluid.
	• Master cylinder piston seals worn, or master cylinder bore is scored, worn or corroded	• Repair or replace master cylinder
Low brake pedal (pedal goes to floor on first application—o.k. on subsequent applications.)	• Disc brake pads sticking on abutment surfaces of anchor plate. Caused by a build-up of dirt, rust, or corrosion on abutment surfaces	• Clean abutment surfaces
Fading brake pedal (pedal height decreases with steady pressure applied.)	• Fluid leak in hydraulic system	• Fill master cylinder reservoirs to fill mark, have helper apply brakes, check calipers, wheel cylinders, differential valve, tubes, hoses, and fittings for fluid leaks. Repair or replace parts as necessary.
	• Master cylinder piston seals worn, or master cylinder bore is scored, worn or corroded	• Repair or replace master cylinder
Decreasing brake pedal travel (pedal travel required for braking action decreases and may be accompanied by a hard pedal.)	• Caliper or wheel cylinder pistons sticking or seized	• Repair or replace the calipers, or wheel cylinders
	• Master cylinder compensator ports blocked (preventing fluid return to reservoirs) or pistons sticking or seized in master cylinder bore	• Repair or replace the master cylinder
	• Power brake unit binding internally	• Test unit according to the following procedure: (a) Shift transmission into neutral and start engine (b) Increase engine speed to 1500 rpm, close throttle and fully depress brake pedal (c) Slow release brake pedal and stop engine (d) Have helper remove vacuum check valve and hose from power unit. Observe for backward movement of brake pedal. (e) If the pedal moves backward, the power unit has an internal bind—replace power unit

TCCA9C01

Troubleshooting the Brake System (cont.)

Problem	Cause	Solution
Spongy brake pedal (pedal has abnormally soft, springy, spongy feel when depressed.)	• Air in hydraulic system	• Remove air from system. Refer to Brake Bleeding.
	• Brakeshoes bent or distorted	• Replace brakeshoes
	• Brakelining not yet seated with drums and rotors	• Burnish brakes
	• Rear drum brakes not properly adjusted	• Adjust brakes
Hard brake pedal (excessive pedal pressure required to stop vehicle. May be accompanied by brake fade.)	• Loose or leaking power brake unit vacuum hose	• Tighten connections or replace leaking hose
	• Incorrect or poor quality brakelining	• Replace with lining in axle sets
	• Bent, broken, distorted brakeshoes	• Replace brakeshoes
	• Calipers binding or dragging on mounting pins. Rear brakeshoes dragging on support plate.	• Replace mounting pins and bushings. Clean rust or burrs from rear brake support plate ledges and lubricate ledges with molydisulfide grease. NOTE: If ledges are deeply grooved or scored, do not attempt to sand or grind them smooth—replace support plate.
	• Caliper, wheel cylinder, or master cylinder pistons sticking or seized	• Repair or replace parts as necessary
	• Power brake unit vacuum check valve malfunction	• Test valve according to the following procedure: (a) Start engine, increase engine speed to 1500 rpm, close throttle and immediately stop engine (b) Wait at least 90 seconds then depress brake pedal (c) If brakes are not vacuum assisted for 2 or more applications, check valve is faulty
	• Power brake unit has internal bind	• Test unit according to the following procedure: (a) With engine stopped, apply brakes several times to exhaust all vacuum in system (b) Shift transmission into neutral, depress brake pedal and start engine (c) If pedal height decreases with foot pressure and less pressure is required to hold pedal in applied position, power unit vacuum system is operating normally. Test power unit. If power unit exhibits a bind condition, replace the power unit.
	• Master cylinder compensator ports (at bottom of reservoirs) blocked by dirt, scale, rust, or have small burrs (blocked ports prevent fluid return to reservoirs).	• Repair or replace master cylinder CAUTION: Do not attempt to clean blocked ports with wire, pencils, or similar implements. Use compressed air only.
	• Brake hoses, tubes, fittings clogged or restricted	• Use compressed air to check or unclog parts. Replace any damaged parts.
	• Brake fluid contaminated with improper fluids (motor oil, transmission fluid, causing rubber components to swell and stick in bores	• Replace all rubber components, combination valve and hoses. Flush entire brake system with DOT 3 brake fluid or equivalent.
	• Low engine vacuum	• Adjust or repair engine

TCCA9C02

Troubleshooting the Brake System (cont.)

Problem	Cause	Solution
Grabbing brakes (severe reaction to brake pedal pressure.)	• Brakelining(s) contaminated by grease or brake fluid	• Determine and correct cause of contamination and replace brakeshoes in axle sets
	• Parking brake cables incorrectly adjusted or seized	• Adjust cables. Replace seized cables.
	• Incorrect brakelining or lining loose on brakeshoes	• Replace brakeshoes in axle sets
	• Caliper anchor plate bolts loose	• Tighten bolts
	• Rear brakeshoes binding on support plate ledges	• Clean and lubricate ledges. Replace support plate(s) if ledges are deeply grooved. Do not attempt to smooth ledges by grinding.
	• Incorrect or missing power brake reaction disc	• Install correct disc
	• Rear brake support plates loose	• Tighten mounting bolts
Dragging brakes (slow or incomplete release of brakes)	• Brake pedal binding at pivot	• Loosen and lubricate
	• Power brake unit has internal bind	• Inspect for internal bind. Replace unit if internal bind exists.
	• Parking brake cables incorrectly adjusted or seized	• Adjust cables. Replace seized cables.
	• Rear brakeshoe return springs weak or broken	• Replace return springs. Replace brakeshoe if necessary in axle sets.
	• Automatic adjusters malfunctioning	• Repair or replace adjuster parts as required
	• Caliper, wheel cylinder or master cylinder pistons sticking or seized	• Repair or replace parts as necessary
	• Master cylinder compensating ports blocked (fluid does not return to reservoirs).	• Use compressed air to clear ports. Do not use wire, pencils, or similar objects to open blocked ports.
Vehicle moves to one side when brakes are applied	• Incorrect front tire pressure	• Inflate to recommended cold (reduced load) inflation pressure
	• Worn or damaged wheel bearings	• Replace worn or damaged bearings
	• Brakelining on one side contaminated	• Determine and correct cause of contamination and replace brakelining in axle sets
	• Brakeshoes on one side bent, distorted, or lining loose on shoe	• Replace brakeshoes in axle sets
	• Support plate bent or loose on one side	• Tighten or replace support plate
	• Brakelining not yet seated with drums or rotors	• Burnish brakelining
	• Caliper anchor plate loose on one side	• Tighten anchor plate bolts
	• Caliper piston sticking or seized	• Repair or replace caliper
	• Brakelinings water soaked	• Drive vehicle with brakes lightly applied to dry linings
	• Loose suspension component attaching or mounting bolts.	• Tighten suspension bolts. Replace worn suspension components.
	• Brake combination valve failure	• Replace combination valve
Chatter or shudder when brakes are applied (pedal pulsation and roughness may also occur.)	• Brakeshoes distorted, bent, contaminated, or worn	• Replace brakeshoes in axle sets
	• Caliper anchor plate or support plate loose	• Tighten mounting bolts
	• Excessive thickness variation of rotor(s)	• Refinish or replace rotors in axle sets

TCCA9C03

Brake Light Switch

REMOVAL & INSTALLATION

▶ See Figure 1

1. Disconnect the negative battery cable.
2. Remove the drivers side hush panel/sound insulator.
3. Detach the switch electrical connector.
4. If equipped, unfasten the retaining nut from switch.
5. Remove the switch from the retainer by grasping it and pulling it toward the rear of the car.

To install:
6. Insert the brake light switch into the retainer until the switch body seats on the retainer or install the retaining nut.
7. Adjust the brake light switch, as follows:
 a. Pull the brake pedal upward against the internal pedal stop. The switch will be moved in the retainer providing proper adjustment.

➡Proper switch adjustment is achieved when no clicks are heard as the pedal is pulled upward and when the brake lights do not stay on without brake application.

8. Attach the switch electrical connector.
9. Install the hush panel/sound insulator.
10. Connect the negative battery cable.

1 Brake pedal mounting bracket
2 TCC and cruise control switch
3 Stoplamp switch
4 Stoplamp switch terminals
5 Brake pedal assembly
6 TCC and BTSI connector

Fig. 1 The brake light switch is mounted on the brake pedal

Master Cylinder

REMOVAL & INSTALLATION

Except Anti-Lock Brakes

▶ See Figures 2, 3, 4, 5 and 6

1. Disconnect the negative battery cable.
2. Using a suitable tool, (a clean turkey baster works well) drain some of the fluid from the master cylinder reservoir.
3. Unplug the electrical connector from the fluid level sensor on the master cylinder.
4. Place a number of cloths or a container under the master cylinder to catch the brake fluid. Disconnect and plug the brake lines from the master cylinder; use a flare nut wrench if one is available.

✳ WARNING

Brake fluid eats paint. Wipe up any spilled fluid immediately, then flush the area with clear water.

5. Unfasten the nuts attaching the master cylinder to the booster or firewall.
6. Remove the master cylinder from its mounting studs and from the vehicle.

To install:
7. Attach the master cylinder to the booster with the nuts. Tighten to 20–30 ft. lbs. (27–45 Nm.).
8. Unplug the lines, then connect them to the master cylinder. Tighten to 10–15 ft. lbs. (13–20 Nm.).
9. Attach the fluid level sensor electrical lead.
10. Bleed the brakes, as outlined in this section.
11. Connect the negative battery cable.

Power Brake Booster

REMOVAL & INSTALLATION

▶ See Figure 7

➡It is not necessary to remove or disconnect the master cylinder from the vehicle in order to remove the vacuum booster. However, if both the vacuum booster and master cylinder are to be removed, remove the master cylinder first.

1. Disconnect the negative battery cable.
2. Unfasten the master cylinder-to-booster retaining nuts.
3. Separate the master cylinder from the booster. Move the master cylinder forward just enough to clear the studs on the vacuum booster. This will flex the brake pipes slightly; be careful not to bend or distort the pipes.

Fig. 2 Detach the fluid level sensor electrical connector

Fig. 3 Placing rags under the brake lines will catch any brake fluid that spills out when the lines are disconnected

Fig. 4 Unfasten the attaching nuts, then remove the master cylinder from the vehicle

1 Master cylinder mounting nut
2 Master cylinder assembly
3 Brake pipe tube nut

87959010

Fig. 5 Master cylinder mounting—vehicles without ABS

1 FLUID LEVEL SENSOR
2 PROPORTIONER VALVE CAP
3 PROPORTIONER VALVE CAP O-RING
4 PROPORTIONER VALVE PISTON SPRING
5 PROPORTIONER VALVE PISTON
6 PROPORTIONER VALVE SEAL
7 RESERVOIR TO BODY O-RING
8 MASTER CYLINDER RESERVOIR COVER
9 MASTER CYLINDER RESERVOIR DIAPHRAGM
10 MASTER CYLINDER RESERVOIR
11 MASTER CYLINDER BODY
12 SECONDARY PISTON SPRING
13 SPRING RETAINER
14 PRIMARY SEAL
15 SECONDARY PISTON
16 SECONDARY SEAL
17 PRIMARY PISTON
18 PISTON RETAINER
19 SPRING PIN

87959011

Fig. 6 Exploded view of a master cylinder assembly

4. Disconnect the vacuum hose from the vacuum check valve.
5. Unfasten the booster retaining nuts.
6. Disconnect the vacuum booster pushrod from the brake pedal inside the car. Tilt the entire vacuum booster slightly to work booster pushrod off the pedal clevis pin without putting undue side pressure on the pushrod.
7. Remove the booster from the vehicle.

To install:
8. Position the booster in the vehicle.
9. Connect the booster pushrod to the brake pedal. Tilt the entire booster slightly to work the booster pushrod onto the pedal clevis pin without putting undue pressure on the pushrod. Use your left hand to align the pushrod with the pedal and push together.

1 Pushrod
2 Master cylinder
3 Booster
4 Nut, 27 Nm(20 lbs. in.)
5 Nut, 27 Nm(20 lbs.in.)

87959012

Fig. 7 Vacuum (power brake) booster mounting—1994 vehicle shown

10. Install the booster attaching nuts, then tighten them to 20 ft. lbs. (27 Nm).
11. Connect the booster vacuum hose to the vacuum check valve.
12. Position the master cylinder to the booster and install the retaining nuts.
13. Connect the positive battery cable
14. Connect the negative battery cable.

Proportioning Valves and Failure Warning Switch

These parts are installed in the master cylinder body on all models except those equipped with the 1985–86 V6 engine. On these models the proportioning valve and the brake pressure differential warning switch is located to the left frame rail below the master cylinder.

REMOVAL & INSTALLATION

Proportioning Valves

▶ See Figure 8

1. Remove the proportioner valve caps. It may be necessary to remove the master cylinder reservoir.
2. Remove and discard the valve cap O-rings.
3. Remove the proportioner valve piston springs, then remove the valve pistons using needle-nose pliers. Be careful not to scratch or damage the piston stems.
4. Remove the valve seals from the proportioner valve pistons.
5. Clean all parts in clean denatured alcohol, then dry with compressed air. Inspect the valve pistons for corrosion or deformation and replace if necessary.

To install:
6. Lubricate new proportioner valve cap O-rings and valve seals with the silicone grease given in the repair kit. Also, lubricate the stem of the proportioner valve pistons.
7. Place new proportioner valve seals on the proportioner valve pistons with the seal lips facing upward toward the proportioner valve cap.
8. Position the proportioner valve pistons and seals into the master cylinder body.
9. Place new proportioner valve cap O-rings in the grooves in the proportioner valve caps.
10. Install the valve caps in the master cylinder body, then tighten the caps to 20 ft. lbs. (27 Nm).
11. If removed, install the master cylinder reservoir.

Fluid Level Switch

▶ See Figures 9 and 10

1. Disconnect the negative battery cable.
2. Detach the electrical connector from the fluid level switch.
3. Using needle-nose pliers, compress the switch locking tabs at the inboard side of the master cylinder reservoir and remove the switch.

To install:
4. Press the fluid level switch into the master cylinder reservoir until it snaps into place.
5. Attach the switch electrical connector.
6. Connect the negative battery cable.

1 Proportioner valve cap assembly
2 O-ring
3 Spring
4 Proportioner valve piston
5 Proportioner valve seal

87959013

Fig. 8 Removal of the proportioner valves—1994 vehicle shown

1 Fluid level sensor
2 Master cylinder reservoir

87959014

Fig. 9 The fluid level switch is mounted in the master cylinder reservoir

1 Fluid level sensor
2 Master cylinder reservoir
3 Master cylinder body

87959015

Fig. 10 Remove the switch by using needle-nose pliers to compress the switch locking tabs

Brake Hoses and Pipes

Metal lines and rubber brake hoses should be checked frequently for leaks and external damage. Metal lines are particularly prone to crushing and kinking under the vehicle. Any such deformation can restrict the proper flow of fluid and therefore impair braking at the wheels. Rubber hoses should be checked for cracking or scraping; such damage can create a weak spot in the hose and it could fail under pressure.

Any time the lines are removed or disconnected, extreme cleanliness must be observed. Clean all joints and connections before disassembly (use a stiff bristle brush and clean brake fluid); be sure to plug the lines and ports as soon as they are opened. New lines and hoses should be flushed clean with brake fluid before installation to remove any contamination.

REMOVAL & INSTALLATION

▶ **See Figures 11, 12, 13 and 14**

1. Disconnect the negative battery cable.
2. Raise and safely support the vehicle on jackstands.
3. Remove any wheel and tire assemblies necessary for access to the particular line you are removing.
4. Thoroughly clean the surrounding area at the joints to be disconnected.
5. Place a suitable catch pan under the joint to be disconnected.
6. Using two wrenches (one to hold the joint and one to turn the fitting), disconnect the hose or line to be replaced.
7. Disconnect the other end of the line or hose, moving the drain pan if necessary. Always use a back-up wrench to avoid damaging the fitting.
8. Disconnect any retaining clips or brackets holding the line and remove the line from the vehicle.

➡️If the brake system is to remain open for more time than it takes to swap lines, tape or plug each remaining clip and port to keep contaminants out and fluid in.

To install:

9. Install the new line or hose, starting with the end farthest from the master cylinder. Connect the other end, then confirm that both fittings are correctly threaded and turn smoothly using finger pressure. Make sure the new line will

TCCA9P09

Fig. 11 Use a brush to clean the fittings of any debris

TCCA9P10

Fig. 12 Use two wrenches to loosen the fitting. If available, use flare nut type wrenches

TCCA9P11"

Fig. 13 Any gaskets/crush washers should be replaced with new ones during installation

TCCA9P12

Fig. 14 Tape or plug the line to prevent contamination

not rub against any other part. Brake lines must be at least 1/2 in. (13mm) from the steering column and other moving parts. Any protective shielding or insulators must be reinstalled in the original location.

** WARNING

Make sure the hose is NOT kinked or touching any part of the frame or suspension after installation. These conditions may cause the hose to fail prematurely.

10. Using two wrenches as before, tighten each fitting.
11. Install any retaining clips or brackets on the lines.
12. If removed, install the wheel and tire assemblies, then carefully lower the vehicle to the ground.
13. Refill the brake master cylinder reservoir with clean, fresh brake fluid, meeting DOT 3 specifications. Properly bleed the brake system.
14. Connect the negative battery cable.

Bleeding The Brake System

The hydraulic brake system must be bled any time one of the lines is disconnected or any time air enters the system. If a point in the system, such as a wheel cylinder or caliper brake line is the only point which was opened, the bleeder screws downstream in the hydraulic system are the only ones which must be bled. If however, the master cylinder fittings are opened, or if the reservoir level drops sufficiently that air is drawn into the system, air must be bled from the entire hydraulic system.

If the brake pedal feels spongy upon application, and goes almost to the floor but regains height when pumped, air has entered the system. It must be bled out. If no fittings were recently opened for service, check for leaks that would have allowed the entry of air and repair them before attempting to bleed the system.

As a general rule, once the master cylinder (and the brake pressure modulator valve or combination valve on ABS systems) is bled, the remainder of the hydraulic system should be bled starting at the furthest wheel from the master cylinder and working towards the nearest wheel. Therefore, the correct bleeding sequence for 1982–91 vehicles is:
- master cylinder
- modulator or combination valve (ABS vehicles only)
- right rear wheel cylinder
- left front caliper
- left rear wheel cylinder
- right front caliper

The correct bleeding sequence for 1992–94 vehicles is:
- master cylinder
- modulator or combination valve (ABS vehicles only)
- right rear wheel cylinder
- left rear wheel cylinder
- right front caliper
- left front caliper

Most master cylinder assemblies on these vehicles are NOT equipped with bleeder valves, therefore air must be bled from the cylinders using the front brake pipe connections.

** CAUTION

If the vehicle has anti-lock braking, do not use this procedure without first reading the information on ABS system bleeding found later in this section. Improper service procedures on Anti-Lock Braking Systems (ABS) can cause serious personal injury. Refer to the ABS service procedures.

MANUAL BLEEDING

▶ **See Figures 15 and 16**

For those of us who are not fortunate enough to have access to a power bleeding tool, the manual brake bleeding procedure will quite adequately remove air from the hydraulic system. The major difference between the pressure and manual bleeding procedures is that the manual method takes more time and will require help from an assistant. One person must depress the brake pedal, while another opens and closes the bleeder screws.

➡ In addition to a length of clear neoprene bleeder hose, bleeder wrenches and a clear bleeder bottle (old plastic jar or drink bottle will suffice), bleeding late-model ABS systems may also require the use of one or more relatively inexpensive combination valve pressure bleeding tools (which are used to depress one or more valves in order to allow component/system bleeding). To fully bleed the late model ABS systems, a scan tool should also be used to run the system through functional tests.

1. Deplete the vacuum reserve by applying the brakes several times with the ignition **OFF**.
2. Clean the top of the master cylinder, remove the cover and fill the reservoirs with clean fluid. To prevent squirting fluid, and possibly damaging painted surfaces, install the cover during the procedure, but be sure to frequently check and top off the reservoirs with fresh fluid.

** WARNING

Never reuse brake fluid which has been bled from the system because the old fluid may be contaminated with moisture and/or debris

3. The master cylinder must be bled first if it is suspected to contain air. If the master cylinder was removed and bench bled before installation it must still be bled, but it should take less time and effort. Bleed the master cylinder as follows:
   a. Position a container under the master cylinder to catch the brake fluid.

** WARNING

Do not allow brake fluid to spill on or come in contact with the vehicle's finish as it will remove the paint. In case of a spill, immediately flush the area with water.

   b. Loosen the front brake line at the master cylinder and allow the fluid to flow from the front port.
   c. Have a friend depress the brake pedal slowly and hold (air and/or fluid should be expelled from the loose fitting). Tighten the line, then release the brake pedal and wait 15 seconds. Loosen the fitting and repeat until all air is removed from the master cylinder bore.
   d. When finished, tighten the line fitting to 20 ft. lbs. (27 Nm).
   e. Repeat the sequence at the master cylinder rear pipe fitting.

➡ During the bleeding procedure, make sure your assistant does NOT release the brake pedal while a fitting is loosened or while a bleeder screw is opened. Otherwise, air will be drawn back into the system.

4. Check and refill the master cylinder reservoir.

➡ Remember, if the reservoir is allowed to empty of fluid during the procedure, air will be drawn into the system and the bleeding procedure must be restarted at the master cylinder assembly.

5. On late model ABS equipped vehicles, perform the special ABS procedures as described later in this section. On 4 wheel ABS systems the Brake Pressure Modulator Valve (BPMV) must be bled (if it has been replaced or if it is suspected to contain air) and on most Rear Wheel Anti-Lock (RWAL) systems the combination valve must be held open. In both cases, special combination valve depressor tools should be used during bleeding and a scan tool must be used for ABS function tests.
6. If a single line or fitting was the only hydraulic line disconnected, then only the caliper(s) or wheel cylinder(s) affected by that line must be bled. If the master cylinder required bleeding, then all calipers and wheel cylinders must be bled in the proper sequence.
7. The proper sequence for 1982–91 vehicles is:
   a. Right rear
   b. Left front
   c. Left rear
   d. Right front
8. The proper sequence for 1992–94 vehicles is:
   a. Right rear
   b. Left front
   c. Right front
   d. Left front
9. Bleed the individual calipers or wheel cylinders as follows:

a. Place a suitable wrench over the bleeder screw and attach a clear plastic hose over the screw end. Be sure the hose is seated snugly on the screw or you may be squirted with brake fluid.

➡ Be very careful when bleeding wheel cylinders and brake calipers. The bleeder screws often rust in position and may easily break off if forced. Installing a new bleeder screw will often require removal of the component and may include overhaul or replacement of the wheel cylinder/caliper. To help prevent the possibility of breaking a bleeder screw, spray it with some penetrating oil before attempting to loosen it.

b. Submerge the other end of the tube in a transparent container of clean brake fluid.

c. Loosen the bleed screw, then have a friend apply the brake pedal slowly and hold. Tighten the bleed screw to 62 inch lbs. (7 Nm), release the brake pedal and wait 15 seconds. Repeat the sequence (including the 15 second pause) until all air is expelled from the caliper or cylinder.

d. Tighten the bleeder screw to 62 inch lbs. (7 Nm) when finished.

10. Check the pedal for a hard feeling with the engine not running. If the pedal is soft, repeat the bleeding procedure until a firm pedal is obtained.

11. If the brake warning light is on, depress the brake pedal firmly. If there is no air in the system, the light will go out.

12. After bleeding, make sure that a firm pedal is achieved before attempting to move the vehicle.

PRESSURE BLEEDING

▶ See Figure 17

For the lucky ones with access to a pressure bleeding tool, this procedure may be used to quickly and efficiently remove air from the brake system. This procedure may be used as a guide, but be careful to follow the tool manufacturer's directions closely. Any pressure bleeding tool MUST be of the diaphragm-type. A proper pressure bleeder tool will utilize a rubber diaphragm between the air source and brake fluid in order to prevent air, moisture oil and other contaminants from entering the hydraulic system.

1. Install Pressure Bleeder Adapter Cap J 35589 or equivalent, to the master cylinder.

2. Charge Diaphragm Type Brake Bleeder J 29532 or equivalent, to 20–25 psi (140–172 kPa).

3. Connect the line to the pressure bleeder adapter cap, then open the line valve.

4. Raise and safely support the vehicle.

5. If it is necessary to bleed all of the calipers/cylinders, the following sequence should be used for 1982–91 vehicles:
- Right rear
- Left front
- Left rear
- Right front

6. The following sequence should be used for 1992–94 vehicles:
- Right rear
- Left rear
- Right front
- Left front

7. Place a proper size box end wrench (or tool J 21472) over the caliper/cylinder bleeder valve.

8. Attach a clear tube over the bleeder screw, then submerge the other end of the tube in a clear container partially filled with clean brake fluid.

9. Open the bleeder screw at least ¾ of a turn and allow flow to continue until no air is seen in the fluid.

10. Close the bleeder screw. Tighten the rear bleeder screws to 62 inch lbs. (7 Nm) and the front bleeder screws to 115 inch lbs. (13 Nm).

11. Repeat Steps 6–9 until all of the calipers and/or cylinders have been bled.

12. Carefully lower the vehicle.

13. Check the brake pedal for sponginess. If the condition is found, the entire bleeding procedure must be repeated.

14. Remove tools J 35589 and J 29532.

15. Refill the master cylinder to the proper level with brake fluid.

16. DO NOT attempt to move the vehicle unless a firm brake pedal is obtained.

A Tube must be submerged in brake fluid
1 Bleeder wrench
2 Tube
3 Caliper

87959019

Fig. 15 Attach a clear plastic hose to the screw and submerge the other end in a transparent container of clean brake fluid

87959020

Fig. 16 It's often helpful to attach the bleeder bottle to the frame using an old coat hanger

J 35589

1 Master cylinder reservoir

87959021

Fig. 17 View of the pressure bleeder adapter cap installed on the master cylinder

DISC BRAKES

▶ See Figure 18

✳ CAUTION

Brake pads may contain asbestos, which has been determined to be a cancer causing agent. Avoid inhaling any dust from any brake surface. Never clean the brake surfaces with compressed air! When cleaning brake surfaces, use a commercially available brake cleaning fluid.

Brake Pads

REMOVAL & INSTALLATION

▶ See Figures 19 thru 25

1. Using a clean turkey baster or equivalent, siphon ⅔ of the brake fluid from the master cylinder reservoir.

2. Loosen the wheel lug nuts, then raise and safely support the vehicle.

1 Mounting bolt & sleeve
  assembly
2 Bushing
3 Outboard shoe & lining
4 Wear sensor
5 Inboard shoe & lining
6 Boot
7 Piston
8 Piston seal
9 Bleeder valve
10 Caliper housing
11 Bleeder valve cap

87959022

Fig. 18 Exploded view of a typical front disc brake caliper and pad assembly

3. Remove the tire and wheel assembly.

4. Using a C-clamp, bottom the piston in its bore for clearance to remove it from the rotor.

5. Remove the caliper, as described later in this section.

6. Use a suitable prytool to disengage the buttons on the shoe from the holes in the caliper housing, then remove the outboard shoe and lining.

7. Remove the inboard shoe and lining.

8. Prior to installing new shoes and linings, wipe the outside surface of the boot clean with denatured alcohol.

To install:

9. Use a large C-clamp to compress the piston back into the caliper bore. Be careful not to damage the piston or boot with the C-clamp.

10. After bottoming the piston, lift the inner edge of the boot next to the piston and press out any trapped air. The boot must lie flat.

11. Install the inboard shoe and lining by snapping the shoe retaining

spring into the piston inside diameter. The shoe retainer spring is already staked to the inboard shoe. After installing the shoe and lining, make sure the boot is not touching the shoe. If there is contact, reseat or reposition the boot.

12. Install the outboard shoe and lining with the wear sensor at the trailing edge of the shoe. During forward wheel rotation, the back of the shoe must lay flat against the caliper.

13. Install caliper, as outlined later in this section.

14. Install the tire and wheel assembly.

15. Carefully lower the vehicle, then fill the master cylinder to the proper level.

16. Push the brake pedal down firmly three times to seat the linings.

INSPECTION

▶ **See Figure 26**

➡**Always replace all pads on both front wheels at the same time. Failure to do so will result in uneven braking action and premature wear.**

1. Inspect the brake linings approximately every 6,000 miles (9,000 km) or whenever the wheels are removed.

2. Check both ends of the pad and the lining thickness on the inner shoe to make sure it is wearing evenly.

➡**Some inboard shoes have a thermal lining against the shoe, molded integrally with the lining. Do not confuse this lining with uneven inboard-outboard lining wear.**

3. Whenever the thickness of the lining is worn to the wear indicator, replace the pads on both sides.

Brake Caliper

▶ **See Figures 27 thru 33**

➡**Always replace the brake calipers on both front wheels at the same time. Failure to do so will result in uneven braking action and premature wear.**

87959023

Fig. 19 Front disc brake components after removing the wheel and tire assembly

87959024

Fig. 20 Use a C-clamp to compress the caliper piston

1 Outboard shoe & lining
2 Caliper housing

87959025

Fig. 21 Disengage the buttons on the shoe from the holes in the caliper housing to remove the outboard shoe and lining

87959026

Fig. 22 Remove the outboard brake pad from the caliper, then . . .

87959027

Fig. 23 . . . remove the inboard brake pad

1 Inboard shoe & housing
2 Piston
3 Caliper housing
4 Shoe retainer spring

87959028

Fig. 24 Install the inboard shoe and lining, then . . .

REMOVAL & INSTALLATION

1. Using a clean turkey baster or equivalent, remove about ⅔ of the brake fluid from the master cylinder.

2. Loosen the wheel lug nuts, then raise and safely support the vehicle.

3. Remove the tire and wheel assembly.

4. Sometimes it is helpful to reinstall two of the lug nuts to hold the rotor to the hub and bearing assembly.

5. Push the piston into the caliper bore to provide clearance between the brake pads and the rotor as follows:

a. Install a large C-clamp over the top of the caliper housing and against the back of the outboard shoe.

b. Slowly tighten the clamp until the piston is pushed into the caliper bore enough slide the caliper off of the rotor.

6. If the caliper assembly is being removed from the vehicle for overhaul, unfasten the bolt attaching the inlet fitting, then plug the exposed fitting to prevent contamination. If just the pads are being replaced, there is no need to disconnect the inlet fitting.

7. Unfasten the caliper mounting bolt and sleeve assemblies. Some vehicles have a rubber cap over the retaining bolt which must be removed first.

8. Lift the caliper off of the rotor. If the caliper is not being removed for overhaul, suspend it from the strut with a wire hook.

9. Inspect the mounting bolts, sleeves and bushings for damage and replace as necessary.

To install:

10. Liberally coat the inside of the bushings with silicone grease.

11. Position the caliper over the rotor into the knuckle, then fasten the mounting bolt and sleeve assemblies. Tighten to 38 ft. lbs. (51 Nm).

12. If removed, connect the inlet fitting. Tighten to 32 ft. lbs. (44 Nm).

13. Remove the two nuts retaining the rotor to the hub, then install the wheel and tire assembly. Only hand-tighten the lug nuts at this time.

14. Carefully lower the vehicle, then tighten the lug nuts to 103 ft. lbs (140 Nm).

1 Outboard shoe & lining
2 Wear sensor
3 Caliper housing

87959029

Fig. 25 . . . install the outboard shoe and lining

87959030

Fig. 26 Measuring the brake pad thickness to see if the pads need to be replaced

87959024

Fig. 27 Use a C-clamp to carefully bottom out the piston to provide clearance for removal

87959031

Fig. 28 If the caliper is being removed for overhaul, unfasten the bolt attaching the fluid line, then plug the line

87959032

Fig. 29 Some vehicles have a cap over the retaining bolt which must be removed to access the bolt

87959033

Fig. 30 Unfasten, then remove the caliper mounting bolts and sleeves

87959034

Fig. 31 Lift the caliper off of the rotor

87959035

Fig. 32 If the caliper is not being removed for overhaul, suspend it with a retaining strap or piece of wire from the strut

ADD SILICONE GREASE TO I.D. OF BUSHING

1 Mounting bolt & sleeve assembly
2 Bushing
3 Caliper housing

87959036

Fig. 33 Lubricating the cavity of the caliper

15. Fill the master cylinder to the proper level, and bleed the brakes if the inlet fitting was removed. Recheck the fluid level.

OVERHAUL

▶ **See Figures 34 thru 41**

➡**Some vehicles may be equipped dual piston calipers. The procedure to overhaul the caliper is essentially the same with the exception of multiple pistons, O-rings and dust boots.**

1. Remove the caliper from the vehicle and place on a clean workbench.

✳✳ CAUTION

NEVER place your fingers in front of the pistons in an attempt to catch or protect the pistons when applying compressed air. This could result in personal injury!

➡**Depending upon the vehicle, there are two different ways to remove the piston from the caliper. Refer to the brake pad replacement procedure to make sure you have the correct procedure for your vehicle.**

2. The first method is as follows:
   a. Stuff a shop towel or a block of wood into the caliper to catch the piston.
   b. Remove the caliper piston using compressed air applied into the caliper inlet hole. Inspect the piston for scoring, nicks, corrosion and/or worn or damaged chrome plating. The piston must be replaced if any of these conditions are found.
3. For the second method, you must rotate the piston to retract it from the caliper.
4. If equipped, remove the anti-rattle clip.
5. Use a prytool to remove the caliper boot, being careful not to scratch the housing bore.

6. Remove the piston seals from the groove in the caliper bore.
7. Carefully loosen the brake bleeder valve cap and valve from the caliper housing.
8. Inspect the caliper bores, pistons and mounting threads for scoring or excessive wear.
9. Use crocus cloth to polish out light corrosion from the piston and bore.
10. Clean all parts with denatured alcohol and dry with compressed air.
To assemble:
11. Lubricate and install the bleeder valve and cap.
12. Install the new seals into the caliper bore grooves, making sure they are not twisted.
13. Lubricate the piston bore.
14. Install the pistons and boots into the bores of the calipers and push to the bottom of the bores.
15. Use a suitable driving tool to seat the boots in the housing.
16. Install the caliper in the vehicle.
17. Install the wheel and tire assembly, then carefully lower the vehicle.
18. Properly bleed the brake system.

Brake Disc (Rotor)

REMOVAL & INSTALLATION

▶ **See Figure 42**

➡**You should always replace the rotors on both front wheels at the same time. Failure to do so will result in uneven braking action and premature wear.**

1. Raise and safely support the vehicle. Remove the tire and wheel assembly.
2. Push the piston into the caliper bore to provide clearance between the brake pads and the rotor as follows:

TCCA9P01
Fig. 34 For some types of calipers, use compressed air to drive the piston out of the caliper, but make sure to keep your fingers clear

TCCA9P02
Fig. 35 Withdraw the piston from the caliper bore

TCCA9P03
Fig. 36 On some vehicles, you must remove the anti-rattle clip

TCCSA9P04
Fig. 37 Use a prytool to carefully pry around the edge of the boot . . .

TCCA9P05
Fig. 38 . . . then remove the boot from the caliper housing, taking care not to score or damage the bore

TCCA9P06
Fig. 39 Use extreme caution when removing the piston seal; DO NOT scratch the caliper bore

Fig. 40 Use the proper size driving tool and a mallet to properly seal the boots in the caliper housing

Fig. 41 There are tools, such as this Mighty-Vac, available to assist in proper brake system bleeding

Fig. 42 Removing the rotor from the hub

a. Install a large C-clamp over the top of the caliper housing and against the back of the outboard shoe.

b. Slowly tighten the clamp until the piston is pushed into the caliper bore enough slide the caliper off of the rotor.

3. Unfasten the caliper mounting bolts, then carefully remove the caliper (along with the brake pads) from the rotor. Do not disconnect the brake line; instead, wire the caliper out of the way with the line still connected.

4. Remove the rotor by simply pulling it off of the hub and bearing assembly.

5. The installation is the reverse of the removal procedure.

INSPECTION

Check the disc brake rotor for scoring, cracks or other damage. Rotor run-out should be measured while the rotor is installed, while rotor thickness/thickness variation may be checked with the rotor installed or removed. Use a dial gauge to check rotor run-out. Check the rotor thickness to make sure it is greater than minimum thickness and check for thickness variations using a caliper micrometer.

Thickness Variation

1. Measure the thickness at four or more points on the rotor. Make all measure measurements at the same distance in from the edge of the rotor. Use a micrometer calibrated in ten-thousandths of an inch.

2. A rotor that varies in thickness by more than 0.0005 in. (0.013mm) can cause pedal pulsation and/or front end vibration during brake applications. A rotor that does not meet these specifications should be resurfaced to specifications or replaced.

Lateral Run-out

1. Remove the wheel and tire assembly.
2. Fasten the lug nuts to retain the rotor.
3. Secure a dial indicator to the steering knuckle so the indicator button contacts the rotor at about 0.5 in. (13mm) from the outer edge of the rotor.
4. Set the dial indicator to zero.
5. Turn the wheel one complete revolution and observe the total indicated run-out.
6. If the run-out exceeds 0.0031 in. (0.08mm), resurface or replace the rotor.

REAR DRUM BRAKES

▶ See Figures 43 and 44

✳✳ CAUTION

Brake shoes may contain asbestos, which has been determined to be a cancer causing agent. Never clean the brake surfaces with compressed air! Avoid inhaling any dust from any brake surface! When cleaning brake surfaces, use a commercially available brake cleaning fluid.

Brake Drums

REMOVAL & INSTALLATION

▶ See Figure 45

1. Raise and safely support the vehicle.

➡ Matchmark the relationship of the wheel to the axle flange and the brake drum to the axle flange to insure proper wheel balance during installation.

2. Remove the wheel and tire assembly.
3. Remove the drum.
4. If the drum is difficult to remove, make sure the parking brake is released, then back off the parking brake cable adjustment. If necessary, use a rubber mallet to tap GENTLY around the inner drum diameter of the spindle. Be careful not to deform the drum by tapping too hard.
5. Inspect the drum for scoring, cracking or grooving. Replace if necessary.

1 RETURN SPRING	11 PRIMARY SHOE AND LINING	21 BOLT
2 RETURN SPRING	12 SECONDARY SHOE AND LINING	22 BOOT
3 HOLD DOWN SPRING	13 ADJUSTING SCREW SPRING	23 PISTON
4 BEARING SLEEVE	14 SOCKET	24 SEAL
5 HOLD-DOWN PIN	15 PIVOT NUT	25 SPRING ASSEMBLY
6 ACTUATOR LINK	16 ADJUSTING SCREW	26 WHEEL CYLINDER
7 ACTUATOR LEVER	17 RETAINING RING	27 BACKING PLATE
8 LEVER RETURN SPRING	18 PIN	30 SHOE RETAINER
9 PARKING BRAKE STRUT	19 PARKING BRAKE LEVER	32 ANCHOR PIN
10 STRUT SPRING	20 BLEEDER VALVE	33 SHOE PADS (6 PLACES)

∗LUBRICATE WITH THIN COATING OF 1052196 LUBRICANT OR EQUIVALENT

Fig. 43 Exploded view of the rear drum brake system components (drum removed)

1 Brake spring remover and installer
2 Brake spring pliers
3 Brake drum/shoe clearance gage
4 Brake spring remover and installer

87959061

Fig. 44 Some special tools are required when servicing brake drums

To install:

6. Install the drum aligning the marks made during removal.
7. Using the marks previously made, install the tire and wheel assembly.
8. Carefully lower the vehicle, then tighten the lug nuts to 103 ft. lbs. (140 Nm).

INSPECTION

1. Inspect the brake drum for scoring, cracking or grooving. Light scoring of the drum not exceeding 0.020 in. (0.51mm) in depth will not affect brake operation.
2. Inspect the brake drum for excessive taper and out-of-round. When measuring a drum for out-of-round, taper and wear, take measurements at the open and closed edges of the machined surface and at right angles to each other.

Brake Shoes

❋❋ CAUTION

Brake shoes may contain asbestos, which has been determined to be a cancer causing agent. Never clean the brake surfaces with compressed air! Avoid inhaling any dust from any brake surface! When cleaning brake surfaces, use a commercially available brake cleaning fluid.

INSPECTION

1. Remove the wheel and drum.
2. Inspect the shoes for proper thickness. The lining should be at least $\frac{1}{32}$ in. (0.8mm) above the rivet head for riveted brakes and $\frac{1}{16}$ in. (1.6mm) above the mounting surface for bonded brake linings.
3. Inspect the linings for even wear, cracking and scoring. Replace as necessary.

REMOVAL & INSTALLATION

◆ **See Figures 46 thru 56**

➡ **The brake shoes should be replaced in axle pairs. Failure to replace the component in pairs may cause unequal braking action and premature wear.**

1. Raise and safely support the vehicle.
2. Remove the tire and wheel assemblies, then remove the brake drum.

➡ **If unsure of spring positioning, finish one side before starting the other and use the untouched side as a guide.**

87959043

Fig. 45 Remove the brake drum by simply pulling it off

87959044

Fig. 46 Use a commercially available spray cleaner to remove brake dust from the components

87959045

Fig. 47 Use a suitable tool to remove the return springs

87959046

Fig. 48 Unfasten the primary return spring, then . . .

87959047

Fig. 49 . . . remove the secondary return spring

87959048

Fig. 50 Use the brake tool to compress the hold-down spring and twist the plate to free the pin

Fig. 51 Once the pin and slot on top of the spring plate are aligned, separate the hold-down spring and pin

Fig. 52 Lift up on the actuator lever and remove the return spring, then . . .

Fig. 53 . . . remove the actuator link

Fig. 54 Remove the brake shoe assembly which is held together by the lower spring

Fig. 55 Exploded view of the drum brake components

1 Hold down spring
2 Bearing sleeve
3 Hold down pin
4 Actuator lever
5 Secondary shoe and lining

Fig. 56 View of the bearing sleeve location

3. Using tool J 8049, J 29840 or equivalent brake spring remover and installer, unfasten the primary and secondary shoe return springs from the anchor pin, but leave them installed in the shoes.

4. Remove the hold-down springs, and pins using suitable pliers or brake tool.

5. While lifting up on the actuator lever, remove the actuator link.

6. Remove the actuator lever, lever return spring and the bearing sleeve.

7. Remove the parking brake strut and spring.

8. Remove the brake shoes, which are held together by the lower spring, after disconnecting the parking brake cable from the backing plate.

9. Disconnect the adjusting screw assembly and adjusting screw spring from the brake shoes.

10. Remove the retaining ring, pin and parking brake lever from the secondary brake shoe.

11. Lift the wheel cylinder dust boots and inspect for fluid leakage.

12. Thoroughly clean and dry the backing plate.

To install:

13. Remove, clean and dry all parts still on the old shoes with denatured alcohol. Lubricate the star wheel shaft threads and transfer all the parts to the new shoes in their proper locations.

14. To prepare the backing plate, lubricate the bosses, anchor pin and parking brake actuating lever pivot surface lightly with brake lubricant GM part no. 1052916, or equivalent.

15. Install the parking brake lever on the secondary shoe with the pin and retaining ring.

16. Install the adjusting screw assembly and adjusting screw spring on the shoe and lining assembly.

17. Position the shoe and lining assemblies after attaching the parking brake cable.

18. Spread the shoes apart, install the parking brake strut and strut spring. The end without the strut spring should engage the parking brake lever and secondary shoe and lining. The end with the strut spring should engage the primary shoe and lining.

→In the next step, the bearing sleeve must be installed between the secondary and lining and the actuator lever. Refer to the accompanying figure.

19. Install the bearing sleeve, actuator lever and lever return spring.

20. Install the hold-down pins and springs.

21. Fasten the actuator link on the anchor pin. While holding up the lever, fasten the actuator link into the lever.

22. Secure the shoe return springs, using tool J 8057 or equivalent pliers.

23. Adjust the brakes using the procedure located in this section.

24. Aligning the marks made during removal, install the brake drum.

25. Install the tire and wheel assembly.

26. Carefully lower the vehicle, then tighten the lug nuts to 103 ft. lbs. (140 Nm).

27. Adjust the parking brake, as outlined later in this section.

ADJUSTMENT

The drum brakes are designed to self-adjust when applied with the car moving in reverse. However, they can also be adjusted manually. This manual adjustment should also be performed whenever the linings are replaced.

1982–86 Vehicles

♦ **See Figure 57**

1. Raise and safely support the vehicle.

2. Remove the tire and wheel assembly.

3. Remove the drum, then measure the inside diameter of the brake drum with a drum-to-brake shoe gauge, J 21177-A or equivalent.

4. Position the tool on the brake linings, as shown in the accompanying figure, with the setting obtained in Step 3 and adjust the brake shoes so that the lining contacts the inside part of the tool.

5. Use a punch to knock out the stamped area on the brake drum. If this is done with the drum installed on the car, the drum must then be removed to clean out all metal pieces. After adjustments are complete, obtain a hole cover from your dealer (Part no. 4874119 or the equivalent) to prevent entry of dirt and water into the brakes.

6. Use an awl or an adjusting tool especially made for the purpose to turn

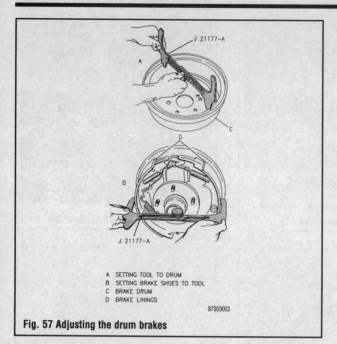

A SETTING TOOL TO DRUM
B SETTING BRAKE SHOES TO TOOL
C BRAKE DRUM
D BRAKE LININGS

87959003

Fig. 57 Adjusting the drum brakes

the brake adjusting screw star wheel. Expand the shoes until the drum can just barely be turned by hand.

7. Back off the adjusting screw 12 notches. If the shoes still are dragging lightly, back off the adjusting screw one or two additional notches. If the brakes still drag, the parking brake adjustment is incorrect or the parking brake is applied. Fix and start over.

8. Install the hole cover into the drum.

9. Check the parking brake adjustment.

➡**On some models, no marked area or stamped area is present on the drum. In this case, a hole must be drilled in the backing plate:**

10. All backing plates have two round flat areas in the lower half through which the parking brake cable is installed. Drill a ½ in. (13mm) hole into the round flat area on the backing plate opposite the parking brake cable. This will allow access to the star wheel.

11. After drilling the hole, remove the drum and remove all metal particles. Install a hole plug (Part no. 4874119 or the equivalent) to prevent the entry of water or dirt.

12. Install the brake drum and the wheel and tire assembly, then carefully lower the vehicle.

1987–94 Vehicles

▶ **See Figure 57**

1. Raise and support the vehicle safely.

2. Matchmark the relationship between the wheel to the axle flange to insure proper balance upon reassembly, then remove the tire and wheel assembly.

3. Matchmark the relationship of the drum to the axle flange, then remove the brake drum.

4. Measure the drum inside diameter using brake shoe gauge J 12177–A, or equivalent.

5. Turning the star wheel, adjust the shoe and lining diameter to be:
   • 0.050 in. (1.27mm) less than the inside drum diameter for each wheel for 1987–90 vehicles.
   • 0.030 in. (0.76mm) less than the inside drum diameter for each wheel for 1991–94 vehicles.

6. Install the drums and wheels, aligning the previous marks.

7. Carefully lower the vehicle.

8. Tighten the wheel nuts to 100 ft. lbs. (136 Nm).

9. Make several alternate forward and reserve stops applying firm force to the brake pedal until ample pedal reserve is built up.

Wheel Cylinders

REMOVAL & INSTALLATION

▶ **See Figures 58, 59, 60, 61 and 62**

1. Raise and safely support the vehicle.

2. Remove the tire and wheel assembly.

3. Following the procedures located in this section, remove the brake drum and brake shoes (if necessary for access).

4. Unfasten the inlet brake fluid line, then cap the line to prevent contamination from entering.

5. If necessary for access to the cylinder, remove the hub and bearing assembly. On some vehicles, you must loosen the hub assembly bolts and slide the hub forward for additional clearance to remove the wheel cylinder.

6. Clean any dirt from around the wheel cylinder.

➡**On some vehicles, you will need a #6 Torx® driver to remove the wheel cylinder bolts.**

7. To remove the round retainer type cylinders, insert two awls or pins into the access slots between the wheel cylinder pilot and the retainer locking tabs. Bend both tabs away simultaneously. The wheel cylinder can be removed, as the retainer is released.

8. To remove the bolted wheel cylinders, unfasten the wheel cylinder bolts, then remove the cylinder from the backing plate.

To install:

9. Apply a very thin coating of silicone sealer to the cylinder mounting surface.

10. For round retainer type wheel cylinders, position the cylinder and hold it in place with a wooden block between the cylinder and the axle flange. Carefully seat the new retainer clip, using a 1⅛ in. 12-point socket and socket extension (to help preserve your fingers). The socket is used to assure that the retainer seats evenly.

11. For bolt type wheel cylinders, position, install the cylinder to the backing plate and fasten the attaching bolts. Tighten to 15 ft. lbs. (20 Nm).

12. Uncap, then connect the brake line to the wheel cylinder. Tighten the inlet tube nut to 17 ft. lbs. (23 Nm).

87959056

Fig. 58 Remove the brake drum, then remove the brake shoes if necessary for access to the wheel cylinder

87959055

Fig. 59 Disconnect and plug the brake line from the rear of the backing plate

Awls

Wheel cylinder retainer

87959057

Fig. 60 Two awls may be used to bend the retainer stubs, releasing the wheel cylinder

13. If removed, install the hub and bearing assembly. Tighten to 43 ft. lbs. (58 Nm).

14. Install the brake shoes, if removed, and the brake drum.

15. Install the tire and wheel assembly.

16. Carefully lower the vehicle, then tighten the lug nuts to 103 ft. lbs. (140 Nm).

17. Properly bleed the hydraulic brake system.

OVERHAUL

▶ **See Figures 63 thru 72**

Wheel cylinder overhaul kits may be available, but often at little or no savings over a reconditioned wheel cylinder. It often makes sense with these components to substitute a new or reconditioned part instead of attempting an overhaul.

If no replacement is available, or you would prefer to overhaul your wheel cylinders, the following procedure may be used. When rebuilding and installing wheel cylinders, avoid getting any contaminants into the system. Always use clean, new, high quality brake fluid. If dirty or improper fluid has been used, it will be necessary to drain the entire system, flush the system with proper brake fluid, replace all rubber components, then refill and bleed the system.

1. Remove the wheel cylinder from the vehicle and place on a clean workbench.

2. First remove and discard the old rubber boots, then withdraw the pistons. Piston cylinders are equipped with seals and a spring assembly, all located behind the pistons in the cylinder bore.

3. Remove the remaining inner components, seals and spring assembly. Compressed air may be useful in removing these components. If no compressed air is available, be VERY careful not to score the wheel cylinder bore when removing parts from it. Discard all components for which replacements were supplied in the rebuild kit.

4. Wash the cylinder and metal parts in denatured alcohol or clean brake fluid.

1 Bleeder valve   4 Seal
2 Boot   5 Spring assembly
3 Piston   6 Wheel cylinder body

87959058

Fig. 61 Exploded view of the wheel cylinder components

1 Socket extension
2 1-1/8 in., 12 pt. socket

87959059

Fig. 62 If equipped with a round retainer type wheel cylinder, use a socket extension to seat the retainer

TCCA9P13

Fig. 63 Remove the outer boots from the wheel cylinder

TCCA9P14

Fig. 64 Compressed air can be used to remove the pistons and seals

TCCA9P15

Fig. 65 Remove the pistons, cup seals and spring from the cylinder

TCCA9P16

Fig. 66 Use brake fluid and a soft brush to clean the pistons . . .

TCCA9P17

Fig. 67 . . . and the bore of the wheel cylinder

TCCA9P18

Fig. 68 Once cleaned and inspected, the wheel cylinder is ready for assembly

TCCA9P19

Fig. 69 Lubricate the cup seals with brake fluid

⁑ WARNING

Never use a mineral-based solvent such as gasoline, kerosene or paint thinner for cleaning purposes. These solvents will swell rubber components and quickly deteriorate them.

5. Allow the parts to air dry or use compressed air. Do not use rags for cleaning, since lint will remain in the cylinder bore.

6. Inspect the piston and replace it if it shows scratches.
7. Lubricate the cylinder bore and seals using clean brake fluid.
8. Position the spring assembly.
9. Install the inner seals, then the pistons.
10. Insert the new boots into the counterbores by hand. Do not lubricate the boots.
11. Install the wheel cylinder.

TCCA9P20

Fig. 70 Install the spring, then the cup seals in the bore

TCCA9P21

Fig. 71 Lightly lubricate the pistons, then install them

TCCA9P22

Fig. 72 The boots can now be installed over the wheel cylinder ends

PARKING BRAKE

Cables

♦ **See Figures 73 and 74**

REMOVAL & INSTALLATION

Front Cable

1. For vehicles through 1988, block the drive wheels and place the gear selector in **Neutral**.

2. Remove the center console as detailed in Section 10.
3. Disconnect the parking brake cable from the lever.
4. Remove the cable retaining nut and the bracket securing the front cable to the floor panel.
5. Raise the car and loosen the equalizer/adjustment nut.
6. Loosen the catalytic converter shield, then remove the parking brake cable from the body.
7. Disconnect the cable from the equalizer, then remove the cable from the guide and the underbody clips.

1 Front parking brake cable
2 Right parking brake cable
3 Left parking brake cable
4 Clip
5 Insulator
6 Parking brake lever
7 Bolts - 25 Nm (18 lbs. ft.)
8 Floor console assembly
9 Rear mounting bracket
10 Equalizer
11 Adjustment nut
12 Retainer
13 Clevis
14 Parking brake cable assembly
15 Nut - 28 Nm (21 lbs. ft.)

87959062

Fig. 73 Parking brake cable routing and lever removal and installation—1993 Sunbird shown

1 Front parking brake cable
2 Right rear parking brake cable
3 Fuel tank strap
4 Left rear parking brake cable
5 Parking brake lever
6 Cable retainer
7 Insulator
8 Equalizer
9 Axle assembly

87959063

Fig. 74 Parking brake cable routing and lever removal and installation—1994 Cavalier shown

To install:

8. Position the cable to the equalizer, guide and underbody clips.

9. Install the parking brake cable to the body and tighten the catalytic converter shield.

10. Tighten the equalizer nut.

11. Install the cable retaining nut and the bracket securing the front cable to the floor panel.

12. Connect the parking brake cable to the lever.

13. Install the center console as detailed in Section 6.

14. Adjust the parking brake cable, as outlined in this section.

Right and Left Rear Cables

1. Raise and safely support the vehicle.

2. Back off the equalizer/adjustment nut (must be separated from the threaded rod if removing the right cable) until the cable tension is eliminated.

3. Remove the tires, wheels and brake drums.

4. Insert a a suitable prytool between the brake shoe and the top part of the brake adjuster bracket. Push the bracket to the front and then release the top brake adjuster rod.

5. Remove the rear hold-down spring. Remove the actuator lever and the lever return spring.

6. Remove the adjuster screw spring.

7. Remove the top rear brake shoe return spring.

8. Unhook the parking brake cable from the parking brake lever.

9. Depress the conduit fitting retaining tangs and then remove the conduit fitting from the backing plate.

10. Remove the cable end button from the connector.

11. Depress the conduit fitting retaining tangs and remove the conduit fitting from the axle bracket.

To install:

12. Install the conduit fitting to the axle bracket.

13. Install the cable end button to the connector (left side only).

14. Install the conduit fitting to the backing plate.

15. Hook the parking brake cable to the parking brake lever.

16. Install the top rear brake shoe return spring.

17. Install the adjuster screw spring.

18. Install the rear hold-down spring. Install the actuator lever and the lever return spring.

19. Install the top brake adjuster rod.

20. Install the tires, wheels and brake drums.

21. Adjust the parking brake cable, as outlined in this section.

ADJUSTMENT

▶ **See Figure 75**

1. Adjust the rear brakes, as outlined in this section.

2. Slowly pull the parking brake lever upward until 5 rachet clicks are heard.

3. Raise and safely support the vehicle.

➡**To prevent damage to the threaded parking brake adjusting rod when servicing the parking brake, clean and lubricate the exposed threaded on each side of the nut.**

4. Tighten the adjusting nut until the left rear wheel can just be turned backward using two hands, but is locked in forward rotation.

5. Release the parking brake.

6. Rotate the rear wheels, they should turn freely in either direction with no drag.

7. Carefully lower the vehicle.

Fig. 75 Parking brake cable adjustment

ANTI-LOCK BRAKE SYSTEM (ABS)

Description and Operation

The Anti-lock Braking System (ABS) was first introduced on J-body cars in 1992. ABS provides the driver with 3 important benefits over standard braking systems: increased vehicle stability, improved vehicle steerability, and potentially reduced stopping distances during braking. It should be noted that although the ABS-VI system offers definite advantages, the system cannot increase brake pressure above master cylinder pressure applied by the driver and cannot apply the brakes itself.

The ABS-VI Anti-lock Braking System consists of a conventional braking system with vacuum power booster, compact master cylinder, front disc brakes, rear drum brakes and interconnecting hydraulic brake lines augmented with the ABS components. The ABS-VI system includes a hydraulic modulator assembly, Electronic Control Unit (ECU), Electronic Brake Control Module (EBCM) or Electronic Brake and Traction Control Module (EBTCM) (these are all different "Computer Control Modules" which differ depending upon vehicle year and application), a system relay, 4 wheel speed sensors, interconnecting wiring and an amber ABS warning light.

The ECU/EBCM/EBTCM monitors inputs from the individual wheel speed sensors and determines when a wheel or wheels is/are about to lock up. The ECU/EBCM/EBTCM controls the motors on the hydraulic modulator assembly to reduce brake pressure to the wheel about to lock up. When the wheel regains traction, the brake pressure is increased until the wheel again approaches lock-up. The cycle repeats until either the vehicle comes to a stop, the brake pedal is released, or no wheels are about to lock up. The ECU/EBCM/EBTCM also has

the ability to monitor itself and can store diagnostic codes in a non-volatile (will not be erased if the battery is disconnected) memory. The ECU/EBCM/EBTCM is serviced as an assembly.

The ABS-VI braking system employs 2 modes: base (conventional) braking and anti-lock braking. Under normal braking, the conventional part of the system stops the vehicle. When in the ABS mode, the Electromagnetic Brakes (EMB) action of the ABS system controls the two front wheels individually and the rear wheels together. If the one rear wheel is about to lock up, the hydraulic pressure to both wheels is reduced, controlling both wheels together.

BASIC KNOWLEDGE REQUIRED

Before using this section, it is important that you have a basic knowledge of the following items. Without this basic knowledge, it will be difficult to use the diagnostic procedures contained in this section.

Basic Electrical Circuits—You should understand the basic theory of electricity and know the meaning of voltage, current (amps) and resistance (ohms). You should understand what happens in a circuit with an open or shorted wire. You should be able to read and understand a wiring diagram.

Use Of Circuit Testing Tools—You should know how to use a test light and how to use jumper wires to bypass components to test circuits. You should be familiar with the High Impedance Multimeter (DVM) such as J 34029–A. You should be able to measure voltage, resistance and current and be familiar with the meter controls and how to use them correctly.

ONBOARD DIAGNOSTICS

The ABS-VI contains sophisticated onboard diagnostics that, when accessed with a bidirectional scan tool, are designed to identify the source of any system fault as specifically as possible, including whether or not the fault is intermittent. There are 58 diagnostic fault codes to assist the service technician with diagnosis.

The last diagnostic fault code to occur is identified, specific ABS data is stored at the time of this fault, and the first five codes set are stored. Additionally, using a bidirectional scan tool, each input and output can be monitored, thus enabling fault confirmation and repair verification. Manual control of components and automated functional tests are also available when using a GM approved "Scan" tool. Details of many of these functions are contained in the following sections.

ENHANCED DIAGNOSTICS

Enhanced Diagnostic Information, found in the CODE HISTORY function of the bidirectional scan tool, is designed to provide the service technician with specific fault occurrence information. For each of the first five (5) and the very last diagnostic fault codes stored, data is stored to identify the specific fault code number, the number of failure occurrences, and the number of drive cycles since the failure first and last occurred (a drive cycle occurs when the ignition is turned **ON** and the vehicle is driven faster than 10 mph). However, if a fault is present, the drive cycle counter will increment by turning the ignition **ON** and **OFF**. These first five (5) diagnostic fault codes are also stored in the order of occurrence. The order in which the first 5 faults occurred can be useful in determining if a previous fault is linked to the most recent faults, such as an intermittent wheel speed sensor which later becomes completely open.

During difficult diagnosis situations, this information can be used to identify fault occurrence trends. Does the fault occur more frequently now than it did during the last time when it only failed 1 out of 35 drive cycles? Did the fault only occur once over a large number of drive cycles, indication an unusual condition present when the fault occurred? Does the fault occur infrequently over a large number of drive cycles, indication special diagnosis techniques may be required to identify the source of the fault?

If a fault occurred 1 out of 20 drive cycles, the fault is intermittent and has not reoccurred for 19 drive cycles. This fault may be difficult or impossible to duplicate and may have been caused by a severe vehicle impact (large pot hole, speed bump at high speed, etc.) that momentarily opened an electrical connector or caused unusual vehicle suspension movement. Problem resolution is unlikely, and the problem may never reoccur (check diagnostic aids proved for that code). If the fault occurred 3 out of 15 drive cycles, the odds of finding the cause are still not good, but you know how often it occurs and you can determine whether or not the fault is becoming more frequent based on an additional or past occurrences visit if the source of the problem can not or could not be found. If the fault occurred 10 out of 20 drive cycles, the odds of finding the cause are very good, as the fault may be easily reproduced.

By using the additional fault data, you can also determine if a failure is randomly intermittent or if it has not reoccurred for long periods of time due to weather changes or a repair prior to this visit. Say a diagnostic fault code occurred 10 of 20 drive cycles but has not reoccurred for 10 drive cycles. This means the failure occurred 10 of 10 drive cycles but has not reoccurred since. A significant environmental change or a repair occurred 10 drive cycles ago. A repair may not be necessary if a recent repair can be confirmed. If no repair was made, the service can focus on diagnosis techniques used to locate difficult to recreate problems.

Diagnostic Procedures

▶ **See Figures 76, 77, 78, 79 and 80**

When servicing the ABS-VI, the following steps should be followed in order. Failure to follow these steps may result in the loss of important diagnostic data and may lead to difficult and time consuming diagnosis procedures.

1. Connect a bidirectional scan tool, as instructed by the tool manufacturer, then read all current and historical diagnostic codes. Be certain to note which codes are current diagnostic code failures. DO NOT CLEAR CODES unless directed to do so.

2. Using a bidirectional scan tool, read the CODE HISTORY data. Note the diagnostic fault codes stored and their frequency of failure. Specifically note the last failure that occurred and the conditions present when this failure occurred. This last failure should be the starting point for diagnosis and repair.

3. Perform a vehicle preliminary diagnosis inspection. This should include:

a. Inspection of the compact master cylinder for proper brake fluid level.

b. Inspection of the ABS hydraulic modulator for any leaks or wiring damage.

c. Inspection of brake components at all four (4) wheels. Verify no drag exists. Also verify proper brake apply operation.

d. Inspection for worn or damaged wheel bearings that allow a wheel to wobble.

e. Inspection of the wheel speed sensors and their wiring. Verify correct air gap range, solid sensor attachment, undamaged sensor toothed ring, and undamaged wiring, especially at vehicle attachment points.

f. Verify proper outer CV-joint alignment and operation.

g. Verify tires meet legal tread depth requirements.

4. If no codes are present, or mechanical component failure codes are present, perform the automated modulator test using the Tech 1® or T-100® to isolate the cause of the problem. If the failure is intermittent and not reproducible, test drive the vehicle while using the automatic snapshot feature of the bidirectional scan tool.

Perform normal acceleration, stopping, and turning maneuvers. If this does not reproduce the failure, perform an ABS stop, on a low coefficient surface such as gravel, from approximately 30–50 mph (48–80 km/h) while triggering any ABS code. If the failure is still not reproducible, use the enhanced diagnostic information found in CODE HISTORY to determine whether or not this failure should be further diagnosed.

5. Once all system failures have been corrected, clear the ABS codes. The Tech 1® and T-100®, when plugged into the ALDL connector, becomes part of the vehicle's electronic system. The Tech 1® and T-100® can also perform the following functions on components linked by the Serial Data Link (SDL):

- Display ABS data
- Display and clear ABS trouble codes
- Control ABS components
- Perform extensive ABS diagnosis
- Provide diagnostic testing for intermittent ABS conditions

6 WAY EBCM HARNESS CONNECTOR

PIN	CIRCUIT NO.	COLOR	CIRCUIT
C	1284	DK GRN	REAR MOTOR HIGH
D	1285	ORN	REAR MOTOR LOW
E	1281	PNK	L/F MOTOR LOW
F	1280	BLK	L/F MOTOR HIGH
G	1283	BLK	R/F MOTOR LOW
H	1282	PPL	R/F MOTOR HIGH

2 WAY EBCM HARNESS CONNECTOR

PIN	CIRCUIT NO.	COLOR	CIRCUIT
A	1633	RED	SWITCHED BATTERY INPUT
B	251	BLK/WHT	GROUND

87959068

Fig. 76 EBCM 6 and 2-way connectors—vehicles with and without the Enhanced Traction System (ETS)

PIN	CIRCUIT NO.	COLOR	CIRCUIT
1	OPEN		NOT USED
2	800	TAN	SERIAL DATA LINK
3	OPEN		NOT USED
4	1289	LT BLU	R/F ABS SOLENOID
5	830	LT BLU	L/F WHEEL SIGNAL HIGH
6	873	YEL	L/F WHEEL SIGNAL LOW
7	882	BRN	R/R WHEEL SIGNAL HIGH
8	883	WHT	R/R WHEEL SIGNAL LOW
9	872	DK GRN	R/F WHEEL SIGNAL HIGH
10	833	TAN	R/F WHEEL SIGNAL LOW
11	885	RED	L/R WHEEL SIGNAL LOW
12	884	BLK	L/R WHEEL SIGNAL HIGH
13	17	WHT	BRAKE SWITCH INPUT
14	41	BRN	SWITCH IGNITION
15	1440	ORN	B+ FEED
16	OPEN		NOT USED
17	OPEN		NOT USED
18	OPEN		NOT USED
19	1286	LT GRN	L/F EMB
20	1287	GRY	R/F EMB
21	849	PNK	BRAKE FLUID LEVEL SWITCH INPUT
22	1632	PNK	ENABLE RELAY CONTROL
23	OPEN		NOT USED
24	1288	DK GRN	L/F ABS SOLENOID

87959069

Fig. 77 EBCM 24-way electrical connector—vehicles without the Enhanced Traction System (ETS)

PIN	CIRCUIT NO.	COLOR	CIRCUIT
1	800	TAN	SERIAL DATA
2	1289	LT BLU	R/F ABS SOLENOID CONTROL
3	830	LT BLU	L/F WHEEL SIGNAL HIGH
4	873	YEL	L/F WHEEL SIGNAL LOW
5	882	BRN	R/R WHEEL SIGNAL HIGH
6	883	WHT	R/R WHEEL SIGNAL LOW
7	872	DK GRN	R/F WHEEL SIGNAL HIGH
8	833	TAN	R/F WHEEL SIGNAL LOW
9	884	BLK	L/R WHEEL SIGNAL HIGH
10	885	RED	L/R WHEEL SIGNAL LOW
11	OPEN		NOT USED
12	OPEN		NOT USED
13	17	WHT	BRAKE SWITCH INPUT
14	41	BRN	SWITCHED IGNITION
15	1440	ORN	BATTERY FEED
16	OPEN		NOT USED
17	1286	LT GRN	L/F EMB CONTROL
18	1287	GRY	R/F EMB CONTROL
19	849	PNK	BRAKE FLUID LEVEL SWITCH INPUT
20	1632	PNK	ENABLE RELAY CONTROL
21	OPEN		NOT USED
22	1288	DK GRN	L/F ABS SOLENOID CONTROL
23	OPEN		NOT USED
24	OPEN		NOT USED

87959070

Fig. 78 EBTCM 24-way electrical connector—vehicles with the Enhanced Traction System (ETS)

Fig. 79 ABS wiring diagram (page 1 of 2)

Fig. 80 ABS wiring diagram (page 2 of 2)

Each test mode has specific diagnosis capabilities which depend upon various keystrokes. In general, five (5) keys control sequencing: "YES," "NO," "EXIT," "UP" arrow and "DOWN" arrow. The F0 through F9 keys select operating modes, perform functions within an operating mode, or enter trouble code or model year designations.

In general, the Tech 1® has five (5) test modes for diagnosing the antilock brake system. The five (5) test modes are as follows:

MODE F0: DATA LIST—In this test mode, the Tech 1® continuously monitors wheel speed data, brake switch status and other inputs and outputs.

MODE F1: CODE HISTORY—In this mode, fault code history data is displayed. This data includes how many ignition cycles since the fault code occurred, along with other ABS information. The first five (5) and last fault codes set are included in the ABS history data.

MODE F2: TROUBLE CODES—In this test mode, trouble codes stored by the EBCM, both current ignition cycle and history, may be displayed or cleared.

MODE F3: ABS SNAPSHOT—In this test mode, the Tech 1® captures ABS data before and after a fault occurrence or a forced manual trigger.

MODE F4: ABS TESTS—In this test mode, the Tech 1® performs hydraulic modulator functional tests to assist in problem isolation during troubleshooting. Included here is manual control of the motors which is used prior to bleeding the brake system.

Press F7 to covert from English to metric.

DISPLAYING CODES

▶ **See Figures 81, 82, and 83**

Diagnostic fault codes can only be read through the use of a bidirectional scan tool. There are no provisions for "Flash Code" diagnostics.

CLEARING CODES

The trouble codes in EBCM memory are erased in one of two ways:
1. Tech 1® "Clear Codes" selection.
2. Ignition cycle default.

DTC	DESCRIPTION
14	Electronic Brake Control Relay Contacts Circuit Open
15	Electronic Brake Control Relay Contacts Circuit Shorted to Battery
16	Electronic Brake Control Relay Coil Circuit Open
17	Electronic Brake Control Relay Coil Circuit Shorted to Ground
18	Electronic Brake Control Relay Coil Circuit Shorted to Battery or Coil Shorted
21	Left Front Wheel Speed = 0 or Unreasonable
22	Right Front Wheel Speed = 0 or Unreasonable
23	Left Rear Wheel Speed = 0 or Unreasonable
24	Right Rear Wheel Speed = 0 or Unreasonable
25	Left Front Excessive Wheel Speed Variation
26	Right Front Excessive Wheel Speed Variation
27	Left Rear Excessive Wheel Speed Variation
28	Right Rear Excessive Wheel Speed Variation
36	Low System Voltage
37	High System Voltage
38	Left Front EMB Will Not Hold Motor
41	Right Front EMB Will Not Hold Motor
42	Rear ESB Will Not Hold Motor
44	Left Front Channel Will Not Move
45	Right Front Channel Will Not Move
46	Rear Axle Channel Will Not Move
47	Left Front Motor Free Spins
48	Right Front Motor Free Spins
51	Rear Motor Free Spins
52	Left Front Channel in Release Too Long
53	Right Front Channel in Release Too Long
54	Rear Channel in Release Too Long
55	EBCM Malfunction
56	Left Front Motor Circuit Open
57	Left Front Motor Circuit Shorted to Ground
58	Left Front Motor Circuit Shorted to Battery or Motor Shorted
61	Right Front Motor Circuit Open
62	Right Front Motor Circuit Shorted to Ground
63	Right Front Motor Circuit Shorted to Battery or Motor Shorted
64	Rear Motor Circuit Open
65	Rear Motor Circuit Shorted to Ground
66	Rear Motor Circuit Shorted to Battery or Motor Shorted
67	Left Front EMB Circuit Open or Shorted to Ground
68	Left Front EMB Circuit Shorted to Battery or Driver Open
71	Right Front EMB Circuit Open or Shorted to Ground

87959077

Fig. 81 List of ABS Diagnostic Trouble Codes (DTCs)—vehicles without ETS

	DIAGNOSTIC TROUBLE CODE AND SYMPTOM TABLE
72	Right Front EMB Circuit Shorted to Battery or Driver Open
75	Serial Communication Malfunction
76	Left Front Solenoid Circuit Open or Shorted to Battery
77	Left Front Solenoid Circuit Shorted to Ground or Driver Open
78	Right Front Solenoid Circuit Open or Shorted to Battery
81	Right Front Solenoid Circuit Shorted to Ground or Driver Open
82	Calibration Malfunction
86	EBCM Turned "ON" the Red Brake Warning Lamp
91	Open Brake Switch During Deceleration
92	Open Brake Switch When ABS Was Required
93	DTCs 91 or 92 Set in Current or Previous Ignition Cycle
94	Brake Switch Contacts Always Closed
95	Brake Switch Circuit Open
96	Rear Brake Lamp Circuit Open

87959078

Fig. 82 List of ABS Diagnostic Trouble Codes (DTCs)—vehicles without ETS, continued

DIAGNOSTIC TROUBLE CODE	DESCRIPTION
14	Electronic Brake Control Relay Contacts Circuit Open
15	Electronic Brake Control Relay Contacts Circuit Shorted to Battery
16	Electronic Brake Control Relay Coil Circuit Open
17	Electronic Brake Control Relay Coil Circuit Shorted to Ground
18	Electronic Brake Control Relay Coil Circuit Shorted to Battery or Coil Shorted
21	Left Front Wheel Speed = 0
22	Right Front Wheel Speed = 0
23	Left Rear Wheel Speed = 0
24	Right Rear Wheel Speed = 0
25	Left Front Excessive Wheel Speed Variation
26	Right Front Excessive Wheel Speed Variation
27	Left Rear Excessive Wheel Speed Variation
28	Right Rear Excessive Wheel Speed Variation
32	Left Front Wheel Speed Sensor Circuit Open or Shorted to Battery/Ground
33	Right Front Wheel Speed Sensor Circuit Open or Shorted to Battery/Ground
34	Left Rear Wheel Speed Sensor Circuit Open or Shorted to Battery/Ground
35	Right Rear Wheel Speed Sensor Circuit Open or Shorted to Battery/Ground
36	Low System Voltage
37	High System Voltage
38	Left Front EMB Will Not Hold Motor
41	Right Front EMB Will Not Hold Motor
42	Rear ESB Will Not Hold Motor
44	Left Front Channel Will Not Move
45	Right Front Channel Will Not Move
46	Rear Axle Channel Will Not Move
47	Left Front Motor Free Spins
48	Right Front Motor Free Spins
51	Rear Motor Free Spins
52	Left Front Channel in Release Too Long
53	Right Front Channel in Release Too Long
54	Rear Channel in Release Too Long
55	EBTCM Malfunction
56	Left Front Motor Circuit Open
57	Left Front Motor Circuit Shorted to Ground
58	Left Front Motor Circuit Shorted to Battery or Motor Shorted
61	Right Front Motor Circuit Open
62	Right Front Motor Circuit Shorted to Ground
63	Right Front Motor Circuit Shorted to Battery or Motor Shorted
64	Rear Motor Circuit Open
65	Rear Motor Circuit Shorted to Ground
66	Rear Motor Circuit Shorted to Battery or Motor Shorted
67	Left Front EMB Circuit Open or Shorted to Ground
68	Left Front EMB Circuit Shorted to Battery or Driver Open
71	Right Front EMB Circuit Open or Shorted to Ground
72	Right Front EMB Circuit Shorted to Battery or Driver Open
75	Serial Communication Malfunction
76	Left Front Solenoid Circuit Open or Shorted to Battery
77	Left Front Solenoid Circuit Shorted to Ground or Driver Open
78	Right Front Solenoid Circuit Open or Shorted to Battery
81	Right Front Solenoid Circuit Shorted to Ground or Driver Open
82	Calibration Malfunction
86	EBTCM Turned "ON" the Red "BRAKE" Warning Lamp
91	Open Brake Switch During Deceleration
92	Open Brake Switch When ABS Was Required
93	DTCs 91 or 92 Set in Current or Previous Ignition Cycle
94	Brake Switch Contacts Always Closed
95	Brake Switch Circuit Open
96	Rear Brake Lamp Circuit Open

87959A79

Fig. 83 List of ABS Diagnostic Trouble Codes (DTCs)—vehicles with ETS

These two methods are detailed below. Be sure to verify proper system operation and absence of codes when clearing procedure is completed.The EBCM will not permit code clearing until all of the codes have been displayed. Also, codes cannot be cleared by unplugging the EBCM, disconnecting the battery cables, or turning the ignition **OFF** (except on an ignition cycle default).

Tech 1® "Clear Codes" Method

Select F2 for trouble codes. After codes have been viewed completely, Tech 1® will ask, "CLEAR ABS CODES"; ANSWER "YES." Tech 1® will then read, "DISPLAY CODE HIST. DATA?" "LOST" if the codes have been cleared or "NO" to clear the codes. Answer "NO" and codes will be cleared.

Ignition Cycle Default

If no diagnostic fault code occurs for 100 drive cycles (a drive cycle occurs when the ignition is turned **ON** and the vehicle is driven faster than 10 mph or 16 km/h), any existing fault codes are cleared from the EBCM memory.

INTERMITTENT FAILURES

As with most electronic systems, intermittent failures may be difficult to accurately diagnose. The following is a method to try to isolate an intermittent failure especially wheel speed circuitry failures.

If an ABS fault occurs, the ABS warning light indicator will be on during the ignition cycle in which the fault was detected. If it is an intermittent problem which seems to have corrected itself (ABS warning light off), a history trouble code will be stored. Also stored will be the history data of the code at the time the fault occurred. The Tech 1® must be used to read ABS history data.

INTERMITTENTS AND POOR CONNECTIONS

Most intermittents are caused by faulty electrical connections or wiring, although occasionally a sticking relay or solenoid can be a problem. Some items to check are:

1. Poor mating of connector halves, or terminals not fully seated in the connector body (backed out).
2. Dirt or corrosion on the terminals. The terminals must be clean and free of any foreign material which could impede proper terminal contact.
3. Damaged connector body, exposing the terminals to moisture and dirt, as well as not maintaining proper terminal orientation with the component or mating connector.
4. Improperly formed or damaged terminals. All connector terminals in problem circuits should be checked carefully to ensure good contact tension. Use a corresponding mating terminal to check for proper tension. Refer to "Checking Terminal Contact" later in this section for the specific procedure.
5. The J 35616–A Connector Test Adapter Kit must be used whenever a diagnostic procedure requests checking or probing a terminal. Using the adapter will ensure that no damage to the terminal will occur, as well as giving an idea of whether contact tension is sufficient. If contact tension seems incorrect, refer to "Checking Terminal Contact" later in this section for specifics.
6. Poor terminal-to-wire connection. Checking this requires removing the terminal from the connector body. Some conditions which fall under this description are poor crimps, poor solder joints, crimping over wire insulation rather than the wire itself, corrosion in the wire-to-terminal contact area, etc.
7. Wire insulation which is rubbed through, causing an intermittent short as the bare area touches other wiring or parts of the vehicle.
8. Wiring broken inside the insulation. This condition could cause a continuity check to show a good circuit, but if only 1 or 2 strands of a multi-strand type wire are intact, resistance could be far too high.

Checking Terminal Contact

When diagnosing an electrical system that uses Metri-Pack 150/280/480/630 series terminals (refer to Terminal Repair Kit J 38125–A for terminal identification), it is important to check terminal contact between a connector and component, or between inline connectors, before replacing a suspect component.

Frequently, a diagnostic chart leads to a step that reads "Check for poor connection." Mating terminals must be inspected to ensure good terminal contact. A poor connection between the male and female terminal at a connector may be the result of contamination or deformation.

Contamination is caused by the connector halves being improperly connected, a missing or damaged connector seal, or damage to the connector itself, exposing the terminals to moisture and dirt. Contamination, usually in underhood or underbody connectors, leads to terminal corrosion, causing an open circuit or an intermittently open circuit.

Deformation is caused by probing the mating side of a connector terminal without the proper adapter, improperly joining the connector halves or repeatedly separating and joining the connector halves. Deformation, usually to the female terminal contact tang, can result in poor terminal contact causing an open or intermittently open circuit.

Follow the procedure below to check terminal contact.

1. Separate the connector halves. Refer to Terminal Repair Kit J 38125–A, if available.
2. Inspect the connector halves for contamination. Contamination will result in a white or green buildup within the connector body or between terminals, causing high terminal resistance, intermittent contact or an open circuit. An underhood or underbody connector that shows signs of contamination should be replaced in its entirety: terminals, seals, and connector body.
3. Using an equivalent male terminal from the Terminal Repair Kit J 38125–A, check the retention force of the female terminal in question by inserting and removing the male terminal to the female terminal in the connector body. Good terminal contact will require a certain amount of force to separate the terminals.
4. Using an equivalent female terminal from the Terminal Repair Kit J 38125–A, compare the retention force of this terminal to the female terminal in question by joining and separating the male terminal to the female terminal in question. If the retention force is significantly different between the two female terminals, replace the female terminal in question, using a terminal from Terminal Repair Kit J 38125–A.

ABS Service

PRECAUTIONS

Failure to observe the following precautions may result in system damage.
• Performing diagnostic work on the ABS-VI requires the use of a Tech 1® Scan diagnostic tool or equivalent. If unavailable, please refer diagnostic work to a qualified technician.
• Before performing electric arc welding on the vehicle, disconnect the Electronic Brake Control Module (EBCM) and the hydraulic modulator connectors.
• When performing painting work on the vehicle, do not expose the Electronic Brake Control Module (EBCM) to temperatures in excess of 185°F (85°C) for longer than 2 hours. The system may be exposed to temperatures up to 200°F (95°C) for less than 15 minutes.
• Never disconnect or connect the Electronic Brake Control Module (EBCM) or hydraulic modulator connectors with the ignition switch **ON** or damage to the system will occur.
• Never disassemble any component of the Anti-Lock Brake System (ABS) which is designated non-serviceable; the component must be replaced as an assembly.
• When filling the master cylinder, always use Delco Supreme 11 brake fluid or equivalent, which meets DOT-3 specifications; petroleum-base fluid will destroy the rubber parts.

Electrical Connectors

▶ See Figure 84

Some ABS-VI components are equipped with electrical connectors using a Connector Position Assurance (CPA) lock.
1. Remove the lock before separating the electrical connectors.
2. Be careful not to damage the locking pin during removal.
3. Make sure that the rubber connector seal is in place on the connector before and after connection.
4. Always install the lock after the connection is made.

1 CONNECTOR POSITION ASSURANCE (CPA) • MAKE SURE SEAL IS IN PLACE ON CONNECTOR

87959084

Fig. 84 View of ABS electrical connectors with a CPA lock

ABS Hydraulic Modulator Assembly Bleeder Valves

REMOVAL & INSTALLATION

▶ See Figure 85

1. Remove the bleeder valve or valves.
2. Install the bleeder valve, then tighten to 65 inch lbs. (7 Nm).

Fluid Level Sensor

REMOVAL & INSTALLATION

▶ See Figure 86

1. Disconnect the negative battery cable.
2. Detach the electrical connection from the fluid level sensor.
3. Remove the fluid level sensor, using needle-nose pliers to compress the switch locking tabs at the inboard side of the master cylinder.

To install:
4. Insert the fluid level sensor unit until the locking tabs snap in place.
5. Attach the sensor electrical connector.
6. Connect the negative battery cable.

Enable Relay

REMOVAL & INSTALLATION

▶ See Figure 87

1. Disconnect the negative battery cable.
2. Detach the electrical connection.

3. Unfasten the retainer on the bracket, then slide the relay off the bracket.
To install:
4. Slide the relay onto the bracket and make sure the retainer locks the relay to the bracket. Fasten the retainer.
5. Attach the electrical connection.
6. Connect the negative battery cable.

ABS Lamp Driver Module

REMOVAL & INSTALLATION

1. Disconnect the negative battery cable.
2. Remove the right side lower sound insulator panel.
3. Slide the glove box all the way out or remove it completely.
4. The lamp driver module is above the cruise control module taped to the instrument panel harness and is light green in color.
5. Open the connector and slide the circuit board out of the connector.
To install:
6. Install the circuit board to the connector.
7. Reposition the connector to the instrument panel harness and make sure it is retaped in place.
8. Slide the glove box back into the dash or reinstall the screws, if removed.
9. Install the right side lower sound insulator panel.
10. Connect the negative battery cable.

ABS Hydraulic Modulator/Master Cylinder Assembly

REMOVAL & INSTALLATION

▶ See Figure 88

➡ To avoid personal injury, use the Tech 1® scan tool to relieve the gear tension in the hydraulic modulator. This procedure must be performed prior to removal of the brake control and motor assembly.

1. Disconnect the negative battery cable.
2. Disengage the two solenoid electrical connectors and the fluid level sensor connector.
3. Detach the 6-pin and 3-pin motor pack electrical connectors.
4. Wrap a shop towel around the hydraulic brake lines, then disconnect the four brake lines from the modulator.

➡ Cap the disconnected lines to prevent the loss of fluid and the entry of moisture and contaminants.

5. Unfasten the 2 nuts attaching the ABS hydraulic modulator/master cylinder assembly to the vacuum booster.
6. Remove the ABS hydraulic modulator assembly from the vehicle.
To install:
7. Install the ABS hydraulic modulator assembly to the vehicle. Secure using the two attaching nuts and tighten to 20 ft. lbs. (27 Nm).

1 Bleeder valves

87959083

Fig. 85 Location of the ABS hydraulic modulator assembly bleeder valves

1 Fluid level sensor

87959085

Fig. 86 Location of the fluid level sensor

1 Bolt screw	4 Dash panel
2 Enable relay	5 EBCM
3 Clench nut	

87959086

Fig. 87 Unfasten the retaining screw, then remove the relay from the bracket

Fig. 88 View of the ABS hydraulic modulator/master cylinder assembly—1994 vehicle shown

1 Solenoid electrical connectors
2 Fluid level sensor connector
3 Motor pack connectors
4 Hydraulic brake pipes (4)
5 Master cylinder attaching nuts (2)
6 Hydraulic modulator and master cylinder assembly
7 Vacuum booster

87959087

8. Uncap and connect the 4 brake pipes to the modulator assembly. Tighten to 13 ft. lbs. (17 Nm).
9. Attach the 6-pin and 3-pin electrical connectors.
10. Engage the fluid level sensor connector and the two solenoid electrical connections.
11. Properly bleed the system, as outlined later in this section.
12. Connect the negative battery cable.

ABS Control Module

Depending upon vehicle year and application this control module is referred to as the Electronic Control Unit (ECU), Electronic Brake Control Module (EBCM) or Electronic Brake and Traction Control Module (EBTCM).

REMOVAL & INSTALLATION

▶ **See Figure 89**

1. Disconnect the negative battery cable.
2. Detach the control module (ECU/EBCM/EBTCM) electrical connectors.
3. Unfasten the hex head screws attaching the ECU/EBCM/EBTCM to the dash panel.

4. Remove the module from the dash panel.
To install:
5. Ensure that the three plastic grommets are properly located.
6. Position the ECU/EBCM/EBTCM to the dash panel, aligning the screw holes.
7. Fasten the retaining hex head screws attaching the module. Tighten the screws to 17 ft. lbs. (21 Nm).
8. Attach the electrical connectors.
9. Connect the negative battery cable.

Speed Sensors

REMOVAL & INSTALLATION

Front Wheel Speed Sensors

▶ **See Figure 90**

1. Disconnect the negative battery cable.
2. Raise and safely support the vehicle.
3. Detach the front sensor electrical connector.
4. Unfasten the retaining bolt, then remove the front wheel speed sensor. If the sensor will not slide out of the knuckle, remove the brake rotor and use a blunt punch or equivalent to push the sensor from the back side of the knuckle.

➡ **If the sensor locating pin breaks off and remains in the knuckle during removal, remove the brake rotor and remove the broken pin using a blunt punch. Clean the hole using sand paper wrapped around a screwdriver or other suitable tool. NEVER attempt to enlarge the hole.**

To install:
5. Position the front wheel speed sensor on the mounting bracket.

➡ **Make sure the front wheel speed sensor is properly aligned and lays flat against the bracket bosses.**

6. Install the retaining bolts. Tighten to 107 inch lbs. (12 Nm).
7. Attach the front sensor electrical connector.
8. Lower the vehicle.
9. Connect the negative battery cable.

Rear Wheel Bearing and Speed Sensor Assembly

▶ **See Figure 91**

➡ **The rear integral wheel bearing and sensor assembly must be replaced as a unit.**

1 EBCM electrical connectors
2 Hex head screws
3 EBCM

87959088

Fig. 89 Electronic Brake Control Module (EBCM) mounting

1 Knuckle
2 Front wheel speed sensor attaching bolt
3 Front wheel speed sensor
4 Front wheel speed sensor electronic connector

87959090

Fig. 90 Location and mounting of the front wheel speed sensor

1 Rear sensor electrical connector
2 Sensor retaining bolts (4)
3 Sensor retaining nuts (4)
4 Bolt removal access hole
5 Drum brake assembly
6 Rear integral bearing and speed sensor assembly

87959091

Fig. 91 The rear wheel speed sensor and bearing are integral; they are replaced as a single unit

1. Disconnect the negative battery cable.
2. Raise and safely support the vehicle.
3. Remove the rear wheel and tire assembly.
4. Remove the brake drum.
5. Detach the rear sensor electrical connector.
6. Unfasten the bolts and nuts attaching the rear wheel bearing and speed sensor assembly to the backing plate. Rotate the axle flange to align the large hole with each bolt. Remove the bolt while holding the nut.

➡️**With the rear wheel bearing and speed sensor attaching bolts/nuts removed, the drum brake assembly is supported only by the brake line connection. To avoid bending or damage to the brake line, do not bump or exert force on the assembly.**

7. Remove the rear wheel bearing and speed sensor assembly.
To install:
8. Install the rear wheel bearing and speed sensor assembly by aligning the bolt holes in the wheel bearing and speed sensor assembly, drum brake assembly and rear suspension bracket.
9. Fasten the attaching bolts and nuts. Rotate the axle flange to align the large hole with each bolt location. Install the bolt while holding the nut. Tighten to 37 ft. lbs. (50 Nm).
10. Attach the rear speed sensor electrical connector.
11. Install the brake drum and the rear wheel and tire assembly.
12. Carefully lower the vehicle.
13. Connect the negative battery cable.

ABS Hydraulic Modulator Solenoid

REMOVAL & INSTALLATION

▶ **See Figure 92**

1. Disconnect the negative battery cable.
2. Detach the solenoid electrical connector.
3. Unfasten the Torx® head bolts, then remove the solenoid assembly.
To install:
4. Lubricate the O-rings on the new solenoid with clean brake fluid.
5. Position the solenoid so the connectors face each other.
6. Press down firmly by hand until the solenoid assembly flange seats on the modulator assembly.
7. Install the Torx® head bolts. Tighten to 40 inch lbs. (4.5 Nm).
8. Attach the solenoid electrical connector. Make sure the connectors are installed on the correct solenoids.
9. Properly bleed the brake system.
10. Connect the negative battery cable.

Filling and Bleeding

✳✳ WARNING

Do NOT allow brake fluid to spill on or come in contact with the vehicle's finish as it will remove the paint. In case of a spill, immediately flush the area with water.

SYSTEM FILLING

The master cylinder reservoirs must be kept properly filled to prevent air from entering the system. No special filling procedures are required because of the anti-lock system.

When adding fluid, use only DOT 3 fluid; the use of DOT 5 or silicone fluids is specifically prohibited. Use of improper or contaminated fluid may cause the fluid to boil or cause the rubber components in the system to deteriorate. Never use any fluid with a petroleum base or any fluid which has been exposed to water or moisture.

BLEEDING THE ABS HYDRAULIC SYSTEM

Before bleeding the ABS brake system, the front and rear displacement cylinder pistons must be returned to the topmost position. The preferred method uses a Tech 1® or T-100® scan tool to perform the rehoming procedure. If a Tech 1® is not available, the second procedure may be used, but it must be followed EXACTLY.

Rehome Procedure

WITH TECH 1® OR T-100® (PREFERRED METHOD)

1. Using a Tech 1® or T-100® (CAMS), select "F5: Motor Rehome." The motor rehome function cannot be performed if current DTC's are present. If DTC's are present, the vehicle must be repaired and the codes cleared before performing the motor rehome function.
2. The entire brake system should now be bled using the pressure or manual bleeding procedures outlined later in this section.

WITHOUT TECH 1® OR T-100®

➡️**Do not place your foot on the brake pedal through this entire procedure unless specifically instructed to do so.**

This method can only be used if the ABS warning lamp is not illuminated and not DTC's are present.
1. Remove your foot from the brake pedal.
2. Start the engine and allow it to run for at least 10 seconds while observing the ABS warning lamp.
3. If the ABS warning lamp turned "ON" and stayed "ON" after about 10 seconds, the bleeding procedure must be stopped and a Tech 1® must be used to diagnose the ABS function.
4. If the ABS warning lamp turned "ON" for about 3 seconds, then turned "OFF" and stayed "OFF," turn the ignition **OFF**.
5. Repeat Steps 1–4 one more time.
6. The entire brake system should now be bled by following the manual or pressure bleeding procedure.

Pressure Bleeding

▶ **See Figures 93 and 94**

➡️**The pressure bleeding equipment must be of the diaphragm type. It must have a rubber diaphragm between the air supply and the brake fluid to prevent air, moisture and other contaminants from entering the hydraulic system.**

1. Clean the master cylinder fluid reservoir cover and surrounding area, then remove the cover.
2. Add fluid, if necessary to obtain a proper fluid level.
3. Connect bleeder adapter J 35589, or equivalent, to the brake fluid reservoir, then connect the bleeder adapter to the pressure bleeding equipment.
4. Adjust the pressure bleed equipment t o 5–10 psi (35–70 kPa) and wait about 30 seconds to be sure there is no leakage.
5. Adjust the pressure bleed equipment to 30–35 psi (205–240 kPa).

✳✳ WARNING

Use a shop rag to catch the escaping brake fluid. Be careful not to let any fluid run down the motor pack base or into the electrical connector.

6. With the pressure bleeding equipment connected and pressurized, proceed as follows:
   a. Attach a clear plastic bleeder hose to the rearward bleeder valve on the hydraulic modulator.
   b. Slowly open the bleeder valve and allow fluid to flow until no air is seen in the fluid.
   c. Close the valve when fluid flows out without any air bubbles.
   d. Repeat Steps 6b and 6c until no air bubbles are present.
   e. Relocate the bleeder hose on the forward hydraulic modulator bleed valve and repeat Steps 6a through 6d.
7. Tighten the bleeder valve to 80 inch lbs. (9 Nm).

1 Solenoid lip seal
2 Solenoid assembly
3 TORX® head bolt
4 Hydraulic modulator
5 Solenoid electrical connector

87959092
Fig. 92 ABS modulator solenoid mounting

* USED WITH PRESSURE BLEEDING PROCEDURE ONLY

1 Pressure bleeder adapter - J 35589
2 Rearward bleeder valve
3 Bleeder wrench
4 Forward bleeder valve
5 Plastic bleeder tube

87959093
Fig. 93 ABS pressure bleeding compo-nents

87959094
Fig. 94 Position a shop rag to catch escap-ing brake fluid

8. Proceed to bleed the hydraulic modulator brake pipe connections as follows with the pressure bleeding equipment connected and pressurized:

   a. Slowly open the forward brake pipe tube nut on the hydraulic modulator and check for air in the escaping fluid.

   b. When the air flow ceases, immediately tighten the tube nut. Tighten the tube nut to 18 ft. lbs. (24 Nm).

9. Repeat Steps 8a and 8b for the remaining three brake pipe connections moving from the front to the rear.

10. Raise and safely support the vehicle.

11. Proceed, as outlined in the following steps, to bleed the wheel brakes in the following sequence: right rear, left rear, right front, then left front.

   a. Attach a clear plastic bleeder hose to the bleeder valve at the wheel, then submerge the opposite hose end in a clean container partially filled with clean brake fluid.

   b. Slowly open the bleeder valve and allow the fluid to flow.

   c. Close the valve when fluid begins to flow without any air bubbles. Tap lightly on the caliper or backing plate to dislodge any trapped air bubbles.

12. Repeat Step 11 on the other brakes using the earlier sequence.

13. Remove the pressure bleeding equipment, including bleeder adapter J 35589.

14. Carefully lower the vehicle, then check the brake fluid and add if necessary. Don't forget to put the reservoir cap back on.

15. With the ignition turned to the **RUN** position, apply the brake pedal with moderate force and hold it. Note the pedal travel and feel. If the pedal feels firm and constant and the pedal travel is not excessive, start the engine. With the engine running, recheck the pedal travel. If it's still firm and constant and pedal travel is not excessive, go to Step 17.

16. If the pedal feels soft or has excessive travel either initially or after the engine is started, the following procedure may be used:

   a. With the Tech 1® scan tool, "release" then "apply" each motor 2–3 times and cycle each solenoid 5–10 times. When finished, be sure to "apply" the front and rear motors to ensure the pistons are in the upmost position. DO NOT DRIVE THE VEHICLE.

   b. If a Tech 1® is not available, remove your foot from the brake pedal, start the engine and allow it run for at least 10 seconds to initialize the ABS. DO NOT DRIVE THE VEHICLE. After 10 seconds, turn the ignition **OFF**. The initialization procedure most be repeated 5 times to ensure any trapped air has been dislodged.

   c. Repeat the bleeding procedure, starting with Step 1.

17. Road test the vehicle, and make sure the brakes are operating properly.

Manual Bleeding

♦ See Figure 95

1. Clean the master cylinder fluid reservoir cover and surrounding area, then remove the cover.

2. Add fluid, if necessary to obtain a proper fluid level, then put the reservoir cover back on.

3. Prime the ABS hydraulic modulator/master cylinder assembly as follows:

   a. Attach a bleeder hose to the rearward bleeder valve, then submerge the opposite hose end in a clean container partially filled with clean brake fluid.

   b. Slowly open the rearward bleeder valve.

   c. Depress and hold the brake pedal until the fluid begins to flow.

   d. Close the valve, then release the brake pedal.

   e. Repeat Steps 3b–3d until no air bubbles are present.

   f. Relocate the bleeder hose to the forward hydraulic modulator bleeder valve, then repeat Steps 3a–3e.

4. Once the fluid is seen to flow from both modulator bleeder valves, the ABS modulator/master cylinder assembly is sufficiently full of fluid. However, it may not be completely purged of air. At this point, move to the wheel brakes and bleed them. This ensures that the lowest points in the system are completely free of air and then the assembly can purged of any remaining air.

5. Remove the fluid reservoir cover. Fill to the correct level, if necessary, then fasten the cover.

6. Raise and safely support the vehicle.

7. Proceed, as outlined in the following steps, to bleed the wheel brakes in the following sequence: right rear, left rear, right front, then left front.

   a. Attach a clear plastic bleeder hose to the bleeder valve at the wheel, then submerge the opposite hose end in a clean container partially filled with clean brake fluid.

   b. Open the bleeder valve.

   c. Have an assistant slowly depress the brake pedal.

   d. Close the valve and slowly release the release the brake pedal.

   e. Wait 5 seconds.

   f. Repeat Steps 7a–7e until the brake pedal feels firm at half travel and no air bubbles are observed in the bleeder hose. To assist in freeing the entrapped air, tap lightly on the caliper or braking plate to dislodge any trapped air bubbles.

8. Repeat Step 7 for the remaining brakes in the sequence given earlier.

9. Carefully lower the vehicle.

10. Remove the reservoir cover, then fill to the correct level with brake fluid and replace the cap.

11. Bleed the ABS hydraulic modulator/master cylinder assembly as follows:

   a. Attach a clear plastic bleeder hose to the rearward bleeder valve on the modulator, then submerge the opposite hose end in a clean container partially filled with clean brake fluid.

   b. Have an assistant depress the brake pedal with moderate force.

   c. Slowly open the rearward bleeder valve and allow the fluid to flow.

   d. Close the valve, then release the brake pedal.

   e. Wait 5 seconds.

   f. Repeat Steps 11a–11e until no air bubbles are present.

   g. Relocate the bleeder hose to the forward hydraulic modulator bleeder valve, then repeat Steps 11a–11f.

12. Carefully lower the vehicle, then check the brake fluid and add if necessary. Don't forget to put the reservoir cap back on.

1 Bleeder valves

87959095

Fig. 95 ABS hydraulic modulator/master cylinder bleeder locations

13. With the ignition turned to the **RUN** position, apply the brake pedal with moderate force and hold it. Note the pedal travel and feel. If the pedal feels firm and constant and the pedal travel is not excessive, start the engine. With the engine running, recheck the pedal travel. If it's still firm and constant and pedal travel is not excessive, road test the vehicle and make sure the brakes are operating properly.

14. If the pedal feels soft or has excessive travel either initially or after the engine is started, the following procedure may be used:

a. With the Tech 1® scan tool, "Release" then "Apply" each motor 2–3 times and cycle each solenoid 5–10 times. When finished, be sure to "Apply" the front and rear motors to ensure the pistons are in the upmost position. DO NOT DRIVE THE VEHICLE.

b. If a Tech 1® scan tool is not available, remove your foot from the brake pedal, start the engine and allow it run for at least 10 seconds to initialize the ABS. DO NOT DRIVE THE VEHICLE. After 10 seconds, turn the ignition **OFF**. The initialization procedure most be repeated 5 times to ensure any trapped air has been dislodged.

c. Repeat the bleeding procedure, starting with Step 1.

15. Road test the vehicle, and make sure the brakes are operating properly.

BRAKE SPECIFICATIONS
All measurements in inches unless noted

Year	Model	Master Cylinder Bore	Brake Disc Original Thickness	Brake Disc Minimum Thickness	Brake Disc Maximum Runout	Brake Drum Diameter Original Inside Diameter	Brake Drum Diameter Max. Wear Limit	Brake Drum Diameter Maximum Machine Diameter	Minimum Lining Thickness Front	Minimum Lining Thickness Rear
1982	All	0.940	0.885	0.830	0.004	7.88	7.93	7.90	0.030	0.030
1983	All	0.940	0.885	0.830	0.004	7.88	7.93	7.90	0.030	0.030
1984	All	0.940	0.885	0.830	0.004	7.88	7.93	7.90	0.030	0.030
1985	All	0.874	0.885	0.815	0.002	7.88	7.93	7.90	0.030	0.030
1986	All	0.874	0.885	0.815	0.002	7.88	7.93	7.90	0.030	0.030
1987	All	0.874	0.885	0.815	0.002	7.88	7.93	7.90	0.030	0.030
1988	All	0.874	0.885	0.815	0.002	7.88	7.93	7.90	0.030	0.030
1989	All	0.874	0.885	0.815	0.002	7.88	7.93	7.90	0.030	0.030
1990	All	0.874	0.885	0.815	0.002	7.88	7.93	7.90	0.030	0.030
1991	All	0.874	0.806	0.736	0.002	7.88	7.93	7.90	0.030	0.030
1992	All	0.874	0.806	0.736	0.002	7.88	7.93	7.90	0.030	0.030
1993	All	0.874	0.806	0.736	0.002	7.87	7.93	7.90	0.030	0.030
1994	All	0.874	0.806	0.736	0.002	7.87	7.93	7.90	0.030	0.030

91139C01

EXTERIOR 10-2
DOORS 10-2
 REMOVAL & INSTALLATION 10-2
 ADJUSTMENTS 10-2
HOOD 10-2
 REMOVAL & INSTALLATION 10-2
 ALIGNMENT 10-3
TRUNK LID 10-3
 REMOVAL & INSTALLATION 10-3
 ADJUSTMENTS 10-3
HATCHBACK ASSEMBLY 10-3
 REMOVAL & INSTALLATION 10-3
 ADJUSTMENTS 10-4
LIFT GATE (STATION WAGON) 10-4
 REMOVAL & INSTALLATION 10-4
GRILLE 10-4
 REMOVAL & INSTALLATION 10-4
OUTSIDE MIRRORS 10-5
 REMOVAL & INSTALLATION 10-5
ANTENNA 10-6
 REPLACEMENT 10-6
FENDERS 10-6
 REMOVAL & INSTALLATION 10-6
CONVERTIBLE TOP 10-6
 TOP REPLACEMENT 10-6
 MOTOR REPLACEMENT 10-9
SUNROOF 10-9
INTERIOR 10-10
INSTRUMENT PANEL AND PAD 10-10
 REMOVAL & INSTALLATION 10-10
CONSOLE 10-11
 REMOVAL & INSTALLATION 10-11
DOOR PANEL 10-12
 REMOVAL & INSTALLATION 10-12
DOOR LOCKS 10-14
 REMOVAL & INSTALLATION 10-14
FRONT DOOR GLASS 10-14
 REMOVAL & INSTALLATION 10-14
REAR DOOR GLASS 10-15
 REMOVAL & INSTALLATION 10-15
FRONT WINDOW REGULATOR AND
 MOTOR 10-15
 REMOVAL & INSTALLATION 10-15
REAR WINDOW REGULATOR 10-16
 REMOVAL & INSTALLATION 10-16
WINDSHIELD AND FIXED GLASS 10-16
 REMOVAL & INSTALLATION 10-16
 WINDSHIELD CHIP REPAIR 10-16
INSIDE REAR VIEW MIRROR 10-17
 REPLACEMENT 10-17
FRONT SEAT 10-17
 REMOVAL & INSTALLATION 10-17
REAR SEAT CUSHION 10-19
 REMOVAL & INSTALLATION 10-19
POWER SEAT MOTORS 10-19
 REMOVAL & INSTALLATION 10-19

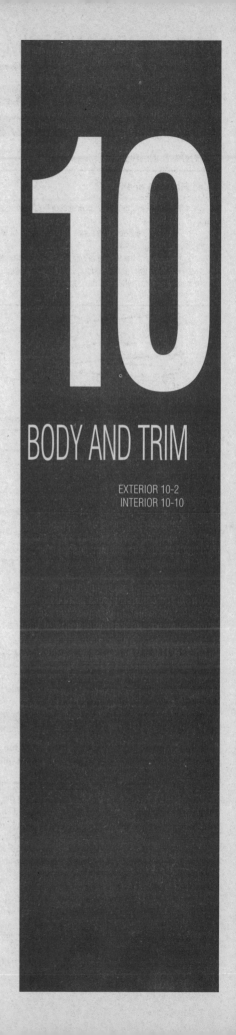

10

BODY AND TRIM

EXTERIOR 10-2
INTERIOR 10-10

EXTERIOR

Doors

REMOVAL & INSTALLATION

▶ **See Figures 1 and 2**

1. On doors equipped with power operated components proceed as follows:

    a. Remove the door trim panel, insulator pad (if so equipped), and the inner panel water deflector.

    b. Disconnect the wiring components inside the door.

    c. Remove the rubber conduit from the door, then remove the wiring harness from the door through the conduit access hole.

87950001

Fig. 1 You can use this tool to remove the spring

1	UPPER HINGE STRAP—BODY SIDE
2	HINGE PIN
3	UPPER HINGE STRAP—DOOR SIDE
4	HOLD OPEN SPRING
5	LOWER HINGE STRAP—DOOR SIDE
6	HOLD OPEN LINK
7	LOWER HINGE STRAP—BODY SIDE

87950002

Fig. 2 View of the door hinge assembly—1994 vehicle shown

2. Tape the area (on the door pillar and body pillar) above the lower hinge with fabric tape.

✳✳ CAUTION

Before performing the following step, cover the spring with a towel to prevent the spring from flying out and possibly causing personal injury!

3. Insert a suitable, long, flat bladed tool under the pivot point of the hold-open link and over top of the spring. The tool should be positioned so as not to apply pressure to the hold-open link. Cover the spring with a shop cloth and lift the tool to disengage the spring. The spring can also be removed by using tool J-28625, or equivalent, door hinge spring compressor tool. The tool is stamped right side and left side. For all the J-cars the tool stamped, "left side" is used to service the right side hinge spring. The tool stamped, "right side" is used to service the left hand hinge spring.

    a. Install the two jaws of the tool over the spring. The jaw with the slots slides over spring at the hold-open link. The jaw with the hole fits over the spring at the bubble on the door hinge pillar.

    b. Install the bolt to the jaws of the tool and tighten to compress the spring.

    c. Remove the tool and spring from the door hinge assembly. Do not remove the spring from the tool.

4. When removing the hinge pin, save the "barrel" clips as follows:

    a. Using two, suitable, flat bladed tools, spread the clip enough to move the clip above the recess toward the pointed end of the pin.

    b. As the pin is removed, the clip will ride the shank of the pin and fall free.

    c. Reinstall the clips onto the pins before installing the door.

5. With the aid of a helper to support the door, remove the lower hinge pin, using a soft headed hammer and locking type pliers. The helper can aid in removing the hinge pin by raising and lowering the rear of the door.

6. Insert the bolt into the hole of the lower hinge to maintain door attachment during upper hinge pin removal.

7. Remove the upper hinge pin in the same manner as the lower. Remove the bolt from the lower hinge and remove the door from the body.

To install:

➡ **Before installing the door, replace the hinge pin clips or reuse the old clips as explained in the removal procedure.**

8. With the aid of a helper, position the door and insert a bolt in the lower hinge hole.

9. The upper hinge pin is inserted with the pointed end up. The lower hinge pin is inserted with the pointed end down. With the door in the full open position, install the upper hinge pin using locking-type pliers and a soft headed hammer. Use a drift punch and hammer to complete pin installation.

10. Remove the screw from the lower hinge and install the lower hinge pin. The use of the special tool J-28625 or equivalent is the recommended method for installing the hinge spring.

✳✳ WARNING

If the spring is installed before installing the upper hinge pin, damage to the hinge bushings may result!

11. If the spring was removed using a long, flat bladed tool, install the spring as follows:

    a. Place the spring in tool J-28625 or equivalent.

    b. Place the tool and spring in a bench vise.

    c. Compress the tool in a vise and install the bolt until the spring is fully compressed.

    d. Remove the tool with the compressed spring from the vise and install in the proper position in the door lower hinge. The slot in the jaw of the tool fits over the hold-open link. The hole in the other jaw fits over the bubble.

    e. Remove the bolt from the tool to install the spring.

    f. Remove the tool from the door hinge. (The tool will fall out in three pieces). Cycle the door to check spring operation.

12. If tool J-28625 or equivalent was used to remove the spring, follow Steps d, e, and f above to install the spring.

13. Remove the tape from the door and body pillars.

14. On the doors with power operated components, install all previously removed parts.

ADJUSTMENTS

1. Adjust the door so that the door-to-body and lock-to-striker align properly.

2. The hinge-to-door bolts may need to be loosened to adjust the alignment properly.

Hood

REMOVAL & INSTALLATION

▶ **See Figure 3**

1. Raise the hood and install protective coverings over the fender areas to prevent damage to the painted surfaces and mouldings.

2. If equipped, detach the underhood wire.

3. Unfasten the retainers, then remove the insulator.

Fig. 3 Unfasten the retainers, then remove the hood insulator

1	HOOD PANEL
2	INSULATOR
3	RETAINER

4. Remove the hood latch striker.
5. Matchmark the position of the hinge on the hood to aid alignment during installation.
6. Have an assistant support the front of the hood, remove the hinge-to-hood screws/bolts on each side of the hood, then grasp the rear of the hood and remove it from the vehicle.

To install:
7. Position the hood, using the alignment marks made when removed.
8. Install the hood-to-hinge bolts snug, but do not fully tighten.
9. Fasten the hood latch striker.
10. Install the insulator and secure with the retainers.
11. If equipped, attach the underhood wire.
12. Remove the protective covering from the fenders.
13. Inspect for proper hood alignments and adjust as necessary, as outlined in this section.
14. Tighten the bolts to 20 ft. lbs. (27 Nm).

ALIGNMENT

To raise or lower the rear of the hood to achieve alignment with the rear of the fenders, proceed as follows:
1. Loosen, but do not remove the bolts on one side.
2. Reposition the hood. Tighten the bolts to 20 ft. lbs. (27 Nm).
3. If necessary, repeat the procedure on the other side of the hood.
To raise or lower the front of the hood to achieve alignment with the front of the fenders, proceed as follows:
4. Close the hood securely.
5. Determine the amount of adjustment necessary.
6. Open and support the hood.
7. Adjust the front bumpers by:
• Turning clockwise to lower the bumper
• Turning counterclockwise to raise the bumper

Trunk Lid

REMOVAL & INSTALLATION

2 and 4-Door Sedans

▶ See Figure 4

The trunk lid hinge is welded to the body and bolts to the lid.
1. Prop the trunk lid open and place protective coverings over the rear compartment to protect the paint from damage.
2. Matchmark the location of the hinge-to-trunk lid bolts, then detach the electrical connections and wiring from the lid (if equipped).
3. Using an assistant (to support the lid), unfasten the hinge-to-lid bolts, then remove the lid from the vehicle.
4. To install, reverse the removal procedures. Adjust the position of the trunk lid to the body.

1	REAR COMPARTMENT LID
2	REAR COMPARTMENT LID HINGES
3	HINGE-TO-LID ATTACHING SCREWS (2) 11 N·m (97 lbs. in.)

Fig. 4 Trunk lid-to-hinge attachment

ADJUSTMENTS

Fore and aft adjustment of the lid assembly is controlled by the hinge-to-lid attaching bolts. To adjust the lid, loosen the hinge-to-lid attaching bolts and shift the lid to the desired position, then tighten the bolts. To increase opening assist, use tool J-211412-1 or equivalent and move the torque rods one step toward the rear of the vehicle. To decrease opening assist, move the torque rods one step toward the front of the vehicle.

Hatchback Assembly

REMOVAL & INSTALLATION

▶ See Figure 5

1. Prop open the lid and place protective coverings along the edges of the lift window opening (to protect the paint from damage).
2. Where necessary, disconnect the wire harness from the lift window.
3. While a helper supports the lid, use an awl or flat bladed tool to remove the clips on the gas supports and pull the supports off the retainer studs.
4. Close the lift window assembly.
5. Remove the rear upper garnish moulding at the rear of the headlining.
6. Remove the nuts retaining the lift window/hatchback to the body.
7. With the aid of a helper, remove the lift window assembly from the body.
8. Installation is the reverse of removal.

Fig. 5 View of the hatchback gas support

➡The gas support assemblies are attached to the lid and the body and are secured by retaining clips and/or bolts.

ADJUSTMENTS

The rear compartment lift window assembly (hatchback) height, fore and aft and side adjustments are controlled at the hinge to body location. This area of the body has oversize hinge attaching holes in addition to the hinge to body shims. Adjustment at the hinge location must be made at the lower panel by adjusting the rubber bumpers. The retaining bolts holding the hinge to body should be tightened to 15–20 ft. lbs. (20–27 Nm).

Lift Gate (Station Wagon)

REMOVAL & INSTALLATION

▶ See Figures 6 and 7

1. Prop open the lift gate and place protective coverings along the edges of the lift gate opening (to protect the paint from damage).
2. Where necessary, disconnect the wire harness from the lift gate.
3. While a helper supports the lid, use an awl or flat bladed tool to remove the clips on the gas supports and pull the supports off the retainer studs.

Fig. 6 View of the station wagon lift gate gas supports—1982–88 vehicles

1. Compartment lid
2. Hinge pin
3. Retaining ring
4. Rod

87950010

Fig. 7 Station wagon lift gate hinge pin (right side shown)—1982–88 vehicles

4. Use a ³⁄₁₆ in. (5mm) diameter rod to remove the hinge pins from the hinges. Place the end of the rod against the pointed end of the hinge pin; then strike the rod firmly to shear the retaining clip tabs and drive the pin through the hinge. Repeat the same thing on the opposite side hinge and with the aid of a helper remove the lift gate from the body.
5. To install, reverse the removal procedure. Prior to installing the hinge pins, install new retaining clips in the notches provide in the hinge pins. Position the retaining clips so that the tabs point toward the head of the pin.

➡The gas support assemblies are attached to the lid and the body and are secured by retaining clips and/or bolts.

Grille

REMOVAL & INSTALLATION

➡The following procedure includes removal of the front end panel.

Cavalier

1982–87 MODELS

1. Open the hood.
2. Remove the headlamp bezel screws (there are usually 2 each).
3. Remove the bolt at each fender-to-front end panel at the upper corner near the headlamp.
4. Disconnect the turn signal lamp socket and head lamp wiring.
5. Unfasten the screw at each turn signal housing, then remove the housings.
6. Remove the bolt from the panel-to-radiator support located below the turn signal housing area.
7. Unfasten the nut at the panel to the inner fender.
8. Remove the two nuts attaching the bumper end cap to the panel at each side.
9. Remove the three bolts at the baffles located at the radiator support.
10. Transfer the headlamps and grille.
11. Installation is the reverse of the removal procedure.

1988–90 MODELS

▶ See Figure 8

1. Remove the grille push-in retainers, then remove the grille panel from the vehicle.
   To install:
2. Position the grille panel to the headlamp and grille mounting panel.
3. Install the push-in retainers in the following sequence:
   a. Top center retainer
   b. Both upper outer retainers
   c. Both bottom retainers

1991–94 MODELS

1. Unfasten the grille retaining screws.
2. Remove the grille panel.

1. Headlamp & grille mounting panel
2. Grille
3. Push-in retainer (5)

87950043

Fig. 8 View of the grille removal and installation—1988–90 Cavalier

To install:

3. Position the grille panel to the headlamp module assembly.
4. Install the retaining screws and tighten to 13 inch lbs. (2 Nm).

Sunbird, Cimarron, Skyhawk, Firenza

▶ See Figures 9, 10, 11 and 12

On these models please refer to the illustrations. Beginning in 1990, the Sunbird has a separate grille similar to that of the Cavalier, refer to those procedures for removal and installation.

Outside Mirrors

With the remote control door outside mirror, the remote control mirror cable must be disengaged from the door trim assembly on the standard trim styles to permit trim panel removal.

On custom trim styles the remote control mirror cable must be disengaged from the upper trim panel and the upper trim panel must be removed to permit lower trim panel removal.

1. Front end panel (fascia)
2. Retainer
3. Reinforcement assembly
4. Screw (9)
5. Nut (16)
6. Screw (6)
7. Moulding
8. Grille (l.h. shown)
9. Screw (16)
10. Nut (15)
11. 3mm max compression

87950045

Fig. 9 Front end panel and grille assembly—Firenza

1. Grille
2. Headlamp housing panel
3. Headlamp molding
4. Screw (3)
5. Screw (3)
6. Screws (4)

87950046

Fig. 10 Radiator grille mounting—1985 Cimarron

1. Nut (2)
2. Screw (2)
3. Screw (2). Torque to 4 N·m (35 lbs. in.)
4. Front end panel
5. Screw (2). Torque to 4 N·m (35 lbs. in.)
6. Push-in retainer

87950048

Fig. 11 Front grille opening panel—1990–92 Sunbird, except LE

1. Filler
2. Screw (2). Torque to 1.5 N·m (14 lbs. in.)
3. Screw (3). Torque to 1.5 N·m (14 lbs. in.)
4. Filler nuts (3)
5. Grille opening cover
6. Push-in retainer (2)

87950049

Fig. 12 Front end panel—1990 Sunbird LE

Refer to the illustrations for both custom trim and standard trim.

➡**The mirror glass face may be replaced by placing a piece of tape over the glass then breaking the mirror face. Adhesive back mirror faces are available.**

REMOVAL & INSTALLATION

▶ See Figures 13 and 14

1. From the inside of the door remove the retaining screw.
2. Remove the outside mirror escutcheon by pulling inward.
3. For manual mirrors, remove mirror control handle/knob and remove escutcheon.
4. If equipped with power mirrors, detach the electrical connector.
5. Remove the gasket, then unfasten the retaining nuts and remove the mirror from the door.

To install:

6. Install the mirror to the door and secure with the retaining nuts. Tighten the nuts to 45 in. lbs. (5 Nm).
7. Install the gasket and, if equipped with power mirrors, attach the electrical connector.
8. Slide the escutcheon onto handle shaft and install handle.
9. Snap the escutcheon into place and install the retaining screw.

Fig. 13 Unfasten the retaining screw, then . . .

Fig. 14 . . . remove the outside mirror bezel/escutcheon

Antenna

REPLACEMENT

1. Unscrew the antenna mast, nut and bezel from on top of the fender.
2. Lift the hood and disconnect the antenna cable from the bottom of the antenna base.
3. Remove the two antenna retaining screws from inside the fender.
4. Installation is the reverse of the removal procedure. Make sure all connections are tight.

Fenders

REMOVAL & INSTALLATION

▶ See Figure 15

➡ Use masking tape and heavy rags to protect the painted surfaces around the fender area. This procedure will help avoid expensive paint damage during fender removal and installation.

1982–88 Vehicles

1. Remove the lower air deflector.
2. Unfasten the three front end attaching screws. The grille must be removed for access to the top screw.

1	FENDER ASM.
2	SHIM (AS REQ'D.)
3	FENDER ASM.
4	INNER FENDER PANEL
5	AIR DEFLECTOR (SIDE)
6	LOCATING STUD
7	REINFORCEMENT ASM.
8	FRT. END PANEL
9	FENDER
10	INNER FENDER PANEL
11	RETAINER
12	RETAINER
13	SPLASH SHIELD
14	SKIRT
15	SPLASH SHIELD
16	LWR. SUPPORT
17	BODY SIDE MOLDING
18	WHEEL OPENING MOLDING
19	SIDE MARKER LAMP

Fig. 15 Front fender assembly mounting—all models similar

3. Remove the rocker panel molding if equipped, then unfasten the lower rear attaching screw. Note the number and location of shims for installation.
4. Remove the wiper arms and cowl vent assembly. The two screws at the inside edge of hinge at the cowl are hidden.
5. If removing the fender that has the antenna, remove the antenna mast, nut and two retaining screws from fender. Allow the antenna housing to fall, the antenna will stay in the car.
6. Unfasten the top fender attaching screws, then remove the fender assembly. Remove the inner fender panel and all attached parts and transfer onto new fender.
7. Installation is the reverse of the removal procedure.

1989–94 Vehicles

1. Remove the wiper arm assemblies, the shroud panel retaining screws, the washer nozzle hose, then remove the shroud panel.
2. Remove the side marker lamp.
3. Remove the front end panel.
4. If equipped, remove the rocker panel molding.
5. Raise and safely support vehicle on jack stands.
6. Remove the tire and wheel assembly, unfasten the attaching bolts and/or retaining clips from inner wheel housing, then remove the wheel housing.
7. Noting the number and location of any shims, remove the upper and lower fender attaching bolts and shims.
8. Remove the fender and transfer remaining parts onto the new fender.
9. Installation is the reverse of the removal procedure.

Convertible Top

TOP REPLACEMENT

▶ See Figures 16 thru 25

1. Install a spacer stick between the No. 3 and No. 4 bow to keep the No. 4 bow in position.

2. Remove the rear belt moldings by removing the attaching screws from rear compartment drain trough. Remove the quarter belt moldings by unfastening the screws and attaching nuts from the rear compartment and underneath the right and left sides of folding top well.

3. Apply a protective cover on the rear deck surface and quarter panel painted areas.

4. Using a sharp grease pencil, mark the location of the complete belt tacking strip (upper edge) on outer surface of top cover.

5. Raise the top to a suitable working height. Remove the front No. 1 bow seal and retainers. Detach welt assembly and top cover from the No. 1 bow.

1 QUARTER PANEL BELT MOLDING CAP	6 RETAINER
2 ISOLATOR	7 SCREW
3 MOLDING ASSEMBLY BACK BELT	8 MOLDING QUARTER PANEL BELT
4 BACK BELT MOLDING CAP	9 MOLDING ASSEMBLY QUARTER BELT FRONT
5 SCREW	10 NUT

87950063

Fig. 16 Convertible quarter and back belt moldings

QUARTER FLAPS

TACKING STRIP

87950064

Fig. 17 Convertible top tacking strip and quarter flaps

1 Dowel pin
2 Set screw
3 Latch hook
4 Welt assembly

87950065

Fig. 18 Convertible top cover and welt assembly

VIEW A

CABLE—SIDE RETENTION

VIEW B

87950066

Fig. 19 Location of the side retention cables

1 ADHESIVE	9 REAR RAIL RETAINER
2 FRONT CENTER RAIL SEAL	10 REAR RAIL SEAL
3 FOAM TAPE	11 CENTER RAIL SEAL
4 CENTER RAIL JOINT SEAL	12 FRONT RAIL RETAINER
5 CENTER RAIL RETAINER	13 FRONT RAIL & NO. 1 BOW SEAL
6 PROTECTIVE CAP	
7 CABLE & SPRING ASSEMBLY	
8 FRONT CENTER RAIL SEAL	

87950067

Fig. 20 Exploded view of the convertible seal assemblies

1 FEATURE STRIP	
2 FEATURE STRIP RETAINER	
3 CAP (END)	

87950068

Fig. 21 Location of the feature strip and strip retainer

6. Unfasten the attaching screw from the rear of each side retention cable. Remove the cable forward end from the hole in front rail.

7. Remove the screws from the lower end of each rear retention cable and rear listing pocket. To ease the removal of rear retention cable screw, raise the top off windshield header. Pull the cables through listing pockets from the upper end.

8. Raise the top and remove the rear rail seals and retainers.

9. Detach the top cover flaps from front rail and rear rail.

10. Remove the feature strip cap (end), feature strip and retainer. Remove the top cover from the No. 4 bow.

11. At underside of the No. 2 and 3 bows, unfasten the screws securing listing pocket top retainers and remove the retainers.

12. Disconnect the top cover from rear belt tacking strip. Note the location and spacing of staples before removing them.

13. Mark the location of rear window outer panels along balance of rear belt tacking strip, and the No. 4 bow (upper and lower edge).

14. Recheck the tack strip location markings on rear window assembly. Remove stay pads and rear window assembly from the rear belt tacking strip and the No. 4 bow. Note the location and spacing of staples before removal.

15. Use a sharp grease pencil and mark the location of all belt molding attaching holes on the lower edge of tacking strip or on quarter panels.

To install:

16. Transfer the reference marks from removed rear window assembly as follows:

| 1 | RETAINER TOP LISTING |
| 2 | LISTING POCKET |

87950069

Fig. 22 Unfasten the listing pocket top retainer screws, then remove the retainers

1	SPACER STICK
2	STAY PAD—SIDE
3	BACKLITE ASSEMBLY WITH ZIPPER
4	TACKING STRIP
5	NO. 4 BOW

87950070

Fig. 23 Installation of the rear window assembly in the convertible top

87950071

Fig. 24 Marking the convertible top cover forward edge

| 1 | FABRICATED SPACER STICK | | 2 | SIDE STAY PAD | | 3 | RIVET |

87950072

Fig. 25 Convertible side stay pads and spacer

a. Place the new rear window assembly on a clean covered work bench with inner surface down.

b. Position the removed rear window assembly over new one, carefully align the upper window with the lower one.

c. While holding both together securely, carefully lay out the trim material of both and transfer the rear window assembly reference marks along bottom portion of tacking strip.

d. Reverse the rear window assemblies by placing the new rear window assembly over the original as described above.

e. Check the location of reverence marks. If any difference is noted, the average between the two is the correct reference to use. Mark the corrected references clearly. Trim off the excess material beyond the ½ in. (13mm) allowance along the bottom and transfer the center mark from bottom center of removed rear window assembly to new one. Transfer of the reference marks must be done correctly for best results and minimum rework.

17. Lock the top to windshield header and install spacer sticks between the No. 4 bow and and rear rail. Spacer stick should be installed between No. 4 bow and rear rail back face. The purpose of the spacer sticks is to hold the No. 4 bow in its most rearward position, keeping tension on the top stay pads during the rear window assembly and top cover installation to belt tacking strips.

18. Position and center the new rear window assembly to the No. 4 bow according to reference marks and center notch. Using heavy duty ⅜ in. (9.5mm) stainless steel staples, staple the rear window assembly to the No. 4 bow. Staple from center to ends. Avoid stretching, but keep the material flat during stapling.

19. Position and center the new rear window assembly to the rear tacking strip according to reference marks and center notch. Staple the rear window assembly to tacking strip as follows:

a. Pull rear window assembly down over the tacking strip to remove all fullness and staple the rear window assembly to the tacking strip. Staple from center to each end of the rear window assembly.

b. Apply downward tension to the rear window assembly at each point of staple installation.

✳✳ WARNING

Excessive heat may cause damage to the rear window. Extreme care should be exercised when following this procedure.

c. After rear window has been properly secured, trim off all excess material at the rear tacking strip. Staple stay pads to the No. 4 bow and belt tacking strip and remove the spacer sticks. If wrinkles are present following installation, apply heat to the rear window surface using a hot air gun. The hot air gun should be held about 2 in. (51mm) from the rear window and moved in a circular motion.

20. Transfer the reference marks from the removed top cover to the new one as follows:

a. Place the new top cover on a suitable clean surface, with inner surface of cover down.

b. Position the removed top cover over the new one.

c. Carefully align the rear window opening upper corners and the rear quarter upper corners of both covers. Secure both covers together at these locations.

  d. Carefully lay out trim material of quarter area of both covers.

  e. Transfer location marks for tacking strip.

  f. Then reverse position of the covers by positioning the new cover over the original as described above.

  g. Recheck location of reference marks. If any difference is noted, the average between the two is the corrected reference to use. Mark the corrected references clearly.

  21. Install the No. 2 and No. 3 bow top cover retainers into the new top cover listing pockets.

  22. Install the side retention cables into the new top cover side rail listing pockets. A length of welding rod or equivalent wire can be used to pull the cable through side rail listing pocket.

  23. Position the top cover over framework. The top cover may require some lateral stretching along the rear bow to achieve proper fit of quarter flaps to the rear side rails and to remove fullness from the top cover valance over rear window.

  24. Secure the No. 2 and 3 bow top cover retainers to the No. 2 and 3 bows.

  25. Raise the top slightly off the windshield header. Attach the rear end of side retention cables to the rear side rail with attaching screw. Then apply a forward on the cables and install forward end of cables into the keyhole slots in the front side rail.

  26. Install the rear retention cables into the rear listing pockets. Secure the lower ends of the cables and listing pockets to the quarter inner reinforcement with screws.

  27. Install the center top cover rear valance over the No. 4 bow. Pull the top cover rear valance over No. 4 bow to remove all fullness from the rear valance. Staple the top cover to the No. 4 bow, starting at center and working towards each end. Avoid excessive stretching, but keep the material flat during stapling. Staples must be installed in a straight line in the center of No. 4 bow. Staples outboard of the seams should not be more than 2 in. (51mm) apart.

  28. Apply adhesive to cementing surfaces of the rear side rail and to quarter flaps. Align the quarter flap seam with the edge of rear rail to remove all fullness from the rear top cover. With the quarter flap seam aligned with each rear rail, install a screw at belt tacking strip, then cement the quarter flaps securely in place.

  29. Install the side rail seal assembly to help maintain position of the quarter flaps.

  30. Lock the top to the windshield header. Pull top cover straight forward at the seams to desired top fullness and align the top cover seams with the notches in No. 1 bow. While maintaining tension on cover over the top of No. 1 bow, make pencil mark on the cover outer surface along the forward edge of top No. 1 bow.

  31. Raise the top off header to a suitable working height. Apply adhesive such as 3M 0864 or equivalent, to cementing area of the top No. 1 bow, surface of top cover and to front corner flaps. Pull top cover ¼ in. (6mm) past the reference point over the No. 1 bow and secure.

  32. Trim the excess material to retaining screw holes for front rail and No. 1 bow seal.

  33. Lower the top and lock to windshield header. Check appearance of the top trim, top operation and locking action of the top. If additional tension is needed in the top cover, repeat step 30 and pull the top cover farther forward. Staple and recheck the top for proper appearance and operation.

  34. Align the welt assembly to No. 1 bow. Fold the vinyl flap back over the welt bulb and staple into position.

  35. Apply adhesive to the stapled edge of the welt assembly and fold the vinyl flap over stapled surface of welt assembly.

  36. Carefully align the front rail retainers. Secure in position with attaching screws.

  37. Apply weatherstrip adhesive to the retainer inner surface. Attach the front rail and No. 1 bow seal assembly to the front rail retainer and across the No. 1 bow. Secure the seal to the No. 1 bow with attaching screws.

  38. Lock the top to the windshield header. Staple the top cover to the belt tacking strip starting at the rear rail and working rearward. Apply downward pressure to top cover at each point of staple installation. Avoid excessive stretching, but keep the material flat during stapling.

  39. Install a pierce hole in the top material and tacking strip at each out board end of the No. 4 bow for feature strip and cap.

  40. Install the rear bow feature strip retainer, feature strip and end caps using a clear silicone sealer.

  41. Cut or pierce holes in the top cover and rear window assembly along the tacking strip for belt molding attaching studs and install belt moldings.

  42. When complete, the folding top cover should be free from wrinkles and draws. Clean up top material and car as necessary.

MOTOR REPLACEMENT

▶ **See Figure 26**

If any parts of the motor and pump assembly are found to be inoperable, it is recommended that the entire unit be replaced with a new motor and pump assembly.

  1. Make sure the convertible top is in the full up position.

  2. Disconnect the negative battery cable.

  3. Remove the partition in the rear compartment to expose the motor/pump unit.

  4. Disconnect the wiring harness, then remove the ground wire attaching screw and ground wire.

  5. Place absorbent rags below hose connections and at the end of the fluid reservoir.

  6. Vent the reservoir by removing then installing the filler plug.

  7. Disconnect the hydraulic lines and cap open fittings to prevent leakage of fluid. Use a cloth to absorb any leaking fluid. Remove the motor/pump unit.

To install:

  8. Fill the reservoir unit with DEXRON IIE® transmission fluid. Position the motor/pump unit in place.

  9. Attach the hydraulic hoses, ensuring that each hose assembly has a seal ring in place. Connect the wiring harness, ground wire and attaching screw.

  10. Connect the negative battery cable and operate the top through its up and down cycles until all the air has been bled from the hydraulic circuit.

  11. Check connections for leaks and recheck the fluid in the reservoir. Level should be even with fill hole, install plug.

1. MOTOR PUMP ASSEMBLY
2. FILLER PLUG ADAPTER
3. BYPASS VALVE
4. HOSE
5. HYDRAULIC FLUID CONTAINER
6. TREE TYPE CLIP

VIEW A

87950075

Fig. 26 Location of the convertible top motor

Sunroof

The vista vent is a hinged window panel mounted to the roof of the vehicle. The vista vent is opened by moving the latch release handle forward and up to lock it in this position. When open, the rear of the window is raised about 1½ in. (38mm).

The vista vent can also be removed completely. First open the panel as previously described. Then press the latch handle release tab and lift the panel up and back to disengage the front hinges. To reinstall the vista vent, position the forward edge of the opening. Line up the hinge blades with the hinge slots and engage completely. If hinge binds in slot, reposition the panel in opening, DO NOT FORCE! Depress the latch release tab and engage striker bar into latch recess. Rotate handle down and back to lock in the closed position.

✳✳ CAUTION

Never attempt to remove the roof panel while the vehicle is being driven! The panel may either fly off or fall inside which may cause damage or personal injury.

Instrument Panel and Pad

REMOVAL & INSTALLATION

1982–88 Vehicles

▶ **See Figures 27, 28 and 29**

1. Disconnect the negative battery cable.
2. Remove the left side instrument panel hush panel.
3. Remove the lower steering column trim cover and A/C outlet.
4. Remove center A/C duct and right close out panel (2 clips hold the A/C duct in the center). Disconnect the courtesy light.
5. Unfasten three steering column-to-instrument panel bolts and lower the steering column.
6. Remove the glove box door and trunk release switch, if so equipped.
7. Unfasten the two radio-to-instrument panel screws, then detach the electrical connectors and antenna lead from radio.
8. Remove the four cluster to instrument panel screws, disconnect the speedometer cable and remove the screw from the speed sensor.
9. Unfasten the three heater A/C control-to-instrument panel screws. Remove clip and screw securing the bowden cable to heater door.
10. Remove trim plate at right of steering column (spring clip attachment).
11. Detach the lighter connector. Remove headlamp switch knob and the trimplate at the left of the steering column. Unfasten the plastic nut at the headlamp switch, then remove the switch.
12. Remove rear defogger switch, if so equipped. Remove ashtray assembly and ashtray light. Remove hood release cable handle. There is one screw and a plastic nut securing the handle.
13. Remove defroster grilles by carefully prying them up, then unfasten the four screws at defroster outlets.

1	DASH PANEL
2	WELD NUTS
3	CENTER REINF.
4	PAD ASM.
5	SNAP-IN CLIPS
6	R.H. LOWER I.P. TRIM PLATE
7	L.H. LOWER I.P. TRIM PLATE
8	I.P. TRIM PLATE
9	TORX SCREW
10	HUSH PANEL
11	STEERING COLUMN TRIM COVER

Fig. 28 Instrument panel and trim plate—1982–88 vehicles

Fig. 29 Instrument panel pad mounting—1982–88 Type 10 vehicles

14. Unfasten the retaining screw, then remove the convenience center, then unfasten the two nuts and screw holding the instrument panel harness and bulk head connector. Remove the brace-to-glove box screw.
15. Remove the nuts at either side of the instrument panel carrier at the lower back of panel, then detach the electrical connectors (The instrument panel duct work must be removed from harness).
16. Remove the carrier and lay on seat. Remove A/C ductwork, screws and clips attaching the wiring harness to carrier.
17. Remove the radio speakers and grilles.
    To install:
18. Install the radio speakers and grilles.
19. Install the carrier. Install A/C ductwork, screws and clips attaching the wiring harness to carrier.
20. Fasten the nuts at either side of instrument carrier lower back of panel and attach the electrical connectors.
21. Install the convenience center and secure with the retaining screw, and fasten the instrument panel harness and bulk head connector with the 2 nuts and screw. Install the brace-to-glove box screw.
22. Install the defroster grilles by snapping them into place, and fasten the four screws at defroster outlets.
23. Install rear defogger switch, if so equipped. Install ashtray assembly and ashtray light. Install hood release cable handle and secure with the screw and plastic nut.
24. Attach the lighter connector. Install headlamp switch knob and trimplate at left of steering column. Install the switch, Fasten the plastic nut at headlamp switch.
25. Install the trim plate at right of steering column and secure with the spring clip attachment.
26. Fasten the three heater A/C control-to-I.P. screws. Install clip and screw securing bowden cable to heater door.

LEFT SIDE A/C **RIGHT SIDE A/C**

LEFT SIDE—HEATER **RIGHT SIDE—HEATER**

1	ACCELERATOR ROD	
2	DASH MAT	6 A/C HEATER DUCT
3	CARPET	7 ACCELERATOR ROD
4	I.P. PAD	8 INSTRUMENT PANEL
5	ECM BRACKET	9 CARPET
		10 DASH MAT
		11 I.P. PAD
		12 BRACKET
		13 SUPT I.P. PAD
		14 ECM
		15 AIR DISTRIBUTION DUCT

Fig. 27 Remove the left side hush panel—1982–88 vehicles

27. Connect the speedometer cable and fasten the screw in speed sensor. Fasten the four cluster-to-instrument panel screws.

28. Attach the electrical connectors and antenna lead to radio. Install the 2 radio-to-I.P. screws.

29. Install the glove box door and trunk release switch, if so equipped.

30. Raise steering column, then secure with the three steering column-to-instrument panel bolts.

31. Install center A/C duct and right close out panel (2 clips hold the A/C duct in the center). Connect the courtesy light.

32. Install the lower steering column trim cover and A/C outlet.

33. Fasten the left side instrument panel hush panel.

34. Connect the negative battery cable.

1989–94 Vehicles

▶ **See Figure 30**

1. Disconnect the negative battery cable.

2. Remove the right and left sound insulators, steering column filler and the right and left instrument panel trim plates.

3. Remove the console housing and glove box door.

4. Remove the heater and A/C control head. For details, please refer to the procedure in Section 6 of this manual.

5. Remove the convenience center. Disconnect the forward lamp harness and engine harness from bulkhead.

6. Remove the bulkhead from cowl. Remove the hood release handle (retained by two set screws), and defroster grilles.

7. Unfasten the four upper instrument panel retaining screws located in defroster duct openings. Remove the two lower corner instrument panel retaining nuts.

8. Remove the screw from the instrument panel brace at left side of instrument panel compartment opening.

9. For vehicles equipped with a manual transaxle, unfasten the two nuts securing the wire harness to the neutral start switch.

10. Unfasten the three steering column retaining bolts. There are two at the instrument panel pad and one at the cowl and lower steering column.

11. Pull the instrument panel assembly out far enough to disconnect the ignition switch, headlamp dimmer switch and the turn signal switch. Tag and detach all other electrical wiring connectors, vacuum lines and radio antenna lead to remove the instrument panel assembly.

12. Remove the instrument panel with wiring harness attached.

To install:

13. Position the instrument panel to the cowl and attach all electrical connectors and vacuum hoses.

14. Install the three steering column retaining bolts. Install the screw into instrument panel brace at left side of instrument panel compartment, then tighten to 57 inch lbs. (6 Nm).

15. Fasten the two lower corner instrument panel retaining nuts, then tighten to 12 inch lbs. (2 Nm). Install the four screws through defroster ducts into cowl, then tighten to 12 inch lbs. (2 Nm).

16. For vehicles equipped with a manual transaxle, install the two lower nuts securing the wire harness to neutral start switch.

17. Install defroster grilles, hood release handle, bulkhead and forward lamp and engine harness into bulkhead.

18. Install convenience center, heater A/C control assembly and glove box door.

19. Fasten the console housing, right and left trim plates and the steering column filler.

20. Secure the the left and right sound insulators.

21. Connect the negative battery cable.

Console

REMOVAL & INSTALLATION

▶ **See Figures 31 thru 38**

➡ **Some of these steps may not be applicable for all vehicles.**

1. Disconnect the negative battery cable.

2. Block the drive wheels of the vehicles, then place the gear selector/shift lever in the neutral position. Apply the parking brake.

3. Remove the accessory trim plate from the console housing. Remove the console trim plate.

4. Open the front ashtray, then remove the ashtray, and unfasten the screws (some models use Torx® screws) under the ashtray.

5. If necessary for console removal, remove the radio and the A/C and heater control.

6. If necessary, unfasten the console-to-instrument panel retaining screws.

7. For vehicles through 1992, if equipped with an automatic transaxle, gently pry out the emblem in the center of the shift knob, then remove snapring securing knob. Lift trimplate assembly out by pulling front end up first and disconnect wire harness.

8. On vehicles through 1992, equipped with a manual transaxle, remove the shift knob by removing the set screw under the knob or unscrewing the knob, as applicable. If necessary, detach the electrical connector

9. If necessary, unfasten the screws under the trim plate, then remove rear ashtray and remove the screw(s) under the ashtray.

10. On vehicles equipped with a manual transaxle, remove the screw under parking brake handle and 2 screws at sides of console in rear.

11. If necessary, unfasten the retaining screws in the console rear storage compartment.

```
1  DASH PANEL
2  NUT
3  SCREW – 2 N·m (19 LBS. IN.)
4  NUT
5  I/P SUPPORT BRACKET
6  SCREW – 9 N·m (80 LBS. IN.)
7  INSTRUMENT PANEL
8  I/P TIE BAR
9  SCREW – 1.4 N·m (12 LBS. IN.)
   A  TIGHTEN 1ST
   B  TIGHTEN 2ND
   C  TIGHTEN 3RD
   D  TIGHTEN 4TH
```

VIEW A

87950081

Fig. 30 Instrument panel mounting—1994 Cavalier shown

87950090

Fig. 31 Remove the front ashtray, then . . .

87950091

Fig. 32 . . . unfasten the retaining screws located under the ashtray

87950092

Fig. 33 Remove the shifter knob, then remove the trim plate and shifter boot

Fig. 34 Be sure to detach any necessary electrical connectors

Fig. 35 Unfasten the rear ashtray retaining screws, then . . .

Fig. 36 . . . remove the rear ashtray from the console

Fig. 37 After removing the ashtray, unfasten the retaining screws

Fig. 38 Unfasten any remaining retaining screws, then lift the console from the vehicle. Be sure to detach any electrical connectors

12. Unfasten any remaining screws, then lift the console up and detach any electrical connectors and out of the vehicle.

13. Installation is the reverse of the removal procedure.

Door Panel

REMOVAL & INSTALLATION

▶ See Figures 39 thru 48

A one piece trim panel is used on styles with standard trim. The custom trim has an upper metal trim panel. The one piece trim hangs over the door inner panel across the top and is secured by clips down the sides and across the bottom. It is retained by screws located in the areas of the top front of the panel assembly.

1. Remove all door inside handles.

➡Removing a window crank handle (with a retaining clip inside the handle) without a special tool can be a problem. An alternative method is to take a clean shop towel and wedge it between the window crank handle and the door panel. Move it up, while pulling it from left to right, as in a sawing motion working the clean shop towel until the retaining clip comes free.

2. Remove the door inside locking rod knob.

3. Unfasten the screws inserted through the door armrest and pull the handle assembly into the door inner panel or armrest hanger support bracket.

Fig. 39 The window crank handle may be removed with a clean shop towel

Fig. 40 Use a suitable tool to remove the trim "buttons", then . . .

Fig. 41 . . . remove the armrest retaining screws

Fig. 42 Unfasten the retaining screw, then . . .

Fig. 43 . . . remove the inside door handle trim piece

Fig. 44 Use of this special tool is the preferred method to remove the window crank handle

Fig. 45 Remove the window crank handle, then . . .

Fig. 46 . . . remove the washer from the door panel

Fig. 47 A trim panel remover tool is very helpful to disengage the retainers when removing the door panel

Fig. 48 Common front door trim panel retention and fastener locations

4. On styles with remote control mirrors assemblies, disengage the end of the mirror control cable from the bezel on the standard trim, or from the upper trim panel on the custom trim. On custom trim, remove the upper trim panel.

5. On styles with power window or door lock controls located in the door trim panel, disconnect the wire harnesses at the switch assemblies. On the four door sedan and the two door hatchback, remove the switch cover by pushing down at the switch area and pulling down at the bottom of the cover. The switch and base may be removed from the trim with the cover removed.

6. Remove the remote control handle bezel screws.

7. Unfasten the screws used to hold the armrest to the inner panel.

8. Remove the screws and plastic retainers from the perimeter of the door trim using tool BT-7323A or equivalent and a screwdriver. To remove the trim panel, push the trim panel upward and outboard to disengage from the door inner panel at the beltline.

9. On styles with an insulator pad fastened to the door inner panel, use tool J-21104 or equivalent to remove the fasteners and the insulator pad.

10. On styles with the water defector held in place by fasteners, use tool BT-7323A or equivalent to remove the fasteners and the water deflector.

11. On styles with the armrest bracket riveted to the inner panel and installed over the water deflector, drill out the armrest bracket rivets using a $\frac{3}{16}$ in. (5mm) drill bit.

To install:

12. To install the insulator pad or water deflector, locate the fasteners in the holes in the door inner panel and press in place. Replace all tape which may have been applied to assist in holding insulator pad or water deflector in place. Where necessary, install the armrest support bracket over the water deflector and onto the door inner panel using $\frac{3}{16}$ in. x $\frac{11}{32}$ in. (5mm x 9mm) rivets.

13. Before installing the door trim panel, check that all trim retainers are securely installed to the assembly and are not damaged. Replace retainers where required.

14. Attach all electrical components.

15. To install the door trim panel, locate the top of the assembly over the upper flange of the door inner panel, inserting the door handle through the handle slot in the panel and press down on the trim panel to engage the upper retaining clips.

16. Position the trim panel to the door inner panel so the trim retainers are align with the attaching holes in the panel and tap the retainers into the holes with the palm of your hand or a clean rubber mallet.

17. Install all previously removed items.

Door Locks

REMOVAL & INSTALLATION

▸ See Figures 49 and 50

1. Raise the window to the full up position.
2. Remove the inside door trim panel.
3. Detach the water deflector enough to access the lock actuator.
4. Disconnect the outside handle-to-lock assembly rod.
5. Disconnect the lock cylinder-to-lock assembly rod.

6. Disconnect the inside handle-to-lock assembly rod.
7. Unfasten the lock assembly screws/bolts and remove the lock from the door. If equipped, detach the electrical connectors.

To install:

8. Attach the electrical connector (if equipped), position the lock assembly to the door and install the retaining screws/bolts. Tighten the screws/bolts to 62 inch lbs. (7 Nm). Do NOT overtighten.
9. Attach the outside handle to the lock assembly rod.
10. Connect the lock cylinder to the lock assembly rod.
11. Connect the inside handle to the lock rod and inside locking rod.
12. Fasten the water deflector.
13. Install the inside door trim panel.

Front Door Glass

REMOVAL & INSTALLATION

Except Convertible

1. Raise the door window to the full up position and remove the door trim panel and water deflector.
2. Unfasten the bolts holding the front glass retainer to the door inner panel and remove the retainer through the rear access hole. Lower the glass to approximately 3 in. (76mm) above the beltline.
3. Rotate the glass forward to disengage the window regulator roller from the sash channel.
4. Lower the glass into the door to disengage the rear guide (on the glass) from the rear run channel.
5. Using care, raise the glass while tilting forward and remove the glass inboard of the upper frame.

To install:

6. Tilt the front edge of the glass downward to locate the glass in the door.
7. Apply pressure rearward and snap the glass rear guide into the rear run channel.
8. Lower the glass to about 3 in. (76mm) above the beltline and install the widow regulator roller to sash channel.
9. Run the glass to the full up position.
10. Place the front glass retainer in position and install the bolts.
11. Check the window to make sure it operates correctly, then install the remaining trim parts.

Convertible

▸ See Figure 51

1. Remove the door trim panel, sound absorber, armrest bracket and water deflector.

1 INSIDE LOCK KNOB ROD	6 ELECTRICAL CONNECTOR	11 ACTUATOR
2 RIVET	7 BELLCRANK ROD	12 INSIDE LOCK KNOB ROD
3 ACTUATOR	8 GUIDE CLIP	13 CLIP
4 BELLCRANK	9 RIVET (3)	14 RIVET (2)
5 RIVET (2)	10 BELLCRANK	

87950111

Fig. 49 Front door lock bellcrank and actuator—1992 vehicle shown

1 HANDLE ASSEMBLY—INSIDE	6 LOCK ASSEMBLY
2 ROD—LOCK REMOTE CONTROL TO LOCK	7 ROD—INSIDE LOCKING TO LOCK
3 ROD—OUTSIDE HANDLE TO LOCK	8 ROD—INSIDE LOCKING TO ACTUATOR
4 HANDLE ASSEMBLY—OUTSIDE	9 ACTUATOR ASSEMBLY—ELECTRIC LOCK
5 LOCK SCREWS (3)	10 KNOB—INSIDE LOCKING

87950113

Fig. 50 Rear door lock system—1992 vehicle shown

1. Front glass run channel
2. Front up stop
3. Catch—front up stop
4. Glass retainer
5. Bushing
6. Cam assembly door glass
7. Front stabilizer
8. Glass assembly
9. Rear stabilizer
10. Guide block
11. Rivets—regulator
12. Rivets—regulator motor
13. Rear up stop block
14. Rivets—rear cam assembly lower
15. Attaching nuts inner panel cam door reinforcement

87950115

Fig. 51 Front door glass and related hardware—convertible

2. Position the glass so that the up stop spanner nut on the glass is visible through the access hole.

3. Using tool J-22055 or equivalent, remove the spanner nut, bushing and stop from the glass.

4. Position the glass so the spanner nuts are visible through the access hole.

5. Remove the spanner nuts and bushings.

6. Loosen the upper stabilizers.

7. Disengage the glass from the studs on the sash where the spanner nuts were removed.

8. Lower the regulator to the full-down position.

9. Grasp the glass and pull the glass up, with the front of the glass tilted down and remove the glass.

10. Installation is the reverse of removal. Before installing trim parts, check the window operation for proper alignment and adjust as needed.

Rear Door Glass

REMOVAL & INSTALLATION

▶ **See Figure 52**

➡**If equipped, the stationary vent assembly must be removed with the rear glass assembly as a unit.**

1. Remove the door trim panel and the water deflector.

2. Lower the glass to the full down position.

3. Remove the screws at the top of the division channel.

4. Unfasten the bolt holding the vent glass support at the belt.

5. Remove the screws at the rear of the door face holding the bottom of the division to the door.

6. Push the stationary vent assembly down and forward to disengage the vent assembly from the run channel. Now that the vent assembly is inboard of the door frame, lift up until the vent assembly is stopped against the door glass.

7. Raise the door glass 6–8 in. (152–203mm) and tilt the whole assembly rearward and disengage the roller from the glass sash channel.

To install:

8. Place the rear door glass in the vent division channel.

9. Load the rear window and vent assembly by lowering the assemblies through the door belt opening. Rotate the glass forward to engage the regulator roller in the glass sash channel. Reposition the vent glass into the door frame.

10. Install the screws at the top of the division channel.

11. Fasten the screws at the rear face of the door holding division and lower support in place.

12. Fasten the bolt securing the division channel support at the belt.

13. Replace all previously removed trim.

1. Rod—remote control to lock
2. Handle—inside lock remote control
3. Filler—sealing strip—front
4. Knob—inside lock
5. Retainer—glass front run channel
6. Regulator assembly
7. Actuator assembly—door lock
8. Glass down stop
9. Handle—window regulator
10. Shoe—inside locking rods
11. Rod—inside lock to actuator
12. Rod—inside lock knob to lock
13. Rod—outside handle to lock
14. Filler—sealing strip rear
15. Support—vent glass
16. Vent assembly—stationary
17. Bell crank
18. Glass assembly
19. Handle—outside glass
20. Glass guide
21. Glass sash channel
22. Lock assembly

87950116

Fig. 52 Rear door glass and related hardware

Front Window Regulator And Motor

➡**The following procedure includes both manual and power window regulator removal and installation. Besides the regulators, window motors and rollers including the washer and pin are serviced separately.**

REMOVAL & INSTALLATION

Except Convertible

▶ **See Figures 51 and 52**

1. Remove the door trim panel and the water deflector.

2. Raise the glass to the full up position and tape the glass to the door frame using fabric tape.

3. Punch out the center pins of the regulator rivets using a ¼ in. (6mm) drill bit. On electric regulators, drill out the rivets supporting the motor to the door inner panel.

4. Move the regulator rearward and disconnect the wiring harness from the motor, if so equipped. Disengage the roller on the regulator lift arm from the glass sash channel.

5. Remove the regulator through the rear access hole.

6. Using a ³⁄₁₆ in. (5mm) drill bit, drill out the motor attaching rivets and remove the motor from the regulator, if so equipped.

To install:

7. If so equipped, attach the motor to the regulator using a rivet tool and ³⁄₁₆ in. (5mm) rivets or ³⁄₁₆ in. (5mm) nuts and bolts.

8. Place the regulator through the rear access hole into the door inner panel. If an electric regulator is being installed, connect the wire connector to the motor prior to installing the regulator in the panel.

9. Locate the lift arm roller into the glass sash channel.

10. Using rivet tool J-29022 or equivalent, rivet the regulator to the inner panel of the door using ¼ in. x ½ in. (6mm x 13mm) aluminum peel type rivets (part No. 9436175 or equivalent). If a rivet tool is not available, use the following nut and bolt method:

   a. Install U-clips on the regulator and motor (if so equipped), at the attaching locations. Be sure to install clips with clinch nuts on the outboard side of the regulator.

   b. Place the regulator through the rear access hole into the door inner panel. If an electric regulator is being installed, connect the wire connector to the motor prior to installing the regulator in the panel.

   c. Locate the lift arm roller into the glass sash channel.

   d. Align the regulator with the clinch nuts to the holes in the inner panel.

   e. Attach the regulator and motor to the door inner panel with ¼ in. screws. Tighten the screws to 90–125 inch lbs. (10–14 Nm).

11. If an electrical window regulator is being installed use a rivet mentioned in step 10 to rivet the regulator motor to the door inner panel.

12. Replace all previously removed parts.

Convertible

1. Remove the door trim panel, sound absorber, armrest bracket and water deflector.

2. Using a ¼ in. (6mm) drill bit, drill out the rivets supporting the motor to the door inner panel.

3. Disconnect the electrical connector from the regulator motor.

4. Support the door glass in the full-up position, using rubber wedge door stops.

5. Remove the nuts holding the cam assembly door reinforcement to the inner panel and remove the cam assembly.

6. Remove the bolt holding the upper portion of the rear cam assembly to the inner panel.

7. Using a ³⁄₁₆ in. (5mm) drill bit, drill out the rivets, holding the lower section of the rear cam assembly to the inner panel.

8. Remove the up stop from the rear cam assembly.

9. Remove the rear cam assembly through the access hole.

10. Disengage the regulator from the glass sash channel and remove the regulator through the access hole.

When removing the electric motor from the regulator, the sector gear must be locked in position. The regulator lift arm is under tension from the counterbalance spring and could cause personal injury if the sector gear is not locked in position.

11. If equipped with an electric window regulator and you wish to remove the motor from the regulator proceed as follows:

    a. Drill a hole through the regulator sector gear and backplate and install a bolt and nut to lock the sector gear in position.

    b. Using a ³⁄₁₆ in. (5mm) drill bit, drill out the motor attaching rivets and remove the motor from the regulator.

    c. To install the motor to the regulator use a rivet tool J-29022 or equivalent and install ³⁄₁₆ in. (5mm) rivets or ³⁄₁₆ in. (5mm) nuts and bolts. Remove the bolt and nut used to secure the sector gear in position.

To install:

12. Make sure the regulator is in the full up position.

13. Install the regulator arm rollers to the glass sash channel.

14. Install the rear cam assembly using ³⁄₁₆ in. (5mm) aluminum peel-type rivets making sure to install the up stop in the cam assembly.

15. Connect the electrical connector to the motor on the regulator.

16. Engage the roller on the regulator lift arm in the cam assembly door reinforcement.

17. Install the cam assembly door reinforcement to the inner panel.

18. Align the attaching holes in the regulator with the holes in the inner panel.

19. Install the regulator to the inner panel, using a rivet gun and ¼ in. x ½ in. (6mm x 13mm) aluminum peel type rivets.

Rear Window Regulator

➡The following procedure includes both manual and power window regulator removal and installation. Besides the regulators, window motors and rollers including the washer and pin are serviced separately.

REMOVAL & INSTALLATION

1. Remove the door trim panel and the water deflector.

2. Raise the glass to the full up position and tape the glass to the door frame using fabric tape.

3. Punch out the center pins of the regulator rivets using a ¼ in. (6mm) drill bit. On electric regulators, drill out the rivets supporting the motor to the door inner panel.

4. Disconnect the wiring harness from the motor, if so equipped. Disengage the roller on the regulator lift arm from the glass sash channel.

5. Remove the regulator through the rear access hole.

6. Using a ³⁄₁₆ in. (5mm) drill bit, drill out the motor attaching rivets and remove the motor from the regulator, if so equipped.

To install:

7. If so equipped, attach the motor to the regulator using a rivet tool and ³⁄₁₆ in. (5mm) rivets or ³⁄₁₆ in. (5mm) nuts and bolts.

8. Place the regulator through the rear access hole into the door inner panel. If an electric regulator is being installed, connect the wire connector to the motor prior to installing the regulator in the panel.

9. Locate the lift arm roller into the glass sash channel.

10. Using rivet tool J-29022 or equivalent, rivet the regulator to the inner panel of the door using ¼ in. x ½ in. (6mm x 13mm) aluminum peel type rivets (part No. 9436175 or equivalent). If a rivet tool is not available, use the following nut and bolt method:

    a. Install U-clips on the regulator and motor (if so equipped), at the attaching locations. Be sure to install clips with clinch nuts on the outboard side of the regulator.

    b. Place the regulator through the rear access hole into the door inner panel. If an electric regulator is being installed, connect the wire connector to the motor prior to installing the regulator in the panel.

    c. Locate the lift arm roller into the glass sash channel.

    d. Align the regulator with the clinch nuts to the holes in the inner panel.

    e. Attach the regulator and motor to the door inner panel with ¼ in. screws. Tighten the screws to 90–125 inch lbs. (10–14 Nm).

11. If an electrical window regulator is being installed use a rivet mentioned in step 10 to rivet the regulator motor to the door inner panel.

12. Replace all previously removed parts.

Windshield and Fixed Glass

REMOVAL & INSTALLATION

If your windshield, or other fixed window, is cracked or chipped, you may decide to replace it with a new one yourself. However, there are two main reasons why replacement windshields and other window glass should be installed only by a professional automotive glass technician: safety and cost.

The most important reason a professional should install automotive glass is for safety. The glass in the vehicle, especially the windshield, is designed with safety in mind in case of a collision. The windshield is specially manufactured from two panes of specially-tempered glass with a thin layer of transparent plastic between them. This construction allows the glass to "give" in the event that a part of your body hits the windshield during the collision, and prevents the glass from shattering, which could cause lacerations, blinding and other harm to passengers of the vehicle. The other fixed windows are designed to be tempered so that if they break during a collision, they shatter in such a way that there are no large pointed glass pieces. The professional automotive glass technician knows how to install the glass in a vehicle so that it will function optimally during a collision. Without the proper experience, knowledge and tools, installing a piece of automotive glass yourself could lead to additional harm if an accident should ever occur.

Cost is also a factor when deciding to install automotive glass yourself. Performing this could cost you much more than a professional may charge for the same job. Since the windshield is designed to break under stress, an often life saving characteristic, windshields tend to break VERY easily when an inexperienced person attempts to install one. Do-it-yourselfers buying two, three or even four windshields from a salvage yard because they have broken them during installation are common stories. Also, since the automotive glass is designed to prevent the outside elements from entering your vehicle, improper installation can lead to water and air leaks. Annoying whining noises at highway speeds from air leaks or inside body panel rusting from water leaks can add to your stress level and subtract from your wallet. After buying two or three windshields, installing them and ending up with a leak that produces a noise while driving and water damage during rainstorms, the cost of having a professional do it correctly the first time may be much more alluring. We here at Chilton, therefore, advise that you have a professional automotive glass technician service any broken glass on your vehicle.

WINDSHIELD CHIP REPAIR

♦ **See Figures 53 thru 67**

➡**Check with your state and local authorities on the laws for state safety inspection. Some states or municipalities may not allow chip repair as a viable option for correcting stone damage to your windshield.**

Although severely cracked or damaged windshields must be replaced, there is something that you can do to prolong or even prevent the need for replacement of a chipped windshield. There are many companies which offer windshield chip repair products, such as Loctite's® Bullseye™ windshield repair kit. These kits usually consist of a syringe, pedestal and a sealing adhesive. The syringe is mounted on the pedestal and is used to create a vacuum which pulls the plastic layer against the glass. This helps make the chip transparent. The adhesive is then injected which seals the chip and helps to prevent further stress cracks from developing. Refer to the sequence of photos to get a general idea of what windshield chip repair involves.

➡**Always follow the specific manufacturer's instructions.**

Fig. 53 Small chips on your windshield can be fixed with an aftermarket repair kit, such as the one from Loctite®

Fig. 54 To repair a chip, clean the windshield with glass cleaner and dry it completely

Fig. 55 Remove the center from the adhesive disc and peel off the backing from one side of the disc . . .

Fig. 56 . . . then press it on the windshield so that the chip is centered in the hole

Fig. 57 Be sure that the tab points upward on the windshield

Fig. 58 Peel the backing off the exposed side of the adhesive disc . . .

Fig. 59 . . . then position the plastic pedestal on the adhesive disc, ensuring that the tabs are aligned

Fig. 60 Press the pedestal firmly on the adhesive disc to create an adequate seal . . .

Fig. 61 . . . then install the applicator syringe nipple in the pedestal's hole

Inside Rear View Mirror

REPLACEMENT

The rear view mirror is attached to a support which is secured to the windshield glass. This support is installed by the glass supplier using a plastic-polyvinyl butyl adhesive.

Service replacement windshield glass has the mirror support bonded to the glass assembly.

Service kits are available to replace a detached mirror support or install a new part. Follow the manufacturer's instructions for replacement.

Front Seat

REMOVAL & INSTALLATION

▶ See Figures 68, 69 and 70

1. Operate the seat to the full-forward position. If a six way power seat is operable, move the seat to the full-forward and up positions. To gain access to the adjuster-to-floor pan retaining nuts, remove the adjuster rear foot covers or carpet retainers.

2. Remove the track covers where necessary, then remove the rear attaching nuts. Remove the front foot covers, then remove the adjuster-to-floor pan front attaching nuts.

TCCA0P09

Fig. 62 Hold the syringe with one hand while pulling the plunger back with the other hand

TCCA0P10

Fig. 63 After applying the solution, allow the entire assembly to sit until it has set completely

TCCA0P11

Fig. 64 After the solution has set, remove the syringe from the pedestal . . .

TCCA0P12

Fig. 65 . . . then peel the pedestal off of the adhesive disc . . .

TCCA0P13

Fig. 66 . . . and peel the adhesive disc off of the windshield

TCCA0P14

Fig. 67 The chip will still be slightly visible, but it should be filled with the hardened solution

87950133

Fig. 68 Unfasten the retaining nuts, then . . .

87950134

Fig. 69 . . . remove the seat track covers

87950135

Fig. 70 Unfasten the seat-to-floor retaining bolts, then remove the seat from the vehicle

3. On seats with power adjusters, tilt the seat rearward and disconnect the feed wire connector.

4. Remove the seat assembly from the car.

5. To install the seat assembly reverse the removal procedure. Tighten the seat adjuster-to-floor pan attaching bolts or nuts to 21 ft. lbs. (28 Nm).

Rear Seat Cushion

REMOVAL & INSTALLATION

▶ **See Figure 71**

1. Remove the rear seat cushion attaching bolts, located at the center of the right and left sections of the rear seat cushion.

2. Lift the cushion upward and remove from the vehicle.

3. To install, reverse the removal procedure. Tighten the seat cushion attaching bolts to 14–20 ft. lbs. (19–27 Nm).

Power Seat Motors

REMOVAL & INSTALLATION

1. Remove the front seat assembly and place upside down on a clean surface.

2. Disconnect the motor feed wires from the motor.

3. Remove the nut securing the front of the motor support bracket to the inboard adjuster and withdraw the assembly from the adjuster and the gear nut drives.

Fig. 71 Rear seat cushion mounting points

4. Disconnect the drive cables from the motor and complete the removal of the support bracket with motors attached.

5. Grind off the peened over ends(s) of the grommet assembly securing the motor to the support and separate the motors from the support, as required.

6. To install, reverse the removal procedure except as noted:

a. Drill out the top end of the grommet assembly using a ³⁄₁₆ in. (5mm) drill.

b. Install the grommet assembly to the motor support bracket and secure the motor to the grommet using a ³⁄₁₆ in. (5mm) rivet.

GLOSSARY

AIR/FUEL RATIO: The ratio of air-to-gasoline by weight in the fuel mixture drawn into the engine.

AIR INJECTION: One method of reducing harmful exhaust emissions by injecting air into each of the exhaust ports of an engine. The fresh air entering the hot exhaust manifold causes any remaining fuel to be burned before it can exit the tailpipe.

ALTERNATOR: A device used for converting mechanical energy into electrical energy.

AMMETER: An instrument, calibrated in amperes, used to measure the flow of an electrical current in a circuit. Ammeters are always connected in series with the circuit being tested.

AMPERE: The rate of flow of electrical current present when one volt of electrical pressure is applied against one ohm of electrical resistance.

ANALOG COMPUTER: Any microprocessor that uses similar (analogous) electrical signals to make its calculations.

ARMATURE: A laminated, soft iron core wrapped by a wire that converts electrical energy to mechanical energy as in a motor or relay. When rotated in a magnetic field, it changes mechanical energy into electrical energy as in a generator.

ATMOSPHERIC PRESSURE: The pressure on the Earth's surface caused by the weight of the air in the atmosphere. At sea level, this pressure is 14.7 psi at 32°F (101 kPa at 0°C).

ATOMIZATION: The breaking down of a liquid into a fine mist that can be suspended in air.

AXIAL PLAY: Movement parallel to a shaft or bearing bore.

BACKFIRE: The sudden combustion of gases in the intake or exhaust system that results in a loud explosion.

BACKLASH: The clearance or play between two parts, such as meshed gears.

BACKPRESSURE: Restrictions in the exhaust system that slow the exit of exhaust gases from the combustion chamber.

BAKELITE: A heat resistant, plastic insulator material commonly used in printed circuit boards and transistorized components.

BALL BEARING: A bearing made up of hardened inner and outer races between which hardened steel balls roll.

BALLAST RESISTOR: A resistor in the primary ignition circuit that lowers voltage after the engine is started to reduce wear on ignition components.

BEARING: A friction reducing, supportive device usually located between a stationary part and a moving part.

BIMETAL TEMPERATURE SENSOR: Any sensor or switch made of two dissimilar types of metal that bend when heated or cooled due to the different expansion rates of the alloys. These types of sensors usually function as an on/off switch.

BLOWBY: Combustion gases, composed of water vapor and unburned fuel, that leak past the piston rings into the crankcase during normal engine operation. These gases are removed by the PCV system to prevent the buildup of harmful acids in the crankcase.

BRAKE PAD: A brake shoe and lining assembly used with disc brakes.

BRAKE SHOE: The backing for the brake lining. The term is, however, usually applied to the assembly of the brake backing and lining.

BUSHING: A liner, usually removable, for a bearing; an anti-friction liner used in place of a bearing.

CALIPER: A hydraulically activated device in a disc brake system, which is mounted straddling the brake rotor (disc). The caliper contains at least one piston and two brake pads. Hydraulic pressure on the piston(s) forces the pads against the rotor.

CAMSHAFT: A shaft in the engine on which are the lobes (cams) which operate the valves. The camshaft is driven by the crankshaft, via a belt, chain or gears, at one half the crankshaft speed.

CAPACITOR: A device which stores an electrical charge.

CARBON MONOXIDE (CO): A colorless, odorless gas given off as a normal byproduct of combustion. It is poisonous and extremely dangerous in confined areas, building up slowly to toxic levels without warning if adequate ventilation is not available.

CARBURETOR: A device, usually mounted on the intake manifold of an engine, which mixes the air and fuel in the proper proportion to allow even combustion.

CATALYTIC CONVERTER: A device installed in the exhaust system, like a muffler, that converts harmful byproducts of combustion into carbon dioxide and water vapor by means of a heat-producing chemical reaction.

CENTRIFUGAL ADVANCE: A mechanical method of advancing the spark timing by using flyweights in the distributor that react to centrifugal force generated by the distributor shaft rotation.

CHECK VALVE: Any one-way valve installed to permit the flow of air, fuel or vacuum in one direction only.

CHOKE: A device, usually a moveable valve, placed in the intake path of a carburetor to restrict the flow of air.

CIRCUIT: Any unbroken path through which an electrical current can flow. Also used to describe fuel flow in some instances.

CIRCUIT BREAKER: A switch which protects an electrical circuit from overload by opening the circuit when the current flow exceeds a predetermined level. Some circuit breakers must be reset manually, while most reset automatically.

COIL (IGNITION): A transformer in the ignition circuit which steps up the voltage provided to the spark plugs.

COMBINATION MANIFOLD: An assembly which includes both the intake and exhaust manifolds in one casting.

COMBINATION VALVE: A device used in some fuel systems that routes fuel vapors to a charcoal storage canister instead of venting them into the atmosphere. The valve relieves fuel tank pressure and allows fresh air into the tank as the fuel level drops to prevent a vapor lock situation.

COMPRESSION RATIO: The comparison of the total volume of the cylinder and combustion chamber with the piston at BDC and the piston at TDC.

CONDENSER: 1. An electrical device which acts to store an electrical charge, preventing voltage surges. 2. A radiator-like device in the air conditioning system in which refrigerant gas condenses into a liquid, giving off heat.

CONDUCTOR: Any material through which an electrical current can be transmitted easily.

CONTINUITY: Continuous or complete circuit. Can be checked with an ohmmeter.

COUNTERSHAFT: An intermediate shaft which is rotated by a mainshaft and transmits, in turn, that rotation to a working part.

CRANKCASE: The lower part of an engine in which the crankshaft and related parts operate.

CRANKSHAFT: The main driving shaft of an engine which receives reciprocating motion from the pistons and converts it to rotary motion.

CYLINDER: In an engine, the round hole in the engine block in which the piston(s) ride.

CYLINDER BLOCK: The main structural member of an engine in which is found the cylinders, crankshaft and other principal parts.

CYLINDER HEAD: The detachable portion of the engine, usually fastened to the top of the cylinder block and containing all or most of the combustion chambers. On overhead valve engines, it contains the valves and their operating parts. On overhead cam engines, it contains the camshaft as well.

DEAD CENTER: The extreme top or bottom of the piston stroke.

DETONATION: An unwanted explosion of the air/fuel mixture in the combustion chamber caused by excess heat and compression, advanced timing, or an overly lean mixture. Also referred to as "ping".

DIAPHRAGM: A thin, flexible wall separating two cavities, such as in a vacuum advance unit.

DIESELING: A condition in which hot spots in the combustion chamber cause the engine to run on after the key is turned off.

DIFFERENTIAL: A geared assembly which allows the transmission of motion between drive axles, giving one axle the ability to turn faster than the other.

DIODE: An electrical device that will allow current to flow in one direction only.

DISC BRAKE: A hydraulic braking assembly consisting of a brake disc, or rotor, mounted on an axle, and a caliper assembly containing, usually two brake pads which are activated by hydraulic pressure. The pads are forced against the sides of the disc, creating friction which slows the vehicle.

DISTRIBUTOR: A mechanically driven device on an engine which is responsible for electrically firing the spark plug at a predetermined point of the piston stroke.

DOWEL PIN: A pin, inserted in mating holes in two different parts allowing those parts to maintain a fixed relationship.

DRUM BRAKE: A braking system which consists of two brake shoes and one or two wheel cylinders, mounted on a fixed backing plate, and a brake drum, mounted on an axle, which revolves around the assembly.

DWELL: The rate, measured in degrees of shaft rotation, at which an electrical circuit cycles on and off.

ELECTRONIC CONTROL UNIT (ECU): Ignition module, module, amplifier or igniter. See Module for definition.

ELECTRONIC IGNITION: A system in which the timing and firing of the spark plugs is controlled by an electronic control unit, usually called a module. These systems have no points or condenser.

END-PLAY: The measured amount of axial movement in a shaft.

ENGINE: A device that converts heat into mechanical energy.

EXHAUST MANIFOLD: A set of cast passages or pipes which conduct exhaust gases from the engine.

FEELER GAUGE: A blade, usually metal, or precisely predetermined thickness, used to measure the clearance between two parts.

FIRING ORDER: The order in which combustion occurs in the cylinders of an engine. Also the order in which spark is distributed to the plugs by the distributor.

FLOODING: The presence of too much fuel in the intake manifold and combustion chamber which prevents the air/fuel mixture from firing, thereby causing a no-start situation.

FLYWHEEL: A disc shaped part bolted to the rear end of the crankshaft. Around the outer perimeter is affixed the ring gear. The starter drive engages the ring gear, turning the flywheel, which rotates the crankshaft, imparting the initial starting motion to the engine.

FOOT POUND (ft. lbs. or sometimes, ft.lb.): The amount of energy or work needed to raise an item weighing one pound, a distance of one foot.

FUSE: A protective device in a circuit which prevents circuit overload by breaking the circuit when a specific amperage is present. The device is constructed around a strip or wire of a lower amperage rating than the circuit it is designed to protect. When an amperage higher than that stamped on the fuse is present in the circuit, the strip or wire melts, opening the circuit.

GEAR RATIO: The ratio between the number of teeth on meshing gears.

GENERATOR: A device which converts mechanical energy into electrical energy.

HEAT RANGE: The measure of a spark plug's ability to dissipate heat from its firing end. The higher the heat range, the hotter the plug fires.

HUB: The center part of a wheel or gear.

HYDROCARBON (HC): Any chemical compound made up of hydrogen and carbon. A major pollutant formed by the engine as a byproduct of combustion.

HYDROMETER: An instrument used to measure the specific gravity of a solution.

INCH POUND (inch lbs.; sometimes in.lb. or in. lbs.): One twelfth of a foot pound.

INDUCTION: A means of transferring electrical energy in the form of a magnetic field. Principle used in the ignition coil to increase voltage.

INJECTOR: A device which receives metered fuel under relatively low pressure and is activated to inject the fuel into the engine under relatively high pressure at a predetermined time.

INPUT SHAFT: The shaft to which torque is applied, usually carrying the driving gear or gears.

INTAKE MANIFOLD: A casting of passages or pipes used to conduct air or a fuel/air mixture to the cylinders.

JOURNAL: The bearing surface within which a shaft operates.

KEY: A small block usually fitted in a notch between a shaft and a hub to prevent slippage of the two parts.

MANIFOLD: A casting of passages or set of pipes which connect the cylinders to an inlet or outlet source.

MANIFOLD VACUUM: Low pressure in an engine intake manifold formed just below the throttle plates. Manifold vacuum is highest at idle and drops under acceleration.

MASTER CYLINDER: The primary fluid pressurizing device in a hydraulic system. In automotive use, it is found in brake and hydraulic clutch systems and is pedal activated, either directly or, in a power brake system, through the power booster.

MODULE: Electronic control unit, amplifier or igniter of solid state or integrated design which controls the current flow in the ignition primary circuit based on input from the pick-up coil. When the module opens the primary circuit, high secondary voltage is induced in the coil.

NEEDLE BEARING: A bearing which consists of a number (usually a large number) of long, thin rollers.

OHM: (Ω) The unit used to measure the resistance of conductor-to-electrical flow. One ohm is the amount of resistance that limits current flow to one ampere in a circuit with one volt of pressure.

OHMMETER: An instrument used for measuring the resistance, in ohms, in an electrical circuit.

OUTPUT SHAFT: The shaft which transmits torque from a device, such as a transmission.

OVERDRIVE: A gear assembly which produces more shaft revolutions than that transmitted to it.

OVERHEAD CAMSHAFT (OHC): An engine configuration in which the camshaft is mounted on top of the cylinder head and operates the valve either directly or by means of rocker arms.

OVERHEAD VALVE (OHV): An engine configuration in which all of the valves are located in the cylinder head and the camshaft is located in the cylinder block. The camshaft operates the valves via lifters and pushrods.

OXIDES OF NITROGEN (NOx): Chemical compounds of nitrogen produced as a byproduct of combustion. They combine with hydrocarbons to produce smog.

OXYGEN SENSOR: Use with the feedback system to sense the presence of oxygen in the exhaust gas and signal the computer which can reference the voltage signal to an air/fuel ratio.

PINION: The smaller of two meshing gears.

PISTON RING: An open-ended ring with fits into a groove on the outer diameter of the piston. Its chief function is to form a seal between the piston and cylinder wall. Most automotive pistons have three rings: two for compression sealing; one for oil sealing.

PRELOAD: A predetermined load placed on a bearing during assembly or by adjustment.

PRIMARY CIRCUIT: the low voltage side of the ignition system which consists of the ignition switch, ballast resistor or resistance wire, bypass, coil, electronic control unit and pick-up coil as well as the connecting wires and harnesses.

PRESS FIT: The mating of two parts under pressure, due to the inner diameter of one being smaller than the outer diameter of the other, or vice versa; an interference fit.

RACE: The surface on the inner or outer ring of a bearing on which the balls, needles or rollers move.

REGULATOR: A device which maintains the amperage and/or voltage levels of a circuit at predetermined values.

RELAY: A switch which automatically opens and/or closes a circuit.

RESISTANCE: The opposition to the flow of current through a circuit or electrical device, and is measured in ohms. Resistance is equal to the voltage divided by the amperage.

RESISTOR: A device, usually made of wire, which offers a preset amount of resistance in an electrical circuit.

RING GEAR: The name given to a ring-shaped gear attached to a differential case, or affixed to a flywheel or as part of a planetary gear set.

ROLLER BEARING: A bearing made up of hardened inner and outer races between which hardened steel rollers move.

ROTOR: 1. The disc-shaped part of a disc brake assembly, upon which the brake pads bear; also called, brake disc. 2. The device mounted atop the distributor shaft, which passes current to the distributor cap tower contacts.

SECONDARY CIRCUIT: The high voltage side of the ignition system, usually above 20,000 volts. The secondary includes the ignition coil, coil wire, distributor cap and rotor, spark plug wires and spark plugs.

SENDING UNIT: A mechanical, electrical, hydraulic or electro-magnetic device which transmits information to a gauge.

SENSOR: Any device designed to measure engine operating conditions or ambient pressures and temperatures. Usually electronic in nature and designed to send a voltage signal to an on-board computer, some sensors may operate as a simple on/off switch or they may provide a variable voltage signal (like a potentiometer) as conditions or measured parameters change.

SHIM: Spacers of precise, predetermined thickness used between parts to establish a proper working relationship.

SLAVE CYLINDER: In automotive use, a device in the hydraulic clutch system which is activated by hydraulic force, disengaging the clutch.

SOLENOID: A coil used to produce a magnetic field, the effect of which is to produce work.

SPARK PLUG: A device screwed into the combustion chamber of a spark ignition engine. The basic construction is a conductive core inside of a ceramic insulator, mounted in an outer conductive base. An electrical charge from the spark plug wire travels along the conductive core and jumps a preset air gap to a grounding point or points at the end of the conductive base. The resultant spark ignites the fuel/air mixture in the combustion chamber.

SPLINES: Ridges machined or cast onto the outer diameter of a shaft or inner diameter of a bore to enable parts to mate without rotation.

TACHOMETER: A device used to measure the rotary speed of an engine, shaft, gear, etc., usually in rotations per minute.

THERMOSTAT: A valve, located in the cooling system of an engine, which is closed when cold and opens gradually in response to engine heating, controlling the temperature of the coolant and rate of coolant flow.

TOP DEAD CENTER (TDC): The point at which the piston reaches the top of its travel on the compression stroke.

TORQUE: The twisting force applied to an object.

TORQUE CONVERTER: A turbine used to transmit power from a driving member to a driven member via hydraulic action, providing changes in drive ratio and torque. In automotive use, it links the driveplate at the rear of the engine to the automatic transmission.

TRANSDUCER: A device used to change a force into an electrical signal.

TRANSISTOR: A semi-conductor component which can be actuated by a small voltage to perform an electrical switching function.

TUNE-UP: A regular maintenance function, usually associated with the replacement and adjustment of parts and components in the electrical and fuel systems of a vehicle for the purpose of attaining optimum performance.

TURBOCHARGER: An exhaust driven pump which compresses intake air and forces it into the combustion chambers at higher than atmospheric pressures. The increased air pressure allows more fuel to be burned and results in increased horsepower being produced.

VACUUM ADVANCE: A device which advances the ignition timing in response to increased engine vacuum.

VACUUM GAUGE: An instrument used to measure the presence of vacuum in a chamber.

VALVE: A device which control the pressure, direction of flow or rate of flow of a liquid or gas.

VALVE CLEARANCE: The measured gap between the end of the valve stem and the rocker arm, cam lobe or follower that activates the valve.

VISCOSITY: The rating of a liquid's internal resistance to flow.

VOLTMETER: An instrument used for measuring electrical force in units called volts. Voltmeters are always connected parallel with the circuit being tested.

WHEEL CYLINDER: Found in the automotive drum brake assembly, it is a device, actuated by hydraulic pressure, which, through internal pistons, pushes the brake shoes outward against the drums.

ABS CONTROL MODULE   9-25
   REMOVAL & INSTALLATION   9-25
ABS HYDRAULIC MODULATOR ASSEMBLY BLEEDER VALVES   9-24
   REMOVAL & INSTALLATION   9-24
ABS HYDRAULIC MODULATOR/MASTER CYLINDER
 ASSEMBLY   9-24
   REMOVAL & INSTALLATION   9-24
ABS HYDRAULIC MODULATOR SOLENOID   9-26
   REMOVAL & INSTALLATION   9-26
ABS LAMP DRIVER MODULE   9-24
   REMOVAL & INSTALLATION   9-24
ABS SERVICE   9-23
   PRECAUTIONS   9-23
ACTUATOR (SLAVE) CYLINDER   7-26
   HYDRAULIC SYSTEM BLEEDING   7-26
   REMOVAL & INSTALLATION   7-26
ADJUSTMENTS   7-2
   LINKAGE   7-2
AIR CLEANER   1-17
   REMOVAL & INSTALLATION   1-17
AIR CONDITIONING COMPONENTS   6-11
   REMOVAL & INSTALLATION   6-11
AIR CONDITIONING SYSTEM   1-31
   PREVENTIVE MAINTENANCE   1-31
   SYSTEM INSPECTION   1-32
   SYSTEM SERVICE & REPAIR   1-31
AIR POLLUTION   4-2
ALTERNATOR   2-12
   DIAGNOSIS   2-12
   REMOVAL & INSTALLATION   2-13
ALTERNATOR PRECAUTIONS   2-12
ANTENNA   10-6
   REPLACEMENT   10-6
ANTI-LOCK BRAKE SYSTEM (ABS)   9-19
AUTOMATIC TRANSAXLE   7-27
AUTOMATIC TRANSAXLE (FLUIDS AND LUBRICANTS)   1-39
   DRAIN & REFILL (INCLUDES PAN & FILTER SERVICE)   1-40
   FLUID RECOMMENDATION   1-39
   LEVEL CHECK   1-39
AUTOMATIC TRANSAXLE ASSEMBLY   7-29
   ADJUSTMENTS   7-32
   REMOVAL & INSTALLATION   7-29
AUTOMOTIVE EMISSIONS   4-3
AUTOMOTIVE POLLUTANTS   4-2
   HEAT TRANSFER   4-2
   TEMPERATURE INVERSION   4-2
AVOIDING THE MOST COMMON MISTAKES   1-2
AVOIDING TROUBLE   1-2
BACK-UP LIGHT SWITCH   7-3
   REMOVAL & INSTALLATION   7-3
BASIC ELECTRICAL THEORY   6-2
   HOW DOES ELECTRICITY WORK: THE WATER ANALOGY   6-2
   OHM'S LAW   6-2
BASIC FUEL SYSTEM DIAGNOSIS   5-2
BASIC OPERATING PRINCIPLES   9-2
   DISC BRAKES   9-2
   DRUM BRAKES   9-2
   POWER BOOSTERS   9-3
BATTERY   1-20
   BATTERY FLUID   1-20
   CABLES   1-21
   CHARGING   1-22
   GENERAL MAINTENANCE   1-20
   PRECAUTIONS   1-20
   REPLACEMENT   1-22
BATTERY CABLES   6-7
BLEEDING THE BRAKE SYSTEM   9-8
   MANUAL BLEEDING   9-8
   PRESSURE BLEEDING   9-9
BLOWER MOTOR   6-9
   REMOVAL & INSTALLATION   6-9

MASTER

INDEX

BLOWER SWITCH 6-11
    REMOVAL & INSTALLATION 6-11
BODY LUBRICATION 1-44
    ACCELERATOR LINKAGE 1-45
    DOOR HINGES 1-44
    HOOD LATCH & HINGES 1-44
    PARKING BRAKE LINKAGE 1-45
    TRANSAXLE SHIFT LINKAGE 1-44
BOLTS, NUTS AND OTHER THREADED RETAINERS 1-7
BOTTOM FEED PORT (BFP) INJECTION SYSTEM 5-18
BOTTOM FEED PORT FUEL INJECTORS 5-19
    REMOVAL & INSTALLATION 5-19
BRAKE CALIPER 9-10
    OVERHAUL 9-12
    REMOVAL & INSTALLATION 9-11
BRAKE DISC (ROTOR) 9-12
    INSPECTION 9-13
    REMOVAL & INSTALLATION 9-12
BRAKE DRUMS 9-13
    INSPECTION 9-14
    REMOVAL & INSTALLATION 9-13
BRAKE HOSES AND PIPES 9-7
    REMOVAL & INSTALLATION 9-7
BRAKE LIGHT SWITCH 9-5
    REMOVAL & INSTALLATION 9-5
BRAKE MASTER CYLINDER 1-42
    FLUID RECOMMENDATION 1-42
    LEVEL CHECK 1-43
BRAKE OPERATING SYSTEM 9-2
BRAKE PADS 9-9
    INSPECTION 9-10
    REMOVAL & INSTALLATION 9-9
BRAKE SHOES 9-14
    ADJUSTMENT 9-15
    INSPECTION 9-14
    REMOVAL & INSTALLATION 9-14
BRAKE SPECIFICATIONS 9-28
BUY OR REBUILD? 3-56
CABLES 9-18
    ADJUSTMENT 9-19
    REMOVAL & INSTALLATION 9-18
CAMSHAFT 3-49
    BEARING REPLACEMENT 3-50
    REMOVAL & INSTALLATION 3-49
CAMSHAFT CARRIER COVER 3-15
    REMOVAL & INSTALLATION 3-15
CAMSHAFT POSITION (CMP) SENSOR (ELECTRONIC ENGINE
    CONTROLS) 4-17
    OPERATION 4-17
    REMOVAL & INSTALLATION 4-17
CAMSHAFT POSITION SENSOR (DIRECT IGNITION SYSTEM AND
    ELECTRONIC IGNITION SYSTEMS) 2-10
CAMSHAFT SPECIFICATIONS 3-2
CAMSHAFT SPROCKET 3-47
    REMOVAL & INSTALLATION 3-47
CAPACITIES 1-50
CARBURETED FUEL SYSTEM 5-2
CARBURETOR 5-3
    ADJUSTMENTS 5-3
    MODEL IDENTIFICATION 5-3
    OVERHAUL 5-6
    PRELIMINARY CHECKS 5-3
    REMOVAL & INSTALLATION 5-5
CHARGING SYSTEM 2-20
CHARGING SYSTEM 2-11
CHASSIS GREASING 1-44
CIRCUIT BREAKERS 6-28
    REPLACEMENT 6-28

CIRCUIT PROTECTION 6-27
CLEARING CODES 4-21
CLUTCH 7-23
CLUTCH HYDRAULIC SYSTEM 7-24
    REMOVAL & INSTALLATION 7-24
CLUTCH MASTER CYLINDER (CLUTCH) 7-25
    REMOVAL & INSTALLATION 7-25
CLUTCH MASTER CYLINDER (FLUIDS AND LUBRICANTS) 1-43
    FLUID RECOMMENDATIONS 1-43
    LEVEL CHECK 1-43
CLUTCH SWITCH 7-2
    REMOVAL & INSTALLATION 7-2
COIL SPRINGS 8-14
    REMOVAL & INSTALLATION 8-14
COMPONENT LOCATIONS
    FRONT SUSPENSION COMPONENT LOCATIONS 8-4
    REAR SUSPENSION COMPONENT LOCATIONS 8-13
    UNDERHOOD COMPONENT LOCATIONS 1-16
CONSOLE 10-11
    REMOVAL & INSTALLATION 10-11
CONTROL ARM/SUSPENSION SUPPORT 8-10
    CONTROL ARM BUSHING REPLACEMENT 8-11
    REMOVAL & INSTALLATION 8-10
CONTROL PANEL 6-12
    REMOVAL & INSTALLATION 6-12
CONVERTIBLE TOP 10-6
    MOTOR REPLACEMENT 10-9
    TOP REPLACEMENT 10-6
COOLANT TEMPERATURE SENDING UNIT 2-18
    REMOVAL & INSTALLATION 2-18
COOLING 1-45
    ENGINE 1-45
    TRANSMISSION 1-45
COOLING SYSTEM 1-40
    DRAIN & REFILL 1-42
    FLUID RECOMMENDATIONS 1-41
    FLUSHING & CLEANING THE SYSTEM 1-42
    LEVEL CHECK 1-41
CRANKCASE EMISSIONS 4-4
CRANKCASE VENTILATION SYSTEM 4-4
    OPERATION 4-4
    REMOVAL & INSTALLATION 4-5
    TESTING 4-5
CRANKSHAFT AND CONNECTING ROD SPECIFICATIONS 3-3
CRANKSHAFT POSITION (CKP) SENSOR (ELECTRONIC ENGINE
    CONTROLS) 4-17
    OPERATION 4-17
    REMOVAL & INSTALLATION 4-17
    TESTING 4-17
CRANKSHAFT POSITION SENSOR (DIRECT IGNITION SYSTEM AND
    ELECTRONIC IGNITION SYSTEMS) 2-10
CRANKSHAFT SPROCKET 3-48
    REMOVAL & INSTALLATION 3-48
CRUISE CONTROL 6-14
CRUISE CONTROL 6-13
CV-BOOT 1-24
    INSPECTION 1-24
CYLINDER HEAD (ENGINE MECHANICAL) 3-32
    REMOVAL & INSTALLATION 3-32
CYLINDER HEAD (ENGINE RECONDITIONING) 3-58
    ASSEMBLY 3-64
    DISASSEMBLY 3-59
    INSPECTION 3-62
    REFINISHING & REPAIRING 3-63
DESCRIPTION AND OPERATION (ANTI-LOCK BRAKE SYSTEM) 9-19
    BASIC KNOWLEDGE REQUIRED 9-19
    ENHANCED DIAGNOSTICS 9-20
    ONBOARD DIAGNOSTICS 9-20

DESCRIPTION AND OPERATION (CHARGING SYSTEM)   2-11
DESCRIPTION AND OPERATION (STARTING SYSTEM)   2-15
DETERMINING ENGINE CONDITION   3-55
   COMPRESSION TEST   3-55
   OIL PRESSURE TEST   3-56
DIAGNOSIS AND TESTING (DIRECT IGNITION SYSTEM AND ELECTRONIC
  IGNITION SYSTEMS)   2-9
   EST PERFORMANCE   2-9
   SYSTEM PERFORMANCE   2-9
DIAGNOSIS AND TESTING (HIGH ENERGY IGNITION SYSTEM)   2-2
   ELECTRONIC SPARK CONTROL (ESC) SYSTEM   2-4
   ELECTRONIC SPARK TIMING (EST) SYSTEM   2-3
   HALL EFFECT SWITCH   2-3
   IGNITION MODULE   2-3
   PICK-UP COIL   2-3
   SECONDARY SPARK   2-3
DIAGNOSIS AND TESTING (TROUBLE CODES)   4-19
   TROUBLESHOOTING   4-19
DIAGNOSTIC PROCEDURES   9-20
   CLEARING CODES   9-22
   DISPLAYING CODES   9-22
   INTERMITTENT FAILURES   9-23
   INTERMITTENTS AND POOR CONNECTIONS   9-23
DIRECT IGNITION SYSTEM (DIS) AND ELECTRONIC IGNITION (EI)
  SYSTEMS   2-7
DISC BRAKES   9-9
DISCONNECTING THE CABLES   6-7
DISTRIBUTOR   2-6
   INSTALLATION IF THE ENGINE WAS DISTURBED   2-7
   REMOVAL & INSTALLATION   2-6
DISTRIBUTOR CAP AND ROTOR   1-27
   INSPECTION   1-27
   REMOVAL & INSTALLATION   1-27
DO'S   1-6
DON'TS   1-6
DOOR LOCKS   10-14
   REMOVAL & INSTALLATION   10-14
DOOR PANEL   10-12
   REMOVAL & INSTALLATION   10-12
DOORS   10-2
   ADJUSTMENTS   10-2
   REMOVAL & INSTALLATION   10-2
DRIVEN DISC AND PRESSURE PLATE/CLUTCH COVER AND
  DISC   7-23
   ADJUSTMENTS   7-24
   REMOVAL & INSTALLATION   7-23
E2SE CARBURETOR   5-10
ELECTRIC COOLING FAN   3-31
   REMOVAL & INSTALLATION   3-31
ELECTRICAL COMPONENTS   6-2
   CONNECTORS   6-4
   GROUND   6-3
   LOAD   6-3
   POWER SOURCE   6-2
   PROTECTIVE DEVICES   6-3
   SWITCHES & RELAYS   6-3
   WIRING & HARNESSES   6-3
ELECTRICAL CONNECTORS   9-23
ELECTRONIC ENGINE CONTROLS   4-11
EMISSION CONTROLS   4-4
ENABLE RELAY   9-24
   REMOVAL & INSTALLATION   9-24
ENGINE (ENGINE MECHANICAL)   3-7
   REMOVAL & INSTALLATION   3-7
ENGINE (FLUIDS AND LUBRICANTS)   1-37
   OIL & FILTER CHANGE   1-37
   OIL LEVEL CHECK   1-37

ENGINE (SERIAL NUMBER IDENTIFICATION)   1-11
ENGINE BLOCK   3-65
   ASSEMBLY   3-68
   DISASSEMBLY   3-65
   GENERAL INFORMATION   3-65
   INSPECTION   3-66
   REFINISHING   3-68
ENGINE COOLANT TEMPERATURE (ECT) SENSOR   4-14
   OPERATION   4-14
   REMOVAL & INSTALLATION   4-14
   TESTING   4-14
ENGINE IDENTIFICATION   1-14
ENGINE MECHANICAL   3-2
ENGINE OVERHAUL TIPS   3-56
   CLEANING   3-57
   OVERHAUL TIPS   3-57
   REPAIRING DAMAGED THREADS   3-57
   TOOLS   3-56
ENGINE/POWERTRAIN CONTROL MODULE (ECM/PCM)   4-11
   FUNCTIONAL CHECK   4-12
   OPERATION   4-11
   REMOVAL & INSTALLATION   4-12
ENGINE PREPARATION   3-58
ENGINE RECONDITIONING   3-55
ENGINE START-UP AND BREAK-IN   3-71
   BREAKING IT IN   3-71
   KEEP IT MAINTAINED   3-71
   STARTING THE ENGINE   3-71
ENTERTAINMENT SYSTEMS   6-14
EVAPORATIVE CANISTER   1-19
   FUNCTIONAL TEST   1-20
EVAPORATIVE EMISSION CONTROL SYSTEM   4-5
   OPERATION   4-5
   REMOVAL & INSTALLATION   4-6
   TESTING   4-6
EVAPORATIVE EMISSIONS   4-4
EXHAUST GAS RECIRCULATION (EGR) SYSTEM   4-6
   OPERATION   4-6
   REMOVAL & INSTALLATION   4-8
   TESTING   4-8
EXHAUST GASES   4-3
   CARBON MONOXIDE   4-3
   HYDROCARBONS   4-3
   NITROGEN   4-3
   OXIDES OF SULFUR   4-3
   PARTICULATE MATTER   4-3
EXHAUST MANIFOLD   3-25
   REMOVAL & INSTALLATION   3-25
EXHAUST SYSTEM   3-52
EXTERIOR   10-2
FASTENERS, MEASUREMENTS AND CONVERSIONS   1-7
FENDERS   10-6
   REMOVAL & INSTALLATION   10-6
FILLING AND BLEEDING   9-26
   BLEEDING THE ABS HYDRAULIC SYSTEM   9-26
   SYSTEM FILLING   9-26
FIRING ORDERS   2-10
FLASHERS   6-29
   REPLACEMENT   6-29
FLUID DISPOSAL   1-36
FLUID LEVEL SENSOR   9-24
   REMOVAL & INSTALLATION   9-24
FLUID PAN AND FILTER   7-28
FLUIDS AND LUBRICANTS   1-36
FOG LAMPS   6-26
   REMOVAL & INSTALLATION   6-26
FRONT AND REAR WHEELS   8-2

INSPECTION 8-3
  REMOVAL & INSTALLATION 8-2
FRONT DOOR GLASS 10-14
  REMOVAL & INSTALLATION 10-14
FRONT HUB AND BEARING 8-11
  REMOVAL & INSTALLATION 8-11
FRONT SEAT 10-17
  REMOVAL & INSTALLATION 10-17
FRONT SUSPENSION 8-4
FRONT SUSPENSION COMPONENT LOCATIONS 8-4
FRONT WINDOW REGULATOR AND MOTOR 10-15
  REMOVAL & INSTALLATION 10-15
FUEL AND ENGINE OIL RECOMMENDATIONS 1-36
  ENGINE OIL 1-36
  FUEL 1-36
FUEL FILTER 1-17
  REMOVAL & INSTALLATION 1-17
FUEL INJECTOR (MODEL 300 AND 500 THROTTLE BODY INJECTION
  SYSTEMS) 5-12
  REMOVAL & INSTALLATION 5-12
FUEL INJECTOR (MODEL 700 THROTTLE BODY INJECTION
  SYSTEM) 5-16
  REMOVAL & INSTALLATION 5-16
FUEL INJECTORS (MULTI-PORT & SEQUENTIAL FUEL INJECTION
  SYSTEMS) 5-23
  REMOVAL & INSTALLATION 5-23
FUEL LINES AND FITTINGS 5-2
FUEL METER BODY 5-13
  REMOVAL & INSTALLATION 5-13
FUEL METER COVER 5-13
  REMOVAL & INSTALLATION 5-13
FUEL PRESSURE REGULATOR (BOTTOM FEED PORT INJECTION
  SYSTEM) 5-20
  REMOVAL & INSTALLATION 5-20
FUEL PRESSURE REGULATOR (MODEL 700 THROTTLE BODY INJECTION
  SYSTEM) 5-17
  REMOVAL & INSTALLATION 5-17
FUEL PRESSURE REGULATOR (MULTI-PORT & SEQUENTIAL FUEL
  INJECTION SYSTEMS) 5-24
  REMOVAL & INSTALLATION 5-24
FUEL PRESSURE REGULATOR/COMPENSATOR (MODEL 300 AND 500
  THROTTLE BODY INJECTION SYSTEMS) 5-13
  REMOVAL & INSTALLATION 5-13
FUEL PRESSURE RELEASE 5-2
FUEL PUMP (MODEL 300 AND 500 THROTTLE BODY INJECTION
  SYSTEMS) 5-11
  REMOVAL & INSTALLATION 5-11
  TESTING 5-11
FUEL PUMP (MODEL 700 THROTTLE BODY INJECTION
  SYSTEM) 5-15
  REMOVAL & INSTALLATION 5-15
  TESTING 5-15
FUEL PUMP (MULTI-PORT & SEQUENTIAL FUEL INJECTION
  SYSTEMS) 5-21
  REMOVAL & INSTALLATION 5-21
  TESTING 5-21
FUEL RAIL ASSEMBLY 5-25
  REMOVAL & INSTALLATION 5-25
FUEL SYSTEM PRESSURE RELEASE 5-14
  2.0L OHC ENGINE 5-15
  2.0L AND 2.2L OHV ENGINES 5-14
FUEL SYSTEM PRESSURE RELIEF 5-18
  1992 VEHICLES 5-18
  1993-94 VEHICLES 5-19
FUEL TANK 5-27
FUSE PANELS 6-29
FUSES 6-27
  REPLACEMENT 6-28

FUSIBLE LINKS 6-28
  REPLACEMENT 6-28
GENERAL DESCRIPTION 6-13
GENERAL ENGINE SPECIFICATIONS 3-2
GENERAL INFORMATION (DIRECT IGNITION SYSTEM AND ELECTRONIC
  IGNITION SYSTEMS) 2-7
  SYSTEM COMPONENTS 2-8
GENERAL INFORMATION (ELECTRONIC ENGINE CONTROLS) 4-11
GENERAL INFORMATION (HIGH ENERGY IGNITION SYSTEM) 2-2
  HEI SYSTEM PRECAUTIONS 2-2
GENERAL INFORMATION (MULTI-PORT & SEQUENTIAL FUEL INJECTION
  SYSTEMS) 5-20
GENERAL INFORMATION (SUPPLEMENTAL INFLATABLE RESTRAINT
  SYSTEM) 6-7
  DISABLING THE SYSTEM 6-9
  ENABLING THE SYSTEM 6-9
  SERVICE PRECAUTIONS 6-8
  SYSTEM COMPONENTS 6-8
  SYSTEM OPERATION 6-7
GENERAL INFORMATION (TROUBLE CODES) 4-18
  DASHBOARD WARNING LAMP 4-19
  LEARNING ABILITY 4-19
GENERAL RECOMMENDATIONS 1-45
GRILLE 10-4
  REMOVAL & INSTALLATION 10-4
HALFSHAFTS (AUTOMATIC TRANSAXLE) 7-32
HALFSHAFTS (MANUAL TRANSAXLE) 7-10
  CV-JOINT OVERHAUL 7-12
  REMOVAL & INSTALLATION 7-10
HALL EFFECT SWITCH 2-6
  REMOVAL & INSTALLATION 2-6
HANDLING A TRAILER 1-45
HATCHBACK ASSEMBLY 10-3
  ADJUSTMENTS 10-4
  REMOVAL & INSTALLATION 10-3
HEADLIGHT SWITCH 6-21
  REMOVAL & INSTALLATION 6-21
HEADLIGHTS 6-22
  HEADLIGHT AIMING 6-23
  REMOVAL & INSTALLATION 6-22
HEATER CORE 6-11
  REMOVAL & INSTALLATION 6-11
HEATING AND AIR CONDITIONING 6-9
HIGH ENERGY IGNITION (HEI) SYSTEM 2-2
HITCH WEIGHT 1-45
HOOD 10-2
  ALIGNMENT 10-3
  REMOVAL & INSTALLATION 10-2
HOSES 1-23
  INSPECTION 1-23
  REMOVAL & INSTALLATION 1-23
HOW TO USE THIS BOOK 1-2
IDLE AIR CONTROL (IAC) VALVE 4-13
  OPERATION 4-13
  REMOVAL & INSTALLATION 4-14
IDLE SPEED AND MIXTURE ADJUSTMENTS 1-29
  CARBURETED ENGINES 1-29
  FUEL INJECTED ENGINES 1-29
IGNITION COIL 2-4
  REMOVAL & INSTALLATION 2-4
  TESTING 2-4
IGNITION COIL ASSEMBLY 2-9
  REMOVAL & INSTALLATION 2-9
IGNITION LOCK CYLINDER 8-21
  REMOVAL & INSTALLATION 8-21
IGNITION MODULE (DIRECT IGNITION SYSTEM AND ELECTRONIC
  IGNITION SYSTEMS) 2-9
  REMOVAL & INSTALLATION 2-9

IGNITION MODULE (HIGH ENERGY IGNITION SYSTEM) 2-6
    REMOVAL & INSTALLATION 2-6
IGNITION SWITCH (INSTRUMENTS AND SWITCHES) 6-22
IGNITION SWITCH (STEERING) 8-19
    REMOVAL & INSTALLATION 8-19
IGNITION TIMING 1-28
    GENERAL INFORMATION 1-28
    INSPECTION & ADJUSTMENT 1-29
INDUSTRIAL POLLUTANTS 4-2
INSIDE REAR VIEW MIRROR 10-17
    REPLACEMENT 10-17
INSPECTION 3-52
    REPLACEMENT 3-54
INSTRUMENT CLUSTER 6-19
    REMOVAL & INSTALLATION 6-19
INSTRUMENT PANEL AND PAD 10-10
    REMOVAL & INSTALLATION 10-10
INSTRUMENTS AND SWITCHES 6-19
INTAKE MANIFOLD 3-20
    REMOVAL & INSTALLATION 3-20
INTERIOR 10-10
INTERMEDIATE SHAFT 7-8
    REMOVAL & INSTALLATION 7-8
JACKING 1-47
JUMP STARTING A DEAD BATTERY 1-46
JUMP STARTING PRECAUTIONS 1-46
JUMP STARTING PROCEDURE 1-46
KNOCK SENSOR (KS) 4-18
    OPERATION 4-18
    REMOVAL & INSTALLATION 4-18
LIFT GATE (STATION WAGON) 10-4
    REMOVAL & INSTALLATION 10-4
LIGHTING 6-22
LOWER BALL JOINT 8-8
    INSPECTION 8-8
    REMOVAL & INSTALLATION 8-8
MACPHERSON STRUTS 8-5
    OVERHAUL 8-6
    REMOVAL & INSTALLATION 8-5
MAINTENANCE INTERVALS 1-48
MAINTENANCE OR REPAIR? 1-2
MANIFOLD ABSOLUTE PRESSURE (MAP) SENSOR 4-16
    OPERATION 4-16
    REMOVAL & INSTALLATION 4-16
    TESTING 4-16
MANIFOLD AIR TEMPERATURE (MAT)/INTAKE AIR TEMPERATURE (IAT)
  SENSOR 4-15
    OPERATION 4-15
    REMOVAL & INSTALLATION 4-15
    TESTING 4-15
MANUAL TRANSAXLE 7-2
MANUAL TRANSAXLE (FLUIDS AND LUBRICANTS) 1-38
    DRAIN & REFILL 1-38
    FLUID RECOMMENDATIONS 1-38
    LEVEL CHECK 1-38
MASTER CYLINDER 9-5
    REMOVAL & INSTALLATION 9-5
MECHANICAL FUEL PUMP 5-2
    REMOVAL & INSTALLATION 5-2
    TESTING 5-3
**MODEL 300 AND 500 THROTTLE BODY (TBI) INJECTION
  SYSTEMS 5-10**
MODEL 700 THROTTLE BODY INJECTION (TBI) SYSTEM 5-14
**MULTI-PORT (MFI) & SEQUENTIAL (SFI) FUEL INJECTION
  SYSTEMS 5-20**
NATURAL POLLUTANTS 4-2
NEUTRAL START/BACK-UP LIGHT SWITCH 7-28
    REMOVAL & INSTALLATION 7-28

OIL PAN 3-38
    REMOVAL & INSTALLATION 3-38
OIL PRESSURE SWITCH 2-18
    REMOVAL & INSTALLATION 2-18
OIL PUMP 3-41
    REMOVAL & INSTALLATION 3-41
OUTSIDE MIRRORS 10-5
    REMOVAL & INSTALLATION 10-5
OXYGEN (O2) SENSOR 4-13
    OPERATION 4-13
    REMOVAL & INSTALLATION 4-13
    TESTING 4-13
PARKING BRAKE 9-18
PCV VALVE 1-18
    REMOVAL & INSTALLATION 1-18
PICK-UP COIL 2-5
    REMOVAL & INSTALLATION 2-5
PISTON AND RING SPECIFICATIONS 3-5
POWER BRAKE BOOSTER 9-5
    REMOVAL & INSTALLATION 9-5
POWER SEAT MOTORS 10-19
    REMOVAL & INSTALLATION 10-19
POWER STEERING PUMP (FLUIDS AND LUBRICANTS) 1-43
    FLUID RECOMMENDATIONS 1-43
    LEVEL CHECK 1-43
POWER STEERING PUMP (STEERING) 8-23
    REMOVAL & INSTALLATION 8-23
    SYSTEM BLEEDING 8-24
PROPORTIONING VALVES AND FAILURE WARNING
  SWITCH 9-6
    REMOVAL & INSTALLATION 9-6
QUICK-CONNECT FITTINGS 5-2
    REMOVAL & INSTALLATION 5-2
RACK AND PINION UNIT 8-23
    REMOVAL & INSTALLATION 8-23
RADIATOR 3-29
    REMOVAL & INSTALLATION 3-29
RADIATOR FAN TEMPERATURE SWITCH 2-18
    REMOVAL & INSTALLATION 2-18
RADIO RECEIVER/TAPE PLAYER/CD PLAYER 6-14
    REMOVAL & INSTALLATION 6-14
READING CODES 4-20
REAR AXLE/CONTROL ARM 8-15
    REMOVAL & INSTALLATION 8-16
REAR DOOR GLASS 10-15
    REMOVAL & INSTALLATION 10-15
REAR DRUM BRAKES 9-13
REAR HUB AND BEARING 8-16
    REMOVAL & INSTALLATION 8-16
REAR MAIN SEAL 3-50
    REMOVAL & INSTALLATION 3-50
REAR SEAT CUSHION 10-19
    REMOVAL & INSTALLATION 10-19
REAR SUSPENSION 8-13
REAR SUSPENSION COMPONENT LOCATIONS 8-13
REAR WINDOW REGULATOR 10-16
    REMOVAL & INSTALLATION 10-16
REAR WINDOW WIPER MOTOR 6-18
    REMOVAL & INSTALLATION 6-18
REGULATOR 2-14
    REMOVAL & INSTALLATION 2-14
RELIEVING FUEL SYSTEM PRESSURE (MODEL 300 AND 500 THROTTLE
  BODY INJECTION SYSTEMS) 5-10
    1985-86 2.0L (OHV) 5-10
    EXCEPT 1985-86 2.0L (OHV) ENGINES 5-10
RELIEVING FUEL SYSTEM PRESSURE (MULTI-PORT & SEQUENTIAL
  FUEL INJECTION SYSTEMS) 5-21
    1.8L AND 2.0L OHC ENGINES 5-21

1992 2.0L (VIN H) ENGINES 5-21
2.8L AND 3.1L ENGINES 5-21
ROCKER ARM (VALVE) COVER 3-13
   REMOVAL & INSTALLATION 3-13
ROCKER ARMS AND PUSHRODS 3-16
   REMOVAL & INSTALLATION 3-16
ROUTINE MAINTENANCE 1-15
SENDING UNITS AND SENSORS 2-18
SERIAL NUMBER IDENTIFICATION 1-11
SERPENTINE DRIVE BELTS 1-23
   INSPECTION & ADJUSTMENT 1-23
   REMOVAL & INSTALLATION 1-23
SERVICING YOUR VEHICLE SAFELY 1-6
SHOCK ABSORBERS 8-15
   REMOVAL & INSTALLATION 8-15
   TESTING 8-15
SIGNAL AND MARKER LIGHTS 6-25
   REMOVAL & INSTALLATION 6-25
SPARK PLUG WIRES 1-27
   REMOVAL & INSTALLATION 1-27
   TESTING 1-27
SPARK PLUGS 1-24
   INSPECTION & GAPPING 1-25
   REMOVAL & INSTALLATION 1-25
   SPARK PLUG HEAT RANGE 1-25
SPEAKERS 6-15
   REMOVAL & INSTALLATION 6-15
SPECIAL TOOLS 1-4
SPECIFICATION CHARTS
   BRAKE SPECIFICATIONS 9-28
   CAMSHAFT SPECIFICATIONS 3-2
   CAPACITIES 1-50
   CRANKSHAFT AND CONNECTING ROD SPECIFICATIONS 3-3
   ENGINE IDENTIFICATION 1-14
   E2SE CARBURETOR 5-10
   GENERAL ENGINE SPECIFICATIONS 3-2
   MAINTENANCE INTERVALS 1-48
   PISTON AND RING SPECIFICATIONS 3-5
   TORQUE SPECIFICATIONS 3-72
   TUNE-UP SPECIFICATIONS 1-30
   VEHICLE IDENTIFICATION CHART 1-12
SPEED SENSORS 9-25
   REMOVAL & INSTALLATION 9-25
SPEEDOMETER CABLE 6-20
   REMOVAL & INSTALLATION 6-20
SPEEDOMETER, TACHOMETER AND GAUGES 6-20
   REMOVAL & INSTALLATION 6-20
STABILIZER BAR 8-16
   REMOVAL & INSTALLATION 8-16
STABILIZER SHAFT (SWAY BAR) 8-9
   REMOVAL & INSTALLATION 8-9
STANDARD AND METRIC MEASUREMENTS 1-10
STANDARD DRIVE BELTS 1-22
   INSPECTION & ADJUSTMENT 1-22
   REMOVAL & INSTALLATION 1-22
STARTER 2-15
   REMOVAL & INSTALLATION 2-15
   SOLENOID REPLACEMENT 2-18
   TESTING 2-15
STARTING SYSTEM
STARTING SYSTEM 2-15
STEERING 8-17
STEERING COLUMN HOUSING STEERING SHAFT AND IGNITION SWITCH
   HOUSING JACKET BUSHING 8-22
      DISASSEMBLY 8-22
STEERING GEAR 1-43
STEERING KNUCKLE 8-11
   REMOVAL & INSTALLATION 8-11

STEERING LINKAGE 8-22
   REMOVAL & INSTALLATION 8-22
STEERING WHEEL 8-17
   REMOVAL & INSTALLATION 8-17
STRUT CARTRIDGE 8-8
   REMOVAL & INSTALLATION 8-8
SUNROOF 10-9
SUPPLEMENTAL INFLATABLE RESTRAINT (SIR) SYSTEM 6-7
SYSTEM DESCRIPTION (BOTTOM FEED PORT INJECTION SYSTEM) 5-18
SYSTEM DESCRIPTION (MODEL 300 AND 500 THROTTLE BODY
   INJECTION SYSTEMS) 5-10
SYSTEM DESCRIPTION (MODEL 700 THROTTLE BODY INJECTION
   SYSTEM) 5-14
TANK ASSEMBLY 5-27
   MODULAR FUEL SENDER ASSEMBLY REPLACEMENT 5-28
   REMOVAL & INSTALLATION 5-27
TEMPERATURE CONTROL CABLE 6-12
   ADJUSTMENT 6-12
   REMOVAL & INSTALLATION 6-12
TEST EQUIPMENT 6-4
   JUMPER WIRES 6-4
   MULTIMETERS 6-5
   TEST LIGHTS 6-5
TESTING 6-6
   OPEN CIRCUITS 6-6
   RESISTANCE 6-6
   SHORT CIRCUITS 6-6
   VOLTAGE 6-6
   VOLTAGE DROP 6-6
THERMOSTAT 3-18
   REMOVAL & INSTALLATION 3-18
THROTTLE BODY (MODEL 300 AND 500 THROTTLE BODY INJECTION
   SYSTEMS) 5-11
   REMOVAL & INSTALLATION 5-11
THROTTLE BODY (MODEL 700 THROTTLE BODY INJECTION
   SYSTEM) 5-15
   REMOVAL & INSTALLATION 5-15
THROTTLE BODY (MULTI-PORT & SEQUENTIAL FUEL INJECTION
   SYSTEMS) 5-22
   REMOVAL & INSTALLATION 5-22
THROTTLE POSITION (TP) SENSOR 4-16
   ADJUSTMENT 4-16
   OPERATION 4-16
   REMOVAL & INSTALLATION 4-17
   TESTING 4-16
TIMING BELT (ENGINE MECHANICAL) 3-45
   INSPECTION 3-47
   REMOVAL & INSTALLATION 3-45
TIMING BELT (ROUTINE MAINTENANCE) 1-23
   SERVICING 1-23
TIMING BELT COVER 3-42
   REMOVAL & INSTALLATION 3-42
TIMING CHAIN AND SPROCKETS 3-44
   REMOVAL & INSTALLATION 3-44
TIMING CHAIN COVER OIL SEAL 3-44
   REPLACEMENT 3-44
TIMING CHAIN FRONT COVER 3-43
   REMOVAL & INSTALLATION 3-43
TIRES AND WHEELS 1-33
   CARE OF SPECIAL WHEELS 1-35
   INFLATION & INSPECTION 1-34
   TIRE DESIGN 1-34
   TIRE ROTATION 1-33
   TIRE STORAGE 1-34
TOOLS AND EQUIPMENT 1-3
TOOLS AND EQUIPMENT (TROUBLE CODES) 4-19
   ELECTRICAL TOOLS 4-19
   SCAN TOOLS 4-19

TORQUE   1-7
  TORQUE ANGLE METERS   1-10
  TORQUE WRENCHES   1-8
TORQUE SPECIFICATIONS   3-72
TOWING THE VEHICLE   1-46
TRAILER TOWING   1-45
TRAILER WEIGHT   1-45
TRAILER WIRING   6-27
TRANSAXLE (MANUAL TRANSAXLE)   7-4
  REMOVAL & INSTALLATION   7-4
TRANSAXLE (SERIAL NUMBER IDENTIFICATION)   1-15
TROUBLE CODES   4-18
TROUBLESHOOTING CHARTS
  CRUISE CONTROL   6-14
  TROUBLESHOOTING THE BRAKE SYSTEM   9-3
TROUBLESHOOTING ELECTRICAL SYSTEMS   6-5
TROUBLESHOOTING THE BRAKE SYSTEM   9-3
TRUNK LID   10-3
  ADJUSTMENTS   10-3
  REMOVAL & INSTALLATION   10-3
TUBE MODULE ASSEMBLY   5-18
  REMOVAL & INSTALLATION   5-18
TUNE-UP SPECIFICATIONS   1-30
TURBOCHARGER   3-29
  REMOVAL & INSTALLATION   3-29
TURN SIGNAL (COMBINATION) SWITCH   8-18
  REMOVAL & INSTALLATION   8-18
UNDERHOOD COMPONENT LOCATIONS   1-16
UNDERSTANDING AND TROUBLESHOOTING ELECTRICAL
  SYSTEMS   6-2
UNDERSTANDING THE AUTOMATIC TRANSAXLE   7-27
  HYDRAULIC CONTROL SYSTEM   7-28
  PLANETARY GEARBOX   7-27
  SERVOS & ACCUMULATORS   7-27
  TORQUE CONVERTER   7-27
UNDERSTANDING THE CLUTCH   7-23
UNDERSTANDING THE MANUAL TRANSAXLE   7-2
VACUUM DIAGRAMS   4-28
VALVE LASH   1-29

VALVE SPECIFICATIONS   3-6
VEHICLE   1-11
VEHICLE IDENTIFICATION CHART   1-12
WATER PUMP   3-31
  REMOVAL & INSTALLATION   3-31
WHEEL ALIGNMENT   8-12
  CAMBER   8-12
  CASTER   8-12
  TOE   8-12
WHEEL BEARINGS   1-45
WHEEL CYLINDERS   9-16
  OVERHAUL   9-17
  REMOVAL & INSTALLATION   9-16
WHEEL LUG STUDS   8-3
  REPLACEMENT   8-3
WHEELS   8-2
WHERE TO BEGIN   1-2
WINDSHIELD AND FIXED GLASS   10-16
  REMOVAL & INSTALLATION   10-16
  WINDSHIELD CHIP REPAIR   10-16
WINDSHIELD WASHER FLUID RESERVOIR & PUMP   6-18
  REMOVAL & INSTALLATION   6-18
WINDSHIELD WIPER BLADE AND ARM   6-16
  ADJUSTMENT   6-16
  REMOVAL & INSTALLATION   6-16
WINDSHIELD WIPER MOTOR   6-17
  REMOVAL & INSTALLATION   6-17
WINDSHIELD WIPER SWITCH (INSTRUMENTS AND SWITCHES)   6-21
  REMOVAL & INSTALLATION   6-21
WINDSHIELD WIPER SWITCH (STEERING)   8-19
  REMOVAL & INSTALLATION   8-19
WINDSHIELD WIPERS   1-32
  ELEMENT (REFILL) CARE & REPLACEMENT   1-32
WINDSHIELD WIPERS AND WASHERS   6-16
WIPER LINKAGE   6-18
  REMOVAL & INSTALLATION   6-18
WIRE AND CONNECTOR REPAIR   6-7
WIRING DIAGRAMS   6-31